John Franklin Jameson

and the Development of

Humanistic Scholarship

in America

John Franklin Jameson

and the Development of

Humanistic Scholarship

in America

Morey Rothberg, Project Director

EDITORS

Morey Rothberg

Jacqueline Goggin

SPONSORS

The American Historical Association

The Library of Congress

The National Archives

John Franklin
Jameson
and the Development of
Humanistic Scholarship
in America

VOLUME ONE : SELECTED ESSAYS

Edited by Morey Rothberg and Jacqueline Goggin

Foreword by William E. Leuchtenburg, James H. Billington,

and Don W. Wilson

The University of Georgia Press   Athens & London

Funding for this project is provided principally through grants from the

National Endowment for the Humanities and the National Historical Publications and

Records Commission.

E
175.5
J33
A25
1993
v. 1

© 1993 by the

University of Georgia Press

Athens, Georgia 30602

All rights reserved

Designed by Richard Hendel

Set in Palatino by

Tseng Information Systems, Inc.

Printed and bound by Thomson-Shore, Inc.

The paper in this book meets the

guidelines for permanence and durability

of the Committee on Production Guidelines

for Book Longevity of the Council on

Library Resources.

Printed in the United States of America

97 96 95 94 93 C 5 4 3 2 1

FRONTISPIECE

John Franklin Jameson, circa 1930

(National Archives)

Library of Congress Cataloging in

Publication Data

Jameson, J. Franklin (John Franklin),

1859–1937.

John Franklin Jameson and the development

of humanistic scholarship in America /

edited by Morey Rothberg and Jacqueline

Goggin : foreword by William E.

Leuchtenburg, James H. Billington,

and Don W. Wilson.

p. cm.

Includes bibliographical references

and index.

Contents: v. 1. Selected essays.

ISBN 0-8203-1446-3 (v. 1)

1. United States—History.   2. United

States—Historiography.   3. Jameson,

J. Franklin (John Franklin), 1859–1937.

I. Rothberg, Morey.   II. Goggin, Jacqueline

Anne, 1953–   III. Title.

E175.5.J33A25   1993

973—dc20   92-8221

                                                       CIP

British Library Cataloging in Publication

Data available

Contents

Contents

Foreword

Some years ago, at a gathering of historians at Fraunces Tavern in downtown Manhattan, one of my dinner companions, a prizewinning biographer, mentioned a project on which he was working that reminded me of a book that had meant a great deal to me when I was a graduate student. What was the impact on his study, I asked, of the Jameson thesis? "*What*," he replied, "is the Jameson thesis?" "Oh," I answered, "the theme of *The American Revolution Considered as a Social Movement*, probably the best-known piece of writing by John Franklin Jameson." To which he responded, "*Who* is John Franklin Jameson?"

Who indeed? I fear that my acquaintance is not alone in not knowing the answer to that question. Yet Jameson left an extraordinary mark on the historical profession. The recipient of the first doctorate in history conferred by the Johns Hopkins University, one of those who attended the founding session of the American Historical Association at Saratoga in 1884, editor of the *American Historical Review* from its very first issue in 1895 through 1928 (save for a brief interregnum), the first university-trained professor to be elected president of the AHA, Jameson could well claim to be, to borrow a phrase from Dean Acheson, "present at the creation."

Jameson initiated countless historical projects. For nearly a quarter of a century he served as director of the Department of Historical Research in the Carnegie Institution of Washington. At the same time he edited the *AHR*, he served as chairman of the Historical Manuscripts Commission, and he would go on to spark the movement to create a National Historical Publications Commission. He began the practice of publishing the *List of Doctoral Dissertations in History in Progress or Completed at Colleges and Universities in the United States*; and he laid the plans for Charles O. Paullin's great work, *Atlas of the Historical Geography of the United States*, and was its principal supervisor.

His immense contributions, though, could not be cabined within the historical profession. He served as chief of the Division of Manuscripts of the Library of Congress, helped mightily to bring about the American Council of Learned Societies, and secured enactment of a law providing for the construction of the National Archives building in Washington. It was he, too, who acquired a half-million dollar subvention to prepare the manuscript of the *Dictionary of American Biography*. Its second editor, Dumas Malone, expressed doubt that, if Jameson had made all the choices, he would have

xi

admitted to the *DAB* "athletes and dancers, along with occasional gamblers, freaks, and other bizarre characters," but Jameson, he added, "accepted all the editorial decisions with the best of grace and took great pride in the remarkable breadth of view which became so characteristic of the *Dictionary*."

Malone's doubts suggest that, to more than a few, Jameson appeared to be a formidably frosty New England patrician. To young Allan Nevins he seemed, at first glance, "stiffly erect, soberly dressed, deliberate of movement, and austere in manner as in speech." But Nevins, like many others, soon came to know him as not "a bit juiceless or desiccated" but a kindly man forever seeking to be helpful to others, including young people just starting out in the historical profession. Dumas Malone, too, later spoke of "his unending desire to facilitate all scholarship and to be of all possible help to any scholar."

Jameson, for all of his regal bearing, seems not fully to have appreciated his achievements. He did not think he was in the same league with "learned historians." He "could never be," he said, "an excellent historian" nor "a first-rate teacher." A generation after he wrote those words in 1903 he confessed, "I should like to have written learned books myself."

We know better. We know that, quite apart from his pathbreaking *American Revolution Considered as a Social Movement*, he was a superb historian, and that as an advocate and an institution-builder, he was nonpareil. In a tribute that appeared shortly after his death, a note in the *American Historical Review* stated: "We shall not see his like again. . . . He had no predecessor, and he will have no successor." True enough. Yet for those of us who are honored by being elected to follow him in the presidency of the American Historical Association, he is a vivid reminder that, though we cannot hope to match his extraordinary accomplishments, we should, like him, endeavor to hold a large view of our responsibilities. We need to keep in our memory a man who addressed questions of the magnitude of those in "The Present State of Historical Writing in America"; who proposed bold, and still not inconceivable, ventures such as a center for advanced studies for historians in Washington; and who understood the imperative of creating a partnership among historians on college and university campuses and public historians at institutes such as the National Archives and the Library of Congress. In the end, these may be John Franklin Jameson's most important legacies.

WILLIAM E. LEUCHTENBURG
President of the American Historical Association

J. Franklin Jameson came to the Library of Congress in 1928 as chief of its Manuscript Division. He was sixty-nine years old and was acknowledged as the nation's preeminent promoter of scholarship in American history, a reputation he had acquired during a twenty-three-year tenure as director of the Department of Historical Research at the Carnegie Institution of Washington (1905–28), and as the longtime editor of the *American Historical Review*. The Manuscript Division had already amassed a vast array of nationally significant collections, had experience of thirty years administering them, and had become the recognized leader in the field. Herbert Putnam, the librarian of Congress, hoped to find a man who could meet the measure of these collections and initiate new programs that would carry the division beyond its current attainments. J. Franklin Jameson was Putnam's first and only choice.

Jameson once compared the progress of learning to the advance of an army, in which the workers in libraries and other learned institutions led the way "like pickets or scouting parties making a reconnaissance." Picket duty and reconnaissance were congenial duties to Jameson, and his curiosity never dimmed. His search for collections that would add to the store of information about our national past was relentless: it has been estimated that Jameson nearly doubled the holdings of the Manuscript Division in the nine years he served as its chief. When he died in September 1937, his obituary in the *American Historical Review* declared: "He had no predecessor, and he will have no successor." As publication begins of a multivolume edition of J. Franklin Jameson's writings, we at the Library remind our contemporaries of his enduring achievements and express our pride in having the splendid collection of his papers from which much of this edition is drawn.

JAMES H. BILLINGTON
Librarian of Congress

On the east side of the National Archives in Washington is the inscription: "This building holds in trust the records of our national life and symbolizes our faith in the permanency of our national institutions."

It is to the efforts of John Franklin Jameson, more than any other single individual, that we owe the creation of the National Archives and other vital institutions and organizations that preserve our national heritage.

The historian Dumas Malone once said that Jameson was the most learned man in the field of history that he had ever known. Jameson himself described his own role as a maker of "bricks for others to use." Those so-called bricks include, in addition to the National Archives, the American Historical Association, the Department of Historical Research in the Carnegie Institution of Washington, the American Council of Learned Societies, and the National Historical Publications and Records Commission. They amount to no less than the foundation of the American historical profession.

In a career spanning four decades as history professor, director of the Carnegie Institution's Department of Historical Research, editor of the *American*

Historical Review, and chief of the Manuscript Division of the Library of Congress, Jameson was a master planner, lobbyist, administrator, and, in the words of Lyman Butterfield, longtime editor of the *Adams Papers*, an "amiable goad" in the cause of American history.

Jameson was instrumental in helping transform the study of American history from an avocation of gifted amateurs into a profession of scholars. He was a principal catalyst between the world of scholars and the world of corporate philanthropy and government funding.

This magnificent edition of the Papers of John Franklin Jameson, edited with great care and precision by Morey Rothberg and Jacqueline Goggin, provides a documentary record of the establishment of the American historical profession, the growth of professional librarianship, and the evolution of archival management, all seen through the indefatigable efforts of this one remarkable individual.

Jameson died in 1937, the same year that John Russell Pope's splendid building on Constitution Avenue was completed. In the National Archives a bronze portrait plaque pays tribute to the man whose unflagging energies had such importance for the institution and the field of history.

Allan Nevins once remembered Jameson as an austere, shy, reserved gentleman of the "old school," erudite, learned, blessed with refreshing dry humor. Nevins also remembered him as a "slender, frail-looking birch tree rustling with dry leaves." For the National Archives, for the National Historical Publications and Records Commission, for many of America's cultural institutions, Jameson was not a frail birch but solid ironwood.

DON W. WILSON
Archivist of the United States

Acknowledgments

Since the inception of this project in 1984, we have accumulated many debts, more than we can acknowledge here. Our largest debt is to our sponsors and funding agencies, for without their support the project would not have been possible. In January 1984 Morey Rothberg began discussions with Roger A. Bruns of the Publications Program of the National Historical Publications and Records Commission (NHPRC) to determine whether the commission would be interested in funding a project to collect and publish Jameson's letters and other papers. The commission staff endorsed the project and encouraged Rothberg to apply for funding. To secure institutional sponsorship and support for the project, Rothberg and the commission staff began discussions with Samuel R. Gammon, executive director of the American Historical Association (AHA), who in turn raised the idea of the project with Daniel J. Boorstin, the librarian of Congress, and Robert M. Warner, the archivist of the United States. This spirit of cooperation has continued with the current librarian, James H. Billington; and with the current archivist, Don W. Wilson. The AHA agreed to administer the project, the Library of Congress agreed to provide office space and equipment, and funds were received from the NHPRC in June 1984. In 1986 the National Endowment for the Humanities (NEH) awarded its first grant to the project.

Individuals at these institutions deserve special thanks for their willingness to work with us on this collaborative effort. Along with Samuel Gammon, other AHA staff members merit recognition: Jamil S. Zanaildin and his successor as deputy director, James B. Gardner; Eileen Gaylard and her successor as assistant to the executive director, Sharon K. Tune; Kathy Koziara-Herbert, editor of *Perspectives*; and James H. Leatherwood, Randy B. Norell, A. A. Pietropaoli, and Shahin Saidi-Taleb of the accounting department.

At the NHPRC the enthusiasm Roger Bruns displayed for our project was matched by that of his colleagues. Frank G. Burke, Timothy D. W. Connelly, Gerald George, Mary A. Giunta, Sara D. Jackson, Richard Jacobs, Nancy Sahli, Richard N. Sheldon, and Donald L. Singer assisted and advised us at every stage. We thank NEH staff members Margot Backas, Richard Ekman, Kathy Fuller, Alice R. Hudgins, Jack Meyers, Dennis Romano, Gordon B. McKinney, and Douglas M. Arnold.

Individuals and foundations, as well as the NHPRC and the NEH, contributed to the production of this volume. Substantial grants were awarded us by the Morris and Gwendolyn Cafritz Foundation, the Carnegie Institution of Washington, the Lucius N. Littauer Foundation, the Richard Lounsbery Foundation, and the National Home Library Foundation. The Amherst Alumni Association of Philadelphia, the Capitol Historical Society, the Queen Ferry Coonley Foundation, the Cosmos Club, the Edward and Marjorie Goldberger Foundation, the Historical Society of Washington, D.C., and the Johns Hopkins Alumni Association of Washington, D.C., provided additional funds. Martin Atlas, Arthur Berlin, Ray L. Bowers, Patricia Parratt Craig, Charles G. Dobbins, William L. Fox, Mary Ann Guyol, Daniel M. Lundquist, James T. Morris, Jane North, S. Dillon Ripley, Maxine Singer, Douglas Sprunt, and Wilcomb E. Washburn gave generously of their time and attention. We also gratefully acknowledge the financial support and interest of Albert J. Beveridge III, Marvin Bower, Ira V. Brown, John Higham, Douglass E. Kellogg, Irving and Sue Burnett Panzer, William J. Roberts, and Elizabeth Burnett Wiens.

Since 1984 we have had the good fortune to have offices at the Library of Congress. Anyone familiar with the vast collections and staff of the library can appreciate the pleasures we have experienced by being there. John C. Broderick and the professionals under his direction through the Office of the Assistant Librarian for Research Services—Lee Avdoyan, Thomas D. Burney, Edward A. D'Alessandro, Annette L. Hale, Victoria C. Hill, David B. Kresh, Diane N. Kresh, Everette E. Larson, Bruce Martin, Ardie S. Myers, Robert J. Palian, Maurice Sanders, Carolyn H. Sung, Suzanne E. Thorin, and Christopher Wright—provided access to collections and computer data bases, offered reference services, facilitated interlibrary loans, and translated documents.

James H. Hutson and his fine staff of archivists and historians in the Manuscript Division have provided us both a place to work and valuable assistance. The Reading Room staff—Frederick W. Bauman, Jeffrey M. Flannery, John Hackett, Charles J. Kelly, Michael J. Klein, Gary J. Kohn, Janice E. Ruth, and Mary M. Wolfskill—cheerfully responded to requests for manuscript materials. Richard B. Bickel, Paul I. Chestnut, John D. Knowlton, and David W. Wigdor also facilitated our access to collections of documents. Joseph D. Sullivan provided technical assistance. The Letters of Delegates to Congress Project is located in the Manuscript Division, and we thank Gerard W. Gawalt, Ronald M. Gephart, and Paul H. Smith for their advice and assistance in the early stages of our work.

Many other archivists across the country willingly gave us various forms of assistance and advice at crucial points in the project's development. We thank the following archivists and reference librarians: Robert Buckeye, Middlebury College; Margaret N. Burri, Historical Society of Washington, D.C.; Earle Coleman, Princeton University; Daria D'Arienzo, Amherst College;

Jill Erickson, Boston Athenaeum; Bernard R. Crystal, Columbia University; Thomas D. Hamm, Earlham College; Helene Lambert, Amherst College; Martha L. Mitchell, Brown University; Sarah Polirer, Harvard University; Barbara Trippel Simmons, American Antiquarian Society; and Wesley L. Wilson, Enoch Pratt Free Library, who searched collections in their custody for materials on the lectures and essays presented in this volume. For permission to cite materials in their collections, we again thank Margaret N. Burri and Earle Coleman. We also thank Ray L. Bowers, Carnegie Institution of Washington; Thomas F. Harkins, Duke University Archives; John Hoffman, Illinois Historical Survey, University of Illinois; Daniel Meyer, Special Collections, Joseph Regenstein Library, University of Chicago; Harold Miller, State Historical Society of Wisconsin; Julia B. Morgan, Ferdinand Hamburger, Jr., Archives, the Johns Hopkins University; Cynthia Requardt, Eisenhower Library, the Johns Hopkins University; Matthew T. Schaefer, Bentley Historical Library, University of Michigan; and Judith Ann Schiff, Sterling Memorial Library, Yale University. We thank LaWanda Cox for permission to quote from a letter she wrote to the editors in 1986.

We gratefully acknowledge permission to reprint the following essays by John Franklin Jameson:

"The Present State of Historical Writing in America." Reprinted by permission of the American Antiquarian Society.

"The American Acta Sanctorum," "Historical Scholars in War-Time," and a review of Claude Moore Fuess, *Amherst: The Story of a New England College*. Reprinted by permission of the American Historical Association.

"The Need of a National Archive Building." Reprinted by permission of the American Library Association.

"The Arrival of the Pilgrims." Reprinted by permission of Brown University.

"A New American Historical Journal." Reprinted by permission of Duke University.

"The Control of the Higher Education in the United States." Reprinted by permission of Earlham College.

"The Future Uses of History." Reprinted by permission of the Helen Dwight Reid Educational Foundation.

"An Introduction to the Study of the Constitutional and Political History of the States." Reprinted by permission of the Johns Hopkins University Press.

"The Influence of Universities upon Historical Writing." Reprinted by permission of the University of Chicago Press.

Review of James Bryce, *The American Commonwealth*. Reprinted by permission of W. Green and Son, Ltd.

We also acknowledge permission from the University of Pittsburgh Press to quote from James A. Kehl, *Boss Rule in the Gilded Age: Matt Quay of Pennsylvania* (Pittsburgh, 1981). Morey Rothberg expresses his thanks to the American Historical Association, Brown University, and the University of California Press for permission to include in his introduction material that appeared, respectively, in the *American Historical Review*, the *Brown Alumni Monthly*, and the *Public Historian*. He also thanks Ronald Hoffman for permission to incorporate material scheduled to appear in Ronald Hoffman and Peter Albert, eds., *"The Transforming Hand of Revolution": Reconsidering the American Revolution as a Social Movement* (Charlottesville: University Press of Virginia, forthcoming).

We also wish to thank the Catholic University of America Press for permission to incorporate in our bibliography of Jameson's writings information compiled by Donald J. Mugridge and published in *J. Franklin Jameson: A Tribute*, edited by Ruth Anna Fisher and William L. Fox (Washington, D.C., 1965), pp. 103–137. Special thanks is due to the late Francis Christie Elwell Jameson, who gave us permission to print without restriction documents written by his father, John Franklin Jameson.

The editors have made every effort to obtain permission from known copyright holders of any material contained in this volume. Omissions reported to the publisher will be acknowledged in subsequent editions.

Documentary editors have been especially generous with their time. We acknowledge the assistance of the following editors: W. W. Abbot, Ira Berlin, Charles Beveridge, Charlene N. Bickford, Larry I. Bland, Kenneth R. Bowling, James M. Buchanan, John Catanzariti, Jane T. Censer, David R. Chestnutt, Charles T. Cullen, Robert A. Hill, Ronald Hoffman, Patricia G. Holland, Elizabeth S. Hughes, John P. Kaminski, Stuart B. Kaufman, Arthur S. Link, Mary Lynn McCree, Grace Palladino, James R. Perry, Nathan Reingold, Leslie Rowland, and Ronald Zboray.

Our consultations with the historians and editors on our editorial advisory board have ensured that this volume reflects the concerns of scholars from different fields. Margaret S. Child, Mary O. Furner, James H. Hutson, Richard W. Leopold, John Beverley Riggs, Dorothy Ross, Raymond W. Smock, and David D. Van Tassel have assisted us in making crucial editorial decisions and have reviewed in manuscript this volume of Jameson's writings.

We also are indebted to several other scholars. Jack R. Censer, Raymond J. Cunningham, Eugene D. Genovese, Lewis Hanke, John Higham, Michael G. Kammen, Peter Novick, and Charles Royster provided advice and counsel. John L. Thomas and James Hoopes formed an exclusive circle of Jameson enthusiasts when this project was merely an idea. William Dornemann assisted us with translation.

For their work in transcribing documents and in data entry, we thank

Celia R. Gray, Eugene Royal, and Rose Thompson, who often worked under difficult conditions, deciphering illegible handwriting—ours and John Franklin Jameson's.

We also acknowledge the assistance of the University of Georgia Press. Malcolm Call, the director of the Press, provided an early and sustaining source of encouragement. Madelaine Cooke, Karen Orchard, and Debra Winter smoothly shepherded us through the publication process, and we thank them for their patience.

Finally, we thank John Terry Chase, assistant editor from July 1990 to August 1991; and Frank Rives Millikan, NHPRC Fellow in Historical Editing for 1990–91, who were instrumental in getting the manuscript into final shape. The editors are jointly responsible for the selection of documents in the volume, as well as the production of headnotes and annotations, and take full responsibility for any errors or omissions in this volume.

In 1956 Elizabeth Donnan and Leo F. Stock, close associates of John Franklin Jameson for many years, published *An Historian's World: Selections from the Correspondence of John Franklin Jameson* (Philadelphia: American Philosophical Society). Because Donnan and Stock limited themselves to publishing only letters authored by Jameson that had been collected in the John Franklin Jameson Papers at the Library of Congress, their volume, useful as it is in many ways, cannot meet the needs of modern scholars. It focuses much more intensively on Jameson's personal development and is more of a biographical portrait than the present work. Nevertheless, *An Historian's World* is marked by an appreciation of Jameson and a love of scholarship that we can only regard with admiration and respect.

We intend that this documentary edition will be a contribution to American intellectual and social history, as well as to humanistic studies, and additionally that it will be a source of information and stimulation in the ongoing debate among scholars, journalists, politicians, cultural administrators, and the general public about the nature of our collective research enterprise. John Franklin Jameson was a modest man who might have been embarrassed to learn that he has become the focus of so much attention. We hope that, at the very least, he would find our objectives worthy of this exploration of his personal and professional life.

Editorial Methods

The objective of this project is to collect the papers of the American historian John Franklin Jameson (1859–1937) and from these papers edit, annotate, and prepare a selected number of these documents to form the basis for a three-volume documentary history of the American historical profession and of humanistic scholarship in America. The documents in this first volume consist of lectures, speeches, essays, and articles spanning Jameson's career as a scholar, teacher, editor, and cultural administrator. The two volumes to follow consist of correspondence, diary entries, and reports, and are arranged in chronological order.

It becomes clear from the documents that Jameson's concerns ranged well beyond those traditionally assigned to academic scholars. He was passionately interested in the meaning of historical scholarship in particular, and humanistic scholarship more generally, in a scientific age. By publishing Jameson's writings on these subjects, we observe him responding simultaneously to intellectual, personal, social, and professional imperatives, and thereby demonstrating the connection between biography and both social and intellectual history. The historical essays show Jameson to be a pioneer, previously unnoted, in the fields of constitutional and political history, black history, and the history of the South, as well as in the fields of social history and the study of the American Revolution, for which he long ago gained lasting recognition. His discussion of the development of the historical profession and humanistic scholarship, as well as his analysis of higher education and the new university system in America, is less well known, but in these articles and addresses, he mapped out a strategy for promoting the growth of scholarship as a profession. The two succeeding volumes of correspondence and other documents show in detail how he carried out this strategy and provide insights on the meaning of scholarship in contemporary society.

Jameson produced his most substantial work as a scholar of history relatively early in his career and then proceeded to become an administrator, journal editor, and cultural entrepreneur. Partly for this reason, we have arranged the documents in this volume into two groups: scholarship and advocacy. Within each group, the documents are presented chronologically. Whether a particular document is published here for the first time, as in the case of the lectures Jameson presented in 1891 on the history of the South, or reprinted, as is true for his 1907 presidential address to the American Historical Association, we think that its inclusion in the volume helps to understand a significant aspect of Jameson's career. Taken together, the documents we have selected encompass the major cultural, political, and intellectual commitments that Jameson displayed through a lifetime of exhortation and organization.

We have decided not to include *The History of Historical Writing in America* or the complete text of *The American Revolution Considered as a Social Movement*. They are perhaps the two historical works for which Jameson is best known, and both are significant historiographical documents as well. These two books, however, are still in print. Included in this volume are two lectures, on slavery and the West, that Jameson delivered as part of an 1895 series of lectures at Barnard College on the American Revolution as a social movement, which were excluded from the published version in 1926. When these writings are considered along with previously unpublished essays on the origin of political parties in the United States, and on the constitutional and political history of the South, as well as selected published articles on historiography and the historical profession, the reader of this volume has access to most of the information included in the works we have chosen not to print, and also to many elements of Jameson's thinking that have not been previously available to a general audience.

We intend that each of the documents in this volume should be understandable without extensive reference to other documents or sources outside the volume. Each document is introduced by a brief headnote describing the context in which the document was written and the circumstances surrounding Jameson's interest in the subject. We place explanatory material in the notes and rely as much as possible on primary documents—letters, newspapers, and contemporary literature—when annotating documents. We do not cite standard reference works, such as the *Dictionary of American Biography* and *Notable American Women*. Annotation is used to illuminate unclear references to events, individuals, or subjects discussed in the documents. We identify individuals and subjects discussed in the documents as they were known when a given document was written. We have identified authors of books and articles as they identified themselves in print. Individuals are identified only if they were important within the context of Jameson's life and career.

If a document has been published previously, we provide the bibliographical citation. If the source for a document is a manuscript, we identify it by repository, collection, and box number. In headnotes, footnotes, and source identifications, we indicate the nature of the document, whether for example, it is a signed autograph letter (ALS), a typed manuscript (TM), or a typed carbon of a letter (TLc).

We have kept editorial intrusion to a minimum so that the published version of a document mirrors the original as closely as possible. We do not attempt, however, to present the original form of a document. We have brought material added above a line of text or at the margin into the line, placing this material in brackets where necessary to retain the readability of the text. When Jameson introduced bracketed material in a text, we identify this in a footnote. The editors have used brackets in footnotes and in the bibliography to supply additional information about a document.

None of Jameson's spelling, grammar, or punctuation has been altered unless it was necessary for clarity. We place commas and periods inside quotation marks. In his typescript lectures on the constitutional and political history of the South, Jameson often placed the period for parenthetical statements outside the parentheses; we place the period inside the parentheses. In punctuating the source citations for these lectures, Jameson used hyphens and colons interchangeably. We employ colons uniformly and separate citations in a series by semicolons, rather than by colons, as Jameson did. In these lectures, Jameson employed quotation marks as a shorthand symbol following the number in a date, for example, May 2" for May 2nd. We have substituted "nd," "rd," or "th," as indicated, and we have silently deleted these quotation marks in a date where they are clearly superfluous, for example, May 2", 1775.

If punctuation is missing from a text, it has been inserted within braces. Editorial insertions of words that Jameson inadvertently omitted are inserted within braces. Missing characters in words also are corrected by the insertion of the character within braces. We indicate illegible text thus: {illegible}. We have expanded abbreviated titles and subheadings of documents. We have not reproduced strikeovers or crossouts, but we have indicated in a footnote what was changed when this is significant. Typographical and printer's errors, as well as slips of the pen in handwritten documents, have been silently corrected. Ellipsis points have been standardized throughout all the documents.

If a document exists both in manuscript and in published form, the published version of the text is presented; in these instances, we have found no significant differences between the two texts. In the case of previously published essays that include footnotes, we have numbered the footnotes consecutively rather than retaining the original note numbers. When we add explanatory footnotes of our own within a text, we distinguish them from Jameson's notes by placing the note number in braces.

Two documents exist only in drafts that are incomplete. These are "The Origin of Political Parties in the United States," first delivered at Brown University in 1890, and "The Revolution and the West," from the 1895 lecture series "The Revolution as a Social Movement." We note in a document where a section of the text is missing.

Symbols and Abbreviations

A   Autograph; written in author's hand
P   Printed
T   Typed

D   Document
L   Letter
M   Manuscript

c   carbon
t   transcript or copy made at a much later date

S   Signed by author

Standard endnote and footnote abbreviations include:
AD   Autograph document
AM   Autograph manuscript
ALS   Autograph letter, signed by author
TM   Typed manuscript
TLc   Type letter, carbon, unsigned by author

Symbols used to designate repositories in most instances are those listed in Modern Language Association of America, *American Literary Manuscripts: A Checklist of Holdings in Academic, Historical and Public Libraries in the United States* (Austin: University of Texas Press, 1960).

CIW   Carnegie Institution of Washington, Washington, D.C.
CtY   Yale University, New Haven, Connecticut
DLC   Library of Congress, Washington, D.C.
DNA   National Archives, Washington, D.C.
IU   University of Illinois, Urbana
MdBJ   The Johns Hopkins University, Baltimore, Maryland

MiU   University of Michigan, Ann Arbor
NcD   Duke University, Durham, North Carolina
NjP   Princeton University, Princeton, New Jersey
NN   New York Public Library, New York
NNC   Columbia University, New York
RPB   Brown University, Providence, Rhode Island
ViU   University of Virginia, Charlottesville
WHi   State Historical Society, Madison, Wisconsin

OTHER SYMBOLS AND ABBREVIATIONS

AHA   American Historical Association
AHA, *Annual Report*
        Annual Report of the American Historical Association for the Year
AHA Records
        Records of the American Historical Association
AHR   *American Historical Review*
JFJ   John Franklin Jameson
JP   John Franklin Jameson Papers
RG   Record Group

Introduction

Out of the social, cultural, and political mosaic of American history, John Franklin Jameson created an expression of nationhood. During his long and productive career, first as a teacher and writer of American history and then as an editor and cultural administrator, he emphasized the role of history in stimulating a sense of national unity and cultural homogeneity. This sense of shared beliefs was crucial, he thought, to developing an atmosphere of individual self-restraint and communal loyalty in which democracy flourished. Born in a suburb of Boston just before the Civil War, on September 19, 1859, and coming to maturity at a time when ethnic differences and the potential for social conflict became manifest in America and the world, Jameson strove to develop national and international agencies of scholarship. These agencies would mirror political institutions designed to submerge antagonisms in favor of harmony and stability.

In 1905, at the age of forty-six, Jameson gave up a teaching career that had included successive positions at the Johns Hopkins University, Brown University, and the University of Chicago to become the director of an agency he in fact conceived, the Department of Historical Research in the Carnegie Institution of Washington. In this position, which he held for twenty-three years, he initiated or continued a breathtaking array of projects—editorship of the *American Historical Review*, production of guides to foreign archives, campaigns for a national historical publications commission and a national archive building, and a bibliographical guide, *Writings on American History*. He also took on numerous influential assignments within the American Historical Association, the presidency of which he held in 1907. These many activities were but a partial realization of Jameson's vision of a great national historical enterprise emanating from Washington under his leadership.[1]

As Jameson saw an American nation and then a world community arising out of a welter of racial and ethnic groups, so did he envisage a professional community of scholars replacing the eccentric and often ineffectual efforts of individual researchers working in virtual geographic and intellectual isolation from one another. His vision paralleled that of leading academic scholars and university administrators as part of what the sociologist Magali S. Larson has termed a "collective mobility project" of aspiring professionals in the late nineteenth century.[2] Larson observes that the emergence of large-scale industrial and commercial enterprises relying upon credentialed expertise provided favorable conditions for the creation of university-based professions.[3] Jameson welcomed this development; he made it his life's work to organize historical and humanistic scholars in order to win from industry, private foundations, and government the financial resources previously enjoyed only by wealthy amateurs. These professional scholars, solidly positioned within a highly bureaucratized national society, might lack the spark of genius that Jameson prized in the finest research, but this was an accommodation he made without hesitation; indeed, he could see no alternative.

Although Jameson grew up within a family whose finances were modest—he lived with his parents throughout his four years as an undergraduate at Amherst College and supported the family while teaching at the Johns Hopkins University—he learned early to regard himself as a member of a social and intellectual elite. Frank Jameson traced his lineage through his father, John, to a Scots-Irish emigrant from Ulster, Thomas Jameson, who settled in New Hampshire in 1746. John Jameson's humble origins meant far less to Frank than a love of history and a strong sense of public duty. On his son's twenty-first birthday, John Jameson instructed him to "go forth to your life's work, to your life's battle, not boasting yourself now at the putting on of your armor but living such a life that at its close you may be able to say with Paul 'I have fought a good fight, I have kept the faith.'"[4]

Frank's mother, Mariette Thompson Jameson, was descended from a founder of Woburn, Massachusetts, and she admonished her son while he was still a youth to "associate with those not our equals to benefit them if possible." Frank's unease at socializing with different classes of people distressed her, "for sometimes it is really one's duty to associate with inferiors."[5] As valedictorian of the class of 1879 at Amherst, Jameson reminded the graduating seniors of their responsibility to resolve the great issues of their day, not thinking themselves superior in this work, "but we must feel that we are under stronger obligations to attempt it."[6]

When Jameson enrolled at Johns Hopkins in the fall of 1880, intending to pursue graduate study in history, he entered an environment that encouraged budding scholars to view their work in relation to current political issues. Jameson took up the challenge in the first major paper he wrote as a student in the Hopkins Seminary of Historical and Political Science, the essay "Disturbances in Barbados in 1876." Noting the violent response of poor blacks on the island to the apparent indifference of the planter class to their misery, Jameson considered various modes of governance that might resolve the island's problems and settled on what he termed "an impartial administrative despotism" in which "the two races, each restrained from oppression of the other, may most quickly and happily arrive at the condition in which the establishment of a constitutional government is not only possible, but wise."[7] Jameson's scholarly interest in the West Indies probably was encouraged by a trip his family made there in 1867, when he was seven years old, and during which time he kept a journal.[8]

The guiding principle of historical study in the Hopkins Seminary was the village community theory, which later became known as the germ theory. According to Herbert B. Adams, the seminary's director and associate in history at Hopkins, the beginnings of American political institutions could be found in the structure of English parish assemblies and, beyond the parish assemblies, in the procedures for land distribution followed by "Teutonic farmers" in the village communities of medieval Germany.[9]

Jameson made light of the seminary's obsession with local institutions as a graduate student and later as an instructor at Johns Hopkins following the earning of his doctorate in 1882, the first awarded there in history. He confided to his diary that "our men have received from Adams altogether too one-sided an impulse to study of the local institutions under the Anglo-Saxons. I am going to get over that period in two meetings."[10] Yet Jameson never publicly disavowed the village community theory, and his own writings reflected the same desire to recreate the sturdy spirit of Anglo-Saxon democracy in a society far too ethnically diverse to support such a notion.[11]

The idea of a democratic but deferential society evolving over centuries became, if anything, even more appealing to Jameson as class and ethnic differences made themselves increasingly visible to him. On one occasion in the fall of 1882, Adams adjourned the weekly meeting of the seminary to permit its members to observe a political rally. Jameson left the rally disgusted at what appeared to him the low aptitude of the masses, "but every political meeting I have attended has had the same effect, to shatter my rising respect for the people, in their political capacity, and make me despise them." In 1886 he described Isidor Rayner, a congressional candidate in Baltimore, as "a vulgar, loudly-dressed, dirty young Jew."[12]

Such attitudes made Jameson an unlikely candidate to view with insight the role of common people in history, but a social historian he meant to become. When James Bryce, the British political commentator, suggested to him on a visit to Baltimore in November 1883 that determining the social aspects of politics would prove challenging, Jameson assured himself that this would be his most significant achievement.[13] Prior to this discussion, his extensive reading schedule had led Jameson to discover the works of Henry Buckle and Hippolyte Taine, scholars who in different ways stimulated the study of social history. For Taine, the author of a study on the *ancien régime*, understanding French history prior to the Revolution meant exploring that history from every perspective, immersing oneself in its social texture.[14]

While Taine was passionately engaged with his subject, Henry Buckle, in his *History of Civilization in England*, stood at a distance from the events and people he discussed. Physical and social influences stood far behind intellect as the prime mover in his grand scheme. Around the world nature and mind were at war with each other, but in Europe alone the mind had triumphed.[15] Taine was far superior to Buckle, Jameson concluded, because "he understands and can set forth the course and origins of a popular movement, and the social condition of a whole nation," but it was Henry Buckle whom Jameson more closely resembled in his writings.[16] As Buckle remained an intellectual historian while professing to write social history, so Jameson saw the realm of ideas as a restraining influence on the unpredictable and often undesirable consequences of social movements.

Repeatedly, Jameson's ambition to write the social history of America was thwarted by his obvious distaste for people in the mass and for ethnic groups other than his own. A series of lectures he delivered on state constitutional and political history in January 1885 before the Hopkins Seminary (later published in the university's *Studies in Historical and Political Science*) began provocatively by commenting that "our political histories have for the most part been Iliads; they are filled with the deeds of the chieftains 'wise in council,' 'fertile in devices,' 'kings of men,' . . . while the rest of the well-greaved Achaians stand in their ranks unnoticed and unsung." John B. McMaster's *History of the People of the United States* (1883), if flawed, represented a healthy departure from this practice, Jameson acknowledged, "but the true history of our nation will not be written until we can obtain a correct and exhaustive knowledge of the history of public opinion upon politics, the history of the political views and actions of the average voter."[17] Politics still provided Jameson the essential frame of reference, and the "voter," a statistical entity, was the center of attention rather than the tradespeople, merchants, farmers, and lawyers that Taine embraced.

It was a constitutional and political history of the individual states on which Jameson focused as the subject of what he modestly decided would be his "magnum opus" many years hence.[18] While still an instructor at Hopkins, he began to sketch the outlines of this project, focusing first on the American South. A number of reasons may have encouraged him in this direction. Students from Baltimore, a southern city, made up a sizable proportion of both the undergraduate and graduate students in the early years of the university, and the history of slavery became a subject for investigation in the Hopkins Seminary.[19] Also, the problem of elite rule over a multiracial society, which Jameson had examined in his essay on Barbados, appeared to extend to the post-Reconstruction South.[20]

Jameson left Johns Hopkins and Baltimore in the fall of 1888 for a professorship at Brown, but he took with him his plans for an investigation of southern history, even though he was now considerably further from his sources. He envisaged an edition of the records of the Virginia Company, as well as biographies of John C. Calhoun and Richard Henry Lee.[21] Invited to return to Johns Hopkins in the spring of 1891, Jameson used the occasion to lecture to the Hopkins Seminary on the constitutional and political history of the South and subsequently to travel through the eastern half of Virginia, examining private and public collections of documents.[22]

In these lectures Jameson found once more that it was easier to talk about abstractions than about people. How did it happen, for example, that highly aristocratic Virginia produced a Declaration of Rights, the abolition of entail and primogeniture, and the disestablishment of the Anglican Church? The solution to this apparently contradictory situation was the influence of the Enlightenment, embodied in the words and deeds of Thomas Jefferson.[23] Ideas moved history; at least in Virginia, they were strong enough "to cast off the shackles of oligarchical privilege and base the new government upon the broad foundations of popular support."[24] Speaking the following year on the colonial history of Virginia, first at the Peabody Institute in Baltimore and then before a meeting of the Rhode Island Historical Society, Jameson made plain his belief that even more than Jefferson's statecraft, the secret to success in Virginia politics rested with the existence of a largely rural, homogeneous society of Anglo-Saxon heritage in which mobility between classes coexisted with clearly understood traditions of deference to education and position. He insisted that "towns and trade had little place in Virginia, and the vast majority of the great middle class consisted of yeomen, small planters and farmers. They were a vigorous class of genuine English stock, sturdy and manly, sharing the independent spirit of the richer planters, yet naturally following the lead of the latter in political, as well as in social matters. They were considerably more ignorant than their social superiors, but they had the same generous and hospitable dispositions."[25]

The further west and south one moved from Virginia, the more politically troubling was the history of the region; reason and a common ancestry could not contain the struggle between opposing economic interests. It was actually in the Old Southwest of Alabama, Mississippi, Kentucky, and Tennessee, Jameson discovered, that democracy would be most firmly anchored. Here was the birthplace of Jacksonian democracy, and following Frederick J. Turner's discussion of the frontier, the reason was economic: "In these regions a new type of American humanity was being developed, destined in time to force upon the older portions of the south a democracy more complete than their own, because based upon economic conditions more favorable to pure democracy, and an Americanism more fervent because more perfectly free from economic and mental dependence upon Europe." Left to themselves, the masses displayed both a marvelous zest for democracy and an appalling ignorance of the restraints necessary to prevent freedom from dissolving first into anarchy and then into tyranny. This was the lesson Jameson found in the history of Jacksonian democracy and, more recently, in the amazing growth of Populism, "a movement on the part of masses hitherto but slightly engaged in politics, which threatens to put the conduct of our public affairs into the hands of a vast horde of unintelligent farmers, whose ardency and inexperience combine to put them in the power of loud demagogues and skillful wire-pullers."[26]

Along with his explorations in southern history, Jameson examined the colonial and Revolutionary history of the North. Here, the results were even more distressing to this Brahmin scholar, for the middle colonies especially compelled a recognition of ethnic as well as economic diversity as contributing factors to political development. Reassuringly, he concluded in his 1890 lecture "The Origin of Political Parties in the United States" that party disputes were minimal in his native Massachusetts, which was "unified by severe measures based on the conviction that the interests and wills of individuals must be strictly subordinated to the interest and will of the community." Political conflict was greatest in the colonies of New York and Pennsylvania, both populated heavily by Germans. The Germans in Pennsylvania, "not having inherited traditions of self-government and of Anglo-Saxon modes of political action, were largely indifferent to public affairs, desiring only to be undisturbed and to be prosperous." In colonial New York, Jameson found the same propensity to individual aggrandizement and "a similar dead-weight of non-English population indifferent to large political questions and therefore at the disposal of energetic politicians."[27]

In his investigation of the Revolutionary period, Jameson's intelligence and skill at research repeatedly led him toward conclusions that were profoundly disturbing to his conservative instincts, and probably upsetting to a large segment of the reading public he might address. He had the intellectual audacity to frame the American Revolution as a "social movement" in a series of lectures he delivered at Barnard College in 1895, then drew back in alarm from the contemporary implications of this term. How indeed could the American Revolution be considered a social movement? This had been the fate of the French Revolution, where rebellion against a savagely unjust political and social system had ended in a new era of political tyranny, but the "Anglo-Saxon" who made the American Revolution "had no wish to destroy or recast his social system. He sought for political freedom, but he had no mind to allow revolution to extend itself beyond that limited sphere. As Burke said, he was 'taught to look with horror on those children of their country who are prompted rashly to hack that aged parent to pieces and put him into the kettle of magicians, in hopes that by their poisonous weeds and wild incantations they may regenerate the paternal constitution.'"[28]

Whatever their designs, the leaders of the American Revolution unleashed powerful forces that transformed both the social and political spheres of American life. Echoes of Hippolyte Taine surfaced in Jameson's observation that "the various fibres of a nation's life are knit together in great complexity. It is impossible to sever some without also loosening others, and setting them free to combine anew in widely different forms."[29]

Once again, Jameson confronted a contradiction he could not easily resolve: a peaceful and conservative society of Anglo-Saxon yeomen had generated a revolution that threatened to tear that society apart. The egalitarianism of which Americans boasted, it seems, had been born initially of violent conflict. What did such a discovery reveal about the American past? What did it portend about the future? Perhaps the Populists, that "vast horde of unintelligent farmers," had their own revolutionary tradition to draw upon. What indeed had happened to that "social movement" that there should be such strife in the land now? Jameson did not answer these troubling questions directly, but his reluctance to publish the lectures for over thirty years, and then only when their political implications and personal consequences for him were diminished, suggests a conviction on his part that what the conservative canons of scientific history and his own political beliefs did not permit him to say he might better refrain from acknowledging in print.[30]

When William R. Harper, president of the University of Chicago, invited Jameson in the spring of 1900 to succeed Hermann von Holst as head of the university's history department, Jameson was wary but receptive. After an uncertain beginning, Brown had proved to be a very congenial environment. Harper was considered not only talented and energetic but also prone to shift his enthusiasm from one idea to another and to make unrealistic promises to faculty.[31] The graduate program in history at Brown had faltered, however, as had the career of its controversial president, E. Benjamin Andrews. Brown had ensnared Jameson in a series of parochial disputes over the nature of what remained a small Baptist liberal arts college. In contrast, at the University of Chicago, where Jameson moved in the spring of 1901, the prospects seemed boundless. The questions he would address at Chicago, as well as his audience, would be national in scope.

In his inaugural address as head of the history department, "The Influence of Universities upon Historical Writing," Jameson reminded his audience that academic historians had new responsibilities that separated their work from that of their amateur predecessors. Romantic liberalism had encouraged a style of historical writing that emphasized rhetoric over substance; now, he commented, "old-fashioned whiggery is dead; the political theories that have taken its place borrow their postulates from the domain of physical science." The new "scientific" history embodied the hard judgment that humanity was much more limited in what it could achieve than previous generations had imagined. "Since Darwin," Jameson concluded, "it has been no more possible for the age to produce a crop of Macaulays and Michelets than it is possible for those who picture running horses to expel from their minds what they have learned from Mr. Muybridge's photographs of animal locomotion."[32]

Historians had a responsibility, in Jameson's view, to provide justification for governance by a new national elite. Yet the desire to present a more encompassing portrait of historical reality never deserted him. At Chicago he infused a measure of enthusiasm and scholarly rigor into a department very nearly moribund. He initiated a three-year sequence of courses in historical method, including lectures on the history of historiography and what he termed the "auxiliary sciences" of historical geography, numismatics, paleography, and epigraphy, as well as on historical criticism and bibliography. He offered graduate lecture courses on the history of land policy in America and on the organization of American religion, as well as graduate seminars in American political and constitutional history prior to 1815.[33] He also presented courses on the history of American political parties to 1844, the constitutional history of the states between 1775 and 1830, and the history of the doctrine of states' rights, nullification, and secession.[34] As a teacher, if not as a published scholar, Jameson pursued social history, the history of political institutions, and the role of state and local constitutional history in relation to the history of the American constitution.[35]

Jameson was the first academically trained historian to be elected to the presidency of the American Historical Association. He used the occasion of his presidential address in 1907 to focus the attention of his colleagues on the social implications of American religious history, at that point a topic almost completely neglected by scholars. Historians unwittingly narrowed their perspective through reliance on manuscript and the printed page, he remarked. As long as the American national character was defined solely through literature, scholars were in "constant danger of forgetting how small the literary class is and always has been." Religion, more than any other single element, permeated the lives of Americans generation after generation. The statistics of economic growth supported the structure on which American social history would be built; still, "no view is truthful that leaves out of account the ideals which animated these toiling millions, the thoughts concerning the universe and man which informed their minds." [36]

Jameson recognized that a dramatically transformed political environment worldwide demanded the investigation of historical subjects previously ignored. "What sort of histories will a socialized and internationalized Europe desire?" was the question he posed to the trustees of the Carnegie Institution of Washington in his 1913 address "The Future Uses of History." While political and constitutional history would not lose their significance, social and economic history would rise in importance, because these elements of past societies most nearly correlated with the significant features of the industrial age.[37] An early essay by Ulrich B. Phillips on the "black belt" in the antebellum South, submitted to the *American Historical Review* in 1905, elicited praise from Jameson but also the admonition that the paper's sweeping assertions rested upon a meager foundation of evidence. Its strengths lay "in its last half, where you are able to present out of concrete materials, to which you give references, an interesting demonstration of social and economic transition."[38]

Under Jameson's direction, and with the strong support of Carnegie Institution president Robert S. Woodward, the Department of Historical Research published a guide to the Swiss and Austrian archives that identified significant documents for the history of American immigration, a guide for American repositories containing documents for religious history, and documentary histories of the slave trade and slave laws in the South. It produced the *Atlas of the Historical Geography of the United States*, published by the Carnegie Institution and the American Geographical Society in 1932. Jameson himself edited for the Society of Colonial Dames a volume of documents on the history of privateering and piracy in the American British colonies.[39] In these and in other ways he acknowledged the claims of social, economic, and religious history and provided a foundation for further research that to the present time historians have not fully exploited.

Jameson gained lasting recognition, somewhat against his will, as a historian with the publication in 1926 of *The American Revolution Considered as a Social Movement*. After being invited to address this subject in 1925 as the Vanuxem lecturer at Princeton, Jameson reduced the original six lectures delivered at Barnard College to four. Because the terms of the Vanuxem Foundation required it, the lectures were published the following year.[40]

In the thirty years between Jameson's Barnard lectures and the publication of his book in 1926, the study of the American Revolution and its consequences had been transformed. Younger scholars around the country, unshackled by Jameson's devotion to Brahmin New England, embraced the diversity of American society as they examined its social and political divisions. The theme of class conflict and struggle against privilege, which resonated throughout the Progressive era, animated the most significant historical studies of the Revolution. Clashes within the colonies over race, class, economic and geographical differences, to which Jameson had alluded in his lectures, formed the core of arguments presented in a number of monographs.[41]

As a new generation of scholars revealed a revolutionary society filled with conflict, Jameson largely restated the arguments put forward in his 1895 Barnard lectures. The enumeration of Anglo-Saxon virtues had been deleted, but in its place was the pointed observation that the vigor of the Revolution resided largely "not in the mob or rabble, for American society was overwhelmingly rural and not urban, and had no sufficient amount of mob or rabble to control the movement, but in the peasantry, substantial and energetic though poor, in the small farmers and frontiersmen."[42] The effect of Jameson's eloquent prose and skillful organization of material was to present the Revolution as an intricate tapestry of events, stability and gradual progress in the midst of violent social and political upheaval. It was the American Revolution and the nation as Jameson preferred to see them.[43]

As a young scholar, Jameson was trapped between his desire to explore the social aspects of American political history and his conservative political instincts that appeared to frustrate that ambition. Consequently, he established a career as an institution builder rather than as a writer of historical narrative. He ultimately provided the American historical profession a national structure within which the distinctive elements of race, ethnicity, class, and culture could be investigated by others, since he could not bring himself to attempt this task. In September 1890 Jameson published an article in the *Atlantic Monthly* entitled "The Development of Modern European Historiography." A review of the substantial material and financial support that European governments afforded historians led Jameson to chastise the government of the United States for the relative paucity of its contribution to historical scholarship. Reaching out for that assistance, he noted that nations as well as individual historians benefited from state patronage of research, "for historical work, vividly recalling the glories of the past, has often contributed immensely to the quickening of national patriotism."[44]

Even more significant was a paper Jameson presented in 1890 before the American Historical Association, "The Expenditures of Foreign Governments in Behalf of History." With the publication in 1892 of this paper in the annual report of the association for 1891, he staked out for himself the primary task of finding institutional support for historical research. No European government for which he had information spent so little on maintaining its archives as did the United States, Jameson observed, adding that "it is true that our history is shorter than theirs, but it is also true that our purse is much longer."[45] The federal government was potentially the most important source of funds for history, but state and local societies, as well as learned societies like the AHA, would have to be prodded to do their part. Jameson suggested that the association's annual report, which was published by the federal government as a result of the charter the society received from Congress in 1889, might serve as a vehicle for publishing historical documents that had been properly edited.[46] The executive council of the AHA approved his proposal, but it was not until 1895 that it created a Historical Manuscripts Commission, of which Jameson was appointed the first chairman, "for the preparation or supervision of a calendar of original manuscripts and records of national interest relating to colonial and later history of the United States."[47] Preeminently, the commission's intention was to link and organize the work of libraries, archives, and historical societies, both in this country and abroad.

For all practical purposes, Jameson *was* the Historical Manuscripts Commission, and its chairmanship offered him the means to pursue his study of southern constitutional and political history. Thus, in its annual report of

1897, the commission announced that most of its time and effort during the preceding year had been devoted to collecting the correspondence of John C. Calhoun. "In view of the eminence of that statesman, his long career and varied services, and the relation in which he stands to some of the most vital and dramatic struggles of our national history," the report concluded, "the members of the commission were early convinced that they could perform no service to American history more important" than the publication of the Calhoun correspondence.[48] When this correspondence was published as part of the AHA annual report for 1899, it marked the end of Jameson's tenure as chairman of the Historical Manuscripts Commission, while the volume itself provided a basis of comparison against which to measure succeeding editions of historically significant correspondence.[49] Because Jameson also had been appointed in 1895 as the first managing editor of the *American Historical Review*, a position he held alongside that of chairman of the Historical Manuscripts Commission, it was apparent by the turn of the century that a career unique in the annals of American scholarship was taking shape. By force of argument, ability, and sheer determination, Jameson was drawing together virtually all the elements that now constitute the American historical profession: teaching, research and writing, documentary editing, journal editing, institution building, and advocacy. Indeed, it appeared increasingly that an institutional network and a new profession, rather than a great work of historical synthesis, would be his magnum opus.

The combination of Jameson's accomplishments and activities made him an increasingly influential figure within the historical community. Thus he spoke with particular force in his address "The Functions of State and Local Historical Societies with Respect to Research and Publication" to the 1897 annual meeting of the AHA. Historical societies had failed to look at local history as "American history locally exemplified," Jameson complained. This shortsightedness resulted in part from the failure of the societies to make college professors of history aware of the significance of their holdings. He noted that "the professor is daily occupied with the teaching of general American history. His mind is set on that. He can care little for local history that has not an infusion of that larger element." Moreover, historical societies cut themselves off from academic researchers by restricting themselves to the period in American history up to and including the Revolutionary War. Here again, the explanation was obvious: the society's most venerable patrons wanted it that way. Jameson was sympathetic but stern: "An historical society must not disdain popularity; but it shows a woeful, and to my mind a quite unnecessary, want of courage if it avoids topics of real importance because they are not yet objects of popular interest, or permits popular fancies to divert it from what it really thinks to be its best work." Historical societies might serve both scholar and patron, Jameson urged, through the promotion of economic history, "for there is nothing more certain to interest the business man, that arbiter of all American destinies, than the history of American business."[50]

An opportunity that arose early in 1902 to create an institute for historical research within the newly endowed Carnegie Institution of Washington promised to answer Jameson's desire to unify the historical profession in America, set a single standard of scholarship for each of its members, lift that scholarship out of the parochialism encouraged by geographic isolation, and provide historians in any part of the country with the tools to do research. A plan for this research institute was presented to the Carnegie Institution trustees in 1902 by a committee of the AHA, consisting of Jameson, the patrician historian Charles Francis Adams, Jr., and Andrew C. McLaughlin, professor of history at the University of Michigan. This committee initially had been established to propose ways to utilize the five-thousand-dollar bequest left the AHA by Herbert B. Adams, its longtime secretary.[51] The inspiration and details for the plan were supplied largely by Jameson, who saw in the ten-million-dollar Carnegie endowment a much larger field of action.

Encouraged by Daniel C. Gilman, the Carnegie Institution's first president, to state his objectives, Jameson proposed in January 1902 that the Carnegie Institution take the *American Historical Review* under its wing because this would enable the *Review* to pay leading historians to write articles for it. Articles from these individuals would bring them more securely within the professional fold, while their work would provide an example for younger scholars to emulate. Guides to foreign archives published by the new historical institute would bring to light significant documents for American history, and transcripts of these documents would greatly reduce the need for extended and expensive trips overseas. The institute for historical research would function as a clearinghouse of information for the entire historical profession. A school of history, which Jameson first had designated as the primary beneficiary of the Adams bequest, would be open only to the most highly regarded professors and graduate students. The school would become the vehicle by which the profession's elite stimulated and controlled the lines of research it thought profitable, providing assistance to established practitioners and to students believed most likely to benefit by it.[52]

Along with describing his plans for an institute of historical research in the nation's capital, Jameson gave a detailed resume for the job of director that happened to match his own. As he informed a close confidant, "there is a bee in my bonnet and I cannot dislodge it: the notion, namely, that I should like that post myself." He felt secure in his position at Chicago, but the possibilities of this new job in Washington seemed to outshine even those of a department head in one of the most highly regarded universities in the country: "Its influence on the work of the profession would be great, or might be made so."[53] Much to his disappointment, Jameson was passed over in 1903 for the directorship of what was first the "Bureau," then "Department," of

Historical Research, in favor of his close friend, Andrew C. McLaughlin.[54] In retrospect, it may seem puzzling that Jameson was not chosen as the first director of the bureau, but McLaughlin was the current editor of the *American Historical Review*, which the Carnegie Institution agreed to support, and he along with William M. Sloane of Princeton and George B. Adams of Yale negotiated with John S. Billings, the most influential Carnegie Institution trustee, over the form and purpose of the Bureau of Historical Research. As a trustee of the Johns Hopkins University when Jameson was a student and instructor there in the 1880s, Billings may have known him indirectly, but it is not surprising that McLaughlin, with whom Billings had dealt personally, should have been chosen to organize the Bureau of Historical Research.[55]

When Jameson succeeded McLaughlin at the Carnegie Institution two years later, in the fall of 1905, he lost no time in identifying his priorities. Speaking to the Columbia Historical Society in Washington, D.C., late in 1905, Jameson restated his belief that none of the agencies concerned with history—the federal government as well as state and local historical societies—were proceeding in an orderly and systematic fashion, in contrast to the well-organized efforts of European governments and historical institutions. Attempts by government agencies to publish significant historical documents were "casual and miscellaneous"; historical societies were "prone to publish what seems at the moment most interesting or most available, provided of course it is of date anterior to 1783, at which date for most of them American history comes to an end." Individuals publishing documents exerted much energy to little effect; taken all together, "the result is chaos."[56]

Given the need to establish an agenda, how were these disparate agencies and institutions to proceed? Because Jameson was discussing documentary publications, he logically emphasized the kind of history to which this material seemed to lend itself, that of the great national political figures and the institutions they created. He insisted that "even after the tide has set in the direction of economic and social history strongly, even violently, as is the manner of American currents, even in that socialistic millennium toward which we are no doubt advancing, it is to be hoped that students, however fascinated with the narrative and the theory of social movement, however penetrated with the conviction that economic forces have controlled all human destinies, will yet remember that for the last four hundred years the actual form in which human life has mainly run its course has been that of the nation."[57]

Jameson's position as director of the Department of Historical Research between 1905 and 1928 provided him the perfect vantage point from which he could scan the entire scholarly world in order to see how its different parts might be better coordinated. Indeed, it appears that, increasingly, the scholarly community and the public at large expected him to assume this function. When the American Antiquarian Society marked the opening of its new headquarters and library in October 1910, it turned to Jameson, as well as to Edward Channing of Harvard University and John B. McMaster of the University of Pennsylvania, two senior statesmen of the historical profession, to address the question of the state of historical scholarship in America. The same year, Earlham College, whose president, Harlow Lindley, had studied under Jameson at the University of Chicago, invited the distinguished scholar-administrator to deliver its commencement address, and he responded with a discussion of the control of higher education in America. Both of these statements marked Jameson as a penetrating student of the interplay between scholarship and the increasingly complex institutional world within which it now operated.

In Jameson's view, scholarship would reinforce, and largely benefit from, a national network of institutions and philanthropic activities. There was certainly no escape from coming within the orbit of the modern organizational world. "It may be that our educational life, like our industrial life, must advance by natural and in the end beneficent evolution into stages of greater and greater national consolidation, and that we must reconcile ourselves to the régime of trusts," he noted somberly in his address at Earlham College. "But at all events it is well to see the possible evils, as well as the obvious benefits, inherent in the new order." Chief among these evils was the potentially corrupting effect of corporate influence, but, Jameson concluded, "tyranny for tyranny, one would rather have that of the large-minded New York multimillionaire and his literary or charitable confidants than that of the swelling local magnate, with his narrow horizon, his bigoted dogmatism, his bumptious self-confidence."[58]

Foremost among his many nationalizing activities was Jameson's managing editorship of the *American Historical Review*, a position he had given up in coming to the University of Chicago in 1901, and which he resumed at the Carnegie Institution four years later. While he consulted with the members of his editorial board over which articles the *Review* would accept, he took sole responsibility for turning down potential contributors and displayed little patience with those who questioned his autocratic behavior. The *Review* was "not edited by a town meeting," he explained to board member Edward P. Cheyney, "but it is edited in the interest of all, and I should think that anybody would see that." If some disagreed with him, he professed unconcern, quoting Cromwell, "I know not why they should not be as well at our mercy as we at theirs."[59]

Editing the *Review*, Jameson stressed the significance of national, as opposed to local or regional, history. The author of a paper on alterations in the western boundary of Arkansas, which Jameson at first chose not to examine at all, insisted that his essay was "written primarily from the national view point."[60] The complaint won the paper a reading, but Jameson still declined to publish it because "the history of boundary arrangements is intrinsically one that can hardly be treated in such a manner as to give that readableness which a general historical journal must seek to maintain."[61]

Displaying more tolerance and even encouragement for new approaches to history than was often recognized by his contemporaries, Jameson nevertheless envisaged the historical profession as a hierarchy in which scholars gained both recognition and intellectual latitude as they matured. That he rejected many articles submitted to the *American Historical Review* by younger historians inevitably generated resentment and the suspicion that both the *Review* and the American Historical Association were held hostage by a small clique of conservative men. These suspicions were strengthened by the patronizing attitude that Jameson displayed toward those who criticized his conduct. "Opinions will always differ as to the respective values of experience and of new blood in the management of scientific organizations," he reminded John Latané, a professor at Johns Hopkins, yet those institutions "whose forms of administration have necessarily been a matter of much study to me" consistently favored continuity in office.[62] He tended to shrug off attacks. "I look forward to the time when there will be an increasing, and ultimately irresistible chorus of those who say that Jameson, though well enough in his own day, has become quite impossible now," he admitted in 1913, "but, having no means of support except history, am desirous to postpone the cataclysm as long as possible."[63]

Between 1913 and 1915 a group of insurgent scholars, largely from the West and the South, and led by Latané, the patrician historian Frederic Bancroft, and Dunbar Rowland, the state archivist of Mississippi, charged that the leaders of the AHA, including Jameson, were both autocratic and malfeasant. The membership of the association rejected these charges at its annual meeting in December 1915, but Jameson was embittered. "I do not recognize myself in the printed descriptions," he complained, "but I have read them, all right."[64]

The entry of the United States into the First World War provided Jameson an unexpected opportunity to reassert his leadership over the historical profession. Having watched their public standing fall in relation to that of physical, biological, and social scientists, some academic historians sought to place their discipline at the service of the government as it attempted to rally support for the war effort. It was for just this reason that Jameson convened a meeting of prominent historians in April 1917 at the offices of the Department of Historical Research to organize the National Board for Historical Service.[65] While others directed this agency from his offices, Jameson contributed historical lectures to be delivered in army training camps and edited similar lectures written by other historians.[66] More significantly for historical scholarship, he brought the *Review* under the aegis of the war effort, soliciting articles that, while intended to display scientific neutrality, in fact laid the blame for the war entirely at Germany's doorstep.[67]

Ironically, as Jameson had seen himself rebuked by insurgents within the historical profession for what appeared to be a long career of service, so did his participation in the war effort ultimately bring him public censure. In the spring of 1918 Jameson and Samuel N. Harper, a political science professor and Russian expert at the University of Chicago, were called by the government's Committee on Public Information to certify the authenticity of documents produced by Edgar G. Sisson that indicated German collusion in the ascent of the Bolsheviks to power in Russia. With no expertise and not much hesitation, Jameson joined Harper in declaring most of the documents to be genuine. As a result, he found himself subject to sharp criticism from the *New York Post* and the *Nation*, which judged the documents to be complete forgeries.[68] Any doubts about the authenticity of the documents in Jameson's mind was assuaged by the conviction that the Bolsheviks were capable of anything.[69]

It must have been with a sense of relief that Jameson in the postwar years turned away from internecine struggles among historians, and from public commentators who appeared to him uninformed about politics and unappreciative of his very considerable accomplishments. Instead, he returned to the task around which he had built much of his career: mediating between the realm of ideas and the world of money. The novelty of Jameson's position at the Carnegie Institution matched perfectly the skills that he brought to it. Bringing scholars and their corporate and governmental patrons together required an entrepreneur who understood the patron's desire for rationality and recognition, and who knew as well the impossibility of fitting scholarship precisely within the confines of anyone's organizational chart.[70]

Jameson's immediate concern was the reconstruction of international scholarship in the wake of terrible destruction. The end of the world war found the international scholarly community in ruins. As the only western power that had emerged from the war relatively unscathed, the United States, in Jameson's view, had an obligation to rebuild this community. To this task, Jameson applied himself with a remarkable degree of finesse and political astuteness. Using his extensive organizational contacts, Jameson located entire sets of the *Review* and sent them to European libraries. He solicited work and funds for destitute Viennese archivists to search collections in their custody and to transcribe materials pertaining to American history; in the process, he may have saved some of these individuals from starvation.[71] When Konrad Eubel, a German Franciscan priest and historian, urgently needed funds in 1920 to complete his monumental *Hierarchia Catholica*, a compendium of information about all the significant prelates in the history of Christianity, Jameson suggested to the archbishop of Baltimore that, with postwar Europe devastated, Catholics in America "should take the honor and duty of finishing this great work, one of the glories of Catholic scholarship."[72]

Scholars at home as well as abroad benefited from Jameson's broad interests and seemingly inexhaustible energy, the latter trait especially remarkable for a man who in 1919 turned sixty years old. Carter G. Woodson, the eminent black historian, sought support from the Rockefeller Foundation in 1930 for his efforts in collecting significant manuscripts in black history. At Woodson's request, Jameson advised John D. Rockefeller, Jr., president of the foundation, that Woodson was a distinguished scholar pursuing a significant subject, adding that there existed "a great deal of illustrative material in negro hands which a competent and persuasive negro worker can attain for permanent preservation more easily than any white collector."[73]

As a prime mover behind the establishment of the American Council of Learned Societies in 1920, Jameson proved to be the perfect interlocutor in drawing out the common interests among philologians, historians, archeologists, and others whose thoughts rarely intersected. He was convinced that "in order to vindicate a claim for money, we should have to show in concrete terms, coming down to brass tacks, what we should do with it if we had it." Jameson pressed scholars contemplating such projects as a glossary of medieval Latin to compose "such arguments as first occur to you, together with a few capital instances that would be convincing to the mind of such lawyers or executives or business men as we find on important boards nowadays."[74] In 1926 Jameson persuaded Adolph Ochs, the owner and publisher of the *New York Times*, to underwrite the publication of the *Dictionary of American Biography* through the ACLS with a gift of five hundred thousand dollars. This achievement provoked a colleague to tell Jameson that "had you been willing to enter upon a less glorious career than the one which you chose, you would now have been senior partner in the firm of J. Pierpont Morgan, or else would have owned all the railroads in the country."[75] Jameson envisaged this dictionary as "a work that is monumental in the strict sense of the word" because it would produce "an immeasurable impression upon the American mind, spreading, through means of public and private libraries alike, the sense of what Americans have done in the making of America."[76]

Additionally, in 1926 President Calvin Coolidge signed an Omnibus Public Buildings Act providing one million dollars toward the construction of a national archives building and marking a successful conclusion to nearly twenty years of unremitting effort on Jameson's part to secure this objective.[77] Jameson realized early in his tenure at the Carnegie Institution that only by the most oblique methods could he overcome the conviction held by both elected officials and bureaucrats that scholars were a nuisance to be tolerated at best and ignored if possible.

Agency officials might be willing at first merely to deposit unwanted records in a warehouse, subject to their strict control, he remarked to President William H. Taft's personal secretary in 1910, "but such a régime would not continue many years before the advantages of a centralized archive administration would be apparent and the way would be open to its creation without much friction."[78] In 1930, when Congress was considering legislation to create the National Archives as an independent organization, Jameson reminded a colleague that historical scholars were "a feeble folk, that far more than nine-tenths of all the impulse toward erecting an archive building comes from the business needs of the government, and that all legislation respecting it would be shaped far more by hard-boiled officials of the chief clerk or file clerk variety than by historians."[79]

Occasionally, even Jameson's considerable influence and skill could not prevent government officials from using their authority in a manner that crippled rather than assisted historical research. In 1914 the secretary of the Smithsonian Institution exercised his prerogative as publisher of the AHA's annual report to exclude several essays in American religious and political history that he thought too provocative. Jameson protested in vain against this act of government censorship, confessing to the author of one of the banned articles, "Mexican Feeling Toward the United States in 1846," that "it seems a pity that when Congressmen can say the most irritating things about Mexico day after day, a scientific presentation of Mexican opinion seventy years ago can not be printed for fear of offending their delicate sense of propriety."[80]

Throughout much of his life Jameson maintained a physical presence that was as imposing, even intimidating, as his professional standing. As a college student, his appearance suggested that Jameson was undernourished. When he was a junior at Amherst, he stood six feet tall and weighed just over 141 pounds. His classmates noted in the college yearbook for 1878 that "Jameson has decided not to rent his legs for fish poles."[81] With the passage of time, however, Jameson's well-proportioned figure and disciplined demeanor came to inspire awe even as they hid a thoughtful and generous personality. Waldo G. Leland, Jameson's chief aide for nearly all the years he spent at the Carnegie Institution, recalled in his sketch for the *Dictionary of American Biography* a man whose sharply defined features matched the economy of his thought and speech. As a younger man, Jameson's gray eyes contrasted with the reddish-brown color of his hair, but then complemented the thinning gray hair of his maturity, his once-full beard trimmed to a point. "His habitual expression was austere, cold, even stern," Leland observed, "and belied his true nature, which was revealed by frequent warm and friendly smiles."

This unusual combination of reserve and genuine concern created a profound impression even upon those who made his acquaintance only briefly. A historian who met him at the Library of Congress, when he was chief of the Manuscript Division and she was a graduate student, recalled more than fifty years later "the cordiality of Dr. Jameson's reception of this fledgling, the time that he took to show me the division and some of its collection, the absence of any hint that my intrusion upon him was presumptuous."[82] The members of Jameson's staff at the Department of Historical Research received the same treatment while they worked for him. Upon the publication in 1935 of the fourth and final volume of *Documents Illustrative of the History of the Slave Trade to America*, Jameson informed Elizabeth Donnan, the editor, that in his opinion "there never was a finer piece of work done in the making of any book of documents for American history."[83] Close friends, who were in fact numerous, as well as subordinates knew Jameson as a man who accepted his own foibles, and those of other people, with humor and understanding. "I have acquired a small motor boat, and find that there are '57 varieties' of ignorance regarding its management," he reported in 1917 to an assistant from his summer offices in North Edgecomb, Maine. "I have got so far that I can now avoid two or three of the 57 consequent misfortunes."[84]

The personal cost to Jameson of his staggering list of responsibilities and achievements was an absorption in his work that left little time for relaxation, other than long hikes with his friends George L. Burr of Cornell University and Francis A. Christie of Meadville Theological Seminary, or for his family. His congenial home life required a degree of understanding from his wife, Sara Elwell Jameson, and his two children, Katrina and Francis, that he acknowledged, even if he could not always reciprocate. The youngest of eight children in a family that traced its lineage in America to the Pilgrims on her father's side and to the Dutch in New Netherland through her mother, "Sallie" Elwell was born in Irvington, New Jersey, in 1865 and grew up in Brooklyn. She was a school teacher living at the same rooming house in Providence in which Jameson as a professor at Brown University lodged during the winter of 1891–92. Severely introverted before he met Sara, Jameson was captivated by her. Engaged in the summer of 1892, they were married in Brooklyn in April 1893, and five years later their first child, Katrina, was born.[85]

Jameson indulged both Katrina and his son, Francis Christie Elwell Jameson, born in 1909, but with this permissiveness came the understanding that he had many other claims on his attention. Invited in 1916 to visit Chicago and his longtime friend Andrew McLaughlin, Jameson regretfully declined, citing Katrina's graduation from private school as a more compelling engagement. "I do far too little for my family," he confessed, "see far too little of them, have been too far from acting the part of the ideal parent in my daughter's painful progress in education to feel that I could readily stay away from so important a stage in it, now that she is beginning to make it more of a success."[86]

Accomplishments as an organizer of historical and humanistic research and finally as a writer of history seemingly reinforced in Jameson the conviction he first expressed as an instructor at Johns Hopkins that cooperative scholarship necessarily produced second-rate work, while only individual

genius gave birth to great narrative history. Cooperative ventures, he concluded in 1926, promised at best a summation of previous scholarship rather
than the sources of seminal ideas, while "your big books that treat whole
areas in an even and satisfactory manner have to wait until later, and anyhow
are better done on the spontaneous impulse of individual talent, because
you do not easily coax Pegasus into the harness."[87] But even after he was
forced into retirement in 1928 by John C. Merriam, the unsympathetic pale-
ontologist who succeeded Robert Woodward as president of the Carnegie
Institution in 1920, Jameson discovered that the historical profession, many
of whose members at one time dismissed him as hopelessly antiquarian,
had embraced with fervor the ideal of a standardized historical product that
he put forward in his inaugural address at the University of Chicago over
twenty years earlier. He was saved from both ignominy and financial embarrassment by Herbert Putnam, the librarian of Congress, who invited him
in 1927 to assume the position of chief of the Division of Manuscripts at the
Library and to become the first incumbent of the William Evarts Benjamin
chair in American history. During his tenure the Division of Manuscripts
increased tremendously in the number and size of its collections and in stat-
ure, as the papers of Alexander Stephens, Andrew Carnegie, Admiral John
Dahlgren, Justice Joseph Story, and Joseph Pulitzer, as well as those of abo-
litionists, plantation owners, journalists, and diplomats joined the collected
papers of American presidents and other public figures.[88]

Jameson found himself the object of extended and heartfelt tributes at a
1928 dinner in New York on the occasion of his retirement from the Carnegie Institution.[89] Even more gratifying must have been the invitation from
Arthur M. Schlesinger to compose an introduction to *Historical Scholarship in
America*, a 1932 report of the AHA Committee on Research. From the most
tentative beginnings, he observed, a body of historical literature had developed, "very impressive in quantity and, on the whole, in quality." Yet there
remained for Jameson in this efflorescence of activity, as in the society at
large, an element of disorder that offended his sense of institutional, social,
and cultural discipline. "One would not wish to see research unduly regimented," he pointed out, "but those whom 'this unchartered freedom tires'
will be glad if the present publication leads to a little more careful planning in
the endeavor to see that work is directed toward things that are suffering to
be done, and away from fields already cultivated to the point of diminishing
returns."[90]

At the age of seventy-three, and long since honored with the unofficial
title of "dean of the historical profession," Jameson could no more allow
his sense of rectitude and scholarly mission to lapse than he could cease to
breathe. Unlike many of his colleagues, whose books had been subjected to
analysis and discussion in the pages of the *American Historical Review* and
then set aside in the relentless process of investigation he had fostered,

Jameson's good works—the *Review*, the National Archives, the Carnegie archival guides and documentary editions, the *Atlas* of American history, the *Dictionary of American Biography*, tireless assistance to individual scholars—permeated the atmosphere within which scholars wrote and talked and taught. The nation and the world marked his death on September 28, 1937, with appropriate statements of appreciation—the Columbia historian Evarts B. Greene remarked that Jameson was "so much the centre of the Historical Association and related activities for nearly half a century that it is hard to think of them without him."[91] Yet even his closest associates could comprehend only the smallest part of what Jameson had accomplished, and the same has been true for succeeding generations. We have yet to walk through many of the doors he unlocked; that we can do so at will is John Franklin Jameson's permanent gift to scholarship.

Morey Rothberg

NOTES

1. See Morey D. Rothberg, " 'To Set a Standard of Workmanship and Compel Men to Conform to It': John Franklin Jameson as Editor of the *American Historical Review*," AHR 89 (October 1984): 961.

2. Magali Sarfatti Larson, *The Rise of Professionalism: A Sociological Analysis* (Berkeley and Los Angeles: University of California Press, 1977), pp. 66–80.

3. Larson, *Rise of Professionalism*, pp. 144–45.

4. John Jameson to JFJ, September 19, 1880, ALS, Box 5, JP, DLC.

5. Mariette Jameson to JFJ, January 12, 1880, ALS, Box 5, JP, DLC. See also Morey D. Rothberg, "Servant to History: A Study of John Franklin Jameson, 1859–1937" (Ph.D. dissertation, Brown University, 1982), chapter 1.

6. JFJ, "Buddha," July 3, 1879, AMS, Box 43, JP, DLC.

7. JFJ, "The Disturbances in Barbados in 1876," this volume, pp. 11–12.

8. See [JFJ], diary, February 4–May 1, [1867], AD, Box 1, JP, DLC.

9. Herbert B. Adams, "The Germanic Origins of New England Towns," *Johns Hopkins University Studies in Historical and Political Science* 1 (1882): 8, 18; see also Rothberg, "Servant to History," pp. 45–46.

10. JFJ, diary, September 28, [1883], AD, Box 3, JP, DLC. See also John Higham, *History: Professional Scholarship in America* (1967; reprint ed., Baltimore: Johns Hopkins University Press, 1983), pp. 160–62; Peter Novick, *That Noble Dream: The "Objectivity Question" and the American Historical Profession* (Cambridge, England: Cambridge University Press, 1988), pp. 80–84; and Marvin E. Gettleman, "Introduction," to Gettleman, ed., *The Johns Hopkins University Seminary of History and Politics: The Records of an American Educational Institution, 1877–1912*, 4 vols. (New York: Garland Press, 1987–), 1:60–64.

11. I have found instructive in considering Jameson's intellectual and political beliefs the remarks made by John Higham on September 28, 1987, at a ceremony at the National Archives on the fiftieth anniversary of Jameson's death.

12. JFJ, diary, October 27, [1882], AD, Box 2, JP, DLC; JFJ, diary, October 18, [1886], AD, Box 4, JP, DLC. See also Morey D. Rothberg, "The Brahmin as Bureaucrat: J. Franklin Jameson at the Carnegie Institution of Washington, 1905–1928," *Public Historian* 8 (Fall 1986): 49; and Edward N. Saveth, *American Historians and European Immigrants, 1875–1925* (New York: Columbia University Press, 1948), pp. 14, 15.

13. JFJ, diary, November 26, [1883], AD, Box 3, JP, DLC.

14. Hippolyte A. Taine, *The Ancient Regime*, trans. John Durand (1881; reprint ed., Freeport: Books for Libraries Press, 1972), pp. viii–x, 179–80. See also Rothberg, "Servant to History," pp. 51–52.

15. See Henry Thomas Buckle, *History of Civilization in England*, 2 vols. (New York: D. Appleton and Company, 1876), 1:109–13; see also Rothberg, "Servant to History," p. 52.

16. JFJ, diary, October 19, [1881], AD, Box 2, JP, DLC.

17. JFJ, "An Introduction to the Constitutional and Political History of the States," this volume, p. 18.

18. JFJ, diary, March 15, [1883], AD, Box 3, JP, DLC.

19. John David Smith, *An Old Creed for the New South: Proslavery Ideology and Historiography, 1865–1918* (Westport: Greenwood Press, 1985), chapter 5. In the fall of 1884, thirteen of the thirty graduate students in history at Johns Hopkins came from Maryland, twelve of these from Baltimore. The subject of slavery in the antebellum North stimulated a lively debate in the seminary in the spring of 1885 and a paper on the subject by Jameson. *Johns Hopkins University Circulars* 4 (November 1884): 8–10; JFJ, "What Became of the Northern Slaves?," May 22, 1885, AM, Box 25, JP, DLC. See also Hugh Hawkins, *Pioneer: A History of the Johns Hopkins University, 1874–1889* (Ithaca: Cornell University Press, 1960), p. 271; and James Curtis Ballagh, "The Johns Hopkins University and the South," *Johns Hopkins University Circulars* 20 (January 1901): 23. For this and other related information, I acknowledge the research assistance of Jacqueline Goggin.

20. Jameson explicitly compared the problems Britain experienced in governing Barbadian blacks to those encountered by whites in the American South, although he later regretted introducing this sensitive issue in the seminary. JFJ, "Disturbances in Barbados," this volume, p. 11; JFJ, diary, November 19, [1880], AD, Box 1, JP, DLC.

21. See JFJ, diary, July 6, [1885], AD, Box 3, JP, DLC; JFJ, diary, September 30, [1889], AD, Box 4, JP, DLC; JFJ to John Jameson, April 1, 1888, ALS, Box 8, JP, DLC.

22. Herbert B. Adams to JFJ, May 15, 1890, TLS; July 3, 14, 1890, both ALS,

all in Box 46, JP, DLC; see also [JFJ], "A Little Journey of Historical Research in Eastern Virginia," paper delivered to the Rhode Island Historical Society, February 23, 1892, TM, Box 28, JP, DLC.

23. See Rothberg, "Servant to History," pp. 123–24.

24. JFJ, "Lectures on the Constitutional and Political History of the South," this volume, p. 84.

25. [JFJ], "Virginian History, 1763–1812," lectures delivered at the Peabody Institute, [Baltimore], Jan. 28, Feb. 2, 4, 1892[:] I, "Virginia and the Revolution, 1763–1783," p. 11, AM, Box 28, JP, DLC; see also [JFJ], "A Little Journey of Historical Research," p. 38.

26. JFJ, "Lectures on the Constitutional and Political History of the South," this volume, pp. 144, 160; see also Rothberg, "Servant to History," pp. 124–26; and Rothberg, "To Set a Standard of Workmanship," p. 73.

27. JFJ, "The Origin of Political Parties in the United States," lecture read in Manning Hall, Dec. 1, 1890; Middlebury, Vt., May 6, 1892; this volume, pp. 47, 49–50.

28. [JFJ], "The Revolution as a Social Movement: I, Whigs and Tories," [1895], TM, Box 25, JP, DLC. The manuscript copy of this lecture is fragmentary, making pagination here impractical.

29. [JFJ], "Revolution as a Social Movement."

30. See Rothberg, "Servant to History," pp. 128–29.

31. See John M. Manly to JFJ, September 30, [1900], ALS, Box 111, JP, DLC.

32. JFJ, "The Influence of Universities upon Historical Writing," this volume, p. 270.

33. "The Department of History," in *Annual Register, July, 1901–July, 1902 with Announcements for 1902–3* (Chicago: University of Chicago, [1902]), pp. 209–11.

34. "The Department of History," in *Annual Register, July, 1902–July, 1903 with Announcements for 1903–4* (Chicago: University of Chicago, [1903], p. 237; "The Department of History," in *Annual Register, July, 1903–July, 1904 with Announcements for 1904–5* (Chicago: University of Chicago, [1904]), pp. 231, 234.

35. Rothberg, "Servant to History," p. 203.

36. JFJ, "The American Acta Sanctorum," this volume, pp. 178, 179; see also Rothberg, "Servant to History," pp. 269–70.

37. JFJ, "The Future Uses of History," this volume, p. 314.

38. [JFJ] to Ulrich B. Phillips, November 25, 1905, TLc, Box 265, AHA Records, DLC. See also Ulrich B. Phillips, "The Origin and Growth of the Southern Black Belts," *AHR* 11 (July 1906): 798–816.

39. See Albert B. Faust, *Guide to the Materials for American History in Swiss and Austrian Archives* (Washington, D.C.: Carnegie Institution of Washington, 1916); William H. Allison, *Inventory of Unpublished Material for American Religious History in Protestant Church Archives and Other Repositories* (Wash-

ington, D.C.: Carnegie Institution of Washington, 1910); Elizabeth Donnan, ed., *Documents Illustrative of the History of the Slave Trade to America*, 4 vols. (Washington, D.C.: Carnegie Institution of Washington, 1930–35); Helen H. Catterall, ed., *Judicial Cases Concerning American Slavery and the Negro*, 5 vols. (Washington, D.C.: Carnegie Institution of Washington, 1926–37); Charles Oscar Paullin, *Atlas of the Historical Geography of the United States* (Washington, D.C., and New York: Published jointly by the Carnegie Institution of Washington and the American Geographical Society of New York, 1932); JFJ, ed., *Privateering and Piracy in the Colonial Period. Illustrative Documents* (New York: Macmillan Company, 1923; reprint ed., New York: Augustus M. Kelley, 1970).

40. [JFJ] to Dana Munro, October 22, 27, 1925, both TLc, Box 114, JP, DLC; "Dr. Jameson to Lecture," *New York Times*, November 3, 1925, p. 16, col. 2; JFJ to Merle Curti, November 18, 1936, TLS, Box 21, Merle Curti Papers, WHi.

41. See, for example, J. Allen Smith, *The Spirit of American Government: A Study of the Constitution: Its Origin, Influence and Relation to Democracy* (New York: Macmillan Company, 1907); Charles A. Beard, *An Economic Interpretation of the Constitution of the United States* (New York: Macmillan Company, 1913); Charles H. Lincoln, *The Revolutionary Movement in Pennsylvania, 1760–1776* (1901; reprint ed., Cos Cob: J. E. Edwards, 1968); Carl L. Becker, *The History of Political Parties in the Province of New York, 1760–1776*, Bulletin of the University of Wisconsin 2 (April 1909): 1–319; Arthur M. Schlesinger, *The Colonial Merchants and the American Revolution, 1763–1776* (New York: Columbia University, 1918); James Truslow Adams, *Revolutionary New England* (Boston: Atlantic Monthly Press, 1923); and Arthur Schlesinger, *New Viewpoints in American History* (New York: Macmillan Company, 1922), pp. 160–83.

42. JFJ, *The American Revolution Considered as a Social Movement* (Princeton: Princeton University Press, 1967), p. 18.

43. See Morey Rothberg, "John Franklin Jameson and the Creation of *The American Revolution Considered as a Social Movement*," in Ronald Hoffman and Peter J. Albert, eds., *"The Transforming Hand of Revolution": Reconsidering the American Revolution as a Social Movement* (Charlottesville: University Press of Virginia, forthcoming, 1993).

44. JFJ, "The Development of Modern European Historiography," The *Atlantic Monthly* 66 (September 1890): 332.

45. JFJ, "The Expenditures of Foreign Governments in Behalf of History," in AHA, *Annual Report*, 1891 (Washington, D.C.: Government Printing Office, 1892), p. 43. See AHA, *Annual Report*, 1890 (Washington, D.C.: Government Printing Office, 1891), pp. 9–10, for a notice of Jameson's paper.

46. AHA, *Annual Report*, 1890, p. 10.

47. AHA, *Annual Report*, 1895 (Washington, D.C.: Government Printing Office, 1896), p. 10. The other members of the commission were Douglas Brymner, Talcott Williams, William P. Trent, and Frederick J. Turner.

48. JFJ et al., "Second Annual Report of the Historical Manuscripts Commission of the American Historical Association," in AHA, *Annual Report*, 1897 (Washington, D.C.: Government Printing Office, 1898), p. 401.

49. JFJ, ed., "Correspondence of John C. Calhoun," in AHA, *Annual Report*, 1899, 2 vols. (Washington, D.C.: Government Printing Office, 1900), vol. 2.

50. JFJ, "The Functions of State and Local Historical Societies with Respect to Research and Publication," this volume, pp. 258–60; see also Rothberg, "Servant to History," p. 153.

51. JFJ, Charles Francis Adams, and Andrew C. McLaughlin, "Report of the Advisory Committee on History," in Carnegie Institution of Washington, *Year Book*, 1902 (Washington, D.C.: Published by the Institution, 1903), pp. 226–31; see Rothberg, "Servant to History," pp. 190–91; on the Herbert B. Adams bequest, see JFJ to the Members of the Executive Council of the American Historical Association, November 23, 1901, PL, Box 134, JP, DLC.

52. Daniel C. Gilman to JFJ, January 14, 1902, TLS, Box 86, JP, DLC; JFJ to Gilman, February 14, 1902, TLS, CIW; Rothberg, "Servant to History," pp. 190–91.

53. JFJ to Francis A. Christie, February 15, 1902, TLS, Box 71, JP, DLC.

54. JFJ to Francis A. Christie, March 6, 1903, TLS, Box 71, JP, DLC.

55. See [Andrew C. McLaughlin] to George B. Adams, February 21, 1902, TLc, Box 258, AHA Records, DLC; [McLaughlin] to JFJ, February 21, 1903, TLc, Box 260, AHA Records, DLC; Adams to McLaughlin, March 1, 1903, TLS, Box 259, AHA Records, DLC. In 1905 *AHR* board member Albert B. Hart hinted that Daniel C. Gilman blocked Jameson's appointment. See Hart to George B. Adams, February 16, 1905, TLS, George B. Adams Papers, CtY.

56. JFJ, "Gaps in the Published Records of United States History," *AHR* 11 (July 1906): 818.

57. JFJ, "Gaps in the Published Records of United States History," p. 819.

58. JFJ, "The Control of the Higher Education in the United States," this volume, pp. 287, 288.

59. [JFJ] to Edward P. Cheyney, August 26, 1914, TLc, Box 279, AHA Records, DLC.

60. J. H. Reynolds to JFJ, September 8, 1908, TLS, Box 271, AHA Records, DLC.

61. [JFJ] to J. H. Reynolds, October 28, 1908, TLc, Box 271, AHA Records, DLC.

62. [JFJ] to John H. Latané, February 28, 1914, TLc, Box 280, AHA Records, DLC.

63. [JFJ] to Frederick J. Turner, June 5, 1913, TLc, Box 279, AHA Records, DLC.

64. [JFJ] to Albert B. Hart, January 8, 1916, TLc, Box 286, AHA Records, DLC. On the insurgency, see Frederic Bancroft, John H. Latané, Dunbar

Rowland, *Why the American Historical Association Needs Thorough Reorganization* (Washington, D.C.: National Capital Press, 1915); American Historical Review, *An Historical Statement Concerning the American Historical Review* (Washington, D.C.: American Historical Review, 1915); Rothberg, "Servant to History," chapters 5, 6; Ray Allen Billington, "Tempest in Clio's Teapot," *American Historical Review* 78 (April 1973): 348–69.

65. See [JFJ], "The National Board for Historical Service," *AHR* 22 (July 1917): 918–19.

66. [JFJ] to Frank Aydelotte, August 28, 1918, TLc, Box 31, Records of the National Board for Historical Service, DLC.

67. See Rothberg, "To Set a Standard of Workmanship," p. 971.

68. See Carol S. Gruber, *Mars and Minerva: World War I and the Uses of the Higher Learning in America* (Baton Rouge: Louisiana State University Press, 1975), pp. 151–53; Stephen Vaughn, *Holding Fast the Inner Lines: Democracy, Nationalism, and the Committee on Public Information* (Chapel Hill: University of North Carolina Press, 1980), p. 77; Christopher Lasch, *The American Liberals and the Russian Revolution* (New York: Columbia University Press, 1962), pp. 112–18; and George F. Kennan, "The Sisson Documents," *Journal of Modern History* 28 (June 1956): 130–54.

69. [JFJ] to Samuel N. Harper, December 11, 1918, TLc, Box 31, Records of the National Board for Historical Service, DLC.

70. Rothberg, "Servant to History," p. 174.

71. [JFJ] to H. Nelson Gay, June 26, 1926, TLc, Box 304, AHA Records; Albert B. Faust to JFJ, April 3, 1920, TLS; [JFJ] to Faust, April 6, 1920, TLc, both in Box 82, JP, DLC.

72. [JFJ] to James Gibbons, August 9, 1920, TLc, Box 86, JP, DLC.

73. [JFJ] to John D. Rockefeller, Jr., April 1, 1930, TLc, Box 125, JP, DLC.

74. JFJ to Charles H. Haskins, January 18, 1921, TLS, Box A1, Records of the American Council of Learned Societies, DLC.

75. Edward C. Armstrong to JFJ, November 23, 1926, TLS, Box 416, AHA Records, DLC.

76. "Dictionary of National Biography Has High Aims," *New York Times*, December 21, 1924, sec. 8, p. 7, col. 1.

77. See Victor Gondos, Jr., *J. Franklin Jameson and the Birth of the National Archives, 1906–1926* (Philadelphia: University of Pennsylvania Press, 1981), pp. 164, 166.

78. [JFJ] to Charles D. Norton, November 21, 1910, TLc, Box 57, JP, DLC.

79. JFJ to Evarts B. Greene, March 28, 1930, TLS, Evarts B. Greene Papers, NNC.

80. [JFJ] to Justin H. Smith, October 23, 1914, TLS, Box 128, JP, DLC.

81. JFJ, diary, April 22, [1878], AD, Box 1, JP, DLC; *The Olio*, December 1878, p. 88.

82. LaWanda Cox to Jacqueline A. Goggin and Morey D. Rothberg, Feb-

ruary 24, 1986, TLS in the possession of the John Franklin Jameson Papers Project.

83. JFJ to Elizabeth Donnan, May 9, 1935, TLS, Box 141, JP, DLC.

84. [JFJ] to Frances G. Davenport, July 12, 1917, TLc, Box 74, JP, DLC.

85. Francis C. Jameson, "Our Jamesons in America," June 1970, TM, in the author's possession, p. 6, cited in Rothberg, "Servant to History," p. 115.

86. [JFJ] to Andrew C. McLaughlin, February 28, 1916, TLc, Box 286, AHA Records, DLC; see also Rothberg, "Servant to History," p. 272.

87. [JFJ] to Waldo G. Leland, February 15, 1926, TLt, Box A2, Records of the American Council of Learned Societies, DLC; see also Rothberg, "The Brahmin as Bureaucrat," p. 58.

88. See the report of the Division of Manuscripts in the *Annual Report of the Librarian of Congress* (Washington, D.C.: Government Printing Office, 1929–37).

89. People who attended this banquet on February 24, 1928, were given a program in the form of a miniature issue of the *American Historical Review*. Included in this program was a comment by Carl L. Becker, professor of history at Cornell University. Becker recalled a remark by his mentor at the University of Wisconsin, Frederick J. Turner, that Jameson was "the salt of the earth." To which Becker now added: "No trace of sugar ever discovered." Copy of program in Box 41, JP, DLC.

90. JFJ, Introduction to American Historical Association, *Historical Scholarship in America: Needs and Opportunities: A Report by the Committee of the American Historical Association on the Planning of Research*, this volume, p. 353.

91. Evarts B. Greene to Laurence Larson, October 9, 1937, ALS, Box 1, Laurence Larson Papers, IU.

SCHOLARSHIP

The Disturbances in Barbados in 1876

The Johns Hopkins University Seminary of Historical and Political Science was a focal point for both students and faculty when Jameson enrolled at the university in the fall of 1880. Open only to graduate students and faculty, the seminary began in 1876, the same year that Johns Hopkins was founded. Students met on Saturday mornings in the library of the Maryland Historical Society under the direction of Austin Scott, who had earned his doctorate at the University of Leipzig. According to Herbert B. Adams, Scott's successor as head of the seminary, the weekly sessions consisted of a short lecture by the seminary director, followed by discussion of subjects that the students had been assigned to investigate.[1] In the seminary, Scott emphasized American constitutional history, having assisted George Bancroft in writing his monumental survey. In contrast, the topic in the seminary under Adams was the history of local self-government, which derived from his graduate studies at the University of Heidelberg.[2] It was at a meeting of the seminary in November 1880 that Jameson delivered his first major paper at Johns Hopkins, the essay "Disturbances in Barbados in 1876."

Jameson's interest in the West Indies can be traced back to his childhood. Both his father and grandfather had traveled to the West Indies during the 1850s in search of business opportunities. In 1867, when Jameson was seven years old, the family made a trip to Barbados, Saint Thomas, and Puerto Rico, staying with friends.[3] Since young Jameson had never before traveled outside of New England, the racial configuration of the population on the islands must have been striking to him. In letters to her mother, Mariette Jameson commented extensively on the racial demography, noting the physical appearance, labor conditions, styles of dress, and the social and religious practices of the Barbadian black population. Jameson explored a number of the islands with his father, visiting sugar plantations and estates, and was confronted at every turn by a black majority.[4]

This early exposure to black people and race relations in the West Indies may have prompted Jameson to explore the 1876 riots and the problem of self-government in Barbados for his seminary paper. He interviewed West Indian merchants and visited the British consulate in Baltimore to obtain leads on sources. Jameson conducted most of his research in the Peabody Library, discovering that newspapers provided the best accounts of labor conditions. By examining labor and race relations in the postemancipation period in Barbados, Jameson intended to provide a comparison with the southern United States during the Reconstruction era, "bringing up analogues with many American troubles."[5]

While the seminary itself met on Saturdays, Jameson gave his paper at Hopkins Hall on Friday evening, November 19, 1880, at a meeting of the Historical and Political Science Association. The association began as an adjunct to the seminary in 1877 and was open to the public.[6] Although the economist Henry C. Adams, who presided over the meeting, privately remarked afterward that Jameson had delivered a "very good paper," the latter was dejected because he received no other words of appreciation, and he regretted that he had referred to race relations in the United States.[7]

NOTES

1. Herbert B. Adams, "New Methods of Study in History," *Johns Hopkins University Studies in Historical and Political Science* 2 (1884): 97–99.

2. Adams, "New Methods of Study," p. 101.

3. [JFJ], diary, February 4–May 1, [1867], AD, Box 1, JP, DLC.

4. See the transcriptions Jameson prepared of his mother's letters to Esther Thompson for the period from February through March 1867 in Box 15, JP, DLC.

5. JFJ, diary, November 1, 9, 16, 19, [1880], AD, Box 1, JP, DLC.

6. Adams, "New Methods of Study," p. 131; *Johns Hopkins University Circulars* 1 (December 1880): 83.

7. JFJ, diary, November 19, [1880], AD, Box 1, JP, DLC.

WHEN I ASK your attention for even a few minutes to a violent constitutional struggle in a colony which is about one-sixth as large as Rhode Island, it may seem that I am much exaggerating the importance of what can have been, at best, only a tempest in a teacup. But there are sometimes reasons which make conflicts whose importance, measured in numbers, is very slight, nevertheless deserving of consideration. It is not impossible that the study of the difficulties of Barbados may throw a little light on similar conditions and events in our own and other countries.

The area of Barbados is indeed very small, only 166 square miles, but of this it is said that 93 per cent. is under cultivation, and the exports of sugar, rum, and molasses give the island a commercial importance much out of proportion to its size. But that which, more than anything else, makes Barbados, next to Jamaica, the most important possession of England in the West Indies, is its dense population. On the little island is gathered a population of 170,000, or something over a thousand to a square mile. No country or island in the world, except Malta, has so dense a population. That of Belgium, the most densely peopled country in Europe, is less than one-half as great; that of Massachusetts, the most crowded of the American states, less than one-fourth.

The chief peculiarity of this dense population is that nine-tenths are colored, the proportion of black to white having constantly increased since the abolition of slavery in 1834. Only a small part of the population is gathered in towns, the plantation-system prevailing there, as in the Southern States. Although socially the color-line was always drawn by the whites in the strictest way, and they alone controlled the politics of the colony, yet there had been no serious conflict between the two races either before or after emancipation of the negroes, down to the administration of Gov. Pope Hennessy.

In their relations to the home government, however, the planters of Barbados had, at several periods during the history of the island, shown great impatience of control, and this apparently with less reason than most colonies. The insular history begins with the year 1605, when the crew of the Olive Blossom landed on the island and carved on the bark of a tree the inscription, "James, king of England and of this island." Within comparatively few years the island came to be the seat of a profitable trade. Undoubtedly the finances of this, as of all other colonies in that age, were managed for the benefit of the mother country, but, to offset this, the islanders enjoyed a representative government of an unusually liberal form. But the planters were constantly demanding more, and the successive English administrations doubtless thought that the island caused them more trouble than its size warranted. Many of the demands of the planters were just, especially those relating to commercial restrictions, but they had, and still have, a very

5

deficient sense of their dependence on the great Empire upon whose map their island is only a speck. An islander whose native country is 22 miles long and 12 miles wide, may be very competent to manage its internal affairs, but he can scarcely understand the magnitude of the interests of England, or appreciate the value of its protection to his little island, which, so far as he can see, would be better off if it had as little connection with the home government as, in the opinion of a contemporary Ohio statesman, the United States of America have with "abroad." [1]

The abolition of slavery in the West Indies in 1834, in spite of the large compensation voted by the English Parliament, destroyed the prosperity of the English colonies in general. The negroes, able to earn their own living by half an hour's labor a day, did not care to work on the sugar plantations of their former masters. In Barbados alone this difficulty was not felt. There all the land was already occupied, and the former slaves, unable to get their living by cultivating land not before appropriated, as in the other islands, were obliged to work as paid laborers for the planters. Hence Barbados has suffered no such commercial decline as the other Windward and Leeward Islands.

After the abolition of slavery, the rule of the island remained, as before, in the hands of the whites. The form of government was at that time, and is now, substantially the same as when first established. The lieutenant-governor, who is also governor-in-chief of the Windward Islands, is appointed by the Secretary of State for the Colonies, and is responsible to the Crown. The legislature is bicameral. The upper house, which till 1876 acted also as the governor's council, consists of twelve members, appointed in theory by the home government, but practically selected by the governor himself. The lower house, or Assembly, consists of twenty-four annually-elected members, being two for each of the eleven parishes into which the island is divided, and two for the town of Bridgetown. Though thus closely imitating the constitution of the English Parliament in some of its forms, yet in the character of the constituencies which it represents the Legislative Assembly of Barbados unfortunately has more resemblance to the Duke of Newcastle's House of Commons than to that of the present day. For in a total population of more than 170,000, there are, on account of a property qualification, only about 1350 voters. Of the twenty-four legislators, two who together represent a population of 8000 are chosen by 24 electors, and another representing a constituency of 10,000 by 92. The assembly thus con-

---

{1.} James Abram Garfield (1831–81), congressman from Ohio, opposed President Grant's efforts to annex Santo Domingo. Garfield believed that this expansion would extend to other islands in the West Indies, and he was concerned that the natives of these islands would never be assimilated into American life. See Allan Peskin, *Garfield: A Biography* (Kent, Ohio: Kent State University Press, 1978), p. 338.

stituted is empowered to make laws for the government of the colony, but these must receive the consent of the governor and council, and must within three months be submitted to the home government for its approval.

This was the state of Barbados at the time of the disturbances in 1876. The cause of those disturbances is to be found in the formation of an executive council independent of the legislative council or upper house, and in a project for the confederation of the Windward Islands. The islands of St. Lucia, St. Vincent, Grenada and Tobago, though much smaller than Barbados even, had each a separate and independent government. Each had its governor, its attorney-general, its various courts, and all the officers and machinery of an independent colony, though the governor of Barbados was also governor-in-chief of the whole group. The impolicy of maintaining so many separate and expensive establishments, and the advantages of confederation, had been evident to several successive colonial secretaries. In 1871 the six Leeward Islands were united in such a confederacy. Two years {later} Lord Kimberley, the secretary of state for the colonies, advised Sir Rawson Rawson,[2] then governor of Barbados, to suggest to the Barbadian Assembly that they should appoint delegates to confer with representatives of the other Windward Islands in regard to the formation of a similar confederation of that group. But the governor took no action in the matter.

The Earl of Carnarvon, who succeeded Lord Kimberley in the formation of the Disraeli cabinet of 1874, was, as is well known, a warm advocate of measures of colonial confederation. Soon after the Hon. John Pope Hennessy was sent out as governor of Barbados, in the fall of 1876, he was instructed by the secretary to recommend such a project to the Barbadian assembly. The chief obstacle to such a plan, it was known, was that while Barbados was solvent and prosperous, the other islands were in a bad state financially, and it was feared that the Barbadian planters might oppose the confederation from the belief that it would bring upon them a share of the indebtedness of the other islands, a burden which would much overbalance the advantages derived from a reduction of the expenses of government. To make such a belief impossible, Lord Carnarvon, in a despatch to the governor, stated, with the clearness which was characteristic of all his papers, that "a community of financial arrangements would not be a feature of a confederation, and that, subject to such contributions as it may be agreed to levy for the maintenance of joint public institutions, the revenue and expenditure of each island would be administered separately, as at present."

Another point in regard to which the Colonial Office is always compelled to be careful, is the avoidance of the slightest appearance of coercion. The smaller the colony, the more jealous it is of interference, and the more deli-

{2.} Rawson William Rawson (1812–99) served as governor-in-chief of the Windward Islands from 1869 to 1875.

cate must be the hints as to what course Her Majesty's Government would recommend. In this particular instance, Lord Carnarvon explicitly declared that "Her Majesty's Government could not proceed with any measure of confederation except on the spontaneous request of each Legislature concerned."

One would think that, if an English cabinet officer ever does sleep, Lord Carnarvon might, so far as Barbados was concerned, have slept soundly after sending to the island so apparently unmistakable an explanation of the nature of his project. But the event showed that it was not unmistakable, at least by West Indian planters, for the legislature of Barbados rejected the proposal. Their reasons seem to have been fear of the debts of the other islands, and fear of being coerced, the very apprehensions which Lord Carnarvon had apparently shown to be needless, by his despatch.

According to the instructions and the intentions of the Colonial Secretary, the decision of the Assembly was final. But Gov. Hennessy could not so consider it. He had entered ardently into the Secretary's projects, and was convinced that confederation would not only improve the management of some of the local institutions, but would also, by reducing taxes and encouraging trade and emigration, raise wages and alleviate the misery of the negro population. He took up the cause of the latter with a laudable English desire to help the weaker, but with much less than English discretion, and, in an address to the Assembly, advocated the undoubtedly advantageous but unpopular measure in a more partisan spirit than became the representative of the Crown, and in terms likely to spread among the negroes the notion that the planters were purposely depriving them of the higher wages which would result from confederation. "I feel confident," said he in the course of his speech, "that no intelligent person who loves Barbados will take the serious responsibility of standing between his poorer countrymen and the wise policy of the British Government.{"}

The assuming by the Governor of the attitude of a champion of popular rights against the selfish aristocracy produced an immediate effect. Riots occurred in various parts of the island. The excitable negroes, believing that for all their proceedings they had the authority of the Governor, began setting fire to the cane-fields, on which the prosperity of the colony almost wholly depends, and robbing the provision-grounds. Finally, as one of these mobs was plundering the estate of a planter, the police fired upon it and one man was killed. Two others, on this or other occasions, received wounds from which they died.

Such occurrences seem trifling enough; but they were sufficient to arouse the wildest excitement in Barbados. The hopeless poverty and utter ignorance of the employed encouraged them to all sorts of attacks on property, in the hope of raising wages, and with the belief, frequently expressed by them, that the Governor approved their course. There was even a rumor among them that Mr. Hennessy was in reality Prince Arthur, sent out by the Queen to help their distress. They clamored for confederation with about as much understanding of their object as had the Russian mob which, some years ago, shouted with great enthusiasm for a Constitution, which they supposed to be the name of the Grand Duke Constantine's wife, or those ardent patriots in Missouri, who, it is said, still vote for Jackson.

On the other hand, the planters were even more excited, and with great reason. Not only did the Governor appear to them to be allying himself with the lowest classes, and unscrupulously urging a project intended to deprive them of their constitutional privileges and that commercial prosperity, based on abundance and cheapness of labor, which distinguished them among all the islands of the British Antilles, but they saw the destruction of their crops and the even more alarming prospect of a negro insurrection, a prospect terrifying under any circumstances, but especially where the colored population outnumbered the white in the proportion of nine to one.

Accordingly, the Barbadian press attacked the Governor with a truly insular violence of passion. The "Defence Association" and the planters individually, sent the most alarming, and, as afterward appeared, exaggerated, telegrams to the Colonial Office, and Lord Carnarvon was overwhelmed with requests for the immediate recall of Gov. Hennessy. Although the latter was regarded as having shown considerable indiscretion, and had, in his despatches, depreciated the importance of the conflict, the Secretary wisely declined to remove him at once, quoting in his speech in the House of Lords Mr. Lincoln's saying, that it was unwise "to swop horses while crossing a stream." Additional troops were ordered from Jamaica, Trinidad and Demerara, and the disturbances were soon ended, without their being compelled to fire a single shot. Ninety persons were taken while engaged in rioting; and afterwards, on suspicion of rioting and receiving stolen goods, 320 more. The trials of these prisoners, the unfairness of the insular chief-justice, and the opposition of the Assembly to Lord Carnarvon's action in sending out a special commissioner from England for their trial, furnish curious evidence of the narrowness and wrongheadedness of the colonists.

Thus tranquility was finally restored. Gov. Hennessy was soon transferred to the governorship of Hong Kong, where he has since had similar troubles from the attempt to ameliorate the condition of the natives. Undoubtedly this was his purpose in Barbados, however indiscreet he may have been in carrying it out. But it is not my intention to discuss the comparative merits of Governor and Assembly. Whatever interest the conflict has, lies, as I have said, in the illustrations which it supplies of similar conditions elsewhere. These bear chiefly upon colonial confederation, the influence of a certain sort of political economy on legislation, and the government of a society composed of members of two different races.

And first, in regard to colonial confederation. Proposals of confederation seem likely to become increasingly frequent in the colonial policy of Great Britain. As a rule, they are not well received by the colonists. And we, remembering our origin from certain refractory colonies, are inclined to decide off-hand in favor of the colonists, and to declare that they must be the best judges as to whether confederation would be advantageous to them. Such is the ordinary American view of the case in Canada, South Africa and Australia. The conduct of the Barbadian Assembly tends strongly to disprove such a view. The confederation-plan, which proposed reforms which were neither sweeping nor unreasonable, was carefully explained by the Secretary, as affecting neither the financial nor the constitutional independence of the colony, but the planter-assembly of Barbados blindly voted it down without serious discussion. The arguments for and against confederation in South Africa and Australia are, to be sure, quite different from those applicable to the Windward Islands, and it is not likely that the governing classes in a large colony will be as narrow-minded as in a very small one. But I think that the example of Barbados must convince us, that the politicians of a colony, even when they do not form an oligarchy divided from the mass of the population by distinction of race and color, are so jealous of any interference with that independence which seems to them far more important than good government, that we ought not to consider their judgment on matters of intercolonial policy as the best possible, nor condemn a measure of confederation because it does not meet their approval.

The economic questions involved in the Barbadian conflict are for the most part either too obscure or too peculiar to Barbados to be discussed here. The only matter of the sort to which I wish to call attention, is the influence upon the planters of certain traditional or hereditary economic theories. It was brought out in the strongest manner, in the debates of the Legislative Assembly, that the planters held to the comfortable belief that the over-population of the island, the exceedingly low rate of wages, and the consequent degradation and misery of the laboring classes, were inevitable, and that they, as the employing class, had no other duties toward the employed than to profit as much as possible by the advantages given them by the cheapness of labor. Accordingly, the legislature made almost no effort to improve the economic condition of the laborers, or to reform the well-filled prisons and lunatic hospitals, and in passing a law nominally promoting emigration, practically nullified it by the important exception that no laborers should emigrate. Now it seems to me that this attitude of the colonists is directly traceable to the influence of the perhaps partially misapprehended maxims of the narrowest school of English economists, which led them to believe that the condition of the island which afforded them the largest gains was also the natural one, and that efforts to change it would be fruitless contests against the unchangeable laws of political economy.

But the most important inferences to be drawn from the account I have given relate to the government of inferior races. When in a dependency or province, whose population has previously consisted of two classes, free and servile, whose social, political and civil status are widely different, the civil inequality is suddenly removed by the emancipation of the inferior class, there are four forms under which the general government may order the dependency or province to be ruled. First, it may grant both the franchise and eligibility to office to all of the former slave-class; this was the course followed by the Republican party in the United States. Second, it may continue the former slave-owners in the exclusive possession of both the franchise and eligibility; this was virtually done in Barbados, by a high property-qualification. Third, it may combine extended suffrage with restricted eligibility, allowing both classes to vote, but compelling them to select their representatives from among a number limited by a property-qualification; this form has not been tried, so far as I know. Fourth, it may temporarily take away local self-government, originating the legislation itself, and establishing as executive a governor impartial to the interests of black and white; this was done with excellent results in Jamaica, which has been a Crown colony since the rebellion of 1865.

The first plan is generally regarded as unwise, though whether in the particular instance of the United States the Republican party did wisely in adopting it, to retain its own supremacy, I do not intend, and indeed do not feel able to discuss. But the example of Barbados should, it seems to me, convince us of the futility of expecting good results from the second plan. The planters were regarded, probably with justice, as having accepted the results of the abolition of slavery. But their legislation remained class-legislation, and the recommendations of several successive governors had scarcely any effect in inducing them to consider the claims of the negroes to legislative attention. Making all allowance for those conditions which were peculiar to Barbados, it yet seems impossible to deny that the plan which failed there would, for similar reasons, be a failure elsewhere.

Of the other modes, the history of Barbados affords no illustration. The third might produce good results, if the franchise were gradually extended, and the qualification of the legislators were one of property and not of race, and there were security for fairness of voting. The most prominent objection to it is that the legislators would still be drawn from a class, namely, the wealthy, but this is the case with the English House of Commons. An objection to the fourth, in some cases, is the difficulty of obtaining an impartial executive. But in spite of this difficulty, and in spite of all prejudices in favor of the continuance of constitutional forms, it seems probable that an impartial administrative despotism under the supervision of the imperial legislature, is the government under which, in such cases as that of Barbados, the two races, each restrained from oppression of the other, may most quickly and happily arrive at the condition in which the establishment of a constitutional government is not only possible, but wise.

AM, Box 25, JP, DLC.

An Introduction to the Study
of the Constitutional and Political History
of the States

The historical instruction that Jameson received first as an undergraduate at Amherst College and then as a graduate student at the Johns Hopkins University emphasized the significance of European history over that of American history. Indeed Jameson reminded himself while at Johns Hopkins that he would have to achieve professional success as a student of European history before he could "safely specialize" in American history.[1] But as the son of the Amherst postmaster and, somewhat contradictorily, as a Mugwump reformer who detested the kind of political patronage that provided his father a job, Jameson was intensely interested in the lessons American history could provide for the possibility of political transformation.[2] A staunch Unionist who nevertheless joined other reformers in focusing on state and local politics as a fulcrum for change, Jameson once declared that the "great work" of his life would be a volume on "the constitutional and political history of the *states* of the Union (since 1789 or 1776, i.e.)."[3] He discussed this project with James Bryce, the British political observer, when the latter lectured at Johns Hopkins in 1883. Bryce encouraged him to pursue this neglected subject, although he noted that the states were declining in influence relative to the national government.[4]

With his customary thoroughness and energy, Jameson mapped out a program at Johns Hopkins that would set him on the path to writing his great book. In the fall of 1882, he envisaged a course that he would teach voluntarily, enrolling only the best graduate students and covering "disputed points in American history, the object being that we may once a week get away from all second-hand work and get practice in the use of sources, and that we may come to conclusions, on a few points, that we feel we can rely upon, in spite of the contradictions of party-statements."[5] This course did not materialize, in spite of a conversation in 1884 with Herbert B. Adams, head professor of history at Johns Hopkins, during which Adams seemed to recognize the case Jameson had made for the "usefulness" of American history.[6] Still, Jameson wrote his father that he hoped to inspire the graduate students "to start a boom in my little hobby of state history."[7] Jameson originally prepared the three essays that follow for delivery to the graduate students in the Johns Hopkins Seminary of Historical and Political Science in January 1885. Adams suggested that the essays be included in a volume of the *Johns Hopkins University Studies in Historical and Political Science* devoted to the topic of state political and constitutional history. Despite his conviction that the essays were "far too slight and sketchy," Jameson reluctantly agreed because he was under great pressure to publish in order to strengthen his precarious position at the university.[8]

NOTES

1. JFJ, diary, March 15, [1883], AD, Box 2, JP, DLC.
2. JFJ, diary, May 23, [1884], AD, Box 3, JP, DLC.
3. JFJ, diary, March 15, [1883].
4. JFJ, diary, November 26, [1883], AD, Box 3, JP, DLC.
5. JFJ, diary, November 3, [1882], AD, Box 2, JP, DLC.
6. JFJ, diary, May 23, [1884], AD, Box 3, JP, DLC.
7. JFJ to John Jameson, April 20, 1884, AL, Box 6, JP, DLC.
8. JFJ, diary, January 24, [1885], AD, Box 3, JP, DLC. See also Seminary of History and Politics, Minutes, January 9, 23, 30, 1885, reproduced in Marvin E. Gettleman, ed., *The Johns Hopkins University Seminary of History and Politics: The Records of an American Educational Institution, 1877–1912*, 4 vols. (New York: Garland Publishing, 1987–), 1:129, 137–41.

I

THREE YEARS AGO, when I first visited the library of the Department of State at Washington, the Constitution of the United States was kept folded up in a little tin box in the lower part of a closet, while the Declaration of Independence, mounted with all elegance, was exposed to the view of all in the central room of the library.[1] It was evident that the former document was an object of interest to very few of the visitors of Washington. But when I was last in the library, I learned that the Constitution also was being mounted in order to be similarly placed upon exhibition, because, as I understood it, there was a more general desire to see it. It seemed to me that this incident is typical of a considerable change which the last few years have seen in our way of looking at American history. The interest which during most of the years of the republic has been nearly confined, so far as the popular mind is concerned, to the more dramatic episodes and portions of our history, and has made histories of discoveries, histories of settlements, and pictorial field-books of our various wars the most popular historical works, is now at last being extended to our constitutional and political history, which, with little picturesqueness is yet capable of being, to a mature and thoughtful American mind, of all parts of history the most interesting. Certain states of politics are peculiarly favorable to the production of historical work of a high type. Our politics are now in such a state. Questions necessarily arousing violent partisan passions have no longer the foremost place. The questions which are most prominent, questions of administration and finance, are precisely those to the solution of which history is most directly useful. And not only the quality of the present interest in politics, but its quantity, is favorable to us. The last few years have witnessed, side by side with the incipient decline of the machine politics of the first twelve or fifteen years after the war, a great awakening of interest in politics proper among the more intelligent young men of the country. For instance, at the commencement of one of our largest colleges attended last year, the subjects of one-half of all the orations delivered by the young men were political; five years ago political orations by the students were almost unknown. The times are thus ripe for a more assiduous study of our constitutional and political history. In the present paper and one or two subsequent papers it is intended to point out the importance and urge the cultivation of a singularly neglected portion of that history.

1. These three papers were prepared without any thought of publication for the historical seminary of the Johns Hopkins University, before which they were read on January 9, 23 and 30, 1885; I have thought it as well that they should retain a form which to some extent shows their original purpose. The first of them was read before the American Historical Association at Saratoga, on September 10, 1885.

The history of political institutions and events in the United States is divided into three parts,—national, state, and local. It cannot be asserted that
there is not a great need of good work in the national and local fields, but
something has been done in both. The most neglected field in American
history is the field of state history,—the constitutional and political history
of the individual states. Any bibliography will show that there is an astonishing barrenness even in the case of the older states, whose history might
be supposed to present most of interesting incident to the general reader of
history. An examination of the books themselves will give rise to still further
surprise. Not only are they usually below mediocrity in character, deficient
in research, deficient in perspective, hopelessly myopic and parochial, but
they do not even make an attempt to cover in point of chronology the whole
ground. Almost invariably they are confined to the colonial period and the
revolutionary war. For instance, a certain popular history of Virginia gives
four hundred pages to the colonial and revolutionary period and the civil
war, and about fifty to the period between 1789 and 1861; that is to say, the
author considers one-ninth of his volume a fair proportion to devote to that
period in which the influence of Virginia was greatest, and her history best
worth considering. So it is with the state historians generally. They seem
to belong to that singular class of historical writers who think it advisable
to give no very full account of the recent history of any country, but wiser to
stop the narration of English history at Waterloo, and that of France at the
Revolution, which proclaims the utility of historical study on the ground that
only the study of the past can enable us to understand the present, and then
neglects all that part of the past which is most necessary to an understanding
of the present, namely, the immediate past, thus reversing the laws of perspective by drawing the foreground on the smallest scale. It is to be hoped
that this theory of the importance of all centuries but the nineteenth, if that
can be called a theory which is apparently a feeling based on timidity and
indolence in the presence of new and difficult tasks, will speedily become
obsolete, and that the opposite view, supported by the, at least respectable,
examples of Herodotus, Thucydides and Tacitus, Hooft, De Thou and Father
Paul, will in time prevail. When that view is adopted, the relative importance, in the history of politics, of colonial history and state history will be
appreciated.

It seems the merest commonplace to say that the preservation of due
proportion between the parts in the constitutional history of any country
depends upon a correct sense of the proportions between the various factors
in its constitution. But obvious as this principle is, it is not always applied.
Students know that the part played by the Church in the life of mediaeval
England was far greater than its present part; yet how many of them devote a proportionate amount of attention, in their studies of the history of
England in the middle ages, to its ecclesiastical polity? A similar failure to

make this application seems to be at the bottom of our astonishing neglect of state history. We fail to perceive that the peculiarity of our governmental institutions makes necessary a peculiar distribution of attention in treating of their history, as if, like Samuel's Israelites, we could not get used to the idea of not being governed like the nations around. We know, when we stop to think of it, that our constitutional life has been lived quite as much in the state as in the nation, in the branches as much as in the trunk, that the life of the average citizen has probably more points of contact with the life of the state government than with that of the central government, that indeed there have been times in our history when the latter bore to the former a relation not entirely different from that which the last Carolingians bore to the Dukes of France, Normandy and Lorraine. But when it comes to writing our constitutional history, we neglect all this, and proceed as if the United States were as centralized a unity as modern France. To illustrate this point, let us look a moment at the recent constitutional history of England. The most important constitutional measures of the last sixty years have been, we may say, the parliamentary reform acts of 1832, 1867 and 1884, the municipal corporations reform acts, the new poor law, the removal of Catholic disabilities, the abolition of church-rates, the commutation of tithes, the acts for the organization of elementary education, the reform of the universities, the succession of changes effected in the tenure of land, the ballot act, and the disestablishment of the Irish Church. Now imagine all this legislation transferred to America. A moment's reflection will convince that, with the exception of some minor provisions (such, for instance, as those for redistribution), absolutely every one of these enactments would in this country have been made by state legislatures, or possibly state conventions, and not by the national legislature. And yet the history of the constitutional action of these legislatures and conventions, and the whole course of the constitutional development of all these states during the last hundred years, remains practically unknown to us. Even if the history of the general government were alone worthy of attention, the great influence of the states upon the life of the national constitution would cause them to deserve fuller investigation than they have ever yet received. But as it is, it is no exaggeration to say that the half has not been told us, and that the constitutional history of the United States never has been written, and never will be written until scholars, well-trained in historical learning and mature in political thought, take up the constitutional history of our commonwealths, one by one, and show the world the treasures of political instruction to be derived from them.

More has been said thus far of work in constitutional history than of work in political history, not because of a belief that there is more to be done in the former, but because it is more important to the practical and didactic purpose which has led to the writing and publishing of this paper, the purpose, namely, of urging upon the members of the historical seminary of the

Johns Hopkins University, and then upon other young historical students, the undertaking of some work in this still unharvested field. To write a great constitutional history is no doubt as difficult as to write a great political history, but it is easier to find in the former department minor tasks which may be undertaken in the earlier years of our studies than in the latter, just as pieces of investigation suitable for younger men may perhaps more easily be found in anatomy than in physiology. But the history of state politics must be written; perhaps indeed it is even more urgently needed than the history of state constitutions. For the distortion which its neglect has produced in the popular view of our history is equally great, and there is another reason which may not unreasonably be thought still more important, arising out of still another failure to adjust the composition of our histories to the facts of our government. We have not seen that, where the government is a government of the people, it is essential that the history be the history of the people, that, in fact, the history of a democracy ought not to be an Iliad. Our political histories have for the most part been Iliads; they are filled with the deeds of the chieftains "wise in council," "fertile in devices," "kings of men," or even, in a humbler sphere of usefulness, "good at shouting," βοὴν ἀγαθοί, while the rest of the well-greaved Achaians stand in their ranks unnoticed and unsung. There are signs of a change; McMaster's "History of the People of the United States," with all its faults, is such a sign; its general purpose is most commendable. But the true history of our nation will not be written until we can obtain a correct and exhaustive knowledge of the history of public opinion upon politics, the history of the political views and actions of the average voter. Now these views and actions for the most part appear in a local sphere, and can be exhibited best by the study advocated in this paper, the study of the history of state politics. For instance, suppose that we wish to understand the greatest event of our earlier political history, the gradual triumph of the republican party over the federalists. We shall never acquire a perfect knowledge of that great change, or even of the election of 1800–1801, by studying only those events and those characters which were great enough to occupy a conspicuous place in the wide theatre of national politics. We must go below the surface, and as soon as we go below the surface we find that there are many minor currents, the currents of state life, which have joined to form the great resultant movement. These minor currents, merely eddies sometimes, must be studied. If we are attempting to discover the causes which gave this or that issue to a recent presidential election even, we do not think of being satisfied with an explanation expressed, so to speak, in terms of national politics only; we ask ourselves: What influences worked upon the mind of the average voter in Ohio, leading him, with whom the decision rested, to decide thus? What combinations of circumstances so affected the political molecules in Massachusetts or in Virginia as to give a new complexion to the political tissue? How was New

York carried, and how Pennsylvania? Just so if we are discussing the great political change of eighty years ago. The actions of the leaders are already well known; if the change in the opinion of the mass of voters is to be investigated, it can best be done by the study of local movements. What were the influences that gradually converted the rank and file in Massachusetts and Connecticut? Why did Delaware so long remain Federalist? The answers to such questions as these are not easily obtained. The future historians of our states must not only laboriously ransack the printed histories and annals of states and counties and towns, the archives of the former, and the newspapers of the latter; but if they would get down to the real facts of the political history of the people, they must examine the masses of county and town and court records, and what of private correspondence has been preserved, and leave no stone unturned in the effort to reproduce exhaustively the course of democracy in our country. But the enormous pains required will be well rewarded; for, as the result, we shall have at last the history of the people of the United States, written with some recognition of the fact that our national name is plural.

I shall perhaps be told that the history of the states is so closely bound up with the history of the federation itself, that the former if related apart from the latter is left incomplete and loses half its meaning. I reply that it is equally true that the latter if related apart from the former is left incomplete and loses half its meaning. This is what we have been doing; let us try the effect of light polarized in another plane. Or perhaps it will be said that the states are vanishing quantities. Probably they are; but institutions of the past, even those that are obsolete, are necessary objects of historical investigation if they have been strongly influential in making the present what it is. Nor would it be unreasonable to desire that work upon state history should do something to direct attention more strongly to the importance and value of our state governments, now that the danger from extreme state-rights theories has been succeeded by a pronounced danger from the opposite quarter. Teachers of history will find an increasing number of pupils who intend to engage in politics. Is it not as well to direct their attention to the fields of usefulness which state politics present, a field wherein tangible results can more probably be reached than in the wider arena of national politics, where none but the heaviest cestus has much chance of making itself felt?

II

It is the object of the present paper to present some illustrations of the subject already discussed, drawn from an examination of the constitutions of the states,—more especially those framed during the revolutionary period. One who carries his research little beyond the bare text of these fundamental laws gives, I am aware, but a narrow basis to his study of the constitutional history of our states; yet, if time fails him to exhaust all sources, as his ideals would exact, it may not be entirely unprofitable to him to study one source, provided he bears in mind how partial must be the views thus obtained. For the states have, no less than the general government, unwritten constitutions. The form of our government in 1885 is widely different from its form in 1789; the brief document called the constitution of the United States remains the same. The executive departments have doubled in number. Their heads have decreased in power. The spoils system has risen and declined. The senate, from a small executive council of ambassadors debating with closed doors, has come to have fully the position of an upper house of the legislature. The standing committees of the House and Senate, unknown in the earlier years of the government, have now come to control it. The speaker of the House has become, next to the President, the principal officer of the republic. The electoral college has become an obsolete organ, which either avails nothing, or avails occasionally to disturb and pervert the function which it was originally designed to subserve, like that singular result of evolution, the *appendix vermiformis*, whose only present office is occasionally by obstruction to produce acute peritonitis. Yet of all these momentous changes, every one of which is an important alteration in our constitution, the few pages of print called by that name bear no trace. The same can be said of the real constitutions of the states. But it does not hold true to anything like the same extent. The state constitutions have been for the most part much more detailed, they have been subjected to much more amendment, and have from time to time been replaced by new constitutions. So it is not likely that in the constitutional history of the individual states we shall often find changes so great as those which have been mentioned occurring without leaving some trace in the fundamental document. When we see that of the older states, whose constitutions antedate the beginning of this century, nearly a half retained the same constitutions unsuperseded from that time until after the civil war (three of them indeed until the present time), that the average duration of American state constitutions has been thirty years, while ten of them have lasted more than sixty years, we feel sure that, during the continuance of many of these, changes in the actual form of government, sometimes perhaps changes of importance, have occurred which are not to be found registered in amendments, but must be sought in the statute books, in the law reports, or even traced by means of the newspapers, the daily records of state development. Yet we shall not in most cases go quite wrong if we take into account only the state constitutions and their amendments.

The *formal* aspects of our state constitutions present some points of interest. For instance, it is interesting to observe the evidence of growing stability afforded by the fact that their average duration has been increasing, and not diminishing, as perhaps most persons would suppose. But on the other hand there has been an ominous increase in length. The first of the state constitutions, the New Hampshire constitution of 1776, covers little more than a single page in Major Poore's edition;[2] the constitution of 1875 for Missouri occupies rather more than thirty-three pages; printed in duodecimo it would make a sizable volume. Nor is this tremendous document at all unique; the last constitutions of Maryland, Texas and Arkansas are nearly as long. Indeed, the instruments of government framed since the war are about three times as long as those of the revolutionary period. This change seems due to a desire to include in the constitution a mention of everything, from the name of God, often dragged in in an inappropriate and even silly manner, down to barbed fence-wire, city alley-ways, and historical paintings in state-houses. It is interesting to observe, it would perhaps be not unprofitable to investigate, the growth of this tendency to comprehensiveness, a tendency which is one of the most striking facts in the history of American constitutions, and, one may well think, one of the most deplorable. For when we introduce minor details into such an instrument, we are introducing temporary elements, which will necessitate frequent amendments. And nothing can be more certain than that the practice of frequent amendment must in time impair the reverence with which constitutions ought to be regarded, lower their authority, and introduce into our governments a most undesirable instability.

So much for matters of *form* which admit of profitable study. As to the *substance* of American constitutions, two methods may be pursued. We may follow down the constitutional history of a given state, or we may make a comparative study of the state constitutions of a given period. Perhaps to follow the latter method may most easily serve the purpose of the present paper, which is not to present the results of a careful examination of any portion of history, but to suggest lines of inquiry to others. In the revolutionary period all the states except Connecticut and Rhode Island formed new constitutions. Here, accordingly, the opportunities for a comparative study are full. If I were urging a student to such study, either with a view of producing some contribution to historical science, or simply in order to enlarge his own knowledge, (and for the one purpose or the other, one ought certainly to recommend every student of our constitutional history to pay some attention to this subject), I should say to him, study first of all the declarations of rights which are prefixed to these constitutions, or, in some cases, included in them. For these, more than any other portions, exhibit the principles of the Revolution. We see in them how great was the influence of

{2.} Benjamin Perley Poore, ed., *The Federal and State Constitutions, Colonial Charters, and Other Organic Laws of the United States*, 2 vols. (Washington, D.C.: Government Printing Office, 1878).

the Revolution of 1688; the very words of some parts of the Bill of Rights are again and again repeated. We see everywhere appearing the influence of the contemporary or recent political philosophy of France and England, of Montesquieu especially, and Locke and Rousseau. But besides these influences from England and France, we see the workings of colonial conditions of life; we see what were the grievances that seemed largest to the revolutionary party, the eagerness to provide for the liberty of the subject, the dislike of the military, the odium of general warrants; we see how strong had already become the tendency to democracy. Here, too, we find light thrown upon the progress toward religious equality, toward new relations between church and state.

The comparative study of the forms of government at that time adopted, in obedience to the suggestions of Congress, will prove not less remunerative than that of the declarations of rights. From the year 1776 to the year 1780 an extraordinary amount of attention was given by the inhabitants of the colonies to the then new task of constitution-making; the results, the expedients adopted, now singularly wise, now singularly crude, furnish food for much investigation, thought and comparison. Into such a comparison, however, I shall not enter; for its details would be tedious if expressed with the condensation here necessary.

Again, the subject of the origin of each of these first constitutions is one of the greatest interest, and one which has received surprisingly little attention. Hegel, in criticising Schelling's system, said that in it the absolute was, as it were, shot out of a pistol. It is somewhat so with American state constitutions in most historical works. No considerable effort is made to deduce their origins; they spring full-armed from the heads of Olympian conventions. The investigation is indeed no easy one. The factors of the final result are in general four. First, the constitution of England, or what the fathers thought to be the constitution of England. Second, the political philosophy of the time, prevalent among the people, derived from both England and France. Third, the ideas as to the needed form of government which the leading statesmen really originated and then caused to be adopted. Fourth, the already existing constitutions of the colonies. I do not mean simply the meagre provisions of the charters; for these had undergone a great development, like willow stakes that have been set out, hard and smooth and geometrical, by the shore of the ocean, but have there sprouted and grown into living trees. These constitutions, with their written and unwritten elements, constitute, perhaps, the chief of the factors, certainly the least thoroughly known. At all events, these four are the factors to be considered; and the task is, to discover the proportions in which each is present in the constitution as it came finally from the hands of the state convention. Thus, in the case of Virginia, we know that the preamble to the Declaration of Rights was taken from a draft sent on from Philadelphia by Jefferson, that the declaration itself was written by the admirable George Mason, and but slightly amended in the convention itself. We know that, some months before, Richard Henry Lee and George Wythe had at different times asked the advice of John Adams as to the form of government to be adopted, (as was also done by the patriots of North Carolina and New Jersey), and we have the brief note which he wrote to the one, and the letter afterward written to the other which was printed anonymously as a pamphlet. We have the reply to this contained in the anonymous Address to the Convention, by Carter Braxton, and Patrick Henry's letter, commenting upon the two. We have much interesting information upon the characters and lives of the members in Grigsby's Phi Beta Kappa Address, and we have the Journal of the Convention. With these materials and the manuscript treasures of Washington and Richmond, it ought to be possible for a ripe scholar, who understands well the Virginian character and the signs of those times, and is thoroughly learned in the workings of the institutions of Virginia in the times just previous to the revolution, to effect a satisfactory solution of the profoundly interesting question of the real derivative sources of the Virginia constitution of 1776, to analyze this new compound into its component parts. Such a solution we do not now possess in the case of any of the state constitutions, so far as I know. We have much personal description of the various conventions, much vociferous panegyric of their work. Personal details and vociferous panegyric have played far too large a part in American historiography; the time has come for something more solid. Shall we believe that the new forms of government were called into being by the creative fiat of statesmen (to judge from the language of some historical writers the class of statesmen must have been phenomenally large in 1776, embracing, one would estimate, about one-tenth of the adult male population of America), or shall we set ourselves seriously to study the transition as a piece of sober constitutional history, rejecting, at whatever sacrifice of our feelings, the theory of direct verbal inspiration, and patiently investigating in order to discover exactly how great and of what sort the transition was?

Another matter of great interest and importance, and well deserving investigation, is the influence of the state constitutions upon the formation of the federal constitution. Let us for a moment banish from our minds the history of the last hundred years, and try to realize how new a thing the making of written constitutions then was. If we except the makers of the Instrument of Government and of the Humble Petition and Advice, no body of Englishmen in the mother country had ever done such a thing; no body of Englishmen on this side of the water had ever done quite such a thing, except, in the early days, for very small settlements, until eleven years before the Philadelphia Convention. When, therefore, that convention assembled, virtually the only experience on which the members could draw in prosecuting the work before them was that of the state conventions of the last dozen years. And in those conventions at least a third, very likely a half, of the members of the Philadelphia Convention had taken part. It would be very strange if we did not find many traces of the influence of the discussions and results of these conventions. And in fact these do appear again and again. The Virginia plan read by Governor Randolph, slight sketch as it is, shows the influence of the constitution of his state. The very name of the senate is derived from that constitution. Evidences of such influence naturally enough appear with especial frequency in the details of the provisions adopted or suggested. The Pennsylvanian opposition to a bicameral legislature is such an evidence. Hamilton's (supposed) design of having the senate elected by freeholders only was borrowed from the constitution of his own state. Gorham's suggestion that the appointment of judges by the President be subject to confirmation by the senate was based on arguments from the constitutional history of Massachusetts. Mason and Ellsworth's advocacy of ratification by conventions was founded on recent experience. These instances, taken at random, will perhaps suffice; one could find many more. Indeed, I have even heard it maintained that all those parts of the work of the Convention of 1787 which have proved successful were borrowed from the constitutions of the states, and all those parts which were new have proved failures. As to the first ten amendments to the Federal Constitution, it is unnecessary to do more than allude to the manifest and well-known influence which the Virginia Declaration of Rights and the imitations of it in other states had upon them.

III

In the first of these three papers allusion was made to the desirability of making more effort to get at the real political history of the masses of the American people. It will be generally felt that the principal difficulty in the way of such attempts is the paucity of reliable materials bearing upon the political history of the less articulate classes. The object of the present paper is to give some evidence in support of the opinion that one particular class of sources, perhaps not much regarded hitherto, would on thorough examination be found to yield materials of considerable value for historical work of just this sort. I refer to local records, more especially the town records of the North. The belief has been expressed in a previous paper that much of our national history must be sought in state sources; it is now urged that local sources may be made of great use to the history, in the revolutionary and post-revolutionary periods, of the individual state and thus of the nation. The average political unit of that day wrote few letters, and these said little of politics. The newspapers furnish but a very partial and imperfect reflection of public opinion upon politics. But in the town records we get a genuine, and sometimes a tolerably full expression of the popular mind. Sometimes ill-written, sometimes not perfectly grammatical, they bear evidence upon the very first inspection that they have at least that value which springs from perfect authenticity; that they bring us close to the real thoughts of the people. Seldom indeed do we get so good a chance to see the non-literary classes thus unconsciously self-registered.

It may be thought that these records are full of nothing but parochial matters—the election of hog-reeves, the seats in the meeting-house, the school-house at the north end, the highway by Dea. Smith's house, the minister's salary and firewood. Certainly they do contain much that is trivial. But two things must be said on the other side. In the first place, by combining many such data, obtained from different towns, we get a solid basis not only for a description of society at any given time, but for a description of the constitution, or, at any rate, of those numerous departments of human life which are common to social history and to constitutional history. Thus, it is of no especial consequence how the quarrel between the Rev. Mr. Parsons and his parishioners at Amherst as to his salary turned out; but if we have data from a hundred different towns as to the dealings of ministers and parishioners with each other, we have some evidence which will help us to form an opinion as to the position and power of the ministers in society and in the state.

But, still further, the town records are by no means confined to casting these indirect and side lights upon the history of state and nation. They contain much that bears immediately upon politics of a wider scope—much direct action and expression of opinion. He who thinks this improbable should remember what the towns of New England were. No one who knows them can fail to see that each of them has had an individuality and a life of its own. Mr. Howells has admirably described Lexington, Mass., as a typical New England town; but let no one suppose that Woburn, on the one side, and Arlington, on the other, are towns exactly similar. The very map of the Massachusetts towns, with their singular irregularities and varieties of outline, seems to betoken an individuality on their part which it is difficult to suppose existing in regular square subdivisions designated as township number seven, township number eight, Brandnew County. The old New England towns were not so much subdivisions as component parts of the state, each with a mind of its own; witness the singular theory of town autonomy developed during the Revolution in a part of New Hampshire, as exhibited by Mr. John L. Rice's article in the Magazine of American History for January, 1882. As component parts, with minds of their own, they took an interest in the politics of the state and the continent; and of this interest the town records bear traces in greater or less abundance.

Perhaps I may enforce what I have said upon the first of these two heads by illustrations suggested to me by the records of one New England town, which I examined with great care in the process of preparing a part of them for publication.[3] It was plain enough, for instance, that the fathers of this town had a great reverence for rank and position; thus, titles are at first given carefully and very sparingly, though their number increases gradually, especially after the Revolution. It seemed to me that by putting together incidental touches, here and there occurring throughout these records, I got valuable indications of the original strength and extent of aristocratic influences in the town, and could trace with some degree of exactness the progress of their decline; and it seemed probable that if the records of all the other towns were equally accessible, one might, by combining their data, obtain a firm basis for general conclusions as to the history of the aristocratic factor in the social and political constitution of the whole commonwealth, in short, as to the progress of democracy. Again, it became clear to my mind that the Revolution was, so far as this town was concerned, distinctly a movement of the lower and middle classes. The men who have been hitherto most prominent in the management of town affairs drop into the background. The squires fall under suspicion and disfavor. One is deprived of his arms, with the other the town is involved in litigation. The conduct of the parson is voted inimical to the interests of the United States. A new set of leaders comes forward, men who have hitherto been far from prominent in position, and, one feels sure, men of less education than those who preceded them, for the documents of the town, unconsciously bearing witness of their constructors, become at this time distinctly more illiterate. Of course these hints from one town can give us no valid conclusions. But if such an examination were sufficiently extended, it would, I feel sure, throw valuable light upon the character of the two parties to the great conflict. It would show us what sort of man became a Tory, what sort of man joined the party of revolution, and afford us no inconsiderable help in judging the merits of the two causes. Our conclusions might not at the end be entirely new, but they would be based on testimony for the most part unimpeachable, because unconscious; and this would be no slight advantage. Again, upon the state of society and the political situation a few years later, much light was thrown by the records of this town for the period of Shays' Rebellion, and I presume that other town records would give even more.

As to the second kind of help, that afforded by notices of direct action or expression of opinion upon matters of state or national politics, it is certainly

{3.} In 1884 Jameson published an edition of the town records of Amherst. He began the project in 1883 "quite sure that they ought to be published" and believed "it is a sort of thing that every town ought to have done for it; if all did, it would make a very valuable body of materials for historical work of several kinds." See JFJ, diary, June 11, [1883], AD, Box 2, JP, DLC; and JFJ, ed., *Records of the Town of Amherst from 1735 to 1788*, reprinted from the *Amherst Record* (Amherst: Press of J. E. Williams, 1884).

not so often given. The voice of the town-meeting is seldom heard in these affairs, except at such crises as the Revolutionary period, Shays' Rebellion, the time of strained relations with the Directory, the period of the embargo. But when it does speak, it is always instructive, a truly original and primary expression of public opinion. It may not be useless to attempt to indicate with some particularity the sort of help which can come from this source to the student of state history by a single instance. The example which I shall choose is, the reception by the voters of the proposed constitutions of Massachusetts. It will be necessary first to give a brief outline of the history of those constitutions. At first the province, acting under the advice of the Continental Congress, had governed itself according to the provisions of its old charter, with the substitution of an executive council for the governor and lieutenant-governor. This method of government proving inefficacious, a committee of the General Court was appointed in June, 1776, to prepare a new frame of government; but it did not carry the matter far. In September, and again in the next May, the House recommended their constituents to invest the deputies chosen to the next General Court with power to construct a form of government for the state. In a majority of cases this was done, and in the next session a committee of four members of the Council and eight members of the House was appointed to prepare a constitution. They prepared a draft, which, on being approved by the legislature, was submitted to the people in March, 1778, but was rejected by a vote of about ten thousand to two thousand. In 1779 the vote of the people was taken on two questions;—first, whether they would choose at this time to have a new government at all; second, whether they would empower the legislature to summon a special convention for this purpose. Assent was given, and a convention was called, which met at Cambridge on the first of September. The committee of thirty chosen by it delegated the duty of preparing a draft to a sub-committee of three, and these in turn confided the task to John Adams. The constitution finally prepared was much more largely his work than that of any other man. It was accepted in 1780, and has been in operation ever since, the most durable of all those American constitutions of which its chief author afterward wrote the defence.

Now, what illustrations of these events do the town-records supply? In the first place, we see such towns as Ipswich, Gloucester and Plymouth, already in 1775, urging the framing of a new government or the amendment of the old. When, in October of the next year, the suggestion of the General Court that its members be empowered to frame a constitution is submitted to the town-meetings, the votes of the latter become, in some instances, highly instructive. The town of Norton gives, as its reasons for not consenting to this proposal: "1stly, that the present House and Council were not separately elected by the people for that special purpose, which we think it highly reasonable they should be in a matter of such importance; 2dly, the requisition of the Honorable House being so pregnant with power, we cannot think it will be conducive to the future good of the people to comply with their proposal"; a jealousy, it may be added, quite characteristic of the farmers of old Massachusetts. Andover town-meeting, in its instructions to its representative, alleges still other reasons, that "some of the ablest men, who have a peculiar right to a voice, are absent in the field or at Congress," and that it is no time when "foes are in the midst of us and an Army at our Doors to consider how the country shall be governed, but rather to provide for its defence." "We therefore conclude that to set about the forming a New Constitution of Government at this time is unnecessary, impolitic and dangerous; and it is accordingly our direction that you oppose it with those solid arguments of which the subject is so fruitful, and that you do it vigorously and perseveringly." Lexington expresses its opposition in an able document, which was probably written by the minister; but this will probably be thought too little the spontaneous expression of the popular mind to be here quoted. A vote against which this objection certainly cannot be made is that of the small inland community of Townshend; its very lack of a predicate is sufficient evidence that it is a genuine instance of the kind of expression we are seeking. After refusing the desired permission to the legislature, the town votes "That the act made by the late house respecting representation, by which the privilege of many towns is much enlarged, which we think gives the maritime towns a material advantage over the country towns, as the court is held at that side of the state, by which we think the mercantile part of the state has a dangerous advantage over the land part; we therefore" wish the former mode of representation restored. We see also something of the political character of a "hill-town" in the suggestions which Warwick makes to its representative. They desire that the legislature shall consist of one chamber (one of the coast towns was about the same time instructing its member to make sure that there were two chambers), that each town shall have one member, towns of the largest class not more than four or five, the rest in proportion, that suffrage shall be universal, that a town shall have the right to recall its member at any time on evidence of misconduct, and that at no time shall less than eighty members constitute a house.

Though the quotations made come only from the towns opposed, it will be remembered that these were in a minority. When, however, the projected constitution of 1778 was submitted, its opponents were a majority; the principal objections made were, that it contained no declaration of rights, that it did not secure equality of representation, that it placed no limitation upon the reëligibility of the Supreme Magistrate and the members of the General Court, did not sufficiently ensure the mutual independence of the executive and legislative, nor provide for adequate amendment by the people.

In short, it was thought to be too much what in those days was called "a high-toned government." It appears that the coast towns were almost unanimously opposed to it. Among the farming towns it seems, from the data which I have, to have found favor chiefly with towns of one particular class, namely, ancient and conservative towns which a few years later exhibited a decided disapproval of the plebeian and Adullamite [4] insurrection under Daniel Shays, and after the formation of the national government are found adhering to the Federalist party. I may add that they were in part the same towns that are found gravitating to the Unitarian side in the great theological division a generation later. With a fuller accumulation of facts, it would be interesting to work out the connection which I believe existed between these various predilections.

Both at this and at other times a great difference is noticeable in the degree of interest taken in political matters by different towns and sections of the state. In Hardwick and Rowley nearly all the voters must have been present at the town meeting, (at least in 1780), in the Cape towns but a small proportion. Foremost, perhaps, in interest in politics were the coast towns of Essex County, and here the constitution of 1778 was most decidedly rejected. At Newburyport the town voted that the selectmen should write circular letters to the several towns within the county, proposing a convention of delegates from these towns to consider the proposed constitution. A few refused to send. From the rest, some of the most prominent citizens assembled at Treadwell's tavern, in Ipswich, and instituted an elaborate examination of the intended constitution. A statement of their objections to it, drawn up by Theophilus Parsons, was printed at Newburyport in the form of a pamphlet, entitled, The Result of the Ipswich Convention, and had much influence upon the decisions of the towns. Such county conventions were somewhat frequent in the earlier years of the state, and were a valued means, long since disused, I believe, of collecting and formulating public opinion. A curious feature of the interim between the two attempts of 1778 and 1780, is the rise of a remarkable theory of town autonomy, developed especially in Berkshire county. Thus we find the citizens of Lee voting that they hold themselves "bound to support the Civil Authority of this State for the term of one year and Bound to obey the laws of this State." And a little earlier, Great Barrington votes No, on the question, "Whether, under the situation of this county, not having a new Constitution, and other reasons, the laws of the State ought to operate among us?"

The constitution of 1780, sent forth after longer and calmer deliberation,

---

{4.} Jameson is comparing the confrontation of Daniel Shays with the state militia of Massachusetts to that of David against Saul, the first king of Israel. David was forced to retreat to Adullam and his followers were know as Adullamites.

was received with even more interest and attention. There were few towns in which it was not discussed fully. In many the meetings, adjourning from day to day, examined it clause by clause, assigned parts of it to select committees for more minute examination, and debated at length the amendments which these reported. It gives an instructive idea of the political value of these small communities, to see the little town of Rowley, whose population cannot then have exceeded thirteen hundred, spending several days discussing the new declaration of rights and frame of government, sentence by sentence, in full town-meeting, and recording their opinions of its successive articles in seventy-five separate votes—votes, too, in which the widely-varying numbers pro and con indicate much independence of judgment; or, again, to observe the moderation and practical good sense with which they urge the adoption of the amendments which they have concluded to recommend; or, once more, to see the evidence of interest and information in politics afforded by such votes as that of Ward, an obscure little farming town of scarcely more than four hundred inhabitants, that "we could heartily wish that representation might be weighed by the number of polls, which would be similar to the proceedings of the Honorable Congress and some neighboring well-regulated States, that have been attended with very wholesome effects." The extent to which the towns entered into the business of examining the new constitution may be inferred from the statement that, if my calculations are not incorrect, the number of amendments to it which they proposed must have amounted to something between six hundred and a thousand. Many of these, of course, duplicated each other; but the evidence of political activity throughout the state is none the less convincing.

Interesting deductions could very likely be made from a tabulation of these amendments in detail; I shall only say that, in general, we can perceive a heightening of confidence in government since 1778, and a consequent lessening of the unwillingness to entrust power to it. On the other hand, many of the amendments desired are identical with those for which the insurrectionists of 1786 clamored, such as, for instance, the curious request made by several of the hill-towns, that there should be a probate judge, register of probate, and register of deeds in each town.

The article to which objection was most generally made was the third article of the Declaration of Rights, which invested the legislature with authority to require towns to support public worship by taxation. Perhaps it may not be uninteresting to quote at length, in conclusion, the resolution of one of the towns (Westford) upon the article, as a somewhat more extended specimen than has been given hitherto of the political thought of the masses throughout the state. That it is not more than the expression of the views of the average voter, its style seems to indicate clearly. It is as follows:

"Voted, to object against the third article of the Declaration of Rights, and that for the following reasons, viz., that it is asserted and taken for granted in the premises of said article—'that the Happiness of a people and the good order and preservation of civil government, essentially Depends upon Piety, Religion and morality; and these cannot be generally diffused through a Community but by the Institution of the Public Worship of God, and by publick Instruction in piety, Religion, &c.'— When both antient History and modern athentic Information concur to evince that Flourishing civil states have Existed and still exist without the Legislature's Instituting the Public Worship or Publick Instruction in piety and the Christian Religion; but rather whenever such Institutions fully executed by the civil authority have taken place among a people, instead of promoting essentially their Happiness and the good order and Preservation of civil government, it has, we believe, invariably produced impiety, irreligion, Hypocrisy and many sore and oppressive evils.

"We think the third article, if adopted, will be likely to form such a combination between the Court and Clergy that the libertys of the people will be endangered.

"[Nor are we]{5} Intitled to such a Right as is attributed to the people of the Commonwealth in said article of Investing the Legislature with power to authorize or require the several Towns, Parishes, precincts or other bodies politic or Religious Societies to make suitable provision at their own expense for the institution of the public worship of God, and for the support of the public teachers of piety and religion; because we fully believe that the great Head of the Church has in his gospel made suitable provision for the said Institution of his public worship and for the support of Christian teachers of piety and Religion, and that he has never invested any Commonwealth or Civil Legislature as such, by force and penalty, to carry these aforesaid Institutions into executions,—all attempts of which, we think, tend to encroch on the unalienable Rights of conscience, and to the marring of the true principles of civil government, which last ever ought, in our opinion, to be kept Distinct of Religious gospel institutions. Further, it appears to us that the general principles of civil government, as contained in the Constitution, without the said third article, properly attended to and acted upon, would much better secure and promote the Happiness of the people and the good order and preservation of civil government (which we would ever zealosly promote) than retaining and adopting the said third article."

It may be that the instance which I have chosen, the action of the towns on the state constitutions, is one unusually favorable to my argument because, before the erection of the federal government, the formation of constitutions for the states was a matter of prime importance. It may indeed be that the

{5.} Brackets in original document.

means of investigation which I have been suggesting are neither so novel nor so fruitful as I have believed. But I shall be satisfied if I succeed in drawing increased attention to the main subject of these papers, the careful and scientific study of the constitutional and political history of the individual states.

Johns Hopkins University Studies in Historical and Political Science 4 (May 1886): 181–209.

Review of James Bryce,
The American Commonwealth

Jameson first heard James Bryce lecture at the Johns Hopkins University in 1881 and was impressed by Bryce's "candid" and "moderate" views on British and American political history. Bryce was invited again to lecture at Johns Hopkins in 1883, and Jameson took the opportunity to consult with him. Jameson wanted Bryce's suggestions about his own plans for scholarly research. Bryce encouraged him to study in Europe to gain a broader perspective on politics and thus to focus better on the social aspects of political history. Rather than simply read books on the subject, Bryce urged Jameson to interview politicians and study the political system in operation. Had it not been for his visit to the United States, Bryce admitted that he would not have understood American politics as clearly.[1]

In January 1889 the newly established *Juridical Review*, a Scottish journal, invited Jameson at the suggestion of his friend Albert Shaw to review Bryce's *American Commonwealth* (London and New York: Macmillan and Co., 1888). Jameson readily agreed, even though he was "over burdened with work."[2] In writing this review, Jameson expressed himself more freely in print on contemporary politics than was customary for him. Perhaps he did this because the review was to appear in a new and relatively unknown European publication, and consequently Jameson could anticipate that few American scholars would read it. Upon completing the review, he confided in his diary that Bryce had written a "wonderful book."[3] Jameson dispensed praise sparingly, but he later termed *The American Commonwealth* the "most important book ever written about the United States."[4]

NOTES

1. JFJ, diary, November 21, [1881], AD, Box 2, JP, DLC; JFJ, diary, November 20, 26, [1883], AD, Box 3, JP, DLC.

2. See Albert Shaw to JFJ, January 10, 1889, ALS, Box 127, JP, DLC; JFJ to Shaw, February 28, 1889, ALS, Albert Shaw Papers, NN; photostatic copy in Box 127, JP, DLC.

3. JFJ, diary, January 31, March 14, [1889], AD, Box 4, JP, DLC.
4. Quoted in Leo F. Stock, ed., "Some Bryce-Jameson Correspondence," *AHR* 50 (January 1945): 261.

ONE OF THE THINGS on which an American reviewer of this already-famous work feels impelled first of all to comment is the character of its reception. It is decidedly worthy of note that the book seems to have given rise to equal pleasure and admiration on both sides of the Atlantic. This is not only a high tribute to its qualities, but a significant evidence of an important change of sentiment which has been going on in America during the last twenty or twenty-five years. Before the Civil War, a European book upon America could not easily secure the favour of the American public save by almost unrelieved laudation; national sensitiveness to European criticism was exceedingly acute. But from that tremendous conflict the American nation emerged adult and mature, able to look upon itself and the world around it with more sobriety and discrimination, and to examine its characteristics and modes of life with an externality of view unknown to the preceding generation. Mr. Bryce makes full and free statements of the defective and evil elements in American politics and government. An American who loves his country can hardly fail to rise with deep pain from the reading of some of those chapters in which Mr. Bryce has described systematically the faults and evils which are individually familiar to the reader, but which, thus described, come upon him with cumulative effect. But he is likely, in these days more than ever before, to recognise the justice of what is said thus in friendly criticism, and to prefer the book which gives instruction to that which feeds national vanity. Perhaps, too, it may be assumed that the warm reception with which the book has been received in Great Britain is due not alone to its remarkable excellences, but in part also to an increasing interest in American affairs which begets and is begotten of a kindlier feeling toward the younger English nation than was once entertained or, perhaps, deserved.

But to turn to the book itself. Seldom indeed has any nation received, at the hand of a foreign observer, the gift of a description of its political anatomy and physiology so thoroughly complete and just. America is greatly indebted to Tocqueville's remarkable exposition, written fifty years ago. But Tocqueville's account, acute and thoughtful as it is, is far inferior to Mr. Bryce's in fulness and precision of detail, in the attainment of reality. He often seems a political theorist, drawing illustrations of his theories from American democracy, rather than a student whose thoughts take their origin from things actually observed. In a word, his politics breathe the philosophical spirit, where those of Mr. Bryce breathe the scientific spirit of our time. Rarely, however, has the scientific spirit in politics been so completely followed. Again and again does the American reader—and the more often the better acquainted he is with the institutions of the United States—find himself called upon to marvel, first, at the minute accuracy of the information respecting those institutions displayed by a European writer; again, at the extraordinary completeness of his presentation; and thirdly, at the vigilant discretion with which all non-scientific material has been excluded. This last deserves a moment's special comment. As England grows more democratic, Englishmen grow more and more into the habit of resorting to American experience for examples of political arrangements or results. It must have been obvious to Mr. Bryce that a book like his would be frequently used as an arsenal of political weapons. The temptation to be constantly making applications and pointing morals was therefore strong, and we ought therefore to bestow high praise upon the self-control with which he has avoided this temptation, or perhaps one ought rather to say upon the qualities of mind which made the temptation less strong to him than it would be to thinkers less thoroughly disciplined.

European and American writers have been hampered by two different prepossessions in their treatment of American institutions, and have thereby usually failed to draw a true and well-proportioned picture of the whole system. European writers have brought with them in their minds the general framework or scheme of governmental institutions common to European states, have unconsciously referred American institutions to this scheme, have described as significant those parts which correspond to significant elements in the European scheme, and have taken less interest in other parts and described them but meagrely. In reality, the whole scheme of things is in many ways different in America, and a distorted view is given, unless one recognises this and discards at the outset any prepossession that stands in its way. It is one of the signal merits of Mr. Bryce's book that he has done this. He has given their true place to the governments of the States and the system of party organisation, the two elements in American political arrangements most foreign to European experience. These are elements which occupy a vast space in the actual configuration of affairs, of the latter of which he rightly says that these organisations "form a second body of political machinery, existing side by side with that of the legally constituted government, and scarcely less complicated"; and to them, with the inclusion of local government, he is not wrong in assigning the whole of his second volume. The same rectitude of vision appears also in minor matters.

American writers have not only been led into these errors of inapt classification and disproportionate emphasis, but have been subject to another source of error of their own. This is of the sort which Lord Bacon called *idola fori*.[1] The application of the phrase, "the Constitution of the United

{1.} Sir Francis Bacon, in his *New Organum* (1620), describes four classes of idols. The *idola fori*, "idols of the marketplace," referred to the problem that occurs when language, which Bacon found inexact and misleading, is employed to describe the reality of daily life and commerce. In his view, the real world could be understood only through direct observation. See Norman F. Cantor and Peter L. Klein, eds.,

States," to the particular document in which the brief outline of the federal system is written down, an application which in the minds of most Americans is nearly the exclusive one, has brought it about that American works professedly treating of the American Constitution have, for the most part, been confined to comment on that document. In reality, not only do great portions of the American systems of government lie quite outside the field of that document, as, for instance, the portions spoken of in the preceding paragraph, but even considerable portions of the federal government itself are not mentioned in it, but have grown up either from it or outside of it. Mr. Bryce is among those who have not only perceived this, but perceived it in its full force and extent. In other words, while the distinction he so forcibly points out between rigid and flexible, or written and unwritten constitutions, is a vital one, it is not to be forgotten that, over and above its written constitution, the United States has, if one may so say, a large amount of unwritten constitution; and Mr. Bryce has had a sufficient eye for reality to see and adequately to use this fact.

There are, however, a few matters which one would be glad to see treated with more fulness, especially because of the important place they hold in American political life. One such is the matter of contested elections to legislative bodies. To an Englishman this seems an unimportant matter; and so it would be in the United States if the method of dealing with it were what it should be. It is only the gradual introduction of better methods,— by Mr. Grenville's Act in 1770, by Sir Robert Peel's Act, and by the Act of 1868 referring election petitions to the judges—that has reduced it to unimportance in England. It was not unimportant in the age when Sir Robert Walpole's Ministry fell by reason of defeat on the Chippenham election petition. Now the American House of Representatives and the legislatures of the States are, in this matter, in almost as bad a state as the House of Commons was before the passage of the Grenville Act, when all such cases came before the whole House, and were decided by the House on party motives, so that, as Mr. Lecky says, "A considerable portion of the members of the House of Commons owed their seats, not to the electors, but to the House itself." Something like this is true to-day of American legislative bodies. It is true that a Committee of Elections prepares the case, and often virtually decides it, but that Committee is always as much a partisan body as the whole House before which the case comes for final decision. It is obvious how demoralising an influence in the governmental system must be exercised by even a few cases as these in Federal and State Legislatures; and cases of contested

---

Seventeenth Century Rationalism: Bacon and Descartes (Waltham: Blaisdell Publishing Co., 1969), pp. 191–92; Brian Vickers, *Francis Bacon* (London: Longman Group, 1978), p. 18; and Charles D. Broad, *The Philosophy of Francis Bacon* (New York: Octagon Books, 1976), pp. 48–49.

election occur in greater or less number nearly every year. Mr. Bryce says, speaking of the Federal House of Representatives, "As a member is elected for two years only, and the investigation would probably drag on during the whole of the first session, it is scarcely worth while to dispute the return for the sake of turning him out for the second session" (i. 169, 170). What makes it worth while is the $5000 of salary *per annum*, and the excessively large allowance for "mileage," which sometimes amounts to $1000 more. Instances have therefore been known in which contestants have been seated in the last days of the second and final session, and have then drawn their pay for two years' service to which it is decided that they were entitled.

Something similar may be said of the practice of "gerrymandering." This abuse, dismissed with a sentence, might well have received a greater emphasis; for it has become almost universal, and ingrained into the political habits of the American people at least as firmly as the "spoils" system itself, so that it is a difficult matter to induce the average American voter to see any harm in partisan arrangements of the boundaries of electoral districts, provided it is not pushed to an absurd extreme. It may be worth while to add that Mr. Bryce is slightly in error in his statement of the connection of the gerrymander with Elbridge Gerry, of whom he says that he, "when Massachusetts was being re-districted, contrived a scheme which gave one of the districts a shape," &c. (i. 165). Gerry was governor at the time. The scheme originated in the legislature, and Austin, in his "Life of Gerry," says that the governor advised his party associates in that body against it. The main odium does not belong to him therefore, though it is true that when the bill came up before him he failed to veto it. It is perhaps of interest to know that the first instance of gerrymandering for Congress seems to have been that involved in a redistricting scheme put in operation in Virginia by Patrick Henry, in the autumn or winter of 1788, in order to secure the defeat of James Madison.

A third suggestion may be ventured, ungracious as it seems to find fault with a work for which Americans owe so great a debt of gratitude. It may be observed parenthetically that the reviewer, who desires to find fault with the book, will find himself almost wholly confined to suggesting the inclusion of this or the heightening of that statement (in regard to which the author may very well be supposed to have his own views of fitness or proportion to maintain *per contra*); for as to incorrect statement of important facts, there is hardly an instance of it to be found in the whole three volumes,—a most astonishing thing when one thinks of it. But, after urging that two evils, upon which Mr. Bryce touches, are so pervasive in their effects that the black spots which they represent in the picture might have been made larger, it is pleasant to call attention to a place in which a fuller treatment would have brought better elements of American public affairs into prominence. Of the three departments of government, between which the federal constitutional system attempts so completely to discriminate, Mr. Bryce gives least space to the executive department. This is wholly reasonable, and his treatment of the office of president leaves nothing to be desired. But one would be glad to see him devote a few more pages to the organisation and conduct of the executive departments, beyond the few in which he treats of the members of the cabinet. For, in spite of all the enormous and wide-spread evils with which the spoils system has afflicted the country, and in spite of all the injury it does to the public business, the organisation and management of the executive departments of government is a strong point in the American system, and one which well displays certain of the nation's most noteworthy characteristics. The exclusion of executive officials and especially of cabinet ministers from the legislative bodies is frequently commented on by European observers as weakening the executive, and no one has better stated the evils of this want of close connection between the two than Mr. Bryce. But it has this compensation that it makes it possible to put at the head of a department a man who, though perhaps a poor speaker and little apt successfully to defend the interests of his department in a parliament, may have exceptional gifts for the special business of administration. Such men are more than ordinarily numerous in the United States, and numbers of them have from time to time occupied themselves with its public business. The result is that the organisation of the executive departments is in many respects excellent, and their methods of managing business presents many interesting points capable of generalisation. This is one of the reasons why the unreformed system of appointments to office does not produce as pernicious effects as a European observer would be led to expect. The spoils system is immensely harmful, but the business talents of the nation neutralise its evils to a surprising extent.

It is one of Mr. Bryce's many merits that he so clearly perceives and sets forth the extent to which the defects of American political machinery are in part corrected in practice by the operation of national qualities, without which they would prove disastrous. A description of that machinery, without reference to those compensations, would do America much injustice. It has to be said that the nation often contents itself with crude devices in matters of politics; but it often happens also, that devices which look badly on paper, are made to work fairly well in practice. An instance of this is the elective character of the judiciary in the States. Indeed, Mr. Bryce's treatment of the judiciary is a particularly excellent portion of his book. Especial praise belongs to his luminous exposition of the real character of the judicial function of pronouncing upon questions of constitutionality. His thesis that this is a simple and necessary incident to the function of declaring the law, possessed alike by State and Federal judges, might, did space permit, be re-inforced by a further discussion of the cases in which State Courts pronounced laws unconstitutional before the erection of the federal judiciary.

Trevett v. *Weeden*, if it was such a case, which a Rhode Island critic has recently doubted, was not the first of them. Among the earlier instances was
one, the famous case of *Rutgers* v. *Waddington*, 1784, in which an Act of the
Legislature of New York was declared void, by means of unconstitutionality,
by no higher a Court than that of the mayor of New York city!

Mr. Bryce's description of the organisation of political parties in the United
States, a description filling the second half of the second volume, is especially
worthy of admiration because the American literature of the subject, is so far
as systematic efforts at description are concerned, exceedingly meagre. He
gives practically the first extended treatment of this complex and elaborate
system, and gives it with extraordinary accuracy, comprehensiveness, and
good judgment. His remarks on the history of the parties are excellent, too,
though his introduction disclaims any intention of going fully into historical
matters; and the few little errors which have crept in here and there in the
course of the three volumes occur mostly in matters of history. In respect
to the generalisations with which the author concludes this chapter, some
will be inclined to doubt whether the two parties which may be said to run
through our political history are rightly to be characterised as the parties of
liberty and of order respectively (ii. 340, 341). In some respects the cleavage
coincides with this division, but in some it does not. The identification is
a true one when applied to the times when the party in opposition to the
Democrats was the Federalist party, but less true in the days of the Whig
and Republican parties. Mr. Bryce is right, however, in thinking that there is
a pervasive distinction between the two parties throughout their histories;
indeed there is a distinction so vital that the ordinary division into loose-
constructionist and strict-constructionist, according to attitude toward the
Federal Constitution, is only incidental to it. The term, party of liberty, may
very well stand for the Democratic party, which, during its continuous life of
nearly a century, has had in the main the simple creed of American political
principles—the principles of democracy in the general sense of that word.
The average American has had in quiet times no other articles than these in
his political creed, and has therefore adhered to the Democratic party. But
over against this party of political principles has been set, from time to time,
a party mainly characterised by devotion to the furtherance of political measures, a party of progress, a party seeking definite political changes. In other
words, there have three times arisen from the mass of American democracy
bodies of men united in the purpose to add to or alter our political fabric—the
Federalist, Whig, and Republican—all of whom may, be grouped together
as a party of political measures more securely than as a party of order. The
relation of this party to the constitution is involved in its main purpose. It
is loose-constructionist because it wishes to get certain definite things done,
yet is working under an instrument. What confirms this last deduction is
that all those minor parties in the United States which have been parties of

political measures—parties, that is, of definite, limited programme,—have had loose-constructionist platforms.

It is interesting to note the strong sentiment of admiration and interest which Bryce entertains for Alexander Hamilton, and his feeling that Hamilton's countrymen "seem to have never, either in his lifetime or afterwards, duly recognised his splendid gifts" (ii. 328). It is interesting to note it because one may suspect that there is a special reason why Hamilton should be better appreciated by a European statesman than by his own countrymen. Hamilton was in fact essentially a European statesman. He was of the same school as Bacon, Strafford, Richelieu, Cromwell, Bismarck, the school in whose ideals of government the office of the individual statesman has its highest place, the school of administrative statesmen who would have a nation ruled by the person of weightiest brain. Herein the course of the Federalist party is different from that of all other parties in the history of the United States, that it proposed to itself these European ideals of statesmanship and of political conduct. But in a new country the part played by natural conditions, economic, and other, is proportionally far larger, that played by individual statesmen proportionally far smaller than in Europe. America therefore turned away in large measure from the political ideals of Hamilton and the Federalists, and in the present age it may probably be true of the whole party, as of Hamilton, that a European is likely to appreciate them more highly than Americans do.

The admiration of the reader increases as he enters the third volume, which treats of the nature and action of public opinion, the general characteristics of American democracy, and the social institutions of the United States. These are subjects which call for political generalisations of the highest order, and bring out the best qualities of Mr. Bryce as a political observer. Every page shows comprehensive study, a catholic spirit, and, above all, discrimination and soundness of reflection. Many as are the generalisations which are made in this volume, there are few that will not command the general assent of thinking men, when the form in which they are cast is exactly noted. Mr. Bryce's style is grave rather than brilliant; but it has the precision of statement belonging to scientific writing, and is occasionally warmed with a touch of genuine enthusiasm for what is best in America. Americans will not be slow to recognise this trait, as well as the just faithfulness of portraiture which has made so many pages of the book sad reading to them. They will highly appreciate the friendly spirit which has presided over the making of a book destined long to be the classical description of their public life, and will gladly reward its author with grateful feeling as well as with enthusiastic admiration.

The Juridical Review: A Journal of Legal and Political Science 1 (April 1889): 204–10.

The Origin of Political Parties
in the United States

The Brown University Historical and Economic Association, which Jameson established in the fall of 1888, was modeled after a similar association at the Johns Hopkins University, which sponsored lectures open to the general public.[1] To obtain speakers for the Brown series, Jameson relied largely upon scholars from New England.

The lecture series in the fall of 1890 explored the history of political parties as well as contemporary economic problems. Anson D. Morse, professor of history at Amherst College, spoke on parties during the Federalist era; Andrew D. White, the former president of Cornell University, discussed the influence of the American Revolution on the French Revolution; Charles H. Levermore, professor of history at the Massachusetts Institute of Technology, explored American political history in the era of Andrew Jackson; Elisha B. Andrews, president of Brown University, and Frank W. Taussig, professor of political economy at Harvard University, both spoke on monetary policies.[2]

The lecture that follows was presented first on December 1, 1890, in Manning Hall on the campus of Brown University. In it, Jameson continued the exploration of state and local politics that he began at Johns Hopkins. He delivered this lecture on at least two other occasions. In May 1892 he was the third speaker in a series on political science sponsored by Middlebury College in Vermont; the series included lectures by Andrews and Levermore.[3] Jameson also delivered the lecture in March 1914 at the University of Michigan, where Jesse H. Reeves, a diplomatic historian, noted that Jameson had a "marvelous faculty of compressing an extraordinary amount of unusual information within the compass of an hour, a power that can only come from the ripest sort of scholarship."[4] The text that follows is presented as we believe Jameson delivered it in 1890.

NOTES

1. JFJ to Daniel C. Gilman, July 21, 1888, ALS, Daniel C. Gilman Papers, MdBJ; JFJ, [Report of the Professor of History], in *Annual Report of the Presi-*

dent to the Corporation of Brown University, June 20, 1889 (Providence: [Brown University], 1889), p. 45.

2. See JFJ, diary, October 3, November 23, December 1, [1890], AD, Box 4, JP, DLC; see also Brown University Historical and Economic Association, "Free Public Lectures," flyer, [November 1890], Box 9, JP, DLC.

3. [Middlebury College], "Public Lectures in Political Science," flyer, [April 1892], Box 29, JP, DLC; JFJ to Sara Ellwell, June 17, 1892, TLS, Box 12, JP, DLC.

4. Jesse H. Reeves to Claude H. Van Tyne, March 14, 1914, TLS, Box 1, Claude Van Tyne Papers, MiU; "Economic Lectures," *Providence Journal*, December 2, 1890, p. 10; "The Lecture Course," *Undergraduate* (Middlebury College) 17 (1892): 123–24.

Two hundred years ago William Congreve, in his Epistle to Lord Halifax, exclaimed

"How oft a Patriot's best laid Schemes we find
By *Party* cross'd or Faction undermin'd!"

If we consider the exclamation a moment, we see at once that this is the expression of a feeling respecting parties quite different from that entertained in our own country and time. The modern American would say that while the patriot's best laid schemes might indeed be undermined by factions, as for parties, they were the most likely and obvious means through which to secure the triumph of his beneficent prospects. The truth is that the word has risen to better employment. Its use in the sense of person, indeed, from being so wholly reputable that Bishop Andrews, in preaching of the Crucifixion, could say "it is wee that have pierced the Party this found slave," has become wholly vulgar; but party in the political sense has constantly risen in repute, until it has even, in special cases, become entitled to be modified by the adjectives *grand* and *old*, by which the American mind is wont to express supreme satisfaction in its favorite {missing text}[1]

rules of his word in all their proceedings, so as it might be conceived in charity, that they walked according to their judgments and conscience, and where they went aside, it was merely for want of light, or their eyes were held through some temptation for a time, that they could not make use of the light they had, for in all these differences and agitations about them, they continued in brotherly love, and in the exercise of all friendly offices each to other, as occasion required."[2] In other words, the ideal of those early days was the ideal which the Lay of Horatius attributes to the early days of Rome, when none was for a party and all were for the state.

The history of political parties in the United States is, then, in part the history of a change of ideas. As the English cabinet was at first looked at with disfavor and alarm, and as Sir Robert Walpole indignantly rejected the imputation of being a prime minister, yet cabinet and prime minister are now among the most honorable terms in the political vocabulary, so political parties, at first deprecated, have grown in repute with the growth of the colonies and of the republic. This gives a certain importance to the story of their development down to the time when they become fully organized and permanent. But there is another consideration which may do still more to

{1.} The title page of the lecture ends here. It was filed separately from the remaining pages of the manuscript, and the intervening page or pages of the lecture have not been located.
{2.} The source of this quote has not been identified.

vindicate such a lecture as the present from the charge of mere antiquarian-ism. The growth of thirteen diverse and discordant colonies into one nation was not effected all at once by the framing of a constitution. Indeed, it was not to be brought about by any voluntary alterations of political institutions. To say nothing of the slow and gradual work of time and mutual attrition in furthering uniformity of habits and sentiments in matters outside of politics, there were changes of political thought and habit which were plainly neces-sary. If it was expedient that to the local governments of the states should be added a general government acting throughout the whole area of the Union, it was no less necessary that within the minds of citizens the habit of preoccupation with local affairs should give place to the habit of taking interest in the general affairs of the whole Union, the habit, in the quaint but expressive phrase of post-Revolutionary times, of "thinking continen-tally." But such widening of interest was sure to find expression in new party associations. Into the place of parties and party divisions confined to single colonies came the great national parties and national political divisions. The history of the local parties and of the transition is therefore not an unimpor-tant part of the history of national consolidation, that gradual, and various, and pervasive process of which the half has not been told us.

In spite of that ideal of brotherly love from which the gentle and magnani-mous Governor Winthrop was unwilling to think that his associates ever departed, party divisions in the American colonies sprang up at the very beginning of their history. We may even say that they sprang up before that beginning, for even on the very voyage by which the Sarah Constant, the Godspeed and the Discovery brought the first settlers to the James River, such dissensions broke out that the doughty Captain John Smith had to be put under arrest, and was for a time after the landing not permitted to take his seat in the council. The trouble seems to have been about offices. The connection between party contests and offices was already close. Indeed, that the American office-seeker made his appearance in the very first year of American history is shown by an intercepted letter recently found in the Spanish archives, and written from Virginia in March 1608 by one Perkins to some friend in England. "I pray you will have the goodness," he says, "to negotiate with Sir William Wade, Sir Thomas Smith, . . . and the others, that I be appointed one of the council here in Virginia, as much for my honor as that I may be better able to pay my debts. There are some of the members of the council here who understand state affairs as little as I do, and who are no better than I. It will be a matter of great delight to see coming here so many from our country, so richly gifted and enlightened that I should not be worthy to appear among them!"

So long, however, as the government of Virginia was in the hands of the Virginia Company, party divisions in the colony itself could nowise assume an extensive and hardly a permanent character. In the meetings of the Company itself, in London, party spirit ran high, the king's party and the Parliament party warmly disputing the control of it. But these struggles, highly interesting in themselves, do not strictly fall within our subject. Of definitely formed political parties in Virginia we get hardly a trace until we come to the middle of the century and the times of the Great Rebellion in England. Then we find the political development of Virginia already so far advanced that each of the parties to the great struggle in England finds allies in the colony. These colonial contests have to do with principles and questions affecting the government of Virginia, yet bear some likeness to the contests going on in the mother country. The easy reduction of the colony by the Parliamentary commissioners proves the feeble and lukewarm nature of the royalist principles in Virginia. A greater violence of party feeling is exhibited during the rule of the ensuing governor, Sir William Berkeley, in the famous episode known as Bacon's Rebellion. Here the quarrel arose mainly out of the governor's maladministration, the attempt of the assembly to restrict the suffrage, and certain miseries and misfortunes. It would appear that the followers of Bacon were like those that gathered around David in the cave of Adullam, "everyone that was in distress, and every one that was in debt, and every one that was discontented";[3] but with them were also some of those advocates of colonial and popular liberties who grew more and more numerous and influential among the Virginian planters.

In Maryland, as in Virginia, the first well-defined party contests were excited by and ran parallel with the convulsions of the great civil war in England. But that colony had started with a ground of future dissension which had not existed in Virginia; the antagonism of Catholic and Protestant had added to the mutual hostility of Cavalier and Roundhead. Moreover, that antagonism was the more extreme because Maryland, unlike Virginia, had received a large immigration of Puritans. But, as in Virginia, the contests of the eventful years from 1640 to 1660 were not solely a reflexion of those going on in England; local questions, especially with respect to the powers of the proprietor, were important among the animating causes. After the Restoration, the antagonism of Protestant and Catholic continued. In part, this was simply an American phase of the anti-Catholic excitement which was rife in England in the last years of Charles II, the years of the Popish Plot and the Exclusion Bill. But in part it was occasioned by a fear of danger incidental to the standing menace of the English colonies by the presence of the French power in America. The Protestant party in Maryland feared that in the event of war the Catholics would be disposed to render aid to the great Catholic power of Louis XIV., and regarded the Jesuits as all-too-skillful emissaries of that monarch.

{3.} I Samuel 22:2. See above, p. 29n.

That the most hotly-contested political struggles in the first century of the history of New England were closely connected with the great debate of Royalist and Parliamentarian in Old England is familiar. But the marvelous political activity of the group of colonies had brought about party contests even before that date. In the years from 1632 to 1642 in Massachusetts, it is easy to see that a warm contest was being waged between a high-minded oligarchy, headed by the blameless Winthrop, and intrenched in the board of assistants, and the advocates of popular rights assembled or represented in the General Court. We see, in the religious policy of the state, a party of severity headed by Dudley and a party of leniency headed by Winthrop, though all such differences in early Massachusetts were repressed as much as possible, in order that the Puritan state, face to face with hostile elements without, might not be weakened by manifest internal dissensions. The intimate union of religious and political affairs gave to the gainsaying of Anne Hutchinson and Wheelwright the character of a political party, and caused the decisive defeat of Vane in the election of 1637. The period of the Civil War and the Commonwealth was not in Massachusetts as in the southern colonies a period of more acute party contest. There was no royalist party, and moreover the colony, unified by severe measures based on the conviction that the interests and wills of individuals must be strictly subordinated to the interest and will of the community, was asserted in the determination to maintain itself independent of both the contestants in England. In the confederation called the United Colonies of New England there was a standing party division between the members representing Massachusetts and the representatives of the smaller colonies, Massachusetts attempting to play in the confederation the part which Athens and Prussia have played in more famous leagues, the other colonies opposing. In the discussions which arose, outside the meetings of the commissioners, respecting the foreign policy of the Confederation with regard to the Indians, the French, and the Dutch, we have perhaps the first faint beginning of party divisions transcending the limits of a single colony. Of the smaller colonies, little needs to be said. Connecticut and New Haven were little vexed by party spirit. New Hampshire had much of it, but on a small scale. As for Rhode Island, it is well known that the "lively experiment" which Roger Williams proposed to maintain owed no small part of its liveliness to the vagaries of disputing townships and certain anarchical citizens; but how far parties were definitely formed is, except in a few instances, hard to say.

A new era in the history of parties in New England begins with the arrival of Edward Randolph as royal agent to Massachusetts. In his efforts to break down the charter government, Randolph set himself to call into existence a royal party. The time was ripe for such a movement. Increase of trade and of wealth had relaxed in the minds of many the rigidity of Puritanism. The advocates of the Half-way Covenant had just obtained a signal victory. Religion and politics were so closely united that these could be reckoned on not to support the most extreme pretensions of the ruling set. Randolph in his first letter to the King declared that the generality of the people denounced the arbitrary government and oppression of their magistrates. However exaggerated such a statement might be, he at any rate found it possible to build up a party well-affected to the royal cause, and this was so rapidly furthered by his labors and by the course of events, that in the election of 1684 Bradstreet, the representative of waning Puritanism, polled only 690 votes against 631 for his competitor Danforth. Randolph complacently notes that after the election seventy of the chief merchants and gentlemen, on horseback, escorted the rejected candidates home. It is plain that, though the farmers of the country towns remained constant to the old traditions, the classes who enjoyed wealth, position and European connections, and who had been liberalized by glimpses of the larger world with which commercial Boston had more and more to do, were turning into loyal subjects of the Crown. The foundation of the Tory party was laid.

Meantime other colonies had come into existence,—the Carolinas, New Jersey and Pennsylvania,—and New York and Delaware had been acquired from the Dutch. The whole Atlantic sea-board from Maine to South Carolina was under English power. As the completion of the line by the conquest of New Netherland was an indispensable condition to the future securing of governmental unity, so also it paved the way for united political action. If not united, at any rate uniform, action soon came under the impulse of common grievances and a common opportunity. That opportunity was presented by the Revolution of 1688. The year 1689 saw the first instance of simultaneous action by several colonies toward the same end; in this instance, the expulsion of obnoxious governors and the proclamation of William and Mary.

From the date of the accession of those two monarchs, the party history of the various colonies becomes more uniform. All signs pointed to the eventual advent of colonial union, and thereby of continental parties. Throughout the period from 1690 to 1765 the chief party divisions in all but the two colonies that elected their chief magistrates arose out of disputes between the royal proprietary governors, representative of the Crown or proprietor, and the colonial assemblies, representatives of the people. The record of these disputes makes the time, so far as political history is concerned, the most tedious in the history of the colonies. Milton in his History of Britain scornfully dismissed the wars of the heptarchic period as "battles of the kites and crows"; but modern scholarship sees underlying them the widening of the rule of the local king into the rule of the bretwalda, the widening of the bretwalda's power until he achieves the unity of England. So, if the petty and personal conflicts of colonial governors and colonial assemblies cannot individually claim our attention, we may at least remember that collectively they have an importance in the development of the habit of resistance to trans-Atlantic authority and a high importance in the development of party organization in the United States.

The first part of the eighteenth century was a period of general political indifference in the colonies. To this, in almost every colony, there succeeded a period of petty and harassing disputes between governor and assembly. The royal government in great part had itself to blame for this. It frequently sent out as governors the most worthless members of the nobility, needy adventurers, and men whom corrupt party governments felt obliged to reward. Its obstinate persistence in establishing the Church of England in several colonies alienated large and powerful bodies, such as the Catholics and Quakers of Maryland and the various Dissenters of the Carolinas. Some of the governors, to be sure, were excellent men and able administrators. But even these almost inevitably became odious as the representatives of a government remote and virtually alien. Opportunities for conflict were abundant. Usually the disputes were with regard to the furnishing of money for governmental expenses by taxation. Holding the purse-strings, the assemblies attempted to bring the governor to terms by withholding supplies, especially the governor's own salary, acting therein on the ancient claim of their forefathers in the English Parliament, that redress of grievances should precede grants of supply. Disputes respecting paper-money often had a large share in the troubles, and in these and in not a few other matters the governors seem to have been in the right.

Of all the colonies, these disputes were carried to the greatest length in Pennsylvania and New York. Here party spirit reached its extreme height. Here therefore in the next generation party organization received its most complete development. When General Jackson said, "Sir, I am not a politician, but if I were I would be a New York politician," he was bestowing a commendation which, such as it was, had been deserved long before his time. Throughout our history those two great states, producing very few statesmen, seldom represented in national affairs by superior men, sterile in the development of political principles, have been fertile in skillful politicians, acute political devices, and bitter partisan struggles in which only personal questions have seemed to be in debate. Most of the great abuses in American government have there received their first development, and have thence been imported into the conduct of the federal government. The causes of the peculiar character of party action in New York and Pennsylvania lie far back, in the colonial period, and deserve from us a moment's attention. The leading causes in both were the presence of a large body of indifferent and apathetic voters, and the preoccupation of many others with commercial pursuits in New York also. During the earlier part of the century many thousands of Germans had immigrated into the colony of Pennsylvania. These, not having inherited traditions of self-government and of Anglo-Saxon modes of political action, were largely indifferent to public affairs, desiring only to be undisturbed and to be prosperous. The quarrels of governor and assembly turning mainly upon questions of money and being pushed to their greatest extreme by the assembly when war with the French was on foot, and the government was thereby embarrassed, the Quakers, a large and influential part of the population, averse to both war and taxes but not highly political, formed another important make-weight. When a great portion of the voters are indifferent, then comes the chance of the shrewd politician. Personal politics become the rule. Political contests become violently heated, but not through the ardent discussion of political principles. Such has been from the beginning the political history of Pennsylvania, sober and practical, but contributing little to public thought. If it is a new thing that one of her chief representatives at Washington sits silent in the face of tremendous accusations, it is no new thing that the other sits silent because he has nothing to say.[4]

In the colony of New York there was the same devotion to quiet prosperity, the same inertness on the part of many citizens of English birth, and there was a similar dead-weight of non-English population indifferent to large political questions and therefore at the disposal of energetic politicians. This body included the great mass of the people; the Dutch farmers, and some of the great manorial proprietors, who returned a certain number of members to the assembly, and the foreign settlers, who were very numerous; for New York was from the first noted for its mixture of nationalities, Father Jacques noting as far back as 1644 that eighteen different languages were spoken in or near it. The centre of agitation against the government lay in the group of young men of English race who founded the Whig Club and published the "Independent Reflector." The English officials, on the other hand, and the wealthy Dutch merchants of the city led an exceedingly loyal

{4.} Jameson is referring to Senators Matthew Stanley Quay (1833–1904) and James Donald Cameron (1833–1918). Quay was the subject of a series of articles in the *New York World* in February and March 1890. The articles charged him with numerous instances of accepting bribes and of malfeasance in office. According to Quay's biographer, "every incident in [*World* reporter William S. Bowen's] biographical sketch was reported from the vantage point of the boss's enemies; Bowen simply painted the most lurid picture of financial and political pilfering that could be wrung from the informants' descriptions." Cameron's father, Simon, paved the way for his son's political career, resigning his Senate seat in 1877 so that his son could assume it. Both Quay and Cameron were notorious for their absenteeism while in the Senate. A Philadelphia newspaper complained that "Pennsylvania is now voiceless in the Senate, for neither of its members can advocate, explain or defend any measure in the interest of the State or present in plain and simple English reasons why any particular measure prejudicial to this Commonwealth should not become a law." Editorial, *Philadelphia Press*, January 7, 1892, p. 4, col. 2; see also James A. Kehl, *Boss Rule in the Gilded Age: Matt Quay of Pennsylvania* (Pittsburgh: University of Pittsburgh Press, 1981), pp. 41–42, 138–44.

party, supporting King and governor with ready enthusiasm. But whereas Pennsylvania was the most democratic of all the large colonies, in New York the family influence of the great proprietors played a large part, and the party contests were often almost literally contests between the Schuylers, the Livingstons and the DeLanceys. When the contest with the mother country broke out, the DeLancey or Episcopalian connection became the Tory party, while the Schuyler and Livingston factions, reinforced by the more democratic strength of the Clintons, formed the Revolutionary party.

The Revolution first gave existence to parties extending throughout all America. As we have seen, parties favorable to the royal government and parties opposed to it had existed in each of the colonies before this time but without mutual connection. Common action in the French and Indian War made mutual connection possible. As the royal government advanced to measures more and more unwise and threatening, these popular parties drew more and more closely together, until the Committees of Correspondence finally welded them into one; then the upholders of the royal government in all the colonies were forced to draw more closely together, and the party division of America was complete. So it was in Greece. The increasing aggression of Darius and Xerxes forced into an attitude of mutual support those everywhere in every state who were determined to maintain independence, and the union of these forced concert of action on the part of the medizing Greeks everywhere.[5] Party names for the new arrangements lay ready at hand. Maintaining as the opposition party did the principles of the Revolution of 1688, of which our Revolution was but the extension to America, it was natural that they should appropriate the cherished name of the Whigs, by whom that Revolution, securing the liberty of the subject from the arbitrary oppressions and exactions of kings, had been brought about. After a long period of discredit arising from the old Jacobite intrigues, the Tory name was now, in the period succeeding the fall of Pitt's ministry, rising into renewed favor as attaching to the increasing party known as the "king's friends," which George III was so industriously and shrewdly building up. The name of American Whigs was therefore naturally matched by that of American Tories.

It has for a century been customary in America to speak of the Tories with aversion and even hostility, as of persons who were not only enemies but traitors. It is time that all this should cease. Can men become traitors to a nation which does not yet exist by remaining faithful to a government which has long existed? Why is it customary among us to eulogize the faithfulness of the Union men of West Virginia, of eastern Tennessee and of North Carolina during the late civil war? Is it not because, against the strong

---

{5.} Darius (521–486 B.C.) and his son, Xerxes I (486–465 B.C.), rulers of Persia, unsuccessfully waged war on the Greek city-states of Ionia.

opposition of communities determined to secure independence and set up a new government, they remained firm in allegiance to the old government to which they had long been attached and in devotion to the old flag? But this is precisely what the Tories did. Indeed, the comparison is not sufficiently favorable to them. For, in the first place, the chance that the proposed movement for independence would prove abortive and fail of the justification of success seemed greater than in the case of the Southern Confederacy; and, in the second place, it is well known that much of what is commended as devotion to the Union on the part of the Appalachian mountaineers was merely hostility to the ruling set, the lowland magnates in the Southern states,—and the natural enmity of the frontiersman to whatever government is nearest. It is time that, instead of remembering the Tories with aversion, we should recognize the sincerity of their patriotism, should be touched by the remembrance of their sufferings, and should be ashamed of the ungenerous rapacity and vindictive harshness with which our fathers treated them. No one can read the diary and other writings of the exiled Tory governor Hutchinson without being reminded of Macaulay's Epitaph on a Jacobite, not the best known of his poems, but one in which he for once strikes a deep and genuine note of human feeling.

> "To my true king I offered, free from stain,
> Courage and faith; vain faith, and courage vain.
> For him, I threw lands, honors, wealth away,
> And one dear hope, that was more prized than they
> For him I languished in a foreign clime
> Grey haired with sorrow in my manhood's prime
> Leave on Lavernia Scargill's whispering trees,
> And prized by Arno for my lovelier Teas.
> Beheld each night my home in fevered sleep,
> Each morning started from the dream to weep;
> Till God, who saw me tried too sorely, gave
> The resting-place I asked, an early grave.
> On thou, whom chance leads to this nameless stone
> From that proud country which was once mine own,
> By those white cliffs I never more must see,
> By that dear language which I spoke like thee,
> Forget all feuds and shed one English tear
> O'er English dust.
> A broken heart lies here."

In every discussion of party history, one of the most interesting objects of inquiries is the composition of the parties. What sort of man became a Tory when it finally became necessary to choose sides? What sort of man becomes a Whig? Of course almost all persons who enjoyed offices under the Crown became Tories, and so did most of those merchants who had extensive interests that were imperilled by rebellion. Colonists very recently arrived from England were likely to take the same side. Immigrants from Scotland usually became royalists. The Irish, on the other hand, and those of the Scotch-Irish stock, were warmly on the anti-British side, and this not only because it was anti-British, but also because this poor but sturdy race had mostly settled in the highland districts back from the Atlantic coast, and had the anti-governmental sentiments of American frontiersmen. When the loyalist Galloway, late speaker of the Assembly of Pennsylvania, was examined before a committee of the House of Commons, he was asked the question, "That part of the rebel army that enlisted in the service of the Congress—were they chiefly composed of natives of America, or were the greatest part of them English, Scotch and Irish?" To this he replied, "The names and places of their nativity being taken down, I can answer the question with precision. There were exactly one-fourth natives of America—about one-half Irish—the other fourth were English and Scotch." But his statement is evidently true of the Middle States only, certainly not of New England, where the blood was almost purely English, though such Scotch-Irish as there were, for instance in New Hampshire, were strongly revolutionary. In all the colonies the Germans generally adhered to the party of independence, but not with great ardency. Episcopalians were generally royalists. So were many of the richest farmers. The debtor class were mainly on the side of revolution. And, as is usually the case, that side was more frequently espoused by young men, the conservative cause by their elders. Among all the leaders of the Revolution, very few were forty-five years old in 1775; most were under forty.

If we investigate the Tory party in the several colonies in detail, we are forced to the conviction that, in the northern states generally, it comprised a very great share, probably more than half, of the most wealthy, educated and respectable classes. In New Hampshire the chief party divisions were local, between the men of the old towns in the southeastern part of the state, those of the southern towns immigrants from Massachusetts, and those of the Connecticut Valley, immigrants from the state of Connecticut. The last section were certainly devoted to the Revolution, and so were probably the majority of the other two. But that the exiled Tories comprised a great part of the *elite* of the province is evident from Jeremy Belknap's remark (in 1792) that "The Revolution which called the democratic power into action, has repressed the aristocratic spirit," and still more from his confession that in the new state "the deficiency of persons qualified for the various departments in government, has been much regretted, and by none, more than by those few, who know how public business ought to be conducted."

That a very great proportion of the most honored and respected men in Massachusetts were Tories is well known; e.g., it is said, nearly every physician of repute and all but a few lawyers. But probably few persons suspect the extent to which it is true. The eleven hundred refugees who sailed away with Howe in March 1776 and the thousand or more who followed them carried with them perhaps a majority of the old aristocracy of Massachusetts. The act of banishment of 1778 includes among its three hundred odd names the greater part of those which had been distinguished in the earlier days of the colony, the names of Hutchinson, Oliver, Ruggles, Amory, Brattle, Coffin, Deblois, Faneuil, Gardner, Gray, Hallowell, Pepperrell, Royall, Saltonstall, Sewall, Vassall, and Winslow. The loss of this important element, cultivated, experienced, and public-spirited, was severely felt later a very serious one. It may be said with truth that the Revolution was in Massachusetts a social as well as a political revolution. New strata everywhere came to the surface. In a certain town with whose public records I happen to be familiar, and which seems to be fairly typical, the movement was distinctly one of the middle and lower classes.[6] The men who have hitherto been most prominent in the management of town affairs drop into the background. The squires fall under suspicion and disfavor. One is deprived of his arms, with the other the town is involved in litigation. The conduct of the parson is voted inimical to the interests of the United States. A new set of leaders comes forward, men who have hitherto been far from prominent in position, and, it is plain, men of less education than those who preceded them, for the documents of the town, unconsciously bearing witness of their constructors, become at this time distinctly more illiterate. Toryism, it is interesting to note, was strong in the oldest towns, and in the Old Colony, or the counties of the Plymouth & Bristol.

The Tories of Rhode Island and Connecticut were, like those of Massachusetts, largely recruited from among the most respectable and highly educated classes. Nor need it surprise us that this should be so. The desire to keep all branches of the Anglo-Saxon race in union, the vision of a mighty English empire securely founded upon the parent island and the vast American continent, and ruling India and the islands of the sea, the vision which had kindled to its greatest warmth the imaginative genius of Pitt, was apt to seem most attractive to the most full and cultivated minds! An example of this is before our eyes today. Sir Charles Dilke tells us that in Australia, which with boundless hope and confidence is setting out upon a career of greatness certain in many respects to resemble our own, it is among the leading men, the landholding and commercial classes, that the projects of Imperial Federation find their response; the people at large, on the other hand, the ruling democracies of Australia, pay little heed to appeals to preserve the unity of the British Empire.

{6.} JFJ, ed., *Records of the Town of Amherst from 1735 to 1788*, reprinted from the *Amherst Record* (Amherst: Press of J. E. Williams, 1884).

In Connecticut the Tories were probably more numerous than in any other New England colony. This was probably due to its proximity to New York. That colony was the stronghold of the Tories. With New Jersey and Pennsylvania, it furnished the larger part of the armed bodies of royalists. The bulk of the property-owners in the colony belonged to that party, and it was strong also among the middle classes of the towns and among the country population. On the large manorial estates the tenant farmers sided with their landlords if they took sides at all. The city of New York and the county of Westchester, on the mainland, were ardently Tory, and so were Staten Island and the three counties of Long Island. In Pennsylvania it is probable that during the critical years of the war, at least, the majority of the population was on the side of the Crown, and that majority seems to have included a large portion of the persons of most eminence, as well as many Quakers, insomuch that Congress recommended all the states to seize the papers of the Quaker yearly meetings, and to transmit the political part of their contents to Congress.

In Delaware there were many Tories in the southernmost county. In Maryland there were not a few. In Virginia there seem to have been almost none, and the Virginia aristocracy, full of the spirit of local independence, took quite the opposite side to that espoused by their northern compeers, and this almost unanimously. North Carolina had from the very beginning of its history been torn by internal dissensions, and now was almost evenly divided between Whig and Tory; but of the characteristics of either party it is not easy to discover much, save that from Governor Martin's proclamation of 1775 it is to be inferred that he expected most support for the king's cause from certain of the more western counties. In South Carolina, too, the party divisions were mainly local in their character. Ever since the upland region had been settled, chiefly by that Scotch-Irish stock of which Jackson and Calhoun both sprang, there had been a standing antagonism between the settlers there and the lords of the lowlands, the great rice and indigo planters. Yet when most of the latter threw themselves into the cause of revolution, it was only a part of the former that held aloof; the former Regulators who had opposed the royal government in the uplands now remained neutral for the time being, and so did the Germans. The Scotch-Irish who had come directly into the province, and held their lands on specially favorable royal grants, refused to stir. But those Irish who had migrated from the northern colonies engaged heartily in the Revolutionary cause, and Ramsay tells us that though there were some royalists in every part of the province, there was no settlement in which they outnumbered the friends of Congress excepting the district between the Broad and Saluda rivers. He also tells us that "beside their superiority in numbers, there was an ardor and enthusiasm in the friends of congress which was generally wanting in the advocates for royal government." But later, and especially after the capture of Charleston, the royalist party in both South Carolina and Georgia grew to formidable dimensions, and the war between the two factions was carried on with bitterness and even with ferocity.

It is difficult to give any trustworthy estimate of the respective numbers of Tories and Revolutionaries. In fact, their numbers must have been vastly different at different epochs in the struggle. When war began, the Tories formed probably a minority,—but a very large minority. At its close, it is estimated that those who had fled to New Brunswick and Nova Scotia alone amounted with their families, to not less than 35,000 persons, and the whole number of the refugees to 100,000. With their departure, the story of active Toryism in America, ends; [save that of Boston, two gentlemen, the daughters of the Rev. Mather Byles, a Tory clergyman, continued through their old age even to 1831 to keep the birthday of the King of G.B. George III. and to regard themselves as his subjects].{7}

But even yet we have not reached the full formation of American political parties, organized for the peaceable, or at least usually peaceable, contests of the polls. These could not come until governmental unity had been attained, or was in sight. Neglecting therefore such party divisions as those which revealed themselves in the Continental Congress between delegates who were ready for immediate declaration of independence and delegates who were not yet ready for so decided a step, we pass to the contests of the years 1787–1790 over the work of the Philadelphia Convention. First, however, it is well to premise that, just as minor local party divisions had prepared the way for the Continental schism of Whig and Tory, so in the years preceding 1787 state parties had sprung up, whose cleavage did much to fix the line of division between Federalist and Anti-federalist. That division was preferred in the mutual jealousies of Congregationalists & Episcopalians in N.H. In Massachusetts the name of the Essex Junto, afterward so famous, had already been applied by Hancock as early as 1781. The able group of leaders so denominated represented the commercial interest, and the desire of that commercial interest for stronger government; it was therefore among the origins of federalism. But the votes for governor, from 1780 to 1789, show that a well-defined party contest hardly existed in any year save 1786. In that year came the insurrection of Daniel Shays, which is to be reckoned among the origins of Massachusetts anti-federalism. Rhode Island had the opponents and the advocates of paper money; Connecticut the advocates and the opponents of the Congregational church establishment. In New York the attainder of the DeLanceys and the confiscations of Tory property had removed one great family interest, and the field remained clear for the Schuylers, the Livingstons and the Clintons. Of these the first became the Federalist party in New York. The two latter were temporarily united in support of Anti-federalism

{7.} Brackets in original document.

by Aaron Burr, the father of such as make deals and run primaries. Pennsylvania was given over to vigorous struggles about the state constitution, waged between two parties called the Republicans and the Constitutionalists respectively. Their character is described in the autobiography of Charles Biddle, vice-president of the supreme council of Pennsylvania. "The Republicans," he says . . . "have always been the most wealthy, and generally the most respectable of our inhabitants, but they never make those exertions that are made by the opposite party, especially on the election ground." Here, it is plain, we have the element which subsequently formed the Federalist party in Pennsylvania. The Constitutionalists, on the other hand, zealous supporters of the existing democratic constitution, whom Biddle describes as exceedingly jealous, especially of army men, were evidently soon to become Anti-federalists and Democrats. In states further south, we do not find the existence of definite parties mentioned in these few years.

Beside the facts referred to, we shall find that, without continuity of life from Tory to Federalist, the districts that abounded in Tories in 1775 often abounded in Federalists in 1788. So it was with south-eastern New Hampshire, and with Newport and its island. In Massachusetts, those same ancient towns which had included many Tories were also strenuous in their resistance to the plebeian and Adullamite insurrection of Shays and in 1788 were strong in their advocacy of the new Constitution of the United States. I may add that it is also most often those towns in which, a dozen or twenty years later, in the days of Professor Henry Ware, that the first church became Unitarian. And similarly in other states the connection of Toryism and Federalism is made manifest geographically.

If among mankind at large the most natural party divisions are those between the conservative and the progressive, federal unions have a special basis for party differences, which may or may not coincide with these. They are sure, from the nature of the case, to have a party of consolidation or national union and a party of state-rights. In the chief federal republic existing in 1787, the republic of the United Netherlands, two such parties had been in existence for two hundred years. How much more than this simple issue was involved in the contests of Federalists and Anti-federalists I will not stop to set forth. The principles which were at stake in those contests belong properly to the province of the next lecturer.[8] If I intrude upon his field at all it is to conclude my narrative by displaying not the principles but, in part, the composition of our first two national parties, and their relations to the less extensive or less permanent party divisions which preceded them. This I have chosen to do partly by rough maps of certain of the states,

{8.} Anson Daniel Morse (1846–1916), professor of history at Amherst College, presented the next lecture, "The Federalist Era," on December 8, 1890. See the *Providence Journal*, December 9, 1890, p. 3, col. 7.

upon which are indicated the localities favoring one or the other party in the contest for ratification of the Constitution in 1787 and 1788. Popular votes upon which to base these indications are not in existence. Our only resource is the vote of the representative of the locality in the convention upon the final question of ratification. This is not a certain guide, for in that vote the member may not have represented his constituents; but it will be in the main trustworthy. It should be added that much is known from other sources, respecting the popular attitude toward the Constitution,—that the rich and commercial classes favored it, while the poor and the ignorant opposed, that it was readily accepted by the small states, reluctantly by the large, that the former officers of the Continental army favored it almost to a man, that the minor religious sects viewed it with some distrust, and so forth.

Let us proceed now to our maps.[9] They represent only seven of the states. The conventions of Delaware, New Jersey and Georgia ratified the constitution unanimously, and therefore furnish no guide as to the geographical distribution of public opinion. Materials for a complete delineation in the case of Maryland, Virginia and North Carolina have not been accessible to me. In the states which are represented, districts whose members opposed the new form of government are noted in black, while those which favored it are shaded and regions not settled (i.e. to the extent of two inhabitants to the square mile) are left blank. One general fact is to be noted at the outset. The alluvial districts, the regions of most fertile land, were almost uniformly in favor of ratification, the hilly regions, the watersheds between the fertile valleys, were generally opposed. In New Hampshire all the delegates from the coast towns, almost all those from the valley of the Piscataquis, and many of those around Lake Wainspisagee voted aye. So did almost all the fertile farming towns of the Connecticut valley, and many of those in the valley of the Merrimac. The strength of the opposition lay in the regions of greater altitude or less fertile soil facing the watershed between the Merrimac and the Connecticut, or lying between the Merrimac Valley and the sea. In Massachusetts the Federalist strength came from the coast regions, which were almost entirely of this way of thinking, the more fertile parts of Middlesex and what is now Norfolk County, the fruitful valley of the Connecticut and the valley of the Housatonic, while the fear of strong government came mostly from the hill towns. So it did in Rhode Island, where the map represents the vote of towns in the convention of 1790. Here, however, the Anti-federal strength was reinforced by several coast & valley towns. In Connecticut again, where ratification was carried by an overwhelming majority, that majority rested on the coast-belt and the valleys of the Thames, the Connecticut and the Housatonic, while the minority was derived from a certain portion of the poor hill-towns lying between those valleys. Southward from

{9.} These maps have not survived.

New England, in states where the county-system prevented, representation in the conventions was by counties, not by towns, and the results appear in less detail, but the general fact is much the same. In New York the islands and the more favored half of the lower Hudson valley were Federal, the rest of the state was anti-federal. Delaware, which lies wholly within the alluvial belt and New Jersey, of which the settled portions lie mainly within it, were unanimous in acceptance of the new constitution. Of Pennsylvania the rich farming lands along the Delaware and the Susquehanna and in the fertile region between the two were Federalist, the remaining counties, with a sporadic exception or two, Anti-federalist. The vote for the Maryland convention was very strongly in favor of the new constitution. Since but two counties and a half lay outside the alluvial belt, it is no great exception to our generalization that a large share of the opposition came from the coast counties of Ann Arundel and Harford. But Ann Arundel was carried but narrowly in the elections to the convention, and Annapolis itself was Federal. In Virginia the small counties of the tide-water region were in favor of the Constitution, but not without exceptions, as where the personal influence of Patrick Henry carried Prince Edward adversely, and that of Benjamin Harrison and John Tyler took away Charles City. The same seems to have been true of North Carolina, Iredell and his Federal friends apparently obtaining most of their support from seaboard counties like Chowan, Craven, Onslow and (New Hanover). As for South Carolina, the map shows the plainest and broadest division between upland and lowland.

If we go more into detail we note, in New Hampshire, that the towns in the western valley, settled from Connecticut, followed that state in its approval of the new system. The strong showing for Federalism in the thinly-settled north part of the state is probably in part due to its representation in the convention by certain magnates likely to be more Federal than their constituents. But it is probably due mostly to the desire of those who fronted an alien country to be protected by a strong government, the same impulse which brought Georgia into the Union unanimously. The district of Maine was almost wholly Anti-federal. Elsewhere in Massachusetts the largest element in the Anti-federal strength came from those towns which had but recently been engaged in Shays' Rebellion, that is, from Worcester County and the portions of old Hampshire County east of the Connecticut. The similar insurrections in Ber{k}shire and the discontent arising there from the boundary disputes with New York left a similar legacy of feeling against government, which reveals itself in the marking of westernmost Massachusetts upon the map. A glance at the map of Connecticut shows along its northern border a marked influence of the Shays Rebellion there, in a large amount of Anti-federal sentiment. The lighter spots that here and there appear in the western half of Massachusetts are such as indicate that the oldest towns were Federalist. So were in general the towns where there were many Tories, such as the great maritime towns and those of Plymouth and Bristol Counties, and so was Nantucket, which had been practically neutral during the Revolution. In Rhode Island, if not all the coast towns were Federal, at least all the maritime and commercial towns were. Newport and Bristol counties in the convention of 1790 voted solidly for the new Constitution, and so did Providence and Westerly. I have heard it said that one cause of Rhode Island's temporary rejection of the Union was an unevenness of representation in the deliberating bodies, whereby a popular majority failed to secure its rights. I point out, in passing, that the contrary is true. In the convention which accepted it the votes against it came from towns which in the census of that year had an aggregate population of nearly 36,000, while the votes in its favor came from towns aggregating only 32,000 inhabitants. But in point of fact such an argument is needless, for it is probable that, taking the whole thirteen states together, a universal popular vote, could it have been taken, would have proved adverse to the new plan.

As we enter the Middle States we come into a region where nationality has much to do with the result. If in New York the Dutch farmers were favorable, the Irish and English settlers of the remoter counties were opposed. In Pennsylvania the Germans may have been favorable. But the Irish had much more political activity. The western country was almost wholly in their control. Charles Biddle tells us that so largely, almost exclusively, were the politicians of the Western counties Irish that even those who were not spoke with somewhat of an Irish brogue. Here, in the regions later famous for the Whiskey Insurrection, the new government met with no favor. In the northeasternmost settled part of the state, a region not less rugged and peopled by backwoodsmen not less than the western region, we see a large area of Federalism. This is the mark of the Connecticut Yankees who had settled in Luzerne County and the Wyoming valley. The Quakers, too, were mostly Federalist. The Federalism of Huntingdon County I am at a loss to account for, but I should add that its evidence is in the vote of the Assembly, and not of the Convention, where I believe its vote does not appear.

In Virginia the normal relations of Federal and Anti-federal were disturbed by heightened objections to the new government arising from the fact that Virginia was the greatest of all the states, and felt especially jealous of her independence and especially able to stand alone. Moreover, her aversion to a strong general government had been recently increased by the course pursued by Congress in respect to the right to the navigation of the Mississippi. It is to this last that we must attribute the fact that the delegates from the Kentucky district were unanimously anti-federal. The small and old counties of Virginia were mostly in favor of acceptance, the new counties of large area opposed. The towns were Federal. Fredericksburg, for instance, was Federal, though its county of Spottsylvania was Anti-federal. The southwestern counties and those south of the middle and upper course of the James River were opposed. So were the Virginia Baptists. So were the judges of the general court and the admiralty court, and most of the members of the bar. In North Carolina, debtors and public officers were said to be against Union, the Quakers and the Scotch merchants for it; the western region which afterward became Tennessee was as strongly Anti-federal as Kentucky. Such were the small rivulets of local and temporary interest which joined to make up the great streams of federal and anti-federal feeling. But it should not be forgotten that amid them a great place belongs to the larger motives that for many years were to be fundamental in our politics, on the one hand the desire to preserve local autonomy and individual freedom, and on the other hand the high ambition by founding a more perfect union, to secure to this western world the majestic career of imperial greatness which Bishop Berkeley had prophesied for it.

As the lines were drawn in the momentous conflict of 1788, so in general they were drawn when, a few years later, Thomas Jefferson, calling all Israel to their tents, organized anti-federalism into the Democratic-Republican party. Thus I have brought my narrative down to the time when national parties were fully formed in the United States, and took their places as a recognized and valued adjunct in our political system. It may be that, in entering so far into the curiosities of party history in the times of Tories and especially of Federalists, I have presumed upon too strong an interest in historical detail. If so, the corrective will be supplied by my friend who lectures before you again on next Monday evening, and who will point out the meaning of the battle and the nature of the strategy, where I have been content to catalogue the battalions and to exhibit the seat of war.

AM, Box 28, JP, DLC.

Lectures on the Constitutional and
Political History of the South

Jameson's interest in the South was stimulated while he was a graduate student at the Johns Hopkins University, where the largely southern student body as well as the location of the university in Baltimore invited an investigation of the region's history and politics.[1] In the spring of 1890, while a professor at Brown University, Jameson planned a research trip to Virginia for the following year, complementing the investigation of state political and constitutional history in the North that he had also begun.[2]

It was in connection with his projected trip to Virginia that Jameson wrote to Herbert B. Adams, head of the Seminary of Historical and Political Science at Hopkins, and offered to give a series of lectures to the graduate students in the seminary. Johns Hopkins president Daniel C. Gilman and Adams endorsed the idea as a source of both instruction and inspiration; Gilman suggested that the university begin a series of "Fellowship courses of lectures" and "invite every year some of those who have been on our roll as fellows to come back and allow us to share in the fruits of their after-studies."[3] For this reason, where Jameson calls attention in these lectures to works produced by members of the seminary, we provide full citations. After negotiations with the Hopkins Board of Trustees and Gilman, Adams invited Jameson to present ten lectures on southern constitutional history during the spring of 1891.[4] Jameson presented the lectures between May 6 and May 22 to graduate students in the seminary, undergraduates, and members of the public.[5]

The typed manuscript in the Jameson Papers that forms the basis for the following text is untitled. We have titled it by referring to the correspondence by which arrangements for the lectures were made and to the subject matter covered in the lectures. This text incorporates without comment minor corrections evidently made over a number of years. In the lectures covering the more recent history of the South, Jameson made numerous changes in the text, reflecting his difficulty in maintaining an objective stance in matters of current political interest. Significant alterations of the text are noted.

NOTES

1. See John David Smith, *An Old Creed for the New South: Proslavery Ideology and Historiography, 1865–1918* (Westport, Conn.: Greenwood Press, 1985), chapter 5.

2. Herbert B. Adams to JFJ, May 15, 1890, TLS; July 3, 14, 1890, both ALS, all in Box 46, JP, DLC. See also [JFJ], "A Little Journey of Historical Research in Eastern Virginia," paper delivered to the Rhode Island Historical Society, February 23, 1892, TM, Box 28, JP, DLC.

3. [Herbert B. Adams] to Daniel C. Gilman, May 13, 1890, TL, Daniel C. Gilman Papers, MdBJ; Adams to JFJ, May 15, 1890, TLS, Box 46, JP, DLC; Gilman to JFJ, July 25, 1890, ALS, Box 86, JP, DLC; JFJ to Adams, January 14, 1891, ALS, Herbert B. Adams Papers, MdBJ; Adams to JFJ, April 14, 1891, TLS, Box 46, JP, DLC.

4. JFJ to Herbert B. Adams, July 2, 1890, ALS, Herbert B. Adams Papers, MdBJ; Adams to Jameson, July 3, 14, September 8, 1890, all ALS; Adams to JFJ, November 28, 1890, TLS; and Adams to JFJ, January 9, 1891, TLS, all in Box 46, JP, DLC.

5. See *Johns Hopkins University Circulars* 10 (June, 1891): 130; and the following articles, all in the *Baltimore Sun:* "Southern History: An Interesting Series of Lectures By Professor J. Franklin Jameson," May 7, 1891, p. 6, col. 3; "Constitutions of Southern States," May 8, 1891, p. 6, col. 3; "Southern History: The Constitutions of Maryland, North Carolina and Georgia," May 9, 1891, p. 8, col. 2; "Southern History: Professor Jameson Continues His Lectures at Johns Hopkins University," May 14, 1891, p. 6, col 3; and "Southern History: Professor J. Franklin Jameson on the Period of the Federalists," May 16, 1891, p. 4, col. 5.

I

THE REVOLUTION obviously affords a most appropriate point of time at which to begin such studies as these. It is necessary first however to give ourselves some account of the constitutions of the Southern Colonies and of their political status at the time when that crisis occurred. My first lecture will therefore be devoted to a brief presentation of this subject. I shall begin with Virginia because not only was that colony the oldest of the group, but its constitution seems to have served in large degree as a type and model of those which grew up in the colonies of later date. The historical steps by which the colony of Virginia attained its final shape are probably familiar. The first and second charters of the Virginia Company granted in 1606 and 1609 were followed by an instrument of greater vitality granted in 1612. It provides for institutions of government for the Company itself in London and for the colony in Virginia. The former was to be governed by a Treasurer or President, a Council of twenty four persons meeting and transacting business at frequent intervals and a great and general Court of the Company, or as we should say a general meeting of the stock-holders four times a year. The charter gave to this assembly the power to appoint officers and make laws for the government of Virginia. The governor in Virginia was subsequently given a council to advise him and finally the colonial constitution received its completion by the calling into existence of a colonial assembly, consisting of two deputies or burgesses from each plantation. At first the governor, the council and the burgesses met together in a single body, consulting regarding the public weal and enacting laws, but soon a separation was effected in such manner that the council in its legislative aspect and the assembly formed two houses of a colonial legislature.

Such was the form which the constitution of the colony of Virginia early acquired and such in its main outlines it remained until the time of the Revolution. But what was the origin of this form of government? A recent writer in the Annals of the American Academy of Political and Social Science, Professor William C. Morey, has developed the view which had been suggested before, that one must look for the origins of the constitutions of royal colonies to the constitutions of the chartered companies by which some of the colonies were established. He points out interesting analogies between the form of government of the Virginia Company and the form of government which the colony of Virginia maintained long after the company ended its troubled existence, and he rejects the view that the Virginia constitution of 1621 was modelled after that of the English government. Possibly he is right in this last, but his affirmative arguments seem to be weakened, if one brings into the comparison the constitutions of ancient British colonies which did not go through a period of subjection to the rule of a chartered company.—

(A group of colonies, I may say in parenthesis, whose institutions have received less attention than they deserve from those who inquire into the early history of our royal colonies.) I refer to certain of those present possessions of the British government which were in its possession in the times when our colonial constitutions were taking shape. One, Bermuda, was for a time under the administration of a company in London and it may be urged that the Bahamas also were subject in a considerable degree to the influence of the colonies of the mainland. We may, however, adduce with safety the example of Barbadoes, Jamaica and Antigua. Barbadoes acquired in the Seventeenth Century and still retains a constitution of which the leading features were a governor appointed by the crown, an executive council appointed by the crown and a legislature consisting of the governor, an appointed legislative council and an elective assembly chosen by the free-holders of each parish. Antigua and Jamaica early acquired constitutions even more closely resembling that of our royal colonies, tho' their constitutions no longer remain in their original shape. (Avalle and Parliamentary Return.) In the Seventeenth Century their constitution included a governor, a nominated council, which also acted as an upper house of the legislature, and an assembly elected by the free-holders of the parishes. Now if this form of constitution came into existence in the Seventeenth Century in colonies which had not passed through the experience of subjection to a colonizing company, we must regard the fact as weakening somewhat the force of the arguments which Mr. Morey adduces in favor of ascribing the origin of the colonial constitution of Virginia to the influence of the constitution of the Virginia Company.

Whatever may have been its origin the constitution of Virginia in the year 1774 was one fairly well adapted to the needs of a province of the British crown. At the head of the administration was a governor appointed by the crown and enjoying a salary of seventeen hundred pounds. The governor was not simply the chief executive and the commander of the militia: he had also the powers of a chief justice, a chancellor and a vice-admiral. He had theoretically the right to collate to all benefices, could pardon except in capital cases, summoned, prorogued and dissolved the assembly and exercised, though not without question, a veto upon its legislation. He appointed his council and all officers but the treasurer and the speaker of the assembly, even to appointing the clerks of the assembly. The council consisted regularly of twelve members. Beside their functions in the executive and legislative branches of the government, they, with the governor, constituted the chief law court, and were colonels of the militia in their respective counties, naval officers and collectors of revenue. The house of Burgesses exercised the chief power in legislation and had the exclusive right of levying taxes. It consisted of two members from each county (and in 1774 there were 61 counties) together with one member for the borough of Norfolk, one for Jamestown, one for the city of Williamsburgh and one for the college of William and Mary. It therefore included at the outbreak of the Revolution one hundred and twenty six members. (Hening VIII:305.) A new act respecting the elections to the house had been passed in the session of 1769. This act gave a right to vote at any election of burgesses for any county to any man who had a free-hold estate for his own life or the life of another, or other greater estate in at least fifty acres of land unsettled, or twenty five acres with a plantation and house thereon at least twelve feet square, lying or principally lying in that county, or who possessed a lot or part of a lot in any city or town with a house thereon at least twelve feet square. Penalties were prescribed for freeholders failing to vote. The sheriff caused the ministers of all the parishes to announce the ensuing election immediately after divine service on the preceding Sundays. When election day arrived, if a poll were required, the free-holders were required to vote viva voce at the hustings according to the old English fashion. The privileges of members resembled those of members of the House of Commons. They were paid ten shillings a day and varying allowances for time spent in coming to the sessions and returning. The burgesses chose the treasurer of the colony and their speaker. Until lately these two offices had been united in the hands of the same person, but in 1766, upon the death of John Robinson, who had held both these offices, extensive peculations on his part were brought to light, arising mainly from his practice of lending the monies of the colony to assist his friends in their financial difficulties. His colleagues, unable to take the lenient view of such transactions which has of late been held in respect to a member of one of our legislative bodies, prosecuted their claims upon his estate and separated permanently the offices of treasurer and of speaker.[1] The treasurer henceforth enjoyed a salary of one hundred pounds plus five per cent. of all the monies received by him, the speaker the sum of five hundred pounds sterling.

As for the judiciary system in the year 1765, there were inferior courts known as county courts, sitting once a month at the county towns. Each of these consisted of eight gentlemen of the county appointed as judges by the governor. Quarter sessions were also held at the county towns by the justices of the quorum and by those of the general court on circuit. The local justices of these courts were country gentlemen, for the most part not trained in the

{1.} In March 1891 the *New York Times* ran front-page stories concerning William Herbert, a prominent Delaware politician and former state treasurer. The stories focused on Herbert's use of state treasury funds to make personal loans. After Herbert paid back $90,000 of approximately $124,000 that he had loaned out, the *Times* stated: "His personal honesty is undoubted, and in loaning the State's funds he simply followed a precedent that has been in existence here for years." *New York Times*, "Delaware Funds Missing," March 3, 1891, p. 1, col. 1; "Delaware's Lost Securities," March 4, 1891, p. 1, col. 4.

law. Twice a year at Williamsburgh the general court, consisting of the governor and council sat as a court of oyer and terminer and to hear appeals from the courts below. As an incident to the governor's functions as chancellor and vice-admiral, he and his council also sat as a court of chancery, court of admiralty and a spiritual court. Appeal lay from them to the judicial committee of the Privy Council for all cases involving more than five hundred pounds, but such appeals were expensive and in practice not common.

The local government was, as is familiar, organized upon the county system. There were, to be sure, a few towns, which strenuous efforts of the legislature had not been able to endow with any great vitality or size, and Norfolk had fully the organization of a borough with mayor, recorder, eight aldermen and sixteen common councilmen; but in general Virginia was agricultural and its population rural. The great extent of the alluvial plain and the numerous rivers which made all parts of it accessible to the ships of the London merchants, made unnecessary that concentration of population which was so marked a feature of the settlement of the New England colonies. Being thus left free to do as they would, the early settlers had reverted to the indulgence of that preference which Tacitus ascribes to their Germanic forefathers and "dwelt apart, each by himself, as woodside, plain or fresh spring attracts him." Therefore of the two sets of local institutions which in the England of the Seventeenth Century existed side by side, while the institutions of the township had had almost exclusive sway in the New England colonies, those of county government had received an almost exclusive development in Virginia and in the southern colonies in general. The difference was something more than a difference in area. While in the New England township all affairs of government were discussed by all the freemen and their decisions carried out by officers whom they had themselves elected, in the Virginian county there was no general public discussion and no extensive election of officials and therefore little self-government. The principal officers of the county were appointed by the governor. If the governor was almost always guided by the opinion of the local magnates, this tempered his autocracy with the influence of the few rather than of the many. The form of local government in Virginia was therefore highly aristocratic and confined the administration of local affairs for the most part to the control of the wealthy planters. Highest among the county officers whom the governor appointed stood the lieutenant of the county, who commanded its militia and had in a way a position analogous to that of the lord lieutenant of an English county. The greater portion of the administrative work of the county was, like its judicial work, performed by the justices sitting in the quarter sessions. In 1774 Virginia comprised, of the next sub-division below the county, seventy or eighty parishes governed by elected boards of vestry-men, who beside their important position in church affairs, had very considerable secular functions making returns of births, marriages and deaths, imprisoning for crimes, providing for the maintenance of the poor, apportioning the levy of taxes and appointing minor local officers.

The Church of England had early been established by the colony. Its clergy were provided for by glebes and tithes and from time to time laws of more or less stringency were passed to enforce conformity to it. By the year 1774, however, the number of non-conformists had probably come to equal, if not to exceed the number of adherents of the Established Church. The state of public feeling regarding the parsons is well illustrated by the celebrated case of the parsons, in which Patrick Henry won his first distinction (apparently on the wrong side). [Clergy el. by vestry, Dev Jarratt's life, 80.]

A few more points may perhaps be deserving of mention in order to make more complete the picture of the colonial constitution of Virginia. The attachment to primogeniture and to the system of entails, another mark of an aristocratic organization of society, had been so great that an act of the year 1705 made it impossible to dock entails by fine and recovery; they could be barred only by act of legislature. Many such acts are to be found in the eighth and preceding volumes of Hening. The system of taxation was by a levy of six, eight and nine pounds of tobacco on every "tithable," recently about once in every three years. The regulations respecting slaves had grown somewhat more severe during the period preceding. Slaves going abroad without leave were subject to corporal punishment by the master or overseer of the plantation where found and more than five blacks were not to meet together except for lawful business or for church. There were restrictions upon the hiring out of slaves. When tried for offences punished with life or limb, their trial, though public, was without jury. A slave-owner was not liable to prosecution if his slave died during correction, provided the killing was not wilful. The population of Virginia in 1774 cannot be very closely estimated. In 1782 it was estimated by Mr. Jefferson to include about three hundred thousand free inhabitants and two hundred and seventy thousand slaves.

(Refer to Poore, Hening, Virginia Calendars of State Papers, Burk's "Virginia," Campbell's various works, Papers relating to the History of the Church, Brackett's Essay.)

In respect to the broader features of constitutional and political life a general similarity pervaded all the southern colonies. The governmental institutions which have been described in the case of Virginia and the characteristics of the organization of Virginian society both find a parallel in the other colonies. Especially is this true of Maryland. In respect to the forms of governmental organization it stood perhaps no nearer to Virginia than the colonies lying to the southward: indeed as a proprietary colony it presented some features quite distinct; but climate, natural and other features of physical geography and the economic conditions resulting from them gave to the organization of society in Maryland a form closely resembling that observed in Virginia. Yet, while in Maryland as in Virginia the dominant influence in political affairs lay in the hands of a land-holding aristocracy, the Maryland aristocracy seems to have been less compact, less firmly united and less completely influential than that of Virginia. Side by side with it and rivalling it in influence was a body of energetic and wealthy merchants more considerable than the corresponding class in Virginia; for while Norfolk, the commercial capital of the latter, though of far greater size than its political capital, Williamsburgh, had reached a population of only seven thousand, Baltimore had in forty-four years attained a population of fifteen or twenty thousand inhabitants, so that the commercial element was already large and of great influence in the government of the province. In other respects too the rule of the great land-holders was less complete. On the one hand the powers of the governor had been more fully preserved by reason of the fact that behind him stood, not the crown, but a virtually independent proprietor. For instance, in the government of the church, while the governors of Virginia early lost all substantial power of appointment of rectors, the governor of Maryland freely inducted candidates—and it must be said often most improper candidates—to benefices within the province. (See Papers relating to the History of the Church in Maryland 334–339; The Reverend Jonathan Boucher, "Discourse on reducing the Revenue of the Clergy" in his "View of the Causes and consequences of the American Revolution{.}") To be sure, the authority of the governor was far from remaining uncontested. The correspondence of Governor Sharpe, recently published by the Maryland Historical Society, shows in the most interesting manner the frequency and intensity of the disputes between the governor and the assembly. (See especially, Vol. II, Calvert to Sharpe, 375–387, Sharpe to Calvert, 423–434.) The assembly frequently claimed the rights and privileges of a House of Commons, a claim against which Attorney General Pratt, afterward Lord Camden, pronounced most decidedly in 1759. (Sharpe Correspondence, II: vii.) Nevertheless the powers of the governor remained extensive though less in the hands of Governor Robert Eden than they had been in those of Sharpe. On the other hand, that the rule of the aristocracy was less complete than in Virginia is seen from the vigorous existence of popular meetings in the sub-divisions of the county called "Hundreds." Another sign is seen in the fact that under Maryland law entails could be docked by common recoveries, an easier process than that which, as we have seen, was provided by Virginian law. Perhaps it was in the sphere of local government that the institutions of Maryland differed most signally from those of Virginia. The hundred retained its importance in the smaller province and was essentially the fiscal, military and election district. The manor remained in existence in numerous instances, exhibiting upon the soil of America one of the most picturesque of those survivals of English usage in the local government of the colonies to which this seminary was in its earlier days with so interesting and valuable results devoted. The county indeed was of importance as a judicial district, having also administrative functions of lesser consequence. But for these matters of local government I must be content to refer to the interesting monographs of Mr. Ingle and Mr. Johnson in the first series of the Johns Hopkins Studies and to that of Mr. Wilhelm in the third.[2]

The central government of the province was like that of Virginia with the proprietor substituted for the King. The proprietary governor was assisted in executive matters by an appointed council of twelve members, in legislative matters by that council as an upper house and by a lower house consisting of four burgesses from each of the sixteen counties and two from the city of Annapolis. Elections were triennial. The suffrage, in accordance with the Act of 1716, belonged in each county to all freemen of the county who had in the county a freehold estate of fifty acres, or were residents and had a visible estate of forty pounds. Catholics were excluded from office & vote. The judiciary was organized upon a simple system and seems to have worked in a fairly satisfactory manner, in spite of the general absence of legal attainments among those who occupied the bench. County courts consisting of four or more magistrates appointed by the governor from among the leading gentlemen held quarter sessions. Cases of greater consequence came before the Provincial court, which sat twice a year at Annapolis; but that this more dignified court did not possess great legal learning, in spite of the high standing of the bar in Maryland, may be inferred from the fact that in a reported case of the year 1772, the justices being at a loss to determine the points at issue, sought for the opinions of some of the gentlemen of the bar, who were not engaged in the cause. (I, Harris & McHenry 437{.}) There was also a high court of appeals and a court of chancery composed of the governor and his council. Such matters as in England came before ecclesiastical courts were here adjudged by a prerogative court presided over by the commissary general, from which appeals lay to a court of delegates specially appointed by the governor. (I, Harris & McHenry 409, 509.) The picture which has been given of the constitutional peculiarities of Maryland, needs to be completed by an account of Maryland slavery, but the admirable historical work written upon that subject by a member of this seminary makes it possible for me to refer for a full treatment of this matter to Mr. Brackett's "The Negro in Maryland."[3]

{2.} Edward Ingle, *Parish Institutions of Maryland, with Illustrations from Parish Records* (1883; reprint, New York: Johnson Reprint Corporation, 1979); John H. Johnson, *Old Maryland Manors, with the Records of a Court Leet and a Court Baron* (Baltimore: Johns Hopkins University, 1883); Lewis W. Wilhelm, *Local Institutions in Maryland* (Baltimore: Johns Hopkins University, 1885).

{3.} Jeffrey R. Brackett, *The Negro in Maryland* (Baltimore: Johns Hopkins University, 1889).

In entering North Carolina one comes into a new climate of political conditions. The Philadelphia Convention of 1787, in apportioning representatives provisionally to the various states, assigned to North Carolina a number proportioned to a population of about two hundred thousand. This was in all probability the best estimate then attainable, yet when the census of 1790 was taken Americans were astonished to discover that the population of the state was a little less than four hundred thousand. The fact is significant. Never in the course of her whole history has North Carolina maintained in the opinions of Americans or in the councils of the Union an importance at all proportioned to the magnitude of her population. In part her inhabitants resembled those people who in the Book of Judges are described as dwelling "quiet and secure, after the manner of the Zidonians, and having no dealings with any man." In part, however, it must also be confessed, her history resembles that of the times mentioned in Sacred Writ, when "there was no judge in the land and every man did that which was right in his own eyes." North Carolina in other words had remained from the beginning of her history to the time which we have reached a community large indeed, prosperous and contented and apparently virtuous in private life, but filled with constant dissension, unorganized and in political matters largely impotent. In the very year which we take as the year of our survey there were no superior courts whatever in the province, because the House of Commons refused to pass bills ordaining any such courts save in a form which it was known that the crown, Governor Martin and the Council would not approve. (Martin, II:294–326.) Before this time there had been a supreme court sitting twice annually in the chief town of each of the six districts into which the province was for judicial purposes divided. Municipal courts for each county met at the county towns. In 1774 there were about thirty counties. The lower house consisted of from two to five representatives from each of these (five in the six older or northern counties, two in the newer) together with two members for New Berne and one each for Edenton, Wilmington, Bath & Halifax. A qualification of property in land was required in order to hold office and only freeholders could vote. The upper house consisted of a council of twelve members. (Brickell's North Carolina, 1743.) In 1766 the treasurer began to be appointed by the legislature. Before, the introduction of this practice had been hindered by the fact that the upper and lower house could not agree. (Martin II:222.) The English Church was by law established in North Carolina, but there were few parsons of the Established Church. In 1765 the new governor Tryon urged the passage of a better clergy law. Arguing the necessity of keeping up the Established Church, he declared himself the advocate of toleration, "but observed he had never heard toleration urged in any country as an argument to exempt dissenters from their share of the support of the Established Church." (Martin II:194.) The assembly so far agreed as to pass a law that church wardens should provide a glebe and a salary of one hundred and thirty three pounds thirteen shillings for each minister.

In its main elements the colonial constitution of South Carolina resembled those which have already been described. Perhaps the power of the governor was somewhat more restricted than in Virginia. The council consisted of twelve members but seldom more than four attended the meetings. (Lowndes's Opinion in Drayton I:122.) Drayton declares in his Memoirs (I:238) that in 1775 there were only eight councillors in the province of which number five were not only crown officers but strangers. Ramsey says, "His Majesty's Council for several years had been losing their weight in the government. Their number was small and they were for the most part persons of little influence, unknown to the inhabitants in any other character than that of needy and depending crown officers." Obviously this at once distinguished the council in a considerable degree from that of Virginia. The assembly in the year 1774 consisted of forty nine members, (Ramsay 24) one, two or three being elected from each of the twenty one parishes. South Carolina was somewhat peculiar among American colonies in that ever since 1704 elections had been by ballot. (List in Drayton I:161–162.) Elections were governed by an act of the year 1759 (IV. Cooper's Statutes 99), which restricted the suffrage to free white men, protestants, having a freehold estate in a settled plantation, or one hundred acres of land unsettled, or in towns a freehold estate of sixty pounds value, proclamation money (⅙) 6 s. = $1., in houses, lands or town lots, or who had paid ten shillings, proclamation money, for their own proper tax within the year. A representative was required to have a settled plantation of five hundred acres and twenty slaves, or houses, building or town lots of a thousand pounds, proclamation money. These sums, reduced to sterling, indicate a somewhat extended suffrage. Indeed, I am inclined to doubt, because of several particulars which will be mentioned, the usual opinion that the government of South Carolina was before the Revolution one strongly limited or highly aristocratic. Even the economic basis upon which such constitutions usually rest can hardly have been present, if the opinions of an apparently intelligent observer, the Reverend Alexander Hewit, are to be adopted. After declaring that there are few poor people in the province, he says (Historical Account of the Rise and Progress of the Colonies of South Carolina and Georgia, II:294), "Nor is the number of rich people great, most of them being in what we call easy and independent circumstances. It has been remarked that there are more persons possessed of between five and ten thousand pounds sterling than are to be found anywhere among the same number of people. In respect of rank, all men regarded their neighbor as their equal and a noble spirit of benevolence pervaded the society." The truth is that colonial South Carolina exhibited in many ways the effects and the characteristic virtues arising from town life. Great plantations were present, but there was also a town of high importance ("The City"). It is impossible to account for the hold which Federalism maintained for so many years upon South Carolina, without remembering that the colony and state were not, like the other southern provinces, exclusively agricultural in industries and rural in society. As one instance of the effects of urban life upon the social constitution of the colony one may note that singular abundance of societies formed for mutual support and relief, such as "The South Carolina Society," which in 1776 had a capital of sixty nine thousand pounds, current money. (Hewit II:299.)

The judiciary system of the state had earlier consisted of little else than a court of common pleas, sitting at Charleston, and the usual chancery and admiralty courts. Now, however, the court of common pleas held quarter sessions in the six rural precincts of the colony and an act of 1769 had established six new district courts in the six precincts other than that of Charleston. By that act salaries were given to the assistant judges of the highest court. "The English administration at once," says Drayton (I:150) "caught hold of the opportunity and sent over from England men destitute of support in their own country." The highest ecclesiastical court seems to have been a body of twelve church commissioners seldom assembled, if we may judge from Bullman's Case (Drayton I:142–144.) The Established Church, it may be remarked, maintained a far higher character than was usual in the southern colonies, but its membership seems always to have been a minority of the inhabitants of the province. It was probably the result of their more independent and respectable position that when the Revolutionary struggle broke out, while the Virginian and Maryland ministers were almost all bitter tories, those of South Carolina, as a rule, sided with the Revolutionary Party. For purposes of local government the province was divided into seven precincts and these into twenty five parishes and three townships. The parish usually chose its own rector. The vestry consisted of seven members who were usually chosen yearly by the freeholders and tax-payers of the parish, (Ramage 10–11), another instance of a constitution slightly more democratic than that of Virginia, where the vestry-men at least filled up vacancies in their own body (Channing) and where indeed there was little representation of the people in local government. Much effort had been made to settle townships, yet Beaufort, Purisburgh, Jacksonburgh, Dorchester, Camden and Georgetown were inconsiderable villages of twenty, thirty or forty dwelling houses. Charlestown in 1765 had five or six thousand white inhabitants and seven or eight thousand negroes (Hewit II:289, sqq) and was obviously one of the largest centres of population within the American colonies, apparently exercising a more dominant influence in the affairs of the province than Baltimore did in those of Maryland. The population of the colony must probably have been somewhere between one hundred and fifty and two hundred thousand persons, the whites well mixed of various national elements, progressive, social, public-spirited and intelligent. As for the condition of the slave, see Mr. Brackett's Essay. As near as I can make out, no entails since act 1733, providing ag{ricultural}. stat{istics}. *de donis.* Not arist{ocratic}.

The southernmost of the American colonies still remained exceedingly small, with only a few thousand inhabitants and these more thoroughly dependent upon the royal power than elsewhere, as was natural to a colony which had been so recently founded and had emerged at so late a period from the tutelage of a strong, but excessively paternal body of proprietors. We note for instance, that quite to the contrary of the practice elsewhere observed, even the treasurer and the speaker of the lower house of assembly were appointed by the governor. (Account of executive Officers in Jones II:141–143.) The delegates to the assembly were required to own five hundred acres of land and were chosen by the freeholders, the suffrage being confined to those who were proprietors of fifty acres or a town lot. The province in 1774 consisted of twelve parishes and these were represented in the assembly by about twenty nine members. Courts of the province consisted of the usual series of central courts and county courts.

This rough and rapid survey must suffice as an account of the constitutions of the southern colonies at the time when the Revolutionary struggle broke out. It will be seen that there were strong resemblances in the forms of government then in operation in these five provinces. The control of the royal administration was very much the same in all: in all, local government was organized upon the English county system rather than upon the township system which had received its fullest development in the New England colonies: in all the representatives of the local districts sat in assemblies of substantially similar powers and in all the greater proportion of political power, so far as it was not wielded by officers of the crown imported from England, was in the hands of the well-to-do classes in the community, if not in those of a land-holding aristocracy.

In order to complete the picture with which I have proposed to introduce the studies represented in this course, it would be useful not simply to describe the form of government existing in these five provinces, but also to give a hasty glance at the politics of each and at the constitution of political parties so far as they at that time existed. In Maryland as in Virginia the first well defined party contests were excited by and ran parallel with the convulsions of the great Civil War in England. Throughout the period from 1690 to 1765 the chief party divisions in all these southern colonies, arose out of disputes between the royal or proprietary governors, representative of the crown or proprietor, and the colonial assemblies, representative of the people. Usually the disputes were with regard to the furnishing of money for governmental expenses by taxation. From this arose those divisions of sentiment which in 1775 and 1776 developed into a mutual hostility of Whig and Tory, the first political parties extending throughout all America. In Maryland there was a considerable class so far attached to the royal power as to constitute subsequently the Tory party. In Virginia there seems to have been almost none, and the Virginian aristocracy, full of the spirit of local independence, took quite the opposite side to that espoused by their compeers in New England, and this almost unanimously. North Carolina had from the very beginning of its history been torn by internal dissensions and later was almost evenly divided between Whig and Tory. Of the characteristics of either party it is not easy to discover much, save that from Governor Martin's Proclamation of 1775, it is to be inferred that he expected most support for the King's cause from certain of the more western counties. In South Carolina, too, the party divisions were mainly local. Ever since the upland region had been settled, chiefly by that Scotch-Irish stock of which Jackson and Calhoun both sprang, there had been a standing antagonism between the settlers there and the lords of the lowlands, the great rice—and indigo— planters. Yet when most of the latter threw themselves into the cause of revolution it was only a part of the former that held aloof. The former Regulators who had opposed the royal government in the uplands now remained neutral for the time being and so did the Germans. The Scotch-Irish who had come directly into the province and held their lands on specially favorable royal grants refused to stir; but those Irish who had migrated from the northern colonies engaged heartily in the Revolutionary cause, and Ramsey tells us that though there were some royalists in every part of the province, there was no settlement in which they outnumbered the friends of Congress, except the district between the Broad and Saluda Rivers. He also tells us that "Beside their superiority in numbers there was an ardor and enthusiasm in the friends of Congress which was generally wanting in the advocates for royal government." These facts, to be sure, refer mostly to a later time than that which we have chosen for our survey, yet they serve to show us in part what were the political elements which the Revolution found in existence in the southern colonies of the American Continent.

II. The Revolution and the New Constitutions (South Carolina and Virginia)

Whoever has had the pleasure of reading Mr. Dicey's brilliant Lectures introductory to the Study of the Law of the Constitution will remember the clear manner in which he points out as among the leading political characteristics of the English race the law-abiding quality, the devotion to the rule of law. Never has the statement found more striking exemplification than in the doings of those colonial Englishmen who conducted the American Revolution. The misgovernment of England had come to seem intolerable, but to pass from this to any other state than that in which the law was clear, certain, revered and observed would have been equally intolerable. It was not simply that upon the extinction of the royal governments substitutes were presently found; the law-abiding quality was too deep-seated to admit even of a brief hiatus. Long before the final collapse of the royal governments the institutions were already in operation out of which were to grow the constitutional arrangements of the new era. If it is true of many periods through which we shall pass that the history of the southern states cannot be perfectly related apart from the history of the United States, especially is this true of the period of the first revolutionary movements. That cooperation of colony with colony which Adams's device of the Committee of Correspondence, expanded into a continental system by Dabney Carr and the other Virginian patriots in the spring of 1773, had so admirably maintained, was of the very essence of the movement. Colony reacted upon colony and there was perpetual action and reaction between the Continental Congress and the representative bodies of the individual colonies.

If, however, we separately consider the Southern Colonies, remembering all the time that many of our statements are equally true of the eight colonies to the northward, we are struck first of all by the fact that the law-abiding quality carried with it, as it is wont to do, a high regard for precedent. Little of the action of the revolutionary bodies was without precedent in the historical past of the English-speaking race, and especially was this true in the domain of constitutional movements. The leading feature in the organizations which carried on the revolutionary movement in its earlier stages were Conventions or Provincial Congresses serving as the legislative bodies in each state and Committees or Councils of Public Safety serving as the executive. Precedents for the Convention are well known, but it is not so frequently remembered that even for the Committee of Public Safety there was already in existence an English precedent. The precedents of both Committee and Convention come from that fertile source of republican and revolutionary example to which American students of a hundred years ago seem to have paid much more attention than English students of even recent times have been willing to give—the period of the Commonwealth: the period which Hallam passes over in half a chapter and which Mr. Taswell-Langmead with singular blindness ignores—was at any rate attentively studied by the acute young students of constitutional law who made the American Revolution. In the last days of the English republic, when Richard Cromwell had fallen from power, the executive of England which the officers temporarily set up was a board which received the name, famous in many revolutions since, of the "Committee of Public Safety." The precedent of the Convention was found a little later upon the restoration of Charles II. The initial means of new organization was provided by the summons of a Convention consisting of persons elected by the several constituencies of the realm as for a lawful parliament but incapable of being properly termed a parliament since it had been called without the royal writ; and so the Convention of 1689, summoned by the Prince of Orange, consisted of persons elected in a similar manner on the call of the Prince issued at the recommendation of many lords and ex-members of the House of Commons. Called by a person not constitutionally authorized, this body, though otherwise collected in the same manner as a Parliament, was yet without a shadow of legal authority, was of revolutionary and not of regular origin, and therefore was called a Convention. Now these English bodies took it upon themselves both to settle anew the constitutional bases of the national government and to declare themselves to be Parliaments and act as such in conjunction with the King whom they themselves had called to the throne. This may furnish us with sufficient explanation why the American Conventions of 1776 were far from observing so scrupulously as would now be done the distinction between the revolutionary convention, that is the provisional government, and the constitutional convention. Very few of them satisfied fully the requirements which would now be imposed in order to give validity to the proceedings of a constitutional convention, but it does not follow that in accordance with the opinions held in their own time, their acts were in any way invalidated by these considerations. At any rate the mixture and irregularity seemed to them to be dictated by necessity.

Such were the precedents which lay before the makers of the Revolution and with them were also some colonial precedents, like those of the Massachusetts Conventions of 1689, which deposed Andros. The main cause of revolution was the ill-conduct of the royal government. In each of the southern colonies the governor and council were the representatives of that royal government. The protest against misgovernment therefore naturally took the form of setting up the popular element in the colonial governments as solely entitled to rule. This posture of affairs naturally suggested the analogy of the English conventions which had consisted in the representatives of the nation gathered in absence of the royal government.

It is less to our purpose to trace the collapse of the royal governments than to trace the rise and gradual development of the institutions which were to take their place. In Maryland the mild Governor Eden was gently pushed aside, notified that he was at liberty to depart and quietly suffered in June, 1776, to board a British frigate and carry away with him the last fragment of proprietary government. In Virginia Lord Dunmore made a stiffer resistance to the inevitable; but his removal of the powder at Williamsburgh and his other bits of opposition did not enable him long to maintain a government from which the substantial elements had departed. He too in June, 1775, escaped on board a British war vessel. In North Carolina Governor Martin found considerable support in his efforts to stir up civil war but in the end was compelled to flee. Lord William Campbell, in spite of his recent arrival, in S. Car., his accommodating spirit and even his final efforts to foment opposition, was obliged in the Autumn of the same year to retire on board the Tamar, sloop-of-war, taking the province seal with him. In the ensuing February Sir James Wright, Governor of Georgia, after a brief period of arrest by the Committee of Safety, made his escape also to a British vessel, the common refuge of royal agents on the American coast.

It was in November of 1775 that, upon requests from several colonial conventions, Congress advised those bodies to call a full and free representation of the people, in order to form such a frame of government as in their judgment would best promote the happiness of the people and most effectually secure peace and good order in their provinces during the continuance of the dispute with Great Britain. Later, when it became apparent to all that independence must ensue, on the 10th of May, 1776, Congress adopted a decisive resolution, "That it be recommended to the several assemblies and conventions of the united colonies where no government sufficient to the exigencies of their affairs hath been hitherto established, to adopt such government as shall in the opinion of the representatives of the people best conduce to the happiness and safety of their constituents in particular and America in general." As a rule it was upon this advice that the colonies proceeded to frame for themselves new governments, but on the other hand, one at least of the colonies had already before these last (May) resolutions, formed for itself a constitution, and in all, the steps toward that consummation had been gradually taken during a period of several years preceding. Indeed, with South Carolina (the colony alluded to as having a primacy in this matter) there was a colonial precedent dating from the year 1719, when the Assembly, revolting from the proprietaries, resolved itself into a Convention, elected a governor, chose a council and made themselves masters of the government. That this Convention of 1719 may have formed a connecting link between that of the Prince of Orange in 1688 and those of the revolutionary period may be seen from the following of its resolutions, "Secondly, that the writs whereby the representatives here met were elected are illegal, because they are signed by such a council as we conceive the proprietor has no power to appoint. . . . Thirdly, that we, the representatives, cannot act as an Assembly, but as a Convention delegated by the people." The proceedings also included the subsequently familiar device of an Association (Hewit I:260). The genesis of the revolutionary government began more than a year before the dissolution of the last constitutional legislature and the retirement of the royal governor. On the news of the acts against Boston a meeting of the inhabitants of almost every part of South Carolina was held at Charleston in July 1774. Among its resolutions one provided for the appointment of a committee of ninety-nine to act as a general committee to correspond with the committees of the other colonies and to carry out the other resolutions of the meeting. The legislature in August approved their doings; but legislatures could be dissolved by the governor and in fact his legislature was almost immediately dissolved; therefore to give efficacy to the measures adopted by the Congress at Philadelphia, the General Committee proceeded to convene at Charleston a Provincial Congress. The constitutional Assembly, it has been seen, consisted of only forty-nine members. This new representative body, though similarly elected from the parishes and districts, was to contain more than two hundred. This first Provincial Congress met on January 11, 1775, and again upon the first of June. Just after this latter date the revolutionary organization had been provided with an executive by the choice of a Council of Safety consisting of thirteen members. A Committee of General Security consisting of eleven members was also appointed. In August a new Provincial Congress was chosen to meet Nov. 1. The state of things was now virtually this; that there were in simultaneous existence within the province two governmental organizations, one, the old organization, consisting of the Governor, Council and Assembly, the other, the revolutionary organization, with the Convention for its legislative and the Council of Safety and other committees chosen by the Convention, for its executive. But the progress of revolutionary enthusiasm had paralysed all the muscles of the old organization long before the flight of Lord William Campbell and had caused all the blood that was in the political system to flow through the enlarging channels of the popular system. Thus, legislative, executive and judicial powers were insensibly transferred to the Provincial Congress, Council of Safety and the subordinate committees. (Ramsay I:18, 22–4, 33, 38, 41, 42, 60; Drayton I:231.) The congressional recommendations of November, 1775, coupled with the Act of Parliament of December, confiscating American property and throwing all the colonies out of His Majesty's protection, convinced even those who hitherto had hesitated that America must now take care of herself, and produced a majority for the definite establishment of an independent constitution. The refusal of the judges to exercise their function in the absence of regularly constituted authorities assisted to force on this consummation. In spite of doubts on the part of some members as to their competency to take such action, a constitution was framed by the Provincial Congress and adopted on March 26, 1776. [Committee II. C{harles} C{otesworth} Pinck{ney,} J{ohn}. Rutl{edge,} C{harles} Pinck{ney,} H{enry} Lau{rens,} 2 R{awlins} Lown{des,} 1 Chr{istopher} Gads{den,} Ar{thur} Mid{dleton,} Preamble by Rut{ledge}.] South Carolina was thus the first of the Southern Colonies that formed an independent constitution. The instrument drawn up deviated as little as possible from ancient forms and names. The kingly office was dropped, but for those elements in the colonial constitution which were of royal origin substitutes were found as nearly similar as was practicable. The Congress voted that it should henceforth be called the General Assembly of South Carolina, 30 from Cha{rle}st{o}n, 6 from most par{ishes}., that the General Assembly should elect out of their own body a Legislative Council of thirteen members, that the General Assembly and Legislative Council should jointly choose the President and Commander-in-chief and the Vice-president of the Council, and that there should be a Privy-council, consisting of the Vice-president and six other members chosen, three by the General Assembly and three by the Council. The General Assembly was to consist of the same number of members as the present Congress, to be chosen after the same manner, and to serve two years. The Privy-council were to act as a Court of Chancery. Other judicial officers and the more important executive, military and naval officers were elected by joint ballot of the General Assembly and Legislative Council. This constitution it will be seen differed from the colonial constitution in little else than the addition of an Executive Council and the substitution of election by the legislature for royal appointment in case of the principal executive officers. John Rutledge was chosen President, Henry Laurens Vice-president, William Henry Drayton Chief Justice. From this time forward public business was conducted after the orderly and regular manner that the Anglo-Saxon mind loves. Bills were regularly passed by the two houses and approved by the President, and South Carolina had again secured for itself that supremacy of law in the absence of which men of English race are seldom long content. (Ramsay, I:82–103, 127, 128; Drayton II:171–181.) (See also Gibbes Documentary History of South Carolina, 3 Vols.; Moultrie's Memoirs, I:9–18, 125–138.)

South Carolina must be conceded the priority in the forming of new constitutions; but for all that, greater importance attaches to the work of the Virginia Convention which in June 1776 reported a new constitution for that state. In the first place, Virginia was the largest and most important of the states. It is well to remember by how much it was the largest. No state in the present Union has a population of more than one tenth that of the whole country. At the time of the census of 1790 the population of Virginia equalled twenty one per cent. of the whole population of the United States. Even its free population was of more than one tenth. In the second place, the Virginia constitution was framed with far more deliberate care than that of South Carolina. Thirdly, it was framed by a convention newly summoned, while the South Carolina constitution, as we have seen, proceeded from the Provincial Congress, chosen sometime before. Neither was chosen for that purpose especially. In neither case did these conventions confine themselves to that business alone and in neither case were the constitutions which they prepared submitted to the people for ratification. On these grounds Jameson in his treatise on the Constitutional Convention refuses to either of them the title of a true constitutional convention.[4] From a legal point of view this exclusion may be valid, but historically speaking it is not worth while to

{4.} John Alexander Jameson (1824–90), a Chicago jurist and uncle of John Franklin Jameson, wrote A Treatise on Constitutional Conventions; Their History, Powers, and Modes of Proceeding, 4th ed. (Chicago: Callaghan and Company, 1887).

insist with so much nicety upon the observance of distinctions which arise simply from the more developed thought of subsequent times, after maturer experience of constitutional devices. At present no constitution would be considered valid save one which had been confirmed by a convention chosen especially for that purpose and which had been submitted to the people for ratification; indeed the constitution of 1776 for Virginia was already as early as 1781 attacked by Jefferson, in 1816 (Girardin 150) as being no true constitution. But any one who looks at the matter from an historical point of view will hardly incline to be so exacting. However this may have been, the constitution of Virginia had at any rate no more regular origin than that of South Carolina. And it is also of importance in the fourth place because of the immense influence which certain portions of it have exerted upon American political ideas through all times succeeding.

The process of development by which informal and unauthorized institutions, created spontaneously as a supplement to the perverted royal government, acquired strength and fullness from popular favor until they grew into the recognized and exclusive institutions of government for an independent state, is in the case of Virginia easily to be traced by gradual steps. In the first place, comes the informal gathering of burgesses in the Apollo Room at the Raleigh Tavern after the dissolution of the House by Lord Botetourt in 1769 (Randall I:58). Then came in 1774 a similar gathering after the dissolution by Lord Dunmore. This informal gathering called the first Virginia Convention, to be held at Williamsburg on the first of August. The relation of this Convention to the House of Burgesses which was elected at the same time is made clear from the proceedings of the counties, in which it appears that, though the delegates to both bodies were in all cases the same, the people made the appointment to the Convention in each case a separate act. (Randall I:85–6.) The first Convention met at the appointed time at Williamsburg and thus the germ of a revolutionary government was planted, for this purely voluntary body proceeded to exercise quasi-legislative powers. (Randall I:88; Lee's "R. H. Lee" I:98–9.) Its ordinances and those of the subsequent Conventions fill the first one hundred and fifty pages of Hening's ninth volume. No central executive as yet corresponded to this legislative. Virginia counties soon began to organize Committees of Safety whose powers, not being yet defined, were in practice almost unlimited. (Randall I:99; Girardin 6.) This was the Convention which sent the delegates of Virginia to the first Continental Congress. The second Convention met in Richmond in March, 1775, approved the measures of the Continental Congress, and listened to the most celebrated of Henry's speeches, that in support of his resolutions for embodying and arming the militia. (Tyler's Henry, 118–133.) One of George Mason's letters shows that by this time (No, in 3d Conv.) the Anglo-Saxon desire for the complete maintenance of legislative forms had already asserted itself even in this revolutionary body. "Every ordinance," he writes, "goes through all the formalities of a bill in the House of Burgesses, has three readings, etc. before it is passed and in every respect wears the face of law, resolves as recommendations being no longer trusted to in matters of importance." (Virginia Calendar of State Papers, I:269.) Parties already existed, Pendleton, Wythe, Bland, Peyton Randolph, and R. C. Nicholas, the treasurer, leading the more cautious spirits, while Patrick Henry, Richard Henry Lee, Jefferson, the Pages, and George Mason were the leaders of the more aggressive and democratic wing. Yet substantial harmony prevailed. (Tyler's Henry, 84–5, 121.) In June the regular colonial Assembly held its last session. In July the third Convention met at Richmond and there for the first time was organized a provincial Committee of Safety consisting of eleven gentlemen, charged with the executive duties of the revolutionary government. The ordinance for its establishment and those for regulating the organization of the Convention and of the county committees may be seen in Hening 9:49, 53. The fourth Convention met in December at Richmond and adjourned to Williamsburg. Its chief new contribution to the constitution of Virginia was the providing of three admiralty judges to decide on violations of an ordinance for punishing violations of the Continental Association. Thus we come to the fifth and from a constitutional point of view the most important of these Conventions, that which assembled at Williamsburg on May 6, 1776, charged with the consideration of the two great questions of independence and re-organization, the latter, it should be observed, being taken up before the Congressional resolve of May 10, already alluded to, had reached Williamsburg.

The Convention of 1776 was without exaggeration a highly remarkable gathering of men. Richard Bland, Richard Henry Lee, George Mason, Patrick Henry, Edmund Pendleton, Robert Carter Nicholas, George Wythe, Archibald Cary, and younger men, like Edmund Randolph and James Madison, formed an array of great men sufficient to confer distinction upon any assembly. Mr. Pendleton was chosen President. In his speech upon taking the chair he said among other things, "The administration of justice and almost all the powers of justice have now been suspended for near two years. It will become us to reflect whether we can longer sustain the great struggle we are making in this situation, and the case of criminals confined and not tried and others who may be apprehended pursuant to our laws deserves particular notice." (In all the revolutionary governments it was obviously the judiciary which was weakest.) Before speaking of the actual work of this assembly, it may be well to call attention to the influence upon its deliberations of certain men who were not members, or at least to their attempts to influence its course. Edmund Randolph states (Conway, 28), that Jefferson, then in Congress, urged him to oppose the formation of a permanent constitution for Virginia until the people should elect deputies for that especial purpose, "He attacked the power of the body elected, as he conceived them, to be the

agents for the management of the war, to exceed some temporary regimen."
But Pendleton, Henry and Mason, he says, "saw no distinction between the
conceded power to declare independence and its necessary consequence, the
fencing of society by the institution of government." Jefferson had a further
share in the doings of the Convention. In a letter to Judge A. B. Woodward,
April 13, 1825, he says, "I was then at Philadelphia with Congress and knowing that the Convention of Virginia was engaged in forming a plan of government, I turned my mind to the same subject and drew a sketch or outline
of a constitution, with a preamble, which I sent to Mr. Pendleton, President
of the Convention, on the mere possibility that it might suggest something
worth incorporation into that before the Convention." The letter came virtually too late, "but being pleased with the preamble to mine, they adopted
it in the House by way of amendment to the report of the Committee and
thus my preamble became tacked to the work of George Mason." Jefferson's
draft has recently been discovered and printed. In November, 1775, Richard
Henry Lee had obtained from John Adams his advice upon a new government, embodied in a letter printed in Adams works IV:185. In January, 1776
a letter of Adams to Wythe upon the same subject was by Adams's permission printed by Richard Henry Lee as a pamphlet with the title, "Thoughts
on Government," (Adams IV:193–200) and was highly approved by Henry
in a letter to Adams (I:202). But the opinions of Adams, which in the latitude of Pennsylvania were by many thought too little democratic, found in
Virginia an important opponent in a pamphlet entitled "Address to the Convention of the Colony and Ancient Dominion of Virginia," supposed to have
been written by Carter Braxton. (See Force's Archives IV:VI:748–754.) The
plan ultimately adopted stood between the two, but was much influenced
by that of Adams. Indeed it was based on one published in the Va. Gazette
of May 10, 1776, which is either Adams' plan modified by Lee or drawn up
from Adams' and Lee's together.

On the fifteenth of May the Convention instructed their delegates in Congress to propose the declaration that the United States are free and independent states. The resolution was followed immediately by one appointing
a committee "to prepare a Declaration of Rights and such a plan of government as will be most likely to maintain peace and order in this colony
and secure substantial and equal liberty to the people." (Force 4 VI:1524.) A
large committee was immediately appointed of which the leading members
were Cary, Meriwether Smith, Nicholas, Henry, Edmund Randolph, Bland,
Carrington, George Mason, and James Madison. On the 27th of May the
Declaration was reported. This famous document, in which were summed
up most of the great principles of political liberty for which the English
race through so many ages had contended, and the fundamental doctrines
of American democracy as well, and whose terse and masculine phrases
have so often since been copied, was probably entirely the work of George

Mason. Fifteen articles were adopted from his draft almost unchanged. The one against general warrants and the one declaring for a single government in Virginia were added by the committee. The sixteenth, the broad and striking assertion of the doctrines of religious liberty, was probably amended by Henry from Mason's draft, in which had stood a narrower declaration in favor of toleration. Some of the articles of Mason's declaration were derived from the political ideas of the time, some from the English Bill of Rights of 1689. His provision respecting toleration closely resembles the declaration of the Westminster Assembly upon that subject. In giving to it the wider form which assured to Virginia the honor of setting the example of complete religious liberty, the youthful James Madison seems to have had an important part. The Declaration of Rights concluded, the Convention proceeded to deliberate upon the form of government. The authorship of the original draft of the Virginian constitution of 1776 is uncertain. It is attributed to George Mason, though certain curious considerations of style (the word "judicative") seem to point to another hand in some articles, perhaps that of Meriwether Smith. Far more important however than the authorship is the general tendency of that famous document. The revolutionary movement and the attendant questioning of traditional institutions had carried with them a tendency among even the majority of the Virginian aristocracy to cast off the shackles of oligarchical privilege and base the new government upon the broad foundations of popular support. Most of the members of the committee were by origin genuine aristocrats, but the Virginian aristocracy, with as much unselfishness and enthusiasm as the representatives of the nobility in the States-General of France, though with less of rhetoric and excitement, quietly, though not without much debate, abandoned the ground of aristocratic privilege for the broad principles of democracy. The new constitution provided for a lower House of Assembly whose members were to be elected annually by the people in the proportion of two members from each county with one for Williamsburg and one for Norfolk. [Wm. & Mary not.] The suffrage was left as before. The upper house was to consist of twenty-four members to be elected for four years by the people, one member from each of the senatorial districts into which the several counties should be grouped, one fourth to retire by rotation each year. This body was, I believe, the first among American political bodies to receive the appellation of "The Senate." The lower house had the sole initiative of laws. The chief executive was to be a Governor elected annually by joint ballot of both houses and not to remain in that office longer than three years successively, nor then to be eligible again until after the lapse of four years. He was to be assisted by a Privy-Council of eight members, who, as well as the delegates in Congress and the judges in the several courts, were all to be elected by joint ballot of the two houses. In the judiciary department a Supreme Court of Appeals, a General Court, and chancery and admiralty judges were provided. The Secretary, Attorney General and Treasurer were to be chosen by joint ballot of the two houses; the Treasurer to serve for one year, the rest during good behavior. Such were the outlines of this highly important document, which almost as much as the Declaration of Rights exercised a potent influence in the subsequent constitutional history of America and deserves to be read with the greatest care. The constitution was adopted on June 20, 1776. Immediately the new government was set in operation. Patrick Henry was elected Governor and on the 5th of July the memorable Virginia Convention adjourned. (Rives's Madison, I:122–167; Tyler's Henry, 167–186; Conway's Randolph, 28–34 158–165; Proceedings of Convention in American Archives, IV:VI:1510–1616; Grigsby, "Convention of 1776.") [Hening's Henry. Rowland's Mason.]

The changes thus effected in the ancient constitution of the colony are easily perceived. It was evidently felt to be expedient that the executive functions of the Council and the functions of an upper house, which it had hitherto possessed, should be given hereafter to two bodies; also, that the natural substitute for royal appointments was election of Governor, of Privy-Council and of upper house by the new sovereign, the people of Virginia, either directly or indirectly. Other changes were dictated by the revolutionary spirit or by the principles of popular government embodied in the Declaration of Rights.

III. Constitutional and Political History During the War (Maryland, North Carolina, and Georgia)

The preceding lecture treated of the development of the two new constitutions which stood first in order of time and first in historical importance. That of Maryland has, however, a peculiar interest to many in this audience and deserves attention on other grounds also. At many turns in the correspondence of the Revolution we come upon indications that the political conduct of Maryland was marked by an unusual amount of wisdom and moderation. As a small state it had been somewhat more cautious in committing itself finally to a revolutionary independence than some of the other provinces. Moreover, it is to be remembered not only that the soil of Maryland never felt the pressure of war, but also that nowhere were the relations of the representatives of the province with the royal governor more pacific. Mr. Eden was personally popular and his withdrawal from the province was managed on both sides with great kindliness and real good feeling. Now, just as the democracy of Australia is of a milder type than the democracy of older countries, where it is the child of revolution, so in Maryland the absence of violent conflict between the representatives of the old regime and of the new brought it about that the new regime was accompanied with less of innovation, with less rapid strides in the direction of democracy, and that its installation was conceived with more of moderate wisdom, than in colonies where violent conflicts had excited party animosities.

I pass somewhat rapidly over the earliest stages of the development of the revolutionary constitution. There was no session of the provincial legislature after April, 1774. When in June, 1776, the Governor attempted to summon it anew, the Convention forbade it. The first Convention had been summoned, as elsewhere, upon news of the Boston Port Bill and upon call of a popular meeting at Baltimore. As elsewhere, election to the Convention was carried on after the manner usual in elections to the House of Delegates. A curious fact with regard to them is alleged by a Tory clergyman, Reverend Jonathan Boucher. (Discourses, 367.) "The first popular elections that were made without the authority of law," he says, "were made by a mere handful of the people and those of ordinary character and condition. The County of Prince George's, in which I last resided, was one of the largest, richest and most populous in the settled parts of the rich province of Maryland, and in that, I affirm on my own knowledge, the members to the first Provincial Convention . . . were chosen by three persons only, of no considerable rank or property." However this may be, this Convention and similar successors gradually grew to be the government of Maryland. That of July, 1775, formed (a usual step in the revolutionary movements in each state) an "Association of the Freemen of Maryland." Under this Association the supreme power was vested in the Provincial Convention composed of five delegates from each county, elected to serve for a year. The executive power was entrusted to the Committee of Safety elected by the Convention, consisting of sixteen persons, eight from each shore. For more than a year this was the government of Maryland. I leave undiscussed the gradual progress of public opinion toward independence and the steps taken in concert with the other colonies. I may remark here that I have usually felt it necessary in these lectures, while admitting that the history of the Federal Government is indispensable to the history of the states, for the most part to confine attention to such portions of their constitutional and political history as went on within their own borders, and concerned their own affairs. Until well into June, 1776 (American Archives IV:VI:740) the administration of Maryland clung to the hope of reconciliation. It was only on June 28 that Maryland's delegates were authorized to join in declaring American independence. To this commission was joined, however, a proviso; "Provided, That the exclusive right of regulating the internal government and police of this Colony be reserved to the people thereof." Then followed Maryland's Declaration of Independence, which upon the face of it, I may remark, should apparently be dated July 6, though Maryland historians have usually found reason for dating it July 3. (See Am. Arch. IV:VI:1506; Scharf II:233, Note.) On the 3rd of July at any rate, the representatives of the state proceeded to act upon the matter which they had by their vote on June 28 reserved to themselves. On that day it was "Resolved, That a new Convention be elected for the express purpose of forming a new government by the authority of the people only and indicating and ordering all things for the preservation, safety and general weal of this Colony." Here is seen a distinct progress toward modern ideas of regularity in constitutional conventions. The new Convention was specially summoned for this purpose, though it was intended to govern the state at the same time, and actually did so. The Convention was to consist of four members from each county, two from Annapolis and two from Baltimore. These were to be elected by those persons who under the colonial law hitherto existing had been qualified to vote for delegates, excepting any persons who had been published, by any of the Committees of Observation in the counties, or by the Council of Safety of this colony, as enemies to the liberties of America. (Am. Arch. IV:VI:1496–1498.) That these qualifications were not to be extended upon any principles of revolutionary democracy was made plain when the Convention assembled. The inhabitants of Prince George County had agreed "That every taxable bearing arms, being an inhabitant of the county, had an undoubted right to vote for representatives at this time of public calamity," and in Kent a number of people not qualified to vote for members of the late Convention had prevented the election. The new Convention at once quashed the election in Prince George and in every way showed their determination to maintain strictly the letter of the ordinance. (Am. Arch. V:III:84–86.)

This Convention, which assembled at Annapolis on August 14, 1776, included a very great proportion of the leading men of the colony. From Talbot came Matthew Tilghman, who was chosen President of the Convention: from Dorchester Robert Goldsborough: from Caroline Thomas Johnson: from Saint Mary's George Plater: from Anne Arundel Samuel Chase and Charles Carroll (barrister): from Annapolis William Paca and Charles Carroll (of Carrollton): from Baltimore Jeremiah T. Chase. On August 17 Samuel Chase moved the appointment of a committee to prepare a Declaration, a Charter of Rights and a Plan of Government. Tilghman, Paca, the two Carrolls, Plater, Chase, and Goldsborough were elected and Thomas Johnson was subsequently added after the resignation of Charles Carroll (barrister). The Convention was necessarily occupied with many other matters, but on the 10th of September they brought in a decl{aration}. and? constitution. Some delay was caused by the progress of military preparations: moreover, the Convention adjourned from September 17th to the 30th to give opportunity to take the sense of the people upon these documents. They were then considered on nearly every day from the 10th to the 30th of October, it being even voted on October 14, that in order to expedite the consideration of the Bill of Rights and the form of government, the house should sit while that business was transacting every evening until eight o'clock. (Am. Arch. V:III:90–91, 108, 121, 135.) Among the items of business which intervened was that discussion and assertion of the common right and jurisdiction of the United States over the western lands, which, pursued consistently as a policy by Maryland, proved, as has been shown in Doctor Adams's important pamphlet on "Maryland Land Cessions," to be a most valuable, if not indispensable contribution on the part of Maryland to the foundation of our national Government.[5] The Maryland Bill of Rights was adopted on the 3rd of November, the constitution on the 8th. Whether they were much amended in committee does not appear: at any rate but few changes were made by the house in the papers as reported by the Committee of the Whole. A curious change made in the fifth article of the constitution may be noted in passing. Mr. J. T. Chase, member for Baltimore, proposed a regulation decreasing its representation in the House of Delegates, if its population decreased to a certain amount and increasing it, if it grew more populous. The Convention adopted the first part of the amendment and rejected the second. The Declaration and the Constitution were both long documents. Indeed, Maryland has always had a tendency to extremely long constitutions. The Declaration seems in many respects to have been modelled upon Mason's Declaration and upon the sources of the latter, but added clauses forbidding poll taxes and ex post facto laws and at the last moment inserted in the clause respecting religious freedom the provision that "The legislature may in their discretion lay a general and equal tax for the support of the Christian religion, leaving to each individual the power of appointing the payment of the money collected from him to the support of any particular place of worship, or for the benefit of the poor of his denomination, or the poor in general of any particular county." The Constitution was elaborate. It left the House of Delegates, elections to it and the suffrage practically as they were. Delegates were, however, to have a property qualification of five hundred pounds current money. But as Virginia had done, it separated into two distinct bodies the upper house and the executive Council. The former, here also called "Senate," was to have equal rights with the delegates in legislation, except in the proposal of money bills. It was to be chosen in a peculiar manner. The electors of delegates were once in five years to choose two persons from each county to be electors of the senate. These should meet and choose fifteen senators, nine residents of the western and six of the eastern shore, residents of the state for six years, and having therein real and personal property above the value of one thousand pounds current money. Both houses were annually to choose by joint ballot a Council of five members, qualified as senators. The Governor's qualification was to be twenty-five years of age, to have had five years of residence

{5.} Herbert B. Adams, *Maryland's Influence in Founding a National Commonwealth* (Baltimore: Printed by J. Murphy, 1877); revised version published as *Maryland's Influence upon Land Sessions to the United States* (Baltimore: Johns Hopkins University, 1885).

and to have in the state real and personal property above the value of five thousand pounds current money, one thousand pounds whereof at least to be a freehold estate. Rotation in the governor's office was arranged, as in Virginia. Officers of the army and navy and United States and ministers of the gospel were ineligible to the general assembly or Council. There were to be two Treasurers, one for each shore. The judiciary was to consist of a General Court, taking the place of the Provincial Court, a Court of Chancery, a Court of Admiralty and over all three the Court of Appeals. All the judges were to be appointed by the Governor. (Am. Arch. V:III:136–174.) The constitution thus provided, arranged with more deliberation than had been possible in Virginia (and as has been shown with less of innovation) seems to have been regarded in the United States as a remarkably excellent one. At all events it subsisted with some amendments until 1851. The method of choosing the senate is of particular interest. James Wilson in the Pennsylvania State Convention, December 31, 1789, praises the result as follows; "The Moderation, the Firmness, the Wisdom, the Consistency which have characterized the Proceedings of that Body have been of signal Benefit to the State of whose Government it forms a Part; and have been the Theme of just Applause in her sister States.{"} (Ms. in Hist. Soc. Pa.) The Federalist, also, in a paper written by the least conservative of the three authors, says, after describing the arrangements of the Maryland Senate, "If the Federal Senate, therefore, really contained the danger which has been so loudly proclaimed, some symptoms at least of a like danger ought by this time to have been betrayed by the Senate of Maryland, but no such symptoms have appeared. On the contrary, the jealousies at first entertained . . . have been gradually extinguished by the progress of the experiment and the Maryland Constitution is daily deriving from the salutary operation of this part of it a reputation in which it will probably not be rivalled by that of any state in the Union." It should be added that Chancellor Hanson highly commended the moderation and justice of the government administered by the Convention through the Council of Safety. The transition from this to the new form was effected on March 21, 1777, when Thomas Johnson, Jr. was inaugurated as Governor. The courts of justice went into operation more gradually. Indeed, the Court of Appeals was not completed until December, 1778. This constitution, it may also be noted, was the first American constitution which contained regulations respecting its own amendments, amendments by its terms requiring to be passed by two legislatures in order to acquire validity.

That the constitution of Maryland acquired its highly conservative character by reason of the absence of violent party conflict within its borders is confirmed by observation of the opposite case of North Carolina. Here it was early apparent, not only that the partisans of royal government were nearly as powerful as those of the new system, but that a bitter division existed between those who desired to retain as much as possible of the British forms of government and those who were eager to substitute for them radically democratic institutions. The history of the first Conventions of the province need not detain us. That of 1774 seems to have been organized on much the same basis as the legislature. That of April, 1775 was largely identical with the contemporary provincial legislature, the last which sat in North Carolina. That which sat from August to September, 1775, organized a provisional government differing somewhat in form from that which was created in the other states. The County Committees were left with much the same organization as they had possessed, being elected by the legislature. There was to be a Provincial Council consisting of a chairman and twelve additional members, two from each of the six districts of the state, corresponding thus to the Committees of Safety, or Councils of Safety in the other states; and between these higher and lower bodies there was to be a Committee of Safety consisting of thirteen members in each district. Although in form this was a more developed government than that which was provisionally established in the other states, in reality it is probable that it simply represented the extraordinary tendency of North Carolina politics to local dissension, and the power as a matter of fact remained in the hands of the central body, the so-called Provincial Council. (Jones's Defence of North Carolina 198–206.) The restriction of the right of suffrage to freeholders materially assisted the revolutionary party in Cumberland County, by excluding the poor and unmanageable Highlanders, who were generally guided by some wealthy Tory of their clan. In certain counties in which the lands of Lord Granville were situated, householders were enfranchised. On April 4, 1776, a Provincial Congress assembled. It met at Halifax under the presidency of Samuel Johnston, the leader of the more aristocratic members. On April 12 a resolve was passed empowering delegates in Congress to declare independence but reserving to the colony the sole and exclusive right of forming a constitution and laws for itself.

This might seem to be the proper place at which to say a word respecting the famous resolves of the Mecklenburg Convention. It has been vigorously affirmed and denied that on the 20th of May, 1775, the people of Mecklenburg County passed bold resolutions in favor of independence. I take it that President Welling, in his articles in the "North American Review" for 1874 and in the twenty-first volume of the "Magazine of American History" has effectually disposed of this legend, but in any case it is a matter to which I should be unwilling to devote a great amount of time. It seems to me, in general, that it is an unfortunate thing that so much attention has been given among Americans to the discussion of claims of priority in matters of this sort. The fondness for such things rests upon obsolete views of history. It is no longer held that important movements in history have been, as Schelling said of Fichte's idea of the absolute, "Shot, as it were, out of a pistol." Important movements in the life of nations have usually been slowly prepared and have gradually prevailed, and a student whose mind is fixed upon this gradual development of ideas would be unwilling to attribute great importance to the superficial question of priority in the eventual outward expressions of the movements.

On the next day after meeting April 13, 1776, a committee of the Convention was appointed to prepare a temporary civil constitution. On the 27th some parts of the project were adopted, but on the 30th, the project of a constitution was abandoned, and a new committee appointed to revise the temporary form of government. The reason for this was that an ardent conflict had broken out in the committee upon the main principles upon which a constitution should be formed. Samuel Johnston, the President, Allen Jones and Thomas Jones strongly desired a government of energy and power with restricted suffrage, inviolable independence of the judiciary, permanence of office and the most perfect security of property and all vested rights. Willie Jones and Thomas Person, the leaders of the other party, were urgently desirous of the establishment of a radically democratic form of government. Their contention was, as J. S. Jones says, that "The restriction of the right of suffrage which had prevailed in the political government had given the Tories an opportunity of seducing the non-freeholders to their interest and that an extension of that most delicate and important right to every biped of the forest was the surest means of uniting the voices of the people." About the 18th or 19th of April the radicals prevailed in the committee and it was resolved to establish a purely democratic form of government. President Johnston wrote to Iredell with little hope of a satisfactory constitution, but Thomas Jones arranged an adjustment of the matter which resulted soon in the postponement of a permanent government, and the amendment in some respects of the provisional government. On the 14th of May the Convention adjourned. The Council of Safety recommended to the people to elect delegates to a new Congress appointed to assemble at Halifax on November 12th, which was "Not only to make laws, but also to form a constitution which was to be the cornerstone of all law . . . and according as it was well or ill ordered would tend in the first degree to promote the happiness or misery of the state." Vigorous efforts were made to prevent the return of Mr. Johnston from Chowan County in the coming election and these efforts were successful, but, after all, the constitution which was formed is said to have been more the work of his friend, Thomas Jones, than of any one else. This is attributed to the lack of experience and learning on the part of the Radicals; yet Thomas Jones is said to have been assisted in the matter by Willie Jones, the head of the latter faction. On the 9th of December Johnston writes to Iredell "The constitution is to be adopted today. . . . I am in great pain for the honour of the province; at the same time, when I consider only my own ease and peace I congratulate myself on being clear of any share of the trouble I must have had, if I had been a member. Any one who has the least pretence to be a gentleman is suspected and borne down *per ignobile vulgus*—a set of men without reading, experience or principle to govern them." (J. S. Jones, "Defence of the Revolutionary History of North Carolina," 257–8, 272–92; McRee, "Life of Iredell" I:276–81, 333–9.) The Bill of Rights was in fact ratified on the 17th of December and the Constitution on the 18th, and Richard Caswell was elected Governor. The Bill of Rights did not notably differ from those which had preceded it. The Constitution provided for a legislature in two branches. The Senate was to consist of one member for each county qualified by the possession of three hundred acres of land in fee and elected by citizens having a freehold within the county of fifty acres of land. The House of Commons was to consist of two members for each county and one for each of six towns, elected by all tax-payers and qualified by the possession of one hundred acres in fee or for life. In this respect the result was evidently a compromise between the aristocratic and conservative predilections of the leading landholders and the democratic desires of the Radicals. The elections were to be by ballot. The General Assembly, so constituted, was to elect the judges and Attorney General, who should hold their offices during good behavior and the Secretary, whose term should be three years, and should annually choose a Governor, qualified by a freehold in lands and tenements above the value of one thousand pounds, a Council to consist of seven members, and a Treasurer or treasury. Clergymen were incapable of sitting in the Assembly, or Council of State. Religious freedom was provided. At the last moment Dr. David Caldwell, a Presbyterian member from the upper country, a man of great ability (Caldwell's Life by Caruthers) induced the Convention to insert the provision, "That no person who shall deny the being of God, or the truth of the Protestant religion, or the divine authority either of the Old or New Testament, or who shall hold religious principles incompatible with the freedom and safety of the state, shall be able to hold any office or place of trust or profit in the civil department within this state." (McRee, I:339.) A characteristic provision was that against imprisonment for debt. Schools and universities were provided for and it was enjoined that the future legislature should regulate entails in such a manner as to prevent perpetuities.

The framing and the composition of the constitution of Georgia need not long detain us. The final Convention which assembled at Savannah in October, 1776, occupied much time in deliberation, but the instrument which was prepared was marked by the crudity natural to the constitutional work of a new and frontier province. (See Jones, Ga. II:244, 245, 254–260.) The House of Assembly was arranged to consist of but one house to be composed of ten members from most of the counties, who should be of the Protestant religion and possessed of two hundred and fifty acres of land, or some other property to the amount of two hundred and fifty pounds. White citizens having property to the amount of ten pounds or being of any mechanick trade had a right to vote. Indeed, it was provided that any such person ne-glecting to cast his ballot should be subject to a penalty not exceeding five pounds. The Governor was to be chosen annually by ballot by the house and not to be eligible more than one year out of three and to be assisted by an Executive Council of two from each county subtracted from the members of the House of Assembly. The Council was always to vote by counties and not as individuals and was to examine the laws and ordinances sent them by the House of Assembly and return them in five days thereafter with their remarks thereon. There were to be Superior Courts in the Counties and a Supreme Court consisting of the Chief Justice and certain of the Justices of the county who were elected by the House of Assembly. Juries were to be judges of law as well as of fact. Estates were not to be entailed. The property of persons dying intestate was to be divided equally among their children and no alteration was to be made in this constitution without petitions from the majority of the counties signed in each case by the majority of the voters of the county.

A considerable amount of time has been devoted to a study of the new con-stitutions framed by the Southern States, but not, it is believed, an amount of time at all disproportioned to their importance, which is, in the field to which these lectures are devoted, preeminent. The remainder of the present lecture will be given to an exposition of certain points in the history of these states during the period from the formation of their first constitutions to the virtual conclusion of hostilities. Hostilities upon the soil of the Southern States were practically ended by the surrender of Cornwallis at Yorktown in the Autumn of 1781. Since the Spring of that year had seen a complete ratification of the Articles of Confederation, that year may form a convenient point for the beginning of another lecture. Within the period then concluded only a few points need be treated. A very great part of the energies of the newly formed states was devoted to the prosecution of the war with Great Britain. More especially was this the case from the time of the capture of Savannah by Campbell at the end of the year 1778 and further northward from the capture of Charleston in May, 1780. During the years 1779, 1780 and 1781 all the Southern States with the exception of Maryland, were filled with the terror of British invasion. Their public authorities were straining every nerve to meet the attacks of the royal army. The regular course of con-stitutional and political history was interrupted. One who does not propose to pursue the military history of the Revolutionary War may therefore be justified in singling out from the occurrences of the eventful years 1777 to 1781 those which have most significance for constitutional and political his-tory of the South and treating them, without effecting to relate the irregular transactions of revolutionary governments with the same precision of analy-sis that can properly be applied in the case of governments more peacefully developed.

On several occasions during these years of war, it became necessary in each state, or seemed necessary to the more ardent revolutionaries, to confer extraordinary powers upon certain departments of the executive government in the states. In North Carolina an extraordinary Council was invested with supreme power for a time. In Georgia a Supreme Executive Council at Augusta necessarily assumed extreme powers in 1779. In Virginia this impulse takes form in that project of the Dictatorship, which so strongly excited the alarm and indignation of Mr. Jefferson and received so dramatic a rebuke at the hands of Colonel Archibald Cary. [Henry II:147, 8. See Nation, Feb. 8, 1894.] A feature of state organization to which attention may be called for a moment in passing as having been developed during these years, was the practice of establishing Executive Boards, such as the Navy Board of South Carolina: the Navy Board and Board of Trade in Virginia; the N.C. Board of Trade; Hubbard's Davie, 72. These, like the corresponding boards established by congressional authority, may be enumerated among the sources of the executive departments of the United States Government as established in 1789, (Guggenheimer), though the Boards of Trade were merely offices for procuring supplies for the state. In all the states, as the war progressed and the currency depreciated, the financial efforts to sustain the war grew more and more burdensome, and during British invasion the emboldened Tories engaged in more and more of hostile attacks. The temptation grew strong to make retaliation upon the royalists and at the same time lighten the burden of prosecuting the war by passing acts confiscating the property of Tories, whether actively engaged in hostilities against the American force or simply absenting themselves from the country in its hour of need. Such acts, of greater or less severity, amounting in some cases to odious injustice, were passed by all the states. One curious service which these acts did may for a moment be alluded to. They were preeminently the cause of the first instances in which American Courts exercised their highest function, that of ignoring statutes of the legislature on the ground of unconstitutionality. This function, which, as Mr. Dicey and Mr. Bryce have well shown, is a necessary incident to all American judiciary action, found its first field of exercise in its present shape after the formation of the written constitutions of the states. That these instances were mainly connected with the laws concerning Tories and British creditors is doubtless due in large part to the fact that, while during the years under consideration the Radical or Democratic party had control of the legislatures of the states, the bench in each state was likely to be recruited from a profession always conservative and in the Southern states composed largely of those members of the upper classes who adhered to the more old-fashioned ideas of government. But to this subject I shall recur in a subsequent lecture.

In the political history of Maryland during this period, the most important movement, and a movement of the most momentous consequences, was that which compelled the solution of the question respecting western lands on terms of equality among all the states, by insuring their possession and government by the United States as a whole. But of this matter it is unnecessary for me here to give any account. I may instead refer to Doctor Adams's pamphlet upon the subject. In Virginia very much that is interesting during the period was concerned with the acquisition of the northwestern regions by General George Rogers Clark and the discussion respecting the disposition of the same; but this matter may be reserved for more particular treatment in a later lecture. In the history of the states farthest to the south interest attaches to the attempt of South Carolina to swallow up Georgia in 1777, [Gibbes, Doc. Hist. SC. 1776–1782, pp. 74, 77–87] (Jones, II:275–8){,} and to the divided authority exercised in Georgia during 1779 and '80 by a royalist assembly on the one hand, and two rival revolutionary governments on the other. In South Carolina, however, an event for which a greater importance can be claimed occurred in the year 1778. The constitution of 1776 had been formed, it will be remembered, in advance of the Declaration of Independence. It therefore had somewhat of a provisional quality. After the Declaration it seemed necessary to re-model the form of government. "The elections in every part of the state," says Ramsay, "were conducted on the idea that the members chosen, over and above the ordinary powers of legislators, should have the power to frame a new constitution suited to the declared independence of the state." The confidence reposed in the legislature was not abused. The frame of government which it formed was submitted for the space of a year to the consideration of the people at large and received their implied consent. Besides such verbal changes as that of "colony" to "state" and "president" to "governor," the new instrument established a rotation by limitation of re-eligibility in the offices of Governor, Privy-Councillor, Treasurer, Secretary, etc. Instead of the Legislative Council chosen by the representatives, a Senate was established, consisting of twenty eight members, each upwards of thirty years of age, to be elected by the people in their respective parishes and districts. In the matter of religion, respecting which the Constitution of 1776 had made no provision, that of 1778 put the denominations of Protestant Christians upon an equality, though without despoiling the Anglican Church of its property. A large number of curious regulations of the organization of Protestant societies was also included in the instrument. In March, 1778, the General Assembly and Legislative Council proceeded to give to this new instrument its final sanction, but when it was presented to President Rutledge, he, by virtue of the veto delegated to him by the existing constitution, refused to pass it. He declared that it was impossible for him, without breach of solemn obligations, taken under the Constitution of 1776, to give his sanction to the establishment of a different mode of government. He denied the power of the Legislature to effect changes in the Constitution. "The people," he said, "delegated to us a power of making laws, not of creating legislators, and there can be no doubt that if we have authority to take the right of electing the Legislative Council from that body in which the Constitution placed it and give it to another, we may not only do the like with the right of electing members of the Assembly and members of the Council, but vest the election of both the Assembly and the Council in any other body instead of the people, and the election of the President in some other body than the Council and Assembly." He therefore thought proper to resign the office of President. Arthur Middleton, being chosen, declined on account of similar difficulties in the way of his passing the new Constitution. Rawlins Lowndes, however, being elected on the 19th of March, 1778, gave his assent to the new Constitution. (Ramsay, I:128–39; Moultrie's "Memoirs," I:267–8; letters of Charles Cotesworth Pinckney.) With some difficulties and delays the new government went into operation. (Moultrie, I:278, 279, 282; letters of Charles Pinckney, Senior.) It is interesting to observe with respect to the considerations of constitutional law which President Rutledge adduced, that in 1823, in the case of Athanasius Thomas vs. Chesley Daniel, the Supreme Court of South Carolina, by the mouth of Justice Huger, distinctly affirmed that the first two South Carolina constitutions were merely ordinary statutes, repealable by the General Assembly. (II, McCord's Reports:359–60.)

But by far the most important matters in the constitutional and political history of the Southern States during the period under consideration are to be found, most fully exemplified in the legislative activity of the Virginia Assembly. Retiring from Congress to lead the important movements which he foresaw, Mr. Jefferson devoted himself in the Virginia Assembly to the advocacy of a series of measures of far-reaching consequence, the effect of which was to complete the work of the Virginia Constitution by sweeping away the principal foundations of the aristocratic system and establishing in permanent strength the institutions of American Democracy. The legislative activity of Virginia during that period was of so great influence upon the subsequent legislation of the other states as to be rendered strictly epoch-making. In a common-wealth where all the forces of tradition and many of the forces of economic interest combined to keep in vigorous operation the institutions of aristocracy, the burning democratic, humanitarian, rationalist zeal of one man, upheld by many able associates, sufficed to plant institutions which, spreading everywhere upon Southern soil, grew and grew into greater luxuriance. The most striking fact in the constitutional and political history of the Southern States, as I have said in the remarks introductory to these lectures, was the standing anomaly between a society organized upon aristocratic principles, or at least maintaining such principles in private life and in many departments of public usage, and the warm advocacy of strongly democratic theories. This anomaly was introduced into Southern history by the group of radical reformers in the Virginia Assembly of

October, 1776, headed by Thomas Jefferson. They did not content themselves with such changes as had been made in the fundamental constitution, but proceeded to urge such innovations in the system of Virginian law as would in time bring the rationalism of the eighteenth century, the doctrines of democratic equality and the spirit of devotion to the abstract rights of man to bear with destructive effect upon the most deep-seated peculiarities of the old Virginian social system. But in order to treat of these matters in connection with others which should properly be treated at the same time, it will be best, somewhat in defiance of chronological arrangement, to defer the subject to the next lecture.

IV. The Period of the Confederation

Although the present lecture might most appropriately begin and the last one was understood in most respects to leave off with the year 1784, for convenience of treatment it was thought well to postpone to this lecture the recital of the important legislative activities of Virginia during the years 1776 and 1777. The reason of this will be apparent as we proceed, the legislation of those two years being connected in the closest manner with that of the years 1785 and 1786 and that of the period from 1781 to 1788 in some of the other states. The first Assembly of Virginia under its new constitution convened in October, 1776. Mr. Jefferson, declining an election to Congress, took his seat in the Virginia House of Delegates on the first day of the session. He says in his Memoir, "Our delegation had been renewed for the ensuing year, commencing August 11th; but the new government was now organized, a meeting of the legislature was to be held in October and I had been elected a member by my county. I knew that our legislation under the regal government had many very vicious points, which urgently required reformation and I thought I could be of more use in forwarding that work." In the work of the ensuing session he was very sensibly aided by George Mason, and by George Wythe and strongly opposed in many matters by Edmund Pendleton and Robert Carter Nicholas. Mr. Jefferson thought it best first to attack in detail a few test matters. At once he asked and obtained leave to bring in a bill establishing courts of justice throughout the commonwealth. The next day he obtained leave to bring in a bill to enable tenants in tail to convey their lands in fee simple and another for the revision of the laws. On the 14th he reported the bill in regard to entails, sweeping them all away at once and providing that estates in tail should henceforth be held to be estates in fee simple. This was a change of great consequences in the social and especially in the political organization of Virginia, a step of importance in the process of transmuting Virginian aristocracy into Virginian democracy. Though encountering considerable resistance, the act was passed on November 1,

1776. Meanwhile, however, other measures of Mr. Jefferson had met with a more rapid success. Among them was an act defining treason, one providing for and organization of courts of oyer and terminer and one organizing an admiralty court. The bill for religious freedom by which he intended to carry out that complete equality of religious denominations toward which the sixteenth section of the Virginia Declaration of Rights had been directed, met with only partial success in the form of an act by which dissenters were exempted from levies for the support of the Church. At the same time the glebes and other property of the Church were preserved to it. The question of a general assessment for all religions was deferred and the colonial act making provision for the salaries of the clergy was suspended. Beside these measures and others less successful, Mr. Jefferson proposed and succeeded in securing the passage of a bill for a general revision of the laws by five elected revisors. The choice fell upon Mr. Jefferson, Edmund Pendleton, George Wythe, George Mason and Thomas Ludwell Lee. These very considerable achievements marked the Autumn session of 1776. (Randall I:196–203; Hening, IX:164–75, 202, 218, 226.) Of them all, by far the most important was the statute abolishing entails. It may be well to anticipate here so far as to state the action of the other Southern States in this matter. Maryland, by an act of November, 1782, provided that any person having an estate in tail should have the power to convey it in fee simple. In North Carolina the const. of 1776 had provided that the legislature should regulate entails so as to prevent perpetuities; the act of 1784, regulating descents, of which more later, at the same time converted tenants in tail into tenants in fee simple. In South Carolina, as has already been said in the first lecture, it appears that since the statute of 1733, there had been no entails, and in Georgia there were now no estates in tail, since Georgia had abolished them by a provision in her Constitution in 1777. Thus one of the two chief elements which go to make up a land-law favorable to the development of aristocracy was, within a few years, under the democratizing influence of the Revolution, almost simultaneously abolished in all the Southern States. In the two sessions of the year 1777 provision was made for a Court of Chancery, to consist of three Chancellors, for a General Court, to consist of five Judges and for rotation in the office of delegate to Congress. Among the acts of the sessions of 1778 those of most intrinsic interest are that remarkable, perhaps unique, act of attainder against Josiah Philips, which a former member of this Seminary, Mr. Trent, has so interestingly described, and the memorable statute prohibiting the importation of slaves.[6] (Maryland passed a similar act to this last in 1796.) This year also saw the organization of a Court of

{6.} See William P. Trent, "The Period of Constitution-Making in the American Churches," in JFJ, ed., *Essays in the Constitutional History of the United States in the Formative Period, 1775–1789* (Boston: Houghton, Mifflin Co., 1889), pp. 186–262.

Appeals, but this was better organized at a later time. It had for a time a form curiously resembling the complicated system employed in England in the case of the Court of Exchequer Chamber, but its eventual form was that of a Court embracing the Chancellors and Judges of the General Court and the Judges of the Court of Admiralty. (Randall I:209–15; Hening IX:299, 388, 389, 401, 463, 471, 523, etc.) On a vote respecting one of these judiciary bills the previous question was ordered and the yeas and nays were ordered to be entered on the journal, both which were up to that time rare and perhaps unprecedented in the transactions of Virginian Assemblies. Meantime each session had seen a renewal of the act suspending the statutory provisions for the salary of the clergy. In October, 1780, an act was passed making it lawful for any minister of any society or congregation of Christians to celebrate the rite of marriage. (Hening X:361.) In North Carolina it had already been provided in 1778, that all ministers having the cure of souls could legally perform that rite, whereas the old act of 1766, though extending the permission to Presbyterian as well as Episcopalian ministers, had provided that the fees for the ceremony should be given to the Episcopalian clergyman of the parish. Returning to Virginia: an act of May, 1779, provided for the transfer of the seat of government from Williamsburg to Richmond. This was but the first instance of a general movement. The period between the Revolution and the first years of this century shows in several instances the transference of state capitals in the old seaboard states from the tide-water region to the head of navigation, that is, to the physical boundary line between the lowland and the upland region. This movement, which carried the capital of Pennsylvania to Harrisburg, that of Virginia to Richmond, that of North Carolina to Raleigh, that of South Carolina to Columbia, was but a recognition of the fact that the population of the western parts of these states was increasing in magnitude and asserting, as its activity in the Revolution had seemed to entitle it to assert, a claim to greater power in the administration of the states.

By the resignation of George Mason and the death of Thomas Ludwell Lee, the Committee of Revisors became reduced to three. Having completed their tasks, Jefferson, Wythe and Pendleton brought in, in the Spring of 1779, a report consisting of one hundred and twenty six bills drawn up with great clearness, brevity and precision. They were calculated to work very considerable changes in the administration of the law within Virginia, but only a few of them belong within the sphere of constitutional and political history. Several of them met with immediate success. An act respecting naturalization provided for the acquisition of citizenship by any white persons who should migrate into the state and should, before a Court of Record, give proof that they intended to reside therein and assurance of fidelity to the commonwealth. Maryland in 1779 provided that any foreigner taking an oath of allegiance to that state should be deemed a subject. This liberality

in the matter of naturalization was, it will be remembered, a characteristic
feature of Jeffersonian democracy. A much greater difficulty was encountered by many of the other proposals of the Commission. (Randall, I:216–29.)
Mr. Jefferson becoming governor of the state and being thereafter occupied
in congressional and diplomatic service, little progress was made in pushing
the new laws of the three revisors until in 1784 Mr. Madison, on the expi-
ration of his service in Congress, became again a member of the Virginia
House of Delegates. Under his skilful and consiliatory management rapid
progress was made in the matter. In the session of 1785 thirty-four of the revisors' laws were enacted, in that of 1786 twenty-three more. Mr. Jefferson's
projected law respecting education obtained no success until 1795 and then
only very partial success. The criminal code which he proposed, marked on
the one hand by an enlightened mildness contrasting strongly with the bar-
barity of the contemporary English criminal law, but on the other hand by
many fantastic provisions, received little attention until 1796. Of the laws
which were passed, by far the most important were that respecting religious freedom and that respecting descents. (Hening, XII:84, 138). The bill
for establishing religious freedom provided in most vigorous terms, (though
with a highly rhetorical preamble), that no man should be compelled to frequent or support any religious worship, place or ministry whatsoever, nor
should be in any way molested on account of his religious belief. This law,
it will be remembered, was one of the three achievements which Mr. Jefferson directed to be inscribed upon his tombstone. [See also Rives, I. II. and
Conway 156–165, Hawks, Contrib. to Eccl. Hist.:Va.]

In Maryland, as has already been related, the Constitution of 1776 had left
the Legislature free to impose a general assessment for the benefit of religion,
to be applied in each case to the religion which the tax-payer might prefer.
No such assessment was laid during the time of the war. In May, 1783, Governor Paca recommended it. At the same time the Episcopal Church applied
to the Legislature for incorporation, but succeeded in nothing more than the
passage of an act in 1784, incorporating the Episcopal clergy of the state into
a society for the relief of the wives and children of ministers of that Church.
To anticipate a little, the Legislatures of 1809 and 1810 amended the Constitution by forbidding the levying of any tax for religious purposes. [Hawks,
Cont. to Eccl. Hist.:Md.] North Carolina and South Carolina had by their
constitutions already admitted a perfect or nearly perfect religious freedom.

The Virginian act of 1785 respecting descents was a natural accompani-
ment of Mr. Jefferson's law abolishing entails. Entails and primogeniture are
the natural foundations of aristocracy. The first the assembly destroyed by
the act of 1776; the act of 1785 abolished the other, decreeing that the lands
of a person dying intestate should not go to his oldest son as heretofore, but
should be divided equally among all his children. Judge Benjamin Watkins
Leigh, in an interesting letter to John Taylor {Tyler}, dated August 27, 1832,

and published in the "Virginia Law Journal," Volume IX:199–203, points out that while the English law of descent was admirably adapted to uphold aristocracy and that of Virginia to prevent it, this last was not less true of the law usual in absolute monarchies. So, for instance, that of the Code Napoleon and that of the old Civil Law under the Roman Empire was much the same in its detailed regulations as to descent as that of Virginia. "I have seen," he says, "the Revised Code of Denmark, which begins with the formal declaration that the king is sovereign, lord and master of the lives, liberties and properties of all his subjects; and yet the Danish law of descents is so very like ours that it is hardly possible to doubt that Mr. Jefferson had seen it when he drew the statute of 1785 and in many respects designedly followed its model." Following out, as I have done heretofore, the similar legislation of other Southern States, it is to be remarked: that in 1786 Maryland provided that the lands of an intestate should descend to his children equally. A North Carolina act of 1784 provided for descent to all sons equally and then, in default of sons, to all daughters equally. It was not till 1795 that the North Carolina law put the daughters upon an equality with the sons in the taking of descent to the lands of an intestate. In 1791 South Carolina, abolishing primogeniture, gave to the widow of the intestate one-third of his real estate, the rest being divided equally among his children, and the whole being so divided if there were no widow. The first constitution of Georgia in 1777 had already provided for descent to children in equal shares. By these measures it was, together with those abolishing entails, that the foundation was laid for an eventual democratic organization of society throughout the South. (Rives's "Madison," I:536, 561, 562; R. G. H. Kean, "Thomas Jefferson as a Legislator" in the "Virginia Law Journal" for December, 1887.) By some this sort of legislation was viewed with extreme horror. Even down so late as 1851, Hugh Garland, in his "Life of John Randolph," makes frequent lamentations over this agrarian legislation. Another sort of protest comes from that exceedingly curious book, the "Life of the Reverend Devereux Jarratt." After speaking of the habit in his youth, among the plain people with whom he grew up, of regarding gentlefolk as beings of a superior order, he says, in 1794, "But I have lived to see a vast alteration in this respect and the contrary extreme prevail. In our high republican times there is more levelling than ought to be consistent with good government. I have as little notion of oppression and tyranny as any man, but a due subordination is essentially requisite in every government. At present there is too little regard and reverence paid to magistrates and persons in public office; and whence do this disregard and irreverence originate but from the notion and practice of levelling? An idea is held out to us that our present government and state are far superior to the former, when we were under the royal administration; but my age enables me to know that the people are not now by half so peacefully and quietly governed as formerly; nor are the laws, perhaps by the tenth part, so well executed. And yet I allow the superiority of our present government. In theory it is certainly superior; but in practice it is not so. This can arise from nothing so much as from want of a proper distinction between the various orders of the people." (Pp. 14–5.) So thought the worthy Rector of Bath Parish.

It may be well to conclude our survey of the legislation of the period with a glance at the assemblies themselves. First, as to the elections. "In Virginia," Mr. Madison tells us, "where the elections to the colonial legislature were septennial and the original settlers of the prevailing sentiments and manners of the parent nation, the modes of canvassing for popular votes in that country were generally practiced. The people not only tolerated, but expected and even required to be courted and treated. No candidate, who neglected those attentions, could be elected. His forbearance would have been ascribed to a mean parsimony, or a proud disrespect for the voters." Madison himself, refusing to treat, though elected the first time he offered himself, was refused on the second occasion. Laws ag. treating were pretty generally passed in So. Stat. bet. 1783 & 1800. In general, the period of the Confederation was marked by somewhat the same decline in the character of the state legislatures as appeared in the Continental Congress itself. In Virginia, however, the annual elections sometimes brought together a good collection of members, sometimes a poor. Randolph writes to Jefferson in 1784, "The increase of new members has introduced some of the children of the Revolution who labor to satisfy themselves and disdain dependency on the dictum of any individual or faction. By this means we seem to have obtained another division of party in the Assembly. It was manifest throughout the last session that H——y [7] had one corps, R. H. L.,[8] though absent, another, and the speaker a third. . . . This renders it probable that our friend of Orange will step earlier into the heart of battle than his modesty would otherwise permit, for he is already resorted to as a general, of whom much is preconceived to his advantage." (Conway, 55, 56.) Joseph Jones writes to Madison in 1783, "You cannot well conceive the deranged state of affairs in this country. There is nothing like system; division and embarrassment follow under such a state of things. The two great commanders [Patrick Henry and Richard Henry Lee] [9] make excellent harangues, handsome speeches to their men, but they want executive officers, or should be more so themselves to be useful. Indeed, so far as I am able to judge from the short time I have been here, we are much in want of useful men, who do business as well as speak to it." (Letters of Joseph Jones, 118.) St. George Tucker writes to Theodorick Bland in 1782, "Our Assembly will sit next Monday. The choice of the

{7.} Patrick Henry.
{8.} Richard Henry Lee.
{9.} Brackets in original document.

people in their representatives is much for the better, I am told, through the country generally. The principal changes which I have heard of are certainly so. I wish they may form a house endued with more wisdom, foresight and stability of conduct than have heretofore characterized the assemblies of this country." (Bland Papers, II:79.) Somewhat to a similar purpose, Doctor David Ramsay, of South Carolina, writes to Jefferson in April, 1787, "Our governments in the Southern States are much more quiet than in the Northern, but much of our quiet arises from the temporizing of the legislature in refusing legal protection to the prosecution of the just rights of the creditors." (Bancroft, "Constitution," II:417.) N.C. assemblies frequently characterized by Iredell's correspondents. An effort was made in 1783 by several, who, like Jefferson, had doubted the competence of the legislature to frame the constitution, as had been done in 1776, to summon a constitutional convention, but the scheme was defeated and Virginia went on under the same constitution till 1830. (Rives's "Madison," I:555–60; Letters of Joseph Jones, 108; Bancroft, "Constitution," I:317, 335.)

Only second in importance to the democratic legislation of this period may be set, in the field of constitutional history, the development of what has well been termed "the highest function of the American judiciary." An allusion was made in a preceding lecture to the rise in this period of the judicial practice of declaring acts of the legislature void because of unconstitutionality. It is obvious that, as Mr. Bryce and Mr. Dicey have shown, this is only a natural incident to the position of a judiciary under a constitutional system which is marked by two sorts of laws, the one conceived as of higher authority than the other. Some analogies to this function were presented during the colonial period by the rejection of statutes as contrary to colonial charters. Story, I:120–7, mentions a Connecticut case of this sort where a statute of that colony was declared void for this reason, by the Judicial but exec. Committee of the King's Privy-Council and there may have been such decisions by colonial courts. The first such case subsequent to the Declaration of Independence seems to have been discovered by Doctor Austin Scott in the case of Holmes and Ketcham vs. Walton, a New Jersey case of 1779.[10] The next case seems to have been the Virginia case of Commonwealth vs. Caton et als., (IV. Call, 5), a case argued in November, 1782, before the Court of Appeals. In this case the constitutionality of the treason law of 1776 was discussed in the case of three men condemned for treason by the

{10.} Austin Scott (1848–1922), associate in history at Johns Hopkins and head of the Seminary in History and Politics from 1876 to 1883, delivered a paper at the annual meeting of the American Historical Association in 1886 entitled "The Origin of the Highest Function of the American Judiciary." The paper discussed the case in 1779 of *Holmes and Ketcham* vs. *Walton*. An article based on this paper, "Holmes vs. Walton: The New Jersey Precedent," was published in the April 1899 issue of the *American Historical Review*, pp. 456–69. See also AHA, *Papers* 2 (1887): 45–47.

General Court. It had been provided by the Constitution, that the Governor should have the power to pardon, "except where the prosecution shall have been carried on by the House of Delegates, or the law shall otherwise particularly direct, in which cases no reprieve or pardon shall be granted but by resolve of the House of Delegates." Now the act of 1776 provided that in case of conviction for treason, the Governor should have no right of granting pardon, but might suspend the execution until the meeting of the General Assembly, who should determine whether such person or persons are proper objects of mercy or not and order accordingly. In this case the House of Delegates resolved in favor of pardon, but the Senate refused to concur. The defence declared that the act deprived the Governor of the pardoning power in cases of treason, in which case it was unconstitutional to give it to the whole Assembly. Wythe, Pendleton and the other Judges said that if the act were unconstitutional they would unhesitatingly declare it void. Chancellor Wythe said, "Nay more, if the whole legislature . . . should attempt to overleap the bounds prescribed to them by the people, I, in administering the public justice of the country, will meet the united powers at my seat in this tribunal; and pointing to the Constitution, will say to them, 'Here is the limit of your authority; and hither shall you go, but no farther.' " But the Court decided against the true interpretation, I should think, that the statute was in fact constitutional. (IV. Call, 5: Bland Papers, II:86.) Again in May, 1788, the Virginia Assembly, having passed an act purporting to lay certain additional duties upon the Judges of the Court of Appeals, the Judges met and joined in a remonstrance, that the act of the legislature was unconstitutional. (IV Call, 135.) [J. B. Cutting to Jefferson; Bancroft, Const. II. 473.]

Another of these celebrated cases occurred in North Carolina in the interval between the dates of the two Virginian cases just mentioned. In 1801, in the case of Moore vs. Bradley (II Haywood, 314) the council for the plaintiff, John Haywood, said, "In the year 1785 the Assembly passed an act taking from all persons the right of suing for property sold by commissioners of confiscated estates and of course the right of possession that such persons had. The Judges declared the act invalid and in 1786 the Assembly altered it. On that occasion the legislature concurred at last with the judiciary in the position that the legislature could not deprive any man of his right to property or of his right to sue for it. One of the Judges illustrated his opinion in this manner; "As God said to the waters, 'So far shall ye go and no further,' so said the people to their legislature." Judge Ashe deserves for this the veneration of his country and of posterity." But, while the anecdote is very likely historical, it would appear from the case of Bayard et ux. vs. Singleton, (Martin, 43–4), which seems to be the case referred to, that, while Judge Ashe m-a-y have said it in the May term of 1786, it was in May of 1787 that the Judges did with great reluctance declare, "That by the Constitution every citizen had undoubtedly a right to a decision of his property by a trial by jury," that no act of legislature could take away this right and that the act in question was void. McRee, in his "Life of Iredell," prints the letter Iredell addressed to the public in support of the subordination of the legislature to the authority of the Constitution and the duty and right of the courts to pronounce null and void any acts of the Assembly which were inconsistent with that instrument,—the supreme law of the state. This appeared in August, 1786, and certainly implies that the decision had not yet been rendered at that time. (McRee, II:145–9.) Richard Dobbs Spaight writes in August, 1787, from the Constitutional Convention, expressing his alarm at the decision of the Judges then recently rendered and strongly arguing against it. (McRee, II:169–70.) To this Iredell replies in an admirable letter, in which he states with great exactness the ground upon which such judicial decisions properly rest. His words are of great interest as anticipating the very explanations of Mr. Dicey and Mr. Bryce and penetrating much more deeply into the heart of the matter than has been usual with American writers since. He says, "The Constitution, therefore, being a fundamental law, and a law, in writing, of the solemn nature I have mentioned, . . . the judicial power, in the exercise of their authority, must take notice of it as the ground-work of that, as well as of all other authority; and as no article of the Constitution can be repealed by a legislature, which derives its whole power from it, it follows either that the fundamental, unrepealable law must be obeyed, by the rejection of an act unwarranted by and inconsistent with it, or you must obey an act founded on an authority not given by the people, and to which, therefore, the people owe no obedience. It is not that the judges are appointed arbiters, and to determine, as it were, upon any application, whether the Assembly have or have not violated the Constitution; but when an act is necessarily brought in judgment before them, they must, unavoidably, determine one way or another." (McRee, II:173–6.) Thus it was that the Southern States bore their share in the development of this highly important judicial function.

An important portion of the political history of the Southern States during these years consists in their dealings with the immense difficulties of the questions respecting paper money, which the war had brought upon them. All the Southern States had, during the war, made large issues of paper money. The resumption of specie payments came with great difficulty in the subsequent years, when large portions of the population were burdened with debt, when the financial condition of the states was still far from prosperous, and when commerce had not yet been able to struggle back to its original channels or find out new ones. Maryland, in 1780, took an important step toward the solution of the matter by enacting that all contracts expressed in writing to be in specie, must be paid in specie. In 1782 it enacted a stay law, extending to January, 1784, but a strong, indeed a violent, effort in 1786 to renew issues of paper money, though successful in the Assembly, was fortunately held in check by that senate, whose conservative organization has before been commented upon. Virginia had issued millions of dollars in paper money, which had depreciated until it was declared to be no longer receivable, except for the taxes of the year, and was made redeemable in loan office certificates at the rate of a thousand for one. Like other states, it provided in 1782 a scale of depreciation, so that debts contracted during the six years following the first of January, 1777, might be discharged according to their real value at the time of the original contract. By another statute of 1784 all contracts made after the first of January of that year were to be discharged in the manner specified by the contract. In 1785 an attempt was made to issue more paper money. In 1786 a stronger attempt was headed off by the election of George Mason to the Assembly and the strong efforts of that solid and influential statesman and of Madison, who writes to Washington, "The original object was paper money; petitions for graduated certificates succeeded; next came instalments and lastly a project for making property a tender for debts at four-fifths of its value: all these have been happily got rid of by very large majorities."

North Carolina had, during the war, made extensive issues of paper money. Even after the close of the war, in April, 1783, it issued one hundred thousand pounds more. Suits were suspended for twelve months. In November, 1785, another one hundred thousand pounds was issued, to be lawful tender in all payments whatsoever. So, though letters from members of the conservative circle to which Iredell belonged show that strong protests were made against these legislative acts, North Carolina floundered on, deeper and deeper in the mire of irredeemable currency. South Carolina, in February, 1782, repealed the laws making paper money a legal tender and suspended suits for about a year. In 1783 it established a table of depreciation, as had been done by Virginia. In 1784 the legislature passed an ordinance for the payment of debts in four annual instalments, beginning on the first of January, 1786; but before this, in 1785, a law was passed, authorizing the debtor to tender to the plaintiff any portion of his property, which the creditor must accept at three fourths of its appraised value: at the same time the state prolonged the period of the installments of payments and issued one hundred thousand pounds in bills of credit to be loaned at seven per cent. Georgia also, in 1782, passed a stay law giving extension of two years. In February, 1785, its bills of credit were ordered to be redeemed in specie certificates at the rate of a thousand for one. The next year occurred another issue of bills of credit, but one offering considerable security. (Bancroft's "Constitution," I:235–41.)

Among those activities of the state governments which, directly or indirectly, led toward the foundation of a better Union, two stand especially prominent: their dealings with the problem of the western lands and their efforts for a better regulation of commerce. Maryland had entered into the

Confederation in 1781, on the expectation that the other states would make full cession of their western lands to the United States, and New York had already done so in 1780. In March, 1784, Virginia presented to Congress her cession of her claims to lands north-west of the Ohio, making a liberal reservation of bounty lands for her Revolutionary soldiers and those employed under George Rogers Clark in the conquest of Kaskaskia and Vincennes. Virginia stipulated indemnity for the expenses of that expedition, the security of the French inhabitants of those settlements and, most important provision of all, the eventual erection of the ceded lands into republican states, to be admitted to membership in the Federal Union with the same rights of sovereignty, freedom and independence as the other states. The Massachusetts cession of 1785 and the Connecticut cession of 1786 were followed in 1787 by the South Carolina cession, in 1790 by that from North Carolina, in 1802 by that from Georgia. The last two do not fall chronologically within the scope of the present lecture, yet they may, for convenience, be spoken of here. That of South Carolina is closely connected with the suit between South Carolina and Georgia in relation to their boundaries in the region of the sources of the Savannah. [Stevens, Ga., II. 385–6.] It will perhaps be remembered, that the Federal judiciary, under the Articles of Confederation, included not only a Court of Appeals in prize causes, which was in a way the ancestor of the present Supreme Court, but also a peculiarly organized tribunal for the decision of disputed questions about boundary & jurisdiction between two or more states.[11] This Court sat on only one occasion. It was convened on two others; one of these was the case of boundary dispute between Georgia and South Carolina. The matter was accommodated by agreement between the two states, in accordance with which the boundaries were to extend up the Savannah River, then up the Tugaloo to the southern boundary of North Carolina,—or, if that river did not extend so far, to its northernmost source and thence westward to the Mississippi. Now in 1787, South Carolina ceded to the United States all her claims to territory westward of the meridian of the northernmost source of the Tugaloo. Hildreth declares (III:532), that this grant included nothing, apparently supposing that the northern branches of the Tugaloo in fact extended to the southern boundary of North Carolina, but Mr. W. R. Garrett, in his "History of the South Carolina Cession," among the papers of the "Tennessee Historical Society," shows that, in fact, the state had a valid, though useless, claim to a strip twelve miles wide, extending from the meridian indicated to the Mississippi. The historical importance of the act lay in its being the earliest cession of southwestern lands and being probably designed to exert a moral pressure upon the neighboring states. However this may be, the cession of the western lands, now Tennessee, by

{11.} JFJ, "The Predecessor of the Supreme Court," in JFJ, ed., *Essays in the Constitutional History of the United States*, pp. 1–45.

North Carolina, executed in 1790, was invested with no fewer than ten conditions, which provided that the present land-grants of the state of North Carolina should be respected and under which, in general, terms were made, which vastly diminished the apparent value of the gift. Georgia also stipulated in her cession of 1802 for the reservation of several hundred thousand acres and a sum of one million, two hundred and fifty thousand dollars. Thus the Southern States contributed to the formation of the commonwealths of the South-west, though this was done with far less generosity and under conditions constitutionally less noteworthy than those by which Virginia, New York, and Massachusetts coöperated to lay the foundations of the great North-west.

As to their commercial regulations, one may follow the obscure and confused history of the tariffs and other commercial regulations of the individual states in the period before 1789: in Mr. Willard C. Fisher's paper upon that subject in the 3d volume of the Papers of the "American Historical Association," Pp. 465–93, and the history of the five per cent. impost in Curtis or Bancroft. A more interesting and a more distinctly southern chapter in the development of a more perfect Union through the advancement of better commercial systems is that which relates the history of the conferences of Maryland and Virginia respecting the Potomac and their results. Virginia and Maryland had long felt the need of concerted commercial regulations. As far back as 1774 Washington in the Virginia Assembly had moved a bill empowering a number of subscribers to undertake at their own expense the extension of the navigation of the Potomac from tide-water to Mill's Creek, about a hundred and fifty miles. George Mason and Thomas Johnson of Maryland were prominently interested in the matter at that time, but the war interrupted their projects. The dispute as to the jurisdiction over the Potomac, however, was a question intimately connected with this work of extending its navigation. In December, 1784, Washington was commissioned by his state to go to Annapolis and arrange with Maryland for uniformity of action on the part of the two states in establishing under their authority a company for improving the navigation of the Potomac. The concurrence of Pennsylvania was also desired. Next, in order to define with exactness the respective rights of the two states upon the Potomac, Virginia, in June, 1784, commissioned George Mason, Edmund Randolph, James Madison and Alexander Henderson to frame regulations in the matter in concert with commissioners from Maryland. Thomas Stone, Samuel Chase, Daniel of St. Thomas Jenifer, as commissioners on the part of Maryland, met with Mason and Henderson, at Alexandria, in March, 1785. Miss Rowland, in her article in the "Pennsylvania Magazine of History," Volume XI:Pp. 410–25, and in her "Life of George Mason," has given from original papers an interesting description of the interview. "With only two of the Virginia commissioners present and without any copy of the resolves upon the principal subject," says Mason, in a letter to Madison, "we thought it better to proceed than to disappoint the Maryland commissioners, who appeared to have brought with them the most amicable dispositions and expressed a great desire of forming such a fair and liberal compact as might prove a lasting cement of friendship between the two states, which we are convinced it is their interest to cultivate. We therefore, upon the particular invitation of the General, adjourned to Mount Vernon and finished the business there." They prepared the terms of a compact between the two states for the jurisdiction over the waters between the two, and also took up matters of general policy and recommended to the two states uniformity of commercial regulations and a uniformity of currency. From this compact arranged at Mount Vernon between the commissioners of two Southern States came, as is familiar, the summons of the Annapolis Convention of September 1786, from which in turn proceeded the memorable Philadelphia Convention of 1787. (Bancroft: Rives.)

v. The Southern States and the Constitution of 1787

The framing of the Federal Constitution is a portion of the national history of the United States. The struggles for its adoption are an important portion of state history, not only because the ratification was to be carried out by the action of states, but because the struggles themselves bring to light in an interesting manner the political condition and complexion of the individual states. It is intended then in the present lecture to give a history of the attitude of the several Southern States toward the new Constitution and of their actions upon it.

The Southern States were far from pursuing a uniform policy with respect to the work of the Philadelphia Convention. Their interests were affected by the proposed new institutions of government in various ways. With respect to the arrangements which it effected between the interests of large states and the interests of small states, Virginia and North Carolina were affected by it in one way; Maryland and Georgia in another. The large states, too, might be expected to exhibit and did in fact exhibit a greater reluctance at the thought of seeing their state governments overshadowed, and, as they conceived, swallowed up by a more powerful general government. So far as material interests were concerned, tobacco growing states, like Maryland and Virginia, were affected by the new form of government in a considerably different manner from South Carolina and Georgia, with their rice and indigo plantations. The provision that Congress might not prohibit the slave trade before 1808, but might after that date, had a very different bearing in the minds of statesmen of Virginia, where the slave trade had been already for several years prohibited, and in those of South Carolina and Georgia, where slave importations were still numerous and were regarded as absolutely indispensable to the prosperity of the leading industries. By reason of these diversities of view and of interest, it is impossible to treat of the subject of this lecture as a whole. The attitude and situation of each state must be separately considered and the order chosen will very naturally be that of the ratifications of the Constitution by these five states.

Georgia had been represented in the Federal Convention by four members, William Few, Abraham Baldwin, William Pierce and William Houston, but only Few and Baldwin had signed the instrument. The legislature of Georgia chanced to be in session when the message from Congress, transmitting the document, arrived. In the minds of the people of Georgia the natural objection of an exporting state to the concession of the control of navigation to the Federal Congress and the objection to the eventual prohibition of the slave trade were overruled by the exposed position of the state and its need of protection by a strong government against Spain, which bounded it upon the south along the extensive frontier from the Atlantic to the Mississippi, and against the Indians of the interior. A Convention therefore, was immediately called, which met on Christmas-day of 1787. On January 2, 1788, this Convention unanimously ratified and adopted the proposed Constitution. President Wereat, writing to Congress, says, "We hope that the ready compliance of this state with the recommendations of Congress and of the late National Convention will tend not only to consolidate the Union, but promote the happiness of our common country." (Bancroft, "Constitution," II:253–4; Stevens' "Georgia," II:386–7.) Georgia was thus the fourth state to ratify the Constitution; but her Convention seems without doubt to have been ignorant of the action previously taken in the matter by Delaware, Pennsylvania and New Jersey, on the 7th, 12th and 18th of the month preceding. Indeed, one of Washington's letters, of February 7th, shows that after an interval of five weeks only a rumor of the ratification by Georgia had reached him.

Maryland had had five representatives in the Federal Convention, James McHenry, Daniel of St. Thomas Jenifer, Daniel Carroll, John Francis Mercer and Luther Martin. Of these the first three signed the Constitution, Mercer and Martin refusing. Acc. to J. B. Cutting's letter to Jeff{erson}. (Banc. II. 472–3{.}) Martin sent by Chase interest; some leading men had to stay in Md., to fight in leg{islature}. a paper money craze incited by Chase. In November, 1787, Martin brought before the Legislature in an extensive speech and printed for the benefit of the people, under the title of "Genuine Information," etc. an elaborate statement of his reasons for refusal to join in signing the Constitution. He gave at length a history of the Convention, which is a most valuable source of information respecting its deliberations. He arraigned the Convention for having exceeded its authority, urged the dangers attending so extensive an increase of the powers of the Federal Government and declared his steadfast opposition to the government, which he urged would virtually place the small states in the power of the large ones. Martin was answered by McHenry and on the 27th of November the Legislature voted to call a convention of the people of the state to assemble in Annapolis on April 21, 1788, to consider the new Constitution. (Bancroft, II:278; Scharf, II:542; Elliot's Debates, I:344–89.) During the interval there was much public discussion of the new measure. Washington, who during this month seldom went far from his Virginian farm, watched the proceedings of the state across the river with much interest and, with habitual moderation, exercised an influence in favor of the new form of government. The day before the Convention was to meet, April 20th, he writes to Thomas Johnson, that the adjournment of the Maryland Convention to a later period than the decision of the question in Virginia would be tantamount to the rejection of the Constitution. "I have," he says, "good reasons for this opinion and I am led to believe this is the blow which the leading characters of the opposition in the next state [i.e. South Carolina] [12] have meditated, if it shall be found that a direct attack is not likely to succeed in yours. If this is true, it cannot be too much deprecated and guarded against." (Sparks, IX:345.) [Conway 102, Ran{dolph}. to Mad{ison}. "Chase, Paca; Mercer & L. Martin are elected in Annapolis! Should be Anne Arundel? to the exclusion of all the Carrolls; and that Chase had caused a clerk of his to be elected in another county, which he could not represent."] On the fourth day of the Convention, Saturday, Samuel Chase began a fierce opposition to the new government, declaring that its powers were deadly to the cause of liberty. William Paca asking leave to prepare amendments brought them in the next day and began to read them. But members from almost all the counties declared that they and their colleagues were under obligation to vote for the new Constitution and almost all declared further that they had no authority to propose amendments. Washington writes to Madison, that at this point, "Mr. Chase, it is said, made a display of all his eloquence. Mr. Mercer discharged his whole artillery of inflammable matter; and Mr. Martin I know not what, perhaps vehemence—but no converts were made, no not one." The friends of the new Constitution refused to engage in debate and called for the question of ratification, which on April 26th was carried in the affirmative by sixty-three votes against eleven. Paca's amendments were then referred to a committee. The majority of the committee acceded to thirteen amendments intended to carry out very much the same purposes as those secured by the first ten amendments of the present Constitution. The minority demanded more. The Convention on the 28th summoned the committee. The majority of the committee then determined to make no report of any amendments whatever, even of those which they had almost unanimously agreed to. Their

{12.} Brackets in original document.

reason is stated to have been the belief that this would only involve the Convention in difficulties, give an aid to the opponents of government and have ill consequences in Virginia and the other states which had not ratified. The Convention thereupon dissolved without the recommendation of any amendments whatever. (Bancroft, II:281–4, 465–8; Scharf, 542–6.) The address to the people of Maryland, which the minority of the committee on amendments then published, is printed in Elliot's Debates, Vol. II:507–15, and is the only substitute which that repertory contains for a record of the constitutional debates in Maryland. (Alexander Contee Hanson's pamphlet, "Remarks on the Proposed Plan of a Federal Government by Aristides" is to be found in Mr. Ford's reprint of pamphlet on the Constitution.) The effect of the action of Maryland was regarded as highly beneficial by General Washington. He writes to General Lincoln, "It has been strongly insisted upon by the opponents in the lower and back counties in this state, that Maryland would reject it by a large majority. The result being found so directly opposite to this assertion will operate very powerfully upon the sentiments of many who were before undecided and will tend to fix them in favour of the Constitution." (Sparks, IX:363.)

It is interesting to observe, in those states which did not ratify the Constitution unanimously, the geographical distribution of the votes for and against the new instrument of government. Almost everywhere throughout the United States it is to be observed that the alluvial districts, the regions of most fertile land, were in favor of ratification; wild and hilly regions, the watersheds between the fertile valleys, were generally opposed. The vote of Maryland forms only in part an exception. It is, of course to be observed that we have no popular votes upon which to base our inferences. Our only resource in case of each state is the vote of the representative of the locality in the Convention upon the final question of ratification. This is not a certain guide, for in that vote the member may not have correctly represented his constituents, but it will be in the main trustworthy. Of course we know from other sources that the rich and commercial classes favored the Constitution, while the poor and the ignorant opposed; that the former officers of the Continental Army favored it almost to a man; that the minor religious sects viewed it with some distrust, etc.

The vote of the Maryland Convention falls in general within the line of the observation just made regarding influence of physical geography, but there were important exceptions. Almost all the state lay within the alluvial belt and almost all the representatives of the state, as has been seen, voted in favor of the new Constitution; yet the few counties that lay outside the alluvial belt voted in its favor, and the greater share of the opposition came from members representing the coast counties of Anne Arundel, Baltimore and Harford. But Anne Arundel was carried only narrowly in the elections to the

Convention (Bancroft, II:466) and Annapolis itself was Federal, as likewise Baltimore.

Since the ratification by Georgia, Connecticut and Massachusetts had also given in their adhesion to the new form of government. Maryland was therefore the seventh state. The eighth was South Carolina. At the Federal Convention that state had commissioned John Rutledge, Charles Cotesworth Pinckney, Charles Pinckney and Pierce Butler; all were of strongly Federal sentiments. Edward Rutledge writes to Arthur Lee (Lee's "Arthur Lee," II:315), "We have agreed to send deputies to the Continental Convention. My brother, who is truly Federal, is among the number of gentlemen, none of whom, I am convinced, will yield to him in zeal for Continental measures." All four of the delegates of South Carolina signed the Constitution at Philadelphia; yet in the state there was not inconsiderable opposition from fear of oppressive navigation acts, of restrictions upon slavery and of stricter laws respecting paper money and the payment of debts. On January 16, 1788, the South Carolina House of Representatives took up the question of calling a convention. The debates in the Legislature had a high importance for a somewhat peculiar reason. The chief burden of debate in opposition was borne by Rawlins Lowndes, who declared (Elliot, IV:267), that he should not have an opportunity of speaking in the Convention, because his constituents i.e. the voters of the parishes of St. Philip & St. Michael, Charleston would not elect any person as a member of the Convention, that did not approve of the proposed plan of government. He therefore argued at much length against the Constitution in the Legislature. In the imperfect reports of its debates, which are all that we have, hardly any other opponent appears. Charles Pinckney gave a history of the Convention and an exposition of the character of the new Constitution. Charles Cotesworth Pinckney, John and Edward Rutledge, Doctor David Ramsay, Chancellor Pendleton and others upheld the Federal cause against the objections that the interests of South Carolina would be endangered by the treaty-making power, that the Confederation was "a most excellent Constitution," that danger was to be apprehended from restrictions upon the slave trade and from the power to regulate commerce. Mr. Lowndes was thanked for his opposition by the desire of several members, because it had drawn forth from the other side most valuable information and had afforded the necessary debate. A movement for a recommendation of a second Federal Convention failed. A resolution for a Convention to consider the Constitution was unanimously adopted. In the rivalry between Charleston and Columbia as its place of meeting Charleston won by a single vote. The Convention met on May 13th under the presidency of the Governor, Thomas Pinckney. In the absence of Lowndes the leadership of the opposition fell to Edanus Burke and General Sumter. With similar good feeling to that which had characterized the proceedings in the

Legislature, the Convention discussed for a week the paragraphs of the Constitution, and finally on the 23rd of May, the Constitution was ratified by a vote of one hundred and forty nine in favor to seventy three adverse. (Bancroft, II:285–93; Elliot, IV:249–325 Legislature and Convention.)

An inspection of the vote shows that the line of demarcation between the Federal and the Anti-federal districts was a quite definite one and was in fact that physical line which has already been alluded to. The alluvial lowlands voted almost without exception in favor of ratification; the uplands without exception against it. The opposition of the up-country members came out more powerfully in the vote than in the debate. At several points in the latter we are shown that a decided modesty on the part of country members prevented them from speaking in the presence of the more cultivated and skilful members from Charleston and the vicinity. Indeed, Lowndes, among his apologies for taking up so much of the time of the Legislature, declared that "A number of respectable members, men of good sense, though not in the habit of speaking in public, had requested that he would state his sentiments for the purpose of gaining information on such points as seemed to require it." (See also Doctor David Ramsay's Address to the Freemen of South Carolina on the Federal Constitution, by Civis, reprinted in Ford's Pamphlets on the Constitution.) The South Carolina debates, which were very able, were not represented in the first edition of Elliot. Some citizen of the state prepared and published in 1831 a volume of the debates to supply this omission. Elliot in later editions reprinted this volume.

The State Convention of whose discussions we have the fullest knowledge is that of Virginia; the record of its debates fills the whole of the third volume of Elliot and the many important biographies of Virginians and the collected writings of the most famous among them, furnish abundant materials for relating the history of that Convention. By reason of these things the history of its deliberations has become so well known that I may feel justified in relating the same with little fullness of detail and thereby obtaining space to describe more fully than is possible in the case of the other states, the varying attitudes of public opinion outside the Convention.

Not only is the Virginia Convention the one hitherto most abundantly described, but it was also in several respects the most important of the Southern Conventions. Virginia was the largest of the Southern states and so placed that its absence from the new Union Convention would be severely felt, while on the other hand it had the opportunity, denied to some states, to work toward a separate confederacy with the states lying beyond it. Such a design was definitely formed and traces of it are seen at several points in the history of the struggle. The objections to the new scheme upon general grounds were felt quite as strongly in Virginia as anywhere; in addition, the aversion to a strong central government would be felt with peculiar liveliness by a state itself so powerful, and capable, more than any other, of maintaining an independent existence. Moreover there was much in the independent spirit of the Virginian aristocracy, which made them reluctant to strengthen beyond what was barely necessary the powers of any government to which they would be subject. The principles which George Mason had embodied in the Virginian Declaration of Rights had taken deep hold upon her population, and the democratic spirit and love of freedom which had sustained that Declaration, were strongly alarmed by several features of the new frame of government. A ground of opposition more especially temporary in its nature was also in existence, and has been urged as a chief ground for the opposition of Patrick Henry in particular, who had been known in earlier times as one not averse to a strengthening of the Federal Government and was in later times to reappear as decidedly a Federalist. This motive arose from the negotiations of the Federal Government with Spain, in which it appeared that Jay and the Congress were inclined to forego the navigation of the Mississippi for twenty five or thirty years, as the price of a treaty of reciprocity in commerce between the United States and Spain. This caused immediate alarm. The next legislature of Virginia unanimously resolved, "That God had given the Mississippi to the United States; that the sacrifice of it would violate justice, contravene the end of the Federal Government and destroy confidence in the Federal councils, necessary to a proper enlargement of their authority." Still another motive for opposition peculiarly prominent in Virginia was the dread of the British creditor. The recovery of British debts, though required by the treaty of 1783, had hitherto been prevented by Virginian legislation. The new Constitution would make it impossible to resist such claims and the idea of its ratification, therefore, inspired much apprehension. Mr. Conway quotes a letter of St. George Tucker to his step-sons, one of whom was John Randolph of Roanoke, June 29, 1788, in which he says, "You will have heard that the Constitution has been adopted in this state. That event, my dear children, affects your interest more nearly than that of many others. The recovery of British debts can no longer be postponed, and there now seems to be a moral certainty that your patrimony will all go to satisfy the unjust debt from your papa to the Hanburys. The consequence, my dear boys, must be obvious to you. Your sole dependence must be on your own personal abilities and exertions." (Conway, 106.)

Such were the various political motives working in Virginia at the time of the meeting of the Philadelphia Convention. In that Convention the state was represented by Washington, by its Governor, Edmund Randolph, by John Blair, one of its Chancellors and afterward a Justice of the Supreme Court of the United States, by James Madison, by George Mason, by Chancellor Wythe and by Doctor James McClurg. Henry, Lee and Nelson declined to serve. Wythe, and McClurg did not stay until the end of the Convention. Blair took no part in the debates and Washington, being President of the Convention, spoke but once. Governor Randolph, however, had brought in the original series of resolutions that served as the basis of debate; Madison had had perhaps a more influential part than any one else in the course of them, and Mason, though he had never been connected with the Federal Government in any way and had to 1787, according to Madison, seemed little impressed with either the importance or the proper means of preserving the Confederacy, took a most able, as well as active part in the Philadelphia Convention. Yet, because of some unacceptable changes made at the last, he declined to sign it on the part of Virginia. The instrument was signed by only Washington, Blair and Madison, Randolph also declining to give it his approval. On his way home Randolph writes to Madison, "In Alexandria the inhabitants are enthusiastic and instructions to force my dissenting colleague to assent to a Convention are on the anvil. I wrote to him yesterday, suggesting to him this expedient; to urge the calling of a Convention as the first act of the Assembly; if they should wish amendments, let them be stated and forwarded to the states." (Conway, 95.) The contest was now in fact transferred to the individual states, and the part which Virginia might take was eagerly watched for by observers elsewhere. General Washington, on his return to Mount Vernon, transmitted copies of the Constitution to Henry, Nelson and Harrison, ex-governors of the state, and attempted in many effective, though delicate, ways to further its acceptance. The opponents of the Constitution were not less active, and Washington in a letter to Knox speaks strongly of "the unfair—I might without much impropriety make use of a harsher expression—conduct practiced by the opposition here to rouse the fears and inflame the minds of the people." The General Assembly of the state met at Richmond on October 15, 1787, and the Governor immediately laid before them a copy of the proposed Constitution. It appeared at first that the members of the Legislature were strongly in favor of it, but later the influence of Mr. Henry, Colonel Mason and others brought about a cooler state of mind toward it. Although the Convention was resolved upon and John Marshall's resolution that "The new Constitution should be laid before the Convention for their free and ample discussion," a form which left the door open for amendments was unanimously adopted, the influence of the Anti-federalists induced the postponement of elections to the Convention till March, and of its time of meeting until the beginning of June. Randolph writes to Madison, October 23rd from Richmond, "The first raptures in favor of the Constitution were excessive. Every town resounded with applause. . . . These were the effluvia until the Assembly met. . . . At present the final event seems uncertain. There are many warm friends for taking the Constitution altogether without the alteration of a letter . . . but I suspect the tide is turning. New objections are daily started and the opinions of Mr. Henry gain ground. . . . The poor are generally against it: so are the Judges of the General Court. . . . The people of this town are still in rage for the Constitution." (Conway, 95–7.) In December Madison writes from New

York to Jefferson in Paris, "The body of the people in Virginia—particularly in the upper and lower country and in the northern neck—are, as far as I can gather, much disposed to adopt the new Constitution. The middle country and the south side of James River are principally in the opposition to it. As yet a large majority of the people are under the first description; as yet also are a majority of the Assembly. What change may be produced by the united influence of Mr. Henry, Mr. Mason and the Governor with some pretty able auxiliaries is uncertain. . . . Mr. Henry is the great adversary who will render the event precarious. He is, I find, with his usual address working up every possible interest into a spirit of opposition.

"It is worthy of remark that whilst in Virginia and some of the other states in the middle and southern district of the Union, the men of intelligence, patriotism, property and independent circumstances are thus divided, all of this description, with a few exceptions, in the Eastern States and most of the Middle States are zealously attached to the proposed Constitution. . . . It is not less worthy of remark that in Virginia, where the mass of the people have been so much accustomed to be guided by their rulers on all new and intricate questions, they should on the present, which certainly surpasses the judgment of the greater part of them, not only go before but contrary to their most popular leaders; and the phenomenon is the more wonderful as a popular ground is taken by all the adversaries to the new Constitution." But apparently the facts did not wholly warrant the confidence of Mr. Madison in the probability of a majority for the Constitution, nor the confidence of success which the letters of Washington during the Winter reveal. The General during those months seldom went away from his farm; and he heard, therefore, more than anything else the sentiment of Fairfax County, which was largely by reason of his influence strongly Federal. But meantime elsewhere great influence was being exerted by the printed Objections of the Honourable George Mason to the proposed Federal Constitution, by Edmund Randolph's printed Letter on the Federal Constitution and by the more extensive pamphlet of Richard Henry Lee entitled "Observations leading to a fair Examination of the System of government proposed by the old Convention: in a number of letters from the Federal Farmer." All three of these are to be found reprinted in Ford's "Pamphlets on the Constitution{.}" Henry, too, exhausted his resources of argument and artifice in engaging all sorts of interests and prejudices in the service of the opposition. A friend writes to Madison, speaking of Henry, "That gentleman has descended to lower artifices and management on the occasion than I thought him capable of. . . . If Mr. Innes has shown you a speech of Mr. Henry to his constituents, which I sent him, you will see something of the method he has taken to diffuse his poison. . . . He has written letters repeatedly to Kentucky and . . . the people there are alarmed with the apprehension of their interests being about to be sacrificed by the Northern States. . . . He has found means to make some of the best people here believe that a religious establishment was in contemplation under the new government." (Rives, II:544–5.)

The Legislature adjourning in January, an active canvass soon began in all parts of the state for the elections to take place in March for the Convention, and the canvass soon showed various indications of the development of public opinion. Madison's father writes to him toward the end of January of the adoption of the new Constitution, "I believe there were but four that disapproved of it at first in this county, [Orange];[13] but several being at Richmond with their tobacco at the time the Assembly was sitting and hearing the many objections made to it, altered their opinions and have influenced some others who are no better acquainted with the necessity of adopting it than they themselves, and the pieces published against it have had their intended effect with some others. The Baptists are now generally opposed to it as it is said. Colonel Barbour has been down on Pamunky among them and on his return, I hear, publicly declared himself a candidate; I suppose on the encouragement he met with from the Anti-Federalists." (Bancroft, II:458.) Monroe writes to Madison from Fredericksburg in February, "This new Constitution still engages the minds of people, with some zeal among the partisans on either side. It is impossible to say which preponderates. The northern part of the state is more generally for it than the southern. In this county [Spottsylvania][14] they are against it I believe universally." (Bancroft, II:460.) In the same month Randolph writes to him "The Baptist interest and counties on the south side of James River from Isle of Wight upwards are highly incensed [i.e. excited][15] by Henry's influence and public speeches, whensoever occasion has presented. As to the temper of the north side, I cannot clearly discern it. But upon a review made by Mr. Marshall of their comparative strength, he seems to think that the question will be very nice. The election of Henrico commences on Monday; the persons proposed are Doctor Foushee, Marshall and myself. Nothing but a small degree of favour acquired by me independently of the Constitution could send me; my politics not being sufficiently strenuous against the Constitution. Marshall is in danger; but F. is not popular enough in other sections to be elected, although he is perfectly a Henryite." (Conway, 101.) Carrington early in April writes, "Most of the elections in the upper and some parts of the south side of James River have been made in frenzy, and terminated in deputations of weak and bad men who have bound themselves to vote in the negative and will in all cases be the tools of Mr. Henry." (Bancroft, II:463.) A few days later Randolph writes from Richmond that "A comparison of the intelligence which centres there from the various parts of Virginia persuades me that a majority

{13.} Brackets in original document.
{14.} Brackets in original document.
{15.} Brackets in original document.

lies adverse to the Constitution." (Conway, 101.) The returns from what are now West Virginia and Kentucky were awaited with anxiety. Washington writes to McHenry at the end of April, "The sentiments of the western districts of this state are not yet brought to me however. Independently thereof the majority, so far as the opinions of the delegates are known or presumed, is in favour of the adoption and is increasing; but as the parties from report are pretty equally opposed a small matter cast into either scale would give it the preponderance." When the returns were all in, except those from Kentucky, Madison wrote to Jefferson that it seemed probable though not absolutely certain that a majority of the members elect were friends to the Constitution. "The real sense of the people of the state," he adds, "cannot be easily ascertained, but they are certainly attached and with warmth to a continuance of the Union; and I believe a large majority of the most intelligent and independent are equally so to the plan under consideration. On a geographical view of them almost all the counties in the northern neck have elected Federal deputies; the counties on the south side of James River had pretty generally elected adversaries to the Constitution. The intermediate district is much checquered in this respect. The counties between the Blue Ridge and the Alleghany have chosen friends to the Constitution without a single exception; those westward of the latter have, I am informed, generally, though not universally, pursued the same rule; Kentucky, it is supposed, will be divided." (Rives, II:550, 552.) We may anticipate so far as to say that this final forecast by Madison proved to be very nearly correct. The delegates from the eastern shore, the northern neck, the Shenandoah Valley and the small and old counties of tide-water Virginia, with the exception of four or five counties, voted in favor of ratification when the final test came. Indeed, the exceptions are largely to be accounted for by the personal influence of prominent Anti-Federalists, as in the case of Stafford carried Anti-Federalist by the influence of George Mason and Charles City by that of Benjamin Harrison and John Tyler. The rule that alluvial regions voted in favor of ratification is thus seen to have been followed closely in Virginia also. Some of the middle counties and almost all of the counties south of the upper and middle course of James River voted Anti-Federalist as Madison had predicted. The delegates from Kentucky and from the southern part of what is now West Virginia were almost unanimously Anti-Federal. (Journal of Convention, in Massachussetts State Library.) [Ky 9 to 3, out of 14. J. M. Brown, 106.]

The Virginian Convention assembled in Richmond on June 2, 1789. It consisted of one hundred and seventy members, among whom the principal contestants on behalf of the Constitution were Madison, Randolph, Pendleton and Marshall; in opposition Henry, Mason, Monroe, Grayson, Harrison and Tyler. The sessions, after the first day, were held at the "New Academy on Shockoe Hill," (Elliot, III:36), that is to say, in the buildings of that interesting but short-lived Académie des Sciences et Beaux Arts des États Unis de l'Amérique, which the brilliant Chevalier Quesnay de Beaurepaire so enthusiastically labored to establish, and which, as one of the origins of the University of Virginia Doctor Adams has described in his interesting pamphlet.[16]

The progress of the debates it will not be necessary for us to follow. Henry's leading objections were that the new constitution transformed the old Confederacy into a centralized and densely consolidated government, and gave that government enormous powers over states and individuals, unrestrained by an express guarantee of the rights and liberties of the people of the several states. In defence of these objections he used all the resources of his eloquence and skill, but in the end a decisive vote in favor of ratification was passed by a majority of ten, ayes eighty-nine, nays seventy-nine, and Virginia entered as the tenth state into the more perfect Union.

The last of the Southern states to ratify and the next to the last of the thirteen was North Carolina. The people of that state were strongly jealous of their liberties, apprehensive of consolidation and the coming of Federal tax-gatherers, and suspicious of tendencies toward arbitrary power. Troubles arising out of paper money had disorganized the finances and private fortunes of the state. In some of the western counties there had been almost open insurrections. Under such circumstances the new constitution was extremely unpopular in North Carolina. (Hubbard's "Davie," 92.) The state had been represented in the Federal Convention by Hugh Williamson, Richard Dobbs Spaight, William Blount, William R. Davie and for a shorter period by Alexander Martin. Of these Martin, Spaight and Davie were in favor of the new Constitution. The first news from North Carolina which reached those anxiously waiting to the northward was favorable. (Bancroft, II:446; Sparks, IX:288.) James Iredell, the most eminent of North Carolina lawyers, came out in January with a pamphlet, "Answers to Objections to the New Constitution," reprinted in Ford's Pamphlets on the Constitution. The Assembly, meeting in November, called a Convention to be held in July. The struggle which preceded its first meeting was a bitter one. One of Iredell's correspondents writes that two Anti-Federalists "have joined all the low scoundrels in the county and by every underhand means are prejudicing the common people against the new constitution." Another writes that General S. Person is reported to have said "that General Washington was a damned rascal and traitor to his country for putting his hand to such an infamous paper as the new constitution." In Dobbs County the Federal men, finding that they were in danger of losing their election, knocked to pieces the ballot boxes and destroyed the books. (McRee, II:219, 224, 222; Elliot, IV:35.) The

{16.} Herbert B. Adams, *Thomas Jefferson and the University of Virginia* (Washington, D.C.: Government Printing Office, 1888).

rule as to alluvial lands seems to have held, the Federalists apparently obtaining the most of their support from sea-board counties, like Chowan,
Craven, Onslow and New Hanover. Debtors and public officers were reported as against union; the Quakers and the Scotch merchants in favor of it;
the western region which afterward became Tennessee was as strongly Anti-
Federal as Kentucky. On July 21, 1788, the Convention met at the church in
Hillsborough. The opposition was led, as always, by Willie Jones, the most
influential politician in the state. Aristocratic in his habits and tastes, proud
of his wealth and social position, fastidious in the selection of associates,
he was, nevertheless, ultra-democratic in theory. He was a consummately
dexterous politician; his character, from what we know of it, curiously resembles that of Mr. Jefferson and like him he was little effective in debate.
The course which he intended to pursue was shown at the very beginning
of the session. "Mr. Willie Jones," the record says, "moved that the question
upon the constitution should be immediately put. He said that the constitution had so long been the subject of the deliberation of every man in this
country and that the members of the Convention had had such ample opportunity to consider it, that he believed every one was prepared to give his
vote then upon the question; . . . that as it was a large representation from
this state an immediate decision would save the country a considerable sum
of money; he thought it therefore prudent to put the question immediately."

The Federalists vigorously combatted these economical objections, but
they were unable to dissuade their opponents from the effective tactics of si-
lence. Day after day Davie and others set forth the merits of the new system
with much skill, but they were placed in the awkward position of being compelled to answer the objections which they themselves suggested as having
been made in the state, or as being possible, for their opponents took little
other part in the debate than from time to time to ask captious questions.
The debates doubtless threw much light upon the subject, but they likewise
generated no small amount of heat. In no Convention were personalities so
much used. Finally the Federalists were voted down by a vote of a hundred
and eighty-four to eighty-four, Mr. Jones declaring in substance that North
Carolina could very well afford to wait and could come in when it chose. His
tactics were much influenced no doubt by the movement in New York and
Virginia toward a second general Convention.

It is to be noted as evincing the growth of the American doctrines respecting the position of Conventions as directly representing the sovereign
people, that this Convention voted that the seat of government should be
at or within ten miles of the plantation of Isaac Hunter of Wake County,
Raleigh, virtually an amendment of the constitution. In November, 1789, the
new Convention met, which with a similar sense of the peculiar functions of
the Convention, added Fayetteville to the towns represented in the Assembly, again virtually amending the state constitution. In the new Convention

there was still a violent opposition to the adoption of the Federal Constitution, but finally it was carried by a vote of one hundred and ninety-three
to seventy-five. Thus the last of the Southern States joined the new Union,
seven months after the inauguration of Washington, (McRee's Iredell, II:178–
274; Hubbard's Davie, 90–100). With firmer union began the possibility of
greater unity of action among the southern states, and so of a more unified
political history of the South.

v i . The Period of the Federalists

The setting up of the new Constitution involved on the part of the individual
states, first, a participation in the inauguration of the new government by
choosing electors, senators and representatives, and secondly, an adjustment of the form, or at any rate, of the operations, of their governments into
accordance with the new system. It is my intention to treat of these processes before discussing the course of constitutional and political action on
the part of the Southern group of states under the new Constitution.

The mode by which electors, senators and representatives were to be
chosen was so far left to the states by the Federal Constitution, that great
varieties of system at first prevailed. The Legislature of Maryland, on December 22, 1788, passed an act in accordance with which the state was divided
into six Congressional districts. The six representatives were respectively to
be residents of the district they were to represent, but the voters voted for
the whole six on general ticket. The natural result of this was that six Federalists were elected. In general the Federalist outnumbered the Anti-Federal
vote in the proportion of more than two to one. Washington County, the
most populous, cast 1164 votes for the Federalist candidates and none for the
others. Of the eight electors, five were to be residents of the western shore
and three of the eastern shore. The senators were to be elected by joint ballot
of both houses, one a resident of the eastern, the other of the western shore.
John Henry and Charles Carroll of Carrollton were chosen. The representative of Baltimore was William Smith, "a genuine Federal and merchant of the
first reputation, of an independent fortune and considerable family connections . . . against whom the Anti-Federalists opposed Mr. Samuel Sterrett,
a young gentleman of fair character and respectable connection. The contest
lasted four days (almost the entire time allowed by law) and the Federals
were crowned by conquest, Mr. Smith having at the close of the polls a majority of seven votes." (Baltimore Journal: Scharf, II:548.) The only counties
which cast an Anti-Federal vote were Anne Arundel, Baltimore and Harford.
Prince George's went one way for electors and the other for representatives.
(Votes in Scharf, II:549–50.) (The act of 1788, Chapter X, was altered by acts
of 1790 and 1791.)

Much interest attaches to the story of the election in Virginia. Patrick Henry, foiled in the Convention, zealously worked afterward for a second constitutional convention and for the carrying of extensive amendments. A formal application to Congress for a national Convention was prepared by Henry and adopted by the new House of Delegates in November; the House was wholly under Henry's influence. "In plain English," says Tobias Lear, Washington's private secretary, in a contemporary letter, "he ruled a majority of that Assembly, and his edicts were registered by that body with less opposition than those of the Grand Monarque have met with from his parliaments." When the day came for the election of senators by the Assembly of Virginia, Henry took the unusual course of nominating two persons, Richard Henry Lee and William Grayson, and succeeded in having these two, Anti-Federalists, though moderate ones, elected over Madison by a slight majority. Next followed the arrangements for the choice of representatives. Madison being likely to prove a most formidable upholder of the new government, if chosen to the House, and to make opposition there to the Virginian scheme of extensive amendments, Henry doubtless made efforts to defeat his election. The act of November 20, 1788, divides the counties of Virginia into ten districts and provides that in each the voters shall choose a resident of that district to be their representative in Congress. A famous story has been told about this arrangement. I will give it in the words of Mr. Rives, in his "Life of Madison": "Here again unceasing efforts were made by the Anti-Federal leaders in the Legislature to bar against him every avenue to success. In laying off the state into districts for the elections of representatives ingenious and artificial combinations were resorted to for the purpose of insuring his defeat. The county in which he resided was thrown into association with seven others, five of which, through their delegates in the Convention, had given an undivided vote against the acceptance of the Constitution; another had divided its vote and only one besides the county in which he lived had given an undivided vote for the ratification." (II. Rives, 653.) By all other writers who have mentioned the matter this has been accepted as showing Patrick Henry to have been the father of all those that make gerrymanders; and the facts of historical geography in question seem never to have been subjected to a sufficiently critical examination. The story seems to rest on the authority of contemporary letters of Carrington to Madison, Rives II.654, & of Humphreys to Jefferson (II, Banc., 485), repeated by Jefferson (Works, II:574). But what were the actual facts of the act of apportionment? In the Convention of 1788 thirty-nine counties had voted in favor of ratification, thirty-five against it, and ten had been divided; yet in arranging the ten districts the leaders in the Legislature composed six prevailingly of Federalist counties and four prevailingly of Anti-Federalist counties. As to the particular district in which Madison's county of Orange was situated— it did indeed consist of eight counties, of which five had been hostile to the

Constitution, Orange and one other in favor, and one divided; but though I cannot with convenience take time here to set forth all the circumstances, the fact is that it would have been impossible, without either crossing the Blue Ridge, or constructing a district of extraordinary shape, to throw Orange County into a district prevailingly Federal. The counties bordering it, on its side of the Blue Ridge were prevailingly Anti-Federal, the next outer circle beyond them still more so. His friends, it is recorded, strove to have Fauquier County included, but this would have forced a more unsymmetrical arrangement of districts in northern Virginia, than the arrangement which Henry and his friends carried out; and so the ancient charge of gerrymandering, if not disproved (and arguments assuming the counties to be of equal size [they were nearly so][17] cannot disprove it), must, it seems likely, be relegated to the category of exaggerations arising from party animosity in time of election. Governor Gerry need not, therefore, necessarily be robbed of the credit of his invention. However this may be, Madison had a difficult contest against Monroe and prevailed only after great effort. Of the ten representatives chosen by the state, seven were Anti-Federal, as well as its two senators. (Rives, II:655–7; Bancroft, II:483–9; Garland's John Randolph, I:27–8.)

The North Carolina Assembly in 1789 provided that the state should be divided into five divisions and that the inhabitants of each should choose a representative who was a resident of the district. The representation in the Senate and in the House was pretty evenly divided between the friends and the opponents of the new Constitution. (Acts of 1789, Chap. I, 1790; McRee's Iredell, II:272, 276, 284.) South Carolina had also divided itself into five districts, but without the requirement of residence on the part of candidates. It was provided that, if a candidate were returned for two districts, he should make his choice between them within twenty days. The strong Federal feeling which had existed at the time of the Convention was succeeded by a wave of Anti-Federalism which brought into Congress Edanus Burke, General Sumter and Thomas Tudor Tucker, (Garland, I:27, 28){,} though for the Charleston district the Federalist William Smith was elected. South Carolina provided that presidential electors should be chosen by the Legislature, a practice which the state maintained down to 1860. The senators Pierce Butler and Ralph Izard were Federal. I have not been able to learn the plan followed by Georgia.

Interesting light upon the character of southern elections may be obtained by reading, in the Annals of Congress, the records of early contested election cases in the House of Representatives. Thus in the case of Jackson against Wayne it appeared on the evidence of an army surgeon that he went with a certain Osborne to one of the polling places in Camden County, Georgia. It

{17.} Brackets in original document.

was after dark and the sheriff had adjourned the election. Osborne sent for several of the electors to return, re-opened the poll, inquired the names of those who had not been present during the day and set down their names as having voted, though no ballots were cast. The surgeon asked "the judge if this was the common mode of doing business at elections in Georgia, to which Osborne replied never to mind." Still more humorous is the debate in Trigg vs. Preston, in 1793, a case arising in the southwestern district of Virginia. It came to light that Preston's brother, a captain in the army, had appeared at the polls with sixty or seventy Federal troops, of which he had command, that they had attacked and intimidated voters, and that the election closed with a violent affray between the soldiers and the country people. Mr. Smith of South Carolina argued strongly that the election had not been a fair one. Mr. Smith of Maryland defended the sitting member. "In the elections in an eastern state," he said, "the citizens met in small bodies, and they conducted all business with that order and decency which became the true republican character; but it was the misfortune of the southern states that their citizens assembled in large bodies; the electors of a county meet altogether before the sheriff and give their votes at the same time; . . . hence it appeared . . . that an election in the southern states is nothing but a nursery of superlative mischief. . . . Much had been said about the enormity of knocking down a justice of the peace, and in the report the affair was stated as if the magistrate had been at the court-house in his official capacity. 'Now, sir,' said Mr. Smith, 'In this part of it the report is not fair. The justice of the peace was not there in his official capacity; he was there drunk, sir, and he gave the first blow to the man who knocked him down.' Mr. Smith had by the first accounts of the affair been very much prejudiced against the account of the sitting member, but when he became more closely acquainted with the business, he declared that he had never known an election in the southern states where there was so little mischief. He was sorry for that part of the country, to give this account of it to the eastern members, but in point of common justice to Mr. Preston they ought to be informed that a southern election was quite a different transaction from one of theirs. In the evidence before the house it had been stated that one person had been seen at the court-house with a club under his coat, 'But, sir,' said Mr. Smith, 'I suppose that five hundred of my constituents had clubs under their coats; so that if this be a sufficient reason for putting an end to an election, the committee may begin by dissolving mine. If the committee are to break every election where persons were seen drunk they will have a great deal of work upon hand, sir. In what way were elections for southern members carried on? A man of influence came to the place of election with two hundred or three hundred of his friends and to be sure, they would not, if they could help it, suffer anybody on the other side to give a vote as long as they were there.' " The debate also shows that Mr. Smith of Maryland differed decidedly from

Mr. Smith of South Carolina in his opinion respecting the difference between the alleged statement of the soldiers that they could knock down one of Colonel Trigg's voters and the alleged statement that they would do it. Another member declared that at the election of one of these very Smiths there was a riot, and still worse, this riot was in a church; the riot was raised by a magistrate who with his own hand dragged one of the opposite party out of the church, "and if you want evidence of all this," said the member, "I myself was present and can be a witness."

In the second place the going into operation of the new Constitution placed upon a considerably different basis the political actions of the individual states. This marked an era in state history the importance of which is not easily appreciated at first. The prohibitions upon the states expressed in Article I: Section 10, of the Constitution, made impossible the emission of bills of credit, the making anything but gold and silver coin legal tender, the passing of any law impairing the obligation of contracts and the laying of duties on imports or exports or tonnage; that is to say, the whole financial system of the states was subjected to a complete revolution. It is not easy to discover the manner in which this operated.

In the case of Virginia there is in the Arthur Lee papers, in the Library of Harvard College, a paper, which, if it does not throw a clear light upon this matter, is at any rate of interest as showing the financial system of one of the Southern States just before the adoption of the Constitution. [See also as to this A. Lee's life, II. 334.] It is a statement of the revenues and ordinary expenses of the commonwealth of Virginia for the year 1787. Criticisms by I. Hopkins and Arthur Lee appended to the document make it plain that the figures are not the figures of actual receipts and expenditures but of estimated revenues and of payments due, except certain debt payments; for whereas the figures show a large surplus, it is certain that there was in fact a deficiency that year. However the system is sufficiently shown. The revenues of the state arose from internal taxes, from duties on tonnage and imports, from an export duty on tobacco and from legal proceedings. There was a tax on land and lots of one and a half per cent. ad valorem. Upon each negro of whatever age a tax of twelve shillings was laid, upon whites above the age of twenty one a tax of similar amount; upon horses, mares, mules and colts one of two shillings each; upon neat cattle one of three pence; upon carriages one of six shillings for each wheel. Keepers of ordinaries paid five pounds each for their licence and every billiard table paid fifteen pounds. The schedule is of interest as showing that there were two hundred and thirty seven thousand negroes in the state, one hundred and eighty two thousand horses, four hundred and eighty six thousand neat cattle, fifty seven thousand carriage wheels, two hundred and twenty four inns and eleven billiard tables. Act of 1798 forbade billiards. From all these sources two hundred and fifty three thousand pounds were obtained ostensibly in specie mostly from the land tax and the poll tax on negroes and whites. In addition the duties on tonnage brought in eleven thousand pounds; salt, spirits, wine, malt liquors, cordage, cheese, snuff, sugar and coffee paid twenty four thousand more. Duties of two and two and one half per cent. on nearly a million pounds worth of other imported goods brought in twenty three thousand pounds and a shilling was levied on each seaman entering Virginian ports, for the establishment of a hospital. The export duty on tobacco yielded twenty two thousand pounds and law processes and alienations seven thousand more. Of the net revenue of three hundred and forty thousand pounds alleged, the new Constitution, it will be seen, deprived the state of eighty thousand. At the same time it should be remembered that in providing the Federal Government with an independent income of its own, the Constitution had relieved the individual states from the necessity of paying requisitions for its support. Exclusive of such requisitions, the expenditures of the same year, whether correctly or not, estimated at one hundred and fourteen thousand pounds. Sixty eight thousand of this seems to have been appropriated to interest charges upon the debt, fifteen thousand to the salaries of the fixed officers, nine thousand to the pay and expenses of the Assembly, two thousand five hundred to the members of Congress and the rest to the expenses of justice, military pensioners, the arsenal at Point-of-Fork and to the state boats. The condition of the finances was thoroughly disorderly all through the period of the Confederation. With the coming in of the new government there was some lowering of taxation. (Hening, XIII:29.)

The introduction of the new Constitution induced considerable changes in the constitutions of several of the states. In Georgia (Stevens, II:388–91) the Legislature a few days after ratifying the Federal Constitution named three persons from each county who were to constitute a Convention. This Convention met at Augusta in November and framed a new constitution. Its work was revised by another Convention chosen by the people. This second Convention in January made further amendments, which were submitted to a third Convention, from which in May the new constitution came. It was not in any more direct manner submitted to popular vote. The chief changes which it effected in the constitution of the state consisted in making the Legislature bicameral; henceforth there was to be a senate consisting of one member from each county and chosen for three years. The representatives were, however, chosen annually, each county sending from two to five; for both the senators and for the governor a property qualification was instituted; the governor's term was lengthened to two years. In imitation of the Federal Constitution provision was made for his having a veto to be overridden by a two thirds vote of the legislature. He and the other executive officers were to be chosen by the senate out of three nominees, in each case presented by the house. In general the new constitution differed from the preceding one in creating a stronger, or in the phrase of that day, a "more high-toned" government, but the franchise was extended to all tax-payers. The instrument provided that in 1794 a Convention should assemble to propose amendments; accordingly in 1795 amendments were passed by which the senate was rendered annual; it was provided that the elections by the legislature should be by joint ballot, and that the seat of government should be moved to Louisville. These amendments were not submitted to the people. By 1798 it seemed necessary to make still another constitution for Georgia. Representation in the house was now proportioned to population; importation of slaves was forbidden; it was provided that amendments must be passed by two successive legislatures. This constitution was not submitted to the people. (Stevens, 499–502.) A very prominent part in the discussions of the time in Georgia belonged to the matter of the Yazoo frauds, which have been, I suppose, made sufficiently familiar to the members of the Seminary by Mr. Haskins' investigation.[18] The constitution of 1798? forever prohibited sales of land to individuals or companies before counties were fixed and ordered the land companies' purchase money to be kept in the state treasury at the companies' risk and subject to their order or withdrawal. South Carolina, too, made a new constitution in 1790 and again the influence of the conservative and somewhat aristocratic Philadelphia Convention is seen in the new measures adopted. The senators' term was extended from one year to four years, half going out by rotation every two years. Charleston was given two members; the number of members in the house was greatly diminished; representation of the country districts being diminished more than that of Charleston; the governor's term was extended to two years; the religious qualification for the suffrage was withdrawn; it was provided that amendments to this constitution, in order to be valid, must be passed by two thirds of each house in two successive legislatures. The document was not submitted to the people. It may be noted in passing that the capital having now been transferred to Columbia, two treasurers were appointed after the example of Maryland and North Carolina, one for the upper country residing at Columbia, the other for the lower country residing at Charleston, and the judges of the highest court, after completing their circuit, were to sit for a hearing of appeals at both those towns. In 1808 the system of representation in the lower house was again altered by a singular plan which proportioned the number sent from each district of the state to its population and its payments of taxes in equal degree, each district having one member for every sixty-second part of the population of the state which it contained and one for every sixty-second part of the taxes which it paid. Among several amendments passed by Maryland during the period under consideration the most significant were that making full substitution of affirmation for oath in the

{18.} Charles H. Haskins, *The Yazoo Land Companies* (New York: Knickerbocker Press, 1891).

case of Quakers, Mennonists, Tunkers, Nicolites, or New Quakers, and that of 1799 dividing the counties of the state into small districts for election purposes, the origin of the present system of "election districts."

But it is time to turn to a consideration of the great political movement which marked the last years of the eighteenth Century in the Southern States. I refer to the development and organization of the old Republican, or Democratic-Republican party, under the leadership of Mr. Jefferson. The sources of the variation between the Federalists and the Republicans were various and deep-seated. Among mankind there are likely to be in their relation to political matters some who desire most of all the promotion of regularity and order through efficiency of government and others who care far more for the preservation of individual liberty. Those who dwell in cities the centres of industry and commerce are most likely to adhere to the former view; those who dwell apart, scattered over large areas and engaged in agri-cultural pursuits are likely to care most for personal independence. It has, perhaps, been perceived that in respect to matters of administration,—of financial administration, for instance,—the governments of the Southern States were far from being ideally efficient. It was not desired that they should be. The planter cared far more for his individual freedom than for a vigorous government acting through well-devised machinery. It was likely, then, that in the division between the lovers of liberty and the lovers of order, the South should, in general, belong to the former party. As soon as the new Federal Government went into operation, Secretary Hamilton brought forward a remarkable series of measures by which he designed at once to bring new life to the languishing finances of the United States and to strengthen and consolidate the Federal system at the expense of the states and of the enemies of strong central government. This series of measures naturally alarmed all those throughout the United States who desired that governments should be weak, in order that the rights of individuals might not be infringed. Throughout the agricultural regions of the South the appre-hension was general that these new measures were intended to foster the industrial and commercial interests and regions of America at the expense of the agricultural. The spirit of individualism was aroused. Mr. Jefferson conceived upon his return to New York the belief that in the society which surrounded the new government and to which its destinies were confided there existed, not only a desire, but a definite purpose to alter the institu-tions of the country in favor of monarchy. A strong central government had been brought into operation among a reluctant people and its first opera-tions revived the spirit of separatism. As in the Hebrew Monarchy the rig-orous policy of Rehoboam led the wily Jeroboam to call all Israel to their tents and arouse the elements of opposition and separatism still latent in the imperfectly consolidated kingdom, so Mr. Jefferson, believing the liberties of America to be threatened by the strenuous measures of the imperious

Hamilton, called into operation, as the most available forces of resistance, the anti-governmental feelings of the average American farmer and those powerful sentiments of local patriotism which later took the form of devotion to state rights.

It is worth while to inquire why this work of creating the first American opposition party fell to Mr. Jefferson. In the first place the leader of the anti-monarchical party must almost of necessity come from Virginia or North Carolina. Georgia was too small and remote to have developed statesmen of national reputation; in South Carolina and in Maryland important cities, centres of trade and industry, bound the politics of the most influential circle to the scheme of vigorous measures which Hamilton and the Federalists had developed. The commercial interests of those two states enlisted in their cause the most talented and influential champions. Mr. Jefferson's ideas found ready response among the men of the upland districts of South Carolina, but after all the rule of Charleston and its cultivated and skilful politicians was still secure. In a less degree the same was true of Maryland. In North Carolina many and in Virginia some of the brilliant leaders were by nature or by training attached to the leading notions of Federalism. The Anti-Federalist leaders in North Carolina seem to have been mostly of little influence outside of their own state and of little experience in the larger concerns of the Confederation. Indeed that intensity of local patriotism which made men leaders in the Anti-Federalist cause was of itself likely to insure that they should be if not provincial at any rate better fitted for obtaining great success in the arena of state politics than in that of national politics. So it was for instance in a conspicuous degree with Patrick Henry and so it was with most of the other Anti-Federalist characters of eminence in Virginia. Mr. Jefferson on the other hand, while sharing with all these politicians their ardent devotion to individual liberty and to the doctrines of radical democracy and to local interests, had, beside his great talents and extensive acquirements, a fund of broader experience than others, obtained in the diplomatic service of the Union abroad and in the business of the old Congress and of the new executive government. If he was not a more acute politician than Willie Jones and if he was not a more sagacious statesman than George Mason, he had an adaptation to politics transcending state boundaries which was denied to the former and a disposition to engage in them which was not present in the large but unambitious nature of the latter. It was then Mr. Jefferson, who in 1792 and still more in 1793, when the conflict of British and of French interests and partialities was already acute, marshalled in opposition to the moneyed interests and Eastern and Middle State respectability which supported Hamilton the lively forces of southern whiggery and found for them the readiest and most natural avenue of expression through the legislatures of the individual states. Already in the first days of General Washington's administration the Virginia Legislature had sent up its protest against the measures of assumption. Soon after the Legislatures of Virginia and North Carolina protested against the Senate's oligarchical habit of sitting in secret session. It was not simply the actions of the Federal Executive and the Federal Legislature that aroused alarm; it was in a singular degree aroused by what were esteemed the encroachments of the Federal judiciary. In the debates upon the ratification of the Constitution the powers granted to this branch of the new government had excited an especially ardent opposition and now the public men of the Southern States felt that their worst fears were being realized, when in the case of Chisholm vs. Georgia, the Supreme Court of the United States decided that a State of this Union might be sued by a citizen of another State. This was one of the famous British debt cases and of others as well as of this it may be said that the conduct of the Federal judiciary in enforcing the obligation of the Treaty of 1783, obvious as it seems to us that such was their duty, was one of the prime causes in arousing jealously toward the national government and the determination to oppose every instance of aggression on its part and every effort to extend its powers. So it was, for instance, with the celebrated Virginian case of Ware vs. Hylton, than which perhaps no case in a court of law ever excited more ardent interest among the people of that state.

Exactly what were the steps by which Mr. Jefferson gathered up all this widespread feeling of dissatisfaction and made it the basis of a definitely organized political party in the Southern States remains obscure in the imperfect state of publication of his correspondence. The outward results of the process may be traced in the broadest and most obvious manner, though very roughly, in the electoral votes of 1792, 1796 and 1800, for whereas in 1792 in the Southern States only the votes of Virginia, North Carolina and Georgia went to George Clinton rather than to Adams, in 1796 Jefferson beside obtaining nearly all these and the new votes of Kentucky and Tennessee, won for himself the vote of South Carolina and an important minority of the vote of Maryland and obtained in 1800 the whole vote of every Southern State, except Maryland, of which the electoral college was evenly divided. Still, though this marks a genuine trend of public opinion, it is to be observed that between these two dates, at the election for the Sixth Congress, the Federalists secured seven congressmen out of ten in North Carolina, five out of six in South Carolina and the two of Georgia, besides electing eight out of the nineteen members of Congress from Virginia. This last seems to show about the usual state of parties in Virginia during the last part of Adams' Administration, for in December, 1799, in the Virginia Legislature, Colonel Monroe was elected Governor by one hundred votes to sixty six and a year before the Virginia resolutions were passed by a vote of one hundred and one to sixty three (?).

The Federalist majority in Congress grew more and more aggressive in its policy. In the year 1798 after other measures alarming to those solicitous about individual rights, it passed the Alien and Sedition Laws, statutes open to most serious objection on constitutional grounds and whose passage did more than anything else to bring about the downfall of the Federalist Party. At once there was consultation among the statesmen of the Republican Party as to what form the protest against these measures should take. John Taylor of Caroline wrote to Mr. Jefferson urging the setting up of a separate independence of Virginia and North Carolina, a suggestion which Mr. Jefferson rejected. His own plan, which took form during the Summer of 1798 was that of a formal protest by the state legislatures. The same plan was formed quite as early apparently by John Breckenridge of Kentucky. Mr. Jefferson's first plan was that Virginia and North Carolina should join in the protest, but later apparently on the suggestion of Wilson C. Nicholas, he concluded in favor of Kentucky and entrusted to Breckenridge, then in Virginia, a draft of the resolutions for the purpose indicated. A great deal of light has been thrown upon the history of the Kentucky Resolutions by Miss Sarah M. Randolph's article in the "Nation" of May 5, 1887, Mr. E. D. Warfield's article in the "Nation" of June 2 and his subsequent book on the "Kentucky Resolutions of 1798." I must refer to these for the details of their very interesting researches. As to the different inferences drawn by the two writers it appears to me probable though not certain that Miss Randolph is right in her supposition that the conference at Monticello between Jefferson, Breckenridge and Nicholas, which Mr. Jefferson described in his letter of 1821 to Breckenridge's son, did not in fact take place. The draft, which Mr. Jefferson, under a characteristic injunction of entire secrecy, entrusted to Breckenridge was much modified by the latter before he presented it to the Legislature of Kentucky in November, 1798. The text of the Resolutions, as finally passed, is incorrectly given in almost all documentary sources, including all but the earliest editions of Elliot's "Debates." The true text is given authoritatively by Colonel Durrett in the "Southern Bivouac" for March, 1886, and in the appendix to Shaler's "Kentucky." Of the nine resolutions embodied in Mr. Jefferson's draft, the first seven reappear with almost no change in the Breckenridge series, but for Mr. Jefferson's eighth and ninth resolutions which treated of the necessary remedies, Breckenridge substituted two resolutions considerably milder in tone. The first resolution affirmed the Constitution to be a compact {and} declared "That whensoever the general government assumes undelegated powers, its acts are unauthoritative, void and of no force; that to this compact each state acceded as a state, as an integral party, its co-states forming as to itself the other party; that the government created by this compact was not made the exclusive and final judge of the powers delegated to itself . . . but that as in all other cases of compact among parties having no common judge each party has an equal right to judge for itself as well of infractions as of the mode and measure of redress." But whereas Mr. Jefferson's concluding resolutions declared "That where powers are assumed which have not been delegated a nullification of the act is the rightful remedy; that every state has an actual right in cases not within the compact to nullify of their own authority all assumptions of power by others within their limits" and calls for a committee of conference and correspondence, the resolutions actually passed omitted the declaration as to each state's right to nullify and proposed methods of common action less calculated to remind of Revolutionary times. [Letter from G. Nicholas of Ky to his friend in Va. Lexington, Nov. 10, 1798.] The meaning of the Kentucky Resolutions, and especially the question whether they may rightly be alleged as the basis of the later doctrines of nullification and secession is elaborately discussed in the "Nation" of October 18, November 8, and November 15 of 1883, by President Welling and an editor of the "Nation." It seems that the latter has the best of the argument in affirming, namely, that the real purport of the Resolutions is to declare that a state, regarded as a separate sovereignty and original party to the contract, could nullify laws passed by the Federal government under it, otherwise than by securing repeal through Congressional action or constitutional amendment. In December of this same year the Virginia Legislature passed resolutions of a similar drift, but more moderate expression proposed by John Taylor of Caroline. The Virginia resolutions proceeded from Madison and were more judicious in their declaration of the rights which state legislatures might exercise in judging and opposing constitutional infractions. The Virginia Resolutions affirmed that in case the Federal Government dangerously exceeded the powers given by the Constitution "The states who are the parties thereto have the right and are in duty bound to interpose for arresting the progress of the evil, for maintaining within their own respective limits the authorities, rights, and liberties appertaining to them." How much farther than this some of the Virginians were prepared to go was shown by the act of January 1798 requiring the executive to purchase sites for three arsenals, and upon each to have buildings erected capable of holding ten thousand stand of arms and was empowered to establish a manufactory of arms near Richmond. John Randolph in January, 1817, declared that there was no longer any cause for concealing the fact that these preparations were intended "to enable the state of Virginia to resist by force the encroachment of the then ? administration upon her indisputable rights." In 1799 the Kentucky ? Legislature passed resolutions going practically to the full extent of the trenchant expressions in Mr. Jefferson's original draft. [Warfield, 183{.}] Important as were the consequences of these resolutions, they should be regarded rather as weapons of party warfare vigorously expressing the sentiment of the South than, as they so often have been, put forward as authoritative declarations of American constitutional law. Mr. Madison's instructive letters of 1830, especially that to the editor of the "North American Review," show that he was anxious not to be put in a position of having been the father of the theory of nullification.

The principal political purpose of the resolutions was at any rate achieved. They concentrated and fostered the opposition to Federal measures with such effect that in 1800 throughout the Southern States Mr. Jefferson's triumph was complete, save for half the votes of Maryland. Maryland chose Presidential electors by districts, Virginia, warned by the odd vote of 1796, had provided for election of her twenty one on a general ticket.

VII. The New Regions

That the growth and power of the United States and the destiny of imperial greatness which awaits them have been intimately connected with the possession of the West is familiar. It is doubtful, however, whether the attention of students of American history has been as much directed to the influence and importance of the southwestern regions as to those of the regions which formed the Northwest Territory: but, just as in these days when the control of the country belongs mainly to the North, its political development is being strongly influenced by the ideas and characteristics of the Northwest, so in the earlier days of the Republic, when the influence of the South was always great and often dominant, that influence was in many respects shaped by the ideas, characteristics and interests of the Southwest. We know that it was the influence of the states beyond the mountains that forced Mr. Madison and the Federal Government into the War of 1812, but this is only one salient phase of the larger fact that it was the influence of these states which changed the old Republicanism of 1801 into the new Republicanism of 1817 and the new Democracy of 1829. It is well for us then to turn aside from the history of the five older Southern States and take some survey of these peculiar new frontier communities, which since the Revolution had been developed in the districts beyond the Alleghanies.

The Treaty of 1763 gave to England the territory extending westward from the southern Atlantic coast to the Mississippi River. Within the westward portions of this great region were developed from the times which our narrative has been following the states of Kentucky and Tennessee and the Mississippi Territory. Already, as we have seen, before the new formed Constitution had been ten years in operation the Legislature of Kentucky had taken a most prominent and for the time being decisive part in interpreting the fundamental document and fixing bounds to the aggrandizement of the Federal Government. A community so early exerting so great political power well deserves attentive study. Our survey must be too brief to enable us to enter at all into the details which made the political history of Kentucky so vivid and picturesque with heroic defenders, Indian raids, secret intrigues of Spanish and British emissaries, factional fights and popular agitations.

Our outline of the constitutional history of Kentucky begins with the history of the Transylvania Company. Richard Henderson, of North Carolina, obtaining from the Cherokees a great cession of territory attempted to establish a proprietary colony of Transylvania. With the arrival of the first settlers regular and orderly proceedings began: representatives of the people met at Boonesborough in 1775 and passed such laws as seemed to them necessary. Virginia refused to recognize these proprietors and in 1776 organized this western region as the County of Kentucky. County organization, or at least a Court of Quarter Sessions was at once set up and delegates to the Virginia House of Burgesses were chosen. In 1780 the region was divided into the three counties of Jefferson, Lincoln and Fayette, but the name of the District of Kentucky survived in popular and to some extent in legal usage. Throughout the Revolutionary War the people of Kentucky maintained themselves against English and Indians and were supported by Virginian influence against the ill will of Spain. The population increased and finding its interests but little regarded in the Assembly at Richmond began to moot the question of independent existence. Colonel Benjamin Logan called together the militia officers of the district in consultation at Danville in November, 1784, to discuss the possibility of independent action against an expected Indian assault. Already in 1780 all the inhabitants of Kentucky and Illinois joined in a petition to {the} Continental Congress that it would take proper methods to form them into a separate state. Now the matter seemed more nearly ripe and a Convention of representatives, one from each militia company, was called, which met at Danville in the last days of December, 1784. This recommended a civic Convention which met in May, 1785 and resolved, "That a petition be presented to the Assembly praying that the said district may be established into a state separate from Virginia," and "When ? this district may be established into a state it ? ought to be taken into union with the United States of America and into equal privileges in common with said States." The deputies also took steps toward the summons of a new Convention elected on the basis of equal representation in proportion to population and not by counties, a method less likely to find favor with pioneers. The Convention of August, 1785, strongly represented the difficulties of the situation, the impossibility of efficient action in emergencies on the part of an executive power five hundred miles away across the mountains, of adequate legislative representation and of a satisfactory system of appeals. A memorial to the Legislature was prepared and was favorably heard at Richmond where the Virginia Legislature passed an act erecting the District of Kentucky into an independent State subject to formal approval by the new Convention and the affirmative action of Congress. The new Convention in January, 1787, re-affirmed the desire for separation but too late to secure the consent of Congress before the first of June, 1787, as the Virginian act had provided. It was therefore necessary to pass another act, to hold another Convention and to delay still further the consent of Congress. Meanwhile

Jay's project of conceding to Spain the monopoly of the navigation of the Mississippi in return for concessions on her part aroused great alarm not only in Kentucky, whose prosperity was hereby seriously threatened, but in Virginia. The Virginia Legislature actively protested. General Wilkinson in 1787 began to open up the trade of Kentucky with New Orleans sharing his gains with the Spanish Governor and preparing the way for being bribed himself at a later time. In the discussions upon the Federal constitution a majority of the votes of Kentucky in the Virginia Convention were given adverse and the Mississippi question had a large share in bringing about this attitude. In Congress the protest of Kentucky and Virginia proved successful. Gardoqui's negotiations seemed likely to prove unsuccessful: he therefore took up with the proposals of Colonel George Morgan, respecting the New Madrid Company. He proposed a large colony of American settlers within Spanish territory on the west bank of the Mississippi River with freedom of trade with the Spanish possessions below. This would give Morgan the control of the commerce of {the} West and Wilkinson and Miro labored strongly against it. At last they defeated it, but still Gardoqui hoped that the west might be detached from the Union and drift into some sort of connection with Spain. His hopes were raised by the fact that though John Brown of Kentucky succeeded in June, 1788 in securing action from the Continental Congress toward giving independence to Kentucky, the ratification of the Constitution by the ninth state in a few days brought virtually to an end the powers of the old Congress. Thus the hopes of Kentucky were dashed and the matter was postponed for the consideration of the new Congress. Gardoqui at once attempted in conversation with Brown, to lead him to induce Kentucky, in return for free navigation of the Mississippi, to disengage herself from the inhospitable Union of States. It was vehemently asserted at a later time that Brown and his friends in Kentucky had been engaged in a treasonable conspiracy to effect such a separation: but General John Marshall Brown has argued from documents in the Spanish Archives and other evidence, that the accusation is unfounded. [See also J. M. Green.] Even had it more foundation than appears it is well to remember that schemes for independence of the new Union when it was just coming into existence in 1788 on the part of the remote and neglected inhabitants of the western wilderness cannot be stigmatized as very heinous. Brown for good reasons did not make public Gardoqui's advances, yet promptly communicated them to Madison among others.

The Convention which met in July 1788, though greatly disappointed at the action of Congress and recognizing that their action had deprived them of their expected powers, proceeded in an orderly and patriotic manner, recommending a summons of a new Convention which should be satisfactorily empowered to act with reference to dealings with the new government of the United States. Meanwhile the interval was improved in behalf of Spain by Miro and Wilkinson on the one hand and by Gardoqui and Morgan on the other. Lord Dorchester at the same time sent Colonel John Connelly to intrigue on behalf of Great Britain. The agents of these two powers as well as of France were listened to, but except in the case of a few men seem not to have shaken the intention of the public men of Kentucky to secure the existence of Kentucky as a State of the American Union. In the Convention of November, 1788, however, still further delays were caused by the arguments of some that the Convention did not have power to proceed upon the already given consent of Virginia to frame a constitution and petition Congress for admission to the Union, but that the consent of Virginia must again be obtained. The feeling gained ground that this point of strict legality was well taken, though all parties were averse to delay. Colonel Brown seems to have well shown that neither those of the party with whom Spain attempted to intrigue, nor those of the party who were approached by Great Britain had any other feeling than this. Virginia in December gave her final consent to Kentucky's becoming an independent member of the Union. Still another Convention, now summoned upon what all could agree to be a legal basis met in July, 1789. Disagreement about the terms proposed by Virginia made necessary still another in July, 1790. After so many tedious delays, Congress, February 4, 1791, enacted that Kentucky should be admitted into the Union on the 1st of June, 1792, and a Constitutional Convention in April of 1792 prepared a constitution for the new state.

The new constitution differed in many ways from that of the parent state of Virginia. It was a natural result of frontier life that the value of the individual was strongly accented and that democratic ideas were universally prevalent. It was therefore not unnatural that, instead of having the counties equally represented, the constitution of Kentucky provided that the representatives annually elected should be apportioned to the counties in proportion to their population. The senators, chosen for four years, were to be elected by electors according to the Maryland plan. The governor was chosen by these same electors, also for a period of four years. Traces of the influence of the Federal Constitution are to be seen in his extensive power to nominate officers by and with the advice and consent of the senate, in his possession of the veto power and in the limiting of the same by the possibility of reversal through a two thirds vote of the Legislature. As was natural in a frontier community universal suffrage was to prevail. Elections were to be by ballot. It was also natural that there was to be but one Superior Court of Appeals for both law and equity. The sheriffs were to be elected by the people of the county. The treasurer of the commonwealth was to be chosen by joint ballot of the houses of the Legislature. The bill of rights provided for complete religious freedom and there was provision for a vote in 1797 for or against the summons of a new convention. Especially interesting, however, was the ninth article of the Constitution, containing provisions respecting slavery. There was at the time a very strong movement in favor of general emancipation, in which an especially active part was taken by the clergy of the Baptist and Presbyterian denominations and a very important part in the proceedings of the Convention was assumed by George Nicholas, one of the ablest public men of Virginia, who had recently immigrated into Kentucky. The conditions of frontier life were upon the whole adverse to the continuance of the system of slavery and but for the influence of this new-comer from an older region, it is probable that the beginning at any rate of a system of emancipation might have been made. As it was, the regulations of the Constitution, though mild and humane, nevertheless perpetuated slavery. The Legislature, it was provided, should have no power to pass laws for the emancipation of the slaves, without the previous consent of their owners and the payment of a full equivalent in money. While they should permit owners to emancipate and should have full power to prevent slaves being brought into the state as merchandise or from a foreign country, they should have no power to prevent immigrants into the state from bringing with them their slaves. (Up to this point, General John Marshall Brown, "Political Beginnings of Kentucky": from this point Warfield and Marshall, Collins and Shaler.)

The numerous conventions, the long and varied struggles for the attainment of the position of an independent state, the intrigues of Spain and France and England, had all combined with the naturally vigorous and independent spirit of a frontier population to make the men of Kentucky strongly political. They were an energetic and decided race, more largely perhaps than in any other recruited from the ranks of the disbanded Revolutionary Army. Party politics therefore ran to great extremes in Kentucky. Natural causes combined with the action of the Federal Government to make the spirit of her citizens for the most part strongly Anti-Federal, though the Federal Party made up for its lack of numbers by the violence of its party spirit. The war of the French Republic against the allies, one of whom was Spain, excited great commotions in Kentucky, which Washington's administration controlled with moderation and wisdom. In 1795 intrigues with Spain recommenced, but were soon stopped by the treaty of that year which opened the Mississippi and gave Kentuckians a place of deposit at New Orleans. So great was the reaction caused by this and by the conduct of Genet, that the Federalists were able to elect Humphrey Marshall to the Senate. Their triumph proved very short-lived. Three years later the state uttered, as we have seen, its flaming protest against the Alien and Sedition laws and the Federalist Party in Kentucky became a hopeless and discredited minority. Mr. Warfield quotes from a book of Indiana reminiscences the story of a libel suit in that state, in which it was alleged that the defendant had called the plaintiff "an old Federalist" and an old Kentuckian swore that he considered this libellous, would shoot a man who called him either a horsethief or a

Federalist, would rather be called anything under heaven than a Federalist, regarded a thousand dollars damage as the least measure of damages, considered the term as equivalent to "Tory" or "Enemy of his country" and believed that from the earliest days of Kentucky such had been the common acceptation of the term: and the jury agreed with the witness.

Now the correspondence in the matter of the Kentucky Resolutions shows that while the lower house was unanimous in support of those resolutions, there was considerable dissent in the Senate. A Senate chosen by secondary election for four years could not long be sustained against the strong popular feeling which prevailed. The people in 1798 voted in favor of a new Convention which framed in 1799 a still more democratic constitution. The Senate and the Governor were now to be elected by the people and one fourth of the Senate was to retire by rotation each year. A veto could be overridden by a majority vote and there was to be a new Convention whenever the Legislature and the people so voted. The sheriffs, however, were to be appointed by the Governor on nomination of the County Courts, which consisted after Virginian fashion of justices of the peace appointed by the Governor. In 1801 John Breckenridge, the mover of the Resolutions, chosen by the Legislature itself, took his seat in the Senate, as the successor of Humphrey Marshall, and the democratic revolution in Kentucky was complete.

Southward from Kentucky it will be remembered at the close of the Revolutionary War lay regions still under the control of North Carolina and of Georgia. In the former, now called Tennessee, the first settlements had at the beginning of the Revolutionary War, extended along the Holston and the Watauga and the French Broad and along the western base of the Alleghany Range. In 1777 this western district was erected into a county and soon its settlements extended into the valley of the Cumberland River and to the present site of Nashville. Like the pioneers of Kentucky these remote settlers, several hundred miles from the capital of N.C., unprotected by the state or the United States, compelled to protect themselves against the attacks of Creeks and Cherokees, found very great inconvenience in political arrangements which bound them to a power incapable of efficient exertion in their behalf. The question of separation was mooted. Two Conventions were successively called and in 1786 the settlers proclaimed their independence of North Carolina and assumed to set up the new state of Frankland. The state of North Carolina asserted her jurisdiction and manifested a determination to maintain it. Two parties at once sprang up: two separate governmental systems; two distinct and opposing courts were in operation at the same time. Colonel Sevier, the governor, and Colonel Tipton, leader of the North Carolina party, came into violent collision. The third Convention of Frankland met, enacted laws, levied taxes, and sent a delegate to Congress, but Congress refused to recognize their rebellion and interposed its influence to restore harmony. In 1787 the government of Frankland became extinct. In

1790, as has already been seen, North Carolina ceded all the western territory to the United States. The years '88 and '89 had been in this territory as
in Kentucky marked by much agitation of the Mississippi question and as
a consequence by many Spanish intrigues. In 1790 the Federal Government
established a territorial government for the Southwestern Territory, which, it
will be remembered, included both Tennessee and the narrow strip of land
ceded by South Carolina. The act gave to the inhabitants the same privileges
and the same government which had been provided for the Northwestern
Territory, "except so far as is otherwise provided and [? except for] the conditions expressed in an Act of Congress of the present session entitled 'An
Act to accept Cession of the Claims of the State of North Carolina to a certain District of Western Territory.' " Now that act, reciting and accepting the
North Carolina cession, enacted as its eighth provision, "That the laws in
force and use in the State of North Carolina at the time of passing this Act
shall be and continue in full force within the territory hereby ceded until the
same shall be repealed or otherwise altered by the legislative authority of
the said territory." And so, without express mention of it, Congress failed
to confer upon the Southwestern Territory the priceless boon which it had
conferred upon the Northwest Territory in the famous Sixth Article of the
Ordinance of 1787, "There shall be neither slavery, nor involuntary servitude
in the said Territory, otherwise than in the punishment of crimes whereof
the party shall have been duly convicted." The form of government which
the Southwestern Territory acquired included a Governor, Secretary and
three Judges appointed by the President. When the Territory included five
thousand free adult males it was to have a General Assembly elected by the
adult males having freeholds of fifty acres to serve two years and a Legislative Council, or Upper House of five members, whom the President was to
choose from among ten residents of the district, nominated by the General
Assembly. The Governor, Legislative Council and House of Representatives
were to form the Legislature and the Council and House of Representatives
were to choose a delegate to Congress. The same securities for individual
rights were given as in the Northwest Territory. Previous to the creation of
the Legislature, the Governor and Judges were to make such laws as seemed
necessary. The first governor of the Southwest territory was William Blount,
who was also made Superintendent of Indian Affairs. Knoxville was selected
as the capital and treaties made under the authority of the Federal Government secured the protection of the Territory from the formidable tribes to
the southward during most of the years ensuing. In 1794 the first territorial
legislature was convened. The census which it next year ordered revealing
an adequate population, application was made to Congress for authority
to frame and adopt a State Constitution. The authority was given and in
January, 1796 a Constitutional Convention assembled at Knoxville and after
four weeks deliberation framed a State Constitution. This having been ap-

proved by Congress, the new state was on the 1st of June admitted into the Federal Union as the State of Tennessee. The first constitution of Tennessee was for the reasons already given in the case of Kentucky a considerably more democratic document than that made by North Carolina twenty years before, though it established a small freehold qualification.

It did not differ in many essential particulars from that which has just been described as Kentucky's Constitution of 1799. Both houses of the Legislature were chosen for two years: a greater number of officers was appointed by the Legislature than in Kentucky, and no veto power was conferred upon the Governor. The primitive simplicity of the political arrangements of the State is shown by the provisions that the Legislature should not give the Governor a greater annual salary than seven hundred and fifty dollars, the Judges of the Superior Courts more than six hundred dollars each, nor the Secretary more than four hundred. In spite of the injunction of Article 11 [2?], Declaration of Rights, "That no religious test shall ever be required as a qualification to any office under this State" the second section of Article 8 declared, "No person who denies the being of God, or a future state of rewards and punishments shall hold any office in the civil department of this state," and this anomaly continues in the Constitution of Tennessee to the present time. It will be noted that atheism and heresies as to the future life were not deemed a disqualification for military offices and for the work of fighting Indians. (Const. Ramsey. Am. H. Mag.) (Caldwell.)

What the life of Tennessee was in these early days may perhaps be most easily realized by reading the accounts of it which we obtain incidentally in the first chapters of Parton's and other biographies of Andrew Jackson, just as by the way accounts of Clay's first years in Kentucky will help us to understand the condition of things in that state. Jackson came from Nashville in 1788 to take the office of public prosecutor. The duties appertaining to such an office in a wild frontier country and the character of Jackson himself were such that biographers show us much of the rougher and more turbulent side of Tennessee life. The inhabitants were brave and generous but lawless and violent. Jackson was the first representative in Congress from the new state, succeeded William Blount in 1797 and was in Philadelphia until the ensuing Spring. In '98 he was made Judge of the Supreme Court of Tennessee: in 1800 major general of militia. According to Gallatin and Jefferson he made upon them in Philadelphia the impression of a rough and violent backwoodsman and indeed the contrast was in general a sharp one between the civilization of the cities of the sea-board and that of these new regions beyond the mountains.

The removal of William Blount from the Senate just alluded to opens up another chapter in the history of foreign intrigues in the West. In 1797 a letter of his was laid before Congress from which it would appear that he had been abetting some scheme to be carried out under British auspices for invading the Spanish dominions to the south of the United States. The House presented articles of impeachment against him; the investigation was deferred by his Republican associates and never reached a decision upon its merits, for when the Senate formed itself into a high court of impeachment, Blount's counsel filed a plea denying its jurisdiction on two grounds, first, that senators were not "officers" within the meaning of the Constitution and, second, that Blount, having been already expelled from his seat in the Senate during the preceding session, was not now tryable. The senate sustained the plea to the jurisdiction, though it is not clear whether this was done on one or both grounds.

The boundaries of Tennessee were established as they at present lie; that is to say, its southern boundary was the westward projection of the southern boundary of western North Carolina. The Southwestern Territory had however included also the South Carolina cession. I do not know that any provision was made for the government of that long and narrow strip in the interval between 1796 and 1802.

Southward from the State of Tennessee lay the great region now forming the states of Mississippi and Alabama and the western part of Georgia. The Treaty of 1783, by which Great Britain had acknowledged the independence of the United States, had fixed the line of the thirty-first degree of latitude as the boundary of the United States, from the Mississippi River to the Chattahoochee; but by the treaties of that same year the regions to the south of that line passed from the possession of Great Britain into that of Spain and with Spain the American government had considerable disputes as to the proper boundary of their respective possessions. It had been difficult at the time of the breaking out of war between France and Spain, to prevent some of the western people from making war upon the Spanish possessions, and the Baron Carondelet, Governor of New Orleans apprehended considerable danger from them, which he endeavored to avert by intrigues with Kentucky in 1795. The intrigues were unsuccessful and at the same time Thomas Pinckney scored a considerable success in negotiating at Madrid a treaty with Spain establishing latitude 31° as the boundary and securing to the United States the right freely to navigate the Mississippi River, accompanied by a three years' privilege of deposit at the port of New Orleans, free of duty.

In accordance with the terms of this treaty Spain agreed to surrender to the United States all her posts upon the left bank of the Mississippi above latitude 31°. But when Colonel Andrew Ellicott, accompanied by a small military force, arrived at Natchez as commissioner of the United States to join the Spanish Lieutenant-Governor of that place in determining the line of demarcation, the latter on one pretext after another interposed delays extending to more than a year. Finally, however, in March, 1798, the Spaniards evacuated Natchez and the commissioners of the two countries began running the line eastward from the Mississippi. (Monette; Gayarré; on West

Florida, Forbes's "Sketches of the Floridas," 1821; J. L. Williams, "View of West Florida," 1827.)

Of the vast region extending southward from Tennessee to latitude 31°, four Indian tribes at this time were almost complete possessors. The Creeks held what is now central and southeastern Alabama, the Cherokees the northern portion of that state; in what is now Mississippi the southeastern portion was held by the Choctaws, the northern portion by the Chickasaws. The only portions in which the Indian title had been extinguished were a tract equal to about two or three modern counties, extending along the Mississippi from the mouth of the river Yazoo to the Spanish line in the southwest portion of what is now the State of Mississippi, and a tract of similar size between the rivers Pascagoula and Tombigbee in what is now southwestern Alabama. Here were gathered a few thousand settlers who had in part immigrated into the country in times of British possession before the close of the Revolutionary War and in part had recently come there from the western American states. Both these areas lay within a disputed territory, for all the land from the line of 31° to a line running eastward from the mouth of the Yazoo River, say from Vicksburg to the Chattahoochee, that is to say, the southern third of the two states now situated there, was claimed by both Georgia and the United States. The claim on the part of the United States was that in times when Georgia and the Floridas had both been British territory 1763–83 this region had not belonged to Georgia but to west Florida and that therefore when Great Britain conceded the line of 31° this territory was granted to the United States free from any claim on the part of Georgia. Georgia maintained the opposite view and these lands were included in those western lands, the disposition of which caused so great difficulties and scandals in the government of the state during the last years of the century. (Haskins.) It was urged that she should follow the example of other states in ceding her western lands to the Union. Such a cession she was ready to make, but only on condition of being paid a large sum of money and of the Federal Government's undertaking to extinguish within a limited time the Indian title. In the Spring of 1798 Congress passed an act for the appointment of commissioners to adjust these conflicting claims and to receive proposals from Georgia for the cession of her share of the Southwestern Territory. The same act erected all the territory between the latitude 31° north and a line due east from the mouth of the Yazoo to the Chattahoochee into a government to be called the Mississippi Territory, to be constituted and regulated like the territories previously organized, though without the prohibition of slavery,—this last provision being accepted only after a warm debate. The introduction of slaves from without the limits of the United States into the new territory was, however, forbidden. It was declared that nothing in the act should operate in derogation of the rights of Georgia, but it was held to be clear that pending the settlement of her claims an efficient government for these distant and unprotected settlers should be provided. President Adams appointed as Governor of the new territory Winthrop Sargent, who had formerly been Secretary of the Northwestern Territory; and General Wilkinson, Commander-in-chief of the army, arrived at Natchez at the same time, with the United States troops. In 1799 Governor Sargent laid off two counties in the Natchez district and organized county courts. In 1800 a county was added on the Tombigbee River and by the special favor of Congress the territory was admitted to the second grade of territorial government, involving an elected House of Representatives, before the number of free white males had increased to five thousand. In 1802 Georgia completed her cession and in 1804 the Territory of Mississippi was enlarged to include all the region south of the State of Tennessee. Four-fifths of this extensive territory was still in possession of the four great Indian tribes of the south, which are estimated to have included about seventy-five thousand persons and at least ten thousand warriors. (Monette.) A full and remarkable description of one of these confederacies is to be found in the third volume of the collections of the Georgia Historical Society under the title, "A sketch of the Creek country in the years 1798 and 1799," by Colonel Benjamin Hawkins, formerly senator from North Carolina and, at the dates mentioned, agent of the United States for Indian Affairs. It is evident from his accounts that the Creeks at least had attained a considerable degree of civilization, though the indolent and improvident habits of savage life were hard for the excellent agent to overcome.

At the time when Mr. Jefferson was inaugurated in the Spring of 1801 the southwestern country, it will have been seen, had already entered upon a career full of interest and promise. Two states of rapidly increasing population had come into existence and the occupation of the remoter southwest and of the left bank of the great western stream, had already begun. In these regions a new type of American humanity was being developed, destined in time to force upon the older portions of the south a democracy more complete than their own, because based upon economic conditions more favorable to pure democracy, and an Americanism more fervent because more perfectly free from economic and mental dependence upon Europe.

VIII. The Period of the Old Republicans

The most important and decisive event in the history of the South during the administration of Mr. Jefferson was doubtless the acquisition of Louisiana. Up to the time of the acquisition the area possessed by the United States to the westward of the Southern States already organized, was an area of about 180,000 square miles, while that to the north of the Ohio was of one-third more, or 240,000 square miles. Even of the 180,000 that have been

mentioned, more than one-third was occupied by powerful tribes of Indians, difficult to dislodge, and the area available for settlement, and thus for
additions to the number of Southern States and to the force of the Southern element, was hardly more than one-half as great as in the Northwest;
where, moreover, the savage tribes were less formidable. Therefore, without
the acquisition of Louisiana, the scope and opportunities of the Southern
element in American civilization would have been much less extensive, the
number of the Southern States smaller, and their political influence far less.
The opening up of this great area to Southern settlement is therefore the first
topic of importance which must be treated in today's lecture.

The vast area of Louisiana, which Spain had now possessed since 1762,
was but thinly populated. In the region which now forms the State of Louisiana there were gathered at the time of the cession, according to Spanish authorities, about 40,000 inhabitants; in the regions of Upper Louisiana about
6000 or 7000; in all, the population of the whole region transferred by the
first Consul, was one of about 50,000, including, it is probable, rather more
than 25,000 or 30,000 whites, 2000 free people of color, and 15,000 or 16,000
slaves. Although the government had been for 40 years Spanish, very few
of the inhabitants were of that nation; they were almost altogether French;
in part the descendants of those who had emigrated directly from France; in
part of Acadians. The number of Americans had been increasing of late, and
English and Americans seem to have come to form the greater proportion of
the commercial class in New Orleans and the other towns. The population,
both French and American, seems to have been very ignorant. Not more
than half of the inhabitants of New Orleans, says an intelligent observer,
"Are supposed to be able to read and write, of whom not more than 200,
perhaps, are able to do it well." The French inhabitants were of quick intelligence and had many good qualities, but were marked by little enterprise
or energy, and the constant initiative of government in all public affairs had
not allowed public spirit to grow active among the body of the inhabitants.
The Governor of the Province was appointed from Spain, was usually in
residence but a few years, and had strong temptations to devote that period
to caring for his individual interests rather than for those of the Province.

Lately a separation of functions had occurred between the Governor and
the Intendant. The Governor was to be Chief of the army and militia and
head of the civil government. The Intendant, entirely independent of the
Governor, was to be chief of the departments of finance and commerce, to
exercise judicial powers in cases regarding the revenue of the country, and
to control the land offices. Beside this especial financial check upon the Governor, he was assisted by a Council of 12, which had the right of making
remonstrances to him in regard to the interior government of the Province.
This Council was called the Cabildo, consisting of 12 members chosen from
the most respectable families, but acquiring their position by purchase. They

had the general supervision of the political and other administrations of the City and chose the Alguazil or Sheriff, the Alcalde and the Public Prosecutor. The government of the outlying districts was in the charge of Commandants, appointed by the Governor in each district, and having both civil and military authority. The Governor promulgated ordinances for the good government of the Province, but had no power to assess taxes upon the inhabitants without their consent. As for judicial administration it was in like manner under the charge of the Commandants; at New Orleans under the Alcaldes. The Court of the Intendant had jurisdiction over revenue and fiscal causes; the Alcalde provincial over criminal causes; the highest Court, having jurisdiction throughout the province, was that of the Governor. Small causes are reported to have been decided promptly and justly. In the higher Courts the regular procedure, demanded by more important cases, was that of the civil law. Although the country had been French for so many years, during the 40 years occupation the law had become almost entirely Spanish, and consisted of ordinances formed expressly for the colony, of the famous general code for the Spanish colonies, and of the laws of Spain. Appeal lay to the Court of the Governor at Havana, from this to the Audiencia in Cuba, and from this to the Council of the Indies in Spain. The laws were in general rational, though their administration at times had been severe and at other times lax. But four offences were capital. Serious crimes are said to have been rare. The descent of property in case of persons dying intestate, was after the manner of the civil law; it descended to children in equal shares.

Some such description of the condition and organization of the Province has seemed necessary in order that we may readily understand the ensuing events, and their relation to American history. The story of the cession of the Louisiana territory to the United States has been brilliantly related by Mr. Henry Adams. It is, we may say, one of the last chapters of that long continued duel of the French and English race for the possession of the world outside of Europe, which forms the main theme of Prof. Seeley's Expansion of England. Talleyrand had already, in 1797, formed the scheme of restoring the French cause in that conflict, by reviving the colonial Empire of France and erecting in the New World a Latin Empire, which should serve as a balance to the growing American State, conceived by him as sure to be in general an ally with England. The vast regions, extending from the line of 31° and of the Mississippi southwestward to Cape Horn, were in the possession of Spain, a power incapable of carrying out this design of Latin ambition. Within six weeks after the victory of Marengo, in the summer of 1800, the first Consul, under the influence of these ideas of Talleyrand, instituted negotiations with Spain for the possession of Louisiana. On October 1st, 1800, the treaty of San Ildefonso effected the transfer. The design of the brilliant young soldier, now controlling the destinies of France, was to utilize the period of peace into which he was about to enter by creating in Louisiana a formidable colonial establishment; but the necessary basis of his vast schemes of Colonial Empire was the Island of San Domingo. His generals in that Island succeeded in [?] conquering Toussaint L'Overture, but found a more terrible enemy in the yellow fever, before the ravages of which the armies of the first Consul rapidly disappeared. Just at this time the Government of the United States, alarmed by the closure of the Mississippi, which Morales had effected immediately before the cession to France was to take place, and alarmed still more by the prospect of having for our neighbor in the Southwest, instead of the decrepit power of Spain, the enormously active and energetic power of rejuvenated France, under the wonderful control of Bonaparte, engaged in an effort to prevent by any peaceful means the acquisition of New Orleans. It has well been termed by Mr. Adams a turning point in the career of Bonaparte, who was turned from the peaceful policy which was the best interest of France, by the personal gratifications which his selfish spirit found in the renewal of war. He instantly turned from the scene of the failure in San Domingo, abandoned his whole vast project of colonial empire, and sold to the United States the territory he had but just acquired from Spain.

But if it was a turning point in the career of Bonaparte, it was not less so in the history of the United States, and especially of the South. This was true, first, for the reasons which were mentioned at the start. Another Southern territory, and, eventually, another Southern State, were added. Moreover, hitherto the settled district lying beyond the territories of the four Indian tribes had been a remote outpost, unconnected with other American settlements, whereas it now, as American territory, beckoned on American settlers. The Southwestern regions of Alabama and Mississippi received increasing numbers of population. The desire to extend required the Indians to retire,[19] and finally in 1813 the Creeks rose in arms against the Americans during the War of 1812. The rigorous repression of their rising by Jackson and the men of the Southwest, laid open to American settlement the great and fertile regions which had so long been coveted. This great expansion of the Southern population and consequent increase of Southern power was in great degree due to the transfer to American control of that considerable body of American population in the district around New Orleans.

In the second place this was the first step in that process of aggrandizement of the United States at the expense of Spain, which from this time on, for half a century, formed an important portion of Southern policy. The Spanish Empire in America was vast and unwieldy, like one of those great Galleons which sailed in the Armada to the attack upon England. The quick, active and enterprising Americans pushed their attack upon it with skill and rapidity, and even with somewhat of the unscrupulousness which marked

{19.} "to die" struck through.

the Anti-Spanish activities of the Elizabethan Buccaneers. As the Teutonic conquerors rushed forward to seek the fragments of the collapsing Roman Empire, and as Clive and Dupleix struggled to possess themselves of the spoils of the crumbling Empire of the great Mogul, so southern American politicians of the period from 1800 to 1860 were eager to enlarge the Union at the expense of the extensive but feeble empire which lay before them, occupying vast territories of which it could make but little use. The effect of the presence of these territories upon the imagination of Southern politicians during all this period can hardly be over-estimated; it is to be reckoned among the prime causes of the tendency along the lines of which, in spite of all theories, they steadily advanced; the tendency, namely, to make use of the Federal government to push the interests of the South, and especially the increasing interests which centered around the institution of slavery and bound the economic life of a whole great region to an economic system whose most active demand was for more and more new land.

But thirdly, the acquiring of Louisiana is an event of the first consequence in the history of the South, because it became almost of necessity a turning point in the history of Southern political theory. In the United States, as in all new countries, political history has been dominated by economic needs. The forces of nature, far more than the will of individuals, have directed the destinies of such countries, and ruled in spite of man and his efforts. So it was with the South. The economic necessity of trade to the Southwestward, involving the possession of the mouths of the great rivers, compelled the acquisition of Louisiana. The acquisition of Louisiana worked destruction to the constitutional theories of the interesting school of public thought which had hitherto been dominant in the South. The theories of the Virginian Strict Constructionist School could find no justification for the acquiring of Louisiana without an amendment to the Constitution. Mr. Jefferson acquired Louisiana, extending therein the powers of the Federal Government, and did not follow up this act by even a subsequent obtaining of a permissive amendment by the people. An economic necessity had forced the leader of Virginia Republicanism from the Constitutional ground of strict construction, and from this time on the political theories of the Southern representatives could no longer be what they had been. In one act after another the Federal government placed its authority upon the ground of implied powers and the Republicans were forced to abandon the doctrines which had hitherto been maintained in opposition, save the few thousands who bowed not the knee to Baal, and in the gainsaying of [?] John Randolph withstood President Jefferson and Madison and Gallatin and the great majority who supported them.

It is not solely in the *acquisition* of Louisiana that we may see the beginnings of a new departure in constitutional theory. When it became necessary to provide a government for this new territory and its French population, the first measures taken involved the largest stretch of Federal authority. The form of government which had existed under the Spanish government was temporarily continued. The appointment of all officers of the new territory was given to the President alone, without reference to the Senate. The people, though the treaty had promised them the rights of citizenship, were refused all political rights, and a virtual despotism was set up, on the ground of necessity. Early in 1804 an Act was passed providing a more permanent government for the territory. The country north of the 33rd parallel, which now forms the northern boundary of Louisiana, was entitled the district of Louisiana and subjected to the territorial government of the Indiana territory. The district to the south of that line, called the territory of Orleans, was given for one year a government in which the people of Louisiana had actually no share. The Governor, Secretary, Legislative Council and judicial officers were all to be appointed by the President without consulting the Senate. Even the right to a Jury trial was granted in civil cases only when the matter involved more than £20, and, of criminal cases, only in those involving capital punishment. Whether the power to frame such a statute was rested upon the phrase of the Constitution allowing Congress to make all needed rules and regulations respecting the territory or other property belonging to the United States, or whether it was rested upon the inference that the right of acquiring territory implied the right to govern it (American Insurance Co. vs. Canter), this was surely a striking instance of loose Constructionist Legislation.

The exclusion of the people from political power lasted only a year. In 1805 the territory of Orleans was given a government resembling that of the Mississippi territory, with Governor, Secretary and Judges appointed by the President, but with a Legislature elected by the people of the territory. At the same time the Upper District, called the territory of Louisiana, was separated from Indiana and given an organization of its own, after the type of territorial government which was usually accorded to the least populous territories, that is to say, with Governor, Secretary and three Judges, appointed by the President, and Legislative power vested in the Governor and three Judges. The Act of 1805 had promised that Louisiana should become a State when its population amounted to 60,000, and it was, in 1812, admitted to the Union. The convention which met at New Orleans in the winter of 1811 and 1812 framed a constitution not differing in principle from that usual in Southern States, though slightly more conservative than those framed during the Revolution. The suffrage was confined to those who had paid State taxes, plus those who had purchased lands from the United States. The object of this provision was obviously to give additional power to the American immigrants. Representatives and Senators were required to have a property qualification of land to the value of $500 and $1000 respectively. The Representatives were chosen for two years, the Senators for four years, with

partial renewal every two years; both were chosen by the same body of electors. The people also cast their votes for Governor, but the final choice was
made by the Legislature, which elected one of the two candidates having the
largest popular vote. His term of office was four years, and he was invested
with a veto power, limited in the same manner as that of the President of
the United States.

Not only the Louisiana complications, but many other of the affairs of
public importance during these years, drew the Federal government, and
with it the old Republican party, aside from the practice of Strict Constructionist doctrine. But if the possession of power was immediately effective
in modifying the political theories of the dominant party in the direction of
centralization, this did not interfere with the progress of those Democratic
ideas, which had been equally fundamental in the tenets of that party. Evident progress was made toward universal suffrage in States where this had
not already been established. In 1800 there was vigorous agitation in Maryland in favor of the removal of the property qualification. The House passed
a Bill extending a right of suffrage to every free white male citizen, 21 years
of age, who had resided 12 months in the State and 6 months in the County
prior to the election. The Senate insisted upon an amendment requiring that
the voter should have paid a tax and should have resided two years. It was
contended by the House that this would in reality decrease the suffrage
rather than enlarge it, disfranchising many whose property was greater in
value than that required for the voter, yet lay under the limit of that upon
which taxation was imposed. In 1801 the House again passed its Bill and
threatened the summons of a convention which might alter the constitution
of the Senate. The threat was effective; the Senate passed the Act; in 1802,
it was confirmed, and universal suffrage was established in Maryland, with
the exclusion, however, of all persons not white. In 1810 the property qualifications for State offices, for membership of the Legislature, and for Electors
of the Senate, were abolished. Georgia in 1812 substituted popular election
for election by the General Assembly, in the choice of the Judges of the inferior Courts. In 1810 South Carolina effected a slight re-arrangement of the
suffrage, by excluding from it all paupers, and all non-commissioned officers
and private soldiers of the Army of the United States. Another noteworthy
constitutional amendment on the part of that State was that of 1808, which
based the apportionment of members in the House of Representatives upon
population and property, in an equal degree; it provided that the Legislature
should consist of 124 members and that these should be so apportioned that
one Representative should be sent for every 62nd part of the whole number
of white inhabitants, and one Representative also for every 62nd part of the
whole taxes raised by the State.

This may be as appropriate a place as any in which to mention a fact or two
respecting State taxation and finance at this time. It appears, for instance,

that in 1805, the total amount of appropriations made by the Legislature of South Carolina was $190,000; but $50,000 of this sum was appropriated for opening the navigation of certain rivers, and the usual sum may be reckoned at $140,000; whereas in North Carolina in 1804 the total expense of government was £26,300, (?) 16s., 7p. a modest sum, equivalent to about $66,000. The alarming slave insurrection of 1801 in Virginia and some slight contemporary insurrections in North Carolina, led in both States to somewhat severer slave laws.

Another branch of Legislation, hardly less characteristic of the principles of Jeffersonian Democracy, than its regulations respecting suffrage, were its regulations of the relations between Church and State. In respect to this matter developments of very considerable interest took place in Virginia during these years. It will be remembered that the Act providing for freedom of religion had left to the Episcopal parishes the possession of glebe lands. In the first years of the century the argument gained favor that these, having been conveyed by the people in former times, were more rightly the property of the people than of the church, which now no longer included, as of old, the whole body of the population. Therefore in 1802 an Act was passed which, while not disturbing present possessors, provided for the conveyance of the glebes to the use of the State in any parish whenever a vacancy occurred. The question of its constitutionality was raised and was brought before the Court of Appeals, now organized as a Court of five Judges, with Pendleton as President. One of them did not sit in the cause because he considered himself interested in the decision. Of the rest, three agreed in the view that the Act of 1802 was unconstitutional, and that the glebes belonged to the P{rotestant}. E{piscopal}. Church. After arguments that excited great interest throughout the State, the President of the Court prepared his opinion in writing; but on the night before the opinion was to have been pronounced, Judge Pendleton died, and the judgment of the Court was not delivered. His successor, Judge St. George Tucker, agreed with Judge Spencer Roane, tying the court, and the glebes passed out of the possession of the Church.

The statute inflicted a severe blow upon the Episcopal Church in Virginia at a time when its weakness was very great. In the convention of 1805 Bishop Madison was able to muster but sixteen clergymen and a few laymen, and no conventions were held at all from that time until that held in 1812; indeed, it was not until 1818–19 that any considerable life began to revive within the old church. Bishop Meade tells us that when he was ordained on a Sunday in February, in 1811, at Williamsburg, the congregation consisted of two ladies and fifteen gentlemen, while outside one citizen was filling his icehouse, and the students of William and Mary College were going out with their dogs to hunt. It is well that American students should perceive more fully than they have done, that we should so widen the scope of constitutional study, as to include the history of the constitution of religious bodies within our country. The history of religion during this period, too, is of extreme interest; the student sees amid the religious apathy with which the eighteenth century closed in America, that wonderful outburst of religious enthusiasm which began with the Cane Ridge revival of Tennessee in 1798, and spread thence to Kentucky, to North Carolina, to Western Virginia, and over the whole Union, bringing with it everywhere a remarkable awakening of interest in religion, and many new developments in the organization of religious bodies. These in spite of our divorce of Church and State, are not the less important objects of investigation on the part of the student of constitutional history.

The advance of democratic principles throughout the country may be traced in the history of parties and of elections. In 1800, while most of the South voted for Jefferson and Burr, half the vote of Maryland and a third of the vote of North Carolina went to Adams and Pinckney. In 1804 two of the eleven votes of Maryland went to Pinckney but all the rest of the Southern vote to Jefferson. The result in 1808 was a less complete triumph. Again two of Maryland's votes went to the Federalist candidate, and North Carolina also cast three of its fourteen votes for Pinckney rather than for Madison. In 1812, of Maryland's eleven votes six went to Madison, five to De Witt Clinton. In the period from 1801 to 1814 the congressional elections showed with more distinctness the extent of the Federal strength throughout the South. Probably the Federalism of the Essex Junto nowhere found great favor in the South; but the wiser Federalism of Pinckney and Bayard and John Marshall was of considerable weight in Maryland and South Carolina, with their important commercial interests, and even in North Carolina. There in the elections of 1801, three out of ten were Federalists. In 1802, however, the Legislature re-arranged the districts, and after that there seem to have been never more than two Federalists chosen during the years specified, sometimes only one, while occasionally, the State's delegation to the Congress, was unanimously Republican. (Senator Stone turned an administrationist, by his second wife, of Washington.)

IX. The Period of the New Republicans

During the fifteen years succeeding the conclusion of the war of 1812, the interest of Southern history centres largely in the outlying portions of the extreme South and of the Southwest. Not many events of consequence marked the history of Maryland, Virginia, North Carolina and South Carolina during that period. All four of these States were decreasing in relative importance as the number of new States in the Union was increased. Perhaps most parts of these four States, if they did not decline in respect to prosperity, at any rate, made but little progress during these years. The economic influence of slavery was undoubtedly adverse to any diversification of industries and even to the rapid progress of agriculture itself. Along the Boundary line between free and slave States, the decline in value of lands within the slave States, as compared with lands of the same character over the border in the free states, a disparity which had already been noted in General Washington's time, grew more and more marked; as for instance, upon the boundary line common to Pennsylvania and Virginia. A very considerable movement of population from the worn-out lands of the old States took place. Planters and their families emigrated from them to the fresh and unexhausted lands of Alabama, Mississippi and Tennessee. Mrs. Smedes's Memorials of a Southern Planter describes one interesting instance of such emigration. Moreover, the economic condition of the old Southern States had been very greatly affected by the Embargo. That measure of Mr. Jefferson, which had excited so large an outcry in New England, had probably in the end been far more detrimental to the interests of the Southern States. In New England, it destroyed the commercial towns, to be sure, but it built up manufactures; the result in the South was that capital was drained from that region to establish and maintain the varied manufacturing industries of New England and Pennsylvania. Politically speaking, the victory which Jeffersonian democracy had obtained in 1801 was never reversed, indeed, the remoter Southern States were and remained more democratic in their organization than the older ones in which the doctrine had originated. But with that portion of the Virginia doctrine, which concerned the interpretation of the Constitution, the case was otherwise. The War of 1812, profoundly stimulating the sentiment of nationality, carried still farther the progress of loose constructionist theory in the South, and the old school of Virginian Republicans found itself confronted by a growing body of national Republicans, out of whom was to grow the great Whig party of a later time. With Maryland, Virginia and the Carolinas, we need therefore, for the present time, concern ourselves but little, but may turn to the more vigorous and active[20] communities to the Southwestward. Here were going on those political developments, which in 1829 brought upon the scene of national politics, the new forces of Jacksonian Democracy transforming, whether for good or for ill, the theory of politics and administration which had prevailed during the decorous administrations of the first six Presidents. Here, too, were occurring changes more readily traced from stage to stage in outward effects. General Jackson's victory at Horse-shoe Bend had opened up the Creek Country to settlement by the whites. A treaty of the year 1816, had still further opened the area of possible settlement; then came the massacre of Fort Mimms, the capture of the Negro Fort, and the Seminole War. The action of British adventurers in stimulating, on the part of the Indians, the continuance of hostilities during

{20.} "hostile" struck through.

the years after the conclusion of the second war with England, led Jackson to high-handed measures of retaliation. His seizure of St. Mark's and Pensacola in defiance of all international law, at the bidding of that contempt of Spain, which lay deep in the frontiersman's character, threatened for a time to interrupt the progress of peaceful negotiations for the possession of Florida, with which President Monroe's cabinet was occupied; finally, however, Secretary John Quincy Adams, and the Spanish Minister, Don Luis de Onis, succeeded in arranging the terms of treaty in 1819, by which Florida was annexed to the territory of the United States. The augmentation of the available territory of the United States and of the power of the South, was inconsiderable, positively speaking; but it was of much value to the Southern States to have control of the mouths of the minor rivers which flowed from that territory into the Gulf, as well as of the great river, whose valley had been secured by the treaty of 1803. From the time of this cession and of the chastisement of the Seminoles, expansion Southwestward was steady and rapid. In 1817, Indiana having been admitted into the Union the year before, Mississippi was permitted to assume the powers of a State and was cast into the balance on the Southern side. Another free State having been added by the admission of Illinois in 1818, another slave State was added in 1819, by the admission of Alabama. It will be seen that the general rule of westward development had here been interrupted; Mississippi being settled up to the limit of population thought necessary to a State a little earlier than Alabama. This was partly because, earlier than any considerable settlement of Alabama, some settlements had begun during the period after the Revolution in the regions around Natchez, and partly because, ever since the acquiring of the mouth of the Mississippi in 1803, a powerful current of emigration had flowed down the Mississippi River with results, which could not be so easily attained in the less accessible districts lying west of Georgia. So it was, that in 1817, the Mississippi territory was divided by a line running north and south, and the Western portion was erected into a State under the title of Mississippi, while the Eastern portion received territorial organization as the Territory of Alabama. The Constitution with which Mississippi received admission into the Union shows in several respects the influence upon it of the neighboring new State of Louisiana. The qualification of Representatives and of Senators was expressed in very nearly the same terms. The franchise was extended to all free white male citizens over twenty-one, qualified by a certain residence, who were enrolled in the State Militia or paid State or County taxes. Both House and Senate were chosen by these electors; the former for one year, the latter for three, but renewed by one-third each year. The Governor was chosen by the people for two years, and had a veto power arranged as in the Constitution of the United States and of Louisiana, but had little appointing power. Judges, and almost all the State officers, were chosen by the Legislature. As in the Constitution of Tennessee, it was provided, that no person who denied the being of God, or a future state of rewards and punishments, should hold any office in the civil department of the State; but the provision was not, as in Tennessee, stultified by other provisions; for the phrases of the Bill of Rights, which ensured religious freedom to all, were expressed with considerably more circumspection than in the Tennessee Constitution of 1796. Regulations, restricting divorce were inserted in the Constitution, and the interests of property in slaves were carefully guarded. This seems to have been the first of all Southern Constitutions, which was formally submitted to the direct vote of the people for approval or disapproval. The Alabama Territory at this time contained already a population of 33,000; but immigration was extremely rapid, and before the close of the year 1818, the population had increased to more than 70,000. An application to Congress resulted in the passage of an enabling act, the summons of a convention, the framing of a Constitution, and the admission of the State of Alabama in 1819. Seldom has any State more rapidly increased in population, for in 1820 it contained 128,000 inhabitants and in 1830, 310,000. The Constitution of Alabama provided for universal suffrage; it allowed the Governor's veto to be overridden by the vote of a mere majority of the General Assembly, but in other respects differed hardly at all from the Constitution provided for Mississippi. The two States were in fact very similar in respect to population and status, being, as indeed they are to the present time almost exclusively agricultural and rural communities.

Simultaneously with this great increase in population in the regions between Georgia and the Mississippi River, occurred a considerable movement of population over the great river into the regions near its confluence with the Missouri. Here was now gathered a population which approached the requisite number for admission into the Union as a State, and in the Congressional Session of 1819, a measure looking toward this end was introduced. Most of the population of the Missouri territory was situated northward of the mouth of the Ohio, whose course had hitherto formed the boundary between freedom and slavery, but it was determined to divide the territory at the latitude of 36° 30′ north, which was the westward prolongation of the Southern boundary of Virginia and Kentucky. Hence the question whether the new State should be a free State or a slave State at once attracted deep interest. The House of Representatives, in which the free States predominated, struggled to secure the prohibition of slavery in Missouri. The Senate contended for its maintenance, and so in this Session the Bill fell through. We may take this opportunity to describe the history of the temporary organization. The regions north of the State of Louisiana, it will be remembered, had been organized, in 1805, as the Territory of Louisiana; in 1812 its name was altered to the Territory of Missouri, and it received a higher form of territorial organization with an elective assembly, which in 1816, was still more elaborately organized.

The attempt to admit it as a State having failed in 1819, it was renewed in 1820. In the discussion between the Senate and the House as to the exclusion or permission of slavery within Missouri, a new element was introduced by a simultaneous petition from the inhabitants of the district of Maine, for independence as a State separate from Massachusetts. The result of the discussions was the famous Missouri Compromise of 1820, in accordance with which Maine was admitted as a State, and permission was given for the entrance of Missouri into the Union with the institution of slavery, but with a provision that slavery should be forever interdicted in all other territories of the United States, north of the line of 36° 30'. The Constitution which the convention of Missouri framed in pursuance of this enabling Act, was obnoxious to the Northern members of Congress, in that it forbade the Legislature to interfere with the institution of slavery and required the Legislature to frame laws to prevent free colored people from settling in the State. Upon the former matter Congress in its session of 1821, took no action, but the latter operated to prevent free colored persons, who were citizens of other States, as at that time free blacks in some cases were, from settling in Missouri; it was, therefore, thought repugnant to that provision of the Constitution which secured to citizens of any State all the privileges of citizenship in all other States. In regard to this matter, therefore, it was finally resolved that Missouri should be admitted, on condition that this clause should never be construed to permit the passage of any law, abridging the rights of a citizen of the United States. The assent of Missouri to this condition was to be given by its Legislature, which complied with the act of Congress; at the same time it announced that this was a mere formality, because the Legislature had no power to bind the State in any such manner; so ended the memorable struggle over the admission of Missouri. The settlement which was reached, naturally carried with it the effect of securing slavery in the region between Missouri and Louisiana, now organized into the Territory of Arkansas. It was, of course, also admitted in the other Southern territory of Florida, but in both of these it was many years before the population was sufficiently increased to make possible their admission as States.

Pitiful as the military results of the War of 1812 had been, it had had highly valuable political results in enormously stimulating and strengthening the sentiment of nationality. The administrations of Colonel Monroe and John Quincy Adams saw this sentiment still further developed in most parts of the Union. Even the rise of Jacksonian Democracy, so fatal to many of the best elements in American political life, had the great compensation of bringing with it a remarkable expansion of the sentiment of devotion for the Union, among classes by whom that sentiment had not been actively felt hitherto. A natural result of rapid economic development, of westward expansion, of the growth of new States, and of the quiet character of politics during much of these twelve years, was the steady increase of this sentiment, in all parts of the South. Yet it was the last of these very years which witnessed the consolidation of that strong sentiment in favor of State rights which was henceforward to play so large and so distracting a part in our political history. The causes of this reaction are not wholly easy to trace. It is clear that, as in other movements in American history, economic interests had very much to do in bringing this about. This, at least, was true of the most striking exemplifications of the State Rights theory, which occurred within or near this period, that resistance to the Federal Government offered by Georgia in the case of the Creeks and Cherokees, and that offered by South Carolina in relation to the tariff of 1828. Probably, however, it was preeminently one economic interest, that of slavery, which organized in the South a devotion to State Rights and a tendency to united action in their defence. The most acute contests in behalf of the principles of State Rights have not arisen in cases where the rights of an individual State were threatened, but rather in those where the interests threatened were those of a section or of a group of States geographically contiguous. The sense of peculiar interests surrounding the "peculiar institution" would be sure unconsciously to keep alive and active the sentiment of watchfulness against encroachments. Thus it was that the South was drawn into a more and more united maintenance of strict construction and of State Rights, and into a course of action in reference to Federal politics, of which the bearings were distinctly understood by but few Statesmen, if, indeed, by any, except the wayward but penetrating genius of John Randolph, and the cool farseeing intellect of Calhoun, who, as he sat in the vice Presidential chair during these years of Adams' administration, drank in the doctrines of Southern co-öperation and Southern peril, from the Virginian Senator, whose disorderly harangues he refused to check.— One of these crowning instances of the assertion of State sovereignty falls quite within the period of today's lecture: The contest with Georgia over the Indian lands. It will be remembered, that the Georgia land cession of 1802 had been accompanied by the condition that the United States should extinguish the Indians' title to lands within the bounds' of Georgia, as soon as that could be done peacefully and reasonably. Cession after cession had been made until the Indians refused to sell more, and the Creeks denounced the death penalty against any one who should pretend to negotiate a treaty making further cessions. A treaty was negotiated at Indian Springs in February, 1825, purporting to turn over to the United States all the Creek country in Georgia, and several million acres in Alabama. The Indians repudiated the treaty, and President Adams was unwilling to push the execution of it. In the meantime, however, Georgia had proceeded to take possession of the territory and expel the Creeks. Governor Troup, by proclamation, called upon the Georgians to stand by their arms, and declared his intention to survey the lands in spite of all resistance. The language of the Governor to the President and Secretary of War, was defiant, and even insolent, but the collision

was in the end averted, and the Creeks in Georgia, after renewed negotiations, were induced to make the necessary cession, and retired beyond the
Mississippi. In 1826–27 further trouble arose over claims to the Cherokee
lands in the hilly portions of Georgia. The surveyor of that State attempted
to survey these lands in defiance of Indian remonstrances, and the Governor insisted upon the State's authority to arrest all United States officers
opposing such survey, ordered the militia of the State to hold themselves in
readiness to repel all hostile invasions, and announced that any attempt to
oppose the claims of the State by force would be considered an attack upon
the territory, people and sovereignty of Georgia. Congress sustained the
President in his determination to maintain the treaties of the United States
and four years later Judge Marshall, in the case of the Cherokees against
Georgia, 1831, and Worcester against Georgia, 183{2}, sustained the claims
of the Cherokee nation as just, under the Constitution, and vindicated the
control of the national government over the Indian tribes residing within the
United States. But the action of President Jackson in the matter [?] was not
such as to impose upon the refractory States the authority of the Union, or
to teach by example the completest respect for that authority on the part of
the advocates of State Rights, who accordingly multiplied and grew strong
within the Southern States during these years.

x . The Movements of 1830: Conclusion

It has not been my intention to carry a detailed narration of the history of
the Southern States beyond the year 1830. At this point, therefore, it may
be well to pause and examine the status of the Southern States when that
year arrived. Much the greater portion of the Southern area had by that
time been settled, yet in the States southward and westward of Kentucky,
two-thirds of the area was still in the possession of the Federal government
and presumably not occupied by any considerable population. The census
of that year showed, in the Southern States and Territories, a population of
5,700,000. Virginia still led the rest, with a population of nearly a million and
a quarter; next, as of old, stood North Carolina, whose population amounted
to more than 700,000. Kentucky and Tennessee had populations of little less
than 700,000; South Carolina about 600,000; Georgia, about 500,000; Maryland, which in 1790 had been third among the Southern States, now stood
seventh, with a population hardly more than one-third greater than when
the first national census was taken. Next came Alabama, whose population
had made the astounding growth of 142% during the last ten years. In general, the South had held its own in the growth of population during the ten
years preceding, the average gains over the whole area being almost exactly
one-third, during the decade, as in the Northern States. But these gains were

very unequally distributed; in Maryland, the District of Columbia, Virginia, North Carolina and South Carolina, the increase had been small, ranging from 10% in Maryland to 20% in the District of Columbia; evidently these older portions of the South were far from sharing in the advancing prosperity of the whole Union. In the new States of the South and Southwest, on the other hand, gains far exceeding the average, were observed; 41% in Arkansas, 52% in Georgia, 63% in Tennessee, 80% in Mississippi, 110% in Missouri and, as already said, 142% in Alabama. It was obvious that though Virginia and North Carolina might still lead in point of numbers, the sceptre was passing away from the seaboard States, and being transferred to the new lands southward and westward of the mountains.

More ominous [21] for the future were such figures as indicated the industrial development of the section. The fact that the Southern States, while contributing 40,000,000, out of 74,000,000 of exports, drew in but one-fifth of the 71,000,000 imports of the United States, showed plainly that the devotion of the South to agricultural interests was growing more and more exclusive. Populations of towns showed the same thing. Baltimore had 81,000 inhabitants, New Orleans, 46,000, Charleston, 30,000, Washington, 19,000, Richmond, 16,000, and these were all the cities which in that mass of nearly 6,000,000 of population, exceeded the number of 10,000. That commerce and manufactures had a decreasing share among the interests of the South, and that, in short, all diversification of industries was disappearing, is plainly shown, even if figures were lacking, by the attitude of the Southern States toward the tariff of 1828. Statistics never exerted a due influence over the minds of Southern statesmen. They are, indeed, much less likely to be appreciated as a factor in political discussions in agricultural, than in commercial and manufacturing regions. If the appalling figures of the census of 1850, in respect to population and industries, did not succeed in dissuading the Southern politicians from the hope of successful resistance it is not to be expected that the superficially encouraging figures of 1830 should be thought to give alarming signs of the advance of Northern supremacy. One branch of Southern statistics, however, did have upon the minds of Southern statesmen a constant importance as a source of anxiety, and that was the increase of the slave population. In the whole South, where in 1790, there had been between 600,000 and 700,000, there were now 2,000,000; they constituted a little more than half the population in South Carolina, almost exactly half in Mississippi, Louisiana and Florida; 40% in Virginia, Georgia and Alabama; a third in North Carolina, a fourth in Maryland and Kentucky; a small, but still considerable, figure in Tennessee, Missouri and Arkansas. Maryland was the only State in which the proportion of slaves had decreased since 1790; here their absolute number was exactly the same as then, 103,000. Of

{21.} "ruinous" struck through.

free colored persons there were 100,000 in Maryland and Virginia, slightly more in the former than in the latter, and in all the other Southern States put together, about 66,000. The constitutional provisions respecting emancipation had been of due effect in keeping to a very small figure the number of the free colored in Alabama, Mississippi and Missouri, the last three Southern States admitted. Slaves constituted an increasing portion of the wealth of the Southern States, and formed the basis of its industrial life in a degree constantly increasing, as that industrial life became more and more confined to agriculture, and to agriculture of few and simple crops.

Such was the situation of the Southern States when there came upon the world, both European and American, that mighty movement which in Europe was called the Revolution of 1830. It is not so often remembered as it should be, that that movement did not expend all its strength in promoting the July Revolution of France, and the similar uprisings against despotic Monarchs in other States upon the continent. In England the vigorous, and for a time, alarming struggle for the widening of the Parliamentary franchise by means of the Reform Act, was part and parcel of the same great movement. The waves of this great movement in favor of human liberty, popular rights and democratic principles came also across the Atlantic, and took various forms upon the American shores. There can be no doubt that the swift transformation which the Abolitionist cause underwent about the year 1830, proceeded from the same political ferment which caused the Continental Revolutions of that year. The same spirit found vent in the vagaries which marked the contact of Transcendentalism with the events of practical life; even its socialistic and communistic outgrowths found expression upon American soil in the motley throng of enthusiastic communities. In politics the movement which overthrew [22] Charles X. and the Duke of Brunswick, and which carried through so triumphantly the Whig Reform Bill, found such analogy as was possible upon soil exempt from any such tyranny, in the wonderful wave of democratic enthusiasm, which carried General Jackson to the Presidential chair in 1829.—The events of the present time may help us in part to understand that movement: we are seeing the rapid and astonishing progress of a movement on the part of masses hitherto but slightly engaged in politics, which threatens to put the conduct of our public affairs into the hands of a vast horde of unintelligent farmers, whose ardency and inexperience combine to put them in the power of loud demagogues and skillful wire-pullers. To observe carefully the progress of the Farmers' Alliance in the South in our own time, may help us to understand that extraordinary movement, by which, in the last part of the third decade of this

{22.} "threatened" struck through.

century, a vast mass of ignorant voters newly[23] enfranchised, or if already enfranchised hitherto unpolitical, rushed forward to overthrow an imaginary tyranny, and to renovate[24] American government, in the interest of ideas crude and half understood, but enthusiastically believed in.[25]

It was, then, one of the signs of the times that a more ardent spirit of democracy had rapidly come into existence all over the Union. Its character may be seen in the pages of Tocqueville, whose arrival to America occurred just in time to enable him to observe these new developments. The movement of the democratic masses resulted in many constitutional changes, effected in 1830 and the few years immediately succeeding. Most important of all, probably, was the framing of a new Constitution for Virginia, by the convention of 1829–30. There had long been a standing antagonism between the inhabitants of Eastern and those of Western Virginia, and a strong feeling on the part of the latter that the old Constitution of 1776, was no longer adequate to present conditions. Representation in the Legislature was, it will be remembered, by counties; now the counties of Eastern Virginia were small and of slight population, while those of Western Virginia, were large and populous; an arrangement which put them upon an equality, was offensive to the new democratic spirit. On the other hand, the wealth of the State lay in the Eastern counties and here were held the greatest number of the slaves. The democratic influence therefore, found itself confronted by the interests of property and especially slavery. After a long and bitter struggle the democratic or western element secured the summons of a new convention. This memorable body met at Richmond at the end of the year 1829. Madison, then an old man of 79, performed in this convention his last public service, and the hardly less venerated names of Monroe and Marshall were found in the lists of the convention; Monroe, indeed, was chosen to be its President. The most important of the discussions with which the convention was occupied for the next three months, had relation to the suffrage, and to the representation in the House of Delegates. The suffrage was widened by admitting not only free-holders, but various other classes of the occupants of land, and all tax-paying householders. In respect to the House of Delegates, a compromise was arranged, by which the counties were re-distributed in a manner more nearly proportionate to population, though far from satisfactory to the Western Members. The popular vote as to accepting the new Constitution, which amounted to 26,000 in favor, and 16,000 against, shows how considerable was the dissatisfaction. A serious effort made in the convention to take steps toward emancipation received little support save from

{23.} "merely" struck through.
{24.} "repress it" struck through.
{25.} "who forced belief in it" struck through.

the Western Members. The inhabitants of that region afterward, because of this settled{26} divergence of political character, were separated to form the State of West Virginia.

If the Virginia convention was of greater importance than that of other states then summoned, similar signs of the times in these others were not wanting. Mississippi in 1832 framed for itself a new Constitution, which provided for universal suffrage. Tennessee, in its new Constitution of 1834, abolished the property qualification for Governor and for members of the Assembly, and the free-hold qualification for voters. The suffrage was restricted to white men, but it was provided that no colored man should be disqualified who was competent under existing law to testify in Court against a white man. When, in 1836, a Constitution was framed for the new State of Arkansas, it, as a matter of course, provided for universal suffrage, and for the election of the Governor by the people. Other States, without summoning conventions to effect a comprehensive{27} revision of their Constitutions, passed amendments tending in the same direction as the provisions of which we have been speaking. In 1824, Georgia had provided for the election of its Governor by popular vote; North Carolina did the same in 1835; Maryland in 1837, after which time the old Southern practice that the Governor should be chosen by the General Assembly, continued in conservative Virginia and South Carolina alone. Other amendments effected by North Carolina in 1835, turned likewise in the direction insisted upon by the new democratic spirit.{28} Instead of the arrangement by which each county regardless of its size, was to be represented in the General Assembly by one Senator and two members of the House of Commons. It was now provided that the State should be re-districted for the choosing of Senators and that the counties should be represented in the House of Commons by members, whose number was to be proportionate to their Federal population. The suffrage, however, was not widened, the free-hold qualification of 50 acres being maintained; indeed, in one respect it was narrowed, for it was provided that no free person of colored blood, should vote. Before this time free colored men had enjoyed the franchise as citizens of North Carolina, a point of which prominent use was made in the dissenting opinion{29} in the famous Dred Scott case. In 1837, Maryland passed several highly important amendments. First, it abolished indirect voting for the Senate, and established a Senate consisting of two members from each county, chosen by the people for six years, and renewed by thirds every two years. Here

{26.} "unreasonable" struck through.
{27.} "reasonable" struck through.
{28.} "institution" struck through.
{29.} "party" struck through.

also the members of the House of Delegates were to be chosen by the counties in proportion to their Federal population. The Governor's council was abolished. He was to be chosen by the people alternately from the Eastern, Southern and Northwestern districts of the State. The pro-slavery feeling, which it was not found impossible to reconcile with the principles of the new democracy, found expression in the provision that slavery should never be abolished save by unanimous vote of two successive Legislatures.

At no later time between this and the Civil War were changes of equal moment effected simultaneously, and to the same purpose, in so great a number of Southern States. A general constitutional history of the South as a whole, cannot easily be traced farther, and the number of Southern States, which by 1845 had increased to fourteen, makes it tedious to follow the details of constitutional changes in each one individually. Moreover, from this time on, the interest of Southern history is to be found in the attitude of Southern States and Statesmen toward the Federal Constitution, and in political, rather than in constitutional developments. Even within the years of which we have been speaking, the rapid progress of democracy in the Southern States during the thirties, has not attracted anything like the same attention as the dramatic incident of the struggle of South Carolina against the Federal Government in the Nullification imbroglio[30] of 1832. The history of that conflict[31] is sufficiently well known to all students of the general history of the United States, and the same is true of the struggle a dozen years later for the acquisition of Texas. These two incidents both show in a striking degree the sensitiveness of Southern society to the needs and interests of the institution of slavery; for it is plain, in the one case as in the other, that this lay at the bottom of the constitutional or economic reasonings which were put forth. It is also interesting to observe that in 1832, the lead in the direction of Southern public opinion and political efforts had passed from the ancient dominion into the hands of the more hot-blooded and more energetic politicians of South Carolina. And perhaps we may say, that the history of the movement for the acquisition of Texas shows that a dozen years later the political control of the South was passing from the hands of South Carolina into that of the newer States farther to the West and South—Georgia, Alabama, Tennessee, and Mississippi—at any rate, was being shared by South Carolina with them. And among the leaders in those States, as the struggle between North and South grew more determined, Southern politics fell into the hands of men more and more extreme in their views, after the well known process which Thucydides so acutely pointed out long ago. Especially from 1852, when Clay and Calhoun and Webster simultaneously

{30.} "compromise" struck through.
{31.} "effort" struck through.

disappeared from the scene, we have throughout the South, the rule of a new generation,—the "fire-eating" politicians so-called, under whose guidance the South plunged into the vortex of Civil War.

This progress toward greater severity of devotion to sectional interests, toward more strict and complete party allegiance, is interestingly to be traced in the comparison of electoral votes in the South, in the Presidential elections from 1824 to 1860. In 1824 five Southern States gave their whole vote for Jackson, two for Clay and two for Crawford, while two others, dividing their vote, gave the major part of it to General Jackson. In 1828, under the influence of that wave of democracy which has been described, every Southern State but one, voted for the new popular hero, and even in the remaining one, he obtained five votes out of eleven. But in the elections from 1832 to 1840, inclusive, there was no instance in which the candidate most favored in the South, secured the votes of more than eight-elevenths of the Southern States, and in four out of five the South was almost evenly divided. But when we come to the election of 1852, we find the South suddenly "going solid" in support of the democratic candidate, Pierce carrying twelve States out of fourteen; and in 1856, Buchanan carried thirteen out of fourteen Southern States.

It may be interesting to dwell for a few minutes upon the party history of individual States. Only Virginia, Alabama, Missouri, Arkansas and Texas could boast of having in the elections from 1824 to 1860 never failed to cast a democratic vote. Mississippi was carried for Harrison in the great Whig uprising of 1840. Florida was carried for Taylor, the non-political candidate of the Whigs, in 1848. South Carolina, in 1836, when for the second time she proudly threw away her electoral vote, gave it to a North Carolina Whig senator, Willie P. Mangum. Georgia voted for Harrison in 1840, and for Taylor in 1848. Louisiana did the same, and in 1824 had cast two of her five votes for Adams and not for the hero of New Orleans. Naturally enough the border States, other than Virginia, had a more checkered career than the States farther to the Southward of which we have been speaking. North Carolina and Tennessee voted for the Whig candidates, Harrison, Clay and Taylor, in the three consecutive elections of 1840, 1844 and 1848. North Carolina and Tennessee, alone with Kentucky voted for Scott in 1852. In Kentucky the unbounded influence of Henry Clay carried the State for the Whigs, seven times out of eight in the elections from 1824 to 1852, inclusive, the exception being the tidal wave of 1828. It may be of interest to trace more fully the history of the course of Maryland in Presidential elections. In 1824 the State had eleven electoral votes; seven of these were given for Jackson, three for Adams and one for Crawford. In 1828, Adams received six votes and Jackson five. In 1832 Clay received five votes, Jackson three, and there were two vacancies. In the next four elections, the vote of the State was given completely to the Whigs, to Harrison in 1836 and 1840, to Clay in 1844, and to

Taylor in 1848. Though the State went for Pierce in 1852, and for Brecken-ridge in 1860, in 1856 it voted for Fillmore, and one may fairly speak of it as having, in that instance also, maintained the predilection for the Whig party, which had caused it to give a Whig vote in six out of the seven preceding elections.

Probably historians of the future will look back upon the history of the slavery question, as an episode in our national history,—an episode of enormous consequence, indeed, but still, properly speaking, an episode. It interrupted rather than essentially modified the development of this great Democratic republic. A foreign body had been lodged in our political sys-tem and increased and festered{32} until the acute surgery of Civil War was necessary to remove it. But then the natural evolution of American politics is resumed and it becomes possible for us to link our studies of the present time with studies of that remoter period before slavery became a dominant political force in the South. It is this which invests with a peculiar interest the story of the development of Southern institutions in those earlier times. Going back to those days, we are able in respect to them, to do justice to the Southern element in the growth of the American nation, in ways which have long been made difficult by the bitterness of the struggle between North and South during the period when the South was identified with the cause of slavery. There are many, many portions of Southern history still awaiting fair and thorough treatment. Here, upon the borders of North and South, the conditions are all favorable to the prosecution of this great and engaging task. I shall be happy if in these lectures I have succeeded in so far drawing attention to its interest and importance that some of those who have heard me, whether Northern or Southern, shall be induced to enter seriously upon the cultivation of this rich and largely unharvested field.

TM, Box 25, JP, DLC.

{32.} "flourished" struck through.

The American Acta Sanctorum

Jameson's election in 1907 to the presidency of the American Historical Association was significant in two ways. As the first professionally trained historian to be accorded this honor, Jameson symbolized the triumph of professional and academic concerns over amateur and popular interests within the organization. Consequently, his presidential address distinguished itself from its predecessors in marking out American religious history as a new field of investigation for academic scholars to pursue.

Jameson dismissed organized religion during his adolescence and young adulthood—he decided at fifteen that he did not "like Methodist shouting"—and did not consider himself to be a religious person.[1] But following the intention he expressed as a young instructor at the Johns Hopkins University to become a social historian, he focused on religious activity as a social phenomenon. In a lecture given before the Peabody Institute in Baltimore in 1891, on Virginia in the early national period, Jameson applauded religious belief as a bulwark of political conservatism.[2] At the University of Chicago he taught a graduate course in the spring of 1903 on the social organization of religion in American history.[3] In January 1906 he commissioned William H. Allison, a former student of Jameson's at the University of Chicago, to prepare for the Department of Historical Research a guide to religious manuscripts and archives in America.[4]

Jameson began to write his presidential address in the fall of 1907, soliciting from Hippolyte Delehaye, head of the Bollandist Fathers in Belgium, advice on sources to illustrate that the biographies of saints, published over many years by the Bollandists as the *Acta Sanctorum*, "indirectly contributed to the knowledge of the cultural history of the times to which they refer."[5]

NOTES

1. [JFJ], diary, January 24, [1875], AD, Box 1, JP, DLC.
2. [JFJ], "Virginian History, 1763–1812. IV. Virginia in Power, 1801–1812," AM, pp. 22–23, Box 28, JP, DLC.
3. University of Chicago, *Annual Register, July, 1901-July, 1902 with Announcements for 1902–3* (Chicago: University of Chicago, [1902]), p. 211.
4. [JFJ] to William H. Allison, January 13, 1906, TLc, Box 89, JP, DLC; [JFJ]

to Francis A. Christie, January 13, 1906, TLc, Box 71, JP, DLC. See also [JFJ] to Ernest C. Richardson, January 13, 1906, TLc, Box 124, JP, DLC.

5. [JFJ] to Hippolyte Delehaye, August 22, 1907, TLc, Box 61, JP, DLC; see also "Historians Gather Here Tomorrow," *Wisconsin State Journal*, December 26, 1907, p. 6, col. 4; "Madison Host for Noted Men," *Wisconsin State Journal*, December 27, 1907, p. 1, col. 6.

IT WAS NATURAL, and almost inevitable, that a large part of the literature of the Middle Ages should consist of the lives of the saints.[1] The world was a Christian world. In nearly all countries, most writers were ecclesiastics. In a society unreservedly Christian in theory, the main endeavor of clerical writing would surely be to persuade rough men so to live that at the end they might be added to the joyful company of the elect. The saints were those ascertained by universal judgment or papal declaration to inhabit already the mansions of felicity, where evermore they interceded for the members of the church militant. What more natural than that, for the edification of the latter, clerical authors should recount in detail the lives of those who had fought the good fight, had struggled with success up the thorny pathway, had proved that the sanctified life was not impossible to flesh and blood, even to the ardent flesh and insurgent blood of the Middle Ages? Accordingly we have multitudes of such biographies, whose popularity is attested by the great number of manuscript copies in which some of them have survived even to our own time.

It is well known that, in the relative paucity of materials for many portions of medieval history, these pious narratives have been put to frequent and effective use by historians. Sometimes, since "Even in a palace life may be led well," the saint whose life the historian finds among his materials was himself a man of high position, whose life is an important part of the political history of his country. Such was St. Louis, whose life by the Sire de Joinville is a classical and indispensable part of the record of French national development. Such in a less degree but in a darker country was St. Margaret of Scotland, whose life by Abbot Turgot tells us more of the reign of her husband King Malcolm and of the life of the Scottish nobility and court than we can learn for other parts of that dim century from all other sources put together. That the biographies of statesmen like St. Dunstan and St. Thomas of Canterbury, St. Bernard and St. Eligius, furnish invaluable materials to the historian, requires no demonstration. Other saints, though usually not thus immersed in secular affairs, have nevertheless become so involved in particular episodes that their memoirs become, for the moment, sources of prime importance. We should not willingly part with what we know of the ending of the Babylonish Captivity through the activities of St. Catherine of Siena; in the acts of Saint Demetrius the siege of Thessalonica by the Avars in 597 is so fully recounted as to give us our best details as to the military methods then employed in the siege and defence of fortified places.

Still more obvious and direct is the light which the hagiographers cast on European history when their subjects have borne a leading part in clerical

1. Annual address of the president of the American Historical Association, delivered at Madison, December 27, 1907.

or Christian movements. Biographies like those of St. Cyril and St. Martin, St. Patrick and St. Boniface, are often our chief materials for understanding the conversion of northern and western Europe to Christianity, surely one of the most memorable movements in human history. In the later ages, it is in the lives of St. Francis and St. Dominic and St. Ignatius that we may best study, in their early development, those three organizations which have proved the most potent agencies for maintaining vital Christianity in a world already nominally Christian. Of another variety are the lives or narratives of travelling saints, whose observations are among the chief materials for our knowledge of medieval geography.

Less obvious, but hardly less interesting, is the contribution which the lives of the medieval saints make, indirectly and without intention, to our knowledge of social history. Their authors wrote for purposes of edification and devotion. Often they gave little heed to accuracy of statement; often their clerical prepossessions so beclouded their minds that we cannot trust their testimony in the very matters about which they are most concerned to persuade us. Often, on the other hand, they furnish invaluable testimony about matters respecting which they had no thought of conveying information to any reader. They may falsify the portraits which occupy the foregrounds of their pictures, distort and make unreal the attitudes and actions which their minds are set on delineating; but the background is rendered with photographic fidelity, because depicted automatically and unconsciously. It is as certain that the biographer of St. Gervinus or St. Gingulphus will give us trustworthy data of the manners and customs of his time, as that the great Florentine artists will in the backgrounds of their Biblical pictures afford us veracious glimpses of the Tuscan landscape of the sixteenth century. They could not do otherwise. Thus from the hagiographers we often derive fragments of evidence in social history which we should seek in vain in the professed chronicles.

The pious biographer of the Christian missionary little knew that we should value his incidental touches respecting the heathen quite as much as his labored tribute to his hero, should eagerly take our first glimpse of pagan Sweden through the eyes of St. Ansgar, and treasure what little we can learn of conditions in heathen Germany, beyond the borders of civilization, from the life of St. Boniface written by a simple-minded companion. Nowhere does the student of folklore find fuller data as to pagan superstitions and practices in seventh-century Gaul than in the life of St. Eligius. As of the heathen, so also of those humble and inarticulate classes concerning whose life the chroniclers of the Middle Ages tell us so little. Froissart might think of none but lords and ladies; kings and barons, bishops and abbots, might fill the canvas of Matthew Paris. But the Kingdom of Heaven was a Christian democracy. The Northumbrian peasant, the merchant's son of Assisi, the shepherd girl of Lorraine, might become saints, and their biographies, especially the stories of their childhood and youth, will be sure to convey some precious indications as to the everyday life of the classes from which they sprang. Much of our best knowledge of the situation of the medieval Jews comes from the lives of those sainted children whose blood they were fabled to have shed as a means of keeping their unholy passover—St. William of Norwich or St. Simon of Trent or the holy child of La Guardia.

Since it was ordinarily requisite that sanctity should be attested by miracles, narratives of miracles play a large part in the lives of medieval saints. In these we find many of our best illustrations of medieval conditions and manners, and especially in the stories of miracles of healing. Such stories are full of instruction respecting medieval diseases and medicine, pestilence, manias and hygiene. How, for instance, should we know anything of the use of anaesthetics in the Middle Ages, if it were not recorded for us in the life of one of the saints that "many persons fall asleep after taking a draught of oblivion, which physicians call *letargion*, and are not sensible of incisions in their limbs, or sometimes of burning and cutting in the vital parts, inflicted on them in this state, and on waking from sleep are not aware of what has been done to them"?

Or again, to take the one point of the language used by educated people in England under the first Plantagenets, a question respecting which chroniclers are silent; we have our best indications in the hagiographers. William of Canterbury, in his life of St. Thomas Becket, gives a story concerning Helewisia de Morville, wife of one of St. Thomas's murderers, which represents her, a woman of Norman descent, one hundred years after the Conquest, as using English when calling for her husband's aid to punish a refractory Englishman. "Huwe of Morvill, war, war, Liulf haveth his sword ydrawen," she cries; English was her natural tongue. Again, in Reginald of Coldingham's life of the contemporary hermit St. Godric, it appears that the monks of Durham, though Latin was their ordinary language, conversed in English with St. Godric, who spoke French only by miracle. The Virgin taught St. Godric an English hymn, and this is written down in English in Reginald's book, which was intended for the reading of Hugh de Puiset, bishop of Durham. From a passage in the life of bishop Hugh of Lincoln by the abbot Adam of Eynsham, it appears that St. Hugh, who was a Burgundian by birth, did not understand the English dialects of Kent and Huntingdonshire, but that he was addressed by the natives as if it were naturally to be expected that he should understand what they said.

It would be easy to multiply illustrations of the varied and curious ways in which the lives of the saints light up for us the daily life of the Middle Ages. We see in the biography of St. Elizabeth of Hungary the domestic details of a Thuringian castle and of the hovels in the villages around it. In the life of

St. Thomas Aquinas we see the characteristics of hazing in medieval universities, and later, in that of St. Stanislaus Kostka, we observe how the same
practice was conducted in the college of the Jesuits at Vienna. In the life of
St. Etheldreda we perceive, not without instruction, that a great abbess of
the seventh century allowed herself the luxury of a hot bath only before the
great festivals of the Church, and then made it a demonstration of humility,
by first bathing her nuns with her own hands. The story of the Campanian
farmer complaining to St. Felix of the theft of his oxen, and menacing the
saint, if he does not make good the loss caused by his neglect, or, in the life
of St. Wulfstan, the story of the man who had killed another and "could not
on any terms obtain the friendship, nor by any payment get the pardon," of
the man's relatives, that of his ordering a nut-tree which overhung a church
to be cut down, and of the patron's resisting because he sometimes feasted
or played at dice under its shade, and that of the sacrist who was enjoined to
burn a candle before Wulfstan's tomb for a year, and to repeat fifteen psalms,
for having suffered a book which was in his custody to be stolen, the many
tales of funerals and of church-building, of almsgiving, of impiety—such
stories as these, though individually of little significance, yet when brought
together in sufficient quantity may help us to imagine and to reconstruct
those vanished states of society which the contemporary chroniclers take for
granted.

    Not the least interesting result of such study and combining is the light
which a nation's saints throw on a nation's character. "We live by admiration." However much a saint might feel himself to be a member and a champion of the universal church, he could not escape being a man of his own
country and age; and in the long run those whom time has selected as the
chief saints of a nation have come to that position through a congeniality with
the nation's traits that has brought them its steady and natural veneration. In
St. Louis we see the pattern of French chivalry, fearless and honorable, full
of courtesy and generosity. In Joan of Arc, beatified though not canonized,
we see typified the high spirit of the French nation, its military instinct, its
imaginative heroism, its enthusiasm for ideals, its ardor of self-sacrifice. In
St. Elizabeth of Thuringia we see the type of German domestic and practical
piety; in St. Ignatius and St. Francis Xavier the independence, the reticence,
and the organizing power of the Basque. St. Francis of Assisi, with his sensitive poetic imagination, fresh, simple and childlike, sympathetic with the
poor, joyful in all renunciation, could be no other than the best-loved saint of
the Italians. St. Teresa, ecstatic in her mystical union with God, yet gay and
natural and gifted in practical reforms and other dealings with this world,
is as distinctly the Spaniard as the impulsive, passionate, warm-hearted
Columba is the genuine Irish Celt, while in St. Cuthbert, buoyant, energetic,
the strong walker, the lover of the country and of boyish sports, we see

the genuine Northumbrian. (Where indeed but in Yorkshire would William Paternoster have been struck dumb as a punishment for walking alone with a little girl and not enjoying athletic sports?)

But enough has been said of the profit which historians have been able to draw from the stories of the European saints. It is time to turn to the specific subject of the present address. It has been entitled "The American Acta Sanctorum." Its purpose is to call attention to an analogous body of material which lies at the service of students of American history, and to suggest certain reflections as to its content and use. At first thought, obvious differences strike the mind. The lives of the European saints have for the most part been brought together in comprehensive collections, chief among them the *Acta Sanctorum* of the Bollandist fathers, a stately series of nearly seventy folio volumes, in which the original narratives have been treated with all the resources, and are accompanied with all the apparatus, of modern historical scholarship. The American "Acta Sanctorum," on the other hand, appears in the shape of numberless little books, shabby and faded, printed most often on provincial presses and seldom straying far from the place of origin. Each of them contains an artless biography, composed by some pious friend of the deceased clergyman or other saint, in which his spiritual struggles and triumphs, his labors in the vineyard or sufferings under persecution, are recounted for purposes of edification. Sometimes the little book is an autobiography; and there are a few instances of collective biography, like certain portions of Mather's *Magnalia*. But in general we have only the shabby little provincial books, first and only editions, raw materials of an "Acta Sanctorum," not to be brought together without some difficulty, and nowise provided with a Bollandist apparatus of critical or historical comment. Aside from such differences of form, it must be admitted, as a matter of course, that there are differences of character between the mass of medieval literature we have been considering and any body of Protestant hagiology, mostly lives of married clergymen and laymen living in free modern states; and also that the historian's need of such narratives is less urgent when he is dealing with a period much subsequent to the invention of the printing-press than when he occupies himself with the Dark Ages.

Nevertheless, it may fairly be maintained that the American historical scholar can draw from these ill-printed little memorials of local piety much the same varieties of benefit which his European brother derives from the imposing folios of the *Acta Sanctorum*. In the first place, not a few of our American saints have borne an important part in public affairs. The second book of *Magnalia*, Turell's life of Benjamin Colman, the memoirs of Presidents Wheelock, Stiles and Dwight, of Manasseh Cutler and Bishop Leonidas Polk, are the lives of persons who exerted great and continuous influence on secular movements in their day and generation. Others impinged upon the circle of political life for lesser periods, or afford us occasional but valued glimpses of its events. The autobiography of Rev. Thomas Shepard casts most precious light upon the early migration to Massachusetts Bay, the life of Rev. David Caldwell upon the proceedings of the North Carolina convention of 1789, that of President Manning upon the devious course of Rhode Island in the Continental Congress. One of the best accounts of the sea-fight between the frigates *United States* and *Macedonian* is to be found in an autobiographical book by Samuel Leach. Less important, yet of genuine interest, are the curious account which John Churchman, a Quaker preacher, gives of his appearing before the Assembly of Pennsylvania in 1748 to dissuade it from the support of warlike measures; his narrative of the treaty with Teedyuscung and other Indians at Easton in 1757, at which he was present; and the glimpses which saintly John Richardson gives us of Penn and Baltimore and Lady Baltimore in 1702.

As in the parallel case of the European saints, however, we naturally find fuller light upon those transactions which would fall more distinctly within the usual scope of clerical endeavor. The life of John Woolman is surely one of the classics of our colonial literature, marked by all the beauty of spirit and of phrase which elevation, serenity, the habit of meditation, and intimacy with the Bible could so often confer on the writings of the Quakers; but it is also one of the classics of the early anti-slavery movement, and one of the best and best-known examples of the class which we are describing. The life of good Anthony Benezet, the journals of Bishop Coke, are other examples. The anti-slavery movement is illustrated by passages in a host of such biographies; the temperance movement by others. The essential data regarding the formation in 1826 of the Virginia Society for the Promotion of Temperance, of its local auxiliaries, and of the Georgia State Temperance Society some two years later, are best sought in the biography of Elder Abner W. Clopton.

We have also our saintly travellers, whose roamings over our vast continent have enriched the history of American geography with some of its best materials. What William Rubruk and John of Plano Carpini were to medieval geography, that surely were Marquette and Jogues and DeSmet, Father Francisco Garcés and Father Junípero Serra to the exploration of the United States. But upon hagiology of this class it is superfluous to dwell in this city, in which was prepared for publication Dr. Thwaites's splendid series of the *Jesuit Relations*.[2]

{2.} Reuben Gold Thwaites, ed., *The Jesuit Relations and Allied Documents*, 73 vols. (Cleveland: Burrows Brothers Co., 1896–1901). Thwaites (1853–1913), a newspaper editor and historian, succeeded Lyman C. Draper as secretary and superintendent of the State Historical Society of Wisconsin in 1887 and served until his death. In addition to *The Jesuit Relations*, Thwaites edited the *Original Journals of the Lewis and Clark Expedition*, as well as other volumes on early American history. See Frederick J.

But, as in the European case, many of the most interesting and most valuable bits of historical knowledge which we can obtain from our American saints' lives are conveyed to us by the author without his intending to do anything of the sort. Contemporary biographer or autobiographer, he pictures unconsciously, so far as he pictures it at all, the social *milieu* which he saw before him. His object is to edify, to bring about the conversion of precious souls. If we obtain from his pages anything else than our edification or conversion, it is *"corban, that is to say a gift"*; it has been no part of his purpose to furnish materials for the historian. All the more certain is it that what we thus obtain will be trustworthy evidence, except in so far as some general prepossession of the preacher, for which we can make allowance, shall enter in to darken his picture of the actual unregenerate world.

In one particular our analogy will be found defective. The Protestant world having assumed that since the time of the apostles the mediation of the saints has not had the power of effecting miracles, we shall not find in our American Protestant lives an exact parallel to those miraculous tales which have so large a place in medieval hagiology, and which furnish us so many interesting glimpses into the lives of those mostly humble persons for whose benefit the miracles were wrought. But after all the defect is fairly well supplied. If the Protestant biographer is not disposed to maintain that his hero could work miracles, yet he knows well that God defends his elect, and often interposes through "special providences" to protect clergymen of his favorite denomination. Thus, though miracles performed at the saint's tomb or by his relics are absent, the pages of American hagiology bristle with special providences, by means of which we often penetrate into the obscurity of colonial or frontier life.

As the saints of old, and their biographers, lead us within sight of the heathen of Sweden or of Saxony, or as through the eyes of St. Francis Xavier we view the natives of Goa and Travancore, of the Moluccas and Japan, so by means of the American missionaries we see the Indians of the seventeenth and eighteenth centuries. It is extraordinary, how large a part of our knowledge of their characters and their sociology is derived from the lives or narratives of such men—of Eliot and Brainerd, of the Jesuits of the north and the Franciscans of the southwest. The same is true of the life of the frontier. Few travellers show us so much of the actual conditions of backwoods existence as the itinerant missionaries—of the clearings and the log-cabins, the rude agriculture and the perpetual fevers, the camp-meetings and the Indian depredations, the fraternal kindness and the limitless hospitality. Best of all for our purposes are the Methodist circuit-riders, keen, hearty men, whose outdoor life kept them healthy in mind and body, and whose grasp on the

---

Turner, *Reuben Gold Thwaites: A Memorial Address* (Madison: State Historical Society of Wisconsin, 1914).

real world had never been relaxed by education. As one of them says, who at the risk of his life had ridden the Clarksburg circuit during the Indian wars preceding Wayne's treaty, "To speak in backwoods style, they appeared to be surrounded by a kind of holy 'knock-'em-down' power, that was often irresistible." They were not forever feeling their spiritual pulses and doubting of their own salvation, like some anaemic graduates of theological seminaries whose biographers have deemed them very precious vessels because of the very traits that made them useless; nor were they forever walking in visions, like so many of the Quaker itinerants, whose books are often so beautiful and to the historical inquirer so disappointing. Stout-hearted, downright, muscular, practical, the circuit-rider faced the actual world of the frontier, and saw it clearly. If like Peter Cartwright or Henry Smith he leaves behind him a description of what he saw, we are much the gainers.

But even in the older parts of the country, there have been regions or classes of which we know little unless by chance we find some faint record in the early life of one who rose out of them to saintship. We know well the leaders of Virginia politics and society at the time of the Revolution— every important thought and sentiment of Washington and Jefferson, Madison and Henry. But were it not for what little we can glean from the lives of Rev. Devereux Jarratt and Elder Barton W. Stone, should we know one fact, aside from genealogy and county records, about the poor people of Bath Parish and Pittsylvania County, their sentiments and their opinions? If it were a question of Boeotia or of early Wessex, we should treasure every such fact with minute care. Why should we not treasure with equal zeal the little glimpses into life on West River which are afforded us by the memoirs of Thomas Story, or the quaint pictures which his fellow-Quaker John Richardson gives us of Bermuda and its governor, of Nantucket society at the beginning of the eighteenth century and of its Deborah, Mary Starbuck?

Not less interesting than the occasional glimpses which we obtain into the lives of out-of-the-way communities, or of inarticulate classes not represented in literature, are many passages in the lives of Catholic or Protestant worthies who were not of English descent. They paint for us the obscure processes of Americanization. Quaintly expressed, but typical of American conditions, is the religious experience of Brother Crum, a German Methodist in Maryland. He said, "I prayed in Dutch; I am Dutch; and must get converted in Dutch. These are all English people, and they got converted in English. I prayed and prayed in Dutch, but could not get the blessing. At last I felt willing to get converted in English or Dutch, as the Lord pleased. Then the blessing came, and I got converted in English."

It would not be easy to enumerate all the little ways in which the lives of the American saints may enlarge our knowledge of the social background, the substantial warp of our American fabric. Many saints studied at the small colleges of our early days, many taught in country schools or academies; we can learn something from them, incidentally, of the progress of education. They show us something of slavery. Anthony Jefferson Pearson is warned by his father and, his biographer thinks, might well have been anxious in his own mind, lest his connection with the African Sabbath School in the little town in Tennessee where he is attending college might injure him in the estimation of others. He prayerfully tosses up a coin—it is the year 1831, when extreme reformers had their fullest swing—to determine whether his course through this vale of tears, this solemn period of probation, shall be marked by the moderate use of tea and coffee, or whether he shall confine himself strictly to water. It is not without interest to learn that even in 1817, at Augusta, Georgia, it was already customary for the piano to be drowned by conversation at all tea-parties; and the street cries of early Boston are illustrated by the imitations of them with which a youthful saint awakes from sleep and shows to the ear of her anxious parent and biographer that she has passed the crisis of a dangerous illness. We know what our sensations are on seeing a peach-orchard. What were those of Elder Abner W. Clopton in 1828? "Seeing a flourishing peach-orchard by the road, he felt so sensibly on the consequences which it would produce, that he entered the house of the owner, and warned him, or rather his lady, of the danger of the temptation—expressing his fears that the fruit of that orchard would bring her to widowhood, and her babes to orphanage. In two years his fears were realized." To the elder's mind, a peach-orchard had but one meaning; in that meaning lies the explanation of the western insurrection of 1794.

More broadly speaking, the distilled essence of a multitude of these saintly biographies is able, as in the case of the European nations, to show us something of national character. Certain traits which are characteristic or frequent in the lives of medieval saints are absent or curiously infrequent in those of America. They are not records of austerities and macerations. The Methodist circuit-rider came eating and drinking. The chickens fled at his approach. The American saint has lived his life in the world, not in a monastery. His piety has been a Protestant piety, looking toward edification and sanctification of the human being much more than toward the ceaseless adoration of God, contemplative resignation to his will, mystical absorption in his essence. We find few ecstasies like those of St. Teresa. There is a striking want of poetic or imaginative touches. The American saint may be capable of exalted self-sacrifice, but he does not ceremoniously take Lady Poverty to be his bride. He shows us no parallel to St. Francis preaching to the birds, or singing the praises of the Lord responsively with the nightingales of Assisi. He lives in the dry air of this western world, and shares its active, practical, work-a-day life. He has little depth of thought, little subtlety of theology. The triumphant debates with opponents, which his biographer so often records with admiration, are triumphs of Philistine smartness rather than of candor or elevation or spiritual discernment. But, like his nation, he makes up for lack of depth by dexterity, versatility and practical efficiency. He knows what to do in an emergency, and carries into the life of the circuit-rider, the missionary or the reformer that quickness of invention bred in generations of Americans by the life of the forest or the isolated farmstead. Nowhere in literature will you find a completer manifestation of the universal Yankee, inventive, resourceful, brimming over with energy and enterprise, than in the life of the Rev. Cyrus Hamlin, missionary in Constantinople. Not for him the mere preaching of sermons. He must be up and doing. To give work to his Armenian converts in the time of the Crimean war, he organizes great bakeries which supply the allied armies. He enters into the laundry business, and, when his protégées are halted a moment by the indescribable condition of the soldiers' clothing, he devises machinery to enable them to perform their task. He invents the best cholera mixture ever known in Turkey. He establishes factories wherein some of his people can support themselves by making stove-pipes, instructs others in the manufacture of rat-traps, invents a new kind of coffee-mill, and meantime maintains a theological seminary and founds a college.

The American saints have also imbibed from their native atmosphere a cheerful and hopeful spirit, which not even the extreme rigors of ultra-Calvinism can wholly destroy. They know themselves to be members of a rising empire, in which the common man shall have opportunities he has nowhere enjoyed before. They feel themselves to be in the full stream of progress, and with lusty courage and enthusiasm lay their hands upon the oar. They are like Andrew Marvell's exiles in the "remote Bermudas":

> Thus sung they in the English boat
> A holy and a cheerful note,
> And all the while, to guide their chime,
> With falling oars they kept the time.

Not less characteristic is it that the sense of progress is so often, at any rate among the saints of the nineteenth century, expressed numerically. The dry American mind loves figures. Chiefly occupied with measurable material tasks—the subduing of the wilderness, the bridging of rivers, the laying of railroads, the growing of crops—the American has acquired an inveterate interest in statistic, in the making of a "record," and carries it with him into other than practical concerns. He thinks arithmetically concerning his church, his paintings and his sports. Those who compare American athletics to those of Greece forget that the Greek had no stop-watch, no accurate means of measuring time. Does the American actually love out-of-door sports, the pleasure of the pathless woods, the "breezy call of incense-breathing morn," or does he love numerical records of out-of-door sports? Certainly the crowd in front of the newspaper's tabular bulletin-board seems not less intent than the crowd on the "grand-stand." Certainly there is a deep and widespread interest in the framing of "all-America" nines and elevens, one of the most disinterestedly ideal of all mathematical employments. In a similar spirit, Rev. Peter Cartwright and his fellows do not often fail to let us know the number of those converted at each camp-meeting.

It would be wrong to exaggerate the interest of these little lives of long-forgotten worthies, or the amount which they can yield to the student of American social history or of national psychology. In most of them there are long arid stretches. Most of them are written in the *"patois* of Canaan,"* in the set phrases of obsolete theologies, making difficult or tedious reading for the modern inquirer. If one ventures to insist a little upon their utility to the younger investigator, it is from a sense of a real danger which besets the latter's pathway, the danger of confining himself to the constitutional and political history of America, now so easy to study, and from a consequent desire to urge upon him the claims which American religious history may make upon one who wishes a full understanding of the American character and spirit. One would not wish to trench upon the field so excellently covered by last year's presidential address before this association; and indeed it is obvious that the study of the social history and national psychology of the United States may and must be approached by many pathways.[3] Yet there is something to be said for the contention that, of all means of estimating American character from American history, the pursuit of religious history is the most complete. If we approach the problem through the history of American literature we are in constant danger of forgetting how small the literary class is and always has been. Even if we include the readers as well as the producers, we cannot assume that the traits which are revealed by our literary writings are necessarily those of the nation at large, the obscure, unreading, unprinting majority. The cleverest of books upon our literary history seems often to make defective estimates of our national character for want of access to the minds of these inarticulate ones. What is true of literature, is even more true of philosophy. If we turn to the history of the plastic arts in America, how brief, how limited has been their course. Not through them, surely, can the American spirit be made to yield up its total secret, be appreciated in its general extent. The history of American music is an equally slender stream. Little of American life beyond that of recent years and large cities can be said to be reflected in it. How slight a part music played in the first one hundred and fifty years of our colonial existence, even in the most intelligent of our towns, may be seen by a delicious passage in one of our saintly biographies, Turell's life of Dr. Benjamin Colman. The worthy doctor makes a series of proposals to his Boston congregation and others, advocat-

{3.} Simeon Eben Baldwin (1840–1927) was president of the American Historical Association in 1906. His presidential address, delivered December 26, 1906, was titled "Religion Still the Key to History" and was published in the *AHR* 12 (January 1907): 219–43.

ing that the old psalm-book should be enriched by more modern additions. Among these proposals we find the following, which paints to the life the musical abilities of a Boston congregation, thirty years before the Revolution;

> 8. That with respect such Psalms as Dr. Watts has adapted only to a Tune which our Congregation cannot sing, either we resolve upon learning and bringing into Use among us said Tune, or that a new Metre of such Psalms, or part of them, be attempted as near as we can turn them to his Stile and Manner.

He who would understand the American of past and present times, and to that end would provide himself with data representing all classes, all periods, and all regions, may find in the history of American religion the closest approach to the continuous record he desires. Not that all or even most Americans have been religious, but there have been religious men and women in every class, every period, every subdivision of America, and multitudes of them have left individual or collective records of their thoughts and ways and feelings. Millions have felt an interest in religion where thousands have felt an interest in literature or philosophy, in music or art. Millions have known little of any book save one, and that one the most interesting of religious books, the most influential, the most powerful to mould and transform. Doubtless they were occupied mainly with the tasks of daily life; their achievements in these, and the conflicts of economic interest which accompanied them, may be reduced to solid and instructive statistics, without which social history may become unsubstantial and vague. But no view is truthful that leaves out of account the ideals which animated these toiling millions, the thoughts concerning the universe and man which informed their minds. The Spanish trooper held himself to be ever in the hand of the God of Israel, who guided his chosen people by pillars of fire and of cloud. The Puritan farmer sighted his promised land from the top of Pisgah, and thought of no similitude for his Indian warfare but the smiting of the Hittites and the Jebusites. The imagination of the pioneer mother, making with her baby the weary journey through the western wilderness, had no parallel to dwell on but that of the Flight into Egypt.

Moreover, the history of religion in America holds a peculiarly close relation to the general history of the American spirit from the fact that here, more than elsewhere, the concerns of churches have been managed by the laity or in accordance with their will. If ever anywhere ecclesiastical history can be rightly treated as consisting solely of the history of ecclesiastics, certainly it has not been so in the United States. It has reflected the thoughts and sentiments, not of a priestly caste, but of the mass of laymen. An acute English observer, Bishop Coke, speaking of the able debates he heard at the conference of the Methodist preachers of America in 1792, says, "Throughout the debates they conducted themselves as the servants of the people, and therefore never lost sight of them on any question."

Let us take a few examples. In the psychic life of Europe we recognize the middle portion of the eighteenth century as a time of heightened emotionality. We see this in the *Sturm und Drang* literature of Germany, in Rousseau and the Methodists, in the wave of national feeling that swept William Pitt to supreme power. In treating the European history of that period, we should never think of ignoring phenomena so significant. Ought we then, when we are dealing with the same age in the history of a country which was practically without literature, art or nationality, to ignore the Great Awakening, or to treat it otherwise than as the most important and significant event of its time?

Fifty years later we hear in the spiritual life of Europe another modulation of key, the Romantic Movement. The richer culture of the Old World enables us to trace it in many manifestations, in the shifting of ground from rationalism to mysticism, in the rapid heightening of national feeling, in the abrupt transition from *The Botanic Garden* of Dr. Erasmus Darwin to *Childe Harold* and *The Battle of the Baltic*. Such a wave of feeling, we may be sure, could not fail to transmit itself across the Atlantic, and to be manifested in some form in the America of 1800, still colonially dependent upon the European mind. We do indeed trace a slight romantic movement in American literature, a faint heightening of American patriotism, slowly mustering courage for the War of 1812. But if we would seek the most powerful and pervasive manifestation of the movement, the best analogy which the poverty of American culture permitted, we can find it nowhere else than in the wonderful religious revivals which in those years swept through America, and especially through the forest camp-meetings of the non-literary West. It is a narrow-minded student who pursues with eager interest every tortuous move of Jeffersonian diplomacy but disdains to read of these vital movements, or who fails to perceive how closely and with what equal steps the really great political advances of the Jeffersonian era are accompanied by parallel movements in theology and religion, the growth of the Methodists, Unitarians and Disciples, with their heightened sense of the dignity of human nature and of the importance of fraternal union. Equally limited is the mind which can not find in the early story of Mormonism a prime source of illumination upon the actual mentality of the obscure villagers of 1830.

With a little hesitation, one may take a pregnant example from the history of the latest period. The most interesting American historical biography published in recent years, and one deserving an important place in our "Acta Sanctorum," is the life of Mrs. Mary Eddy.[4] A plea for the study of Ameri-

---

{4.} See Georgine Milmine, "Mary Baker G. Eddy: The Story of Her Life and the History of Christian Science," which appeared in twelve installments during 1907

can religious history by others than young theologues may well take account of the movement which she represents. We have here no concern with the validity or invalidity of its theological or philosophical basis. We are only to consider it, with all proper respect, as a phenomenon in the American history of the last twenty-five years. Great pains have been expended in the effort to separate fact from baseless tradition in the early years of Mohammedanism. We welcome with enthusiasm those wonderful discoveries of early Manichaean manuscripts through which the Prussian Academy's recent explorations in Turkestan have laid before us the development of another great modification of Christianity. But here we have growing up among us, in the full light of day, a new religion with a million adherents, threatening in the early years of the twentieth century as grave an invasion of the domain of traditional Christianity as Joachim of Flora and the Eternal Gospel threatened in the early years of the thirteenth; and how many young doctors of philosophy, concerned with recent history, have made a thorough study of the movement? Yet he who cannot explain it to himself must not pretend that he understands the American society of the last quarter-century—or at any rate the bourgeois society of our long-settled communities; since it is from the bourgeois portions of settled society that new religions are apt to spring.

We are accustomed to adjourn such explanations by saying that it is too soon to make them; and no doubt this is true. Yet certain lines of remark seem already open. We can measure the distance we have come. It is a long remove from the tribal god of the early Puritans, the vertebrate Jehovah, the self-conscious martinet of a troubled universe, to the vague and circumambient deity of Mrs. Eddy, the fluid source of therapeutic beneficence. But it marks a long transition in our social life. The early colonist, his life environed with dangers and studded with marked events, must have on high a conscious and watchful sovereign, ever ready to protect the body and to chasten the soul by drastic interpositions. At the other extreme,

> We sit here in the Promised Land
> That flows with Freedom's honey and milk.

Few of us are ever in personal danger. We have had years of extraordinary prosperity. The comfortable middle-class society of our settled communities has had little occasion to feel the heart-gripping stresses of danger and calamity and remorse. In such a soft society, illness and physical pain easily come to seem the chief evils of life. Consciousness of nerves and conscious-

---

and 1908 in *McClure's Magazine.* Eddy (1821–1910) founded the Christian Scientists' Association in 1876 and three years later chartered the Church of Christ, Scientist. In 1883 she began publishing the *Journal of Christian Science,* which attracted a national following.

ness of the processes of digestion come to take nearly the place which consciousness of sin held in the mind of the seventeenth-century American.
Such a society, the product of peace and industrial prosperity, is sure to
be seized with great power by a religion which cheerfully ignores evil and
which, whatever its claims upon superior intellects, presents itself to the
mass of bourgeois minds as primarily a religion of healing.

Why do not Americans study more intently the age of the Antonines?[5]
There they will find a state of society singularly resembling our own—a
world grown prosperous and soft and humane with long-continued peace
and abounding industrial development, a population formed by the mixture
of all races, in which the ancient stock still struggles to rule and to assimilate,
but is powerless to preserve unimpaired its traditions, a mushroom growth
of cities, a universal passion for organization into industrial unions and fraternal orders, a system in which woman has exceptionally full equality with
man, a society in which the newly rich occupy the centre of the stage, offending the eye with the vulgar display of brute wealth yet pacifying the mind
and heart with the record of numberless and kindly benefactions. In this soft
and genial society, the benign product of world-wide peace and growing
wealth, we may find analogies for almost every phenomenon of present-
day American religion, from the sumptuous ritual of historic churches to
the crude deceptions of vagrant astrologers, from the "timbrelled anthems"
of the Salvation Army to the viscous rhetoric of Christian Science. Isis and
Mithra and the pagan origins of Gnosticism can help us to understand the
swarming religions of Chicago and New York, and through them the society
to which they belong.

To the young teacher or investigator, to whom such discourses as this are
principally or most hopefully addressed, such illustrations may seem far-
fetched and inconclusive. Possibly they are so. But it may be hoped that at
least the main theses of this address may nevertheless receive on the part of
such hearers a careful consideration. In every other period of recorded time,
we know that the study of religion casts valuable light on many other aspects
of history. Why should it be otherwise with the religious history of America?
Unless we are content to confine ourselves to the well-worn grooves of constitutional and political history, and to resign to sciences less cautious than
history the broad story of American culture, why should we not seek light
from every quarter? Most of all let us seek it from the history of American
religion, in the sum total an ample record, even though in parts we have to
compose it like a mosaic from fragments of unpromising material.

AHR 13 (January 1908): 286–302.

{5.} Dynasty of the Roman emperors Antonius Pius, Marcus Aurelius, and Com-
modus, A.D. 138–192. *Cambridge Ancient History*, 12 vols. (Cambridge, England: Cambridge University Press, 1936), 11:325–92.

American Blood in 1775

Jameson first delivered the lecture that follows at Brown University on February 25, 1915, when the university was celebrating its sesquicentennial, but his exploration of the role of ethnicity in American history reflected a lifelong preoccupation as both a scholar and a politically engaged individual with the potential for consensus in a pluralistic democracy.[1] In a series of lectures he delivered on colonial Virginia in 1892, Jameson argued that whites in Virginia, who were united by race and ethnicity, if not by class, perceived that they had opportunities for social mobility and that this racial and ethnic solidarity explained the growth of democracy there from colonial times.[2] In contrast, he explained in his essay "The Origin of Political Parties in the United States" that in colonial New York and Pennsylvania, populated by Germans, Dutch, and other diverse ethnic groups, political relations were difficult, and violent conflicts often erupted between ethnic groups contending for power.[3] His lectures on the American Revolution as a social movement, delivered at Barnard College in 1895, stated that Anglo-Saxons with a deep-rooted respect for tradition and stability prevented that conflict from ending in the tyrannicide of the French Revolution.[4]

Although Jameson largely abandoned his own scholarly career when he came to the Carnegie Institution of Washington in 1905, the influence of ethnicity as an element in history remained a central concern. Believing that the social as well as the political history of America could be enhanced from an investigation of documents in European archives, Jameson emphasized the value of archives in Switzerland as a source of information on immigration.[5]

Because he was "rather fond" of the lecture and had to earn additional money to send his daughter Katrina through college, Jameson offered to present it on two other occasions: in early 1921 at the University of Chicago and during the spring of 1928 at Duke University.[6] Jameson also presented the lecture to the Maryland chapter of the Colonial Dames of America and modified it to interest this audience.[7]

NOTES

1. On the presentation of this lecture at Brown, see Marcus W. Jernegan to JFJ, October 3, 1914, ALS, Box 280, AHA Records, DLC; and Walter C. Bronson to JFJ, March 19, 1915, TLS, Box 63, JP, DLC.

2. [JFJ], "Virginian History, 1763–1812," lectures delivered at the Peabody Institute, [Baltimore], Jan. 26, 28, Feb. 2, 4, 1892: I, "Virginia and the Revolution, 1763–1783," p. 11, AM, Box 28, JP, DLC.

3. JFJ, "The Origin of Political Parties in the United States," this volume, pp. 49–51, 60.

4. JFJ, "The Revolution as a Social Movement. I. Whigs and Tories," [1895], TM, Box 25, JP, DLC.

5. See Jameson's preface to Albert B. Faust, *Guide to the Materials for American History in Swiss and Austrian Archives* (Washington, D.C.: Carnegie Institution of Washington, 1916), p. iii.

6. JFJ to Francis A. Christie, March 22, 1920, TLc, Box 71, JP, DLC; [JFJ] to Andrew C. McLaughlin, December 4, 1920, TLc, Box 110, JP, DLC; [William K. Boyd] to JFJ, February 8, 1927, TLc; and JFJ to Boyd, February 11, 1927, TLS, both in William K. Boyd Papers, NcD.

7. It has not been determined when the lecture to the Colonial Dames was given.

THE OLDER WRITERS upon rhetoric, from Quintilian to Quackenbos, unite in assuring the deliverer of a public address that he may properly begin it by defending his choice of a subject. I must confess to a little difficulty in defending the precise wording of my theme, for the present age dislikes metaphors in titles; but one would not say "American Nationality in 1775," when perhaps there was not an American nationality, and one would not say "the American race," lest one be thought to be talking of the Red Indians, and so the form chosen is "American Blood in 1775," the intention being to discuss the racial or national or linguistic elements of which the population of the United Colonies was at that time composed.

Apart from questions of phraseology, the subject, I hope, needs little defense. It can seem unimportant only to those to whom the whole history of America seems to have little importance. If there are such persons, we may presume that they are not here present. Yet I can well believe that it is true of many persons here present—because it is true of most persons in any American Assemblage—that they are far from having a just and full conception of the enormous importance of American history, the almost unexampled place it holds in the history of the human race. Let me quote the words of one who will not be thought to have had either the professional prepossessions of a student of United States history or the national prejudices of an American. Forty years ago the greatest of English naturalists, with that quiet deliberation which added so much weight to his utterances, said of the essential process in our history, "Looking to the distant future, I do not think that the Rev. Mr. Zincke takes an exaggerated view when he says, 'All other series of events—as that which resulted in the culture of mind in Greece, and that which resulted in the empire of Rome—only appear to have purpose and value when viewed in connection with, or rather as subsidiary to' . . . the great stream of Anglo-Saxon emigration to the west." [1]

It can hardly be provincial arrogance for us to hold an opinion which Darwin held. In respect to numbers of civilized, educated, and prosperous mankind, this is already the greatest of nations. Its total wealth is already much greater than that of any other. The natural resources and opportunities which it has in reserve as means of future progress are still superior to those which lie in the pathway of other nations. It is in truth the most powerful political aggregation the world has ever seen, much more powerful than that Roman Empire which cast its shadow across a thousand years of human history. Though the rate of its advance may not so greatly surpass that of other countries in the future as it has in the past, it needs no power and warmth of imagination, but only plain arithmetic, to discover that on the stage of

{1.} See Charles Darwin, *The Descent of Man, and Selection in Relation to Sex* (1871; reprint ed., Princeton: Princeton University Press, 1981), p. 179.

the twentieth century and perhaps of its successors the American nation is to play the leading part, that this wide domain of ours is to be the chief home, the chief workshop, the chief exercise-ground of civilized mankind, and that the story of our national development and its causes will become, and therefore perhaps has already become, the main concern of history.

If these things are so, it needs no apology that one should try to discover the composition of this chosen people at the time when it began its career as an independent nation. In a sense, it is true, this is to select but one point in an age-long process. The leading fact of American history is that, early in the seventeenth century, a body of people mostly English settled on the edge of the largest piece of unoccupied land in the temperate zones, and has continuously proceeded, aided by constant reinforcements from Europe, to go up against it and possess it. This has been the leading fact not simply because it included a ceaseless process of economic conquest and material expansion, but also because it included a ceaseless process of free immigration, the gradual forming of a nation by voluntary transfer of allegiance, by self-selection. Generation after generation the attraction of free, wide, and hopeful America has been at work on the dense human layers of Europe, breaking up their stratification and drawing myriads of the ambitious to a promised land; and that promised land was not merely a New World in a physical sense but a new human world, where out of the old European materials a new humanity was unceasingly in process of formation.

Yet there is a sense in which we may be justified in selecting one particular epoch of time for examining the composition of this ever-changing American people. Not only is it true that, from 1775 on, the destinies of America were placed in her own hands, but it is also true that there began just then a long period, during which the rate of outside reinforcement of her population became less than either before or after. From the opening of the Revolution to the close of the second war with Great Britain, white immigration was relatively insignificant, and even down to 1832, there was never a year when it is thought to have amounted to eight per cent. of the natural increase of our population. Thus the first sixty years of our existence as an independent nation form a period of something approaching stability in the composition of our people. That period contrasts strongly with the sixty years preceding, which had been marked by a transmarine migration of unusual proportions. It contrasts still more strongly, on the other hand, with the last seventy years, which have seen a transmarine migration, prevailingly German, Irish, and British in the first thirty-five years, prevailingly Italian, Slavonic, and Hebrew in the last thirty-five, so prodigious as to constitute the greatest movement of population which human history records.

I do not pause to dwell upon the good fortune which left this American people substantially unchanged in composition during the first sixty years of its existence as a separate nation. Those were the formative years, extending from the breach with Great Britain through the period of making of new constitutions for states and nation, through the first formation of national parties, through the struggle to escape from complications with Europe during the great European wars, through the final vindication of nationality by the second war with Great Britain, through the growth of democracy, the rule of Jackson, and the development of an American industrial policy. It was our period of adolescence and education. At the end of it, our institutions were fully formed, and no influx of newcomers thereafter could essentially alter them. There are therefore solid reasons for taking the year 1775 when attempting to estimate the American composite at a time when its proportions were especially significant.

When the embattled farmers took their stand at Concord bridge and "fired the shot heard round the world," the Thirteen Colonies apparently contained a population of about two million whites and half a million negroes, nine-tenths of whom were slaves. In 1915 the population of our present area must be just about 100,000,000, of whom 11,000,000 are colored and 89,000,000 white. Of these 89,000,000 whites, the proportion descended from the two million white who were here in 1775 may be computed at 37,000,000. This may be done by the use of three different methods which, worked out independently, give approximately the same result. Fifty-two millions, on the other hand, represent the contribution to our present white population made by those who have arrived in America since 1775. In other words, about three-sevenths of our present white blood springs from the Americans of 1775, while four-sevenths represents immigrants into independent America and the descendants of such immigrants. The older stock, however, as we have seen, had the opportunity to prescribe the forms or moulds in which the total life was to be run.

But what was this older stock? What was in 1775 the composition of American blood? That it was prevailingly English is well known. Some there are who would persuade us that all other elements, whatever their numerical magnitude, were in actual effect insignificant, such was the power of assimilation with which the predominant English element absorbed them into its mass. I do not myself read American history thus; but at the present time, at all events, I am not considering these imponderable relations of the spirit, but only the measurable and numerical facts of demography, stated as exactly as the data permit. The data, it must be remembered, share the grave imperfections of all American statistics which antedate the first federal census, the census of 1790.

From such data as we can gather, it would appear that, of the two millions of white population in 1775, somewhat less than 1,200,000, somewhat less than three-fifths were of English stock. Eighty-odd years before, at the time of the Revolution of 1689, the proportion had no doubt been larger, four-fifths or five-sixths, in a population only a tenth as large, say 215,000. But wave after wave of non-English as well as of English immigration had swept across the Atlantic since that time.

The English immigration may, so to speak, be taken for granted. Little of it had of late come to New England, indeed, where the English population of 1775 was mostly descended from those twenty thousand that had come over, in one great swarm from the English hive, before 1643, when the outbreak of the English Civil War stayed further departures. The numerous progeny of those twenty thousand early comers had so filled the profitable part of the New England area that in the eighteenth century but a small part of the additional immigration came hither, and New England, to some advantage and to some disadvantage, remained overwhelmingly English in stock from 1643 to 1843. But to America at large the stream of English migration flowed continuously.

At the time of which we have chosen chiefly to speak, England had probably a population of about 7,500,000, Ireland of 2,500,000, Scotland of 1,000,000, while on the Continent France had perhaps 20,000,000, Spain 8,000,000 and the German lands 25,000,000. Of all these countries, excepting England, it was doubtless Ireland that had made the largest contribution to the American population. It may fairly be calculated that more than 350,000 persons of Irish birth or extraction inhabited the Thirteen Colonies in 1775, perhaps more than a sixth of their entire white population.

The movement of Irish emigration to the New World had first taken on considerable proportions in 1718, when severe economic pressure, caused mainly by the iniquitous selfishness of English legislation, had persuaded so great an emigration that five shiploads, mostly from the region around Coleraine in the north of Ireland, came into Boston harbor the same summer. They and their successors were widely distributed throughout New England, founding several towns in New Hampshire, Maine, and Western Massachusetts. But Philadelphia was throughout the eighteenth century the chief port of such arrivals, and Pennsylvania both their main abiding-place and the main gateway through which they advanced into other colonies, chiefly by passing down the great valley between the Blue Ridge and the Alleghanies. The back country of Pennsylvania was so full of them that a Pennsylvania politician of the time, Charles Biddle, assures us that all dwellers in that region, at least all politicians, perforce acquired their brogue. A little later, so Tench Coxe tells us, out of 69 members of the state legislature, 28 were Irishmen or sons of Irishmen. It is fair to say that, as we might expect, they were somewhat over-represented in that body. There were but fifteen or eighteen of the assembly who were Germans or sons of Germans, and yet it is certain that, taking the state as a whole, there were more Germans than Irish in Pennsylvania. It is fair to add that the Irish probably had also a representation beyond their numerical ratio in the enlistments in the Continental army.

There is an often-quoted passage bearing on this point, in the examination of Joseph Galloway, a Pennsylvania Loyalist, before the British House of Commons. He was asked the following question: "That part of the rebel army that enlisted in the service of the Congress, were they chiefly composed of natives of America, or were the greatest part of them English, Scotch, and Irish?" Galloway answered, "The names and places of their nativity being taken down, I can answer the question with precision. There were scarcely one-fourth natives of America, about one-half Irish, the other fourth were English and Scotch." It appears later, however, that the data of which he speaks were derived from the registration, not of the whole line, nor even of the whole Pennsylvania line, which had more foreign inhabitants than other states, but merely of those who deserted to Howe and thus came under Galloway's observation. But unquestionably the Irish enlistments in the Continental army were exceedingly numerous.

Of the numbers who had emigrated from Ireland we can get some figures from Arthur Young's *Tour in Ireland*, still more from a work published somewhat later by the best of the Irish statisticians of population before the taking of the first Irish census. It appears that for fifty years there had been an average of four thousand emigrants per annum, which in 1771, 1772, and 1773, had risen to an average of 9500; or more in three years than one per cent. of the population of the island. Most had, I think, sailed from the northern ports, especially from Belfast and Londonderry. Not long after the Revolution Phineas Bond, a native of Philadelphia serving as British consul there, writing to the Duke of Leeds, Foreign Secretary, on the amount of migration then taking place through that port, says, "I have not yet been able to obtain any account of the number of Irish passengers brought hither for any given series of years before the war, but from my own recollection I know the number was very great, and I have been told that in one year 6000 landed at Philadelphia, Wilmington, and Newcastle upon Delaware."

It will be noticed that in all this discussion I have used the simple term Irish, and have avoided the term Scotch-Irish. I trust that the moral courage of my course has been duly appreciated. To go farther, and state, in a public lecture, with or without the possibility of mention in a newspaper, that the mass of these immigrants can or cannot be properly called Scotch-Irish, would be an extreme of temerity, comparable to whistling "Lillibullero" on the seventeenth of March, or wearing green on the twelfth of July.[2] But I

{2.} Lillibullero (the spelling varies), a popular parody and protest ballad of Irish Protestants, originated around 1685 after James II, a Catholic, became king of England. The song satirized the king, his allegiance to Catholicism, and ridiculed Saint Patrick. The seventeenth of March is Saint Patrick's Day. Later in the eighteenth century it acquired political significance as well, as did the color green. As political strife between Irish Catholics and British Protestants escalated in the nineteenth century, the color green became a symbol for an Ireland free from British rule. On July 12, 1912,

should value a reputation for careful use of language more than a reputation for rash courage. I conceive that a person born in Ireland is, with rare
exceptions, Irish. I am aware of the argument that kittens born in an oven
are not loaves of bread, but I judge that, if born in an oven in Ireland, they
may fairly be called Irish kittens. The term Irish has thus a definite meaning;
it appears to me that the term Scotch-Irish has not, and I prefer to avoid it in
the present discussion.

Such was, in the main, the contemporary practice of the eighteenth century. The term Scotch-Irish was not unknown, but the man born in Ireland
usually called himself an Irishman, and those about him did the same. In
1737 persons of such origin formed in Boston a charitable society. The man-
agers were Protestants, and it is supposed to have been five years before
Catholics were first made eligible for membership. Of the 116 persons who
are recorded as members in that earliest period, most bear Scottish names,
some have names that might also be English; but there is also a Dillon, a
Fitzgibbon, a Geoghagen, a Melony, a McMurphy, a Mooney, a Ryan, and
a Walsh, and it called itself the Charitable Irish Society, and its first meeting for organization was held on the seventeenth of March. Similar was the
composition of the analogous society formed in Philadelphia, the Friendly
Sons of St. Patrick.

As to race, an eighteenth-century Irishman might be of Celtic blood, or
Scandinavian, or Norman, or English, or Scottish, or, with less likelihood,
French Huguenot or German. Indeed, since a man usually has two parents,
four grandparents, etc., (though these elementary facts are often forgotten
in discussions of ancestry), the eighteenth-century Irishman might be and
usually was, a mixture of all these stocks. But when the term Scotch-Irish is
used, it is commonly used with an implication that in Ulster all this was not
true, that that northern province was inhabited by a race of men of pure Scottish blood (whatever that may be), who, sternly Protestant, kept themselves
from all mixture with the native Irish, largely in order that their descendants
might be more comfortable in their minds. It may be so; but I cannot help
remembering the mordant satire with which Defoe showed us how

> "with easie search you may distinguish
> Your Roman-Saxon-Danish-Norman English. . . .

Protestants in Belfast staged violent anti-Catholic riots in reaction to the movement
for home rule in Ireland. See Giovanni Costigan, *A History of Modern Ireland* (New
York: Pegasus, 1969), pp. 84, 278, 282; Thomas E. Hachey, *British and Irish Separatism:
From the Fenians to the Irish Free State, 1867–1922* (Chicago: Rand McNally Publishing
Co., 1977), pp. 80–81; Edward R. Norman, *A History of Northern Ireland* (London: Pen-
guin Press, 1971), pp. 248–49; and Albert B. Friedman, ed. *The Viking Book of Folk
Ballads of the English Speaking World* (New York: Viking Press, 1956), pp. 286–88.

Fate jumbl'd them together, God knows how;
What e'er they were, they're True-Born English now."

I remember how large a part of Ulster, perhaps a third, was left by King James to Irish gentlemen and other natives when the plantation was formed, and how large a body of English and Episcopalian occupants came in with the Presbyterian Scots. I remember that at present there is not one county in Ulster that is so much as half Presbyterian, and that a century and more ago there was none in which the Catholics did not outnumber the Protestants three to two, and I doubt if there was ever one that was all Presbyterian or all Scottish. I judge too that the Scottish and English immigrants into Ireland must, like other immigrants, have been mostly young men, and I doubt if, more than other immigrants, they always ignored the attractions of the daughters of the land. The legend of pure Scottish Ishry may not be sounder than that which in 1914 was filling the world with the outraged cry of a united Ulster, a unanimous Ulster represented in Parliament by 18 Conservatives, 17 Nationalists, and 7 Liberals![3]

Yet, while I do not speak of Scotch-Irish, I make no doubt that by far the largest part of the Irish immigration into America was of Protestants from the north of Ireland. It is the uniform testimony of Arthur Young and other writers, that, though the population of Ireland was probably four-fifths Catholic and one-fifth Protestant, few Catholics emigrated, and few Church of England men. The great mass was of Ulster Presbyterians, and of linen-makers. There were also a few thousand Irish Quakers, mostly of English descent. These readily associated themselves with the meetings of Friends in America, and the Presbyterians joined themselves into churches after arrival or even migrated bodily as churches. But the Catholic Irish went without organization, and in America found themselves mostly without churches or priests. It is no wonder if, in the colonial period, they made less impression upon America than their considerable numbers might justify. Perhaps they have made up for it since.

It may be of interest to say a few words as to the means by which we attempt to calculate the proportions that various nations or linguistic stocks bore in the population of 1775. For such purposes in the present time we have easy recourse to the census. But the colonial censuses were few and im-

{3.} Irish Protestant opposition to home rule and a United Ireland under Catholic control peaked in 1914, and a compromise was proposed, whereby Ulster would be excluded from home rule for six years. Although the compromise was accepted by the House of Commons, the House of Lords rejected it and altered the bill so as to indefinitely exclude Ulster from home rule. The outbreak of World War I temporarily ended the struggle and staved off a civil war in Ireland. See Norman, *History of Northern Ireland*, pp. 251–53; and Hachey, *British and Irish Separatism*, pp. 83–86, 93–95.

perfect, and took no note of such data, and even when the federal censuses began, in 1790, it was still a long time before the enumerators were charged to take down the facts respecting foreign nativity or parentage. Under such conditions, the men of the time and the historians of the present day have often been put to odd shifts and expedients in the effort to compute linguistic or national proportions. A Pennsylvania writer of the Revolutionary period attempted to compute the proportion of Germans in the population of his state by gathering statistics as to the relative number of German and English spelling-books and newspapers and other issues from the prolific press of Philadelphia. Often, however, there were good statistics of immigration kept at the seaports from the time when the care of foreign immigrants became a serious concern of the colonial governments. Those of Philadelphia begin somewhat early. A very great proportion of the white immigration into the Middle and Southern colonies consisted of indented servants or redemptioners, persons who, unable to pay their passage-money, agreed with the master of the ship to serve him or his assignee for so many years in recompense. On arrival, if no one redeemed the passenger, the shipmaster sold him to whom he pleased, generally to the highest bidder, who then took his place in the contract. The system was open to the gravest abuses, especially in the case of those passengers who had made no formal and written contract, and early the law stepped in for their protection, and for the regulation of the traffic. Thus there are sometimes lists, and in the case of Pennsylvania large lists, for probably a third of the colonists of the first twenty-five years came in under this arrangement for passage, a half of those who came during the next twenty-five years, and two-thirds of those who came between 1727 and the end of the century. An act of that year, passed in some alarm lest entrance be given to too many aliens, required that German immigrants should take an oath of allegiance which was not required of the Irish, and so there are German lists. In other colonies the newspapers contain so many advertisements of shiploads of servants whose time of service is for sale that they make an important contribution toward a knowledge of the various sorts of immigration.

Another important source is lists of surnames, wherever they can be had in sufficient quantities to be significant. For instance, there are numberless tax-lists of the colonial period, and the tax-gatherer even then found a great many persons. There are lists of soldiers. There are polling-lists from elections. Directories begin later, the first being that of New York for 1786, but this is not too late to cast some light on conditions in 1775. Then there are lists of signatures to certain petitions to the legislatures, which in the case of some highly popular measures embrace many names, for then as now the easiest form of persuasion was to get people to sign a petition. Of course the fundamental fact already alluded to, that a man has two parents, four grandparents, eight great-grandparents, and so on, makes it senseless to tabulate an individual by his surname as thereby included in a linguistic stock to which he may in fact belong to the extent of only a sixteenth or a thirty-second or a still smaller part, though in the strict paternal line. But on the whole and in the large mass, the proportion of persons having German sur-names in any given population represents fairly the proportion of German blood in that population, and then one has only to multiply this number of soldiers or petitioners or heads of families by an appropriate multiplier to translate it into numbers of population, always remembering that colonial families were large; how large upon the average, can be figured from our numerous books of colonial genealogy.

This process of inference from surnames, it should be said, cannot be used in the case of the eighteenth-century Irish, any more than it could be used in the case of the twentieth-century Americans. What is an American name? The natives of Ireland were, as has been explained, a varied composite. For instance, of the major-generals and brigadier-generals of the Continental army, I count nineteen or twenty that were born in Ireland or born in America of Irish parents. Yet eight have surnames that might be either English or Scot-tish, five clearly Scottish, three Celtic Irish, two Welsh, one French. Their speech may have betrayed them, but their names could not.

Yet it might seem that persons of German and other non-British blood might be securely detected by their surnames, and that the proportions of such might readily be discovered by running through long lists of names and noting those which were German or French or of other linguistic character. We have indeed this resource at our disposal, but to suppose that it enables us to compute the full tale of non-English population is quite beside the mark. It is to make no allowance for the inveterate desire of English-speaking persons, and for the acquired desire of those who must make their living among English-speaking persons, to modify these strange patronymics into something rational and intelligible. Those who speak English are not alone in this: there are no more monstrous transformations than those which French clerks in Louisiana parishes operated upon the names of German farmers who settled among them, or than those which Swedish officials on the Dela-ware effected in the case of their English neighbors. But in the main the transformer has been English. Now if a compatriot of Evangeline, in Acadia, named Jacques Esbert is transported to Andover, Mass., and the rude fore-fathers of the hamlet choose to call him Jockey Bear, and his name appears later in tax lists under "B," it is a wise statistician who will know that he is dealing with an Acadian. Not every one will know, and descendants will not always disclose, that Lewis Winthrop was originally Levi Weintraub.[4]

{4.} In a letter written in 1912, Jameson noted that a friend had attended a lec-ture "by one who announced himself under the distinguished name of Winthrop. My friend found him to be of so strongly Jewish appearance that he was moved to

Schleiermacher becomes Slaymaker, Fitzpatrick becomes Fitch, and De Witt becomes Dwight. The immigrant of 1750, unless he went at once to a district filled with men of his nationality, had no more desire than the immigrant of 1915 to be tagged, visibly and forever, with a name which marked him as an alien or seemed ludicrous to Anglo-Saxon ears. It is observable that many of the family names, noted by the census enumerators of 1790, which were fantastic, and most of those which tended to cause a distinct loss of dignity to the bearer, have, in the course of a century, been so modified, with the social advance of the possessors, as to lose their unpleasant characteristics.

Equally natural is the process of translation of foreign surnames. The Frenchman Noel becomes the American Christmas, Zimmermann becomes Carpenter, McGowan becomes Smith. Some years ago the Census Office, after printing lists of the heads of families named in the old schedules of the census of 1790, attempted to compute from an inspection of the names the composition of our then population. They did it with a fatal error. It seems to me certain that, before reasoning back from their figures for 1790 to estimates for 1775, we should greatly need to increase their percentages of non-English population, because apparently they have not made allowance for the habit of translation, in accordance with which many a descendant of the O'Clery's lurks undiscovered among the Clarks, and many a Schwarz among the Blacks. Sir Wm. Johnson was grandson of a McShane. For instance, there was in early times a German peasant named Klein who emigrated to Pennsylvania, and dying left behind him three sons. One preserved the paternal name in its original sound, though he spelled it Cline; the other two translated it, but translated it differently. Therefore from this patriarch have descended three families; the family of Cline, the family of Little, and the family of Small. In this case a tabulation that should proceed by the mere appearance of the surname would underestimate by two-thirds the Teutonism of this worthy tribe. In the Irish case the mere dropping of the Mac and the O may give quite a different aspect to a name: Bryan is not more certainly O'Brien than Claflin is McLoughlin and Morrow McMurrough.

To show the underestimates which may arise from such a method, take the case of Delaware. Our census publication, to which I have alluded, computes its population as 97.7 per cent. from the British Isles, one per cent. Dutch, half a per cent. French, .4 of a per cent. German, all other elements .4 per cent. Now the Swedes lost Delaware in 1655, the Dutch in 1664. The population they had placed there was small, but it had come early and it was prolific. The Swedish settler whose genealogy has been most elaborately traced into subsequent times had in the sixth generation 264 known descendants. So, although when the last Swedish expedition to New Swe-

---

make inquiries, and learned that the man's name was originally Weintraub." [JFJ] to Henry S. Boutell, April 1, 1912, TLc, Box 61, JP, DLC.

den ended, there were probably not a thousand Swedes and Finns in the colony, it is not easy to think that, a hundred and thirty years later, their blood was less than .4 per cent. of Delaware blood. I have had the curiosity to run through the 7500 names in the *Calendar of Delaware Wills, Newcastle County*, whose dates average about 1775, and to search for Swedish names. They have sometimes suffered strange alterations. On seeing the surname Justice, one might think of Justice Shallow and other English justices, and might not imagine that it was Gostafson, the son of Gustavus, in disguise. I find in the list nearly 500 Swedish names, and more than 300 Dutch. If similar proportions held in the other two, less populous, Delaware counties, it may well be that we should rate the Swedish blood in that little state as six or seven per cent., and the Dutch as four or five.

In a lecture given before the Maryland Society of the Colonial Dames of America it would be agreeable if one could make precise statements respecting the composition of the Maryland population in 1776, but I fear that one can not safely venture to be very precise. The census publication to which allusion has already been made attempts to do this for the year 1790, by estimating nationality in accordance with names of heads of families, but the conclusions reached seem to me radically unsound. Its computation is that in 1790 84 per cent. of the population of Maryland was of English origin, 6.5 of Scottish, 2.4 of Irish, and 5.9 of German, no other nationality rising to the amount of 1 per cent. But how in the world one can distinguish definitely, in the run of cases, between English, Scottish and Irish surnames I for one do not see, and I am confident that the proportion of German was greater than 5.9 per cent. It was about 1729 when the first German drifted into Maryland and settled near the Monocacy River. Frederick was laid out in 1745. For forty years before the Revolution, and especially for the last twenty years, there had been a great influx of German population into Frederick county, which then included the whole western part of the province. We have few statistics as to arrivals. A good number of years ago a citizen of Baltimore with a German name rescued from the paper mill two parchment bound volumes entitled "Records of Arrivals and Clearances at the Port of Annapolis." I do not know that there are any others, for Annapolis or for Baltimore, and these two volumes run for only two years, 1753–1755. In those two years however 1060 Germans landed in Annapolis. In a list of accounts for quartering soldiers during the French and Indian War, published in the *Maryland Magazine of History*, and apparently covering the whole province, and constituting as large a list of Marylanders of that time as I have seen anywhere in print, out of about 1750 names 400 are German, but I judge that the quartering of soldiers during that war would have been more largely carried out in Western Maryland than in any other part of the province. In a printed list of associators in Frederick county in the first year of the Revolution, embracing 1558 men, 672 are to my eye German. Therefore I do not trust computations by the census authorities which assign only 5000 heads of families in Frederick in 1790 to the German column out of a total number of 27,000. I do not pretend to have gone over the whole array of Maryland families, 33,000 in number, but, taking columns enough to make a thousand, I have found by careful scrutiny 120 German names, and I think it very likely that in 1790 (which to be sure is not 1775) 12 per cent. of the Maryland population was made up of German. I refuse to guess what portion may have been Irish. I note in the list of 1790 only 36 O's, but there are 700 Mac's, of whom however at least 200 names are plainly Scottish.

Accordingly, the census author's estimate of the German strain in the American population of 1790, the most important of these alien strains, needs, from all other sorts of evidence, to be doubled before one can accept it. The best view as to 1775 is that there must have been somewhere about 225,000 Germans or descendants of Germans in the colonies at that time. The author of whom I have spoken as using the issues of the German press for his basis concluded, a few years later than this, that the number of persons who read or spoke German must be 150,000 or 180,000. In Pennsylvania the natives of Germany and the descendants of Germans constituted a third of the population. Next most numerous were those in New York and Virginia, after them Maryland, then New Jersey and South Carolina. North Carolina had its Lutherans and Moravians, Georgia its Salzburgers. In New England they were few save in a certain district in Maine, where German names, more or less transformed, still abound. The German immigrants to America came chiefly from western Germany, from the Palatinate and the Rhine country and the German cantons of Switzerland, for it must be remembered that in 1775 Germany was but a geographical expression, and that our figures, as a matter of course, are not confined within the bounds of the present German Empire, but include German natives of Switzerland, Bohemia, and Austria. They were Lutherans and German Reformed and Moravians and Mennonites and Catholics and Dunkers and Amish. They were, like the English, of all grades of culture, though its quality was frequently and amusingly underestimated by the colonists of English origin. In Pennsylvania the latter even organized a Society for the Promotion of the Knowledge of God among the Germans! In general, the Germans occupied good farming land, and dwelt at ease, after the manner of the prosperous West-German Bauer of their century.

Another Teutonic nationality, midway between the Germans and English, had in 1775 a large representation in our population. Apparently there had been little reinforcement of the Dutch strain by immigration subsequent to 1664, or after the second and final surrender of New York to the English in 1674. But the Dutch had come early, and though there were most likely not more than 7000 of them at the time of the English conquest, their posterity was large. Probably there were some 150,000 of them in 1775. No doubt we should reckon them third among the non-English elements, next after the Irish and the Germans; and probably the settlers from Scotland, Lowlanders and Highlanders together, would come fourth. The Dutch were chiefly to be found in New York and New Jersey. In the former state, a count of members during four or five legislative assemblies, a few years later, shows 108 Dutch names out of 385—a third or a fourth of the whole, though notoriously the Dutch were less inclined to politics than most other elements of the New York population.

If we imagine that 60 per cent. of the white American blood of 1775 came from England, 17 or 18 per cent. from Ireland, eleven or twelve per cent. from Germany, seven or eight per cent. from the Netherlands, and a small but indefinite percentage from Scotland, we shall probably be not far wrong. Several of the other national contributions present a story of great interest, but it is not likely that any of them amounted to one per cent., though the Swedes and the French may have approached that sum. Of the Swedes we have already spoken. French-speaking Protestants came in the very earliest days of New Netherland, but it is often difficult to distinguish in the records between French Huguenots and Walloons, who were French-speaking Belgians or men from northeasternmost France. Driven out from the southern Netherlands by Spanish persecution and living as refugees in the northern Netherlands or Dutch Republic, they were exceptionally free to migrate, and came in considerable numbers to New Netherland. Many a New York name or ancestor reputed Dutch is in reality Walloon, and may be found in the genealogical records of the Walloon Historical Society at Leiden, in the little old Walloon orphan-house that nestles beside the Pieterskerk and the home of John Robinson. The first minister in New Amsterdam preached in French as well as in Dutch.

The Protestants from France came also as victims of persecution, bringing with them all the energy and sobriety and earnestness that belong to such exiles, a happy brightness more peculiarly French, and the acquired aptitudes and experience of the merchant, the artisan, the city-dweller. Even before the Revocation of the Edict of Nantes not a few of them had come to the English colonies in America. After that even they came in larger numbers, and formed settlements in Massachusetts and Virginia, or joined the urban communities of New York and Philadelphia and Charleston. Everywhere, but especially in South Carolina, they acquired an influence and a leadership far out of proportion to their numbers.

In a land which already contains between two and three of the world's twelve millions of Hebrews, the story of the first arrivals of settlers of that race in America could not lack interest. The tale is romantic in itself, but it has little connection with the later Hebrew immigration, for most of the Jews who came before the Revolution were Sephardim, or Jews of the western ritual and of Spanish and Portuguese origin, while nearly all who have come in since the opening of the nineteenth century have been Ashkenazim, that is, German, Polish, and Russian Jews, of the eastern ritual. The persecuted Jews of Spain and Portugal flocked in great numbers to Holland, the land of religious freedom, for the same reasons which led the Pilgrim Fathers there. Soon after the Pilgrims' migration, the Dutch West India Company conquered Brazil, and under the brilliant rule of Count John Maurice of Nassau made Pernambuco for a brief period a Dutch capital and the chief centre of enlightenment in the New World, as the Amsterdam of Rembrandt and Spinoza's time was in the Old World. Jews flocked thither at once, and had no insignificant share in the prosperity of Brazil. In 1654, when the Portuguese, rallying, drove out the Dutch, they drove out also their Hebrew proteges. Before that year was ended, a barque carrying 27 Jews, who perhaps had come from Pernambuco by way of Curacao or Jamaica, came into the harbor of New Amsterdam. Their names were partly Hebrew, partly Portuguese— Abraham de Lucena, David Israel, Joseph da Costa, David Freira, Asser Levy, and the like. Three or four years later a similar group, with names like Rivera and Lopez and Seixas, came to Newport and established Judaism in Rhode Island. Dr. Ezra Stiles, the Congregationalist minister of Newport, notes in his interesting Literary Diary many talks with Rabbi Isaac Carigal of the Newport synagogue, a learned scholar born in Hebron, and with travelling rabbis from Palestine and Smyrna and Poland. (The rabbi preached in Spanish, by the way.) The figures which Stiles and others have transmitted indicate, at the end of the Colonial period, some 25 Hebrew families in Newport, and similar or not much greater numbers in New York, Philadelphia, Baltimore, Charleston, and Savannah—a few hundreds in all.

Other races, Welshmen, for instance, were not unknown, and quite recently a colony of several hundred laborers from Smyrna and Sicily and Minorca had been brought from the Mediterranean to English Florida by an enterprising Scottish padrone. But for all such small elements it may suffice to quote the statement which Father Isaac Jogues, the Jesuit missionary to the Iroquois, says was made to him by Governor William Kieft at New Amsterdam as early as 1643, "On the island of Manhate, and in its environs, . . . the Director General told me that there were men of eighteen different languages." It was already the melting-pot.

Not the least interesting fact about this congeries of linguistic stocks in the New World is the tenacity with which, in spite of all that made for assimilation, they resisted complete linguistic absorption. Of the speech of the Germans, the so-called Pennsylvania Dutch, still subsisting in dialects that betray original migration from Hesse or the Palatinate or German Switzerland, this permanence is familiar. Quaintly expressed, but typical of the linguistic transition, is the religious experience of Brother Crum, a German Methodist in Maryland. He said, "I prayed in Dutch; I am Dutch; and must get converted in Dutch. These are all English people, and they got converted in

English. I prayed and prayed in Dutch, but could not get the blessing. At last I felt willing to get converted in English or Dutch, as the Lord pleased. Then the blessing came, and I got converted in English." The Huguenot Church in Charleston has, I think, never ceased to hold its services in French. Portions of the minutes of the congregation Shearith Israel, the oldest Hebrew congregation in the United States, were kept in Portuguese till as late as 1745, and I believe the Portuguese ritual is used there to this day. Chief Justice William Smith of New York says, of a period twenty years before the Revolution, that in that colony Dutch was still so prevalent that "sheriffs find it difficult to obtain persons sufficiently acquainted with the English tongue to serve as jurors in the courts of law." Dutch was the speech of Rip Van Winkle's village. Not till the close of the eighteenth century did it give way to English as the prevailing language among the people in the country districts. Enough knowledge of it was left in the times of Van Buren's presidency to permit one of the satirical letters of Major Jack Downing to be written in it, or what passed for it. An elderly man of Dutch name who was a professor at Middletown while I was teaching here at Brown told me that his mother and sisters used to talk Dutch together when they did not wish the children to understand what they said. This would have been about 1830. But my sister-in-law told me the same thing of her mother and aunts, who died forty years ago. Indeed I have heard that Dutch speech still survives in some Catskill villages, two hundred and fifty years after the English conquest. It was not till 1786, a hundred and thirty-one years after the Dutch conquest of New Sweden, that the vestry of Gloria Dei Church in Philadelphia, on a vacancy occurring, declared that the King of Sweden need no longer send out Swedish ministers, as the Swedish language had now become extinct among that congregation.

I do not forget that the most numerous of all the alien elements in the American population, the element most fateful in history, and that which still presents the gravest problems, was the African. Not by voluntary migration and choice of allegiance, but through the unspeakable cruelties and horrors of the slave-trade, no fewer than three million negroes, at the lowest calculation, had been carried away from Africa as slaves before 1776. A third of them, we may suppose, such were the dreadful conditions of the Middle Passage, died upon the voyage, and the number taken to the British West Indies and to the Spanish and French and Dutch possessions was much greater than the number taken to the thirteen continental colonies. But of the latter and their descendants there were more than half a million in these colonies when the whites took arms for liberty. "Is it not amazing," wrote Patrick Henry in 1773, "that at a time, when the rights of humanity are defined and understood with precision, in a country, above all others, fond of liberty, that in such an age and in such a country, we find men professing a religion the most humane, mild, gentle, and generous, adopting a principle as repugnant to humanity, as it is inconsistent with the Bible, and destructive to liberty?" But I have believed that the white immigration and population was a distinct and a sufficient theme for one lecture.

It would be agreeable to say something about the contributions which these various white elements have made to our national growth and civilization, but this also would take us far afield. Much has been heard about it from orators speaking before congresses or societies of this or that variety of American, but too much of it has been marred by the desire to "claim everything," until one who should attend a series of such gatherings would be puzzled to know who in reality it was that constituted the mainspring and mainstay, the main bulwark and leaven and salt and glory of this composite nation. Perhaps he would not be far wrong who should hold its main salvation, the chief source of its greatness, to have been the very fact that it was compounded of all these elements, a mass kept active by the mutual attraction and repulsion and attrition of particles coming from various ingredients in proportions varying from generation to generation.

If, unwilling to ignore entirely the question of quality amid the considerations of numbers with which we have been engaged, we essay some generalizations upon the total character of the early immigrants into America, English and non-English, we are met at the outset by natural but hopeless divergences in our sources of information. The colonist already settled in the promised land had naturally prospered there. He speedily began, like the American of the present day, to think ill of the standards and qualities of the newcomers, and to forget the pit whence he was digged. If the new immigrant was ignorant of English, he was necessarily an ignorant man. The colonist's own forbears, on the other hand, just as surely as the forbears of us who are here gathered together, had been superior persons. But if our evidence comes from the land whence they emigrated, and especially from the intelligent and ruling classes in those countries, they tell another story. To such persons it is natural to wonder why people should leave home, leave a goodly land, and the employ of a most estimable governing class, unless indeed they are by nature idle and discontented. Arthur Young hears everywhere in Ireland the same tale: those who have emigrated have been for the most part the idle and worthless, loose, unemployed, disorderly people, whose departure was no loss to Ireland. (These were those noble Scotch-Irish who by their own admission have been the salvation of America.) No, we shall strive in vain to learn from the opinions of contemporary observers what manner of man the American of 1775 was.

And yet a few facts can be relied on with certainty. For instance, the American people was, and it now is, a transplanted section of the European middle class. It had, and it has, the qualities of a middle-class nation, bourgeois religion, bourgeois standards of education and art, bourgeois or peasant morality. Members of an aristocracy are a small element in any country. There is little to tempt them to emigrate. It was long supposed that the higher planting class who by the natural operation of economic causes became the aristocracy of Virginia could lay claim to a remarkable proportion of aristocratic English blood. But it is now abundantly well known that this was not the case. The largest number of them came from the English merchant class, some from the class of squires, some from that of artisans, some from that of indented servants. Virginia population was like New England population, in respect to aristocratic lineage. If it is true that

> "from yon blue heaven above us bent
> The gardener Adam and his wife
> Smile at the claims of long descent,"

nowhere is it more true than in America. The sky is peculiarly blue, and let us thank God for that; but the blood is not. In respect to genealogy, in fact, all American mankind can, with practical completeness, except for some of the latest arrivals, be divided into two classes: Those who are descended from poor Europeans of the middle class and are aware of the fact, and those who are descended from poor Europeans of the middle class and are not aware of the fact. The latter are, I judge, a little happier. They think perhaps of one ancestor of a certain provincial distinction in the early seventeenth century; they forget that he is their ancestor to the extent of perhaps one 256th part.

On the other hand, colonial America did not as a rule receive the dregs of Europe. The long voyage was a deterrent to those who had not a certain morale. Its perils and discomforts and horrors were such as are not easily realized by a soft generation which thinks it the height of hardship "to come home from Europe in war-time in a steamship with one smokestack when it has been accustomed to four." Then there was the passage-money, six or seven or eight pounds sterling—cash or personal labor—which operated as a property qualification to keep out the poorest. Transported convicts there were, indeed, and their number was considerable, but not such as to effect our main generalization.

It must be remembered that the European middle class of the seventeenth and eighteenth centuries had not the standards of the present day. For instance, hardly one of these Americans of 1775 would have seemed to us clean. Life on the frontier, it must be feared, often realized Hobbes' famous description, in the *Leviathan*, of the life of primitive man, "No arts, no letters, no society, and which is worst of all, continual fear and danger of violent death, and the life of man solitary, poor, nasty, brutish, and short." But even in favored Boston we find Cotton Mather in his *Manuductio ad Ministerium*, advising young candidates for the ministry that it is a good thing each morning to wash the face, especially about the eyes; and I know that there was not in any formal sense a bath-tub in Providence till 1809, when the first coppersmith and plumber came here from England. I sometimes wonder whether, if a Daughter of the American Revolution or a Colonial Dame should meet on the street the ancestor through whom she makes her claims to membership, she would invite him home to dinner. But if she did not, I hold that she would make a mistake. It is possible to lay too much stress on small refinements. I doubt not that Charlemagne lacked something of modern refinement, that Luther was not always presentable, that Peter the Great in respect to table manners left something to be desired. But wildernesses are not conquered or nations founded by the merely presentable. The average male American of 1775 was a *man*, a strong, brave, energetic, resourceful man, who, whatever his limitations of culture, could both carve out his own personal fortunes and entertain high visions of empire.

> "We sit here in the Promised Land
> That flows with Freedom's honey and milk,
> But 'twas they won it for us, sword in hand,
> Making the nettle danger soft for us as silk."

TM, Box 25, JP, DLC.

The Revolution as a Social Movement:
Lectures on Slavery and the West

In the spring of 1895 the New York City–based Lenox Chapter of the Daughters of the American Revolution invited Jameson to deliver a series of lectures on the American Revolution at Barnard College, Columbia University. Over the course of six lectures, Jameson chose to focus on the economic and social aspects of the American Revolution rather than on the political or military, although the latter subjects were considered at length. Held in Hamilton Hall on consecutive Tuesday afternoons from March 12 to April 16, the lectures considered political parties, landholding, business and industry, religion, slavery, and the West.[1]

When Jameson traveled to New York to deliver these lectures, he was under consideration for a three-year professorship in American history at Barnard. Jameson was tempted to leave Brown because, as he told his close friend Francis Christie, the professors at Columbia University had "the future with them, in respect to graduate work, and I should probably have more time for my writing." Columbia, however, refused to raise its initial salary offer of $3,500, the same amount Jameson received at Brown, and the negotiations ended.[2]

A quarter-century later, in 1920, A. Lawrence Lowell, president of Harvard University, invited Jameson to present these lectures again in Boston, in Huntington Hall as part of the Lowell Institute Series from November 9 to November 26.[3] Jameson made significant revisions, discarding entire passages from the 1895 lectures and inserting new material.

In 1925 Dana C. Munro, professor of history at Princeton University, invited Jameson to deliver the Louis Clark Vanuxem Memorial Lectures. Since 1925 marked the sesquicentennial of the American Revolution, Jameson chose to repeat his lectures on the economic and social aspects of the Revolution and delivered four lectures at Princeton from November 9 to November 24.[4] On revising the lectures, he concluded that very little since 1895 had been published on the social and economic aspects of the Revolution.[5] The terms of the lectureship required that the lectures be published, and Jameson indicated years later that it was for this reason only that they appeared in print.[6] Included here is the text for two lectures, those on slavery and on the West in the American Revolution, that were excluded from the Vanuxem lectures and the book that followed.[7] They are presented as Jameson delivered them in 1920. Appended to the text are fragmentary concluding sections to the 1895 lecture on the West. Jameson marked these passages for inclusion in 1920 but undoubtedly modified them in his delivery.

NOTES

1. "Six Lectures on American History," *New York Times*, March 10, 1895, p. 9, col. 6; "A Chair of American History," *New York Times*, March 13, 1895, p. 4, col. 6.

2. JFJ to Francis A. Christie, April 1, 1895, TLS, Box 71, JP, DLC.

3. On the Lowell Institute lectures, see Alfred Johnson to JFJ, December 1, 1920, TLS; and [JFJ] to Johnson, December 4, 1920, TLc, both in Box 99, JP, DLC. See also Lowell Institute, *Eighty-first Annual Report*, August 1, 1921, TMc, Boston Athenaeum, Boston, Massachusetts. All the following articles are from the *Boston Evening Transcript*: "Tories Not as Painted: Professor Jameson Speaks Sympathetically," November 10, 1920, pt. 3, p. 1, col. 3; "How Old Land Laws Faded: Professor Jameson Illustrates the Spirit of Democracy," November 13, 1920, pt. 2, p. 16, col. 1; "Why Slavery Persisted: Britain Largely to Blame, Dr. Jameson's Reminder," November 17, 1920, pt. 2, p. 1, col. 1; "Bishops Were Feared: Prof. Jameson Tells of Early Church Struggles," November 20, 1920, pt. 2, p.1, col. 1; "Early Days of Industry: Professor Jameson Traces American Beginnings," November 24, 1920, pt. 2, p. 1, col. 1; and "Jameson, No Boundary Is Final: Professor Jameson Ardent Disciple of Expansion," November 27, 1920, pt. 1, p. 5, col. 3.

4. [JFJ] to Dana C. Munro, October 22, 27, 1925, both TLc in Box 114, JP, DLC; [JFJ] to Elizabeth Donnan, October 5, 1925, TLc; Donnan to JFJ, October 21, 1925, TLS; and [JFJ] to Donnan, October 22, 1925, TLc, all in Box 78, JP, DLC.

5. [JFJ] to Charles A. Beard, August 10, 1926, TLc, Box 59, JP, DLC.

6. JFJ to Merle Curti, November 18, 1936, TLS, Box 21, Merle Curti Papers, WHi.

7. Louis Clark Vanuxem Foundation, "Public Lecturers," n.d., TM, University Archives, Seeley G. Mudd Manuscript Library, NjP; "Dr. Jameson to Lecture: Princeton Chooses Historian to Conduct Vanuxem Ser :s This Year," *New York Times*, November 3, 1925, p. 16, col. 2; *Princeton University Weekly Bulletin* 15 (November 7, 1925): 1; JFJ, *The American Revolution Considered as a Social Movement* (Princeton: Princeton University Press, 1926).

III. The Revolution and Slavery

FEW THINGS in the history of the United States are more interesting, surely, than the history of the development and extinction of slavery. Here on the soil where free institutions were taking their most remarkable development, for nearly a century we tolerated the strange anomaly of human bondage. A generation from now, when all memory of it has faded away, we shall perceive that the whole history of it was an episode in our life, though an episode of gigantic dimensions. It was like a foreign substance lodged in the body, not natural to its growth, but rankling and festering while the patient tossed and turned in agony, until at last the sharp surgery of civil war had to be invoked in order to dislodge it from the system.

An especial interest attaches to the relations of the American Revolution with slavery, for at this time the contrast between American freedom and American slavery comes out, for the first time, with startling distinctness. It has often been asked, How could men who were engaged in a great and inspiring struggle for liberty fail to perceive the inconsistency between their professions and endeavors in that contest and their actions with respect to their bondmen? How could they fail to see the application of their doctrines respecting the rights of man to the black men who were held among them in bondage far harsher than that to which they indignantly proclaimed themselves to have been subjected by the King of Great Britain? We should, to be sure, remember that their contest was rather for the definite legal rights of Englishmen than for those abstract rights common to all mankind which constituted the platform of the French Revolution. But this does not greatly lessen the anomaly. They did appeal to the general rights of mankind with sufficient frequency and warmth to place in a glaring light the contrast to which we have alluded. Abandoning the hope of clearing them in this easy way, let us then see to an examination of the question, whether the American struggle for liberty did in fact result in any beneficial action upon the subject of slavery.

When the first shots were fired at Lexington, slavery had long had a definite legal existence in every one of the thirteen colonies. But its extent and importance as a factor in the social system differed widely in the different colonies. The climate of New England was not well suited to African slavery. Even more important was that difference between New England and the South, in respect to character of settlement, to which reference was made in the last lecture. The labor of slaves is unintelligent, and therefore wasteful, labor. Hence it is inapplicable to lands like those of New England, where the closest individual attention and skill, such as can be expected of none but one who himself owns the land on which he works, are imperatively required. The theatre on which slave-labor can be most profitably employed is that of the large estate in the level plain, with a simple system of agriculture. An exceptional instance in New England confirms this. The one corner of New England in which farming on large estates was practicable and usual was the Narragansett country, the southernmost part of Rhode Island. Now this was one of the few districts in New England in which the labor of slaves was extensively employed in agriculture. Here slaves were somewhat numerous in country towns. Elsewhere in New England they were chiefly to be found in the larger towns, and perhaps most commonly as house-servants. [J. Ames.] Their numbers were not great,—perhaps 5000 in Massachusetts, 4000 in Rhode Island, 6000 in Connecticut. But Rhode Island and Massachusetts were deeply implicated in the slave-trade. It was the usual course to make a triangular voyage. Molasses was brought from the West Indies to the distilleries of Newport and Boston, to be there converted into rum. A cargo of rum was taken to the west coast of Africa, and there exchanged for negroes, and the negroes were then taken to the West Indies and sold for molasses. Then the same process was repeated. The horrors of that middle passage seem to have been beyond description. Our fullest information regarding it comes from a later time, when these horrors were somewhat mitigated. But even then, beside the ordinary sufferings of slaves torn from their homes, they were packed so closely between decks in the vessels, for greater profit, that as a rule and upon the average one-fourth died upon the voyage. The forbidding of importations into the northern colonies and states did not check these voyages to the West Indies and to the South.

In the South, when the Revolution broke out, there were about a half-million of slaves,—namely, about two hundred thousand in Virginia, a hundred thousand in South Carolina, seventy or eighty thousand each in Maryland and in North Carolina, and a smaller number in Georgia. In South Carolina their number was equal or superior to that of the whites. In the other southern states it was probably not more than half as great in proportion. Perhaps there were twenty-five thousand slaves in New York, ten thousand in New Jersey, and a lesser number in Pennsylvania, where the Quaker influence had been adverse to the growth of the institution. In New York the slaves were to be found mostly along the Hudson River and in the city. In all the southern colonies they were chiefly occupied in agriculture,— in Maryland and Virginia the cultivation of tobacco, in South Carolina and Georgia that of rice and indigo. In the unhealthy rice-swamps their condition was most unhappy.

It would be unjust to regard the colonists as solely to blame for the enormous importation of Africans which had taken place. At first little was said or thought about the matter. But as the numbers of negroes increased, alarms arose, and motives of humanity joined with the prudential motives thus suggested led the wiser colonists to protest. Thus, a famous Virginian magnate, Col. Wm. Byrd, writes in 1736 to Lord Egmont, "I am sensible of many bad consequences of multiplying these Ethiopians amongst us. They blow up the pride, and ruin the Industry of our White People, who seing a Rank of poor Creatures below them, detest work for fear it shoud make them look like Slaves. . . . Another unhappy Effect of Many Negros is the necessity of being severe. Numbers make them insolent, and then foul Means must do what fair will not. We have however nothing like the inhumanity here that is practiced in the Islands, and God forbid we ever shoud. But these base Tempers require to be rid with a tort rein, or they will be apt to throw their Rider. Yet even this is terrible to a good natured Man, who must submit to be either a Fool or a Fury. And this will be more our unhappy case, the more Negros are increast amongst us.

"But these private mischeifs are nothing if compard to the publick danger. We have already at least 10,000 Men of these descendants of Ham fit to bear Arms, and their Numbers increase every day as well by birth as Importation. And in case there shoud arise a Man of desperate courage amongst us, exasperated by a desperate fortune, he might with more advantage than Cataline kindle a Servile War. Such a Man might be dreadfully mischeivous before any opposition could be formd against him, and tinge our Rivers as wide as they are with blood. besides the Calamitys which woud be brought upon us by such an Attempt, it woud cost our Mother Country many a fair Million to make us as profitable as we are at present. It were therefore worth the consideration of a British Parliament, My Lord, to put an end to this unchristian Traffick of making Merchandize of Our Fellow Creatures. At least the farther Importation of them into Our Colonys shoud be prohibited lest they prove as troublesome and dangerous every where, as they have been lately in Jamaica."

But such protests were of no avail against the pressure brought to bear by British merchants engaged in a most profitable commerce. It has been estimated that, during the century preceding the Revolution, British merchants obtained from the slave trade gross returns equal to four hundred millions of dollars. In 1749, to increase the traffic, the slave-trade, previously in the hands of the Royal Africa Company, was thrown open to all English traders. In several instances, colonies passed acts to restrict the importation of slaves, but were rebuked by the Crown. Good General Oglethorpe, the founder of Georgia, says, "My friends and I settled the colony of Georgia, and by charter were established trustees. We determined not to suffer slavery there; but the slave merchants and their adherents not only occasioned us much trouble, but at last got the government to sanction them." In the very year 1776 the Earl of Dartmouth, who had lately been secretary of state for the colonies, wrote to a colonial agent, "We cannot allow the colonies to check, or discourage in any degree, a traffic so beneficial to the nation." In 1772 the House of Burgesses of Virginia sent a petition to the King, requesting that governors should be permitted to give their approval instead of their veto to acts which the House might pass for the checking of the slave-trade, but it was in vain. When Granville Sharpe, the philanthropist, waited on the secretary of state to inquire respecting the fate of the petition, the secretary said that it had been received, but that (he apprehended) no answer would be given. Plainly, then, a great share of the blame for the continuance of the slave-trade rests upon the English government and the English king. I would not lay upon them all the blame, as our fathers sometimes did, for had there been no buyers there could have been no sellers. But I believe it to be a fact that, under the influence of an increasingly adverse public opinion, importations of slaves had been decreasing just before the Revolution, and would have entirely stopped in most if not all of the colonies if it had not been for the interposition of the royal government, exercised through the colonial governors. As we shall see later, the two colonies which before the Revolution forbade importations were precisely the two that elected their own governors, and these were not obliged to send their laws to England for royal approval.

Slavery, then, appeared to be a fixed fact. We must next inquire, what was the status of the slave? Statements conflict. Indeed, the institution was sure to differ from colony to colony, and even from plantation to plantation. Some masters were humane and some were not. In some districts the preponderating numbers of slaves forced the anxious whites into an attitude of greater watchfulness and severity than was thought necessary in others. When, a few years later, a committee of the House of Commons took testimony concerning slavery in the West Indies, these witnesses who had resided both there and in Virginia or Carolina uniformly testified that in both those colonies slave-holders were more humane and slaves happier than in the islands. In view of the fiendish cruelty which the evidence showed to be common among the West Indian planters, this may not seem to be much. But there is also positive evidence of the frequency of humane treatment. An English parson, preaching to a Virginian congregation in 1763, says: "I do you no more than justice in bearing witness, that in no part of the world were slaves ever better treated than, in general, they are in these colonies." Yet, if we reflect upon what, under the best circumstances, must be the results of human bondage, I fear we must think of this commendation as qualified much as Lord Burghley in Queen Elizabeth's time qualified his instructions regarding the torturing of certain prisoners, namely, that it be done "as tenderly as such a thing may be."

In the colonies where there were few slaves, the laws regarding them were not of real severity. Slaves were not allowed to be abroad at night without leave, after certain hours, and it was forbidden to sell liquor to them or trade with them without permission from their masters. A negro who struck a white man might be whipped, and negroes might not be freed if there was danger that this would result in their becoming a charge upon the town.

But, except for one Rhode Island law, there were in New England no provisions for special courts or for different modes of trial in the case of negroes from those used in the case of whites. Of the Middle colonies, New York may serve as a specimen. Here the laws were somewhat more repressive. If four or more slaves were found together without good reason, they might be whipped by a justice's order. Masters might punish their slaves, provided they avoided injury to life and limb. And here we find special courts provided for judging offences committed by slaves. In the case of the graver crimes, the negro's guilt was decided upon by a court consisting of the justices of the peace with the addition of five freeholders. Yet trial by jury was not wholly denied. If the master of the slave was willing to pay the expenses there might be a jury.

In the southern colonies the laws were naturally more severe. In South Carolina and Georgia a slave found away from his town or plantation without a pass from his master, and not in the company of a white man, could be given not more than twenty lashes on the spot. One who assaulted a white might be killed. Male slaves more than seven in number, found travelling together without a white man, might be given forty lashes by anyone who might meet them. Slaves going abroad without leave, in Virginia, might be given ten lashes by the master or overseer of any plantation on which they were found. There were severe restrictions upon their meetings, upon their carrying guns, upon their holding of property, upon their having boats. All these laws were evidently dictated by fear of insurrection. Fear of poisoning led to laws in three of the colonies forbidding any slave to administer any medicines without the master's leave. In South Carolina there was a penalty of one hundred pounds for teaching a slave to write; in Georgia one of twenty pounds for teaching one to write or to read writing. Their offences were tried by special courts like that mentioned in the case of New York, with no permission of a jury, save in Maryland. While there were some provisions for proper food and clothing for slaves, and while in South Carolina a fine was laid on masters who compelled their slaves to work more than fourteen hours a day in winter and fifteen in summer, yet in that colony only heavy fines awaited the master who killed his slave by excessive scourging or on sudden passion or even wilfully, and in Virginia a slave-owner was not liable to prosecution in any way if his slave died under correction without his intending it. In South Carolina and Georgia there was no provision for legal manumission, though in North Carolina and Virginia it was possible and in Maryland comparatively easy.

Such was the condition of the American negro when the struggle for liberty and independence from England was begun. Well might the contrast between all this and the principles of the Revolution strike the reflecting mind. Before inquiring whether it did so, and with what effects upon the condition of the blacks, we may well remember that other influences than those of the American Revolution were abroad at that time in the world which would surely work in some degree against the institution of human slavery. On the one hand Voltaire had raised a powerful, if at times a grating voice in favor of a rational humanitarianism, and Rousseau had poured upon time-worn institutions the active solvent of abounding sentimentality. Quite at an other extreme of human thought from them, Wesley and Whitefield had stirred the English nation into a warmth of religious feeling of which Methodism was only one result. With it came a revived interest in all varieties of philanthropic endeavor. Robert Raikes began the establishment of Sunday schools. John Howard wore out his noble life in efforts for the amelioration of prisons and prisoners. After 2 centuries during which the missionary activities of the Christian Church had been almost entirely confined to its Catholic branch, the Protestants of England and Germany began to take an interest in the cause of foreign missions. Philanthropy was in the air. The last lecture showed how the Americans, in their struggle for *liberty*, were led also, by the spirit of the age, to strive for *equality*. The same spirit forced upon their attention the claims of *fraternity*.[1]

The stirrings of such an impulse had already been for sometime felt in the colonies. During the first part of the eighteenth century there had been little or no protest against slavery in the thirteen colonies, though some voices had been raised against further importations of slaves. But in the middle of the century the hearts of many, especially in the Society of Friends, were stirred up by the earnest appeals of John Woolman, the tender-hearted and saintly Quaker preacher, whose beautiful Journal is so largely a record of anti-slavery activity. Other religious bodies, if less active, furnish some manifestations of the new spirit. In the Church of England, where a generation before the interest in the negroes had been simply an interest in them as heathen and as objects for conversion, now there were evidences of a regard for them as men and as wards of the state and members of society. Rev. Jonathan Boucher, rector in Virginia, in his sermon on the peace of 1763, says: "The united motives of interest and humanity call on us to bestow some consideration on the case of those sad outcasts of society, our negro-slaves; for my heart would smite me, were I not, in this hour of prosperity, to entreat you . . . to permit them to participate in the general joy." Among Congregationalists, Dr. Samuel Hopkins, at Newport, where the slave-trade was important, preached and labored against it with signal effect. A small anti-slavery literature began to grow up. Public bodies began to move. The town-meeting of Worcester, in 1765, instructed their representative to "use his influence to obtain a law to put an end to that unchristian and impolitic

{1.} The previous lecture in 1920 considered the Revolution and the ownership of land.

practice of making slaves of the human species." Boston, in the next two years, passed similar instructions. Virginia's non-importation agreement of 1769 bound the signers to import no more slaves until the obnoxious legislation of the British Parliament was repealed. Another interesting sign of the change of sentiment is the series of remarkable cases in the courts of Massachusetts, beginning in 1766, in which slaves, on arriving at the age of twenty-one, sued their masters for the recovery of their freedom and even for the payment of wages. In several such cases the courts freed the slave, but, though the slave's counsel usually argued that slavery was illegal in Massachusetts, it does not at all appear that the judges so decided. Much influence was exerted in some colonies by Lord Mansfield's decision in the famous case of the negro Somerset, in which he is usually supposed to have decided that slavery could not legally exist upon the soil of England,— though I believe his decision really did not go quite so far as that.

The sentiment hostile to slavery was fortified, in these years, by the progress of revolutionary opinion. The fathers of the Revolution were not slow to see the application of its principles to the question of negro slavery. James Otis, in his famous argument against the Writs of Assistance, is said to have included the poor negro in his wide-sweeping declarations regarding human liberty. If he did not do so on this occasion, he did in 1764. At the Commencement of Harvard College in 1773 two young candidates for the bachelor's degree held a "Forensic Dispute on the Legality of enslaving the Africans," which was printed that same year. In this interesting academic exercise, one of the two young disputants says: "To me, I confess, it is matter of painful astonishment, that in this enlightened age and land, where the principles of natural and civil Liberty, and consequently the natural rights of mankind are so generally understood, the case of these unhappy Africans should gain no more attention,—that those, who are so readily disposed to urge the principles of natural equality in defence of their own Liberties, should, with so little reluctance, continued to exert a power, by the operation of which they are so flagrantly contradicted." His opponent argues for the natural inequality of men, and by implication, for the natural inferiority and subordination of the African. To this he replies, somewhat smartly: "I suppose you will hardly imagine the darkness of a man's skin incapacitates him for the direction of his conduct, and authorizes his neighbors, who may have the good fortune of a complexion a shade or two lighter, to exercise authority over him. And if the important difference does not lay here, it seems not very easy to determine where it does; unless perchance, it be in the quality of their hair; and if the principle of subordination lies here, I would advise every person, whose hair is inclined to deviate from a right line, to be upon his guard. If indeed any should alledge, that they are distinguished by the flatness of their noses, I can't but think this circumstance against them, for if a man is to be led and governed by the nose, it may well be questioned, whether a nose of a different figure would not be better adapted to the purpose."

There is in truth no lack of evidences that the analogy between freedom for whites and freedom for blacks was seen. The town-meeting of Danbury, Conn., for instance, declares that it is "a palpable absurdity, so loudly to complain of attempts to enslave us, while we are actually enslaving others." Even among the blacks, the ironies of liberty and bondage were not unperceived. When the Tory estate of the Vassalls, of Cambridge, was confiscated, and the commissioners were offering the old Vassall homestead at public sale, an old black servant named "Tony" stepped forward and said, "I am no Tory, but a friend of Liberty; having lived on this estate all my life, I do not see why I should be deprived of my dwelling."

But it is surely of more importance as well as of more interest to inquire how far all this was perceived and felt by the leading actors in the Revolution, the great statesmen who had in their hands the control of American affairs in this time of transition. The evidences that shall answer this question I will not take from New England or the Middle States, where slavery was not of great importance and agitation against it did not run counter to preeminent economic interests. I will choose them all from Virginia, for surely examples from a slave state will be more convincing as to the movement of public opinion. The foremost place must surely be given to the striking language of Patrick Henry, used in 1773, when he was immersed in the struggle against Great Britain. It is found in a letter which he wrote to one who had sent him a copy of Anthony Benezet's book on slavery. "Is it not amazing," he says, "that at a time, when the rights of humanity are defined and understood with precision, in a country above all others fond of liberty, that in such an age and in such a country we find men professing a religion the most humane, mild, gentle and generous, adopting a principle as repugnant to humanity as it is inconsistent with the bible and destructive to liberty? . . . Would anyone believe I am the master of slaves of my own purchase! I am drawn along by the general inconvenience of living here without them. I will not, I cannot justify it. However culpable my conduct, I will so far pay my devoir to virtue, as to own the excellence and rectitude of her precepts, and lament my want of conformity to them.—I believe a time will come when an opportunity will be offered to abolish this lamentable evil. Everything we can do is to improve it, if it happens in our day, if not, let us transmit to our descendants, together with our slaves, a pity for their unhappy lot, and an abhorrence of slavery. . . . It is a debt we owe to the purity of our religion, to show that it is at variance with that law which warrants slavery."

Washington gave frequent expression to his desire that slavery should be abolished in Virginia. Jefferson, in his Notes on Virginia, after expressing at length his abhorrence of slavery, says: "Indeed I tremble for my country, when I reflect that God is just, that his justice cannot sleep for ever, that considering numbers, nature and natural means only, a revolution of the wheel of fortune, an exchange of situation, is among possible events, that it may become probable by supernatural interference. The Almighty has no attribute which can take side with us in such a contest. But it is impossible to be temperate, and to pursue this subject through the various considerations of policy, of morals, of history natural and civil. We must be contented to hope they will force their way into everyone's mind. I think a change already perceptible, since the origin of the present revolution. The spirit of the master is abating,—that of the slave rising from the dust; his condition mollifying; the way, I hope, preparing, under the auspices of Heaven, for a total emancipation; and that this is disposed, in the order of events, to be with the consent of the masters, rather than by their extirpation."

George Mason, who was perhaps the wisest Virginian of his time, and was certainly one of the most influential, said in the Federal Convention: "Slavery discourages arts and manufactures. The poor despise labor when performed by slaves. They prevent the emigration of whites, who really enrich and strengthen a country. They produce the most pernicious effect on manners. Every master of slaves is born a petty tyrant. They bring the judgment of heaven on a country. As nations cannot be rewarded or punished in the next world, they must be in this. By an inevitable chain of causes and effects, Providence punishes national sins by national calamities. He held it essential in every point of view, that the general government should have power to prevent the increase of slavery." [{illegible, possibly shorthand} 1773 (Rowland I 404.)]

It may be thought that these are simply the expressions of individuals, and that no organized efforts were made toward the removal or alleviation of slavery. On the contrary the Revolution produced a whole crop of societies formed for these purposes. The first anti-slavery society in this or any other country was formed on the 14th of April, 1775, five days before the battle of Lexington, by a meeting at the Sun Tavern, on Second Street, in Philadelphia. The members were mostly of the Society of Friends. The organization took the name of "The Society for the Relief of Free Negroes unlawfully held in Bondage." In the preamble of their constitution they point out that "loosing the bonds of wickedness and setting the oppressed free, is evidently a duty incumbent on all professors of Christianity, but more especially at a time when justice, liberty, and the laws of the land are the general topics among most ranks and stations of men." The society held four meetings in 1775. The war interrupted its activities. Later they were resumed and regular meetings held, the society now adopting the more comprehensive name of "The Pennsylvania Society for promoting the Abolition of Slavery, and the Relief of Free Negroes unlawfully held in Bondage, and for improving the Condition of the African Race." The New York "Society for Promoting the Manumission of Slaves" was organized in 1785, with John Jay for its first president. In 1787 this society offered a gold medal for the best discourse, at the public commencement of Columbia College, on the injustice and cruelty of the slave-trade, and the fatal effects of slavery. The idea of influencing the college young men is also shown in Mr. Jefferson's plan of sending a copy of his "Notes on Virginia," with its ardent expressions of opinion on slavery, to each student in the College of William and Mary. In 1788 a society similar to these two was founded in Delaware, and within four years there were other such in Rhode Island, Connecticut, New Jersey, Maryland and Virginia, while local societies had sprung up at Washington, Pa., at Wilmington, Delaware, and at Chestertown, at Choptank, and in Caroline County in Maryland. When, a few years later, their numbers were for the first time reported, they averaged two hundred members apiece, and these included many of the most influential citizens of their respective localities. Here, then, were thirteen societies formed for this benevolent purpose between the opening of the Revolution and a few years after its close; and probably there were other local societies the knowledge of whose existence has not come down to us. It will perhaps be noticed that seven of the thirteen were organized in the slave-holding states south of Mason and Dixon's line. Not in vain, then, had the old bell which rang out the glad tidings of the Declaration of Independence borne its inspiring inscription, "Proclaim liberty throughout all the land, to all the inhabitants thereof."

But, it will be asked, perhaps with some impatience, what was actually accomplished? Sad as it is to have to acknowledge that the benefits of liberty were chiefly secured for white men, and that the bright promise of a movement for universal liberty was not fulfilled, I think we shall be able to show that, after all, much was accomplished toward the alleviation of the evil. In the first place, it was possible to check the importation of slaves, with all the attendant horrors of the trans-Atlantic slave-trade, in states where provisions for the actual abolition of domestic slavery were not to be secured. The alarm of those who feared on grounds of public safety the increase of slaves fresh from the savagery of Africa, the cupidity of those who saw the profits of slave-raising likely to be reduced by continued importations, would conspire with the zeal of philanthropists to effect this first stage of progress. The Continental Congress of 1774 had been in session but a few days when they decreed an "American Association," or non-importation agreement, in which one section read: "That we will neither import nor purchase any slave imported after the first day of December next, after which we will wholly discontinue the slave-trade, and will neither be concerned in it ourselves, nor will we hire our vessels nor sell our commodities or manufactures to those who are concerned in it." This was agreed to and signed by all the delegates of all the 12 colonies present, and subsequently ratified by the thirteenth. And this provision, which seems to have been based on the resolutions of

Fairfax County, Virginia, drawn up by George Mason in the preceding July for a committee of which Washington was chairman, the Congress never repealed. Its authority was limited, but it was exerted to the utmost for the better cause. For any other action we must look to the states. Four months before this, in July, 1774, Rhode Island had passed a law to the effect that all slaves thereafter brought into the colony should be free. The influence under which it was passed may be seen from the preamble. "Whereas," it begins, "the inhabitants of America are generally engaged in the preservation of their own rights and liberties, among which that of personal freedom must be considered as the greatest, and as those who are desirous of enjoying all the advantages of liberty themselves should be willing to extend personal liberty to others," etc. It is true, this did not prevent Rhode Islanders from carrying slaves from Africa to other colonies, yet it was a distinct step forward. The same may be said of the similar law passed in October, 1774, by Connecticut. 2d Cont. Cong. Apr. 6, 1776.

In the Library of the Department of State, at Washington, hangs Jefferson's original draft of the Declaration of Independence, an object of eager interest to all visitors. But no part of it, surely, is more interesting than the passage across which the framer drew his pen, and which did not appear in the Declaration as passed. It is the one important change which was made in the original draft before passage. It reads, speaking of the unjust actions of King George: "He has waged cruel war against human nature itself, violating its most sacred rights of life and liberty in the persons of a distant people who never offended him; captivating and carrying them into slavery in another hemisphere, or to incur miserable death in their transportation thither. This piratical warfare, the opprobrium of Infidel powers, is the warfare of the Christian king of Great Britain. Determined to keep open a market where men should be bought and sold, he has prostituted his negative for suppressing every legislative attempt to prohibit or to restrain this execrable commerce." Jefferson relates that this clause was struck out in deference to South Carolina and Georgia, who had no desire to abandon the practice of importations, while others felt that a large share of the blame belonged to the colonies themselves.

Of the states in which slaves formed so large a part of the population that they may fairly be called slave states, Delaware was the first to prohibit importations. This was accomplished by her first state constitution, in the year 1776. Virginia achieved the same result in 1778, by an act of the legislature, and Maryland in 1783. All three of these states prohibited importations not only from Africa or by sea, but also by land from other states. Farther south than this the movement did not extend. North Carolina in 1786 imposed a duty of five pounds on each negro imported, at the same time declaring such importations to be "of evil consequence and highly impolitic," but she did not prohibit them. When, in the Federal Convention which met at

Philadelphia in 1787, the subject of a possible prohibition of the slave-trade by national authority was under consideration, there were but the three southernmost states that had not by state authority forbidden it. But North Carolina, South Carolina and Georgia by insistence succeeded in persuading the New England members to agree to a compromise upon the subject. Hence, the provision in the Constitution that Congress should not for twenty years have power to prohibit the slave-trade, or, in the euphemistic phrase adopted, "the migration or importation of such persons as any of the states now existing shall think proper to admit." So it was 1808 before importations were made entirely illegal. Yet in the gradual confinement of the evil to three states the spirit of the Revolution had surely done a notable work.

But more than this was accomplished. The states in which slaves were few proceeded, directly as a consequence of the Revolutionary movement, to effect the immediate or gradual abolition of slavery itself. Vermont had never recognized its existence, but Vermont was not recognized as a state. Pennsylvania in 1780 provided for gradual abolition, by an act which declared that no negro born after that date should be held in any sort of bondage after he became twenty-eight years old, and that up to that time his service should be simply like that of an indented servant or apprentice. Now what says the preamble of this act? That when we consider our deliverance from the abhorrent condition to which Great Britain has tried to reduce us, we are called on to manifest the sincerity of our professions of freedom, and to give substantial proof of gratitude, by extending a portion of our freedom to others, who, though of a different color, are the work of the same Almighty hand. Evidently here also the leaven of the Revolution was working as a prime cause in this philanthropic endeavor. Four years before, the Declaration of Independence had proclaimed here at Philadelphia the fundamental doctrine of human freedom: "We hold these truths to be self-evident:—That all men are created equal; that they are endowed by their Creator with certain unalienable rights; that among these are life, liberty, and the pursuit of happiness." As a great historian has well said, "the resistless logic of one burning sentence" did more than aught else to bring the American mind to the abolition of slavery.[2] In Massachusetts these very words are held to have played an important part in abolishing that institution. The story is a singular one. In the town of Barre, in Worcester County, there was a slave named Quaco Walker, belonging to a farmer named Nathaniel Jennison. Jennison beat the negro, and the negro then sued him for damages for assault. In the county court the jury decided against the white man, declaring that the negro was free. This was in 1781. The case was appealed to the Superior Court of the state. Here it was urged by the negro's counsel, and the court held, that slavery had been at one blow abolished in Massachusetts

{2.} The source for this quote has not been identified.

by a single clause in the Constitution of the state, then recently adopted. The Constitution had said, in almost the exact words of the Declaration of Independence, "All men are born free and equal." The decision of the court was a remarkable one. Words almost identical with these had been used in the Virginian Constitution, i.e., George Mason's Declaration of Rights, four years earlier; yet no one had ever supposed that the use of these words effected the abolition of slavery in Virginia. Nor is there any evidence that those who inserted this statement in the Constitution of Massachusetts intended it to have such effects as these. Even after the decision by the court there is evidence of slavery still existing, but it could not long survive, and apparently did not. It may be that the decision of the court stretched the law, but it substantially effected the abolition of slavery. Gradually it died out in Massachusetts. Certainly no law was passed to abolish it.

In the New Hampshire Constitution of 1784 similar language regarding human freedom and equality was used. But here the courts held that it simply ensured the freedom of all persons born after that Const. went into effect. [Petition of 19 sl{aves}. N{ew} H{ampshire}. 1779, in M{agazine}. A{merican}. H{istory}. XXI. 63.] Slavery then began to die out, and the census of 1790 showed only 158 in the whole state. In this same year, 1784, Connecticut and Rhode Island passed acts which gradually extinguished slavery. In Rhode Island, all born after the beginning of March, 1784, were to be free, in Connecticut all such were to be free on attaining the age of twenty-five. It was not until 1848 that slavery was finally abolished in Connecticut, and I believe that the last slave in Rhode Island died, a very old man, so late as 1858, but a few years before the civil war. In New York and New Jersey slavery lingered as long as in Connecticut, for the acts providing for gradual emancipation were passed at a later date, in New York in 1799, largely owing to the efforts of Governor John Jay, in New Jersey in 1804. In both cases, it is interesting to note, in view of our present inquiry, it was provided that all slaves should be free who were born after the ensuing Fourth of July. But there was more than this sentimental influence of the Revolution and the Declaration. Though attempts at abolition, made during the Revolutionary period, were unsuccessful, the state of New York emancipated the slaves which it acquired from the confiscated Tory estates, extended to slaves the full privileges of trial by jury, and made easier the process by which owners could free their slaves. In New Jersey there were similar laws passed as to trial by jury and as to manumission. Punishments were also provided for masters who treated their slaves inhumanly or who did not teach the young negroes to read, and for any who should export slaves from the state.

Even in three of the slave states, distinctively so called, the Revolutionary period was marked by legislation intended to mitigate the system, though propositions for its gradual abolition, made in Delaware, Maryland and Virginia, were voted down in all three. In Delaware exportation was forbidden, manumission was made much easier, and trial by jury was afforded for slaves accused of capital crime. In Maryland, petitions for gradual or immediate abolition received careful consideration by the legislature. The votes in different cases show how large was the minority which desired emancipation to take place,—thirty-two to twenty-two, thirty to seventeen, thirty-nine to fifteen. Jefferson states that the sentiment in favor of emancipation was stronger in Virginia than in Maryland. Yet in his own state he found it impracticable to carry through the act for gradual emancipation which he had framed, and a petition to that effect was rejected without an opposing voice. It could hardly obtain a reading, wrote Washington to Lafayette. But this was in 1786, when in many ways the American people had degenerated from the high hopes and the unselfish devotion to ideals which had accompanied the opening years of the war, and the legislatures were far from being what they had been ten years before. Surveying the period as a whole, we see some substantial gains in Va. Juster provisions were made for the trial of slaves. The old law was abrogated which declared that a master should be exempt from prosecution who killed his slave by accident or during correction. Most important of all, an act was passed in 1782 which provided that any owner might, by an instrument properly attested, freely manumit all his slaves, if he gave security that their maintenance should not become a public charge. It may seem but a slight thing, this law making private manumission easy where before it had been difficult. But it appears to have led in eight years to the freeing of more than ten thousand slaves, twice as great a number as were freed by reason of the Massachusetts constitution, and more than there were in Rhode Island and Connecticut together when the war broke out.

In the Carolinas and Georgia, it must be confessed, nothing was done by public action to improve the condition of the slaves or the nature of the system of slavery. Individuals might be well disposed, but the mass of the slave-holders were averse to any change whatever in the existing system. Even if they had been willing to sacrifice the most valuable portion of their property, there remained the great problem of what should be done with such vast hordes of blacks when freed. The problem seemed difficult in Maryland and Virginia. We can hardly wonder that in South Carolina and Georgia it appeared positively insoluble. Then, in a few years (1793) came the invention of the cotton-gin by the ingenious Yankee, Eli Whitney. In a year the export of cotton ran up from 187,000 pounds to 1,600,000 pounds. In another year it went at a bound up to 6,300,000 pounds, and by the closing year of the century it had nearly reached the figure of eighteen million pounds, almost a hundred times what it had been only seven years before. After this there was little use in talking of any serious change in the system of slavery in the cotton-growing states. Nor are we to consider that, without this last complication, the removal of slavery ought to have seemed to the men of the Revolution anything other than a task of the very highest difficulty. With this new difficulty added, the Gordian knot was sure to be drawn tighter and tighter, till only the sword could loosen it.

Looking back over the varied record that has been spread before us, what are we to conclude? That all was not done that might have been done we shall not deny, nor that there was in many places a glaring contrast between the principles avowed by the men of the Revolution and their acts respecting slavery. Yet as we think of the general prohibition of the slave-trade, the promotion by several states of immediate or gradual abolition, the facilitation of private emancipation, and the many acts by which the status of the slave, his position before the law and his protection from inhumanity and injustice were improved, I think we shall be willing to concede that here also the Revolution had effects not unworthy of record and of admiration and gratitude.

v i . The Revolution and the West

In the previous lectures of this course, such topics have been considered as the relation of the Revolutionary movement to slavery and industrial life, to land and religion,—topics plainly within the province of social history. It will seem at first sight that the subject of the present lecture is decidedly of a different class, that it brings us within the domain of political history. It is at any rate not so intended. Though it may sound like a paradox, I believe it would not be wrong to say that such subjects as "The Revolution and New England," "The Revolution and the Middle States," or "The Revolution and the South" would be subjects in political history, while the topic "The Revolution and the West" is a topic in social history, or can be made such. In other words, the relation of the thirteen new-born states to the West was a peculiar one, not only affecting their public life, but also affecting, as an economic fact of vast importance, the private and daily life and thoughts of the mass of men. The whole history, not simply of American politics but of American life, has been made different by the fact that to the west of the old states lay a vast area of unoccupied and fertile land. Suppose the country to have been strictly and permanently bounded on the west by the Alleghanies. It would never have become a great country, at any rate not according to our present standards of greatness, and this is an important political fact. But also, and this I think is of a larger importance, it would soon have ceased to have the characteristics of a new country. A new country is a country in which man has not yet proceeded far in his great task of subduing nature to his uses. That which has kept the United States still young and new has been the possession of a vast amount of virgin soil. The frontier has been pushed steadily westward, but there has always been a frontier (until lately), a borderland between civilization and the wilderness, with that mode of life and that type of character which the frontier brings into existence. There to the westward have ever lain new fields, broad and inviting, always beckoning the American on to new tasks and new opportunities. Those tasks and opportunities have developed a special variety of manhood, independent, resolute, active, full of resources, self-reliant, unmindful of precedents, buoyant and hopeful. Frontier life in one decade is found at Syracuse or at Harrisburg, in the next at Buffalo or at Cleveland, then at Chicago or St. Louis, then in Nebraska, in Wyoming, in Idaho. But always frontier life has existed somewhere. Older communities are one degree removed from it, or two, or perhaps more; but even in the oldest we may find underlying strata which bear the fossil evidences of those primitive conditions. At every stage in the history of American development, there have been in existence at one and the same time communities which felt themselves to be old and new or frontier communities, in which American social development was forever beginning over again. The perpetual presence of these has brought to American society at large a perennial renovation, a breath of fresh air as from a younger world, as if Bond Street and Piccadilly were kept in perpetual neighborhood to the primitive society of the book of Genesis,—to Abraham and Lot, to Lamech and Tubal-Cain. The organization of American life has therefore at all times been characterized by a peculiar fluidity and elasticity. To some these signs of newness are unwelcome. But for my part I hope that those of us who live in the most developed communities, and who therefore may be peculiarly tempted to adopt this attitude, may never lose sight of those attractive and even beautiful traits that have gone along with the newness and crudity of American society. Youth is awkward and ungainly, undeveloped and self-conscious; but its eager hopes and bright aspirations are among the most precious possessions of the race. Michelangelo's David has large hands and feet, but who is unmoved by the figure of the ruddy youth, fresh from the wild pastures and from contact with the elemental forces of nature, going forth, fearless and joyful, to his conflict with the Philistine giant?

But whether we admire or do not admire the qualities of American civilization in their most characteristic expressions, historically there can be no question that, such as they are, they have been in large measure produced by the possession of the great West, and the history of its acquisition and first use becomes an important part of the history of the Revolution as a social movement.

It is well known that the charters of several of the colonies assigned to them territories extending far to the westward of the Alleghanies, and even to the Pacific Ocean. These grants had been environed with intercolonial disputes, and France had totally denied all claim of England to lands beyond the mountains. France had done somewhat more than England to make good her claim to the Mississippi. At all events these inland regions seemed to be in easier communication with the French settlements in Canada above and in Louisiana below than with the English settlements upon the Atlantic, between which and the Ohio valley lay the broad ranges of the Appalachian chain. A collision was inevitable. A spark was thrown to the train by Virginia's expedition across the mountains in 1754, and the first shot in the great Seven Years' War, the gigantic conflict which raged between England and France in Europe, in India, in America and upon the high seas, was fired by a small detachment of Virginian militia, in an obscure skirmish in the forest, under the command of a provincial lieutenant-colonel of twenty-two, named Washington. Five years later the final blow was struck, so far as America was concerned, by the capture of Quebec. Before the treaty of Paris was signed, Pitt had retired from the conduct of affairs. So unmindful were his successors of the interests of the colonies, that they for some time debated whether it were better to retain Canada or the West Indian island of Guadeloupe. (700 sq. mi., now 260,000 pop.) It was remarked that sugar production of Guadeloupe was of more consequence than the Canadian fur-trade. Indeed, something more than indifference to colonial interests must be alleged against those ministers, for it was distinctly argued among them that, if the colonies were relieved from the menace of the French power in Canada and the savage allies of France, they would expand without limit over the continent, become a great nation, do their own manufacturing, and become independent of Great Britain. Despite such narrow views, the ministry retained Canada. English territory was extended to the Mississippi, while all that France had held west of that river was ceded to Spain. But that the narrow views remained, was shown by the conduct of the ministry with regard to the new territory. Of all this vast region, only the present area of Quebec was erected into a province. As to all that lay between the Alleghanies and the Mississippi, it was reserved as crown lands, and to be left, in undisputed possession, to the savages. The king's subjects were forbidden to make any purchases of land from the Indians, and to make any settlements west of the mountains. Any who had already settled to the westward were warned to remove. The protection of the Indians from encroachments was alleged as the reason for thus depriving the colonists of one of the chief gains for which they had helped in the war. A truer reason, it appears, is to be gathered from a report of the Lords of Trade and Plantations in 1772, in which they say, writing to the Privy Council: "We take leave to remind your Lordships of that principle which was adopted by this Board, and approved and confirmed by his Majesty, immediately after the Treaty of Paris, viz.: the confining the western extent of settlements to such a distance from the sea-coast as that those settlements should lie within reach of the trade and commerce of this kingdom . . . and also of the exercises of that authority and jurisdiction which was conceived to be necessary for the preservation of the Colonies in a due subordination to, and dependence upon, the mother country. And these we apprehend to have been the two capital objects of his Majesty's proclamation of the 7th of October, 1763" (that creating the province of Quebec). "The great object of colonizing upon the continent of North America has been to improve and extend the commerce, navigation and manufactures of this kingdom."

But in spite of this advice, settlement was not rigorously excluded, and in the nature of the case could not be, especially after the conclusion of Pontiac's war. Adventurous spirits among the backwoodsmen of Pennsylvania and Virginia made their way into the regions between the mountains and the Ohio River, chiefly into the region now called West Virginia. Hunters had visited it before. Now actual settlers began to come. In 1768 Sir William Johnson, the great Indian agent, gathered together the representatives of the Six Nations and their dependent tribes in a great council at Fort Stanwix, now Rome, N.Y. Three thousand of them came and he made with them a treaty by which, for $6000 in money and goods they transferred to the British government their rights to western Pennsylvania, most of West Virginia and Kentucky. Already some thousands of white men had pushed into the mts., and a number of nameless backwoodsmen had wandered over Kentucky and Tennessee, when, in 1769, Daniel Boone began his more famous explorations of Kentucky. He and his companions and men like him, fearless, enduring, full of resources, eager for adventure and fairly enamored of the wilderness and its free life, acted as the advance-guard of civilization. Pushing through the dark and unbroken forest that stretched its twilight over all the broad belt between the Atlantic settlements and the western prairies, they came forth upon the wide and beautiful plains of the blue-grass region, where the buffalo and elk and deer ranged in numbers beyond all that white men had ever seen before. Inconceivable abundance of game offered easy support and rich gains in peltry. Moreover, the land was quite unoccupied. It was a debatable land between the Cherokees on the south and the Algonquin tribes to the north of the river Ohio, the hunting-ground and fighting-ground of both, but inhabited by neither. In these beautiful and abounding solitudes the frontiersmen found ample scope for their powers as hunters, as adventurers and as Indian fighters. In 1769, too, men began the first settlements upon the Watauga River, in what is now Tennessee, and, unexpectedly finding themselves to be outside the jurisdiction of Virginia, framed for themselves a form of government, the Watauga Association. These were the first that went across the mountains to create an organized community. In 1770 Washington himself went down the Ohio to the mouth of the Kanawha, carefully observing the country, and ever after showed the most intelligent application of the problems of Western development.

After that brief Indian war in 1774 which is commonly called Lord Dunmore's War, but which is perhaps chiefly famous by reason of that favorite declamation of American youth, the Speech of Logan, settlement began in

Kentucky. The first log-cabin was built by James Harrod at Harrodsburg in 1774, the first fort by Boone at Boonesborough in 1775. In the first of these years Parliament took an important step by passing the Quebec Act. This statute enlarged the boundaries of the province of Quebec until it included all the territory north of the Ohio and east of the Mississippi, the modern states of Ohio, Indiana, Illinois, Michigan and Wisconsin. All this was to be under the authority of the governor-general, with no representative assembly. Two hundred and forty thousand square miles of territory which early charters had granted to the old colonies were thus taken from them, and no doubt with a purpose not unconnected with the rise of troubles between the colonies and the mother-country. The old colonies complained of this act for establishing the Catholic religion near them, but the feature of it which has just been alluded to appears not to have attracted forcibly their attention. In 1774 the West was little thought of. Only the more sagacious of the colonists, like Washington, looked far enough into the future to appreciate its importance. But at a later time, when the progress of events had made its value plainer, the Quebec Act was often referred to as if its insidious provisions had been among the causes which had stirred the colonists to resistance and revolution.

There is plainly a very striking contrast between the actual status of the West in 1775 and its potential position in respect to the future of the United States. In the old French settlements of Detroit and in Indiana and Illinois—Vincennes, Kaskaskia, Cahokia, Fort Chartres—there were still perhaps 2000 white inhabitants, with a few hundred negroes, though the major part of the Illinois French had drifted across the Mississippi to the new settlement at St. Louis when the flag of Great Britain supplanted that of France on the east side of the Mississippi as a result of the treaty of 1763. Of this small population that dwelt north of the Ohio River, only a few were of English descent. In Kentucky there were perhaps 300 whites from Virginia and the other sea-coast colonies, in Tennessee perhaps 400, mostly from Virginia and North Carolina. A few hundred Connecticut men, soldiers in the previous war, had founded an ill-fated settlement at Natchez, on the lower Mississippi. Except for these 2 or 3000 whites, the whole region between the Alleghanies and the Mississippi, whether north of the Ohio or south of it, was merely the home of Indians and of wild beasts.

When however we consider what this region has come to mean in the America of the present day—consider, to note but one broad fact, that of our hundred millions of population a third dwells in that area, and that without it we could not have had that other third that dwells beyond the Mississippi—it becomes a matter of great historic interest to inquire, first, how this priceless opportunity for expansion was secured. I touch upon it, merely by way of reminder, will lead us briefly into political and military history, but it is political and military history with direct social consequences.

First as to the political or diplomatic movements. When the Continental Congress sent commissioners to Europe empowered to join with the French in making peace with Great Britain, it instructed them to push the northward boundary of the United States to the Great Lakes and somewhat more, the westward boundary to the Mississippi, the southward boundary to the parallel of 31 degrees of north latitude. But though the United States were allied with France and France was allied with Spain, Spain was no ally of America, and hardly even a friend, standing by the cradle of the infant with great misgivings as to what such births of free states might portend to her own empire in the New World. The enterprising Governor Galvez of New Orleans had taken occasion of the war to capture Baton Rouge and Natchez and Mobile and Pensacola. In his view and that of the other Spanish officials, all the region south of Kentucky and west of the Atlantic portion of Georgia might rightfully be claimed by Spain and left for the present to be occupied by Indians under her protection. France, acting the part of the judicious friend to both parties, proposed a line running southward through what is now eastern Alabama, to the east of which should dwell Indian tribes under the protectorate of the United States, while to the west of it dwelt Indian tribes under the protectorate of Spain. In other words, it was by no means a foregone conclusion that the new republic should set out upon its career with those boundaries—of the Mississippi and 31° north—which she craved and which were so necessary to her future development. On the contrary, to have secured them, even though actual possession of all could not be obtained till 1798, was a very distinct diplomatic triumph.

Not more secure of fulfillment was the American claim to the region north of the Ohio. It is a familiar story, how the British government, for the sake of Canada and the Northwestern fur-trade, endeavored to keep this great area, that now embraces Ohio, Indiana, Illinois, Michigan, and Wisconsin, as a game-preserve for her Indian allies, declaring it all to belong rightfully to Great Britain as having been before the war a part of the great province of Quebec. Spain, too, cast longing eyes on this region that we are now accustomed to call the Old Northwest. In 1781 a Spanish officer, sent out from St. Louis, marched through the Illinois country and captured the nearest British fort, that of St. Joseph in what is now southern Michigan. John Jay, then our representative at Madrid, as soon as he heard of it, wrote to our government hinting that it was done with an intention of establishing for Spain a claim to all that country. Dr. Franklin wrote from Paris: "Are (the Spaniards) to be suffered to encroach on our bounds, and shut us up within the Appalachian mountains? I begin to fear they have some such project." Sure enough, when the negotiations began, Spain made her claim to all the northwest. The French negotiator tried to persuade Jay to consent to this, and with it to the abandonment of the navigation of the Mississippi. He tried likewise to persuade England to insist upon this reduction of American territory, and

England attempted to secure the N.W. for herself. Jay answered: "We shall be content with no boundaries short of the Mississippi." That he and his fellow-commissioners succeeded, here also, in securing to the United States their full opportunity for expansion, was again a great diplomatic triumph. But it is improbable that they would have succeeded in making good their claim if the United States had not been in actual possession of the territory in question, and that they did thus possess it was due to the romantic expedition of George Rogers Clark. So we come from the political to the military history of the West.

Whenever the Revolution should begin, it was certain that such men as were in the West by having come into it from English America would be ardently in favor of the Revolution. They loved freedom, and they had lost all remembrance of Europe and all sympathy with European modes of thought. Gathered from several colonies, the uniform conditions of their life had made them all of similar type, but of a type quite unknown elsewhere. Their intense Americanism would be a fighting force of great effectiveness, and so it proved, not only in the Revolutionary War but again in the War of 1812, into which the United States was carried rather by the ardent Americanism of the West than by any other force. In the difficult and dangerous situation in which they dwelt in 1775, it was not possible for them to abandon their wives and children to the savages while they went to fight upon the remote sea-board; and on the other hand the East and the Congress left them to themselves, to work out their own salvation as best they might. Therefore the official proceedings of Congress and the documents of the Continental army make scarcely any mention of their exploits, and to most persons their achievements in the Revolutionary war remain largely unknown. To anyone familiar with the pages of modern European history, across which march thousands and hundreds of thousands of professional soldiers, with all the pomp and circumstance of war, conducting the regular operations of battle and siege in accordance with scientific principles,—"all the while Sonorous metal blowing martial sounds,"—it seems a strange proposition if one says that, after all due credit given to the work of the American diplomats, hardly any modern campaign of the greatest general or the most numerous army ever achieved results of so vast consequence to the future as were achieved by a little irregular force of less than two hundred undrilled backwoodsmen, commanded by a plain young provincial only twenty-six years old. Yet it is no exaggeration to apply exactly this language to the northwestern expedition of George Rogers Clark in 1778 and 1779.

Imagine the United States setting out upon their career as a nation with the Ohio as their northwestern boundary, and England as their northwestern neighbor. Imagine the difference between their real history and present state on the one hand, and on the other hand what their history and condition would be with the omission of all the teeming millions that fill the northern valley, with the great westward plain in the hands of others, and with the Pacific coast and all opportunity for expansion toward it cut off by alien territory and alien powers. You are imagining a United States cabin'd, cribb'd, confin'd, a United States definitely deprived of that majestic career of imperial greatness which, though we discern its outlines but dimly, constitutes the chief inspiration of all our patriotic thought.

In that day of small things, and in that new and untracked country, in which the foot of man was yet to trace out the paths of future development, the opening up of these boundless possibilities was due, more than to any other one thing, to the bold thought which occurred to one brave young Virginian as he came back along the Wilderness Road from the infant settlements of Kentucky in the autumn of 1777. This young Virginian, George Rogers Clark, had made up his mind that by a bold and sudden movement he could at one stroke secure the whole region to the northwest of the Ohio.

With some aid from Governor Patrick Henry of Virginia, he raised in the West a force of less than two hundred men, floated down the Monongahela and the Ohio for 800 miles, marched overland 100 miles to Kaskaskia, surprised the British garrison, and secured the post without firing a gun. This was on July 4, 1778. Cahokia and Vincennes were obtained with similar ease, and when the British commandant at Detroit recaptured Vincennes and threw into it a considerable British force, Clark surprised and recaptured the town by a February march of 240 miles across frozen fields and through ice-cold rivers—a march so wonderful that I refrain with difficulty from recounting its details. It may be that they are familiar to all, as they should be. I will only quote the modest words of Clark himself, written soon after to his friend George Mason: "If I was sensible that you would let no Person see this relation, I would give you a detail of our suffering for four days in crossing those waters, and the manner it was done, as I am sure that You wou'd Credit it, but it is too incredible for any Person to believe except those that are as well acquainted with me as You are, or had experienced something similar to it."

It may be thought that a disproportionate amount of space has been given to this heroic, but not grandiose, achievement. But if it be remembered that in the area which the young Virginian thus won for the United States twenty million Americans are now living, it may well be concluded that, after all, Marathon and Thermopylae are not more important or more truly interesting than Kaskaskia and Vincennes.

Assuming this great area, southwest and northwest, to have been won by arms and diplomacy, what was to be done with it? The story is in all the school books, how the states were persuaded to cede to the United States their claims to Western lands, and how the Continental Congress resolved to use them mainly as a fund for the benefit of the whole nation, throwing them open to settlement, in small parcels for the most part, and on easy terms. It was agreed that they should be made up into new states, to be admitted into the Union on equal terms with the old states. When one thinks of the status in which other nations had up to that time kept those who had gone out from them as colonists, one easily perceives that this last was a most momentous action, fundamental to the success of our republican experiment.

{The fragments of text that follow appear to have formed a part of the concluding passages of the 1895 lecture series.}

other is the ancient stove which the Duke of Beaufort presented to the Burgesses, and whereof its maker wrote in honest pride to Lord Botetourt that "The elegance of workmanship does honour to Great Britain. It excels in grandeur anything ever seen of the kind, and is a master-piece not to be equalled in all Europe. It has met with general applause, and could not be sufficiently admired."

But quaint old Williamsburg was not the only ancient seat of government that was deserted for a more central spot. In South Carolina the way had been paved for a change by a curious arrangement adopted during the time of the war, whereby there should be a state treasurer for each of the two rival sections of the state, one for the low country at Charleston, and one for the upper country with his office at Columbia. Not long after the war the transition was made absolutely, and the scarlet and purple velvet gowns of the speakers of the two houses were seen no more in the old city by the sea. In North Carolina, where dissensions always flourished, it was found impossible to agree upon any town in the upland region to be the substitute for Newbern as the capital, and so, by way of compromise, it was agreed to erect an entirely new town for this purpose, upon the farm of Isaac Hunter in Wake County. Hence arose the city called after the name of Sir Walter Raleigh, the first colonizer of the state. Georgia, at the same time, by a concession to the up-country members, agreed to move its capital from Savannah, which had been the seat of government from the very beginning of the existence of the colony, back to an insignificant country town called Louisville. New Jersey's capital moved a little distance up-stream, from Burlington to Trenton. But in general there was little desire or occasion for change in those small states which lay altogether or almost entirely in the alluvial belt, like Maryland, Delaware, New Jersey, Rhode Island and Connecticut. Indeed, Connecticut, with two meeting-places for its legislature, and Rhode Island, with five, had already met the difficulty after a cumbersome fashion. New Hampshire occasionally used Exeter as a capital during the war, but did not permanently move from Portsmouth up to Concord until later. Massachusetts did not move her capital, but it is a sign of the same movement that the curious swarm of discontented men who composed Daniel Shays' Rebellion clamored for such a change as one of the articles in their programme.

Before many years the new State House was built, with its imposing dome. It is needless to say that after this, with the visible Hub of the Universe protruding from their town, nothing could ever have induced the Bostonians to consent to such a removal. But see Proc. Am. Antiq. Soc. XI: 513 (1793). It is not straying too far from the Revolution to call to mind the fact that the capital of New York was in 1797 moved up the river to Albany, and that that of Pennsylvania about the same time began its westward march over the hills to Harrisburg, the first stage being to Lancaster.
{Section of text concludes at this point.}

> "With softened eye the westward traveller sees
> A thousand miles of neighbors side by side,
> Holding by toil-won titles fresh from God
> The lands no serf or seigneur ever trod,
> With manhood latent in the very sod,
> Where the long billow of the wheatfield's tide
> Flows to the sky across the prairie wide,
> A sweeter vision than the castled Rhine,
> Kindly with thoughts of Ruth and Bible-days benign."

But there was a trait in the frontiersman which, on the other hand, was for a time to exert an unfortunate influence upon the growth of American life. The frontiersman is of necessity compelled to act by and for himself. Government can do little for him, and presently he finds that he has little use for government. That same rugged independence without which he could not subdue the wilderness, without which, indeed, he could not endure the wilderness, makes him but an intractable member of the body politic. We have seen in our first lecture how decidedly the frontiersmen of 1776 were opposed to the government of Great Britain. But unfortunately the same impulse led them in 1786 to be insubordinate to the government of the United States or that state government which tried to exercise authority over them. We have seen with what entire independence the frontiersmen of Vermont carried themselves with respect to both the Continental Congress and the state governments of New Hampshire and New York. Massachusetts could hardly be said to have frontiersmen in the strict sense. But the lawless insurrection in the western counties, known as Daniel Shays' Rebellion, was a movement of the same sort of which we are speaking. In western Pennsylvania, in western Virginia, and in Kentucky, there were outbreaks of lawlessness or intrigues for separation from the old states, intrigues which were busily fomented by the emissaries of Spain, who would gladly have made the whole Mississippi valley hers. Western North Carolina, the region now called Ten{nessee} {Section of text concludes at this point.}

our fathers were impatient for Texas and Oregon, in the days when the "manifest destiny" of the United States was the American's familiar war-cry. It is not simply annexationist fervor that is upon us, the mere longing for Naboth's vineyard; it is a general eagerness for a further expansion, a wider manifestation of the nation's power. We are undergoing, or entering upon, one of those revivals of militant, not to say bellicose, patriotism which periodically recur in the history of all masculine nations. We hope to annex territory. We build a great navy, and are secretly desirous that it shall do something striking. We wish for a spirited foreign policy. We revive the memory of wars. We talk of subjecting our school-boys to military drill. We grow suspicious of foreign immigration, and talk hysterically of protecting American institutions from a foreign church. We exalt the flag. Even the ingenious author of "Chimmie Fadden" perceives that he can play upon a popular chord if he shows his Mr. Paul inspired to furious wrath and marvellous prowess by an insult to that sacred symbol.[3]

There is a ridiculous side to all this, an element of Jingoism incongruous to the life of a peculiarly peaceful people. But it has also its nobler side, as has every manifestation of ardent patriotism. America were a degenerate land if it had not still the power of rising to new opportunities, if it had not still the spirit of courageous expansion. But it behooves us to be on our guard against the excesses of that spirit, to see to it that our strength does not tempt us to injustice, that our inevitable expansion is carried on peacefully and righteously. Such thoughts may form a fitting conclusion to such a series of lectures as these. "Peace hath her victories not less renowned than war." I have taken peculiar pleasure in turning aside from the military history of the Revolution to show how much of what is best and most characteristic in American civilization owes its origin or introduction to the peaceful endeavors of those who, in those critical years, with no less patriotism than that of the army, devoted themselves to the recasting of American institutions and the improvement of the conditions of American life. Such has been a char-

{3.} Edward Waterman Townsend (1855–1942) created the character of Chimmie Fadden in a series of stories that first appeared in the *New York Sun* and were collected and published in 1895 as *Chimmie Fadden, Major Max and Other Stories* and *Chimmie Fadden Explains, Major Max Expounds*. "Chimmie," or James, Fadden, the narrator of these stories, is a streetwise young servant to Mr. Paul, a New York aristocrat. In one story Mr. Paul explains to Chimmie that there are two types of anarchists: "Dose dat teaches it," as Chimmie recounts, "and dose dat performs it." When he gets to be "King of dis country," Mr. Paul says he will "make a hit wit honest folk by hanging de teachers of nannychism,"which will take care of the performers as well since "dere won't be any to hang." See Edward W. Townsend, *Chimmie Fadden and Mr. Paul* (New York: Century Co., 1902), p. 69; and Frank Luther Mott, *A History of American Magazines, 1885–1905*, 5 vols. (Cambridge: Harvard University Press, 1938–68), 4:196.

acteristic note of American history. That we are capable of gigantic military achievements no one now doubts. But those achievements that have done most to make the history of America a bright page in the annals of mankind have been chiefly the results of peaceful endeavor and of innocent social progress.

TM, Box 25, JP, DLC.

The Arrival of the Pilgrims

President Woodrow Wilson asked that all schools and colleges observe the Pilgrim tercentenary in November 1920, and in response to this request, William H. P. Faunce, president of Brown University, invited Jameson to present an address on the Pilgrims and the Mayflower Compact. The university later arranged for the publication of the address.[1] More than a celebration of the Pilgrims, the essay is a statement of Jameson's fundamental political and cultural beliefs. He delivered this address on November 21, 1920, in Sayles Memorial Hall.

NOTES

1. William H. P. Faunce to JFJ, September 21, 1920, TLS; [JFJ] to Faunce, September 24, 1920, TLc; and Faunce to JFJ, November 26, 1920, TLS, all in Box 63, JP, DLC; "Prof. J. F. Jameson Tells of Pilgrims: High Faith of Fathers Described by Former Brown Professor," *Providence Journal*, November 22, 1920, p. 11, col. 3.

On a Saturday afternoon in November, 1620, on a day that would now be called the twenty-first, a small ship, of one hundred and eighty tons in the reckoning of that time, sailed into the bleak harbor at the extremity of Cape Cod. Today, three hundred years later, at the suggestion of the President of the United States, the event is being commemorated in thousands of American towns and villages. Last summer the initial stages of the same voyage were commemorated with impressive ceremonies by the Dutch at Leyden and Rotterdam and by the English at Southampton and Plymouth. We may well ask the question, and indeed it is the purpose for which we have come together this evening, to ask the question, and if we can to answer it, Why should this event be celebrated so extensively and with so much emphasis at the end of three hundred years?

May I say for myself and for my own simple part in the services this evening that I respond always with great pleasure to every invitation to return to Providence, where during thirteen years it was my happy privilege to teach, where I formed lifelong connections with the best of friends, and where every kindness was constantly bestowed upon me.

I also think it proper to say, that I responded to the invitation of President Faunce with great alacrity because it was based upon a general suggestion made by the President of the United States, that this day should be thus commemorated. To me the suggestion or request comes not only as an official call, but as one strengthened by personal feeling and rooted in old remembrances of my first years in Brown University and of years at the Johns Hopkins University before that. My mind goes back to days now thirty years in the past, but which some of you will well remember, when the Brown University Lecture Association was organized, primarily for the purpose of having lectures in history and political science delivered to members and friends of the University in Manning Hall, and when the most attractive of its lectures were a series on municipal government given by a young professor, of brilliant speech and engaging manners, who from time to time came over for the purpose from Wesleyan University at Middletown.[1] Many were then impressed with his political sagacity as well as with his gifts of exposition, though none, I am sure, of those who met him on these occasions, nor I myself, had any notion of the remarkable career that lay before him. He was my warm friend in those earlier days, and though I have naturally

{1.} The young professor was Woodrow Wilson (1856–1924), a graduate student at the Johns Hopkins University from 1883 to 1885 whose *Congressional Government*, published in 1885, was accepted as his doctoral dissertation. Wilson taught history and political economy at Wesleyan University from 1888 to 1890 and presented three lectures to the Brown University Historical and Economic Association in January and November of 1889. See JFJ, diary, January 11, 17, November 11, [1889], AD, Box 4, JP, DLC.

made no attempt to seek intimacy with him during his years in Washington, and am well aware that these years have been checkered with mistakes
and marred by the operation of one great defect, I can not fail to regard
with deep feeling whatever is said by him from that high office. I can not
fail to regard as invested with special force a request to commemorate the
Pilgrims, that comes from one who has shown himself so great a master of
American history, and who, Southern born and Southern bred, has never
failed to show in his writings acute perception and high appreciation of the
work of Pilgrim and Puritan. I can not fail to remember the exaltation and
devoted feeling with which he has conceived of himself as the continuator
of the Pilgrims' work into the wider sphere of political activity into which
the opening vistas of the twentieth century permit us to look. Here in this
university, where I always thought it the main duty of a professor of history to preach fairness and openness of mind, I of course try to look at his
career with serenity and detachment, to see his record as it is, with all its
blemishes. But as I think of him, prematurely old, stricken, disappointed yet
undismayed, ending a memorable administration in obloquy and with the
appearance, temporary or permanent, of tragic failure, I cannot but think
of the words with which Milton, in the second sonnet to Cyriack Skinner,
speaks of the loss of his eyes:

> Yet I argue not
> Against Heaven's hand or will, nor bate a jot
> Of heart or hope; but still bear up and steer
> Right onward. What supports me, dost thou ask?
> The conscience, friend, to have lost them overplied
> In liberty's defense, my noble task,
> Of which all Europe rings from side to side.

But to ask again our question: Why do we celebrate the arrival of that little
ship, three hundred years ago, in that lonely harbor? Not, surely, because
the event in itself was brilliant or imposing. Bearing its crowded company of
one hundred or one hundred and two passengers the little ship came to an
anchor on that Saturday afternoon. On the next day they kept the Sabbath.
On the Monday some of the men went ashore and did a little exploring.
The eighteen wives, or such of them as were able to stand and walk, also
went ashore, and did their family washing. Eighteen wives, of whom by
the ensuing April only four were still living! Contrast all this with some of
the Spanish landings to the southward—of Cortez, or Pizarro, or de Soto,
when formidable bodies of Spanish infantry, with cavalry and artillery, came
ashore, unfurled with imposing ceremony the royal standard of Castile and
Leon, or the imperial flag of Charles the Fifth, and listened to the reading of
pompous proclamations of their high master,

"All the while
Sonorous metal blowing martial sounds."

It may be that there is something impressive, as certainly there is something pathetic, in the spectacle of those eighteen brave women proceeding with housewifely rigor to that humble Monday duty to which tomorrow eighteen million American women will address themselves with the like faithful ardor, and carrying it through in the chilly air of late November (some of them doubtless getting their death-colds in the process), but it does not make a brilliant or picturesque scene.

Neither do we celebrate the day because the settlement which these devoted men and women came to found attained great physical dimensions, so that their colony became itself, as did the Massachusetts colony, one of the great political entities of this world. It had a brief career of seventy years, and when it was absorbed into its more powerful neighbor, it had not above thirteen thousand inhabitants; nor is the area which it covered, to this day, one of the most important or influential portions of our great republic.

Neither do we celebrate the day because the little band of exiles who then came for the first time into an American harbor, or, in the case of the strongest, set foot for the first time on American soil, were themselves great or brilliant or important personages. A dozen of the men were members of the English middle class, men with some education and some property, substantial yeomen or small merchants but nothing more, and the rest were of even humbler standing, in an age when standing counted far more, far more severely limited men's careers, than it does now.

Here, however, if I may digress for a moment, I should like to draw attention to one aspect of their worldly condition to which I think too little attention has perhaps been given by most of those who have considered their story. I do not think it is customary to give due weight to the fact that most of them had lived for a dozen years in Holland. Those who had migrated to Amsterdam in 1608 and Leyden in 1609, had in England been for the most part dwellers in rural villages or small towns. Not a few of those who hear me may have visited the ancient hamlets of Scrooby and Austerfield from which, or the vicinity of which, a considerable number of them are known to have come. Pleasing villages they are, and must have been in the days of the migration. The little church at Austerfield, in which William Bradford was baptised, is a venerable and beautiful monument of antiquity, coming down in part from the eleventh or twelfth century, and so is the somewhat larger church of Scrooby, almost equally old. They are well adapted to bestow on village minds such enlightenment as comes from old religion, hallowed associations, and long continued peace. The quiet scenery of that somewhat tame portion of the English countryside had also other value and other inspiration. But life in these villages, or the life of humble artisans in

Gainsborough or Boston or Lincoln in the early part of the seventeenth century, was certainly sluggish and contracted and parochial. To migrate from that environment to the two great cities of Holland, and to dwell in the most intellectual of these for a dozen years, close by a university that was already the most famous Protestant university in Europe, would surely have its effect in awakening the Pilgrim mind to wider and more active thought and to more tolerant as well as more ingenious habits of mind.

The Pilgrims themselves were not unaware of some of the mental effects of the transition. Says Bradford:

"Being now come into the Low Countries, they saw many goodly and fortified cities, strongly walled and garded with tropes of armed men. Also they heard a strange and uncouth language, and beheld the differente manners and custumes of the people, with their strange fashions and attires; all so farre differing from that of their plaine countrie villages (wherin they were bred, and had so longe lived) as it seemed they were come into a new world. But these were not the things they much looked on, or long tooke up their thoughts; for they had other work in hand, and an other kind of warr to wage and maintaine. For though they saw faire and bewtifull cities, flowing with abundance of all sorts of welth and riches, yet it was not longe before they saw the grimme and grisly face of povertie coming upon them like an armed man, with whom they must bukle and incounter, and from whom they could not flye; but they were armed with faith and patience against him, and all his encounters; and though they were sometimes foyled, yet by Gods assistance they prevailed and got the victorie."

I do not think that the relative positions of England and the Netherlands in 1609 are rightly understood by most of those who read about the Pilgrims. In 1609, and still more in 1620, Holland, at any rate, the chief and most advanced of the Dutch provinces, was in several respects considerably more advanced intellectually and in point of general civilization than England, Amsterdam rather more the center of the world's enlightenment than London, and certainly the University of Leyden superior to those of Oxford and Cambridge. Quite apart from that transition from the life of small rural villages to that of busy and enterprising cities upon the effects of which Bradford comments, it may be maintained with a good deal of force that migration from England to Holland at just that time was migration from a less civilized to a more civilized country. The Netherlands had a smaller population than England, and they were less rich in natural resources, but during the forty years through which they had been conducting against Spain their war of independence, they had progressed enormously. The very fact of independence had given them wider horizons and new energy. The conduct of their political and economic affairs had been in the hands of city-dwellers, of commercial magnates, with urban minds and that wide knowledge of the world which commerce brings. Their commerce had increased by leaps

and bounds. Their great East India Company and their other trading organizations had already in 1609 begun to flood the country with wealth. Art
and letters were already beginning to take on that brilliant development that
made the years of Prince Frederick Henry the Golden Age of Dutch history. Moreover, the very years which the Pilgrims spent in Leyden were the
twelve years of truce with Spain, during which the advancement of Holland
proceeded at a rate exceptionally rapid, so that whatever advantages she had
in the comparison in 1609 were heightened in 1620, and the Pilgrims during
their sojourn were witnesses of an economic progress and of a social advance
such as has seldom been seen in twelve years of the history of any small
nation. From all quarters of Europe, too, merchants and travellers were constantly bringing fresh varieties of intelligence, whose influence even humble
English artisans in Leyden, or, at any rate, their leaders, could not escape.
Most important of all, the province of Holland was far in advance of other
states of the world in respect to the tolerance of all varieties of religious
opinion. Jewish exiles from Spain and Portugal, orthodox like those who
filled the richest of the world's synagogues (that of Amsterdam), or heretical
like Benedict Spinoza, Socinians from Transylvania or Poland, Greeks and
Russians, Catholics and every variety of Protestant, found here a hospitable
home and an undisturbed opportunity to think and to discourse. The superior tolerance which always marked the Plymouth Colony in contrast to
that of Massachusetts Bay cannot have been due solely to the mild and gentle
character which Brewster and Bradford impressed upon their settlement at
its foundation. In large measure it must have been due to the beneficent
operation upon Pilgrim minds of the intelligent tolerance which they had
seen to prevail under the government of the Dutch magistrates, and from
which they themselves had profited so largely.

Amsterdam in those days was smaller indeed than London, with a population of perhaps 100,000 in comparison with perhaps 250,000 in the English
capital; but it was in just those years a city of more enterprise and energy than
London, expanding with extraordinary rapidity, and reaching out through
commercial channels into all quarters of the globe.

Leyden, on the other hand, was the chief manufacturing town of Holland. Its population in these years was about 60,000. Thus it was much
smaller than London; but very few of the Pilgrims had ever lived in London,
and Leyden was perhaps three times as large as any other English city or
town. The manufacture of cloth was its leading industry, and most of the
Pilgrims, tillers of the soil hitherto, turned their hands to the work of weav-
ing. Handweavers, it is known, are prone to think, and in the atmosphere of
Leyden there was much to stimulate the intellect. A stone's throw from the
social center of the Separatist congregation—the house of their pastor, John
Robinson—stood the chief hall of the University of Leyden, which in the
350 years of its existence has probably maintained a higher average level of

eminence in its professors than any other of the old universities of Europe. Justus Lipsius and Joseph Scaliger, most learned of all men, had taught there just before the Pilgrims' time. Daniel Heinsius and Jacob Arminius were teaching there in their day. We know that Robinson attended the lectures of Arminius, and took part, modestly but effectively, in the debates which raged around that celebrated theologian. It is certain that not only Robinson, but Elder Brewster, who occupied himself with the printing of books, and those who assisted in his printing-house, and especially William Bradford, with his well-trained and open mind, always eager for fuller and better knowledge, must have profited largely by the neighborhood of these brilliant intellectual influences. It is almost equally certain that those influences filtered among the rank and file of the congregation, those humble artisans of whose pleasant and close relations with the people of the city Bradford gives us so agreeable a picture.

"So," says Bradford, "they lefte the goodly and pleasante citie, which had been their resting place near 12 years; but they knew they were pilgrimes, and looked not much on those things, but lift up their eyes to the heavens, their dearest cuntrie, and quieted their spirits."

Some writers have made much larger claims of Dutch influence upon the Pilgrim mind, and through it, upon all America. There have been a few who have even gone so far as to declare with great emphasis that our federal system and our habit of the written constitution, since the English did not have them, must have come to us from the Dutch. It is true that the seven Dutch provinces in 1620 were a confederation, and that that confederation had a written constitution. But surely there is a natural history of federal governments, wherein we see the operation of similar causes producing similar results, without the need of resorting to the hypothesis of imitation. Public men are but little accustomed, unless in some great hurry, to adopt the institutions of another country, but much more likely to seek for expedients that will meet the exigencies which immediately confront them and satisfy the people who have appointed them to legislate. Federal governments come into existence because states or communities hitherto independent feel the need of union, for the sake of greater security or power, but are not yet ready to merge their individuality in that of a unitary state. Because the Australian colonies have come together in a federal commonwealth, shall we conclude that they must have been at some time subjected to powerful Dutch or Swiss influences of which we have not heard before? And as to the written constitution, can we imagine states coming together to form a union and not setting down in writing the terms of their agreement?

Somewhat more of a case may be made out for Dutch influence in the formation of the New England Confederation of 1643, by which the colonies of Massachusetts Bay, Plymouth, Connecticut, and New Haven united for common defence against the Dutch of New Netherland, the French, and the Indians. The prime fact of confederation is seen to have been due to causes obvious enough and which require no supposition of Dutch influence upon the movement in general; and Plymouth, which had had the greatest amount of contact with the Dutch, was the least influential of the four confederates. Some features of the plan, however, may easily be held to show the influence of Dutch models, and there are some portions of the early New England legislation which show that some of the excellencies of the Dutch legal system had not escaped the attention of our early law-makers. But in the main we are to seek the traces of Dutch influence upon the Plymouth mind in a greater mildness and tolerance than was customary among the English, and a greater degree of general intelligence than would be expected, in that age, of peasants who had never strayed far from villages of the English countryside.

A long digression, but it may have helped us to understand better the company of forty-one men and eighteen women that sailed into harbor upon the *Mayflower* that Saturday afternoon in November, 1620, and to appreciate more rightly the nature of the action which those men took that day and which makes it memorable. For, to answer our question, we celebrate the day primarily because it is the three hundredth anniversary of the Mayflower Compact. The day which has been most commonly celebrated in memory of the Pilgrims is the twenty-first of December, as being the day on which their vanguard made its famous landing at Plymouth, but that is perhaps because the habit of observing the day began at Plymouth (in 1769), and to those who instituted the observance there it was natural to commemorate first of all the arrival of the Pilgrims at their ultimate home. The great event, however, the one most invested with significance for the future, was that which took place in Provincetown harbor. Gathering together, presumably in the cabin of the *Mayflower*, they set their hands to what Bradford calls "a combination made by them before they came ashore, being the first foundation of their governmente in this place." It is fitting to repeat the old and familiar text:

"In the name of God, Amen. We whose names are underwriten, the loyall subjects of our dread soveraigne Lord, King James, by the grace of God, of Great Britaine, Franc, and Ireland king, defender of the faith, etc., haveing undertaken, for the glorie of God, and advancemente of the Christian faith, and honour of our king and countrie, a voyage to plant the first colonie in the Northerne parts of Virginia, doe by these presents solemnly and mutualy in the presence of God, and one of another, covenant and combine our selves togeather into a civill body politick, for our better ordering and preservation and furtherance of the ends aforesaid; and by vertue hearof to enacte, constitute, and frame shuch just and equall lawes, ordinances, acts, constitutions, and offices, from time to time, as shall be thought most meete and convenient for the generall good of the Colonie, unto which we promise all due submission and obedience. In witnes wherof we have hereunder subscribed our names at Cap-Codd the 11. of November, in the year of the raigne of our soveraigne lord, King James, of England, France, and Ireland the eighteenth, and of Scotland the fiftie fourth. Anno Dom. 1620."

The origin of this agreement is explained by their chronicler. He says that it was occasioned partly by the discontented and mutinous speeches that some of the strangers amongst them had let fall in the ship, that when they came ashore they would use their own liberty, for none had power to command them, because the patent they had was for Virginia and not for New England, with which the Virginia Company had nothing to do; and partly that their act of agreement might be as firm as any patent, and in some respects more sure.

The meaning of this is, that before their departure from Holland the Pilgrim Company had obtained a patent from the Virginia Company, but now, evidently, were about to settle outside the limits of its jurisdiction. The organization commonly called the Virginia Company had under its charter the right to form settlements and exercise jurisdiction anywhere on the American coast between thirty-five and forty-one degrees north latitude. In 1619 and 1620 the company was much disposed to encourage the formation of what they called "particular plantations," settlements which enterprising individuals, or groups of individuals having a certain unity, agreed to form and maintain at their own expense as organisms subordinate to the chief colonial organization that centered in Jamestown. Several plantations in Virginia had this subordinate character and maintained it for some years. To encourage such increase of population to their thinly settled province, the Virginia Company was well content to recognize in such bodies a certain independence of its regulations and a certain freedom of action. In the Division of Manuscripts in the Library of Congress are preserved, as one of its most treasured possessions, two volumes of the records of the Virginia Company's meetings in these very years from 1619 to 1624. In the record of a meeting in February, 1620, we read, "It was ordered allso by generall Consent that such Captaines or leaders of Perticulerr Plantations that shall goe there to inhabite by vertue of their Grants and Plant themselves, their Tennantes and Servantes in Virginia, shall have liberty till a forme of Government be here settled for them, Associating unto them divers of the gravest and discreetes of their Companies, to make Orders, Ordinances and Constitutions, for the better orderinge and dyrectinge of their Servants and buisines Provided they be not Repugnant to the Lawes of England." Now this order was passed on the very day that the patent to John Pierce and his associates for Plymouth was "allowed and Sealed in viewe of the Courte with a Total approbation."

If the Pilgrims had been able to act under such a patent as this, the patent they brought out with them for instance, they would have been possessed of certain powers of framing rules or orders for their own government, certain powers, that is, of local legislation. If authority derived from the Virginia

Company could not be recognized as valid in forty-two degrees of north latitude, it was natural to substitute for it an authority as closely analogous as possible, and one sufficient for the purposes, authority derived from the common consent of colonists, who, if unable to consider themselves under the jurisdiction of the Virginia Company as they had planned, must then consider themselves as authorized to act in a similar manner under the direct authority of their dread sovereign lord, the king of Great Britain.

That a form of government such as they here instituted was contemplated before they left Holland, is plain from a passage which we find in the final letter of advice which their pastor wrote to the whole company at the time of their departure, and which was carried with them from Delfthaven and read to the assembled colonists at Southampton. Among the many advantages which the Pilgrims had enjoyed at Leyden, some of which have already been mentioned, not the least, perhaps the greatest, was in the possession of so wise and beautiful a spirit as that of John Robinson; for, says Bradford, "besides his singular abilities in divine things (wherein he excelled) he was also very able to give directions in civil affairs, and to foresee dangers and inconveniences; by which means he was very helpful to their outward estates, and was in every way as a common father unto them." Nowhere are his foresight and his wisdom better shown than in that passage of the parting letter read at Southampton which relates to matters of government. It runs as follows:

"Lastly, wheras you are become a body politik, using amongst your selves civill goverments, and are not furnished with any persons of spetiall eminencie above the rest, to be chosen by you into office of government, let your wisdome and godlines appeare, not only in chusing shuch persons as doe entirely love and will promote the commone good, but also in yeelding unto them all due honour and obedience in their lawfull administrations; not beholding in them the ordinarinesse of their persons, but Gods ordinance for your good, not being like the foolish multitud who more honour the gay coate, than either the vertuous minde of the man, or glorious ordinance of the Lord. But you know better things, and that the image of the Lords power and authoritie which the magistrate beareth, is honourable, in how meane persons soever. And this dutie you both may the more willingly and ought the more conscionably to performe, because you are at least for the present to have only them for your ordinarie governours, which your selves shall make choyse of for that worke."

The nature of the Mayflower Compact has often been misjudged. It has sometimes been spoken of as if it established in America an independent republic, and this in spite of the plain acknowledgment of subjection to the king of Great Britain with which the document opens. In reality it was a temporary measure, adopted in order to take the place of a patent whose usefulness was at an end, and perhaps in strictness serving only until the arrival of the *Fortune* a year later, bringing a patent from the Council for New

England differing mainly from the first and discarded patent in its territorial grant. From the date of the arrival of that second patent, the settlers of Plymouth found in it clear authority for the scheme of government which they had already adopted. It grants in terms the authority "by the consent of the greater part of them to establish such laws and ordinances as are for their better government, and the same, by such officer or officers as they shall by most voice elect and choose, to put in execution." The same provision is found in the patent granted to Cushman and Winslow in January, 1623, for the settlement at Cape Ann, and also in the colony patent of 1629, granted by the Council for New England to William Bradford and his associates.

It is true that such an agreement, made under such circumstances, would actually bring into existence a polity different in fact from that which had hitherto been usual in attempts, even English attempts, to establish colonies in America. The usual method, in those times, in instituting government for any place outlying from England, was to entrust the control of affairs to those members of the body whose personal status, whose condition in life, marked them out as beings of a superior order, to whom the right of ruling belonged by the decree of heaven. The English world and every portion of it was to be ruled by noblemen and gentlemen; others were called upon simply to obey their betters and to do their duty in that station to which it had pleased God to call them. But Robinson foresaw and the fact was, that the actual composition of their company, lacking the bright presence of noblemen and gentlemen and unprovided with rulers appointed by the gracious hand of their monarch, would naturally lead them into a polity in which the right to rule was not conferred by previous status, might be lodged in persons of little worldly eminence, but was to be exercised by ordinary men whom ordinary men designated for the purpose and who were to be duly respected for that very reason.

In a sense, this temporary government, with its power to make regulations by common consent, was like that which royal charters conferred upon English municipalities, wherein townsmen, authorized by their charter so to do, made by-laws for their own government and elected officers who were commissioned to enforce them—all under the authority of the British crown. Higher than any powers derived from letters patent, or even from the charter of a colonizing company, was the right of an English subject. "Go where he would, so long as he settled on land claimed by England and acknowledged allegiance to the English crown, the Englishman carried with him as much of the common law of England as was applicable to his station and was not repugnant to his other rights and privileges." The colonist in Virginia and in New Plymouth was guaranteed the possession and enjoyment of all the liberties, franchises, and immunities that he would have had if he had been born in England itself and had continued to dwell there, with the exception, of course, of those which his very distance forbade him to exercise.

But though the Mayflower Compact was a temporary device, and government under it alone continued but a year, the event of its signing is nevertheless of the greatest significance and highly worthy of commemoration. To appreciate what it meant, let us take a glance at the world of 1620 in the light of the years that have succeeded. The civilized world of 1620 was Europe. Through toil and trouble lasting through centuries, European mankind had learned how to abide under orderly government, how to remain at peace most of the time, how to go on year after year, in city and town and village, maintaining the industries and intercourse of civilized life with that fair measure of law-abiding spirit and respect for the rights of others that enables men to prosper, to make at least a living, to dwell in a sense of security, and to give a chance to those forces that make for the improvement of men and communities. But that which lay before the future was the problem of expanding this orderly civilization to the filling of the other great divisions of the world, of America especially and of Africa. It is not too much to say that the chief matter of the three centuries that have since elapsed has been the building up of civilized life in America. I remember that I quoted six years ago in this place a passage from Darwin in which, with that quiet deliberation which gave to his utterances so much of their weight, he said of the essential process in our history, "Looking to the distant future, I do not think that the Rev. Mr. Zincke takes an exaggerated view when he says, 'All other series of events—as that which resulted in the culture of mind in Greece, and that which resulted in the Empire of Rome—only appear to have purpose and value when viewed in connection with, or rather as subsidiary to' . . . the great stream of Anglo-Saxon emigration to the west." [2]

We have here in the United States, and the last few years have made it plain to all mankind, the greatest power the world has ever seen, an aggregation of civilized humanity more important, destined to fill a larger place in history, than the Roman Empire which for more than a thousand years so dominated the minds of men. To the north of us lies a great nation, which is kin to our own and in some respects of orderly submission to self-government surpasses us. Great areas to the southward are filled with republics which less perfectly maintain the ideals of self-government indeed, but which after all, by the influence of those ideals and the pervading sense of common origin, a common religion and language, and a common relation to the civilization of the Spanish peninsula, are preserved in a general state of peace as impressive and almost as complete as the famous Pax Romana, and brightened with hopes of progress which the Roman Empire never acquired.

If from the standpoint of 1620 we could look forward into the three centuries which since have passed, could see that the main movement of the

{2.} See JFJ, "American Blood in 1775," this volume, p. 185.

future would be the occupation of the waste places of the earth, in North America, South America, and Africa, should we not perceive, with trembling apprehension, that all the hope of the future depended upon the question whether the European man could stand the strain of so great a transition? Much of his acquiescence in settled order obviously depended upon the conservative inertia of one who dwells where his fathers dwelt and who has no other institutions than those which have grown up around him in a fixed locality. Could he go forth in masses into the new world and spread over its numerous unoccupied areas, and still retain most of what was valuable in the civilization he had acquired?

The very intelligent counsellors who surrounded the King of Spain foresaw this problem in no small degree, and attempted to solve it in a manner according to their prepossessions. To them it seemed indispensable that Spaniards coming to America, to whatever remote part of it, should not escape from the long arm of the law. They regulated their new world from Madrid and from Seville with minute care and abundant and often wise legislation. They provided administrative machinery marked by much ingenuity, sent out many well-qualified officials, and devised still further machinery for bringing to book those whom they had sent out to administer what they had decreed. It was not all in vain. Spanish administration was far from being a failure. Much in it was excellent, and much that we find defective in the government and procedure of Spanish America of today is in larger degree the effect of predominating Indian blood than of whatever weaknesses there were in the Spanish administrative system.

Nevertheless there was a better way by which the great problem, as momentous as any problem that has lain before the human mind, might be solved. No one would now doubt that the problem of the government of very remote communities is best solved if those communities can be made able and willing to govern themselves. To the Spaniards, the Portuguese, the French, and the Dutch of 1620 such a proposal would have seemed unnatural. Their colonies were to be governed by qualified persons whom they sent out to govern, and in the absence of such important representatives of European authority their colonial communities were usually helpless. But there was something in the Anglo-Saxon, however or whensoever acquired, that enabled him, and has almost always enabled him, to rise to such situations. The Mayflower Compact was but the first of a long line of instances in which that ability to supply the lack of external authority by the assumption of self-government has shown itself. Everyone here present knows how in 1636, when Roger Williams and his associates were establishing the town of Providence on territory which seemed to lie outside the jurisdiction of any constituted authority, they framed and signed a similar agreement, influenced possibly by Williams's residence in Plymouth, but naturally evoked by the circumstances in which he and his companions found themselves. Its text may be compared with that of the compact signed in the cabin of the *Mayflower* sixteen years before.

"We whose names are hereunder written, being desirous to inhabit in the town of Providence, do promise to submit ourselves, in active or passive obedience, to all such orders or agreements as shall be made for public good of the body, in an orderly way, by the major consent of the present inhabitants, masters of families incorporated together into a township, and such others as they shall admit into the same—only in civil things."

Very likely the form of such compacts is in some degree derived from that of the church covenants into which Separatist congregations of that day were accustomed to enter. Possibly there may have been some influence from the form of the so-called "associations," or signed agreements to persevere in a given course of political action, which, in the days before the rise of political parties, had done service on several occasions in English and Scottish history, beginning in England with the Association of 1584, the agreement to oppose and pursue all those who should seek to compass the death of Queen Elizabeth.[3] But the real cause of the framing of such documents was that men of the English race found themselves outside the jurisdiction of constituted authorities, yet, through long habituation to local self-government or to other incidents of settled order in English villages, found it intolerable to be without definite basis for government, and improvised one by common action to take the place of what in those days would more normally have been supplied by the crown, as it had been in the case of Jamestown. Several other agreements of the sort, plantation covenants as they were sometimes called, like that which bound together the settlers at Hampton, New Hampshire, may be found in the early annals of our colonies. At a later period, in the days of the Revolution and later, settlers in Vermont or Kentucky or the Northwest Territory, when they found themselves outside the range of state governments or on land so much in dispute that no state could exercise a recognized authority, formed similar temporary compacts for the government of their own affairs. Later, beyond the Mississippi, claim associations of squatters, communities of miners in valleys inaccessible to the arm of the law, Americans who had gone outside the ascertained boundaries of the United States yet deemed themselves to be still within its protection, have framed similar compacts, by which they have agreed to abide by the decision of the majority and to obey the laws and the magistrates which they themselves have made. The American does multitudes of things by voluntary association or informal agreement which the European expects to see done by governmental regulation or on governmental initiative. By the opening

---

{3.} See JFJ, "The Association," AHA, *Annual Report*, 1917 (Washington, D.C.: Government Printing Office, 1920), pp. 303–12.

years of the twentieth century we have arrived at a period when even college students govern themselves, nay more, when even small boys, *ferae naturae*, govern themselves admirably in organizations of Boy Scouts, and solemnly administer a justice little tempered by mercy—nay, most remarkable of all, when, without compulsion of law or executive order, upon the mere request of a government bureau, nearly every American, for several Sundays, voluntarily deprived himself of the use of gasolene in automobiles, repressing for the common good what is now apparently the chiefest passion of mankind.

Do not understand me to hold that because the Mayflower Compact was the first of a long series of voluntary agreements for self-government it is therefore entitled to such fame and celebration as if it had been the cause of all those that followed. An exaggerated importance has often been attached in American history to the first time that this or that thing was done. The agreement signed in Provincetown Harbor was in a sense casual, as being due to circumstances that had unexpectedly arisen. If the Pilgrims had landed where they had expected to land, there is no reason to suppose that their form of government would have been essentially different, or that they would have been governed otherwise than by laws of their own making, administered by officers of their own choosing. For this we have evidence from their patent and from Robinson's letter. It may be that in a strict legal sense government under the Compact lasted little more than a year. Nor can we think that their agreement stood in a causal relation to all the acts of voluntary association that followed in that age and in subsequent times. But when we reflect upon the enormous importance which has attached, in subsequent American history and in that of the rest of the world, to the principle of self-government, of government based on the consent of the governed, of "government of the people, by the people, for the people," we shall surely think it not only warrantable but imperative that we should celebrate with grateful remembrance the action of those who first established such government on American soil.

We have met, then, to celebrate the slight beginnings of American self-government, the first manifestation in the New World of that spirit of voluntary association, of self-rule, of submission to the majority, of democracy, that has since made the conquest of the continent. Where forty-one sturdy Englishmen subscribed their adherence to these principles in 1620, in 1920 they are the accepted doctrine of a hundred and fifty millions or more in America and of a still greater number in Europe. Democracy at last prevails throughout the world.

In our gratulation over its advances, we must not lose sight of the imperfection with which its principles are carried out. Much of our adherence to those principles is lip-service. Rule by the consent of the governed, we sadly admit, is far from having achieved perfection, either as regards legislation or as regards execution. Neither can we yet pride ourselves on that whole-hearted submission to the rule of the majority which the theory of democracy requires. And of course we have to admit that democracy at its best has faults from which some of the rival forms of government are more free. But on the whole it is clear to us that the government of plain men by plain men, or, to put it better, the government of men by their own wills, in the light of what their own minds conceive to be for their own joint interests, brings juster and happier results in the long run than any other polity. So we rejoice in the triumph of democracy and celebrate with fervent gratitude the day of its beginning in America.

The President, with his habitual discernment in historical matters, has rightly seen that, in the whole story of the arrival of the Pilgrims, it is the signing of the Mayflower Compact rather than any landing on Plymouth Rock, that most calls for commemoration three hundred years after, and President Faunce in asking me to come here and speak has rightly indicated that the beginnings of American self-government are likely to be the main theme of such a discourse. Yet, for my own part, I think I might be quite as much disposed to emphasize and commemorate the moral as the political quality of the Pilgrims' advent. The best institutions that ever were devised will work to good results only when sustained by character. Now just as when we look about us upon the founders of other republics—Mirabeau and Bolívar, let us say, and Gambetta and Lenin—we are filled with gratitude that at the forefront of our national history there stands the incomparable figure of Washington, as a model of unselfish patriotism, of balanced wisdom, and of every public virtue, so it has been of incalculable benefit that we have always seen, at the threshold of our colonial history, such examples of civic virtue, of devotion to ideals, of willingness to make sacrifices for the common good, of fortitude, of gentle forbearance, and above all, of faith in the future and in God's providence, as are shown to us by Bradford and Brewster and Winslow and their humbler companions. We were destined to be a nation of pioneers, breaking fresh ground and subduing the wilderness, first in the Atlantic coastland, then in the uplands of the Alleghenies, then in the boundless West. Each community passing through the pioneer stage, usually to ultimate prosperity, there was always danger that it should succumb to the faults of the pioneer and of the prosperous, the rough and reckless individualism of the former, the selfish materialism of the latter, the conviction of both that property is the main good of life, the rights of property the most sacred interests of the race. No one can measure the extent to which our communities have been saved from such grossness by those of their number who at their founding and throughout their rank development have remembered the story of the Pilgrim Fathers.

" 'Tis not the grapes of Canaan that repay,
    But the high faith that failed not by the way."

We have the clusters of Eshcol in prodigious abundance; can we not preserve also the high faith of the Pilgrims—their faith in the order of the world, their faith in the future, their faith in popular government even when it is administered by a party which is not our own, or by persons whom we ourselves would not have chosen?

Multitudes of writers have attempted to set forth the quality of the Pilgrim story and the Pilgrim character, but after all none has ever set forth that spirit so well as the one who did it first, the admirable governor of the colony, William Bradford. There is a famous passage in his History of Plymouth Plantation that we may well take as exhibiting to us briefly the whole spirit of the Plymouth experiment.

"But hear [here]," [4] he says, "I cannot but stay and make a pause, and stand half amazed at this poore peoples presente condition; and so I thinke will the reader too, when he well considers the same. Being thus passed the vast ocean, and a sea of troubles before in their preparation (as may be remembred by that which wente before), they had now no friends to wellcome them, nor inns to entertaine or refresh their weatherbeaten bodys, no houses or much less townes to repaire too, to seeke for succoure. It is recorded in scripture as a mercie to the apostle and his shipwraked company, that the barbarians shewed them no smale kindness in refreshing them, but these savage barbarians, when they meete with them (as after will appeare) were readier to fill their sids full of arrows than otherwise. And for the season it was winter, and they that know the winters of that cuntrie know them to be sharp and violent, and subjecte to cruell and feirce stormes, deangerous to travill to known places, much more to serch an unknown coast. Besids, what could they see but a hidious and desolate wildernes, full of wild beasts and willd men? and what multituds ther might be of them they knew not. Nether could they, as it were, goe up to the tope of Pisgah, to vew from this willdernes a more goodly cuntrie, to feed their hopes; for which way soever they turned their eyes (save upward to the heavens) they could have litle solace or content in respecte of any onward objects. . . . Let it also be considred what weake hopes of supply and succoure they left behinde them, that might bear up their minds in this sad condition and trialls they were under; and they could not but be very smale. . . . What could now sustaine them but the spirite of God and his grace? May not and ought not the children of these fathers rightly say: Our faithers were Englishmen which came over this great ocean, and were ready to perish in this willdernes; but they cried unto the Lord, and he heard their voyce, and looked on their adversitie, etc. Let them therfore praise the Lord, because he is good, and his mercies endure forever. Yea, let them which have been redeemed of the Lord, shew how he hath delivered them from the hand of the oppressour. When they

{4.} Brackets in original document.

wandered in the deserte willderness out of the way, and found no citie to dwell in, both hungrie, and thirstie, their sowle was overwhelmed in them. Let them confess before the Lord his loving kindnes, and his wonderfull works before the sons of men."

I wish that students in Brown University would make themselves more familiar with the pages of Bradford. I should think it a wholly sufficient result of such an address as this if I could persuade many of them to read at least the first third of his book. In the first place, it is in its way a classic, with a frequent beauty of phrase that springs from the beauty of his spirit, and from his familiarity with what was to him the one great book, though he had read many others. In the second place, the reading of Bradford's history could not fail to correct in their minds that conception of the Pilgrim and the Puritan which so easily comes to us from the newspapers and from still more ignorant writings, in which what was harsh and narrow in the spirit of Puritan and Separatist is so emphasized, so exclusively brought into the foreground, that the result is but a caricature. I do not think it would be easy for any right-minded young man to rise from the reading of Bradford without the conviction that, whatever in seventeenth-century theology or ethics is now obsolete, here is a man with whom one could strike hands, with whom one could walk side by side, who can typify to us a spirit which, *mutatis mutandis*, we should be glad to apply and to see applied in all the communities and all the affairs of this great country, that we may advance into the future with a firm hold on what is best in the past.

Men and women of Providence, the history of the Hebrew nation was sacred history only because the Hebrew thought it so. Are we not as truly a chosen people? I wish that we might impose upon our minds the habit of thinking always of our own wonderful history as a sacred story. I wish that, when we read in the eleventh chapter of the Epistle to the Hebrews that magnificent bede-roll of the great ones of Israel, we should translate it into terms of our own history—should remind ourselves that by faith our elders obtained a good report; that by faith Bradford and Brewster, when they were called to go out into a place which they should after receive for an inheritance, obeyed; and they went out, not knowing whither they went. By faith they sojourned in the land of promise, as in a strange country, dwelling in tabernacles with those who were the heirs with them of the same promise: for they looked for a city which hath foundations, whose builder and maker is God. Therefore sprang there even of these few so many as the stars of the sky in multitude, and as the sand which is by the seashore innumerable. These all died in faith, not having received the promises, but having seen them afar off, and were persuaded of them, and embraced them, and confessed that they were strangers and pilgrims on the earth. For they that say such things declare plainly that they seek a country. And truly, if they had been mindful of that country from whence they came out, they might have had opportunity to have returned: but they desired a better country, that is, an heavenly; therefore God was not ashamed to be called their God; for He had prepared for them a city. And what shall I more say? For the time would fail me to tell of Winthrop and of Williams and of Washington and of Franklin and of Adams and of Hamilton and of Lincoln and of Roosevelt, who through faith subdued kingdoms, wrought righteousness, obtained promises, escaped the edge of the sword, out of weakness were made strong, waxed valiant in fight, turned to flight the armies of the aliens. And these all, having obtained a good report through faith, received not the promise, God having provided some better things for us, that they without us should not be made perfect.

Published by Brown University (Providence, Rhode Island, 1920).

Review of Claude M. Fuess, Amherst: The Story of a New England College

Jameson won acceptance to Harvard College at the age of fifteen but enrolled at Amherst College in 1875 against his own wishes when the family moved to western Massachusetts to improve his father's health.[1] While at Amherst Jameson, like many undergraduates, often made disparaging remarks about his professors.[2] Yet he turned to several of his teachers, especially John W. Burgess and Anson D. Morse, who taught history and political science, for advice about his career as a scholar; Jameson cited Burgess in particular as a model of the committed scholar he decided to become.[3]

Throughout his career, Jameson provided counsel on request to the college.[4] He also remained in close communication with his classmates because of his election in 1879 as class secretary—a position he held for nearly fifty years. From 1882 to 1929 he published a *History of the Class of '79*, which was updated each year with news about the achievements of class members.[5] Thus, when Claude M. Fuess published a history of the college in 1935, Henry E. Bourne, editor of the *American Historical Review*, turned to Jameson, one of the historical profession's most eminent graduates of Amherst College, and asked him to review the book.

NOTES

1. JFJ, diary, May 20, 29, June 1, September 1, [1875], AD, Box 1, JP, DLC.
2. JFJ, diary, September 4, 8, [1875]; January 19, [1878]; February 9, March 2, [1878]; October 2, [1878], AD, Box 1, JP, DLC.
3. JFJ, diary, January 20, March 24, April 30, May 20, 24, [1879]; and July 19, [1880], AD, Box 1, JP, DLC. [JFJ] to Ralph Smith, February 4, 1914, TLc, Box 43, JP, DLC.
4. See George D. Olds to JFJ, July 13, August 17, October 23, 1923, all TLS; [JFJ] to Olds, July 18, August 13, 15, November 6, 1923, all TLc; all in Box 54, JP, DLC; [JFJ], [Address to the Amherst *Student* Breakfast], [July 1, 1884], AM, Box 28, JP, DLC; JFJ, diary, July 1, [1884], AD, Box 3, JP, DLC; JFJ, "A

Possible Enrichment of the Teaching of History," *Amherst Graduates' Quarterly* 16 (February 1927): 67–79.

5. See, for example, *History of the Class of '79* (Worcester: F. S. Blanchard and Co., 1882) and *History of the Class of '79 from 1924 to 1929* (Washington, D.C.: Columbian Printing Co., 1929).

A HISTORY OF a college is written primarily for its alumni.[1] The alumni of Amherst College may well feel gratified, to the point of enthusiasm, that its history has been written with so much fullness of information, so much literary skill, and so just appreciation of personal characters—for Dr. Fuess rightly holds that the history of a college is primarily a history of men. Secondarily, such a book, written appreciatively but without partiality, is of value to students of the history of American education, especially in view of the large part which Amherst men have had in the work of teaching. But even the general student of the history of American life and character, however unconcerned with the traditions of Amherst, may draw much profit from the book, especially from its account of the first sixty years, 1821–1881, because of its vivid exhibition of a type. The character of a college, at least of a college as homogeneous as this one was, is formed much less by professors and presidents, plans and curricula, than by the quality of the homes from which the students come. The Amherst catalogue bore almost none but Anglo-Saxon names. Almost uniformly, the students were of the old New England stock, their parents of middling fortune or less and of fair education or more, church-going people of the Congregational faith, their fathers either farmers in the country or professional men in the towns whose parents had come from the country, their preparation for college acquired in country high schools or old-fashioned academies. Those who founded the college intended that it should perpetuate this type, preserving the standards of Puritanism and of Prae-Hibernian Massachusetts. The record of the struggles and sacrifices made toward these ends by the friends of the infant college is moving and impressive. It may well be instructive, to a generation constantly shown the less amiable aspects of New England Puritanism, to see what it could produce, in the earlier half of the nineteenth century, in fortitude, persistence, public spirit, self-sacrifice, and zeal for education.

AHR 41 (October 1935): 197.

{1.} Claude Moore Fuess, *Amherst: The Story of a New England College* (Boston: Little, Brown, and Company, 1935).

ADVOCACY

The Functions of State and Local Historical Societies with Respect to Research and Publication

Throughout his career, Jameson's appreciation of the role historical societies could play in stimulating scholarship was exceeded only by his disdain for the way in which many of them actually operated. A sense of responsibility compelled him as a graduate student at the Johns Hopkins University to join the Maryland Historical Society, but he concluded in 1884 that his membership was "a waste of money almost entirely."[1] Shortly after joining the faculty of Brown University in 1888 as the professor of history, Jameson became a member of the Rhode Island Historical Society, while criticizing the society for its antiquarian interests.[2] In 1890, when the American Historical Association began to cultivate closer ties with local historical societies, he remarked that while he generally did "not entertain a high opinion of our local historical societies," the influence of the AHA on them would be beneficial for both professionals and amateurs.[3]

Believing that local historical societies collected and published material that documented local history and also contained information of national significance, Jameson took the opportunity of addressing this subject at the 1897 AHA meeting in Cleveland as a member of a panel whose topic was "The Functions of Local Historical Societies." Also on the panel were J. F. Wright, a professor at Oberlin College, who described the operations of the Western Reserve Historical Society where this meeting was held on December 30, 1897; and Reuben G. Thwaites, director of the State Historical Society of Wisconsin.[4]

NOTES

1. JFJ, diary, April 21, [1884], AD, Box 3, JP, DLC.
2. JFJ, diary, October 2, [1888], AD, Box 4, JP, DLC.
3. JFJ to Herbert B. Adams, February 21, 1890, ALS, Herbert B. Adams Papers, MdBJ.
4. AHA, *Annual Report*, 1897 (Washington: Government Printing Office, 1898), p. 8.

THE HISTORICAL SOCIETIES of the United States have many and interesting functions. They must collect and preserve historical material, printed and manuscript, and must maintain libraries and museums, well catalogued and accessible; they must print and publish; they must arouse public interest, and keep alive a patriotic regard for local history; they must take part in celebrations; they must accumulate biographical and obituary records; they must attract money and members. We all know that, considering their resources, they do most of these things exceedingly well. Each of us knows the serious efforts which his own society makes to accomplish these tasks; each of us is under frequent obligations to other societies for the fruits of their zealous and successful labors. The development of their libraries in particular can not fail to excite admiration. It may be said with confidence that there is no other country in the world in which the libraries of historical societies have so important a place as they have among the libraries of the United States.

But, if it is our practice with some regularity to examine the publications of these societies, must we not confess to a considerable degree of uneasiness and disappointment with respect to their performance of this particular function? The more certainly will this be our feeling if it is also our habit to keep an eye on the contemporary publications of the European historical societies. To make the comparison in absolute terms would be obviously unfair. The historical societies of a country like ours ought not to be expected to rival the published work of such organizations as the Société de l' Histoire de France or the Scottish History Society. But even if we avoid the comparison with societies planted in cities so large as Paris or so eminent for literary traditions as Edinburgh, there is still much to mortify and to incite us. The ordinary provincial historical journal of France or Germany is, we are obliged to confess, considerably superior to that of America in scholarship and in the amount of really important contribution to historical knowledge. Doubtless they have the advantage of being able to appeal to a larger body of cultivated and scholarly readers. But at least it will not be thought unfair to compare the present published work of our historical societies with that which they were doing forty years ago. Many of them are now printing a larger amount, some of them are printing work superior in quality, but most of them, it seems to me, are decidedly not showing that improvement in product which might justly be expected in view of the far more advanced state of historical knowledge in the country at large. We have also to remember the superior pecuniary resources of our societies, which form probably the richest body of such societies in the world. Upon a hasty estimate their buildings are certainly worth in the aggregate a million dollars, their libraries nearly or quite that, their endowments another million. So far as publications are concerned, the results are lamentably out of proportion to this gigantic investment.

May we not profitably inquire what have been the leading causes that have kept our societies from attaining that development we should have wished them to attain in respect to their functions of publication and research, and by what means their advancement in these respects might be promoted? It will probably be found that the suggestions here made are applicable rather to the historical societies of the older States, private endowed organizations having few or no statutory duties and public responsibilities, than to those State societies, closely connected with their State governments, upon whose functions Mr. Thwaites can discourse with so preeminent knowledge and authority. And certainly the suggestions are made with full knowledge of the fact that each society has its peculiar needs and duties, and that criticism and suggestion can be expressed only in general terms.

In the first place, should we not all agree that our older historical societies have often seemed to conceive of their respective fields and duties in too narrow, and even parochial, a sense? The reason for their existence is, of course, local history, and they win their public support, their money, and their members by devoting themselves to local history. But there are some topics of local history which are purely local and nothing else, and there are those which, while no less important to the history of the locality, are also of significance with respect to the larger life of the nation. The historical society which devotes itself to the former when it might be doing something to elucidate the latter fails of the best part of its mission. Is a subject in the history of the locality more worthy of the society's time and money because nobody outside of the locality can by any possibility be expected to take an interest in it? On the contrary, it is just these subjects which deaden historical societies. If the State or the locality has any importance whatever which should make it worth while to have its history studied, it is because it has played some part in the life of the world. This is the thing to work at. *Hoc opus, hic labor.* Everyone knows that one of the leading defects of American historical writing has been that the writers knew too little of other history. So it is with local history. Neither men nor societies can hope to deal with it rightly unless their minds are full of American history at large and quick to see the relations of their tasks to that which explains them and gives them meaning. It is just this intelligent appreciation which gives to French local historical journals a large part of that superiority which has been remarked. Nor would the intellectual quickening which would come from such a transfer of attention, such consideration of the real importance of topics, be balanced by any material loss. The interest of local readers and subscribers would be held just as well or better. It should be remembered that things are not as they were fifty years ago. With increase of inter-communication purely local feeling has become less acute. The number of people who care a rush whether the Blue Boar Tavern stood in First street or in Second street, or who can excite themselves over silly questions of local priority in this or that small achievement, has grown considerably smaller and is constantly diminishing. Meanwhile the number of persons who have read a considerable amount of general American history or who take an intelligent interest in it, has greatly increased. It is to these people that societies must, in the long run, make their appeal for pecuniary and other support. It is highly probable that, by avoiding fussy antiquarianism and looking chiefly at the larger aspects of local history, they would accomplish the difficult feat of serving both God and mammon. Not a few of our historical societies consist of two or three hundred sustaining members, who like to help in keeping up such an institution, and who are not without interest in American history, but who never attend the meetings, which have become the exclusive property of a few fossilized antiquarians. Would not fresh life be brought in if the society were to perceive clearly that its field of work is, rightly stated, *American history locally exemplified*?

Another class of persons who ought to be more actively interested in local historical societies is that of college teachers of history. This thought may properly be dwelt upon for a moment, for an insufficient degree of cooperation between the historical professors and the historical societies (a cooperation the promotion of which was at the beginning one of the prime objects of this association) is an evil of serious importance. Its importance cannot be rightly estimated unless we take into account the present stage of historical studies among us and the stage into which we are probably proceeding. Predictions are dangerous. But the intense conflicts of the Reformation brought forward in every country a generation of political historians, an age in which the minds of statesmen turned by a natural attraction toward history. Upon that age ensued, by a natural evolution, an age devoted chiefly to works of erudition, the publication of sources, the labors appropriate to academies and Benedictines. So the storm and stress of the French revolution generated a crop of political historians, the best part of the historical work coming from the hands of public men, like Mackintosh and Macaulay, Guizot and Thiers, Niebuhr and Bancroft and Herculano. There are not wanting signs in England and France, in Germany and America, that we are next proceeding, by a natural evolution, into a period characterized, I will not say by Benedictine achievements, but by extensive documentary publication and other academic labors. For the work of such a period the most appropriate agents in our country are the organized historical societies and the representatives of history in the universities. It would be a thousand pities if they should be allowed to drift apart. Yet they will inevitably do so if the societies are permitted to look upon their tasks of local history with purely local eyes; for the professor is daily occupied with the teaching of general American history. His mind is set on that. He can care little for local history that has not an infusion of that larger element.

It is a part of the same general suggestion if one goes on to say, in the second place, that our historical societies would add greatly to their usefulness if, in their published work and what they do in furtherance of research, they would pay more attention to the more recent periods of American history. Speaking of the older States only, it may almost be said that their historical societies pay twice as much attention to the period of exploration and first settlement as to all the rest of the seventeenth century, twice as much to the period anterior to 1700 as to that from 1700 to 1775, and none whatever to that since the Revolution. However great our passion for origines, can we defend this as rational? If the story of the past has a value because of its influence on the present, can we justify our neglect of that portion of the past which has been most directly influential, the more recent past? The field of colonial origins has been abundantly, almost superabundantly, cultivated. We could get along if for ten years no man printed another account of the early days of New England. Meanwhile how unsatisfactory is, for instance, our knowledge of the constitutions of the colonies in the half century preceding the Revolution, how complete our ignorance of State politics during the thirty years beginning in 1789? Fifty years ago it was perhaps reasonable to stop short with the Revolution. But the Revolution is now fifty years farther away, and surely in the hundred and twenty years since its time many interesting things have happened in the State and the locality as well as in the nation. Doubtless there are many persons to whose dim minds the phrase "American history" brings up instantly and solely the image of the Revolutionary war. Apparently most members of State legislatures belong to this class. But after all it is not to these that the society's publications are chiefly addressed. An historical society must not disdain popularity; but it shows a woeful, and to my mind a quite unnecessary, want of courage if it avoids topics of real importance because they are not yet objects of popular interest, or permits popular fancies to divert it from what it really thinks to be its best work.

This inevitably leads one to say a word concerning genealogies. Rejice aniles fabulas, saith the Scripture—rejice genealogias.[1] It is a ticklish business to take up one's parable against them in these days, when many an historical society is finding that by far the greater number of those who resort to its library come there for no other purpose than to hunt up their genealogies and to prove their right to entrance into the charmed circle of the Sons of This or the Daughters of That. But nevertheless no historical society has a right to use its research and publication funds in furthering the purposes of these people, or, as one society does, to buy almost nothing but genealogies with its library fund. These funds were presumably given to the society for the furtherance of history. To use them for genealogical researches, for the publication or purchase of genealogies, is in almost all cases a gross mis-

{1.} Reject old wives' tales, reject genealogies.

use. The theory is of course that genealogy is an important aid to history. But is it, now and in this country? Volumes upon volumes of it have been printed. Search through the whole tiresome mass, and do you get a handful of historical wheat out of all this chaff, this pitiful accumulation of names and dates? But one answer is possible. The theory is, so far as this country is concerned, a mere superstition, one of Lord Bacon's idola fori.[2] Geography is far more useful to history than genealogy; but what should we think of an historical society that bought nothing but atlases and printed nothing but maps? The addiction of historical societies to genealogies arises not from devotion to the primary and public purposes for which they were instituted, but from a weak desire to placate people who, it is thought, may in time, if sufficiently indulged, turn from their personal and private interest in their ancestry, and begin to take an interest in history. They may, but meantime is American history being rightly used?

To return to more positive suggestions, how neglected is the field of American economic history so far as our societies are concerned! If the world of European historical scholarship is turning more and more to the consideration of that subject, how much more ought this to be the case in a country like ours, a new country, a country in which constitutional and political development, the traditional subjects of historical study, have been at every step conditioned, directed, and controlled by economic factors and the course of economic evolution. But how little has been done in this direction aside from the history of the Federal finances! Here again the course which, on intellectual grounds, is so warmly to be advocated would almost certainly be profitable in a mundane sense, for there is nothing more certain to interest the business man, that arbiter of all American destinies, than the history of American business.

But in all these lines of publishing activity, which recommend themselves to our minds as we survey the field, surely we shall all agree that what is most necessary is not the printing of essays and articles, but the printing of documents and materials. Documentary publication is the work which counts in the long run, the work which gives permanent value to the society's volumes. Look over the volumes published by the societies a generation ago. Nearly all the articles and essays are obsolete or antiquated. Such of them as were ever worth doing will have to be done over again. But the original documents then printed are still valid, still useful. The real glory of an historical society is a series of volumes of important historical documents, original materials selected with intelligence, systematically ordered, edited ably, and with finished scholarship.

{2.} Sir Francis Bacon's *idola fori*, "idols of the marketplace," represented commitment to false ideas that blocked human progress. See Charles D. Broad, *The Philosophy of Francis Bacon* (New York: Octagon Books, 1976), pp. 48–49.

All these counsels are in the last analysis counsels of energy and courage. Energy can not always be commanded; the work of societies must be done by the members it possesses, and fortunate are those who possess a group of active and resourceful members; doubly fortunate if their organization is such as to give the control to these rather than to those who are oldest, or to those who are richest, or to those eminent for something else quite alien to the business of history. But the counsel of courage is for all. Placed in the midst of material influences, our historical societies are charged with immaterial, one may even say spiritual, interests. They must be in and of the world. But they are wanting in insight and in that faith in American humanity which the study of American history should create if they do not believe it safe for them to cherish high and even austere ideals of scholarly endeavor; and they are recreant to their high trust if, having formed such ideals, they fail to pursue them in all the great work that lies before them, confident that before long their communities will appreciate and sustain their efforts. Like all of us in this complex and vulgar world, they must make compromises and adjust themselves with outward cheerfulness to the actual conditions of their life; but at least let them economize their concessions, and keep alive an inward regret and dissatisfaction over every sacrifice of their true ideals.

AHA, *Annual Report*, 1897 (Washington, D.C.: Government Printing Office, 1898), pp. 51–59.

The Influence of Universities
upon Historical Writing

When William R. Harper, president of the University of Chicago, could not obtain Whitelaw Reid, the editor of the *New York Tribune*, to serve as the principal speaker at the university's convocation on December 17, 1901, he invited Jameson to use this occasion to deliver his inaugural address as head professor of the department of history, a position he had assumed the previous April. Notwithstanding the last-minute nature of the assignment, Jameson felt flattered, telling his friend Francis A. Christie that Harper had invited "all the historical people from Tidyuscung to Oscaloosa."[1] As the most distinguished representative of the historical profession in the West, Frederick J. Turner, professor of history at the University of Wisconsin, welcomed Jameson as a worthy successor at Chicago to Hermann von Holst and as "a man trained in the conscientious ideals of New England, broadened and freed from provincialism by his residence at Baltimore, and by his studies of the South, recognized as one of the best informed students of the Middle States."[2]

Jameson found choosing a title for this lecture to be troublesome. He wanted to title his speech "The Effects of the Dominance of Universities on Historical Work," but he sensed that this might be too intimidating a title, and he considered the idea of calling it "The Present State and Prospects of Historical Writing in America."[3] He finally settled on "The Influence of Universities upon Historical Writing."

In this address Jameson expanded the role he had established for himself while an instructor at the Johns Hopkins University as a specialist in the fields of historiography and historical criticism. At Hopkins he insisted that the historical profession's primary responsibilities were to set standards of good scholarship and to organize the tools that scholars needed for research. He worked prodigiously toward these ends at the university. In 1882 he devoted many hours without financial compensation to arranging and cataloging the library of the Swiss jurist Johann Bluntschli when the collection was donated to Johns Hopkins as a bequest. He also wrote a brief note on the collection that he read to the Hopkins Seminary and then published in the university *Circulars*.[4] He constructed an elaborate scheme by which scholarly periodicals would be reviewed as a regular feature of the seminary meetings, and he assumed the role of advisor to the graduate students who arrived at the university after him.[5]

In the fall of 1886 Jameson offered the course "Elements of Historical Criticism," which was designed to "afford the graduate students of history a fuller knowledge of the best methods now employed in critical investigation" through lectures and practical exercises. At the same time he presented a series of public lectures in Hopkins Hall on "the history of historical writing in America from the period of colonization to the present."[6] Several of these lectures were published in a German academic journal in 1889, and then all were published in 1891 as *The History of Historical Writing in America*. In these lectures Jameson concluded that the individual brilliance displayed by George Bancroft, Francis Parkman, and John L. Motley yielded necessarily to the mere competence of the academic historian. "My view is that there will not be produced among us any work of super-eminent genius," he explained, "but that there will be a large amount of good second-class work done."[7] An article Jameson published in 1890 in the *Atlantic Monthly* elaborated on this cycle of historical writing, in which long periods of fact-finding were punctuated by brief bursts of synthesis.[8] His cyclical theory of historiography reappeared in the address that follows, along with a reminder to historians of Jameson's generation that they faced yet another period of careful documentation before the next grand synthesis could be written.

NOTES

1. William R. Harper to JFJ, November 22, 1901, TLS, Box 91, JP, DLC; JFJ to Francis A. Christie, November 24, 1901, TLS, Box 71, JP, DLC.

2. *University Record of the University of Chicago*, 6 (January 1902): 293.

3. JFJ to Christie, November 24, 1901.

4. JFJ, diary, January 5, [1883], AD, Box 2, JP, DLC; JFJ, "An Account of the Contents of the Bluntschli Library as Received in Baltimore," *Johns Hopkins University Circulars* 2 (February 1883): 61–62.

5. JFJ, diary, November 10, [1883], AD, Box 3, JP, DLC; JFJ, diary, February 16, [1883], AD, Box 2, JP, DLC.

6. "Historical and Political Science," *Johns Hopkins University Circulars* 5 (July 1886): 132.

7. JFJ, "Historical Writing in the United States Since 1861: A Public Lecture, Delivered in the Hall of the Johns Hopkins University," *Englische Studien* 13 (1889): 235; JFJ, *The History of Historical Writing in America* (Boston: Houghton, Mifflin and Company, 1891); Morey D. Rothberg, "Servant to History: A Study of John Franklin Jameson, 1859–1937," (Ph.D. dissertation, Brown University, 1982), pp. 79–82. See also JFJ, "Historical Writing in the United

States, 1783–1861: A Public Lecture Delivered in the Hall of the Johns Hopkins University," *Englische Studien* 12 (1889): 59–77.

8. JFJ, "The Development of Modern European Historiography," *Atlantic Monthly* 66 (September 1890): 322–33.

MR. PRESIDENT, Gentlemen of the Board of Trustees and of the Faculties, Fellow-Students, Ladies and Gentlemen:

The President of the University has told me that I may in some degree regard this address as an inaugural discourse, spoken on taking up the chief responsibility for the Department of History. If this is done, it is inevitable that our first thought should be of the eminent scholar who has preceded me in that charge, and whose ill-health and retirement are so deeply regretted both by the friends of the University and by the friends of history. His varied historical learning and the fame and brilliancy of his writings have invested this chair with distinction, have made it a high honor to succeed him, and have set a lofty standard toward which his successor must struggle as he can. But his services to the University were not confined to the department over which he presided. He brought to the general concerns of the institution the influence of a well-stored mind, of a judgment trained in the public affairs of his native country and of a character infused with moral earnestness. Best of all, he brought from his old-world universities that strenuous devotion to simple but lofty ideals of scholarly endeavor which, in the gross air of American daily life, has so often proved a tonic of immeasurable value. I fear that we are sometimes not duly mindful of the great debt which almost every one of our American universities has owed, especially in its earlier years, to some devoted European scholar who has brought over here the altar of his studious faith and set it up in the American marketplace. Uneasy in the harness of our academic routine, not wholly pliable to the conditions of American life, often nevertheless they have stirred as with a trumpet the hearts of young men, often indeed of older men, who might otherwise have fallen before the gilded but hollow images of Baal and Ashtaroth.[1] There are some here present who share with me the bright remembrance of the early days of the Johns Hopkins University—halcyon days of a novel and brilliant educational experiment, in which truly "it was a joy to be alive, and to be young was very heaven." Is it not true that whenever we think of those days there rises always before us the quaint figure of the great Sylvester, moving half unconscious of the world of sense, inhaling with eager zest the rarefied air of the higher mathematics, and holding before us all, for lifelong remembrance, the example of a simple and unswerving devotion to the things of the mind?[2]

{1.} Baal and Ashtareth (plural: Ashtaroth) were the god and goddess of fertility among Canaanite peoples.

{2.} James Joseph Sylvester (1814–97) was a British-born and educated mathematician who was called to the Johns Hopkins University in 1876 upon the recommendation of Joseph Henry and Benjamin Pierce. The oldest member of the faculty, Sylvester nevertheless energized his colleagues with his zeal and enthusiasm for intellectual endeavors in all disciplines. While at Hopkins he edited the *American Journal of Mathematics* from 1878 to 1884.

First of all then, before taking up our main theme, let us acknowledge with gratitude our obligations to the scholarship, the labors and the character of Professor Hermann von Holst, first head of the Department of History in this University, and join in heartfelt sympathy for the physical suffering which has marked his recent years and has compelled his retirement.

The subject on which I have chosen to speak is "The Influence of Universities on Historical Writing." But its importance and its bearings will not be duly appreciated unless for a few minutes we consider in its broad outlines the modern history of our science. Dr. Mark Pattison no doubt exaggerated when he declared that history was one of the most ephemeral forms of literary composition. But certainly it has its fashions. The modern history of its development leads us through several successive phases, widely different one from another; and each of these phases, we soon perceive in our study, comes forward in much the same manner and at nearly the same time in all countries of Europe alike. At one time one type of history is dominant throughout all Europe, at another time another. The types are sharply distinct, and the transition from one to the next is a more than national movement. The mode in which the past is regarded is a pan-European mode, and its changes correspond to a modulation of key in the general thought of Europe.

First, the Renaissance gave history new life, a keener outlook upon the world of the past, a more classical taste in matters of form. But it was the Reformation, and the mighty political and religious struggles which accompanied it, that first brought history into the front rank among the objects of literary endeavor, established it as a fit occupation for great minds, and made it the companion of statesmen. It is not an accident that, in the century extending from 1550 to 1650, the profoundest minds that occupied themselves with the public affairs of England, Raleigh and Bacon, occupied themselves also with history; that among the great historians of each country of the Continent were eminent statesmen like Agrippa d'Aubigné and President de Thou, Hugo Grotius and Paolo Sarpi. Public life amid the volcanic turmoil of the Reformation or the stirring times of Elizabeth had deepened their insight into history. "Whenever," said Niebuhr, who remembered the storm and stress of the French Revolution, "whenever a historian is reviewing past times, his interest in them and sympathy with them will be the deeper the greater the events he has witnessed with a bleeding or a rejoicing heart."

In view of those present-day conditions which we are later to consider, it is especially interesting to observe what came next after this age of statesmen-historians. When statesmen write history, they rely upon native insight and political experience rather than upon closet industry and technical perfection. By and by the age, especially if it is an age of prose, begins to miss something, to become uneasy and critical, and to fear that its historians have been giving it eloquence or poetry or political philosophy rather than the cold facts which it has begun to crave. Now the century from 1650 to 1750 was preëminently an age of prose. It played Wagner to its predecessor's Faust. Regularity and decorum, science and criticism, the flowing wig and the rhymed pentameter put the political historian quite as much out of fashion as Shakespeare and Ariosto. A new age set in, the age of erudition. Boldness and originality and fire departed from history; scholarship and method and labor took their place. All over Europe scholars devoted themselves to the laborious search for additional materials, to the learned toil of investigation and criticism, and to the publication of great series of chronicles and documents. Enormous additions were made to the sum of printed knowledge respecting history. Giants of erudition sprang up almost simultaneously in all countries, Anakim [3] with marvelous digestions, who, like Leibnitz, could sit at their desks for eighteen hours at a stretch, and who piled up for us those mighty pyramids of folios out of which the modern scholar is content to quarry his little whitewashed habitation. When the muse of history became so pedestrian, historical enterprises naturally lent themselves to organized endeavor. Two forms of organization played an important part in the work of erudite publication—academies, historical and general, like the Prussian Academy at Berlin or the Royal Academy of History at Madrid, and communities of monastic scholars like the Bollandist Fathers or the Benedictines of St. Maur. Those who have read Matthew Arnold's essay on the Literary Influence of Academies do not need to be told what effect such establishments would have upon history. They could not give it spirit or genius or the force of new ideas, but they could concentrate educated opinion, they could impose high standards of workmanship, and they could undertake tasks which were beyond the power of individuals— even of eupeptic Anakim. So also of those religious houses where learning flourished. The monastic principles of humility and obedience gave the services of all to some common task, at which the members of the community labored in peaceful seclusion, patiently and self-forgetfully, for the glory of God and of their order. So throughout that prosaic age accomplished hands, individually or in coöperation, were laying up vast stores of historical material for the uses of a generation more creative, more philosophical, better provided with literary genius and with general ideas.

Not delaying to consider that next generation, when Montesquieu, and Turgot, and Voltaire, and Hume, gave history a wider horizon and taught it to seek the great laws of social development, let us pass on to observe the influence of the French Revolution. It is difficult to find measured words in which to express duly the magnitude of that influence upon the generation that succeeded. Here, again, as in the Reformation, old things had passed away, and all things had become new. The problems of human life in the

{3.} The biblical aboriginal giants in Palestine who warred with the Israelites.

present and the past seemed forever different to eyes which had beheld revelations of popular forces so gigantic and so unsuspected underlying the surface of society. A deeper study of history resulted as a matter of course. And here again, as after the Reformation, the study fell mainly into the hands of men conspicuous in public life. It was for the same reason. The events of the French Revolution, as of the Reformation, had been such as to force historical studies upon minds of the very highest class, upon the very directors of national life. And so, in the middle of the nineteenth century, we had again an age of statesmen-historians—Macaulay and Mackintosh, Niebuhr and Grote, Guizot and Thiers and Lamartine. Their characteristic notes were quickness in seizing the traits of a political situation, insight into political motives, sturdy political faith, force of statement, skill and vigor in narration. But as we round the promontory and enter upon the long reach of the twentieth century, we find that this school also has passed away; that other planets rule the hour, and that we are in the midst of still another of those changing phases or fashions or climates through which the art of history has successively passed.

It was promised at the beginning that this perhaps too long survey should have a direct relation to the theme of the hour. I have pursued, in general outline, the orderly development of our science in order to make it clear that each age has its own mode of looking at the past, and to lead up to the assertion, which I make with little hesitation, that in this age the leading influence upon historical writing is that of the university and the university professor. If this be so, the Influence of Universities upon Historical Writing becomes, to those who care for history at all, an important theme. But *is* it so? Or is the notion an extravagant one, born of a pedagogue's desire to exalt the pedagogue's office?

The proposition is one not easy to demonstrate without entering into tiresome lists and summaries. I must, in a certain sense, ask you to take my word for it; yet not without giving a reason. For six recent years it was my juicy task, as editor of a historical review, to go through each number of the *Publisher's Weekly*, its English congener, the *Publisher's Circular*, and the *Wöchentliches Verzeichniss* of the German book-trade, to scan elsewhere the advertisements of publishers for announcements of new historical books, and to examine carefully the contents of a dozen or more historical journals coming from various countries of Europe or America. So far as this could enable one to testify as to what is going on in the historical world, I assert with confidence that nearly all the important historical books which appear in Germany are either written by university professors, or show in the plainest way the impress of the university; that almost as much might be said of France and Italy, of Belgium and Holland; that even in England, preëminently the home of the rich amateur and the private student, a larger fraction than ever before of the annual historical output is due to university and college teachers, or directly traceable to the influence of their work. In the United States much more than one-half of what is substantial in our annual product comes somehow from university or collegiate sources. This is made the more remarkable when we reflect that twenty-five years ago a college professor of history rarely wrote a book, seldom indeed attempted to do anything beyond his daily teaching. Very likely he now tries to do too many other things; but, at any rate, it is well known that if he publishes nothing he is likely to be little esteemed in his profession. So in England. In the eighteenth century the university professors of history, making no pretence of teaching, lived the life of pleasant idleness which Gibbon has so amusingly described in his autobiography. During much of the nineteenth they were often more eminent for many other things than for historical achievement. But of late the university and college teachers have been in many cases the great English historians of our time—Stubbs and Freeman and Gardiner and Seeley—and most of them have really taught, and have exercised an influence which was distinctly of the professorial type.

Our thesis may readily be illustrated in another way. In whose hands are the large enterprises of serious historical publication? Not to speak of Germany and France, where it is a matter of course that they are directed by professors, take an English example. Lord Acton, regius professor at Cambridge, plans a great composite work on modern history. Of the announced contributors almost all are or have been professors. In what previous age would this have been true? The same holds good in America. In all lands professors control the historical societies, direct the journals, and fill the historical libraries with their particular type of composition.

As for the causes of this transition, which has brought history for a time under the domination of the university, no doubt some are special to our science, some general. It would be only natural if political historians, especially political historians of the second rank, should provoke a reaction, if they seemed to rely on insight as too perfect a substitute for the laborious sifting of authorities, or to care more for eloquence than for accuracy, for, after all, men like to have history tell the sober truth. Once the discerning portion of the public is convinced that Carlyle was a little too rhetorical, and a little too easily imposed upon, all his vociferous groanings over the assumed toilsomeness of his research, all his excited posing as the lynx-eyed destroyer of shams, will not save him. Men will read him for his eloquence; but when they wish to know exactly what happened in Cromwell's time or in the French Revolution they will turn to Professor Gardiner or Professor Aulard.

But there are broader reasons than these for the change that has supervened. We may as well confess that we dwell in an age of prose. The world cares far less for eloquence than it did a generation ago. *Assez de la lyre!* it says, as the shouting mob said to Lamartine. It seems to care less for noble sentiments than for scientific facts.

In the seventeenth century the high enthusiasms of the earlier years gave place, long before the century had ended, to the rule of sober reason; after the founding of the Royal Society there would be no more Miltons. So before the close of the nineteenth century we have witnessed, all the world over, the distinct decay of political liberalism, the inspiring creed which prevailed almost everywhere from 1830 to 1870, and on which our fathers founded their hearty enthusiasm for liberty and for democracy. Old-fashioned whig-gery is dead; the political theories that have taken its place borrow their postulates from the domain of physical science. If in times of literary tran-sition it is difficult to say what is cause and what is effect, at least we can perceive that certain phenomena arrive together. The rise of professional or professorial history-writing coincided with the rise of realism in fiction. We may fairly maintain that both had the same cause, a discontent with rhe-torical and imaginative presentations of human life, bred in the minds of a generation to which Darwin and his fellows had taught the cogency and the pervasiveness of scientific laws. Since Darwin, it has been no more possible for the age to produce a crop of Macaulays and Michelets than it is possible for those who picture running horses to expel from their minds what they have learned from Mr. Muybridge's photographs of animal locomotion.[4]

If history is to be thus subjected for a season to the tender mercies of professors, how will it fare? What are the qualities of professors, and espe-cially what are their faults, and how are these working themselves out, or likely to work themselves out, in historical composition? At old Oxford com-mencements it used to be the custom to give to some satirical student the part of Terrae Filius, the son of the earth. His pleasing function it was, in a malicious speech, to amuse the audience by abusing the dons. I should be loth to take upon me the part of Terrae Filius. But indeed it is not necessary. The children of this earth, even those of them who get all their notions of college life from the stage, have abundant opportunities of knowing what are the characteristic faults of professors. As to the way in which these will affect books of history, I suppose we should all be obliged to admit that, in the first place, we must not look to a professorial régime to yield us a rich crop of literary masterpieces. The books may be full of excellent information,

{4.} Eadweard Muybridge (1830–1904) was a British-born pioneer of motion pho-tography. While working as a photographer for the United States Coast Guard and the Geodetic Survey on the Pacific Coast, he was hired by the railroad magnate Leland Stanford to discover by photography whether there was any time when a horse had all four feet off the ground while running. Muybridge demonstrated this to be true and spent the rest of his career photographing animals in motion.

they may even avoid pedantry, but they will not be models or miracles of brilliant style. In the United States, indeed, I fear that many of them will not even be well written. I fear it because I have read a good many doctoral dissertations, and a good many historical articles offered by young *Gelehrten* to an historical review. Almost always these are written in a style "that would have made Quintilian stare and gasp." Indeed, the experienced observer is aware of a distinct dialect, doctor's-dissertation English, a compound made up as are Chinook and Pidgin English, insufficiently studied as yet, but apparently composed of good English, the scholastic jargon of a specialty, and undergraduate slang. It may be that the years will work upon these minds a clarifying process, like that mysterious alchemy which, I am informed, takes medical students mostly wicked and transforms them into doctors mostly good. But at least we must expect that historical productions formed under the influence of universities should be somewhat tame and dry.

The truth is that, of history as of other arts, there is a communicable portion and a portion that cannot be communicated. You can teach your pupils technical perfection in music or painting or sculpture; but you cannot give them genius or originality if they do not possess it. And if you put your arts under the charge of a body of professionals, an Académie des Beaux Arts or a corporation of Meistersingers, what you will mainly promote is technical skill and the vogue of academical tradition. After an age of brilliant amateurs history loses her unchartered freedom and is sent to school, to learn how to read and interpret documents, how to sift and to weigh evidences, how to avoid the blunders of amateurs and the vagaries of rhetoricians. If all this cannot be won without losing from our histories their warmth and light and color, it is a lamentable thing. Warmth and light and color, the statesman's insight and the poet's imagination, all these are qualities which we cannot fail to desire, which we almost have a right to demand, of a historian. But if, as the record of literary history seems to show, all good qualities cannot be had at the same time in the nation's or the world's historians, at least let us not be insensible to the excellences of the present régime, nor to the benefits which we are receiving from it.

Never before were historical books written with more strenuous or more successful endeavor to be accurate. Now it is mere sophistry to deny to accuracy the very highest sort of place among the qualities necessary to an historian. It is vain for critics or prime ministers to proclaim Mr. Froude to us as a great historian, once we have learned that he was constitutionally incapable of making accurate statements. The man in the street knows better. Common sense tells him that history and fiction are two different things, and that if a book of history is not accurate it is, as history, not worth reading.

Again, never before were histories, in the average case among prominent works, based on so thorough research. Never before did they show so great a mastery of the processes of comparison and criticism. Never before, I think we may truly say, were they on the whole so fair. If the atmosphere of universities is too close and too secluded to give a writer all that practical insight into the workings of national life that we might reasonably desire, at least it keeps him in the main from those heats of party passion which so often have disfigured the work of men of genius and experience. If he is a teacher, the influence of that still air is usually fortified by his sense of the teacher's responsibility, which powerfully restrains from partisanship and overstatement. So through all the communicable portions of the historical art run excellent influences from what some might scornfully call the domination of the don.

Neither ought we to rate low the value of those corporate or organized agencies through which donnish public opinion exerts its influence upon history. It will be remembered that in the age of erudition two centuries ago, which in respect to the development of historical writing was in general so like our own, there were two such agencies, the academies and the learned monastic communities. I might liken to the former the numerous historical journals of our time. They are a peculiar feature of our age, almost all being the product of the last half-century. But in their influence they are like those old academies. To evoke originality, to kindle the fires of genius, is not their function; but to regularize, to criticise, to restrain vagaries, to set a standard of workmanship and compel men to conform to it. Learned monastic communities we have not, though indeed our professors are virtually under vows of poverty and obedience, and therefore, perhaps, ought to be under the third monastic vow, that of celibacy. But that which was essential in the work of the Bollandists or the Benedictines of St. Maur was the intimate coöperation of congenial scholars in tasks too large for individual strength; and this we have, repeated, in the constant coöperation of university teachers. The great historical enterprises of Germany and France are carried on by voluntary groups of professors, closely associated, though modern conditions make it unnecessary for them to dwell under the same roof. Almost every country has now its coöperative history in preparation, the work of associated experts. As for America, I think few people appreciate, because it is all so recent, how closely the various professors in each specialty are banded together. In history this is to a peculiar degree the case. The professors of history in the principal universities, the leading spirits of the American Historical Association, are all well acquainted. I might almost say that they are all warm friends. (The very flattering remarks to which I have been obliged to listen from my dear friend Professor Turner this afternoon have given us an extreme example of their mutual kindness.) I can set no limits to the useful services to history that can be rendered by the mutual coöperation of this band of brothers, *Fratres communis vitae.*

It must be confessed that, even in the field of what the French call *oeuvres de Bénédictin*, the prospects of this professorial régime are not all roseate.

The professor is obliged to try to do too many different things. He is far from living his life in a vacuum. Around the still air in which he naturally dwells moves the atmosphere of this world, filled with busy spirits who care not for his ideals. He plans a *magnum opus*. Anon the tempter cometh, and persuades him rather to undertake some little caitiff book of a publisher's devising, utterly unneeded, but eminently vendible. Doubtless, the American publishers hit upon many useful devices; but, on the whole, they may fairly be regarded as the chief enemies of productive scholarship in America. History can never reap the best fruits of such an era as we have been describing unless the professor can steel his heart against their blandishments and against many other mundane solicitations. Can he doubt that those clear voices have been right who in all ages have proclaimed the value of the simple life and of unbought devotion to the austere muse? Can the desire to conform to *bourgeois* standards effectually stifle that prompting which the youthful Milton recorded—"an inward prompting which grows daily upon me, that by labor and intent study, which I take to be my portion in this life, joined with the strong propensity of nature, I might perhaps leave something so written to after times as they should not willingly let it die?"

The influence of universities upon historical writing is beneficent in proportion as universities and university men remain true to the ideals appropriate to their position. An epoch marked by the dominance of that influence has, as we have seen and frankly confessed, its limitations. It may be that it does its most useful work by laying up stores of well-sifted materials which later may be used by masters of synthesis, of a type not yet evolved. Meanwhile, however, the professor may, at all events, feel that in writing or in causing young men to write, or in showing them how others have written, and how they themselves might write, he has under all the limitations a large and satisfying function. In taking the chair of history in a leading university, which radiates light throughout the vast valley destined apparently to be the chief home of civilized man, he must surely feel weighted with heavy responsibility; but he may justly feel inspired by the possibilities of unusual influence in his chosen profession.

University Record of the University of Chicago 6 (January 1902): 293–300.

The Control of the Higher Education
in the United States

As a young instructor at the Johns Hopkins University, nothing distressed Jameson more than the subservient attitude that both the president of the university, Daniel C. Gilman, and Herbert B. Adams, head professor of history, appeared to adopt toward potential benefactors. Adams was wrong, Jameson commented in 1883, in thinking that "it is going to be necessary to do work which will strike a chord in the popular heart of Baltimore in order to succeed and secure advancement." He concluded that a commencement address by Gilman in 1882 was "full of the usual taffy, flattered the Baltimoreans and lugged in religion to please them."[1]

As vigorously as he criticized his superiors for their zealous pursuit of public support, Jameson understood the necessity of cultivating patrons and in fact proved himself to be an adept fundraiser. In February 1888 he solicited money to buy books in southern history for Johns Hopkins. Moving to Brown University as professor of history in the fall of that year, Jameson in 1890 completed a successful subscription drive to buy history books for the university library.[2]

There remained the threat, however, that the nascent class of professional scholars to which Jameson belonged could be held hostage by its dependence upon large sums of money from private patrons. When E. Benjamin Andrews effectively was compelled to resign in 1897 from the presidency of Brown by trustees who feared his liberal economic views would offend potential donors, Jameson authored a faculty "open letter" to the Brown University Corporation in which he asserted his belief that "the life-blood of the university is not money, but freedom."[3] Andrews later withdrew his resignation at the request of the corporation, but the episode undoubtedly did much to persuade Jameson that professional scholars needed funding from sources presumably less sensitive to public opinion than college trustees, such as the large private foundations that emerged after the turn of the century. But as Jameson made clear in the following commencement address to the graduating seniors of Earlham College on June 17, 1910, these foundations, no less than college trustees, might well exact a price for their support.[4]

NOTES

1. JFJ, diary, January 23, [1883], AD, Box 2, JP, DLC; JFJ, diary, June 8, [1882], AD, Box 2, JP, DLC.

2. R. G. Evans to JFJ, February 6, 1888, ALS, Box 19, JP, DLC; JFJ, [Report of the Professor of History], in *Annual Report of the President to the Corporation of Brown University*, June 20, 1889 (Providence: [Brown University], 1889), p. 45; JFJ, [Report of the Professor of History], in *Annual Report of the President to the Corporation of Brown University*, June 21, 1890 (Providence: [Brown University], 1890), pp. 41–42.

3. Benjamin F. Clarke, et al., *An Open Letter Addressed to the Corporation of Brown University by Members of the Faculty of that Institution*, July 31, 1897, p. 11, printed copy in Box 63, JP, DLC. See also the correspondence pertaining to the Andrews controversy in this box.

4. See *Earlhamite* 36 (June 17, 1910): 299.

WITHOUT ATTEMPTING to define too closely the words "college" and "university," we may accept the computation that there are something like five hundred colleges and universities in the United States. Each has its annual commencement, each at least one commencement address. We may compute, then, that since the opening of the present century at least five thousand such addresses, usually upon topics related to the higher education, have been delivered by speakers and endured by audiences; and this is to make no account of the many discourses in the same fertile field which have been presented on other than commencement occasions.

Many quantitative facts of this sort warrant us in concluding that, in general, the American of the twentieth century has for educational discussion the same voracious and insatiable appetite which the American of the seventeenth century had for discussions in theology. It is a creditable, it is indeed a touching trait, for it is connected with that keen interest in the welfare of the younger generation, that hope of parents that by sacrifices they may give the children a fuller career than their own, which shows us that America is still regarded as the blessed land of opportunity.

Yet after such copious floods of discussion as we have calculated, after feasts of educational thought that might well satisfy the most ardent national appetites, is it possible to find any topic of the higher education on which anything worth while can still be said? It is difficult to be sanguine regarding this question. Yet there is always a chance, in any field, that some topic of high and central importance may for special reasons have been much less discussed than others of far inferior significance. I take an illustration from the field of descriptive political science. I well remember that thirty years ago one could nowhere find in print a good detailed description of the American party system and its workings. For ninety years, lawyers and politicians had expanded and debated every minutest feature of our written Constitution. For fifty years that Constitution had been extended in some respects, made waste paper in others, by the operations of the system of party organization. Yet its systematic description waited till the year 1882, when a young Russian Jew, dwelling in Paris, made it the theme of a remarkable dissertation printed in a French review of political science.[1] Then in 1889, Mr. James Bryce, to whose kindly but observant eye we are indebted for so much of our best knowledge of ourselves, published his classical description of the system; and since then we have all understood it.[2]

{1.} Jameson is probably referring to Moisei Ostrogoski, "De l'organization des partis politiques des Etas-Unis," excerpt from the *Annales de l'Ecole libre des Sciences Politiques* (January, April, and October 1888; January 1889). See also Ostrogoski, *Democracy and the Organization of Political Parties*, 2 vols. (New York: Macmillan Co., 1902).

{2.} James Bryce, *The American Commonwealth*, 2 vols. (New York: Macmillan and Co., 1889).

The only obstacle to its comprehension had been the conventional feeling that one had sufficiently described or understood the whole circle of the American governmental system when he had described the document called the Constitution of the United States.

It is always possible that some analogous prepossession in the field of the higher education may have caused us to think of some important division of that great field of knowledge and theory less actively than we might. Rightly or wrongly, I have imagined that for many of us this is true of the very highest portions of the system, and, taking my courage in both hands, I invite you to consider seriously with me the Control of the Higher Education in the United States.

I do not for a minute pretend that this is a wholly neglected theme. Yet I think I see some reasons why less may have been said about it than its gravity warrants. The speaker on academic themes is usually a man occupying an academic position. It is natural for him to refrain from much public discussion of boards of trustees and other instruments of academic control, lest his remarks may seem to have chiefly a local or personal application. May I explain that, while in my time I have taught twenty-three years in three different universities, I have now, and for five years have had, no connection whatever with any? I hope I do not need to add that I have neither sought nor obtained any knowledge of the organization or operations of superior control in this college. What shall be said will be said upon the general problem, because it is believed to be worth thinking about, with no thought of local application anywhere, and also with every endeavor to avoid paradox and exaggeration on any side, though this may mean the avoidance of pungency and picturesqueness of style.

In speaking of the control of the higher education, in a preliminary manner, a few minutes ago, we have already mentioned trustees. It is natural in America to think of them first in such a connection. It seems to us axiomatic that each institution of learning should consist of a teaching body of relatively specialized experts, ruled over by a body of men whom we may fairly call amateurs in educational matters, and who are understood to represent this institution's public. But that this is the ideal or inevitable arrangement is in fact very far from axiomatic. It is distinctly open to discussion. In reality, we are so accustomed to it that few persons appreciate how anomalous and peculiar it is. In few other countries has anything of the kind ever been developed. In Germany and France, the lands where the university has had the maximum of reputation and influence, it would be deemed a very strange thing to subject the learned faculties who have made the fame of Göttingen or the Sorbonne to the governance of a body composed, let us say, of several rich manufacturers, several eminent lawyers, two or three doctors of divinity, a bishop perhaps, a retired judge, and one or two railroad magnates.

Equally strange would such a system seem at Oxford or Cambridge, where the academic dons themselves have for centuries exercised over the colleges a government unquestioned, and over the universities a rule interfered with at rare intervals by Parliament and never by the public.

What are the reasons for this wide divergence of opinion? Let us not jump to the conclusion that America is wholly wrong about it, however strong may be the presumption on the side of countries more experienced in the pursuits of learning. In France, Germany and England, excepting the recent English provincial establishments, the universities do not look to the general public for their financial support, and therefore see no reason why the general public should be represented in their management. In the case of the German and French universities, supported by the state, a certain measure of control is exercised by the state through the minister of public instruction, but it is not such as seriously to interfere with the autonomy of the professorial body, to whom from ancient times the interests of the higher education have in the main been intrusted. A parallel case would be that of such of our universities as are state-supported, if above their faculty stood alone the state superintendent of education, and if, perhaps we ought to add in order to make the parallel with France and Germany more exact, our state superintendents of education were somewhat less of politicians than they now are, and somewhat more of scholars. In point of fact, these American state institutions also have regents, closely corresponding to trustees, chosen by the people, or appointed by those who are chosen by the people, and therefore likely in a very real sense to represent popular opinion. Accordingly in this case also we have the same singular organization—a body of scholars, and over them a body of amateurs representing the public.

Such an organization has some very real merits, and in some situations it is indispensable. Many an infant college, which has since done noble work, would have perished in its early struggles for existence if it had not been watched over by faithful and devoted members of its particular public, denominational or local, who knew how to adapt it to the needs of that public better than could academics imported from elsewhere. In the maturer years of an institution, the chief uses of the trustee system are three in number. In the first place, even a very miscellaneous collection of amateurs will usually have, when acting collectively, a fuller sense of the needs of a given community or section than a body of teachers and professional scholars. There have been educational institutions whose faculties have been no more in touch with the modern life of America than the inmates of a Buddhist monastery. Trustees on the other hand will usually be very distinctly in touch with the public and with the alumni, and may therefore be able to correct the vagaries of cloistered scholars, who, breathing "the still air of delightful studies," may lack contact with the actual world. The greatest mathematical genius who has ever taught in an American class-room opened a fresh section of one of his lectures by announcing enthusiastically, "Gentlemen, I shall now show you a beautiful theorem of my own, which has never been polluted by being put to any practical use." Such idealism is of priceless value, but a faculty composed entirely of such spirits would be the better for control by worldly amateurs, "Blest with plain reason and with sober sense."

In the second place, trustees are or may be highly useful in the prudential management of the finances of a college, skilful and experienced in the making of investments, careful and practical in expenditure. Thirdly, trustees have an important function in the collection of money, whether from individuals or from representative legislatures, and in the case of privately endowed or denominational institutions often do much to direct students as well as endowments toward that in which they are especially interested.

All this is familiar ground. I believe that the defects of the system are much less familiar, much less thought upon. Its leading defect may be described in a brief phrase as lying in the amateurishness of such a system of control. The higher education has become a particularly specialized business. The outsider does not know the ropes; how can he safely navigate the ship or even supervise its navigation? The reason why the public thinks it possible is a curious one, and goes far back into our national history. In every part of America the earlier stage of existence has been pioneer life, with its many exigencies which each pioneer had to meet for himself as best he could. This has bred self-confidence, resourcefulness, and wonderful versatility; the true American is nowhere at a loss for an expedient. But it has also bred a universal habit of underestimating the value of special training. It is not so very many years ago that a Senator of the United States importuned the President to displace the head of one of our great scientific offices, a man of national reputation in his special field, in order to give the post to one of the Senator's own constituents. "But," said the President, "your man doesn't know anything about the subject." "Oh well," said the Senator, "he's a smart fellow, and he will catch on." The scientist was removed, the versatile and adaptable genius was appointed.[3] I could tell ludicrous tales of the ignorance he showed at first. Perhaps he "caught on" later, but it would seem that there must have been a certain loss of momentum in that office.

The universal Yankee, who could turn his hand to any invention or pursuit, the "hired man" on the farm who could make almost anything with a jack-knife, has been an interesting and even an impressive figure in our

{3.} In a letter Jameson wrote to a friend in 1907, he stated that this exchange took place between Senator Stephen B. Elkins, a Republican from West Virginia, and President William McKinley, when Elkins proposed George M. Bowers to be Commissioner of the Bureau of Fisheries. [JFJ] to Carl R. Fish, November 4, 1907, TLc, Box 83, JP, DLC. See also the *Official Congressional Directory* (Washington, D.C.: Government Printing Office, 1907), p. 268.

history. But we are now getting to be an older and a less simple nation. The pioneer stage of existence is passed. It is time that we showed a greater appreciation of the value of specialized intelligence and professional training. Indeed, we are already showing high appreciation of its value in all matters that touch our pockets. In the industrial world the trained expert is duly esteemed, well paid, listened to with deference. Why should it be otherwise in the field of the higher education? Why, in the things of the mind, do we so enormously value the "prominent citizen?" America might well be termed "the land of the prominent citizen." He is the ultimate arbiter of all American destinies. Once let a man somehow achieve the proud position of a "prominent citizen," and his opinions on the opera, on sculpture, earthquakes, Shakespeare, forestry, Nicaragua, and pasteurization, at once assume high importance, and are printed in the newspapers as authoritative.

Now it will not be seriously maintained that trustees of colleges and universities are usually experts in the field of the higher education. Of a certain board of trustees, more than twenty in number, I for several years knew the greater number; there were only two of them, beside the president, whose opinion I should ever have thought of asking upon any educational matter. How should it be otherwise? What pains do trustees take to inform themselves broadly in the general field? Meeting on the street one day a friend of mine, an excellent young lawyer, who had just been elected a trustee of his Alma Mater, I congratulated him upon his election. "Well, I don't know," said he, "why should I accept it? What can I do that is at all useful?" The chance to give advice to a trustee was not to be lost. "Do one thing," I said, "which no other member of the board has ever done! Read the annual reports of five presidents of other universities!" If he took my advice, I doubt not he became a shining authority in the board. But what should we think of a railroad director who read no annual reports of any road but his own? And yet the president of an important educational institution lately told me that he was sure very few of his trustees read the whole of his own annual report, though it is seldom more than twenty pages long, and to my thinking is most excellent reading.

The truth is, that if you attempt to compose a board of trustees of the usual "prominent citizen" material, you will have a collection of men most of whom are already trustees and directors in so many other undertakings that they cannot possibly give to the affairs of your institution enough time to enable them to become expert in the understanding thereof. When the board of trustees of a new institution was announced, I asked an experienced university president, who happened to be near at hand, what he thought of it. He said, "It looks like a good board, but is not; they are on the average too old, and too much immersed already in other things." Distinction had been sought rather than real efficiency. I afterward learned that it had proved difficult to hold even the executive committee of that board together for a meeting of an hour and a half.

Under such conditions, we must expect that the merit which in the first place was claimed for amateur body of rulers, that they are closely in touch with public or local sentiment, will be in large degree neutralized by the fact that they are not, and cannot be expected to be, in touch with the methods and processes of superior education. It is sometimes thought that in recent years a great improvement has been effected through the modern practice of alumni representation, now systematically invoked in many institutions. There can be no question as to the value of alumni trustees in respect to working loyally for Alma Mater and endeavoring to make grateful return for happy years spent under her roof-tree. Moreover, since most alumni are young alumni, and it must always be so, the trustees whom they will choose will be marked by much more of youthful enthusiasm, much more of intelligent sympathy with the young, than can be expected from the middle-aged or older varieties of "prominent citizen." But if we are speaking of being in touch with the methods and processes of superior education, or acquainted with recent advances in them, a discriminating judgment will bear in mind that very few alumni keep abreast with these movements of progress; nearly all retain merely the standards of the time when they were in college, and some part of the acquisitions then made. The case was put pungently by a professor in a college where of late years special efforts have been made to exact more performance from the students than was required in the past. He said: "In those easy-going days our standards were so low that no one is justified in regarding the opinions of our alumni as the opinions of educated men; they simply do not look at things from that point of view." An extreme case, no doubt, or a statement colored by professorial fondness for tart epigram. Yet in the matter of intercollegiate athletics, the wild exaggeration of which has in so many colleges forced every intellectual interest into a subordinate position and made their actual life a quaint burlesque of the life educational, it is notorious that young alumni, as a rule, hold a less sane view of the relative values of these things than the undergraduates themselves. The undergraduates cannot wholly escape the haunting thought that after all studies have some importance. The young alumnus has too often escaped from that thought forever. But he can come back to the football game. He can enjoy a victory. And if it is his one annual opportunity to enjoy anything connected with Alma Mater, he can be exceedingly indignant when frivolous considerations of the intellectual life are allowed to interfere with his pleasure.

Altogether, then, our amateur governing bodies, however constituted, have their defects and disadvantages on the side of educational management. Perhaps the system would not have been so uniformly maintained among us, nor so long, if most of our colleges had not been established as denominational concerns, whose course, it was felt, needed to be constantly and carefully watched in a particular interest.

On the side of financial administration the case should be clearer. The typical professor, as we see him on the stage or in our novels, blinking, forgetful, unworldly, absorbed in Greek roots (I know not why it is always Greek roots, a matter in which I never knew even a professor of Greek to take much interest), is not a man to whom to entrust investments and securities. But on the other hand the superior qualifications of men of affairs are in college finance often neutralized by the fact that they are men of too many affairs. It is not in insurance companies alone that one can find dummy directors. Perhaps too the typical professor of the drama is less abundant than is thought. Of late years a large group of national scientific societies has sprung up, whose affairs are managed almost solely by professors. They may fairly be taken as examples of professorial management. Financially they seem to be as solvent, and as prudently administered, in their small way, as the colleges, several of whom, as we know, have come to grief through negligence in supervision.

As for the third important function which our boards of trustees may usefully perform, that of collecting money for the college or university which they serve, it is to be feared that it is so often left to the president that I might more appropriately leave it to be spoken of in connection with that particular factor in academic control. The president of one of the large provincial university-colleges in England told me that in taking the position he made it an absolute condition of his acceptance that he should not be expected to have anything to do with the collection of funds. That, he told the trustees, was to be solely their affair. What chance would this eminent scientific man have had of election to the presidency of an American college and the conduct of its purely educational interests, if he had thus pointedly disclaimed all relation to its financial concerns? The answer may be found in the story of a small college of which I once knew, where pecuniary difficulties accumulated till it seemed that the one resource was an appeal to a well-to-do farmer who was known to have entered the college for $75,000 in his will. With the consent of his chief trustees, the president hired a buggy, drove out to see the intending benefactor, and obtained his consent to an arrangement whereby the bequest of $75,000 was to be commuted into $40,000 in cash. So healthy and well-preserved was the benefactor that the bargain seemed to the president an excellent one, invested with all the proverbial advantages of the bird in the hand. But the next week the farmer died. Then it was found that he had destroyed the will, but had taken no steps toward making the gift! The trustees called for the president's resignation. He had not "made good." He had failed in that which was deemed the most essential of his functions.

All things considered, we shall feel sure that trustees, if they give a proper amount of attention to the task, can manage the financial affairs of a college better than professors, while in its educational affairs the evils of amateur control remain those which have been in part described. "Well," it will be said, "what have you to propose by way of remedy? Would you abolish the trustee system and leave colleges and universities to the sole administration of their faculties?" So violent a breach with our American traditions is not to be contemplated. One reason if no other seems conclusive against it, namely, that we could not be satisfied to have our professors voting money to themselves, either in salaries or in appropriations for the work of their departments. Even when congressmen have voted themselves increase of salary, it has not bred universal contentment. But may we not, now that we have come to be an older country and our colleges and universities have passed most of the crises of youth, take a fresh view of the mutual relations of faculty and trustees, and, recognizing the peculiar merits and uses of each, not their pioneer but their actual and modern uses, attempt a more rational adjustment of those relations?

The present is a favorable time for such inquiries. Desire to share in the benefits of the Carnegie pension fund is causing many colleges to secure alterations in their charters.[4] Such movements should be accompanied by much more discussion of the ideal organization of boards of trustees and of their relations to faculties than I have seen in the public prints. In any such readjustment of those relations, I hold it to be of fundamental importance that the ideas of superior and inferior should be given up; that in their place we should have the idea of close co-operation between two bodies of co-equal power and dignity and mutually complementary qualifications; that the incompetence of amateurs to judge of educational matters and to administer them in detail should be frankly recognized; and that the powers and responsibilities of the bodies of professors should be considerably enlarged. If they are not fit to deal with larger matters of college policy than have com-

{4.} In 1905 Henry S. Pritchett, the president of the Massachusetts Institute of Technology, convinced Andrew Carnegie to fund a program to advance and improve higher education and to begin a pension system for college professors. Carnegie endowed a pension plan, which became the Foundation for the Advancement of Teaching, with ten million dollars in United States Steel bonds. To be eligible for a pension, a professor had to teach at a private institution that was free from religious sponsorship and the students enrolled had to be high school graduates. Initially, only 52 of 421 colleges and universities qualified for membership in the Carnegie plan. However, many institutions that were ineligible took the necessary steps to reform curriculum, entrance requirements, and religious sponsorship, in order to join the Carnegie plan. See E. Richard Brown, *Rockefeller Medicine Men: Medicine and Capitalism in America* (Berkeley, Los Angeles and London: University of California Press, 1979), pp. 53–54, 143.

monly been entrusted to them, they are not the sort of men to whom the higher education in America should be committed. In their selection, and in that of presidents, and in a score of other university functions, let there be close co-operation between the two bodies, by means of joint committees or otherwise. The old notion, that it would impair the dignity of a board of amateur trustees, marked by the usual rapidity, short-sightedness and self-complacency of the successful American "business man," to consult with the "hired men" of the academic staff, must go by the board if we are to have real efficiency. Have a body of teachers who are worth consulting, and then have regular and frequent means of joining them in consultation with your financial and regulating, but never administering, board of trustees. Let the latter be always a small body, that it may meet often and become thoroughly familiar with the college business. Finally, let it be deemed a breach of faith to accept the honor of election to a board of trustees and then not perform with assiduity and singleness of purpose a trustee's duties.

The measure of control over the higher education exercised in our country by boards of trustees or regents is however, as is familiar, complicated by the existence and the singular prerogatives of the American university or college president. No peculiarity of the American educational system has oftener excited the attention of foreign observers than this functionary, so widely differing from that resplendent but powerless figure-head, the *rector magnificus* of a Continental European university. His great powers, moreover, as has often been observed, are all the growth of the last thirty years. A generation ago, the president of an American college was an academic doge, mildly presiding over the deliberations of a body in which he assumed to count but as one member. Today, when successful, he is a czar, whose despotism is not even tempered by assassination. By the acquiescence of trustees, who too often deal with the college through him alone, he has in many cases come to be the sole appointing power, the originator of all important policies, the decider of all important questions. I have known, in one important institution, of a whole year's series of faculty meetings in which not one significant thing was done but to give each week a formal ratification to the acts of the president or a perfunctory assent to what he termed proposals.

Has the American college president too much power, or has he not? Those who hold that he has not, point usually to the superior effectiveness with which one man can act, as compared with the lamentable slowness of old-fashioned faculty meetings. It is perfectly true that faculty meetings are sometimes desperately futile. Professorial salaries are not such as to command in the case of every professor a wide range of scholastic, pedagogic, and also executive talents. But are we sure that the rise of the president to almost supreme power has been due solely to a conviction that only thus can the highest interests of education be truly subserved? It is to be feared that considerations more mundane have entered in. Let us take a leaf out of a familiar chapter in the history of early political institutions. What causes brought it about that the loose preeminence of the tribal chieftain was supplanted by the more rigid rule of the king? It is well known that kingship arose out of warfare, the need for unified control making itself felt when the tribe was hard pressed in the struggle for existence, or immersed in competitive conflicts for the good things of this earth. Forty years ago, one college competed to but a slight degree with another. Each had its local clientele, and was measurably secure from invasion. But increasing ease of communication and the general widening of local horizons have broken down all such protection. Some colleges have had to fight for their lives. Many have felt that success consisted in increasing their number through a competitive struggle with what are called rival institutions. Now no one who thinks his college a good one can fail to wish that it may extend its influence. But when one hears of an institution that pays its president $5,000 per annum, while it pays its professors $1,500 and spends $500 per annum on its library (almost always the weakest spot in an American college), one cannot help thinking that in that board of trustees commercial standards prevail, that the president is paid so well because he is, speaking after the manner of men, a "hustler," can hustle for money, can hustle for students, and can enable Monohippic University to beat Vociferus College. Is this the true spirit which should animate the educational world? The thoughtful trustee should think of himself and his associates not solely as the guardians of an individual college, but also as being, in a very real sense, trustees for the highest interests of education in America. They should think of other colleges not as rivals, but as partners and allies in a noble endeavor;

"For we were bred upon the selfsame hill,
Fed the same flocks by fountain, shade and rill."

They should choose a man president for other reasons than because he can talk successfully with millionaires, or write ingratiating letters to promising young athletes in preparatory schools. In shaping his powers, they should ask themselves, not what arrangements will best secure the kind of success most valued in the business world, but what will work best toward the complete and rounded education of young men and young women. The end in view is the training of these young people toward balanced wisdom and varied usefulness. For its attainment, all the best thought of the best obtainable teachers may well be invoked, even though the process of bringing it into action involve some loss of visible speed.

No doubt it is best that one man should be the chief representative of the institution before the public. No doubt it is best that one man should be in a position to reconcile or adjust the conflicting claims of professors and departments, and to look out for those interests which will not be cared for by any one department. No doubt it is best that the president should be the one regular means of communication between individual teachers and the board of trustees. Ill fares the college where professors are encouraged, or find it profitable, to go privately and singly to the trustees. But on the other hand well would it be for many a college if inter-communication of views between the trustees and the faculty as a whole were more constant, or if regular opportunities of common consultation were provided, through joint committees or otherwise, whereby the qualities and acquirements appropriate to both groups of guardians might be brought to bear simultaneously on college problems.

The president's functions in the choosing of teachers ought also to be large, but they should by no means be those of absolute power. Not a few colleges and universities, and many departments in them, have been completely rejuvenated by the action of a clear-sighted president, who saw what elements of usefulness or vigor were lacking in the existing group, and resolutely supplemented their deficiencies by appointing men whom they, settled upon the lees of tradition and self-complacency, would never have known or admitted that they needed. Yet it is impossible to suppose that in the usual case a president can be so familiar with the growth of all specialties and the qualities of all available young men that he can make a better choice without the aid of the appropriate portion of his faculty than with it. If it be so, that he can, either he or his predecessors have made choice of poor material. Finally, it is in general impossible not to suppose that we have been laying too heavy a burden on our presidents, when we see how difficult it is to fill their places, how extraordinary a combination of desirable qualifications is enumerated whenever a new choice is to be made.

Ten years ago one would have said that the subject of the control of the higher education in America was exhausted whenever one had sufficiently discussed faculty, trustees and president. But in our day two higher terms in the ascending series have been added, by the creation of the Carnegie Foundation for the Advancement of Teaching and of the General Education Board, both armed with ample resources.{5} It is in both cases too soon to estimate properly the kind and extent of the influence to be exerted on the higher education by these benefactions. Such gifts, however beneficent in the long run, seldom operate precisely as was at first contemplated. The former is the organization for maintaining Mr. Carnegie's scheme for the pensioning of professors. Plainly it was not at all intended as an organ of control, yet inevitably it has developed in that direction. If retiring allow-

{5.} The General Education Board was created in 1903 with an endowment of one million dollars from John D. Rockefeller primarily to assist southern educational institutions. The scope soon was expanded to include medical schools throughout the United States. See Raymond B. Fosdick, *The Story of the Rockefeller Foundation* (New York: Harper Brothers, 1952), pp. 9, 96.

ances are to be systematically awarded only to professors who have served in real colleges not under denominational control, it becomes necessary to define what is a real college, and what is to be understood by denominational control. Backed by a sufficient sum of money to be distributed, the former definition becomes an effective standardization of colleges, with rewards for conformity to the standards, the latter a potent discourager of denomination-alism. I have heard it maintained, perhaps somewhat cynically, that these by-products of the benefaction will be its chief results, while the pensions will be gradually discounted by the universities and colleges in the making up of their salary lists. However this may be, the raising of colleges to higher standards of scholarship is doubtless a beneficent operation.

But these are high powers of control, and they are vested in a controlling body which, whatever its excellences, was not chosen for such a purpose, but for the management of a pension system. Since vacancies in that body are to be filled by co-optation, such control as it exercises over the colleges will be an extraneous control. It is true that the presidents of the chief univer-sities will be likely always to constitute, as they constitute now, the leading element in this controlling body, and that body will always try to choose wise men as their administrative officers, in whom a perilous discretion, and even the power to wreck struggling universities, must perforce be vested. But wise men are not always chosen to such positions; and those who have witnessed with pain the jealousies, the consuming zeal for their own houses, which our competitive régime has bred in some of our university presidents, will not look forward with entire complacency to this process of standardiza-tion. High standards imposed from without, by a body which can penalize for infractions, are better than low standards; but they are not so good as high standards developed from within (if we could have them) and adapted by wise men (else they are perhaps not high) to the needs of the local situa-tion. It may be that our educational life, like our industrial life, must advance by natural and in the end beneficent evolution into stages of greater and greater national consolidation, and that we must reconcile ourselves to the régime of trusts. But at all events it is well to see the possible evils, as well as the obvious benefits, inherent in the new order.

Something the same is true of the General Education Board. Surely its operations have been in the main, and in the main will be, beneficent and permanently valuable. Yet the power to use fifty million dollars or more in promoting education is a great power. Those who administer such a fund have in their hands the future of many institutions. Who will they be, and what will be their ideals? It is impossible to believe that they will ever use their power otherwise than in the advancement of what they believe to be high purposes; the history of American endowments warrants no con-trary expectation. It is impossible to suppose that, because the money comes from New York capitalists, or a New York capitalist, the trustees will ever consciously administer their trust in the interest of capitalism. Yet the fact remains that they will always and inevitably be persons of the sort who are normally and naturally trusted by New York capitalists. That this should fix their point of view and determine the standards by which they will act and by which they will try the actions of others, is practically inevitable. But in a country in which public interests are with such difficulty conserved when they come into conflict with capitalistic interests, in which the most powerful popular leader since Lincoln (I speak as one whose sole concern is history; perhaps I should say the most powerful popular leader we have ever had) has barely been able to check, if indeed he has checked, the drift toward plutocracy; in which the strongest political party the world ever saw (I speak as one who was never a member of any political party) has for more than thirty years maintained an apparently unshakable alliance with the wielders of corporate millions—in such a country, to say that an important engine of educational control will be managed by persons acceptable to leaders in capitalistic circles is to express no slight limitation upon its highest usefulness. Even if the question of capitalism were left out of account, the standards of the General Board will be the standards of educated gentlemen of New York City, never wholly able to appreciate the differing needs of Arkansas and Oklahoma as they may be appreciated by the man born on the spot. This also will seem an important limitation to one who values the flexibility which American education arrangements, like American state legislation in general, have derived from home rule.

But the heyday of home rule, like that of the independent producer, has passed.

> "The old order changes, yielding place to new,
> And God fulfills himself in many ways,
> Lest one good custom should corrupt the world."

Flexibility and local adaptation were too often purchased at the price of narrow provincialism. And even in the matter of capitalism, the danger of its sway over our colleges was not first brought into existence by the creation of the General Education Board. Many a college has been cursed with a local benefactor who has felt no doubt that his few thousands of contribution entitled him to lay a heavy hand on the substance of instruction, and to see to it that no idealistic teachings impaired the market value of the silver shrines of Diana. Tyranny for tyranny, one would rather have that of the large-minded New York multimillionaire and his literary or charitable confidants than that of the swelling local magnate, with his narrow horizon, his bigoted dogmatism, his bumptious self-confidence. Test their relative openness of mind, if you choose, by attempting to talk of socialism, almost certainly the world's future régime, with the one set or with the other. It is remarkable how little the American benefactor has consciously interfered with academic freedom of utterance; but the instances which you will recall will mostly have proceeded from the big man of a small city.

But the catalogue of dangers and cautions respecting the control of the higher education is by no means exhausted when we have enumerated or discussed all the forms in which control is consciously exercised. The rapid growth of manufacturing and other corporate enterprises since the Civil War, and the consequent fact that most college gifts bestowed during that period have come from such sources, have surely brought it about unconsciously that the whole field of American industrial organization has been treated with a little less frankness in college class-rooms, or on college platforms, than would otherwise have been the case; perhaps somewhat less freely in colleges and universities resting upon private endowments than in those supported by public taxation.

And then we have, ever present, resting upon us like the pressure of the atmosphere, the right of public opinion. It is well that it should be so. All honor to those free spirits who, defying public opinion or ruffling the ortho-doxy of their time, have stirred men, even by exaggeration and paradox, to unwonted thought. But, speaking generally, the professorial chair is not the place for the prophetic temperament. It is the usual business of colleges to teach young minds, not that which temporarily seems true to the indi-vidual teacher, but either that which, in St. Augustine's phrase, has been believed always and in all places and by all men, or at least that which has commended itself to a considerable minority.

But on the whole there is less danger that academies will be controlled too little by the force of popular thought than that they will be controlled by it too much. The cruder and more Philistine varieties of public opinion are always in evidence, and are more urgent for compliance than are the judg-ments of the wise. Especially crude and especially vociferous is newspaper opinion. Intellectual men despise our newspapers, save a few exceptional sheets, to an extent far beyond what they deem it prudent to express. They see them to be sensational, unscrupulous, and ill-informed, "written," as Lord Salisbury said, "by office-boys for office-boys," and on the average not so good in 1910 as they were in 1880. They are in no danger of mistaking the utterances of such sheets as *vox Dei*. But there is some real danger that cloistered academics may mistake them for that *vox populi* a reasonable com-pliance with which is usually proper. Newspapers, it is maintained, are sure to reflect public opinion, because it is their most profitable course to do so. This is to overlook an important consideration. Their main purpose, often their sole purpose, is to sell the paper. More papers are sold if you represent the public mind as in a state of great excitement than if you represent it as being in a condition of calmness. For all its froth, the American people is in times of crisis exceptionally self-controlled. It may be asserted with confidence, that no other nation in the world could have passed with so little disturbance through so formidable a crisis as that involved in the disputed presidential election of 1876–1877, and perhaps none would have sustained itself so well through such a blow as the assassination of Lincoln. Yet he who should rely on our newspapers as his evidence of public opinion in critical times, such as for instance those of April, 1898, or November, 1907, would conceive of our nation as quite given over to the most violent forms of hysteria, when in reality behind a large part of the alleged phenomena there lay little else than the chronic desire of newspaper publishers to gather in the pennies. If our colleges are to be controlled by American public opinion, as to a considerable extent it is proper that they should be, at least let them appeal from the newspaper caricature of Philip drunk to the living reality of Philip sober.[6]

Those who are about to graduate, and for whom, I am well aware, this occasion was primarily intended, will perhaps be wondering whether all these considerations of the control of the higher education in America have any immediate, direct, and practical significance for themselves. Not immediate, it is true; not direct, in the case of most alumni and alumnae. But surely the higher concerns of a college have practical significance in the future for those who have enjoyed its benefits in the immediate past. The man or woman who accepts an education from the hands of an endowed institution and then feels no desire to do anything for it later, when he shall be able, is a man or woman whom it is a pity to have educated. To contribute in any important degree to its endowments may never be within his power. But at the least he can work for it, directly or indirectly. That he may work for it intelligently, and with a proper comprehension of what it is trying to do, he ought to be, all his life, to some extent a student of American higher education, learning what is done here, reading and observing as to what is done elsewhere, and thinking as to what might be done, what might be done better, what ought to be done. In the control of any college, in the

---

{6.} The source of this metaphor is Valerius Maximus, *Facta et Dicta Memorabilia* (ca. A.D. 15), book 6, chapter 2. A translation of this work published in 1678 includes the following passage: "A Woman of another Countrey intrudes, among so many Men; who being undeservedly condemned by King *Philip* in his drink; *I would appeal to* Philip, said she, *but it must be when he is sober.* The smart sentence rows'd him; and by her present courage she compelled the King to examine the business more finely, and to give a juster Sentence." [Quintus Valerius Maximus], *Romae Antiquae Descriptio. A View of the Religion, Laws, Customs, Manners, and Dispositions of the Ancient Romans, and Others: Comprehended in Their Most Illustrious Acts and Sayings Agreeable to History* (London: Printed by J.C. for Samuel Speed, 1678), p. 268. We acknowledge the assistance of Lee Avdoyan of the Library of Congress in bringing this work to our attention.

shaping of its destinies, in the securing of its truest success, its graduates, whether through organized or unorganized means, play inevitably an important part. It is yours to see that, by acquiring all appropriate knowledge and wisdom, you fit yourselves to render to Alma Mater an intelligent and patriotic service.

Earlham College Bulletin 7 (August 1910): 3–27.

The Present State of Historical Writing in America

For the annual meeting of the American Antiquarian Society on October 19, 1910, which also marked the dedication of its new building, society president Waldo Lincoln invited Edward Channing, professor of history at Harvard University, John B. McMaster, professor of history at the University of Pennsylvania, and Jameson to assess contemporary American historical writing. Jameson preferred to limit his discussion to the implications for scholarship of cooperation between historical societies and disliked the notion of preceding his older, more illustrious colleagues on the program.[1] Nevertheless, on this occasion he assumed the role of featured speaker, with Channing and McMaster largely reinforcing the points he made regarding the progress of historical scholarship in the United States.

NOTE

1. Waldo Lincoln to JFJ, May 27, 1910, ALS; [JFJ] to Lincoln, June 2, 1910, TLc; Lincoln to JFJ, June 13, 1910, TLS; [JFJ] to Lincoln, June 21, 1910, TLc; Lincoln to JFJ, September 14, 1910, TLS; [JFJ] to Lincoln, October 7, 1910, TLc; and Lincoln to JFJ, October 10, 1910, TLS; all in Box 109, JP, DLC.

THE PRESENT STATE of Historical Writing in America is a large subject. It is natural, when this Society stands so near to the hundredth anniversary of its foundation and is upon the threshold of a new building and, as we all hope, of a new stage in its activities, that the President should wish to mark the transition from the old conditions to the new by a thoughtful consideration of the actual status in America of that study to which the Society is dedicated. Such thought may enable us to enter upon the new era with a full consciousness of the setting in which this organization is to play its part, the *terrain* in which it is to manoeuvre. The metaphors imply that the Society is not to drift, but to make a conscious and deliberate effort to relate its activities to the present status of historical science in this nation, and by such effort to advance that status. Yet how many difficult questions must be answered before we can fully describe this present condition of things, this stage of advancement which it is so important for us to understand! Merely to enumerate some of them may be somewhat profitable and impressive, but it will be obvious that no one brief paper can go far toward making real to us the whole circle of what we think to survey. What stage of progress have we reached in the accumulation of printed materials for history in our libraries, or of unprinted materials in our archives? How largely have the latter been reduced to order and made ready for the use of scholars? How much have we done in the publication of documentary materials, what remains undone, and how well are we doing such work? What is the quantity and what the quality of our output of historical monographs? What is upon the average the mental calibre and what the training of those who make them? How do we stand with respect to the publication of histories of a higher order, marked by literary sense or the effort to generalize? How deep or how copious is American thought on the theoretical or philosophical aspects of history? How largely have our historical workers pursued, or appreciated, or been affected by, the advances made in the many other sciences to which history is more or less related? What are the present purposes, nature, and effects of American historical teaching, elementary, secondary, collegiate, or university, which after all represents far more than nine-tenths of the total effort expended on history in this country? In our universities, what is the status of research? How are our historical societies and journals performing their functions? What is the character of those books of history which most hold the public attention—so far as the public attention can be said to be held by any books whatever? What sort or quality of history is presented to the popular mind in the ten-cent magazines and the newspapers, which now constitute almost the sole reading-matter of American mankind?

  Not one of these questions is easy to answer, yet all must be answered before we can adequately picture to ourselves the present state of historical writing in the United States. It is vain to make any attempt this morning to pursue them all, but it may not be vain to have enumerated them; for if then we perforce narrow the scope of the present paper to a consideration of a manageable portion of the whole field, we shall nevertheless do this with some consciousness of the relation which that portion bears to the whole unmanageable total.

In selecting a part of the field, it is natural for me to think of that which is represented by organized activities in the pursuit of history, partly because I have been for some years occupied with a corner of that lesser portion, rather than with literary histories, and have no doubt that

> My nature is subdued
> To what it works in, like the dyer's hand;

and partly because it is much easier to make general and summary statements concerning the results of organized historical work than concerning those more various and literary activities and products which spring from the free spirit of the individual historical worker. We can apply the pedometer and the stop-watch to Pegasus in harness much more easily than to Pegasus in spontaneous aviation.

How then do we Americans stand with respect to organized historical work? The question may be answered by comparison with our status at some period in the past, by comparison with the stage of progress exhibited by the chief European nations, or by comparison with some ideal which, given our opportunities and our resources, we should be expected to have reached. It may also be answered by consideration of the various forms in which, in any country, historical work is usually found organized, the chief typical organizations for the pursuit of our study. If we choose to subdivide and classify, we may speak of the historical work of governments, of societies, of professional journals, of universities and colleges, and of co-operative organizations formed for the production of a given work. At all events these have been in this country the most significant forms in which historical work has been organized.

Intelligent democratic governments will usually show more tendency to subsidize such publications as make immediate appeal to the mass of mankind, such as will rapidly inform or educate great numbers of readers, than such as make their appeal to the few, teach the teachers of teachers, or lay secure foundations, far below the surface, for the best work of future generations. Relatively to the resources of the country, our federal government turned out better historical work seventy years ago in the days of President Sparks's volumes and the folio "American State Papers," than it has in more recent years, when it has become more perfectly democratic.[1] But never did

---

{1.} Jared Sparks, ed., *The Writings of George Washington*, 12 vols. (Boston: American Stationer's Company, 1834–37); *The Works of Benjamin Franklin*, 10 vols. (Boston:

any government in the world's history pour forth such a mass of information regarding any great series of events, nor scatter the volumes of information so freely, as did our government in the case of the 128 volumes of the "Official Records of the War of the Rebellion." It is hardly less characteristic that our government historical volumes, whether well or ill executed, have been brought out casually and sporadically, with no previous and expert effort to form a comprehensive and systematic plan. A clerk of a committee thinks it would be an excellent thing to have a compilation of documents on the history of a given matter, and that he is the ideal man to prepare it. He readily persuades his chairman, the chairman somewhat less readily persuades the committee, the committee perhaps persuades Congress, and we have one more historical "pub. doc.," possibly in several volumes, possibly worth having, but very likely not half so useful to the cause of history as twenty other compilations that could be suggested. Efforts to improve this course of procedure, to provide the government with a steady supply of expert advice on documentary historical publications, are under way, and a bill is before Congress, but its fate is of course by no means certain.[2] Under the present system, or want of system, in selecting what shall be done and who shall do it, our government's historical publications are, on the average, not only far inferior to those of Great Britain, France, Germany, and Austria, but even to those of small countries like Belgium, the Netherlands, Switzerland, and Denmark.

In respect to our State governments, a various tale is to be told. Many of our newer states, in the West and South, are putting forth most creditable work, worthy of being compared with what countries of equal population and resources in Europe accomplish. Examples are Wisconsin,—a commonwealth having perhaps the most enlightened and progressive government

---

Hilliard, Gray, and Company, 1836–40); *Correspondence of the American Revolution*, 4 vols. (Boston: Little, Brown, and Company, 1853). The *American State Papers*, 38 vols. (Washington, D.C.: Gales and Seaton, 1832–61), covered foreign relations, Indian affairs, commerce and navigation, military affairs, and public lands.

{2.} In December 1909 Congressman Samuel McCall, chairman of the House Library Committee, introduced at Jameson's request H.R. 15428, which established a national historical publications commission. Hearings were held in January 1910, but the bill never came to a vote. See *Congressional Record*, 61 Cong., 2d sess., p. 180 (December 15, 1909); and a copy of H.R. 15428, 61 Cong., 2d sess., in Percy Scott Flippin, comp., "The Archives of the United States Government: A Documentary History, 1774–1934," 24 vols. (National Archives), 11:146. See also Committee on the Library, House of Representatives, *Commission on National Historical Publications*, 61st Cong., 2d sess., 1910, H.R. 1000, p. 3, copy in Box 115, JP, DLC; Morey D. Rothberg, "Servant to History: A Study of John Franklin Jameson, 1859–1937" (Ph.D. dissertation, Brown University, 1982), pp. 243–45; and Alan Harvey Ginsberg, "The Historian as Lobbyist: J. Franklin Jameson and the Historical Activities of the Federal Government" (Ph.D. dissertation, Louisiana State University, 1973), pp. 53–54.

in the United States,—Iowa, Illinois, North Carolina, and Virginia. These
States and some others have put their historical work into the hands of
persons who know not only how such things should be done, but also
what is worth doing, facing with fresh and open minds the question, What
has been really important in the development, social, economic and political, of a nineteenth-century democratic community? Most of the older and
richer State governments of the northeast, on the other hand, have steadily
maintained antiquated and conventional views as to what is worth while in
documentary historical publication. That of Massachusetts has for fifty years
displayed the most astonishing indifference to her history, publishing almost
nothing out of the rich stores of her archives, in a period in which a dozen
American States and nearly a dozen European countries have revolutionized
the writing of their histories by extended and judicious publication of fresh
original materials. Other of the eastern States have continued to putter with
muster-rolls and the military records of wars already well known, quite as if
no breath of new life had swept across the historical field since the early days
of Victoria and Van Buren. Here again a defective organization is frequent,
while in the West and South large results have been derived by either one of
two excellent modern systems, that of the state-supported historical society,
best exemplified in Wisconsin, or that of the state historical commission or
department, exemplified by North Carolina and Mississippi.

On the whole it is our historical societies that have made the largest gains
in productivity during the last twenty-five years. The number of those which
are in active existence is very great, probably more than two hundred, a far
larger number than those of Great Britain, and perhaps as large as that of
the strictly historical societies of France or of Germany. The number of members is still more impressive. There are ten thousand members of historical
societies reported in Pennsylvania alone. The pecuniary resources of these
societies are also great. No doubt they form the richest body of such societies
in the world. Their buildings are certainly worth in the aggregate as much
as two million dollars, their libraries more than a million, their endowments
something between one and two millions. Doubtless the work which they
are doing, in the way of research and publication, is not always in full proportion to their wealth, but it is very much better than it was twenty-five
years ago. They are less inclined to print essays written by their members,
often discursive or of temporary utility, more inclined to print documentary
materials, which will have in the future the same original value they have
at present. The number of members sufficiently educated in history to insist
on good workmanship in the published products of the society has greatly
increased. This is especially true in the eastern States. The number has also
greatly increased of those who, having a keen practical eye to the uses of
history, make or sustain the societies' efforts to direct attention toward those
elements in state or local history which have the highest degree of real im-

portance. Such members, persons who see state or local history in its broad relations to national history, and disregarding tradition take up those topics that promise most in the way of fresh and vital instruction, are naturally more numerous among the more open-minded men of the West. The eastern societies are still prone to pursue a certain number of conventional themes—the early voyages, the Indians, the battles of the Revolution, the interminable biographies of deceased members. They are also, as we should expect, little inclined to lift their eyes over their own state borders and take broad national views. In five years of work in Washington, so circumstanced that I am likely to know of historical researches undertaken in national archives or library, I have hardly known an instance in which the publishing authorities of any eastern historical society have set on foot any serious researches in those great and rich repositories. Seldom indeed do they touch the period since 1783.

Nevertheless much has been gained. Twenty-five years ago the publications of most of our historical societies seemed, at least to impatient young minds, hopelessly provincial and unscholarly. But we were then just at the beginning of a new period in all our historical work. The preceding generation had felt the influence of the best European standards in the domain of historical literature, ours was to feel it in the domain of historical criticism. Prescott and Motley were of the school of Thierry and Mignet, Bancroft a disciple of Heeren; we were to be followers of Ranke. A generation of criticism of sources could not fail to have its effect on societies largely devoted to their publication. Exactness of text, minute care in annotation, adequate attention to bibliography, elaborateness of indexing, characterize the volumes put forth by most of our historical societies, even though sometimes they are applied to materials of trivial importance, hardly worth the pains expended upon them.

Besides this improvement in method on the part of our state and local historical societies, we are to note the growth in recent years of many historical organizations whose scope is national. Foremost among these is the American Historical Association, founded in 1884, and already the largest, and presumably the most useful, historical society in the world. Others, while not limited geographically in their scope, are devoted to the American history of a single religious denomination. It is noteworthy that the American Jewish Historical Society and the corresponding Catholic organization have been much more fruitful of good works than the historical societies founded in the various Protestant bodies, which have hardly awakened to the value and interest attaching to American religious history.

Another interesting growth of recent years is the group of organizations devoted to the history of the various ethnic elements which have entered into the population of the United States—such as the German American Historical Society, the excellent Swedish Colonial Society, and that larger association for Scandinavian-American history which seems now to be in process of formation. No one who appreciates how important it is to the American life of these newer elements that they should remember and respect the culture they brought with them, can fail to regard these as among the most useful of our historical societies. Useful to their members, they are capable of being doubly useful to the rest of us, who are prone constantly and enormously to underestimate all but the English element in American development, prone to take the view assumed by the London paper of August, 1909, which thanked Heaven that the North Pole, though unhappily not discovered by an Englishman, had yet been discovered by an Anglo-Saxon— meaning the celebrated Dr. Cook, *geboren* Koch!

In our survey, then, of the present state of historical writing among us, we may look with legitimate complacency upon the stage of development which our historical societies have attained. It is true that there are at least forty historical societies in Europe which are doing work of a grade hardly attained by more than two or three of ours. It is disquieting that in so rich a country there should not be a larger number of well-to-do amateurs engaged in the work of these societies, which normally would attract the interest of well-to-do amateurs in a very high degree—so at least one would expect, and so it has been in other countries and periods. But the disinclination of the American rich to intellectual production is evinced in many another field, and at all events the outlook for our societies is in most ways encouraging.

Of our historical journals most of the same things are to be said which have been said of the societies. Nearly all of them, indeed, are organs of particular societies, and cannot be expected to rise in quality, or in influence upon other historical work, above the grade fixed for them by the qualities of the societies from which they spring. I may be permitted to say much the same of the general organ of the profession, the "American Historical Review." Without denying or palliating faults in the editing, one may safely say in general terms that it is about what the status of historical science among us permits it to be. Its chief articles seem to me to compare favorably with those in some of the better sort of European journals. Its reviews of books are inferior. In the first place, we have not developed so large a class of persons who, whether they themselves write or not, are accomplished judges of what historical books should be. In the second place, there are many subjects or fields, especially in European history, in which no American has acquired a large amount of expert knowledge, partly because our remoteness from European archives and libraries has made it a difficult matter to acquire such familiarity, except in fields for which the sources have to a great extent already been published. Finally, there is the well-known excess of our national amiability, heightened in the case of the historical profession by the friendly and truly fraternal feelings which frequent meetings in the sessions of the American Historical Association, and frequent participation in common tasks for its service, have engendered. It is a beautiful trait, rooted in benign conditions of social development, but it stands in the way of incisive criticism. I should be sorry to see our *Gelehrten* speaking of each other as the Germans still sometimes do, but if they would be more rigid in their standards and more plain-spoken in their criticisms, they would do more to improve American work.

When we come to speak of the American universities as part of our machinery for historical production, it is impossible to repress a certain feeling of disappointment. Thirty years ago, when the Johns Hopkins University was beginning its extraordinary mission in the higher education, and graduate work in the United States was in its infancy, we all felt that a historical professor had it as one of his normal functions to produce historical books at frequent intervals, and that the young man whom he was training in the preparation of a doctoral dissertation was, in the normal case, producing simply the first in a long series of historical monographs. Time and the vast hordes of youths eager to acquire collegiate education (or of parents eager to pay for it) have somewhat undeceived us. The truth is, that more than half of our historical professors do not produce anything at all, and most of the others produce only very slowly: and the doctoral dissertation, instead of being the first in a long series of *Arbeiten*, has been in more than nine cases out of ten, by actual calculation, the young man's sole and last contribution to his science. Doubtless the prime duty of a college teacher is to teach, and the multitudes clamoring more or less actively for historical instruction should receive it; but one cannot resist the wish that the young teacher might, like the young oyster, be carried by artificial means across that critical period of danger to his life which ensues when he is first compelled to go forth into a world of pressure and struggle.

The authorities of universities still appreciate that original research is necessary to the mental health of professors and to their highest usefulness as teachers, and are in some degree aware that, from the point of view of the nation at large, it is a pity that so large a body of persons specially trained for historical investigation should be debarred from it; but there seems to be little chance of immediate remedy in the case of most teaching professors. Meanwhile, however, some of the most enterprising of the western State universities, taking a leaf out of their experience in the sustaining of agricultural and other scientific research, have begun an interesting experiment by the appointment of men who are not expected to teach, but to occupy themselves with historical researches deemed especially useful to the State. Much may be done by such especial foundations; but it will be remembered that bright expectations of the same sort were entertained concerning fellowships thirty years ago, when they were first installed in our system.

Last among the forms of organized historical work to be considered is the general history produced by co-operation. Not unknown in previous

centuries, this *genre* of historical composition has especially flourished during the last generation. Spain, France, England, Germany, the Netherlands,
Denmark, Mexico, all have furnished excellent examples. Twenty-five years
ago the United States provided an elaborate one in Justin Winsor's "Narrative and Critical History," and has not surpassed it since. The merits to
be expected from such undertakings, in an age of specialization, are obvious. As literary products, as efforts toward the profounder interpretation of
the national life, they are sure to suffer from the prescription of uniformity
among their component parts. They will usually succeed better in the sum-
ming up of results already achieved by the writers of monographs than in
the pioneer work of developing new thoughts or opening up new fields of
research.

In non-literary labors, however, in the plodding mechanical work of bringing additional bodies of material to the knowledge of students or making
them accessible in print, there is a far greater field for co-operative endeavor
than is commonly realized. This is a subject especially deserving the attention
of American historical societies. We are a nation notoriously apt for organization. Our librarians, our scientific men, our teachers, have shown conspicuous success in bringing about valuable results through co-operation. The
more plastic historical organizations of our western States have lately shown
their ability to unite by engaging in a most interesting common task, the
making of a calendar of all the papers in the French archives relating to the
history of the Mississippi Valley—a task transcending the scope of any one
of these organizations, yet which would bring almost unlimited duplication
and waste if each should attempt independently to perform its own local part
of the whole. The historical societies of the East have hitherto shown almost
no sign of the ability or the wish to co-operate, though it would be easy to
name a score of undertakings which especially invite co-operative labor. To
take an imaginary instance, yet not wholly imaginary, let us suppose that
one of the New England societies or states possesses a part of the essential
materials for the study of the regime of Andros and Dudley, another society,
another portion, and so on. Can anyone commend a procedure whereby
each society, without concert with the others, publishes (or neglects to publish) solely the fragments of the whole mass which it happens to have in its
building? Can the historian be well served by the result—one part printed
on one system in 1850, let us say, another part printed on another system
in 1900, a third part still reposing in manuscript, and all parts treated on
the basis of the accident of possession? It is but an ideal illustration, but the
principle is a practical one, of frequent application. Situated as the American
Antiquarian Society is with respect to the more local historical societies of
the eastern States, it is ardently to be hoped that, in the new era opening
before it, a considerable part of its duty may be felt to be the promotion of
broad-minded and active co-operation among its fellow societies.

The picture I have attempted to draw of the state of organized historical work among us is not altogether a gratifying one. But I am much attached to that saying of Bishop Butler, "Things are as they are, and the consequences of them will be what they will be; why then should we deceive ourselves?" I see no occasion in these matters to be either optimist or pessimist. Much better and more rational than either, is to be a meliorist, believing that conditions are improving, doing one's part to make them improve.

Proceedings of the American Antiquarian Society, n.s., 20 (October 1910): 3–14.

The Future Uses of History

When this address was presented in December 1912 on the eve of the tenth anniversary of the creation of the Department of Historical Research in the Carnegie Institution of Washington, Jameson could have been credited with establishing the institutional framework for the promotion of historical research. More than a dozen publications initiated by Jameson or his predecessor as director, Andrew C. McLaughlin, had appeared under the auspices of the department, thousands of archival documents had been identified as important for research, and several edited collections of historical documents were nearing completion and publication.[1] Yet these achievements were not without cost, for Jameson constantly struggled to convince his benefactors of the practical uses of history.

Because the Carnegie Institution trustees, largely businessmen and scientists, failed to understand the nature of historical research, they hesitated to provide Jameson with funds to publish guides to European archives that contained significant documents for American history.[2] In time, he succeeded in publishing these guides to archives in Paris, Madrid, Saint Petersburg, Mexico City, and other foreign cities; however, he was unable to convince the trustees to continue funding the publication of *Writings on American History*, an invaluable bibliographical guide begun by McLaughlin.[3] He managed to do this, instead, through private subscriptions and sometimes by advancing the necessary funds out of his own pocket.[4]

As Jameson points out in the lecture that follows, the Department of Historical Research was isolated geographically as well as intellectually within the Carnegie Institution. While administrators and other department heads had offices in the Institution headquarters building on Sixteenth and P streets, NW, the Department of Historical Research occupied a suite some distance away in the Woodward Building in the center of downtown Washington. Jameson was fortunate to have a strong supporter in Robert S. Woodward, president of the Carnegie Institution between 1904 and 1920.

Woodward usually invited heads of departments in the physical sciences to present the Annual Trustees Lecture at their December board meetings. Believing that the trustees would "be glad to have a change of intellectual diet," Woodward invited Jameson to lecture in 1912 on the work of the Department of Historical Research, and Jameson took the opportunity to enlighten the trustees and encourage their support for his projects.[5]

NOTES

1. Carnegie Institution of Washington, *Year Book*, 1913 (Washington, D.C.: Published by the Institution, [1914]), pp. 157–58.

2. [JFJ] to Robert S. Woodward, February 1, 1906, TLt, Box 67, JP, DLC; John Beverley Riggs, "The Acquisition of Foreign Archival Sources for American History to the Year 1940" (Ph.D. dissertation, Yale University, 1955), pp. 181–84.

3. See [JFJ] to Albert B. Hart, December 10, 1906, TLc, Box 138, JP, DLC.

4. [JFJ] to the Macmillan Company, June 20, 1910, TLc, Box 111, JP, DLC; JFJ to the Contributors to the Fund for the Maintenance of "Writings on American History," January 25, 1930, TLS, Librarian's Office Records, RPB; JFJ to Henry L. Koopman, August 6, 1929, TLS, Librarian's Office Records, RPB.

5. Robert S. Woodward to JFJ, December 23, 1911, TLS; and [JFJ] to Woodward, December 26, 1911, TLc, both in Box 67, JP, DLC.

IN THE Church of Rome there is a class of titular bishops, employed rather in ecclesiastical business than in pastoral care, who usually have no actual dioceses, but are given titles derived from cities once obedient to Rome, but long since possessed by the Mohammedan or other unbeliever.[1] For such prelates the style, bishop of such and such a place "in the regions of the unbelieving," *in partibus infidelium*, has till lately been the official designation.

I often think that the director of a department of historical research in this scientific city of Washington is a bishop *in partibus infidelium*. Perched in airy isolation upon the eleventh floor of the Woodward Building, he has no foot of ground that he can call his own temporal domain. As his glance goes forth over the neighboring houses, and over the monstrous cornice of the Southern Building, he sees a city rich in beauty and in historical associations, pulsating with political and social life, supplied in unexampled measure with the materials for American history, yet whose intellectual circles are almost as exclusively devoted to the worship of physical science as ever were the Ephesians to the cult of Diana.

In such an atmosphere, the bishop *in partibus* may on several grounds feel warranted in supposing that the work and objects of his department are not well known. It has put forth no effort to describe them to persons not members of the historical profession. It offers nothing spectacular or even striking to the public eye. It has made no notable discoveries, and has no intention of making any. If any such should ever occur, they will come unsought, as incidents to the single-minded and austere prosecution of the department's real purposes.

What then are those purposes? It is, perhaps, useful to remind the hearer, first of all, that historical work consists of four processes: first, the finding of the documents or other materials that have come down from past times and bear testimony of the events or themes that should be treated; secondly, the critical sifting of these documents, the laying of them in order, the preparation or publication of them for use in telling truly, completely and in proper perspective, the tale that they should tell; thirdly, the writing of monographs or special works on subjects of limited scope; and, fourthly, the composition of general histories. These four processes are, if we may put our classification into a metaphor, the work of the prospector, the work of the quarryman, the work of the mason, and the work of the architect respectively.

Now the writing of general histories, and even of historical monographs, is as a rule best left to individual initiative, to the free exercise of those gifts of insight, of judgment, of imagination, of sympathy, and of power of interpretation, which can neither be commanded at will nor with entire success

1. Lecture before the Trustees of the Carnegie Institution of Washington, December 12, 1912.

be organized. For an endowed department of historical research the proper tasks must be the humbler labors of search and of criticism—the finding of historical materials, the critical testing of their origin and value, the bringing them together, in their proper relation to materials already known, and the publication of them or of guides to them. Such tasks are usually too expensive for the individual, but they are relatively simple, they are to be executed by processes sufficiently well known and in accordance with rules securely established, and they call for the skill of the practised mechanic rather than for the genius of the architect, for the patient steadiness of the plough-horse rather than for the wings of Pegasus.

In the sanctum of the bishop *in partibus* already referred to, there hangs as almost its sole adornment a photograph of that painting of Raphael's commonly called the School of Athens. Below, in the foreground, the geometer and the geographer and other pursuers of earthly arts are seen plying their half-mechanical vocations, but the pyramid of figures rises through forms identified with higher and higher realms of thought, and culminates with divine philosophy in the persons of Plato and Aristotle. The picture hangs there to remind the delver in the earth of the heights to which others may ultimately carry the materials and the thoughts of which he is the humble purveyor.

Sometimes, it must be confessed, it seems a far cry from the immediate work of the day to its final uses, from the editing of documents or the listing of archives to the glowing—or if not glowing let us hope at least veracious—pages of the future historian. Long confinement at hard labor in the subterranean caverns of history may leave one out of touch with the world of sunlight. That close atmosphere has doubtless its particular dangers, its special diseases, like that caisson-disease which afflicts the subaqueous workers in compressed air. It is good for the mine-foreman and his gnomes to emerge occasionally into the fresh upper air, to see in what direction the winds of contemporary intellectual life are blowing, to look around at the structures into which the products of their delving are to enter.

In this belief I ask you to join me in considering, not so much the details of the work of my department, as the reason for its existence and the general direction which it should follow. I name as my subject "The Future Uses of History."

It is easy to say that prophecy is vain, and literary prophecy the most insecure of all. Twenty-two years before the French Revolution, David Hume declared that the writings of Rousseau had once for all been "consigned to perpetual neglect and oblivion." The same acute critic declared confidently that posterity would regard Hume's "Douglas" as the chief of English tragedies. But reluctant as any historical student must be to assume the totally different functions of the prophet, it is not difficult to show that, if it is his business to occupy himself chiefly with the raw materials of history, he must inevitably try to peer forward somewhat into the future of the historical art. He has no other course. The "Guide to the Materials for American History in the Public Record Office of Great Britain," of which we published a volume the other day, is not intended for the benefit of the historian whose book is published to-day or tomorrow. It comes too late for him. He will say of it as the Abbe Vertot, author of a once famous "History of the Siege of Malta," said when new materials were shown to him which upset his narrative before it was published, "Monsieur, mon siège est fait." Several years must pass before any considerable portion of the materials we have listed at the Public Record Office has been examined by historical students, still more years before the fresh facts in them have found their way into historical monographs or articles, still more before they are incorporated into the general histories.

In the field of history, indeed, the advancement of learning may be likened to the advance of an army. The workers in organized institutions of research must go before, like pickets or scouting parties making a reconnaissance. Then, after some interval, comes the light cavalry of makers of doctoral dissertations, then, the heavy artillery of writers of maturer monographs, both of them heavily encumbered with ammunition trains of bibliography and footnotes. Then comes the multitudinous infantry of readers and college students and school children, and finally, like sutlers and contractors hovering in the rear, the horde of those that make text-books. It may be twenty years before new facts discovered, or the elimination of ancient errors, find place in the historical books prepared for the general reader. At all events, the conductor of the reconnaissance must have his eye on the future, rather than the immediate, needs of his profession, and must constantly make such forecast of them as he can. And so he is, perforce, obliged to think of the Future Uses of History, not necessarily with ambitious straining toward an impossible degree of foresight, but at least with sober endeavor to see what can be seen.

As human life in the future will be partly like human life in the past and partly different, so the usefulness of history to future purposes will be partly the same as it has hitherto manifested and partly different. First, leaving aside for the moment all its applications, its independent value as a discipline will surely never cease. The severity of its methods, its merciless sifting and dissection, and comparison of human statements, will always make it the invaluable foe of credulity, the steady propagator of that methodical doubt on which enlightenment so largely depends. It cannot fail to be in the future, as it has been in the past, one of the principal promoters of fairness of mind, that chief lubricant of human affairs. Indeed, in the graded schools beyond which only a small fraction of our population ever proceeds, it is the one study which teaches children anything of the minds and characters of their fellow-beings. These are important considerations, if we are willing to look out of our study-windows and to think of history, not as the property of a small guild of professional colleagues, but as the rightful heritage of millions. For my own part, I do not hesitate to say that in our country the chief use of history is to give young women—I say young women because young men will not read—to give American young women, earlier than life can give it, some knowledge of human nature.

But it will be said that these are vague considerations, on which it would be difficult to erect a program. As historians have usually construed their task, it has been to study, not simply human nature and the general course of its workings in actual life, but specifically the manner in which organized human nature has acted. Human beings have been organized in various ways, and many forms of history have been devised to correspond. Most conspicuously, they have been organized in political states, and political histories have, therefore, been the histories most abundantly written. But whatever the particular variety, the main reason for writing has lain in the conviction that from the history of an organization in the past one could learn what would be useful toward its guidance in the present and future.

History has risen or fallen in popularity as there has been greater or less belief that the past had valuable lessons to teach. If it is the nurse of statesmanship, if it is philosophy teaching by examples, if it shows the ways of God to man, it is well worth pursuing. In the days between the Reformation and the Peace of Westphalia it was so regarded. "Histories make men wise," said Lord Bacon. "To despise them," said Luther, "is not only a coarse Tartaric and Cyclopean barbarism, but also a devilish senselessness, whereby the devil would more and more extinguish the right knowledge of God." Never, on the other hand, did the esteem of history sink lower than in France in the time of the Revolution, when, it was held, old things had passed away and all things had become new, and the politician's great duty was to cut loose from the abhorred and despised past of the Middle Ages and bring the Golden Age into immediate existence.

> "The world's great age begins anew,
> The golden years return;
> The earth doth like a snake renew
> Her winter weeds outworn;
> Heaven smiles, and faiths and empires gleam
> Like wrecks of a dissolving dream."

On the whole, however, men have speedily returned to the opinion, and we may expect them to adhere to it, that history has much light to cast on the problems of statesmanship. It is easy to say that no two ages or countries, no two states of society, no two combinations of events, are ever precisely alike. No doubt one of the chief uses of history itself is to prevent us from being taken in by historical parallels. Caesar had his Brutus and Charles I his Cromwell, but in a modern historical seminar, Patrick Henry would find difficulty in proving that all that had anything to do with George III.

But that history can be misused is no argument that it is useless. Its lessons are not ready in tabloids, predigested for immediate consumption by the inquiring statesman. Its oracles require interpretation, or modification to fit new circumstances. No two cases in history are alike. But no two voyages are alike, yet we prefer a skipper who has voyaged before. No two political campaigns are alike, but it is not customary to trust the management of a new candidacy to one who has never before gone through a political campaign. So of the nation or the race. John Selden put the matter rightly. The passage is in his *History of Tythes*: "The neglect or only vulgar regard of the fruitful and precious part of it [antiquity] which gives necessary light to the present in matter of state, law, history, and the understanding of good authors, is but preferring that kind of ignorance which our short life alone allows us before the many ages of former experience and observation, which may so accumulate years to us as if we had lived even from the beginning of time."

As we are helped in respect to shaping our personal course into the future by all the various knowledge of mankind that we have gained by the experience of life, some of it knowledge that we could state in formal propositions, some of it knowledge that lies implicit in our minds as the foundation of tact, so the uses of history to the public man or to the voter lie partly in formulated conclusions or opinions, partly in less tangible gains—in a heightened sense of what is expedient for man, or for the particular nation or community whose history one has tried to understand, in a more acute judgment as to what will succeed. At the basis of our confidence lies the belief, which the last half-century's studies have converted into settled doctrine, that the whole civilization of the present has its roots deep in the past, and can never be understood except by entering deeply into the study of origins. The stream of history is a stream of causation. The spacious fabric that lies before us, woven for us on the roaring loom of time, gray and dull in some lights or aspects, shot with gleams of splendor when seen in others, is composed of threads drawn from every age of the past.

Not one of these influences or survivals can be rightly understood except by considering its entire setting, and thus we are led into the study of all past ages. The Balkan situation of 1912 demands for its sympathetic comprehension not only a close study of ethnological characters in some of the most intricately mixed populations of Europe, but a knowledge of five hundred years of Turkish history, a thousand years of Bulgarian and Servian history, more than sixteen hundred of Rumanian and Greek. The American negro, the Russian Jew, the many other ethnic elements which go to make up our wonderfully composite population, each requires the patient mastery of a separate history for its proper understanding.

History must be studied in order that we may comprehend how the evolution of human elements and institutions has been brought about, a process radically different from the evolution of animal forms, and consisting mostly in changes of place, in the replacing of one generation by another, and above all in the substitution of new habits of action and thought for earlier ones. But if this were all, the American would have little need to study any but American history, and, in lessening degree as he went backward, those ages of European history from which concrete and definite elements have passed over into the American fabric.

In reality there are two ways in which history enables us to understand the present, and the tracing of origins and transmissions and survivals is but one of them. There is a sense in which we know things only by comparison, can know the present state of civilization in any country only as we appreciate how and wherein it might have been different. Many a statement as to cause and effect in the evolution of society in any given country can be exploded or modified by a glance at the differing manner in which the same forces have worked out under differing circumstances elsewhere. Much of what we deem to have been logically inevitable in the history of the feudalism of the Middle Ages in Europe is seen not to have been true of Japanese feudalism. The elaborate civilizations of Greece and Rome deserve the child's attention, among other reasons, precisely because they are not those of the generations immediately preceding and leading up to his own. There is a provincialism in respect to time as narrowing as the provincialism of space, and one of the chief uses of history is to guard us from it.

The platform orator confidently puts forward the protective tariff as the true source of American high wages. You may give him pause if you point out to him that American wages were high before there was a protective tariff. Henry Wansey, a Wiltshire clothier, who traveled about the United States before even the act of 1790 could have had much effect, declares his belief that manufactures could not succeed in America because of the scarcity and high price of labor.

If not an orator, a highly oratorical historian, unfortunately much read, draws our attention to striking contrasts between the institutions of America and those of England, and urges us to believe that the origins of the former are in the main not English, but Dutch.[2] We do not have an established church. Democratic equality prevails among us. We have a written constitution, a President, a legislature much differing from Parliament. Primogeni-

{2.} See Douglas Campbell, *The Puritan in Holland, England, and America: An Introduction to American History*, 2 vols. (New York: Harper and Brothers, 1893).

ture is unknown among us. Deeds and mortgages are recorded in public offices. Our system of local government is simple. Religious liberty, the freedom of the press, the use of the written ballot, and the modern system of prison management were all fully established in America long before they came into vogue in England. Therefore, says our writer, American institutions, at least these typical ones, must have come from some third country, to wit, from Holland. But a very little historical thinking leads us to ask whether Australia has ever been to any powerful degree subjected to the influences of the Dutch. Here also is a land without established churches, and in which religious liberty, freedom of the press, and democratic equality have long prevailed. The individual colonies, and the Commonwealth of Australia, have written constitutions. The organization of the colonial legislatures is of a more modern type than that of the legislature in England, and the system of local government is simpler. Primogeniture is unknown. The administration of prisons has been in accord with modern notions. The registration of land titles is more highly developed than in the United States, and the arrangements with regard to the written ballot are those which we have at last copied. Now if all these things are not and cannot be of Dutch origin in Australia, neither are they, in the main, in America. The simple truth, of course, is, that most of these differences between English and American institutions are most naturally explained as resulting from the widely different conditions presented by virgin soil, new settlement, absence of traditions, or other historic accidents.

Or again, our platform orator, perhaps, assures us that an antipathy of the white man toward the negro is a natural instinct, implanted by God in the white human breast, so that racial antagonisms are a part of the divine order of the universe. If our historical studies of the negro and of slavery have been confined to the United States and to the Anglo-Saxon, as unfortunately those studies too often are, we may see no course but to acquiesce in the orator's deductions. But if we are able to bring into the comparison the history of the negro in Brazil, where the sentiment alluded to does not exist, we shall see that it is not the fatal product of nature, but the deciduous fruit of history.

Now this use of history, to enrich our intelligence concerning what is before us by including alien institutions and remote civilizations in the circle of our thinking, by the comprehension of a wider variety of social and political forms and events than has underlain our own national development, is a use unaffected in the main by the changes which our own age or nation may undergo. The student of the political and social sciences—the economist, the philologian in the broader sense of that term, the student of legal and religious ideas—will never find direct observation of present phenomena sufficient for their purposes, but will continue in the future, as they have so largely done during the past fifty years, to seek in the rich laboratory of history the materials for sounder conclusions than to-day's phenomena alone can give.

But as to the other chief use of history, to show how the present world has come to be what it is, we must expect that, while remaining generically the same, it shall take on new forms as the social complex changes. It need not surprise us if history once more transforms itself. It has done so again and again. Dr. Mark Pattison declared that history was one of the most ephemeral forms of literature. Without quite subscribing to this dictum, we may readily point out that since the Renaissance history, like other forms of literature, has had its well-defined phases, has passed through several distinct climates of ideas. First came the classicizing historians of the Renaissance, then the memoir-writers of the age of religious wars, then in each country the statesmen-historians of the early seventeenth century, then everywhere those giants of learning, prodigies of documentary collection and publication, who two hundred years ago were making the great age of erudition. Next came the philosophical historians of the school of Turgot and Hume, applying general ideas and ruling the mid-eighteenth century; then the eclipse of history by the French Revolution; then in the period of Restoration and Romanticism, its return into the hands of statesmen and publicists; then the heyday of the critical school, the searchers of documents, the disciples of Ranke, to whose synagogue most of us still belong; and latterly, outside of Anglo-Saxondom at least, a new school of synthetic philosophers and sociological psychologists, speaking what to old ears seems a new language, quite as much the dialect of thermodynamics or of pathology as of history.

Generally speaking, these successive changes of attitude on the part of history have been conscious or unconscious attempts to adapt it to the uses of successive states of society. Every age has its own problems. Each looks to history for help in solving them, because it believes, as Burke said, that the individual's private stock of reason is too small to trade upon, and that he would do better to avail himself "of the general bank and capital of nations and of ages." But each asks its own questions of the oracle, and we are to expect that the next generation, the immediate future, will make other demands upon the records of the past than those which have been made by our own day and generation. If then we are working at all for the future, we must ask ourselves what the future will be like.

To such a question it is foolish to attempt an extensive or detailed reply. There is much, however, to convince us that, broadly speaking, we are approaching the end of one of the great epochs in human history and the beginning of another. The period which is ending has lasted somewhat more than four centuries. It may be called the era of great national states, as the five hundred years which preceded it may be called the era of small feudal states. Shortly before the discovery of America, powerful economic influences, aided by a group of vigorous and ambitious monarchs and statesmen, replaced feudal anarchy by centralized despotism, and welded the discordant fragments of mediaeval Europe into a dozen capacious, strong, and durable kingdoms. For four hundred years this has been the main form or mould in which Europe has been organized. For four hundred years the main subject of European history has been the organized and separate doings of a dozen large nations and their mutual interaction. The peace of Europe seemed to lie in the balance of power among these national states.

But throughout most of these four centuries the conditions of life in western and central Europe changed comparatively little in things essential. Napoleon's army could not invade Italy with much greater celerity than that of Charles VIII under similar leadership might have done. The peasant of a Yorkshire village in 1789 had seen no more of Frenchmen than his predecessor of 1689. His parson had been educated by the same classics as the parson of a hundred years before, his militiaman used the same weapons, his shoemaker the same tools. Western Europe was in the main

> "A sleepy land where under the same wheel
> The same old rut would deepen year by year;
> Where Aylmer follow'd Aylmer at the Hall
> And Averill, Averill at the Rectory."

The Industrial Revolution has changed all that. Coal and iron and steam, the railroad and the steamboat and the telegraph, have knit all Europe together into one complex but compacted whole. Adrianople is nearer to St. James's Palace in 1912 than Calais was in 1800. Forty international congresses take place every year. More treaties are signed in a month than in the sixteenth century were signed in a decade. When France and Germany seem likely to be dragged into war by the conflict of financial and commercial interests in Morocco, the socialists of both countries organize simultaneous anti-militarist demonstrations, in which millions of workingmen take part, and warfare is averted. The peoples of Europe are usually in quite as close and cordial relations as those of the American States were in 1786.

In military, diplomatic, and some political aspects it may still be proper to think of Europe chiefly as a system of great national states. But in nearly every other aspect it is plain that the Age of Nations is approaching its end. The nation is ceasing to be the leading form of the world's structure; organizations transcending national boundaries are becoming more and more numerous and effective. We are advancing into a new world which will be marked by cosmopolitan thought and sentiment, by economic systems more and more socialistic in character, and by institutions increasingly internationalized; and signs are not wanting that among the historians of Europe there are those who will supply the new internationalized and socialistic Demos with the historical information which his new purposes will require.

Meantime it is equally true, though true under other forms, that for

America also the last four hundred years have constituted a distinct era now coming to a close. It is the great and memorable era of free land. Hitherto free land has been our basis. "Land!" was the first cry of the storm-tossed mariners of Columbus. For three centuries the leading fact of American history has been that soon after 1600 a body of Europeans, mostly Englishmen, settled on the edge of the greatest piece of unoccupied agricultural land in the temperate zone, and proceeded to subdue it to the uses of man. For three centuries the chief task of American mankind has been to go up westward against the land and to possess it. Our wars, our independence, our state building, our political democracy, our plasticity with respect to immigration, our mobility of thought, our ardor of initiative, our mildness and our prosperity, all are but incidents or products of this prime historical fact.

It has been a wonderful process. Future ages, remoter from it than we, will see more clearly the high poetic quality in this ceaseless pressure and surge of half-conscious millions, led forward by dim, high impulses to enter the promised land and to prepare it to be the chief home of civilized mankind. "By faith they sojourned in the land of promise, as in a strange country, dwelling in tabernacles," and "died in faith, not having received the promises, but having seen them afar off, and were persuaded of them, and embraced them, and confessed that they were strangers and pilgrims on the earth."

But all this, which has allied our simple annals with the Odyssey and the Book of Genesis, is now a closed or closing chapter. The era of free land is over. Practically all the usable agricultural land, except that which is also forested, has now passed out of the hands of the federal government. That government has disposed of two thousand million acres of public lands; but from 1900 to 1910 the total area of farms increased only four per cent. For nearly three centuries our prevailing practice was the ownership of the land by him that worked it, and our democracy rested largely on the opinion that this was the ideal régime; now three-eighths of our farms are operated by tenants. Half our population is now urban within the census definition, where in 1790 all but three per cent. was rural; meanwhile, our exports of manufactures have more than quadrupled in twenty years. In short, we have ceased, almost suddenly ceased, to be a new country—that is to say, a nation which has taken but the first steps in the subduing of nature to the uses of man—and have become an old country.

Can it be supposed that so great and so dramatic a transition, which has transformed the organization of our economic life and of our political parties, shall have no effect upon the questions which men ask concerning the past? Nothing can be more certain than that history must be prepared to respond to new demands. I do not think so ill of my profession as to suppose that American historians will not make gallant and intelligent attempts to meet the new requirements.

What sort of histories will a socialized and internationalized Europe desire? What information regarding the past will be demanded by a socialized, probably in some sense socialistic, America? Surely the old varieties of history will continue, partly because of human inertia, partly because they ought to continue. Even a world without kingdoms must know the history of kingdoms. Even the drum and trumpet historian, so much reprobated of late, has his place. If we can thoroughly know the present only by contrast and comparison, if we are to steer clear of a provincial habit of mind respecting our own age, we shall think that wars and political machinations that have been important in their day are important in history. Because the automobile is becoming the leading feature of our scenery, we are not warranted in thinking that the one really important event in Napoleon's time was the invention of Trevethick's traction-engine.

Yet surely man will wish to know concerning the past a thousand things of which in former times annalists were incurious. Social and economic history will surely assume a greater place than political history. Where hitherto men have interrogated the past concerning the doings of generals and politicians, they will be more prone to interrogate it concerning the holdings of public and private land, the course of prices, the migrations of settlers and of crop-areas, the rise of trade-unions, the development of new religions, the status of the negro, the advance of education or of missions or of the spirit of toleration.

In an advancing world, the power of thought increases. We must expect that the men of the future will be more curious than we have been respecting the history of thought, of thought as manifested in philosophy and the advance of science, in religion and poetry, in industrial and social programs, in newspapers and the drama. A world that is increasingly ruled by public opinion will wish to know more of the history of public opinion. It will care more about the psychology of the Crusaders' motives than about their deeds of arms, more about the religion of the Visigoths than about the succession of their kings.

A socialized and internationalized Christendom will particularly desire light on the history of national character and of all that has gone to make it up. The advocates of universal peace, whom it is customary in some quarters to stigmatize as "well-meaning," are not deceived in thinking that they have with them, on the whole, the mightiest forces of the new industrial world. It is profitable to modern business and to modern labor alike, to extend that sympathetic comprehension of nation by nation which makes warfare increasingly distasteful, and of that comprehension there is no better nourisher than the study of history.

No doubt many questions will be asked of history which history cannot answer. Past ages have left record of such things only as seemed to them important. If the inventor of gunpowder or of paper could have foreseen its total significance, he would not have left us to grope so dimly in the search for its origins. It would interest us immeasurably to know the fact with certainty, if the decline of the Roman Empire was due to the spread of malaria, but we cannot find all the evidence we would. But the questioning will continue. History that is worth while will be pursued with increasing eagerness. Men will increasingly perceive that our ability to transform the world of society is enhanced by our sense of the transformations it has already undergone, our belief in the possibility of changing it.

These are some of the traits of history's usefulness in the future. These are some of the possibilities and probabilities concerning its development which ought to be born in mind by those who plan for, and work in, an endowed department of historical research. Imperfect as our vision into the future is and must be, by using it as well as we can we shall be enabled better to serve the needs of the historians who shall come after us and enter into our labors. Comforted by this reflection we may retire once more into our subterranean caverns.

History Teacher's Magazine 4 (February 1913): 35–40.

The Need of a National Archive Building

Shortly after becoming director of the Department of Historical Research in the Carnegie Institution of Washington in the fall of 1905, Jameson began a campaign to educate legislators, cabinet officials, and government bureaucrats about the need for a national archive building that would store the government's historically significant records and make them available to scholars. In March 1903, as part of an omnibus Public Buildings Act, Congress had provided for the acquisition of a plot of land for this structure on Eighteenth and Nineteenth streets, between E and F streets, but had made no appropriation to draft architectural plans. Jameson turned for assistance to the American Historical Association, which in 1908 created a committee on the archives, made up of Jameson, Alfred T. Mahan, a retired rear admiral and the author of *The Influence of Sea Power upon History, 1660–1783*, and John B. McMaster, professor of history at the University of Pennsylvania. Jameson was the only active member of this committee, but it gave him institutional standing, he explained in 1919, "whenever there seemed to be any question of what business I, as an outsider to the government, had to meddle in the matter" of a national archive building.[1] Every year from 1908 to 1913, at its annual meeting, the AHA passed resolutions and memorials requesting congressional action to appropriate funds for this building.

A consummate politician, Jameson cultivated the friendship of Senator Miles Poindexter and Congressman Morris Sheppard, who individually introduced legislation in 1913 that eventually resulted in the drafting of architectural plans for the building. Using the press to inform public opinion, Jameson also garnered support from patriotic societies, such as the Sons and Daughters of the American Revolution, as well as from professional societies, asking them to lobby Congress.[2]

In January 1914 Victor H. Paltsits, chairman of the AHA's Public Archives Commission, suggested that Jameson address the American Library Association when it met in Washington that spring. Jameson presented the speech on May 26, 1914, at Continental Hall. In response, the ALA passed a resolution endorsing the need for a national archive and called on Congress to pass an appropriations bill to fund the drafting of architectural plans.[3] Subsequently, Congress appropriated five thousand dollars toward this end. George B. Utley, secretary of the ALA, arranged for the publication of Jameson's speech in the organization's bulletin and provided Jameson with fifty copies to assist in his lobbying efforts.[4]

NOTES

1. [JFJ] to Henry B. Gardner, January 22, 1919, TLc, Box 57, JP, DLC. See Victor Gondos, Jr., *J. Franklin Jameson and the Birth of the National Archives, 1906–1926* (Philadelphia: University of Pennsylvania Press, 1981), p. 10.

2. See, for example, Jameson's 1911 address to the Daughters of the American Revolution, in the *Proceedings of the Twentieth Continental Congress of the Daughters of the American Revolution, Washington, D.C., April 17–22, 1911* (Washington, D.C.: Published by the Congress, 1911), pp. 90–93.

3. Victor H. Paltsits to JFJ, January 21, March 9, 1914, both ALS; [JFJ] to Paltsits, January 23, May 12, 19, 1914, all TLc; all in Box 117, JP, DLC; Edwin H. Anderson to JFJ, February 7, 1914, TLS; [JFJ] to Anderson, February 10, 1914, TLc; both in Box 53, JP, DLC.

4. George B. Utley to JFJ, May 11, June 15, 1914, both TLS; [JFJ] to Utley, June 5, 1914, TLc; all in Box 53, JP, DLC; JFJ to Francis A. Christie, May 28, 1914, TLS, Box 71, JP, DLC. See also Gondos, *Birth of the National Archives*, pp. 63–69.

ENGLAND, SCOTLAND, IRELAND, France, Belgium, the Netherlands, Spain, Portugal, Prussia, Austria, Hungary, Switzerland, Italy, Denmark, Sweden, Norway, Russia, Roumania, Canada, Mexico, Cuba, Colombia— every one of these countries has a national archive, in which all or most of its older records and papers are stored. The presumption must be that there is some merit in the idea of a national archive building. Apparently the burden of proof is on anyone who says that the United States, not the poorest of these countries and we fondly imagine not the least enterprising, ought not to have one. In reality, no one says this. The obstacle is not opposition, but negligence and inertia, only to be overcome by convincing wise men and influential societies of the need of a federal archive establishment and asking them to help forward the movement toward such a consummation.

The evolution of national archives has in most cases a definite and regular natural history. At first, each government office preserves its own papers. By and by the space available for such documents becomes crowded. The oldest of them, seldom referred to, are sent away, to attics or cellars or vacant rooms in the same or other buildings, it matters little where, in order to make room for the transaction of current business. By and by historians arise. They insist that these dead files are full of historical information, that they are a valuable national asset, that it is shameful to neglect them. At the same time, administrators discover that, whenever administration depends upon the careful study of previous experience, it is inconvenient to have the papers recording that experience scattered through many unsuitable repositories, neglected and unarranged. Then begins a movement for a national archive building, a determination to erect a structure ideally adapted for the storage of documents and their preservation in accessible order and to gather into that one fit place the records which hitherto have lain neglected in a multitude of unfit places. Before the passage of the Public Records Act of 1838, and the consequent erection of the Public Record Office in London, the records of the British government were stored in some sixty different places in that city, some of them atrociously unfit. The building of that admirable repository and its successive enlargements have led to the concentration, under one roof, of the records of nearly all branches of the British administration down to within thirty or forty years of the present time.

The British instance represents a very high degree of concentration. In some other countries, where individual executive departments had long since solidified their respective archives and given them a scientific organization, these collections, instead of being merged in the national archives, have been allowed to maintain a separate existence. Thus in Paris, alongside the Archives Nationales, we find the very important separate establishments of the Archives of the Ministries of Foreign Affairs, of War, and of Marine, while at Berlin and Vienna, outside the Staatsarchive, the war departments have independent archives of great importance. Most European ministries, however, retain in their own hands only papers of recent date.

In any grading of archives by the extent to which concentration has been carried, Great Britain and Canada would stand at the highest end of the scale, while the United States would represent the lowest and simplest stage of development. Here in the national capital it has been the practice, from the beginning, that each bureau or division of an executive department should keep its own records and the papers which flow into it in the course of administrative business. Only one department has undertaken to concentrate its archives, the War Department, nearly all whose records and papers have been combined into one collection, under the custody of the adjutant-general. As for federal archives outside Washington, such as the records and papers of custom houses and army posts, no effort has been made to concentrate them. They remain where they always have been, if indeed they remain at all. While every European government has now adopted the policy of transferring from its embassy or legation here in Washington to its home archives all but the last few years' accumulation of papers, our policy, or more correctly, our practice, has been to leave all the archives of embassies, legations, and consulates where they are—with effects which can easily be estimated in view of another of our "policies," that of not having permanent homes for our legations in foreign parts.

In Washington the results of what may be called the bureau system of archive management have been exceedingly unhappy. In the first place, it has produced an excessive number of systems of management. To keep a bureau's papers in an order that he who devised it has thought suitable to its business may not seem to be an evil. But the business of bureaus changes, and bureaus are divided and consolidated and extinguished and shifted from department to department, and the result is sometimes an awkward mixture of systems, some of which were amateurish when devised, many of which have become antiquated since that time. But a greater evil than that of having thirty or forty different filing-systems is that of having more than a hundred different repositories. This would not be so great an evil if we had always one variety of papers, and the whole of that variety in one place; but this is wonderfully far from being the case. Let us take for instance those papers which relate to the history of the government of territories before their admission as states of the Union. The administration of the territories was in the hands of the Department of State till 1873, after that in those of the Department of the Interior. There is no portion of the archival papers of the federal government which is more sought for by historical investigators than these, for the energetic western historical societies find them a copious source of knowledge for the earlier periods. But papers of this sort cannot be found in Washington without special guidance. Many, perhaps most, territorial papers of date anterior to 1873 are at the State Department, but some of them are in the Bureau of Indexes and Archives, some in the Bureau of Rolls and Library, and no man can discern or declare how the line of classification is drawn. Of later papers, many are in the files of the Secretary of the Interior. For years there was an informal dispute between the two departments as to the transference of certain masses of territorial papers in 1873, the Department of State maintaining that they had been transferred, the Interior Department, more correctly, that they had not. Many territorial papers, of great historical importance, are in the files of the Senate and House of Representatives. Some have been transferred from the latter to the Library of Congress. Others are in the Stygian darkness of the General Land Office files, others in those of the Treasury Department, in those of the Indian Office, in those of the inspector-general of the United States army, or in the enormous archives of the adjutant-general.

But dispersion is not the only, or the worst, evil that has flowed from the present system, or want of system, whereby each bureau is in the main left to keep its own papers. It is 125 years since some of these bureaus and divisions were founded. In much less than 125 years a bureau will accumulate enough records and papers to occupy more than all the space originally assigned to it. Those least needed are packed away, in attics and in cellars, over porticoes and under stairs, in closets and in abandoned door-ways, till a building is so full that it will hold no more, if any proper space is to be reserved for the work of officials and clerks. Then warehouses, in almost no case fireproof, are rented to contain the overflow. The Treasury Department has to rent an additional warehouse every five or ten years, merely to hold the fresh accumulation of its papers. Not a mile from this spot, for instance, there is a warehouse in which papers of the Treasury Department have simply been dumped on the floor—boxes, bundles, books, loose papers— till the pile reaches well toward the ceiling; and no man knows what it contains, or could find in it any given book or paper. For quarters of this sort, in buildings usually unsafe and always unsuitable, the government pays each year, counting only the space devoted to storage of records and papers, rentals aggregating between $40,000 and $50,000, more than the interest it would pay on a million. For that sum an excellent archive building could be erected, capable of housing not only all these papers which departments have stored outside their walls, but also all the dead files which occupy space and impede business within the departmental buildings themselves.

These are general statements. Let us mention specific instances. The librarian who is "doing" the sights of Washington may be interested to know, as he gazes at the beautiful proportions of the Treasury Building, that in its attic story several miles of wooden shelving contain old Treasury papers, closely packed together and dry as tinder, which up to the present time have not succumbed to spontaneous combustion under our August sun. If he pauses for a moment to look with pleasure at the sunken fountain at the north end of the Treasury, it may augment his pride in the ingenuity of his government to know that a portion of its Treasury archives is stored in chambers constructed around the substructure of the fountain. If by mistake he goes to the old building of the Corcoran Art Gallery instead of the new, he will be compensated by the unusual sight, in the basement, of a body of governmental records so stored that in a dry season they can be consulted by any person wearing rubber overshoes, while in a wet season they are accessible by means of some old shutters laid on the basement floor. At the General Land Office (really the worst case of all) he may see a body of archives representing the titles to four hundred million acres of formerly public but now private lands, stored in a place not, I think, as fit for the purpose as the average librarian's coal-cellar—certainly not as fit as mine. If he goes into the Pension Office building, he will find the rich and interesting archives of the Indian Office stored in the court-yard. As he looks at the small dome that surmounts the House wing of the Capitol, he may reflect with pleasure that the old files of the House of Representatives are stored, in open boxes, in a manner not unlike that formerly followed by country lawyers, in the stifling heat of the space between roof and ceiling of the dome.

Danger of destruction by fire is constant under such circumstances. It is surprising that fires have not been more frequent. But they have occurred several times in former years, and only last summer a fire in the building of the Geological Survey burned up papers which it had cost $100,000 to produce. There are half a dozen places in Washington where, if an extensive fire should break out, it might in a few hours, by burning up the documents with which claims against the government are defended, cause the government to lose several times the cost of a good national archive building.

Probably there is no repository for government papers in Washington, except the Division of Manuscripts in the Library of Congress, which is strictly fireproof in the fullest sense; but danger from fire is not the only peril to which archives are now exposed. Some of the places where they are stored are damp. In others there is local dampness from steam pipes and leaky roofs. In many there is injury from dust and dirt, in nearly all the grossest overcrowding. As to search and use, it is sometimes impossible, usually difficult. So dark are many repositories that when Messrs. Van Tyne and Leland were preparing their Guide to the Archives of the Government in Washington, an electric searchlight was a necessary part of their equipment.[1] Armed with this, they could read the labels on the bundles or the legends on the

{1.} Claude Halstead Van Tyne (1869–1930) and Waldo Gifford Leland (1879–1966) prepared their *Guide to the Archives of the United States in Washington* (Washington, D.C.: Carnegie Institution of Washington, 1904) under the direction of Andrew C. McLaughlin, Jameson's predecessor at the Department of Historical Research.

backs of bound volumes, whenever these had not rotted off from dampness
or excessive dryness. By way of contrast to the literary search-rooms in the
Public Record Office in London or the Archives Nationales in Paris, in which
fifty or a hundred historical scholars can work amid conditions resembling
those which you, ladies and gentlemen, offer to readers in your libraries, the
courageous student of this country's history is fortunate if, after the volume
or bundle has been dragged from its darksome lair, an obliging clerk—and
nearly all government clerks in Washington are obliging—clears upon some
heavily burdened desk or table a space two feet square which the student
can use for the study of his documents.

To me, and to many of those who hear me, the main reason for interesting ourselves in the problems of a national archive building is that present
conditions interpose almost intolerable obstacles to the progress of history.
We may reasonably expect that this should also seem to legislators a serious
matter. An enlightened government, a government whose success depends
on the intelligence of public opinion, cannot afford to be indifferent to the
advancement of historical knowledge. The government of the United States
should do far more for it than it does. It would be a perfectly justifiable expenditure if on this ground alone, merely as the first step toward a proper
cultivation of the national history, our government should spend $1,000,000
or $1,500,000 in erecting a perfect archive building, in which the historian
could find and use his materials. But as the actual world goes, we are to
expect business considerations to have greater weight than the interests of
history. Very well. Put the matter on that ground. Is it good business for a
government to spend $50,000 a year for rental of bad quarters, when for the
same sum capitalized it could build magnificent quarters with much greater
capacity? Is it good business for a government that can borrow at three
per cent to pay rentals of ten per cent? It certainly is not thought so when
the question is one of building local post-offices. The trusts and other great
business corporations think it indispensable to have the most modern filing-
systems installed in fireproof buildings. To neglect such precautions may
some day cost them too much; to be unable to find papers quickly would
cost them too much every day. But the greatest of all American business
organizations is the Treasury Department of the United States. Its papers
accumulate at the rate of 25,000 cubic feet per annum. It needs at this moment not less than 600,000 cubic feet of space in a modern archive building.
What has it, this greatest of business concerns in the most businesslike of
countries? It has an attic with miles of wooden shelving on which its papers
crumble and fall to pieces from heat, and a sub-basement in which they rot
to pieces from dampness. It rents two floors and part of another floor in a
storage warehouse on E Street, a warehouse on New York Avenue, part of a
building on C Street, part of a building on Fourteenth Street, part of a building on F Street. Two of these it will soon give up, happy to use instead the

cast-off building of the Bureau of Engraving and Printing. It uses the basement of the old Court of Claims building and a part of the old Post-Office building, and has filled the old Winder building with files until it was forced to stop because the floors could not safely bear any more weight. If a paper more than forty years old, of certain sorts, is desired, it may take several days to find it. I do not need to ask whether this is intelligent and economical administration. I have wished merely to emphasize the thought that, if this national archive building comes into existence, as surely it some time will, it will be brought into being, less by the clamor of historians, a feeble folk relatively, than by the steady and powerful pressure of administrators, worried beyond endurance by the increase of files and painfully conscious of the drag which primitive methods of storage impose on the progress of government business.

Administrative eagerness to find a remedy has sought more than one outlet. One is the destruction of useless papers, but this is only a partial remedy. It is perfectly true that many papers of little or no worth beyond the year of their origin have been preserved. One might wish that some of these were burned up. Under existing conditions, as I have shown, some of them are likely to be. But a conflagration cannot be expected to make an intelligent selection of material, and government officials, for that matter, cannot do it perfectly. We have statutes for the destruction of useless papers, but they are very loose in comparison with those of Europe, and give no security that papers useless for administration but valuable for history will be preserved. Not so many years ago, ten tons of Confederate records were barely rescued from the paper-mill, and the schedules of the earlier censuses, though since then the latter have formed the basis of valued historical publications.

Another expedient that has been occasionally suggested has been the transfer of "dead files" to the Library of Congress. It needs but a little thought upon considerations of space to show the futility of such a plan. Where should the Library of Congress find space for two or three million cubic feet of archive material? Some might say that at least such papers as are historically important might be sent to the Library. But, quite apart from the fact that this offers no relief to the government, which as we have seen is the greatest sufferer from the present conditions, it is impossible to accept the underlying assumption that there is a small and perfectly distinguishable portion of the government archives which is historically important, while the rest is not. A jury of the most experienced historians would be the first to declare that no one can tell what the historians of the next age will value as materials, and the first to protest against a process of tearing away certain papers, assumed to be historical, from the remaining series with which they have been associated and which help to explain their origin. Moreover, library administration is one thing, and archive administration, especially for purposes of government business as distinguished from purposes of history,

is a quite different thing. The present Librarian of Congress could administer an archive alongside his library, indeed could administer forty archives,
because he could administer anything.[2] But that hardly covers the point.
Essentially a librarian's business is different from an archivist's business; no
national government combines the two, and anyhow, a makeshift transference of a small part of the government's archives to the Library of Congress
would be no real solution of the difficulties.

The only satisfactory and proper means of escape from the present dis-
graceful conditions is that which other nations have adopted, the erection of
a national archive building in this city, of a size sufficient to contain all the
papers that all the executive departments and the Senate and House of Representatives may send to it, and with a large allowance for future growth.
Essentially a honeycomb of stacks resembling those of a library, it should
have an initial capacity of three million cubic feet, and should be built on a lot
of land large enough to admit of extension to nine million without exceeding
the height usual among our government buildings. The prediction can be
made with confidence, and is supported by the experience of other nations,
that while executive officers may at first transfer somewhat sparingly the
records and papers they have long had nominally under their control, they
will not take long to discover that needles can be more quickly found in
a needle-shop than in a haystack; and as the advantages of an orderly archive come to be appreciated, more and more of the archival papers will be
transferred to the new establishment.

Yet, though it shall be large, our national archive building need not be
alarmingly expensive. No ornate palace should be contemplated. If the ex-
terior is to suit the contents, it should be plain, yet it may easily be beautiful.
I know from the word of a friend that the greatest architect of the last generation said that he should like nothing better than to try his hand on a national
archive building. At a cost well inside fifty cents a cubic foot, or $1,500,000
for a building of the dimensions I have described, it should be possible for
the United States to have the finest archive building in the world, perfect in

---

{2.} Jameson had great respect for Herbert Putnam (1861–1955), who became the
Librarian of Congress in 1899. Under Putnam's predecessor, Ainsworth R. Spof-
ford, many library acquisitions were never unpacked, accessioned, or cataloged. The
only catalog access to the library's book collection was through the author's name.
Putnam's first goal was to improve book cataloging, and he succeeded in implement-
ing a system that is still in use. Another major achievement was a national interlibrary
loan system. Under Putnam's direction, the Library of Congress expanded beyond
its original function as a legislative reference service to become a national research
institution and a permanent custodian of America's cultural heritage. See Paul M.
Angle, The Library of Congress (Kingsport: Kingsport Press, 1948); and John Y. Cole, For
Congress and the Nation: A Chronological History of the Library of Congress (Washington,
D.C.: Government Printing Office, 1979).

every appointment, based on the best experience of Europe, and adequate for every purpose of the immediate future. This is the end toward which we ought to aspire and labor.

Into the details of the construction of such a building and of the organization of an archive establishment there is no time to enter. They are abundantly set forth in Mr. W. G. Leland's masterly article entitled "Our national archives: a programme," in the American Historical Review for October, 1912.

Efforts to secure such a building as I have in general terms described have not been lacking, nor are they a thing of yesterday. As far back as 1878, the quartermaster-general of the army recommended the erection of a "hall of records" for preservation of the records of the executive departments not required for daily reference, and drafted a plan for the proposed structure. That was thirty-six years ago. Since then there has perhaps been only one year in which the erection of a national archive building has not been pressed upon the attention of Congress, with greater or less urgency, by one or other members of the cabinet. At least fifty bills on the subject have been introduced in Congress. Nearly all have found permanent resting-places in the pigeonholes of committees. On two occasions, in 1881 and in 1902, the Senate passed bills providing for an archive building; but the House took no action on them. Finally, in 1903, after an agitation covering a quarter of a century, Congress authorized the purchase of a site for such a building. The site was purchased, but has since been assigned to another building. Meanwhile, within the thirty-six years during which this agitation by executive departments has been going on, Congress has expended at least $250,000,000 for public buildings, and $200,000,000 of that sum for local post-offices, courthouses and customhouses.

In recent years, the agitation has been taken up by various societies of patriotic intention. Nearly six years ago the American Historical Association addressed Congress on the subject, appointed a committee, arranged for useful hearings, and has continued to press the matter upon successive Congresses. Many chapters of the Daughters of the American Revolution have taken part in the endeavor. Recently the National Society of the Sons of the American Revolution has taken it up with much energy. The Public Buildings Act of March 3, 1913, authorized the Secretary of the Treasury to make plans for an archive building; but Congress made no appropriation of money for the planning, and without it nothing could be done. The result of thirty-six years of agitation can be summed up by saying that an item of $5,000 for the making of such plans, in the provisional manner in which alone they can be made before a site is selected, is now before the House Committee on Appropriations, as a part of the Sundry Civil Appropriations bill. Its fate will be known in a few days. This result, after thirty-six years of entreaty and appeal along lines of argument which were obvious thirty-six years ago and in thirty-six years have not been confuted, seems somewhat meagre. But I remember that it was about 1616 when one Francis Bacon recommended the establishment of a General Record Office for the kingdom of England and about 1856 when the first section of that building was erected. Two hundred and forty years, for a thing for which that capacious mind foresaw all the convincing arguments in 1616! We have still some time. Two hundred and forty years from 1878 would bring us only to 2118 A.D. But can we not beat the English record? Can we not, by keeping public opinion alive on a subject of so much importance from the historical and the governmental points of view, carry this great national undertaking along steadily through the stages of making plans, acquiring a site, and constructing the building, and have an archive to be proud of before we have here a national calamity resembling, but with perhaps larger proportions, the great fire at Albany?[3]

Bulletin of the American Library Association, 8 (July 1914): 1–7.

{3.} In the early morning of March 29, 1911, a fire broke out in the New York State Library, destroying thousands of rare documents and books. The exact cause of the fire was never determined, but speculation at the time suggested that defective electrical wiring may have been the source. See the following articles in the *Albany Evening Journal*: "Capital Fire Causes Loss of Millions," March 29, 1911, p. 1, col. 1; "State Library Loss by the Fire Was Tremendous," March 29, 1911, p. 12, col. 1; "Smoke Still Pours Forth from the Capital Ruins," March 30, 1911, p. 1, col. 1; and "Many Priceless Records Saved," March 31, 1911, p. 2, col. 1.

Historical Scholars in War-Time

At Jameson's invitation, a select group of historians met at the Carnegie Institution in Washington, D.C., in April 1917 and formed the National Board for Historical Service.[1] Jameson suggested in a circular to prospective participants that through an organization of historians "all this store of competence and patriotic good will, instead of running to waste lying untouched, might be systematically drawn upon to meet actual needs, felt or unfelt, of the government, or the public."[2] The NBHS sponsored lecture series for the military and the general public, prepared articles for mass circulation magazines, collected research materials, and provided information to federal government agencies during World War I.[3] Not all historians agreed with the goals of the NBHS. William L. Westermann, of the University of Wisconsin, opposed what he perceived to be an overzealous response of historians to the war effort and participated only "to put the damper upon possible tendencies . . . to pervert historical teaching and the meaning of history."[4]

NOTES

1. "National History Conference: Washington, D.C., April 28–29, 1917: Docket," TM, Box 25, Records of the National Board for Historical Service, DLC; see also [JFJ], "The National Board for Historical Service," *AHR* 22 (July 1917): 918–19.

2. [JFJ] to George M. Dutcher, et al., April 20, 1917, TLc, Box 25, Records of the National Board for Historical Service, DLC.

3. Waldo G. Leland to JFJ, July [7], 1917, TLS, Box 105, JP, DLC; [JFJ] to Walter Gilbert, October 2, 1918, TLc, Box 68, JP, DLC; [JFJ] to Robert S. Woodward, January 20, 1920, TLc, Box 68, JP, DLC; JFJ to Woodward, January 7, 1918, TLS, CIW. See also Carol Gruber, *Mars and Minerva: World War I and the Uses of Higher Learning in America* (Baton Rouge: Louisiana State University Press, 1975), chapter 4; George T. Blakey, *Historians on the Home Front: American Propagandists for the Great War* (Lexington: University Press of Kentucky, 1970), chapters 2 and 3.

4. [William L. Westermann] to Ralph V. D. Magoffin, July 10, 1917, TLt, Box 5, Records of the National Board for Historical Service, DLC; see also Gruber, *Mars and Minerva*, p. 127.

Apart from such services as can be rendered equally well by any other able-bodied or intelligent man, what can the "history man" do for his country in time of war, of things for which he is especially fitted by his professional acquirements and habits of mind? Many historical scholars, with the summer vacation before them, are asking the question, of themselves or of others. Many have not found a satisfying answer. It seems relatively easy for the scientist to provide himself with a task that offers good prospects of direct usefulness. He can invent a new range-finder or a new explosive. He can improve the quality of optical glass. He can seek new sources of potash. He can make two potatoes grow where one grew before. And, what is quite as important, the public and the authorities are abundantly aware of the usefulness of what he is doing, while both are prone to regard the historian as occupied only with the dates and details of remote transactions having no relation to the fateful exigencies of the present day.

Against such an opinion the mind of the virile historical student protests with all his might. What is more essential to the successful prosecution of a great national war than an enlightened, unified, and powerfully-acting public opinion? Why is France so heroically strong a combatant, and Russia, with four times the population, so weak? All the munitions that could be piled on the banks of the Dvina or the Sereth could not give military strength to a nation that does not know its own mind, to a population in which, outside a small percentage, public opinion has no existence. The American gun may be the best that science can make it, the man behind it unsurpassed in quality, but how long will he persist in his fearful struggle if the people at home do not see why he should?

But how can public opinion in America be enlightened, homogeneous, and powerful, in a crisis which is in the plainest way the product of historic forces, if it is not informed in the facts and lessons of history? It is notorious how large a part, in giving to German public opinion its marvellous unity and cohesion, has been played by the chauvinistic history lessons of the German schoolmaster. Heaven forbid that we should imitate the chauvinism; the American enters the war distinctly as a citizen of the world. Rather, he enters the war with that intention; but to make him truly such a citizen requires an enormous expansion of his political education, a quick shift of his point of view, rapid reinforcements to his knowledge of European conditions. In the supply of such knowledge, vital alike to intelligent prosecution of the war and to intelligent assistance in the settlement of peace, the historian cannot doubt that his part may rightly be a large one, seeing how largely those European conditions are results of history, inexplicable without its light.

Such a state of the facts calls loudly upon the historical scholar to come out from his cloistered retirement and to use for the information of the public whatever knowledge of European history he may possess—and to use it energetically and boldly. He is conscious of its imperfection; he is accustomed to write slowly, supporting every sentence with a foot-note; he is already, as his daily duty, pressing excellent historical information, by refined methods, upon youthful minds, and hopes thus to ensure that the next generation shall be more historically minded, better fitted for citizenship of the world. But meanwhile the war is to be won or lost, the future peace of the world ensured or jeopardized, by the adult generation now on the scene. Let him come out into the market-place, and make his voice heard by the men of his own age. If they do not receive his message with the docility with which he is accustomed to see it received by his undergraduates, so much the better for him. His training being what it has been, he is much less likely to be found offering worthless wares with bold presumption than to be keeping valuable knowledge to himself, with needless modesty, "And that one talent that is death to hide, Lodged with him useless."

If, for instance, the historical student knows more than most of his fellow-citizens about the history of Servia and its neighbors, or that of Poland or Belgium or Alsace-Lorraine; if his historical studies have brought him that knowledge of Russian character and its possibilities which many would be glad to possess; if his familiarity with recent Austro-Hungarian history enables him, better than others, to estimate the centrifugal and centripetal forces in the Dual Monarchy; if he has studied with some care the history of German economic policy in general, or of the Bagdad Railway in particular, of the Social Democratic party in Germany, of the workings of the imperial constitution, or of the character and results of German rule over non-German populations; if he can show how great alliances against aspiring *Weltmächte*—against Charles V., Louis XIV., Napoleon—have worked in the past, what can be expected of them in the way of unity, what can not; if he knows the history of Pitt's subsidies, or of neutral export of munitions to belligerents; if he can so set forth the condition of Europe after Waterloo as partially to illuminate the dark questions of recovery after universal war; if he can cast historical light on the problems of American Christian missions in the Turkish Empire or of Japanese encroachments in the Pacific—let him by all means, "by printing, writing, or advised speaking," bring his knowledge forward, for the information of a public which eagerly desires to act with intelligence. Many other topics, instructive in war-time, will occur to the historical mind as the changing phases of the war develop.

Still more urgent are the reasons, and much wider the opportunities, for the exercise of the same function in the field of American history. If in the actual warfare of the trenches, under conditions so different from those of previous wars, we must be chiefly guided by the experience of those who for three years have been sustaining the conflict, yet in the thousand-and-one matters that must be transacted on this side of the ocean, on the soil of the United States and among the masses of its people, no experience can be so helpful to American action as American experience, whenever any that is apposite can be adduced. It is easy to say that times, methods, and the nation itself have changed, that the conditions of our present warfare are unprecedented, that we must look at the facts as they are, not as they once were. Yet in all these problems of legislation and execution that lie before us, some of the elements are permanent; some of the methods used in former wars worked well or ill for reasons still operative. Neither ingenuity nor experience is alone sufficient, for man or nation; he is best guided who makes use of both. At all events, history *will* be invoked, whatever we do, is being invoked every day, and if the public is not guided by sound historical information, it will be guided by unsound. When the bill for a selective draft was under debate in Congress, several members of that body sought to adduce our experience with conscription in the Civil War, but it was plain, even to Congress, that they did not know what that experience was. If persons of adequate historical knowledge would seasonably inform them and the public as to the actual merits and demerits of the Committee on the Conduct of the War, as to the experience of the United States with political generals, with army contractors during the Civil War, with "conscientious objectors," with newspaper disclosures of military information, with pension frauds, with the income tax, they might be sure that much of the seed sown would fall on good ground.

The final application of the lessons of experience lies mostly in other hands than those of the historian. His function, as historian, may be confined to the presentation of correct historical information, and it is not for an historical journal to offer advice as to how he or others may apply it. Yet the historian is also a citizen, and as such is entitled to speak his mind upon the issues of the hour. It is for him to judge, according to personal and local circumstances, whether he will do most good by speaking or writing solely as an historian, presenting the facts of history without suspicion of *Tendenz,* or by using them in advocacy of policies which he feels impelled and qualified to defend. The main matter is, that he shall not be withheld, by needless modesty or by timidity, from making use, in one helpful way or another, of such knowledge of the past as he may possess. If he has better knowledge than his fellows, or knows better how with brief labor to acquire it, upon the bond and treasury-note operations of the Civil War, upon its varying effects on wages and prices respectively, upon the blockades and other commercial restrictions of Napoleonic times, upon the history of German or Irish or Polish opinion in the United States, or even upon minor topics like the Sanitary Commission or the Christian Commission or the New England Loyal Publication Society, by all means let him speak up. Anything that helps the public to see the present conflict in a wider perspective is an aid toward intelligent national conduct in war-time. If the cloistered student has never had the habit of addressing the general public, it is no matter; it will do him good to try.

As to the means and methods, they are many—books, pamphlets, articles in magazines and newspapers, lectures and addresses. Especially let it be remembered that the great metropolitan magazines and dailies are by no means the only agencies by which American public opinion is formed. The professor may have, or may easily obtain, access to the columns of papers more local in circulation, and through editorial or other articles may take part in the great work of informing local opinion, which everywhere has its peculiar qualities and needs, qualities and needs which he perhaps understands better than they can be understood by writers in some distant metropolis. As for speaking, a little thought will show him that, with our numberless summer schools and teachers' institutes and similar assemblies, there is no lack of opportunities for laying good history before interested audiences.

If the historical scholar finds no chance to do any of these things, at the least he can encourage and advise neighboring librarians and historical societies in respect to the collecting of materials upon the war, to the end that the future historian may find the means for treating it with all possible breadth of view and in all its varying aspects; for the historical scholar of the present day should surely be better able than others to foresee what kinds of material, economic and social as well as political and military, will be desired by those who come after.

But in respect to all these methods of approach, the historical scholar would do well to communicate first with the National Board for Historical Service, whose character and operations are described on other pages,[1] and who are desirous and prepared to be of use in respect to all the lines of activity which have been indicated above. The address of its secretary is, Mr. Waldo G. Leland, 1133 Woodward Building, Washington, D.C.

AHR 22 (July 1917): 831–35.

{1.} See [JFJ], "The National Board for Historical Service," pp. 918–19.

A New American Historical Journal

In October 1916 William S. Robertson and Charles E. Chapman, delegates that year to the American Congress of Bibliography and History in Buenos Aires, announced in the *American Historical Review* their desire to discuss at the annual meeting of the American Historical Association the establishment of a journal in Ibero-American history.[1] Chapman, an assistant professor of history at the University of California, sought Jameson's advice on the matter after this declaration was published, and the latter proved instrumental in organizing support for the proposal.

Jameson's cosmopolitan outlook and training at the Johns Hopkins University inclined him to view American history in the context of European and even world history; consequently, he gave priority while director of the Department of Historical Research in the Carnegie Institution of Washington to the discovery of documents in Spanish and Latin American archives that shed light on American history. Under his supervision, guides to the archives of Spain and Cuba, begun under his predecessor, Andrew C. McLaughlin, were completed, while Jameson himself commissioned Herbert E. Bolton, professor of history at Stanford University, to produce a guide to the Mexican archives.[2] When Roger B. Merriman, a history professor at Harvard University, expressed doubt that a journal of Latin American history could succeed, Jameson counseled him that "a journal far from perfect might be a valuable means of fostering interest in the subject and might enable it to reach a higher level more rapidly than it would without such an instrument."[3]

Chapman was both energetic and unorthodox in seeking support for the prospective journal. While the project was still embryonic, he solicited an endorsement from President Woodrow Wilson, listing Jameson as a reference without the latter's knowledge. Still, Jameson was warmly encouraging when Wilson requested his opinion in December 1916; Chapman was "a straightforward and disinterested man, and in this present undertaking concerning a Spanish-American historical journal, has no personal or ulterior motives." The need for this journal arose out of the great increase in scholarship in the field of Latin American studies, he added, and was "also in a high degree a matter of public spirit, as a thing that will help increase mutual understanding and good feeling between intelligent people in the United States and in the Spanish-American countries." Subsequently, Wilson provided the desired endorsement, making liberal use of Jameson's description.

Chapman read Wilson's statement at the AHA meeting in December, and then printed it on the first page of the *Hispanic American Historical Review*, as it came to be titled, when the journal appeared in February 1918.[4] In addition to guiding Chapman on the art of organizing a session on the proposed journal at the AHA meeting—"Don't try to hurry the thing along. Above all, don't discuss now who shall be managing-editor or members of the Board of Editors"—Jameson agreed to serve on a nominating committee to suggest the composition of the editorial board. In February 1918 the newly constituted editorial board of the *Hispanic American Historical Review* chose one of its own members, James A. Robertson, as the journal's first managing editor.[5]

NOTES

1. William S. Robertson and Charles E. Chapman, "Communication" to the Managing Editor, *American Historical Review* 22 (October 1916): 217; Charles E. Chapman, "The Founding of the Review," *Hispanic American Historical Review* 1 (February 1918): 9, 10.

2. Carnegie Institution of Washington, *Year Book*, 1905 (Washington, D.C.: Published by the Institution, 1906), p. 234; and Herbert E. Bolton, *Guide to Materials for the History of the United States in the Principal Archives of Mexico* (Washington, D.C.: Carnegie Institution of Washington, 1913).

3. [JFJ] to Roger B. Merriman, December 13, 1916, TLc, Box 112, JP, DLC.

4. Charles E. Chapman to Woodrow Wilson, November 24, 1916, TLS, Woodrow Wilson Papers, DLC,; Wilson to JFJ, November 27, 1916, TLS; and [JFJ] to Wilson, December 5, 1916, TLt; both in Box 135, JP, DLC; [Wilson] to Chapman, December 6, 1916, TLc, Wilson Papers, DLC; see also Chapman to JFJ, December 9, 1916, TLS, Box 93, JP, DLC.

5. [JFJ] to Charles E. Chapman, December 11, 1916, TLc, Box 70, JP, DLC; "Minutes of a Conference on the Foundation of a Journal of Latin-American History, Held at Cincinnati, December 29, 1916," in AHA, *Annual Report*, 1916 (Washington, D.C.: Government Printing Office, 1917), p. 284; Chapman, "Founding of the Review," p. 20.

THE FRIENDS OF a general historical journal like the *American Historical Review* might be excused if in its earliest years they devoted all their superfluous energies to making it as good and as successful as possible, and gave little thought to the problem or possibility of establishing other historical journals in the United States. But now that it is twenty-two or twenty-three years old, and, through whatever troubles of adolescence, has attained its majority, it is natural to consider with open mind the question, what would be the ideal set of organs through which American historical scholarship and American interest in history should express themselves.

The answer should be widely different from that which alone was possible in 1895. That there has been an enormous improvement in the quality of American historical scholarship since those days it would be unwise to affirm, though some improvement has no doubt taken place; but certainly the quantity of our historical output has greatly increased, and it is far more diversified. One through whose hands all important new American books of history then passed, on their way from publisher to reviewer, as similar volumes of the present day pass now, well remembers how often it happened—much oftener than it happens in these days—that after ardent thinking he was obliged to conclude, concerning some book on a quite special subject, that no one in America had qualified himself to review with authority a book in that particular field. Where perhaps some thirty different subjects for doctoral dissertations were being worked upon in 1895, four hundred are being investigated in the present academic year. Whole areas of human history, such as the history of the ancient world, to which American historical scholars were then giving almost no attention, are now being cultivated with ardor by groups of able and learned young men and women.

Meanwhile the wealth of the country, too, and the circle of cultivated readers, have grown with much rapidity. It can no longer be pretended that the country is too backward or too poor to sustain the most expensive undertakings of scholarship. It is abundantly able to support them in rich variety. Indeed, it must speedily awaken to the duty of doing so in much larger measure than heretofore. The resources out of which Europe has in the past sustained the enterprises of scholarship, whether through the hands of governments or of societies or of subscribers, have suffered losses of unparalleled magnitude through four years of the most extensive and destructive warfare ever known. All the apparatus of civilization will feel the disastrous effects for many years, and in particular it will be impossible for Europe to maintain the apparatus of scholarship on any such scale as hitherto. The United States is the richest of countries, and, in any probable event of the great war, will emerge from it far less damaged in resources than any of the nations of Europe. It will be her opportunity and her privilege to step into the breach, to do what one young nation can do to repair the losses, and to take upon herself the leading part, if not in performing the finest labors of scholarship, at least in their sustainment.

What then, in this present-day America of richer and more diversified historical studies, should be the ideal organization of such studies? Or, to consider only one modest subdivision of so large an inquiry, what arrangement would ideally meet her developing needs in respect to regular organs of publication? Individual books will be published in abundance through the usual channels of trade, with profit or loss, most likely the latter, to the author. But much good matter will always appear in the "transactions" or annual volumes of societies, and much in periodicals. The latter as a rule do more toward keeping interest in history or parts of history alive than can be done by volumes frequently or less regularly appearing. Their reviews of books and their pages of news encourage development by bringing constantly before the minds of readers and workers the higher sort of scholarly standards, the advances marked by recent publications, the evidence of professional solidarity, the "aid and comfort" which resides in the sense of not working alone.

The healthiest and most well-rounded development of historical science in the United States would require, first, the existence of one or more general historical journals of high quality; secondly, a multitude of local historical journals, cultivating restricted fields, but not provincial in quality; and thirdly, a considerable number of ably-conducted special journals, whose fields are restricted not by geographical boundaries but by concentration on particular portions or aspects of history.

Such in fact is, or was before the war, the status of Europe in respect to historical periodicals. Each of the more important countries had long had one or more general journals, among which the *Revue Historique* would commonly be rated as the best. Each country, but especially France and Germany, abounded in local or regional journals, most often conducted by men capable of looking outside the boundaries of the locality and of relating its history intelligently to the history of the nation or of the world. Such were or are the *Forschungen zur Brandenburgisch-Preussischen Geschichte*, the *Annales de Bretagne*, the *Archivio della Reale Società Romana di Storia Patria*. But there have also been many organs of special historical learning, often international in character and support, sometimes multilingual in contents, which formed media of communication between savants in various lands whose lives were devoted to individual periods or parts or phases of the field of history— *Revue d'Histoire Ecclésiastique, Revue d'Histoire Diplomatique, Revue de l'Orient Latin, Revue des Études Juives, Revue des Études Napoléoniennes, Byzantinische Zeitschrift, Archiv für Papyrusforschung, Ephemeris Epigraphica*, journals of military and naval and economic and legal history, of ancient history and the history of art or of commerce; their name is legion and their pages are a delight to the lover of learning.

In the first of these two directions America has already attained a more than merely respectable development. To the older journals like the *Pennsylvania Magazine of History* and the Virginia, South Carolina, and Maryland journals of similar name, the last few years have seen the addition of journals of excellent quality and much promise, for the history of Michigan, Wisconsin, Minnesota, Tennessee, and Georgia. At least twenty states have good periodicals of this character, and there are a few excellent journals of regional history.

As for the other variety of historical journal which under normal growth of our science we should expect to appear, the journal neither local nor completely general but dedicated to a special historical field, signs are not wanting that the time is ripe for its emergence. Whether because a general journal, however catholic in intention, can give no very ample amount of space to any one specialty, or for whatever other reason connected with increasing interest and increasing production, the American votaries of particular cults in history have in several instances laid plans for the creation of special organs, and in some cases have called them into existence. In April, 1915, there appeared under the auspices of the Catholic University of America the first number of the *Catholic Historical Review*, an excellent journal, devoted to the history of the Catholic Church in America. It is conducted with much energy and intelligence, has contained many valuable and interesting articles, and has done much to stimulate the many local Catholic historical societies, and to create in them the sense of solidarity and the belief that they have an important mission to be fulfilled by common action. It were much to be desired that the Protestant churches, with their greatly superior wealth and resources, would do half as much for the ecclesiastical and religious history of the United States as is being done, through this journal and otherwise, by the American Catholics. In January, 1916, appeared the first numbers of two other historical quarterlies, representing two widely different specialties, the *Military Historian and Economist* and the *Journal of Negro History*, both of which have since led prosperous careers and have greatly increased the interest of students in two highly important fields of historical inquiry.

Several other fields might be named in which America could probably sustain, or in a few years will be able to sustain, a special historical journal. It ought to be possible before long to maintain a journal of legal history, perhaps of economic history. Still nearer at hand may such a result be in the case of ancient history. That is a specialty which has of late advanced rapidly in the United States. How it can continue to do so in a Greekless land, apparently soon to become also a Latinless land, is a mystery; but the attraction of the subject for the American mind, and especially of the history of the Roman Empire, with its social problems so like our own, has been abundantly and increasingly manifest in recent years.

But of all the departments of history that America might conceivably furnish with a special historical periodical, there is none that has made greater advances in recent years, none that is now in a course of more rapid development, than that which the *Hispanic American Historical Review* has taken for its province. So at least it appears to one whose duty requires him to take passing note, if no more, of all the historical volumes and monographs and articles that the country produces. If such a one looks back ten years, he is astonished at the development which this variety of historical work has attained among us, at the number of competent and active workers who in that brief period have come forward. When it is remembered that more than a third of the area of the United States was once under the dominion of Spain, and that the rest has during three centuries had large relations with Spanish and Portuguese America, it seems fairly obvious that Hispanic American history should be largely cultivated among us, and that many able young scholars should arise to devote themselves zealously to it; but such a thought was not widely entertained ten years ago. How much has been contributed toward this result by the efforts of particular institutions, such as the universities of California and Texas, by the work of individual teachers like those who have been made advisory editors of this journal, or by the hospitable aid and kindly encouragement afforded to young students from our country by eminent historical scholars of Spain, of Portugal, and of Hispanic America, this is not the place to enquire. It suffices to rejoice in the growth and expansion noted, to applaud the impulse, nowise too ambitious, which has led to the foundation of this *Review*, to wish it all success, to expect for it the unselfish aid of all who are strongly interested in its special field, and to promise, on behalf of those to whose interest that field is less central, the hearty co-operation that so loyal a fraternity as the body of American historical scholars is sure to afford.

Hispanic American Historical Review 1 (February 1918): 2–7.

Documentary Historical Publication:
What the United States Government Should Do

From the time he was an instructor at the Johns Hopkins University, Jameson exploited the documentary resources of the federal government and lobbied both elected officials and department administrators to make these resources available in published form. In 1886 he sought the permission of Congress to edit the records of the Virginia Company, in the possession of the Library of Congress, for publication by Houghton Mifflin.[1] Jameson failed to obtain permission, but the vision of a uniform procedure for publishing government documents continued to occupy his attention for the next half century.

In 1890 Jameson compared the expenditures of the federal government on historical publications with those of foreign governments and found that while the United States displayed a degree of liberality in publishing the voluminous records of the Civil War, it did so at the expense of producing presidential and other significant correspondence. "We desire a comprehensive and well arranged scheme of government publication," he informed the American Historical Association. "We should perceive that we can not have it save by means of some permanent institution through which expert opinion can be brought to bear, not simply at the beginning, or by occasional advice, but all the time."[2]

Jameson repeated his call for a national historical publications commission in an address in the fall of 1905 to the Columbia Historical Society of Washington, D.C., shortly after assuming the direction of the Department of Historical Research in the Carnegie Institution of Washington, and again in 1909 as part of a report issued by the Keep Commission, a panel appointed by President Theodore Roosevelt to examine, among other things, the procedures through which the government printed its historically significant records. "It is no part of our purpose to enlist the Government in extravagant schemes," he explained in the introduction to the report, "our desire is rather to pave the way to a procedure whereby, without greater expenditure upon documentary historical publications than at present, a product may be secured which will meet more fully the needs of the Government, of historians, and of the public, and be a source of credit to the nation."[3]

In a 1923 address to the Carnegie Institution trustees, Jameson urged publication of the correspondence of the early British ministers to the United

States.[4] In that lecture as well as in the 1927 address to the American Historical Association that follows, he emphasized the significance of a comprehensive documentary record as the basis for an informed and rational discussion of both national and international politics. "Impoverished as many of the European governments are," he told the federal government's chief budget officer in 1925, "they know that they must continue to enlighten their peoples, and that knowledge of the history of their country is one of the surest foundations for an intelligent patriotism."[5] This address was presented as part of a panel discussion on "Governmental Support of Historical Endeavor" on December 30, 1927.[6] In the program for the meeting, Jameson's contribution is titled "What Can Be Done in the Future." Also on the panel, chaired by Benjamin F. Shambaugh of the State Historical Society of Iowa, were Waldo G. Leland, representing the American Council of Learned Societies, who spoke on government support for history abroad; and John C. Fitzpatrick, assistant chief of the Division of Manuscripts in the Library of Congress, who discussed the historical activities of the federal government to that time.

NOTES

1. JFJ to William Sewell, December 16, 1886, TLS, RG 46 (U. S. Senate, Committee on the Library), DNA.

2. JFJ, "The Expenditures of Foreign Governments in Behalf of History," in AHA, *Annual Report*, 1891 (Washington, D.C.: Government Printing Office, 1892), p. 43; for a notice of Jameson's address to the AHA in 1890, see the *Annual Report* for that year (Washington, D.C.: Government Printing Office, 1891), pp. 9–10.

3. U.S. Senate, *Message from the President of the United States, Transmitting a Report by the Committee on Department Methods on the Documentary Historical Publications of the United States Government, Together with a Draft of a Proposed Bill Providing for the Creation of a Permanent Commission on National Historical Publications*, 60th Cong., 2d sess., S. Doc. 714, February 11, 1909, p. 38. See also Jameson, "Gaps in the Published Records of United States History," *AHR* 11 (July 1906): 817–31; and Morey D. Rothberg, "Servant to History: A Study of John Franklin Jameson, 1859–1937" (Ph.D. dissertation, Brown University, 1982), p. 239.

4. [JFJ], "The Approach to Diplomatic History Illustrated by the Correspondence of the Early British Ministers to the United States," November 20, 1923, TM, Box 62, JP, DLC.

5. [JFJ] to Herbert M. Lord, October 26, 1925, TLc, Box 49, JP, DLC.

6. See the combined *Annual Report* of the AHA for 1927 and 1928 (Washington, D.C.: Government Printing Office, 1929), pp. 35, 46.

IT IS ALWAYS PLEASANT to see one's prophecies verified. One who prophesied, immediately after the World War and the Russian Revolution, that one effect of those prodigious events would surely be a great increase of interest in the world's history, can not fail, such is our poor human nature, to experience a paltry pleasure from the fulfillment of his prophecy, in addition to the more elevated joy that comes from seeing his beloved study more widely pursued and esteemed. Twenty-five years ago the work which I have always thought to be the most talented historical book ever produced in America had, I believe, in a dozen years from its publication, been sold to the extent only of some 600 sets;[1] in our time a posthumous work of the same gifted writer, largely historical in its character, has sold to the number of more than 40,000 copies.[2] A brilliant but by no means brief and light Outline of History has been bought and read by at least a hundred thousand Americans.[3] Even the widespread conflict, now actively waging, as to whether our school histories shall be written by historians or by aldermen, is a pleasing sign of increased interest in our national history.[4] And anyone

{1.} Henry Adams (1838–1918), author of *History of the United States During the First Administration of Thomas Jefferson*, 2 vols. (New York: Charles Scribner's Sons, 1889); and *History of the United States During the Second Administration of Thomas Jefferson*, 2 vols. (New York: Charles Scribner's Sons, 1890). Jameson regarded Adams as "the foremost of our historical writers" and asserted that it was a "privilege" to know him. He was especially impressed with both the research and writing style that Adams displayed; he remarked in 1918 that Adams "never thought that he ought to print a bibliography in his great *History*, and he introduced no footnote references but what were strictly necessary, knowing that the general reader would assume that he had performed the ordinary duties of research (though never likely to know how conscientiously he had performed them)." See [JFJ] to Waldo G. Leland, November 21, 1910, TLc, Box 102, JP, DLC; [JFJ] to Worthington C. Ford, March 27, 1916, TLc, Box 84, JP, DLC; and [JFJ] to Homer C. Hockett, April 25, 1918, TLc, Box 94, JP, DLC.
    {2.} Henry Adams, *The Education of Henry Adams: An Autobiography* (Boston: Houghton Mifflin, 1918).
    {3.} H. G. Wells, *The Outline of History, Being a Plain History of Life and Mankind* (New York: Macmillan Co., 1920).
    {4.} William Thompson, mayor of Chicago, appointed lawyer John J. Gorman to investigate the history textbooks being used in the Chicago public schools. The investigation led to charges that the school superintendent, William H. McAndrew, had adopted pro-British textbooks, *The American People* and *American History*, written by David Muzzey. The mayor disliked Muzzey's coverage of the American Revolution and argued that it was unpatriotic. Superintendent McAndrew was suspended and put on trial before the Board of Education. The conflict received widespread publicity. The Veterans of Foreign Wars and the American Association for the Recognition of the Irish Republic supported Thompson's views. Thompson also accused the American Library Association of being pro-British because it promoted history textbooks that he found offensive. On December 4, 1927, the American Historical Association's

who looks over, in magazine or newspaper, the autumnal advertisements of our publishers, sees at a glance that the proportion of historical books is far greater than it ever was before in our lifetime. Most of these books are poor flashy things, with catchpenny titles and sensationally colored text, but they have been put together in order to meet a real want, and testify to a pathetic desire of multitudes to know more about history.

With such a state of the public mind, what is the duty of the United States government in the premises? Has it any duty? It is recognized that it has a duty to defend the country, and $700,000,000 per annum are cheerfully spent in preparation for defensive warfare. What is spent by the federal government to promote the civilizing of the American mind is insignificant in comparison. Some years ago the late Professor Rosa, of the Bureau of Standards, prepared an ingenious diagram showing in visible proportions the classes of government expenditure. My remembrance is that all that could fairly be reckoned as spent on the increase of knowledge or the advancement of American civilization figured as not more than two per cent. of the whole. And if one were to ask what part of this meagre two per cent. the government spends on the history of the nation that sustains it, the answer must be that it is considerably less than a thousandth part of one per cent. of the whole. Comparison with the budgets of other countries is difficult and insecure, but it is perfectly plain that the governments of Great Britain, France, and Germany, despite post-war conditions, spend far more for historical research, archives, and publication than our government does. It seems plain that the government of the Netherlands, a country with a fifteenth of our population, spends much more for history than the government of this great land. Even Switzerland, a country having a thirtieth of our population and having notoriously the most economical of national governments, usually surpasses

---

executive council passed a resolution introduced by its Committee on History Teaching in the Schools condemning Mayor Thompson's actions. At the annual meeting in December the association endorsed the actions of the executive council. For detailed coverage of the controversy, see the *Chicago Tribune*, October 20–November 7, 1927; for the response of historians, see "Attacks Thompson for History Fight," *New York Times*, December 5, 1927, p. 25, col. 6; "Historians Hit False Patriotism: Demands to Alteration of the Truth Held Harmful to Love of Country," *Washington Star*, December 29, 1927, p. 1, col. 7, and p. 2, col. 1; "Noted Historians Warn of Dangers in Thompson Drive: Association Demands Teaching in Regard to Fact, Not Patriotism," *Washington Post*, December 30, 1927, p. 5, col. 1. For other public responses, see the following *New York Times* articles for 1927: "Chicago on Trial," editorial, October 1, p. 18, col. 4; "Name Officers to Aid Irish Republicans," October 3, p. 18, col. 6; "McAndrew Assailed on His Record Here," October 14, p. 6, col. 1; "Veterans Attack New History Work," October 17, p. 2, col. 5; "Mencken Aloof in McAndrew Case," October 19, p. 4, col. 5; "Says Britain Seeks to Conquer America," October 20, p. 2, col. 1; "Irish of Boston Hear Thompson Hit British," December 5, p. 25, col. 6.

us. Half a dozen of our individual states surpass the federal government in expenditure for history. Or again, make the comparison with what the United States government does for science. Congress willingly spends great sums of money for research in the physical sciences. The money value of geology, of entomology, of aerostatics, of industrial standards, of botanical and chemical research, is easily perceived, and the perception elicits abundant appropriations. The value of an understanding of human action is not so easily perceived or estimated. The last time I had occasion to appear before an Appropriations Committee on behalf of this Association, I showed diagrams wherein what our government spent for history in the preceding year was represented by a black line a few inches long, duly compared with somewhat longer black lines showing what some of our states spent in that way, and what was similarly spent by several foreign governments, but as to a comparison with what our government was spending for investigations in science, I was obliged to tell them that I could not show the comparison because the wall of the committee room would not admit of lines twenty or thirty feet long. The figures for that year ran about twenty-six thousand dollars for history and twenty-one millions for science.

And what is this subject to which Congress has shown itself thus indifferent? It is the story of the genesis and development of the greatest political, economic, and social power the world has ever seen, a power far more formidable, and very likely destined to be more influential, than that Roman Empire that cast its shadow across a thousand years of human history, and without good knowledge of which the subsequent world of human action can never be understood.

I am not expected to be precise as to how much the United States government ought to spend for United States history, but nothing can be more certain than that it ought to spend a great deal more. Let us turn from the question of how much, to the question of what things, it ought to do. In a brief paper, general indications are more appropriate than specific suggestions of programme. In an audience of the American Historical Association, I do not need to say that it is not the proper function of governments or endowed institutions to produce histories or historical monographs. Heaven will raise up historians if the government will print the materials or even show them what materials there are and where. Its historical publications should be of two varieties: guides to historical material and textual publications of documents. When we have our magnificent new National Archive Building, as we shall have in a few years, its usefulness to historians will depend in large degree on the extent to which that establishment is enabled to provide them with lists and calendars and indexes showing them in detail the wealth of historical material that will be contained within its walls. Again, the rich treasures of the Division of Manuscripts in the Library of

Congress call loudly for a provision of lists and calendars and indexes many times more ample than all that has thus far been supplied.

As for the textual publication of documentary historical materials, which we should gladly see carried to a much greater extent, it is obvious that the federal government should not undertake projects that properly belong within the jurisdiction of the individual states and will be better executed there. It must in the main operate in the period since 1775. But in the colonial period, beside those papers that illustrate only the history of individual colonies or states, there are whole series whose publication would illuminate the history of America in general. Take for instance the Calendar of State Papers, Colonial.[5] It has now reached the year 1714. At the rate at which it progresses in the hands of the Public Record Office, which brings out about one year of the eighteenth century in each year of the twentieth, it will be two generations before the American Revolution is reached. The United States government, making a fresh beginning with the year 1765 and the Stamp Act, could readily undertake a series of Public Record Office papers bearing on the history of the struggle for independence. If it contained only the correspondence of the Secretary of State with the colonial governors in that period and of the Secretary of State, the War Office, and the Admiralty with military and naval commanders, it would make a priceless addition to our knowledge of the Revolution.

It is plain, too, that among the methods by which the two-hundredth anniversary of the birth of George Washington should be commemorated, one mode should be the publication of a comprehensive and definitive edition of his correspondence and writings; but this, it is a pleasure to note, is already in contemplation, to be executed by the most competent of all hands.[6]

For the period from 1789 to 1829 it is the custom of many minds to rest content with the imposing folio series of the American State Papers.[7] It is not always appreciated that that magnificent printers'-job, so creditable to the young government of a century ago, after all consisted in nothing more than the reprinting of such pieces as the earlier Congresses had chosen,

{5.} Public Record Office, *Calendar of State Papers, Colonial Series* (London: Her Majesty's Stationery Office, 1860–1969).

{6.} Albert Bushnell Hart (1854–1943), historian at Harvard University, directed a committee to celebrate the bicentennial of George Washington's birth in 1732. The committee sponsored lectures, museum exhibits, parades, and publications, one of which was John C. Fitzpatrick, ed., *The Writings of George Washington from the Original Manuscript Sources, 1745–1799*, 39 vols. (Washington, D.C.: Government Printing Office, 1931–44).

{7.} *American State Papers*, 38 vols. (Washington, D.C.: Gales and Seaton, 1832–61), covered foreign relations, Indian affairs, commerce and navigation, military affairs, and public lands.

somewhat casually and without plan, to set forth in print for the purposes of the day. They are therefore anything but an even and rounded compilation of the important official materials for the history of our first forty years under the Constitution, as they are often supposed to be. If anyone wishes to be convinced of this, let him see how much of a history of the military and naval operations of the War of 1812 he can make out from those venerated pages.

The insufficiency of the American State Papers is especially notable in the field of diplomatic history. The series called American State Papers, Foreign Relations, contains only a fraction of the significant papers illustrative of our earlier years of diplomatic intercourse which are preserved in the archives of the Department of State; and of the papers which are therein printed many are injured as historical evidence by unmarked suppressions that were deemed expedient at the time when a given White Book was first presented to the public.[8] While total publication of the diplomatic correspondence, either of the period from 1789 to 1828, or of the period from 1828 to 1861, may be thought an extravagant undertaking, certainly the State Department ought to be given the means to carry forward that full publication of Instructions to ministers abroad, from 1789 to 1889, which Secretary Hughes instructed his Department to prepare for publication, but which has halted ever since for want of money. Instructions do not tell the whole story, but their publication will give securely its outlines, and would be a great boon to the student, and if so, ultimately a boon to the public; for surely the wise conduct of our foreign relations depends greatly on a proper knowledge of our past policy on the part of the general public.

It may seem a counsel of perfection, which it would be unreasonable to expect our government to realize, if one were to urge that there should also be publication of diplomatic material from foreign archives, that will show how our controversies appeared from the point of view of those with whom we were negotiating. Yet the suggestion that our government should print, for instance, much of the correspondence which Foreign Secretaries in London had with British ministers in Philadelphia or in Washington is not fantastic, but wholly rational. Most books of diplomatic history have been written in the archives of the Foreign Office of the country in which they were produced, or from materials emanating thence, with little consultation of the other contending or contracting party. But to hear both parties is the ABC of historical criticism. *Audi et alteram partem.* Hear the other party not only in the sense of listening to his representations because fairness requires it, but also in the sense of "listening in" upon his consultations with those of his own side, of overhearing what they say to each other when no Ameri-

{8.} The White Book is an official position paper issued by the State Department on a specific topic, but it is not a serial publication. The name derives from the soft white cover that accompanies the paper.

can is present. The editors of government publications have naturally not often sought to supplement their own papers by materials drawn from the chanceries of their rivals. Characteristically, it is especially the Swiss and Dutch, with their cosmopolitan outlook, that have done this in the largest proportion. Professor Colenbrander, for his great series of Gedenkstukken, illustrative of Dutch history from 1795 to 1840, ransacked the Foreign Office archives of Paris, London, Berlin, and Petersburg alike. It would greatly illuminate our early diplomatic history if a similar process should be followed in some government publication of ours, if, for instance, we should print the exchanges across the ocean between the British Foreign Secretary and George Hammond or Anthony Merry or Francis James Jackson or Charles Bagot or Stratford Canning—the instructions from the secretary, the answering despatches from the minister. There would be no difficulty in any European archives, down at least to the time of the Civil War, in printing this correspondence in all its fullness. Whether Downing Street or the Quai d'Orsay has or has not cherished deep and dark designs against the liberty of America, whether the policy of Great Britain or France or Spain toward our country has been selfish or magnanimous, or in whatever proportions it has been the one or the other, it is better that opinion on the subject should rest on evidence rather than on suspicion. If we can make the grounds of European action as well known to present-day readers as they were to the actors themselves, we do not need to foresee what conclusions will be drawn from the evidences presented, so complete must be our confidence that increase of understanding brings increase of good-will among men.

Furthermore, there are several important Presidents or statesmen—Van Buren or Johnson, for instance—whose papers are preserved in the Library of Congress in a copious mass, from which selection should be made of the most important for serial publication. Voluminous as is the mass of military and naval material which the government has printed in the Official Records of the Civil War, little has been done with what we may call the civil papers of that period, of the Confederacy, and of the years of Reconstruction. Little has been done by documentary publication to illustrate the history of the Treasury's operations, yet there is much in the correspondence of the Treasury that the student of economic history would find exceedingly useful, much also for the student of the history of commerce in the consular correspondence of the Department of State. With the decided tendency of modern times toward economic and social history, large services might be rendered to the historian by extensive publication of documents respecting geographic development and exploration, respecting the public lands, respecting agriculture and transportation and the postal system.

But one man would make one list of desiderata, and another man another. Far more important than any individual suggestions of programme is a careful consideration of methods by which a governmental programme repre-

senting the best thought of many minds might be constructed. As one reflects upon the notable series of government historical publication which
Mr. Fitzpatrick has set forth one can not fail to observe that, impressive as
it is, it shows no evidence of a general and rational plan.[9] In fact there
has been no general or rational plan. As a rule government historical publications have come into existence because some one more or less casually
thought of them, perhaps some clerk of a committee of Congress, and the
clerk persuaded his chairman that such a publication would be a good thing,
and the chairman persuaded his committee, and the committee persuaded
Congress. The undertakings have, as a rule, no relation to each other, and
often very little relation to the primary and most severely felt needs of the
historical student. We ought to do better about this. We ought to have a
general plan, and therefore we ought to have some responsible and relatively permanent body charged with the duty of making a general plan and
supervising its execution.

A striking example of the way not to produce a rationally composed series
of historical publications is furnished by the historical sections of the War
and Navy Departments. In each of these departments there has been, since
the World War, an historical section. But anything in the nature of consecutive achievement or continuous progress has been made impossible by the
mechanical operation of laws and regulations that, whenever an officer has
been detailed to the work of the historical section and has remained with
it three years or less, calls him away to his regiment or to sea service, and
substitutes a new officer, with new plans and new methods. I believe that,
in each of these departments, the historical section has had four successive
heads in ten or twelve years. It is not their fault, but the fault of the system,
that, nine years after the war, our governmental contribution to its military and naval history consists of little else than a few meagre professional
pamphlets. The contrast between this slight output and the 23 handsome
volumes of the British Official History of the War, the 12 volumes of the Australian Official History, the four stout volumes already put forth by the German Reichsarchiv, and the nine splendid quartos already published by Les
Armées Françaises de la Guerre, is such as might well make the American
student hang his head in shame. At all events, it is a convincing illustration

{9.} John Clement Fitzpatrick (1876–1940) wrote or edited the following government publications: *Journals of the Continental Congress, 1774–1789*, 34 vols. (Washington, D.C.: Government Printing Office, 1904–37), vols. 28–31; *Calendar of the Correspondence of George Washington*, 4 vols. (Washington, D.C.: Government Printing
Office, 1915); *List of the Washington Manuscripts from the Year 1592 to 1775* (Washington,
D.C.: Government Printing Office, 1919); *Notes on the Care, Calendaring and Arranging
of Manuscripts* (Washington, D.C.: Government Printing Office, 1913); and *The Writings of George Washington from the Original Manuscript Sources*, 39 vols. (Washington,
D.C.: Government Printing Office, 1931–44). See *AHR* 45 (July 1940): 1004–05.

of the thesis that no satisfactory results can be expected in the absence of any sustained plan or permanent planning organization.

What our government needs, in order to meet the wants of students and the public by a rationally devised system of historical publication, is a planning and supervising commission of experts. Why not? Almost every important government in Europe has such a commission of historical experts to organize its series of historical volumes and supervise their execution. As might be expected, the Dutch have the best-planned of such commissions— a commission of professional historical scholars, who 25 years ago began with a careful survey of the documentation of their national history, framed intelligent plans for filling gaps or meeting conspicuous needs, and since then have gone steadily forward with the execution of the programme then laid down.

Nineteen years ago a committee of members of this society, appointed by President Roosevelt—Mr. Worthington Ford, Gen. Charles Francis Adams, Admiral Mahan, Professors Andrews, Dunning, Hart, McLaughlin, Turner, and Jameson, made just such a careful survey, suggested a programme of government publication, and recommended the establishing of a permanent unpaid commission.[10] There was a hearing before a House committee, and there the matter ended. Congress never paid any further attention to any of the recommendations, and the committee's full and careful report slumbers in the files of the printed Congressional documents.

The bill for the creation of an archive establishment, recently introduced in the Senate by Senator Fess and now in the hands of the Library Committee, provides for an advisory commission on historical publications of archive material, consisting of the Director of the Archives, the Archivist, the chief of the Division of Manuscripts in the Library of Congress, the chief of the historical section of the War Department General Staff, the superintendent of records in the Navy Department, and two members of the American Historical Association, chosen by the Director from among members who are or have been members of the Executive Council.[11]

{10.} U.S. Senate, *Message from the President of the United States . . .* , February 11, 1909.

{11.} On December 6, 1927, Senator Simeon Davidson Fess (1861–1936), a Republican from Ohio and a former student under Jameson at the University of Chicago, introduced Senate Bill No. 1169, providing for the establishment of both the National Archives and a National Historical Publications Commission. This legislation failed to pass, but a proviso for the historical publications commission was incorporated into legislation passed in 1934 creating the National Archives as a federal agency. See S. 1169, 70th Cong., 1st sess., December 6, 1927; [JFJ] to Simeon D. Fess, June 23, 1926, TLc, Box 57, JP, DLC; [JFJ] to Fess, November 13, 1922, TLc, Box 82, JP, DLC; [JFJ], "Organization of National Archives: Memorandum for Senator Fess," [1932], TM, Box 190, JP, DLC; and Donald R. McCoy, *The National Archives: America's Ministry of Documents, 1934–1968* (Chapel Hill: University of North Carolina Press, 1978), p. 10.

It would be better if the number of historians in the commission were greater, but it is not practical to ask for it. But at any rate the devising of the programme of publication should not be left to the archivists. In every country of Europe the tendency of archivists, left to their own devices, is to give the foremost position to those classes of documents which have most occupied their attention, which usually means those which have given them the most trouble, either because hardest to read or for some other reason not connected with primary historical values. Look at the one great country in Europe which does not trust these matters to a commission of historians, Great Britain, where the whole series familiar under the general name of Calendars is planned solely by the Deputy Keeper of the Public Records and his staff. What is the composition of that series? Nearly 32 per cent. of the volumes are of medieval materials, nearly 32 per cent. of the sixteenth century, nearly 32 per cent. of the seventeenth, 5 per cent. of the eighteenth, and never a volume to help anyone who is interested in any portion of English history subsequent to 1776. No such state of things could have come into existence if the provision of materials for the use of historians had been confided, as in countries on the Continent, to a committee of historians.

To sum up: we need a great deal more of historical publication on the part of the government, we need to have it so planned as to meet real wants of historians, and to that end we need to have a permanent planning body in which historians shall be strongly represented.

TMS, Box 28, JP, DLC.

Introduction to *American Historical Association,*
Historical Scholarship in America:
Needs and Opportunities

In 1931 the American Council of Learned Societies awarded the American Historical Association one thousand dollars to hold a series of meetings to plan for future research. A committee was created, headed by Arthur M. Schlesinger, and expected to hold conferences on research in ancient, medieval, and modern history, as well as in American history. After the conferences were held, Schlesinger, in consultation with the AHA executive council, asked Jameson to set "forth the important place of history in American education and scholarship" in an introduction to the final report of the committee. On receiving Jameson's contribution, Schlesinger remarked that "the bulk of the publication will seem an anti-climax."[1]

Despite past controversy over Jameson's dominant position within the American historical profession, Schlesinger wanted his imprimatur on the committee's report. Until his death in 1937, Jameson continued to provide both advice and direction to historians and his colleagues in related disciplines. The statement that follows gave increased legitimacy to the notion of a recognized elite setting the agenda for all scholarly practitioners.

NOTE

1. Dexter Perkins to the Executive Council of the American Historical Association, February 4, 1931, TLS; Arthur M. Schlesinger to JFJ, April 7, 1931, TLS; [JFJ] to Schlesinger, February 1, 1932, TLc; Schlesinger to JFJ, February 4, 1932, TLS; and Schlesinger to JFJ, March 10, 1932, TLS, all in Box 51, JP, DLC.

OLDEST OF THE humanistic sciences, and the one that has had the fullest and most various development, history has always and inevitably rested on investigation. That it stands in constant and vital need of varied researches is no new thought. The first meaning of the word history was the search for knowledge, and the delectable writer who first gave it the form we best know spent many preliminary years of travel in the incessant asking of questions and acquiring of information. Neither is it a new thought that, for the most intelligent achievement on a large scale, there is much use for organized and corporate planning of historical researches. All historians since the seventeenth century who have occupied themselves with periods prior to that time have had occasion to be grateful to the well-planned researches and editions which monastic discipline and corporate enthusiasm enabled the Maurist Benedictines and other scholarly organizations of that age of erudition to execute.

The historical writing of the nineteenth century was, however, in the main, and because of its character, based on individual researches. Certainly this was the case in the United States, where the best of our historical writers did each for himself all the spade-work necessary to the elaboration of his particular theme, with an expenditure of time and money and labor which they might partly have been spared by a better public provision of guides and textual sources. Such provision was, it is true, not wholly absent. The federal government, in the period between 1816 and 1850, had under the influence of heightened national feeling published original historical material ("source-material" in the Teutonized academic dialect of later times) in an amount distinctly creditable to a young republic with revenues so limited. Several states had done the like. More than a score of state historical societies came into existence before the date last named, and as many more in the next thirty years, and their publications made large additions to the materials available to the writer on American history. Even the colleges had by 1880 begun to believe that their students should receive real instruction in history.

Yet one who remembers well the status of history in America in that year can testify that the word research, now so constant in the education vocabulary and so lightly applied to the humblest varieties of fact-finding, was then never heard on any campus. There were at that time eleven professors of history in the United States; only four of them ever wrote and published history. Professors of history taught their classes; they were a quite distinct set from the writers of history, who were for the most part well-to-do cultivated amateurs—a class of historical workers which, we must regretfully admit, has not in the ensuing fifty years increased in anything like the same proportion as the wealth and population of the country.

But presently there came a change. Young American scholars trained in the historical methods of the German seminar came back to teach in American universities and colleges. Others imbibed under the inspiring teaching of Henry Adams at Harvard, or under C. K. Adams at Michigan, the sense of the necessity of studying history from the original sources, or the conviction that some amount of occupation with research was the best means of keeping the teacher's mind alive and vivifying his instruction. The Johns Hopkins University, dedicated primarily to research and the training of young men for research—an entirely novel dedication in that day—began instruction in 1876; and some new ingredient in the *Zeitgeist*, or in the academic atmosphere, brought it about that other universities speedily caught the enthusiasm for graduate instruction, for the professional training of college and university teachers, and thereby for that introduction to the processes of investigation without which the teacher is ill qualified for independent thinking.

It is not fanciful to regard the year 1884 as something of an era in the remarkable development which history has undergone in the United States during the past fifty years. In that year was published the first volume of Justin Winsor's *Narrative and Critical History of America*. Readers of the present day, who have been accustomed to use those volumes as a matter of course, and along with them a multitude of other bibliographical guides, since published, can form no just notion of the difference between working at American history in the days before the appearance of Winsor's volumes and working at it with the aid of the critical chapters in which he had amassed so prodigious and so complete an exposition of what had thus far been published in their field.

Still more epoch-marking was the foundation, in September of the same year, of the American Historical Association. The importance of that event has lain in several particulars. First, in order of time, it brought into mutual acquaintance a group of men who, though occupied with the same field of study, seldom had personal knowledge of each other. The subsequent incorporation of the society by act of Congress and its affiliation to the Smithsonian Institution gave it a governmental status which has been of much value to its work. Its peripatetical habit of holding its annual meetings in various cities, over a wide geographical range, has brought to historical students in different regions the point of view of those who are occupied with the history of Europe or with the larger aspects of the history of our own country, and has helped to emancipate the former class from parochial views or from preoccupation with the history of their single states or regions. As numbers have increased, from the original 41 to the present membership of more than 3700, and resources have increased with them, the existence of this organization has made possible a multitude of good works for the advancement of "American history and history in America" (the charter's phrase). In 1895, by creating its first standing committee, the Historical Manuscripts Commission, it began a long series of volumes of original material previously unpublished. Its Public Archives Commission has published inventories of the archives of nearly all the states, and has exerted a strong influence toward better treatment and preservation of archival material. Its bibliographical committees have valiantly aided research, especially of late by the preparation of its *Guide to Historical Literature*. It has made large investigations of the teaching of history, in this and other countries, and has seriously influenced it. It has sustained the *American Historical Review*, and taken a fruitful part in the work of the International Committee of Historical Sciences.

But perhaps there was no more important result of the formation of that society in 1884 than the creation in the United States of an historical profession, as a body conscious of corporate unity, power and responsibilities. Of the dozen or fifteen professors of history teaching in 1884, there were hardly two that knew more than one or two of the others. The college professor's loyalties were to his college, and many a college had little more relation to the general world of scholarship than if it had been a Buddhist monastery. Now nearly all professors have a twofold loyalty, to the college in which they teach and to the profession to which they consciously belong. It is, of course, not in history alone that this beneficent expansion of mind has taken place. The organization of the American Historical Association in 1884 was but one of a dozen or more instances in which, between 1869 and 1894, the votaries of this or that academic subject, scientific or humanistic, drew together by the formation of national societies. It was an important general movement, the value of which to the intellectual life of America has perhaps not yet been duly estimated.

It has been natural to dwell at disproportionate length upon the history of this one historical society, partly because it is national, partly because it is the one which is responsible for the preparation of this book; but it would be much less than just to ignore the contributions to the advancement of historical research made by other societies, not only state societies, of the type already mentioned, but societies devoted to the history of a particular religious body, or science, or department of culture, or societies of teachers of history in an individual region. Of special institutions or departments for historical research unconnected with teaching, we have had little experience, but it seems not improper to mention, as distinctive, the effort made by one such department to pave the way toward a completer and more systematic exploitation of the materials for American history preserved in foreign archives and libraries.[1]

1. The activities and accomplishments of the Department of Historical Research of the Carnegie Institution, referred to here, are recorded in the Institution's *Year Books*,

It is the belief of the present writer that more fruitful advances in historical investigation could be made in institutes specially endowed for the purpose, in which an historical board of strategy or individual strategist, unencumbered by teaching, could plan what seems best and get it done, than in the historical departments of American universities, where such progress is impeded by the distractions of teaching and by all manner of mundane solicitations. But we have the universities, and have not the institutes, nor the House of Solomon that Bacon envisaged; and every millionaire knows about universities and their needs, or can easily be told about them, while the advancement of learning, pure and simple, has few friends to plead or hear its cause.

And so it is our universities that must be, for the present, the chief homes of productive scholarship in history. Their total product is very impressive in quantity and, on the whole, in quality. It is true that it is very miscellaneous. One would not wish to see research unduly regimented, but those whom "this unchartered freedom tires" will be glad if the present publication leads to a little more careful planning in the endeavor to see that work is directed toward things that are suffering to be done, and away from fields already cultivated to the point of diminishing returns. It is also true that, as things stand, historical research in the universities of the United States means, in the majority of cases, the making of doctoral dissertations. One takes more pleasure in aiding the work, and certainly in reading the product, of researches that spring from the native compulsion of the ardent unpaid mind that pursues investigations because it "can no other," than in those that are carried on solely in response to an academic requirement. But there is no help for this. The student will not be indifferent to the ineluctable logic of: no dissertation no degree, no degree no "job." The professor cannot release him from the obligation, though it seems as if he might sometimes be persuaded that dissertations half as long would serve equally well the purposes for which dissertations were invented and are exacted. (Would that the requirements as to French and German were administered with the same rigor!) So the *doctorandi* publish books, while the professors publish articles.

But the object of these introductory pages is not to set forth doctrine respecting research, which is much better done in the pages that follow, but merely to sketch some aspects of the development it has undergone in the United States during one student's recollection. It is an inspiring and en-

---

beginning in 1903. In all too brief recapitulation the *Year Book for 1930–31*, p. 142, says: "Source materials have been unearthed in the United States and Europe; they have been sorted, digested, their whereabouts and content made known by guides and calendars; and a great number of documents of outstanding importance have been printed, annotated and explained in the critical light of modern scholarship"—A.M.S.

couraging record—hundreds at work where hardly more than a score were at work fifty years ago, and at work with better resources, better instruments and better, or at any rate better-furnished, minds.

American Historical Association, *Historical Scholarship in America: Needs and Opportunities. A Report by the Committee of the American Historical Association on the Planning of Research* (New York: Ray Long and Richard R. Smith, 1932), pp. 3–11.

Bibliography

The following is a comprehensive bibliography of the scholarly and professional writings of John Franklin Jameson. Also listed are selected secondary writings on Jameson. We have excluded writings published in this volume, as well as undergraduate essays. This bibliography expands the compilation of Jameson's works prepared by Donald J. Mugridge and published in *J. Franklin Jameson: A Tribute*, edited by Ruth Anna Fisher and William L. Fox (Washington, D.C.: Catholic University of America Press, 1965), pp. 103–37. Principally we have added works inadvertently omitted by Mugridge, as well as unpublished writings.

1881

The Dutch West India Company. Seminar paper, ca. 1881, AM, Box 25, JP, DLC.

The Municipalities of England. Seminar paper, Johns Hopkins University, ca. 1881, AM, Box 25, JP, DLC.

The Attacks on the Wage-Fund Theory. Seminar paper, Johns Hopkins University, January 10, 1881, AMS, Box 25, JP, DLC.

New York City Government. Paper read at Historical and Political Science Association, [Baltimore], March 18, 1881, AM, Box 25, JP, DLC.

1882

History of the Class of '79. Worcester, Mass.: F. S. Blanchard and Co., 1882. Between 1882 and 1929 Jameson, as class secretary, produced ten reports and two supplements.

The Origin and Development of the Municipal Government of New York City. I, The Dutch Period. *Magazine of American History* 8 (May 1882): 315–30. II, The English and American Period. *Magazine of American History* 8 (September 1882): 598–611.

Magazine of American History. Seminar paper, Johns Hopkins University, May 12, 1882, AM, Box 25, JP, DLC.

Review, unsigned, of *Edward the III*, by W. Warburton (Chicago: Charles Scribner's Sons, 1882). *Baltimore Day*, October 25, 1882, p. 2.

On the Revue Historique and Other French Historical Periodical Literature in the

Johns Hopkins University Library. Seminar paper, Johns Hopkins University, October 27, 1882, AM, Box 25, JP, DLC.

1883

Bibliography of James Monroe, and the Monroe Doctrine. In *James Monroe in His Relations to the Public Service During Half a Century, 1776–1826*, by Daniel Coit Gilman. Boston: Houghton, Mifflin and Co., 1883. Pp. 253–80.

An Account of the Contents of the Bluntschli Library as Received in Baltimore. *Johns Hopkins University Circulars* 2 (February 1883): 61–62.

Montauk and the Common Lands of Easthampton. *Magazine of American History* 9 (April 1883): 225–39.

1883–1884

Review of *The Development of Constitutional Liberty in the English Colonies of America*, by Eben Greenough Scott (New York: G. P. Putnam's Sons, 1882). *Historische Zeitschrift* 51–52 (1883–84): 190–91.

Review of *English Colonies in America: Virginia, Maryland, and the Carolinas*, by J. A. Doyle (New York: Henry Holt and Co., 1882). *Historische Zeitschrift* 51–52 (1883–84): 559–61.

Review of *History of the Formation of the Constitution of the United States of America*, vols. 1 and 2, by George Bancroft (New York: D. Appleton and Co., 1882). *Historische Zeitschrift* 51–52 (1883–84): 189–90.

1884

Records of the Town of Amherst, from 1735 to 1788. Reprinted from the *Amherst Record*. Edited by JFJ. Amherst, Mass.: Press of J. E. Williams, 1884.

Lectures on the Science of Physical Geography in Its Relation to History. Undergraduate course delivered at Hopkins Hall, Johns Hopkins University, January–April 1884, AMS, Manuscript Department, ViU.

Review of *Pedagogical Library, vol. 1. Diesterweg's Methods of Teaching History, with Papers by Professors Herbert B. Adams, C. K. Adams, John W. Burgess, E. Emerton, and Mr. T. W. Higginson* (Boston: Ginn, Heath and Co., 1884). *Johns Hopkins University Circulars* 2 (April 1884): 84.

[Address to the Amherst *Student* Breakfast]. [Amherst], [July 1, 1884], AM, Box 28, JP, DLC.

1885

Review of *The Hessians and Other German Auxiliaries of Great Britain in the Revolutionary War*, by Edward J. Lowell (New York: Harper and Brothers, 1883). *Historische Zeitschrift* 53 (1885): 182–83.

Review of *A History of the People of the United States, from the Revolution to the Civil War*, vol. 1, by John Bach McMaster (New York: D. Appleton and Co., 1883). *Historische Zeitschrift* 53 (1885): 381–82.

Review of *History of the United States of America Under the Constitution*, vols. 1 and 2, by James Schouler (Washington, D.C.: W. H. and O. H. Morrison, 1880–82). *Historische Zeitschrift* 53 (1885): 183–84.

Review of *The Life of James Buchanan, Fifteenth President of the United States of America*, by George Ticknor Curtis (New York: Harper and Brothers, 1883). *Historische Zeitschrift* 53 (1885): 185–86.

What Became of the Northern Slaves? Seminar paper, Johns Hopkins University, May 22, 1885, AM, Box 25, JP, DLC.

The Records of the Virginia Company. Paper delivered to the Historical and Political Science Association, [Baltimore], November 20, 1885; and to the Rhode Island Historical Society, [Providence], November 27, 1888, AM, Box 28, JP, DLC.

1887

William Usselinx, Founder of the Dutch and Swedish West India Companies. AHA, *Papers*, vol. 2, no. 3. New York: G. P. Putnam's Sons, 1887. Pp. 149–382.

Review of *New York in the Seventeenth Century*. Address given by Viktor Precht at the March 19, 1884, meeting of the German Social-Scientific Society of New York (New York: Cheronny Printing and Publishing Company, 1884). *Historische Zeitschrift* 57–58 (1887): 179–80.

Review of *Albert Gallatin*, by John Austin Stevens (Boston: Houghton, Mifflin and Co., 1884). *Historische Zeitschrift* 57–58 (1887): 189–90.

Review of *Alexander Hamilton*, by Henry Cabot Lodge (Boston: Houghton, Mifflin and Co., 1882). *Historische Zeitschrift* 57–58 (1887): 182–83.

Review of *Andrew Jackson as a Public Man*, by William Graham Sumner (Boston: Houghton, Mifflin and Co., 1883). *Historische Zeitschrift* 57–58 (1887): 184–85.

Review of *Daniel Webster*, by Henry Cabot Lodge (Boston: Houghton, Mifflin and Co., 1883). *Historische Zeitschrift* 57–58 (1887): 189.

Review of *James Monroe in His Relations to the Public Service During Half a Century, 1776–1826*, by Daniel Coit Gilman (Boston: Houghton, Mifflin and Co., 1883). *Historische Zeitschrift* 57–58 (1887): 187–88.

Review of *John Randolph*, by Henry Adams (Boston: Houghton, Mifflin and Co., 1883). *Historische Zeitschrift* 57–58 (1887): 185–87.

Review of *John C. Calhoun*, by Hermann von Holst (Boston: Houghton, Mifflin and Co., 1882). *Historische Zeitschrift* 57–58 (1887): 183–84.

Review of *John Quincy Adams*, by John T. Morse (Boston: Houghton, Mifflin and Co., 1882). *Historische Zeitschrift* 57–58 (1887): 180–82.

Review of *Montcalm and Wolfe*, vols. 1 and 2, by Francis Parkman (Boston: Little, Brown and Co., 1884). *Historische Zeitschrift* 57–58 (1887): 180.

Review of *Thomas Jefferson*, by John Torrey Morse (Boston: Houghton, Mifflin and Co., 1883). *Historische Zeitschrift* 57–58 (1887): 188–89.

Lectures on the History of Historical Writing in America. Delivered in Hopkins Hall, Johns Hopkins University, January–February 1887, AMS, Box 32, JP, DLC.

1888

The United States One Hundred Years Ago. Series of articles, unsigned, *New York Times*: March 4, 1888, p. 10, col. 4; March 11, 1888, p. 10, col. 4; March 18, 1888, p. 10, col. 2; March 25, 1888, p. 10, col. 5; and April 1, 1888, p. 10, col. 5.

Review, unsigned, of *Half-Hours with American History*, vols. 1 and 2, by Charles Morris (Philadelphia: J. B. Lippincott and Co., 1887). *Independent* 40 (May 3, 1888): 560.

Review, unsigned, of *The English Colonies in America: The Puritan Colonies*, vols. 1 and 2, by J. A. Doyle (New York: Henry Holt and Co., 1887). *Independent* 40 (June 7, 1888): 720–21.

Review, unsigned, of *A Library of American Literature from the Earliest Settlements to the Present Time*, vols. 1–4, compiled and edited by Edmund Clarence Stedman and Ellen MacKay Hutchinson (New York: Charles L. Webster and Co., 1888). *Independent* 40 (July 19, 1888): 912.

1889

The Old Federal Court of Appeal. AHA, *Papers*, vol. 3, no. 2. New York: G. P. Putnam's Sons, 1889. Pp. 381–92.

The Predecessor of the Supreme Court. In *Essays in the Constitutional History of the United States in the Formative Period, 1775–1789*, edited by JFJ. Boston: Houghton, Mifflin Co., 1889. Pp. 1–45.

Historical Writing in the United States, 1783–1861. *Englische Studien* 12 (1889): 59–77.

Historical Writing in the United States since 1861. *Englische Studien* 13 (1889): 230–46.

The Political History of Greece in the Fifth Century, B.C., and Its Relations to Literary History. Paper read to the Greek Club, [Providence], November 2, 1889, AM, Box 28, JP, DLC.

1890

Did the Fathers Vote? *New England Magazine* n.s. 1 (January 1890): 484–90.
The Development of Modern European Historiography. *Atlantic Monthly* 66 (September 1890): 322–33.
An Early Briton. *Chautauquan* 12 (October 1890): 24–28.
Amherst in the Faculties of Other Institutions. *Amherst Student* 24 (October 18, 1890): 30–31.
Virginia and New England. Review of *The Genesis of the United States*, vols. 1 and 2, by Alexander Brown (Boston: Houghton, Mifflin and Co., 1890). *Atlantic Monthly* 66 (November 1890): 700–707.
The Spanish Historians. Lectures delivered to the Rhode Island Women's Club, [Providence], November 5, 1890; and December 3, 1890, AM, Box 28, JP, DLC.

1891

The History of Historical Writing in America. Boston: Houghton, Mifflin and Co., 1891.
The Expenditures of Foreign Governments in Behalf of History. AHA, *Annual Report*, 1891. Washington, D.C.: Government Printing Office, 1892. Pp. 31–61.
An English Sea-Rover. *Chautauquan* 13 (April 1891): 21–25.
Lowell and Public Affairs. *Review of Reviews* 4 (October 1891): 287–91.
Greek History in the Fourth Century, B.C. Paper read before the Greek Club, [Providence], November 7, 1891, AM, Box 28, JP, DLC.

1892

Virginian History, 1763–1812. Lectures delivered at the Peabody Institute, [Baltimore], January 28, February 2, 4, 1892, AM, Box 28, JP, DLC.
A Little Journey of Historical Research in Eastern Virginia. Paper delivered to the Rhode Island Historical Society, [Providence], February 23, 1892, TM, Box 28, JP, DLC.
Aristotle in the Middle Ages. Paper read before the Greek Club, [Providence], March 26, 1892, AM, Box 28, JP, DLC.
Two Virginians. *Atlantic Monthly* 70 (September 1892): 407–14.
Differences of National Character Between the Greeks and the Romans, and the Effects to Be Seen in Latin Literature. Paper read at the Greek Club, [Providence], November 12, 1892, TM, Box 28, JP, DLC.

1893

On a Certain Passage in the Coplas of Don Jorge de Manrique. Paper read to the Historical Group, [Providence], February 4, 1893, TM, Box 28, JP, DLC.

Virginian Voting in the Colonial Period, 1744–1774. *Nation* 56 (April 27, 1893): 309–10.

Greek History and the Constitution of the United States. *Chautauquan* 17 (June 1893): 285–89.

1894

Dictionary of United States History, 1492–1894. Boston: Puritan Publishing Co., [1894].

Papers from the Historical Seminary of Brown University. Edited by JFJ. Nos. 1–10. Providence: 1894–99.

The Origin of the Standing Committee System in American Legislative Bodies. *Political Science Quarterly* 9 (June 1894): 246–67. Also in AHA, *Annual Report*, 1893. Washington, D.C.: Government Printing Office, 1894. Pp. 391–99.

1895

Greek Athletes and Greek Poetry. Paper read before the Greek Club, [Providence], February 16, 1895, TM, Box 28, JP, DLC.

The Flag's First Trip Around the World. Paper read at the meeting of the Rhode Island Society of Colonial Dames, [Providence], June 14, 1895, TM, Box 28, JP, DLC.

American Historical Review. Managing editor, JFJ. 1 (October 1895) through 6 (July 1901). 11 (October 1905) through 33 (July 1928).

1896

Introduction to *A History of France*, by Victor A. Duruy (New York: Thomas Y. Crowell and Co., 1896), pp. vii–xii.

Diary of Edward Hooker, 1805–1808. Edited by JFJ. AHA, *Annual Report*, 1896. Washington, D.C.: Government Printing Office, 1897. Pp. 842–929.

Letters of Stephen Higginson, 1783–1804. Edited by JFJ. AHA, *Annual Report*,. 1896. Washington, D.C.: Government Printing Office, 1897. Pp. 704–841.

Review, unsigned, of *The Pilgrim Fathers of New England and Their Puritan Successors*, by John Brown (New York: F. H. Revell, 1895). AHR 1 (April 1896): 541–42.

[Bibliography of] Proceedings, etc., of Early Party Conventions. *AHR* 1 (July 1896): 760–71.

1896–1897

Letters of Phineas Bond, British Consul at Philadelphia, to the Foreign Office of Great Britain, 1787–1794. Edited by JFJ. I, AHA, *Annual Report*, 1896. Washington, D.C.: Government Printing Office, 1897. Pp. 513–659. II, AHA, *Annual Report*, 1897. Washington, D.C., Government Printing Office, 1898. Pp. 454–568.

Report on Spanish and Dutch Settlements Prior to 1648. In *U.S. Commission to Investigate and Report upon the True Divisional Line Between the Republic of Venezuela and British Guiana*. Vol. 1. Washington, D.C.: Government Printing Office, 1896–97.

1896–1899

Reports of the Historical Manuscripts Commission of the American Historical Association, JFJ, chairman. Nos. 1–4, 1896–99, in AHA, *Annual Reports*, 1896–99, as follows:

1. *Annual Report*, 1896. Washington, D.C.: Government Printing Office, 1897. Pp. 463–1107. Report proper, pp. 467–80.
2. *Annual Report*, 1897. Washington, D.C.: Government Printing Office, 1898. Pp. 397–679. Report proper, pp. 399–403.
3. *Annual Report*, 1898. Washington, D.C.: Government Printing Office, 1899. Pp. 565–708. Report proper, pp. 567–72.
4. *Annual Report*, 1899. Washington, D.C.: Government Printing Office, 1900. Vol. 2.

1897

The Colonial Assemblies and Their Legislative Journals. Collected by JFJ. AHA, *Annual Report*, 1897. Washington, D.C.: Government Printing Office, 1898. Pp. 403–53.

Graduate Studies in History at Brown University, 1887–1897. [Providence: Brown University, 1897.] Copy in Box 63, JP, DLC.

John Lothrop Motley. In *Library of the World's Best Literature, Ancient and Modern*, edited by Charles Dudley Warner. New York: R. S. Peale and J. S. Hill, [1897]. Vol. 18, pp. 10373–80.

President Andrews and the Situation at Brown. *Review of Reviews* 16 (September 1897): 310–16.

The Early Political Uses of the Word *Convention*. American Antiquarian Society. *Proceedings*, n.s. 12 (October 1897): 183–96. Also in *AHR* 3 (April 1898): 477–87.

Review, unsigned, of *American History Told by Contemporaries*, vol. 1, by Albert Bushnell Hart (New York: Macmillan Co., 1897). *AHR* 3 (October 1897): 166–67.

1898

Remarks by Prof. J. F. Jameson, of Brown University. AHA, *Annual Report*, 1898. Washington, D.C.: Government Printing Office, 1899. Pp. 73–76. Comment on papers by Charles M. Andrews, "American Colonial History, 1690–1750," and by Herbert L. Osgood, "Study of American Colonial History."

Review, unsigned, of *American History Told by Contemporaries*, vol. 2, by Albert Bushnell Hart (New York: Macmillan Co., 1898). *AHR* 4 (October 1898): 168–69.

1899

Correspondence of John C. Calhoun. Edited by JFJ. AHA, *Annual Report*, 1899. 2 vols. Washington, D.C.: Government Printing Office, 1900. Vol. 2.

1900

Letters of Ebenezer Huntington, 1774–1781. [Edited by JFJ.] *AHR* 5 (July 1900): 702–29.

Diary of John Harrower, 1773–1776. [Edited by JFJ.] *AHR* 6 (October 1900): 65–107.

1901

Review, unsigned, of *American History Told by Contemporaries*, vol. 3, by Albert Bushnell Hart (New York: Macmillan Co., 1901). *AHR* 6 (April 1901): 590–91.

Letters on the Nullification Movement in South Carolina, 1830–1834. [Edited by JFJ.] I, *AHR* 6 (July 1901): 736–65. II, *AHR* 7 (October 1901): 92–119.

Letters of Dr. Thomas Cooper, 1825–1832. [Edited by JFJ.] *AHR* 6 (July 1901): 725–36.

1902

Studies in the History of the Federal Convention of 1787. AHA, *Annual Report*, 1902. Washington, D.C.: Government Printing Office, 1903. Vol. 1, pp. 87–167.

The Johns Hopkins Anniversary. *Dial* 32 (March 1, 1902): 143–46.

On Teaching Pupils to Be Fair. Paper delivered at North Central History Teachers Association, [Chicago], March 29, 1902, TM, Box 28, JP, DLC. Published in *Proceedings of the North Central History Teachers Association, 1899–1904* (Chicago: Published by the Association, 1904), pp. 21–23.

Review of *The Writings of James Madison*, edited by Gaillard Hunt, vols. 1–2 (New York: G. P. Putnam's Sons, 1900–1901). *AHR* 7 (April 1902): 573–75.

Review of *American History Told by Contemporaries*, vol. 4, by Albert Bushnell Hart (New York: Macmillan Co., 1901). *AHR* 7 (April 1902): 609.

Review of *Essays in Historical Criticism*, by Edward Gaylord Bourne (New York: Charles Scribner's Sons, 1901). *AHR* 7 (July 1902): 745–47.

Review of *The Writings of James Monroe*, edited by Stanislaus Murray Hamilton, vol. 5 (New York: G. P. Putnam's Sons, 1901). *AHR* 7 (July 1902): 781–83.

A Letter of Alexander H. Stephens, 1854. Edited by JFJ. *AHR* 8 (October 1902): 91–97.

1903

Portions of Charles Pinckney's Plan for a Constitution, 1787. Edited by JFJ. *AHR* 8 (April 1903): 509–11.

Review of the Naval Miscellany, edited by John Knox Laughton, vol. 1 (London: Navy Records Society, 1902). *AHR* 8 (April 1903): 532–34.

Review of *The Writings of James Madison*, edited by Gaillard Hunt, vol. 3 (New York: G. P. Putnam's Sons, 1902). *AHR* 8 (April 1903): 559–61.

St. Eustatius in the American Revolution. *AHR* 8 (July 1903): 683–708.

Review of *The Writings of James Monroe*, edited by Stanislaus Murray Hamilton, vol. 6 (New York: G. P. Putnam's Sons, 1902). *AHR* 8 (July 1903): 781–82.

Professor von Holst as a Historian. *University Record of the University of Chicago* 8 (October 1903): 156–60.

1904

Review of *The Cambridge Modern History*, vol. 7, *The United States* (New York: Macmillan Co., 1903). *AHR* 9 (January 1904): 365–69.

Review of *The Writings of James Monroe*, edited by Stanislaus Murray Hamilton, vol. 7 (New York: G. P. Putnam's Sons, 1903); and *The Writings of James Madison*, edited by Gaillard Hunt, vol. 4 (New York: G. P. Putnam's Sons, 1903). *AHR* 9 (April 1904): 577–79.

On Certain Relations Between Political Geography and History. Lectures delivered at the Naval War College in Newport, Rhode Island, August 11–12, 1904, TM, Box 28, JP, DLC.

1905

Report of J. Franklin Jameson, general editor of the *Original Narratives of Early American History*. AHA, *Annual Report*, 1905. Washington, D.C.: Government Printing Office, 1906. Pp. 51–59.

Notice of *The Writings of James Madison*, edited by Gaillard Hunt, vol. 5 (New York: G. P. Putnam's Sons, 1904). *AHR* 10 (April 1905): 691–92.

The Age of Erudition. *University Record of the University of Chicago* 10 (July 1905): 19–28. Also published in *Representative Phi Beta Kappa Orations* (Boston: Houghton, Mifflin Co., 1915), pp. 326–43.

1906

Papers of Dr. James McHenry on the Federal Convention of 1787. [Edited by JFJ.] *AHR* 11 (April 1906): 595–624.

Gaps in the Published Records of United States History. *AHR* 11 (July 1906): 817–31.

Journal of John Mair, 1791. [Edited by JFJ.] *AHR* 12 (October 1906): 77–94.

Letter of Grant to His Father, on the Capture of Vicksburg, 1863. [Edited by JFJ]. *AHR* 12 (October 1906): 109.

Letter of Stephen R. Mallory, 1861. [Edited by JFJ.] *AHR* 12 (October 1906): 103–9.

Letters of Jefferson to Marbois, 1781, 1783. [Edited by JFJ.] *AHR* 12 (October 1906): 75–77.

Project of Latin-American Confederation, 1856. [Edited by JFJ.] *AHR* 12 (October 1906): 94–103.

1906–1917

Original Narratives of Early American History. JFJ, general editor. 19 vols. New York: Charles Scribner's Sons, 1906–17. For the volumes edited individually by JFJ, see 1909, 1910, and 1913.

1906–1928

Carnegie Institution of Washington. Department of Historical Research. Annual Report of the Director, J. Franklin Jameson. Extracted from the *Year Books* of the Carnegie Institution, vols. 5–27.

1. *Annual Report*, 1906–19. 14 vols. in 1. Washington, D.C.: [Published by the Institution], 1907–20.

2. *Annual Report*, 1919–28. 8 vols. in 1. Washington, D.C.: [Published by the Institution], 1920–28.

1907

Gilman v. McClary: A New Hampshire Case of 1791. [Edited by JFJ.] *AHR* 12 (January 1907): 348–50.

Intercepted Letters of Virginian Tories, 1775. [Edited by JFJ.] *AHR* 12 (January 1907): 341–46.

Letter of John Marshall to James Wilkinson, 1787. [Edited by JFJ.] *AHR* 12 (January 1907): 346–48.

Letters of Thomas Newe from South Carolina, 1682. [Edited by JFJ.] *AHR* 12 (January 1907): 322–27.

Narrative of a Voyage to Maryland, 1705–1706. [Edited by JFJ.] *AHR* 12 (January 1907): 327–40.

The Catholic Mission in Maryland, 1641. [Edited by JFJ.] *AHR* 12 (April 1907): 584–87.

Edmund Randolph on the British Treaty, 1795. [Edited by JFJ.] *AHR* 12 (April 1907): 587–99.

Virgil Maxcy on Calhoun's Political Opinions and Prospects, 1823. [Edited by JFJ.] *AHR* 12 (April 1907): 599–601.

1909

U.S. Committee on Department Methods. *Message from the President of the United States Transmitting a Report by the Committee on Department Methods on the Documentary Historical Publications of the United States Government, Together with a Draft of a Proposed Bill Providing for the Creation of a Permanent Commission on National Historical Publications.* Washington, D.C.: Government Printing Office, [1909]. 60th Cong., 2d Session, Senate Doc. 714. Jameson wrote the introduction and conclusion to this report, and edited the contributions of a panel of specialists, including Charles M. Andrews, Andrew C. McLaughlin, William A. Dunning, Albert B. Hart, Alfred T. Mahan, Frederick J. Turner, Charles F. Adams, Jr., and Worthington C. Ford.

Narratives of New Netherland, 1609–1664. Edited by JFJ. New York: Charles Scribner's Sons, 1909. A volume of the Original Narratives of Early American History series.

The American Historical Association, 1884–1909. *AHR* 15 (October 1909): 1–20.

Review of *The Federal and State Constitutions, Colonial Charters, and Other Organic Laws of the States, Territories, and Colonies Now or Heretofore Forming the United States of America,* vols. 1–7, edited by Francis N. Thorpe (Washington, D.C.: Government Printing Office, 1909). *AHR* 15 (October 1909): 153–55.

[Letter from John Jameson, Butteville, Marion Co., Oregon, to His Younger Brother, Edwin Jameson, August 17, 1852.] Communicated by JFJ. *Oregon Historical Society Quarterly* 10 (December 1909): 390–95.

1910

Johnson's Wonderworking Providence, 1628–1651. Edited by JFJ. New York: Charles Scribner's Sons, 1910. A volume of the Original Narratives of Early American History series.

Letters of John Bridge and Emmanuel Altham. Edited by JFJ. Massachusetts Historical Society, *Proceedings,* 1910–11. Boston: [Published by the Society], 1911. Vol. 44, pp. 178–88.

[Statement on Committee on National Archives.] AHA, *Annual Report,* 1910. Washington, D.C.: Government Printing Office, 1912. Pp. 313–14.

Letter of John Quincy Adams, from Ghent, 1814. [Edited by JFJ.] *AHR* 15 (April 1910): 572–74.

Letter of Major-General Johann Kalb, 1777. [Edited by JFJ.] *AHR* 15 (April 1910): 562–67.

Letter of the Marquess of Rockingham Respecting Defense Against John Paul Jones, 1779. [Edited by JFJ.] *AHR* 15 (April 1910): 567–71.

Letter of William Henry Trescot on Reconstruction in South Carolina, 1867. [Edited by JFJ.] *AHR* 15 (April 1910): 574–82.

Letters of Toussaint Louverture and of Edward Stevens, 1798–1800. [Edited by JFJ.] *AHR* 16 (October 1910): 64–101.

1911

Letters of William T. Barry, 1806–1810, 1829–1831. [Edited by JFJ.] *AHR* 16 (January 1911): 327–36.

Review of *The Writings of James Madison, 1819–1836,* vol. 9, edited by Gaillard Hunt (New York: G. P. Putnam's Sons, 1910). *AHR* 16 (April 1911): 675.

Address to the Daughters of the American Revolution. Delivered in Memorial-Continental Hall, [Washington, D.C.], April 19, 1911. In *Proceedings of the Twentieth Continental Congress of the Daughters of the American Revolution, Washington, D.C., April 17–22, 1911.* [Washington, D.C.: Published by the Congress], 1911. Pp. 90–93.

The First American Discoveries in the Antarctic, 1819. [Edited by JFJ.] *AHR* 16 (July 1911): 794–98.

Records of the Settlers at the Head of the French Broad River, 1793–1803. [Edited by JFJ.] *AHR* 16 (July 1911): 791–94.

Senator Few on the Second Session of the First Congress, 1790. [Edited by JFJ.] *AHR* 16 (July 1911): 789–90.

1912

Introduction to *Providence in Colonial Times,* by Gertrude Selwyn Kimball. Boston: Houghton, Mifflin Co., 1912. Pp. xv–xxi.

Review of *The Swedish Settlements on the Delaware: Their History and Relation to the Indians, Dutch and English, 1638–1664*, by Amandus Johnson (Philadelphia: University of Pennsylvania Press, 1911). *AHR* 17 (January 1912): 381–83.

Debates on the Declaratory Act and the Repeal of the Stamp Act, 1766. Contributed by Charles H. Hull and Harold W. V. Temperley. Introductory note by JFJ. *AHR* 17 (April 1912): 563–86.

Journal of William K. Beall, July–August 1812. [Edited by JFJ.] *AHR* 17 (July 1912): 783–808.

Diary of Thomas Ewing, August and September 1841. [Edited by JFJ.] *AHR* 18 (October 1912): 97–112.

1913

[Statement on National Archives.] AHA, *Annual Report*, 1913. 2 vols. Washington, D.C.: Government Printing Office, 1913. 1:267–68.

Journal of Jasper Danckaerts, 1679–1680. Edited by Bartlett Burleigh James and JFJ. New York: Charles Scribner's Sons, 1913. A volume of the Original Narratives of Early American History series.

Correspondence of the Russian Ministers in Washington, 1818–1825. [Edited by JFJ.] 1. *AHR* 18 (January 1913): 309–45. 2. *AHR* 18 (April 1913): 537–62.

The International Congress of Historical Studies held at London. *AHR* 18 (July 1913): 679–91.

Notes of Colonel W. G. Moore, Private Secretary to President Johnson, 1866–1868, contributed by St. George L. Sioussat. [Annotations supplied by JFJ.] *AHR* 19 (October 1913): 98–132.

Reasons for Studying American Religious History. Paper delivered at the 1913 meeting of the American Historical Association in Charleston, S.C., December 29, 1913, TM, Box 28, JP, DLC.

1914

The History of Historical Societies. Address by Dr. J. Franklin Jameson at the Seventy-fifth Anniversary of the Georgia Historical Society. Savannah: Morning News Print, 1914.

Journal of Jean Baptiste Truteau on the Upper Missouri, "Primiere Partie," June 7, 1794–March 26, 1795. [Edited by JFJ.] *AHR* 19 (January 1914): 299–333.

Typical Steps of American Expansion. *History Teacher's Magazine* 5 (February 1914): 39–43.

Estimates of the Value of Slaves, 1815. [Edited by JFJ.] *AHR* 19 (July 1914): 813–38.

Letters relating to the Negotiations at Ghent, 1812–1814. [Edited by JFJ.] *AHR* 20 (October 1914): 108–29.

1915

American Historical Review. An Historical Statement Concerning the *American Historical Review*. Washington, D.C.: American Historical Review, 1915.

Letters from Lafayette to Luzerne, 1780–1782. [Edited by JFJ.] 1. *AHR* 20 (January 1915): 341–76. 2. *AHR* 20 (April 1915): 577–612.

The Meeting of the American Historical Association in Chicago. *AHR* 20 (April 1915): 503–27.

The Meeting of the American Historical Association in California. *AHR* 21 (October 1915): 1–11.

1916

The Meeting of the American Historical Association at Washington. *AHR* 21 (April 1916): 441–67.

1917

The Association. AHA, *Annual Report*, 1917. Washington, D.C.: Government Printing Office, 1920. Pp. 303–12.

The Meeting of the American Historical Association at Cincinnati. *AHR* 22 (April 1917): 509–34.

Protocols of Conferences of Representatives of the Allied Powers Respecting Spanish America, 1824–1825. [Edited by JFJ]. *AHR* 22 (April 1917): 595–616.

The National Board for Historical Service. [Note by JFJ.] *AHR* 22 (July 1917): 918–19.

Paris in 1870: Letters of Mary Corinna Putnam. [Edited by JFJ]. *AHR* 22 (July 1917): 836–41.

Kearsage and Alabama: French Official Report, 1864. [Edited by JFJ.] *AHR* 23 (October 1917): 119–23.

1918

In Memoriam: Henry Adams. AHA, *Annual Report*, 1918. 2 vols. Washington, D.C.: Government Printing Office, 1921. 1:71–72.

The American Minister in Berlin, on the Revolution of March 1848. [Edited by JFJ.] *AHR* 23 (January 1918): 355–73.

The Confederacy and the Declaration of Paris. [Edited by JFJ.] *AHR* 23 (July 1918): 826–35.

The River Platte Voyages, 1798–1800. [Note appended by JFJ.] *AHR* 23 (July 1918): 816–25.

1919

Amherst Petition on the Embargo, 1808. Massachusetts Historical Society, *Proceedings*, 1918–19 Boston: [Published by the Society], 1919. Vol. 52, pp. 161–63.

[The Archives of] the United States of America. In *British and Allied Archives During the War*. Royal Historical Society, *Transactions*, 4th series, 2 (1919): 37–40.

Report of Committee of Council to Act on Report of Committee on American Scientific and Educational Interests in the Ottoman Empire. AHA, *Annual Report*, 1919. 2 vols. Washington, D.C.: Government Printing Office, 1923. 1:77–78.

Diary and Memoranda of William L. Marcy, 1849–1851. [Note appended by JFJ]. *AHR* 24 (April 1919): 444–62.

Diary and Memoranda of William L. Marcy, 1857. [Edited by JFJ.] *AHR* 24 (July 1919): 641–53.

1920

John Clark of the Mayflower. Massachusetts Historical Society, *Proceedings*, 1920–21. Boston: [Published by the Society], 1922. Vol. 54, pp. 61–76.

Final Report of the Chairman on the London Headquarters of the Association. AHA, *Annual Report*, 1920. Washington, D.C.: Government Printing Office, 1925. P. 100.

Report of Committee on National Archives. AHA, *Annual Report*, 1920. Washington, D.C.: Government Printing Office, 1925. P. 88.

Henry Adams and Garibaldi, 1860. [Edited by JFJ.] *AHR* 25 (January 1920): 241–55.

Scholars of the World Form a Union. *New York Post Magazine*, March 6, 1920, p. 7.

The Arrest of Professors Fredericq and Pirenne. *AHR* 25 (April 1920): 446–47.

The American Council of Learned Societies. *AHR* 25 (April 1920): 440–46.

The American Historical Review, 1895–1920. *AHR* 26 (October 1920): 1–17.

The Meeting of the American Historical Association at Cleveland. *AHR* 25 (April 1920): 369–90.

Spanish Policy Toward Virginia, 1606–1612; Jamestown, Ecija, and John Clark of the Mayflower. [Edited by JFJ]. *AHR* 25 (April 1920): 448–79.

An International Council of Scholars. *Review of Reviews* 61 (May 1920): 526–27.

Letter of Daniel Webster, 1833. [Edited by JFJ.] *AHR* 25 (July 1920): 695–97.

Letter of William Wirt, 1819. [Edited by JFJ.] *AHR* 25 (July 1920): 692–95.

1921

The Meeting of the American Historical Association at Washington. *AHR* 26 (April 1921): 413–39.

Memoir of Charles McCarthy. May 10, 1921, TM, Box 109, JP, DLC. Published in

McCarthy of Wisconsin, by Edward A. Fitzpatrick. New York: Columbia University Press, 1944. Pp. 14–15.

Review of *A Hidden Phase of American History: Ireland's Part in America's Struggle for Liberty*, by Michael J. O'Brien (New York: Dodd, Mead and Co. 1920). *AHR* 26 (July 1921): 797–99.

Journal of a French Traveller in the Colonies, 1765. [Edited by JFJ.] 1. *AHR* 26 (July 1921): 726–47. 2. *AHR* 27 (October 1921): 70–89.

The Anglo-American Conference of Professors of History. *AHR* 27 (October 1921): 58–63.

1922

In Memoriam: James Bryce. AHA, *Annual Report*, 1922. 2 vols. Washington, D.C.: Government Printing Office, 1926. 1:95–96.

Report of Committee on the Documentary Historical Publications of the United States Government. AHA, *Annual Report*, 1922. 2 vols. Washington, D.C.: Government Printing Office, 1926. 1:71.

Report of the Committee on the National Archives. AHA, *Annual Report*, 1922. 2 vols. Washington, D.C.: Government Printing Office, 1926. 1:170.

Report of Committee on the University Center for Research in Washington. AHA, *Annual Report*, 1922. 2 vols. Washington, D.C.: Government Printing Office, 1926. 1:70.

Statement of JFJ on Public Archives Commission. AHA, *Annual Report*, 1922. 2 vols. Washington, D.C.: Government Printing Office, 1926. 1:160–63.

Washington in 1834; Letter of Robert C. Caldwell. [Edited by JFJ.] *AHR* 27 (January 1922): 271–81.

The Meeting of the American Historical Association at St. Louis. *AHR* 27 (April 1922): 405–25.

Lord Sackville's Papers Respecting Virginia, 1613–1631. [Edited by JFJ.] 1. *AHR* 27 (April 1922): 493–538. 2. *AHR* 27 (July 1922): 738–65.

1923

The American Historian's Raw Materials. Ann Arbor: University of Michigan, 1923.

Privateering and Piracy in the Colonial Period. Illustrative Documents. New York: Macmillan Co., 1923.

Report of the Committee on the Documentary Historical Publications of the United States. AHA, *Annual Report*, 1923. Washington, D.C.: Government Printing Office, 1929. Pp. 89–92.

Report of the Committee on National Archives. AHA, *Annual Report*, 1923. Washington, D.C.: Government Printing Office, 1929. Pp. 79–80.

Report of the Committee on the University Center for Research in Washington.

AHA, *Annual Report*, 1923. Washington, D.C.: Government Printing Office, 1929. Pp. 86–87.

The University Centre for Research in Washington. *AHR* 28 (January 1923): 259–62.

The Meeting of the American Historical Association at New Haven. *AHR* 28 (April 1923): 417–39.

A Pure History Law. *AHR* 28 (July 1923): 699–701.

Letters of Robert Biddulph, 1779–1783. Introduction by Violet Biddulph; annotations by JFJ. *AHR* 29 (October 1923): 87–109.

Masson, Marjorie, and JFJ. The Odyssey of Thomas Muir. *AHR* 29 (October 1923): 49–72.

The Approach to Diplomatic History Illustrated by the Correspondence of the Early British Ministers to the United States. Lecture delivered at the Carnegie Institution of Washington, November 20, 1923. TM, Box 62, JP, DLC.

1 9 2 4

Report of the Anglo-American Conference of Professors of History. AHA, *Annual Report*, 1924. Washington, D.C.: Government Printing Office, 1929. Pp. 93–94.

Report of the Committee on the Documentary Historical Publications of the United States Government. AHA, *Annual Report*, 1924. Washington, D.C.: Government Printing Office, 1929. Pp. 84–85.

Report of the Committee on the National Archives. AHA, *Annual Report*, 1924. Washington, D.C.: Government Printing Office, 1929. Pp. 78–79.

The Assassination of President Lincoln, 1865. [Edited by JFJ.] *AHR* 29 (April 1924): 514–17.

Henry W. Hilliard to James Buchanan, 1858. [Edited by JFJ.] *AHR* 29 (April 1924): 613.

The Meeting of the American Historical Association at Columbus. *AHR* 29 (April 1924): 423–48.

On the Journals of the House of Representatives, 1836. [Edited by JFJ.] *AHR* 29 (April 1924): 510–12.

Note: Papers of Count Tisza. [Edited by JFJ.] *AHR* 29 (April 1924): 522.

Papers of Count Tisza, 1914–1918. [Edited by JFJ.] *AHR* 29 (January 1924): 301–15.

W. E. Gladstone to Sir Frederick Bruce, 1866. [Edited by JFJ.] *AHR* 29 (April 1924): 517–18.

William Lattimore to His Constituents, 1805. [Edited by JFJ.] *AHR* 29 (April 1924): 506–10.

Marbois on the Fur Trade, 1784. [Edited by JFJ.] *AHR* 29 (July 1924): 725–40.

Dictionary of Biography Has High Aims. *New York Times*, December 21, 1924, sec. 8, p. 7, col. 2. Article contains extended statement by Jameson on the proposed *Dictionary of American Biography*.

1925

Report of the Board of Editors of the American Historical Review. AHA, *Annual Report*, 1925. Washington, D.C.: Government Printing Office, 1929. Pp. 70–71.

Report of the Committee on the Documentary Historical Publications of the United States Government. AHA, *Annual Report*, 1925. Washington, D.C.: Government Printing Office, 1929. Pp. 97–98.

Report of the Committee on National Archives. AHA, *Annual Report*, 1925. Washington, D.C.: Government Printing Office, 1929. P. 79.

From the Autobiography of Herschel V. Johnson, 1856–1867. [Edited by JFJ.] *AHR* 30 (January 1925): 311–36.

The Escape of Louis Philippe, 1848. [Edited by JFJ.] *AHR* 30 (April 1925): 556–60.

The Meeting of the American Historical Association at Richmond. *AHR* 30 (April 1925): 451–77.

Autobiography of Omar ibn Said, Slave in North Carolina, 1831. [Edited by JFJ.] *AHR* 30 (July 1925): 787–95.

Talleyrand and Jaudenes, 1795. [Edited by JFJ.] *AHR* 30 (July 1925): 778–87.

1926

The American Revolution Considered as a Social Movement. Princeton: Princeton University Press, 1926.

Report for the Delegates in the American Council of Learned Societies. AHA, *Annual Report*, 1926. Washington, D.C.: Government Printing Office, 1930. Pp. 105–6.

Report of the Committee on the Documentary Historical Publications of the United States Government. AHA, *Annual Report*, 1926. Washington, D.C.: Government Printing Office, 1930. Pp. 77–78.

Report of the Committee on the National Archives. AHA, *Annual Report*, 1926. Washington, D.C.: Government Printing Office, 1930. Pp. 69–70.

Despatches of Castelnau de la Mauvissiere (on Frobisher, Gilbert, de la Roche, Drake), 1577–1581. [Edited by JFJ.] *AHR* 31 (January 1926): 285–96.

A Confederate Private at Fort Donelson, 1862. [Edited by JFJ.] *AHR* 31 (April 1926): 477–84.

The Meeting of the American Historical Association at Ann Arbor. *AHR* 31 (April 1926): 415–42.

1927

Major-General Henry Lee and Lieutenant-General Sir George Beckwith on Peace in 1813. [Edited by JFJ.] *AHR* 32 (January 1927): 284–92.

A Possible Enrichment of the Teaching of History. *Amherst Graduates' Quarterly* 16 (February 1927): 67–79.

The Meeting of the American Historical Association at Rochester. *AHR* 32 (April 1927): 429–54.

Introduction to a Bibliography of the History of the United States. International Committee of Historical Sciences, *Bulletin* vol. 1, pt. 2 (June 1927): 226–29.

Despatches from the United States Consulate in New Orleans, 1801–1803. [Edited by JFJ.] 1. *AHR* 32 (July 1927): 801–24. 2. *AHR* 33 (January 1928): 331–59.

1927–1928

Report of the Delegates of the American Council of Learned Societies. AHA, *Annual Report*, 1927–28. Washington, D.C.: Government Printing Office, 1929. P. 180.

1928

A Provisional List of Printed Lists of Ambassadors and Other Diplomatic Representatives. International Committee of Historical Sciences, *Bulletin* vol. 1, pt. 4 (March 1928): 475–90.

Letters of a West Pointer, 1860–1861. [Edited by JFJ.] *AHR* 33 (April 1928): 599–617.

The Meeting of the American Historical Association at Washington. *AHR* 33 (April 1928): 517–43.

Henry J. Raymond on the Republican Caucuses of July 1866. [Edited by JFJ.] *AHR* 33 (July 1928): 835–42.

Jefferson to William Short on Mr. and Mrs. Merry, 1804. [Edited by JFJ.] *AHR* 33 (July 1928): 832–35.

Review of *Histoire et Historiens depuis Cinquante Ans: Bibliotèque de la Revue Historique*, vols. 1 and 2 (Paris: Felix Alcan, 1927). *AHR* 34 (October 1928): 92–93.

1929

The International Historical Congress at Oslo. *AHR* 34 (January 1929): 265–73.

1929–1937

Annual Reports of the Chief, Division of Manuscripts. Included in the *Annual Report of the Librarian of Congress*. Washington, D.C.: Government Printing Office, 1929–37, as follows: 1929, pp. 45–75; 1930, pp. 61–94; 1931, pp. 53–86; 1932, pp. 33–60; 1933, pp. 25–40; 1934, pp. 32–45; 1935, pp. 30–45; 1936, pp. 30–45; 1937, pp. 30–40.

1930

Ephraim Douglass Adams. AHA, *Annual Report*, 1930. 4 vols. Washington, D.C.:
  Government Printing Office, 1931. 1:48–49.
Notes from the Archives of Scotland Concerning America. AHA, *Annual Report*,
  1930. 4 vols. Washington, D.C.: Government Printing Office, 1931. 1:97–122.
The London Expenditures of the Confederate Secret Service. [Edited by JFJ.] *AHR*
  35 (July 1930): 824.

1931

Introduction. In *Persecution and Liberty; Essays in Honor of George Lincoln Burr*. New
  York: Century Co., 1931. Pp. xv–xviii.
Preface. In *Essays in Colonial History Presented to Charles McLean Andrews by His
  Students*. New Haven: Yale University Press, 1931. Pp. ix–xiii.
Review of *The Adams Family*, by James Truslow Adams, (Boston: Little, Brown,
  and Co., 1930). *AHR* 36 (January 1931): 410–12.

1932

Introductory Preface. In *The Harkness Collection in the Library of Congress. Calendar
  of Spanish Manuscripts Concerning Peru, 1531–1651*, edited by Stella R. Clemence.
  Washington, D.C.: Government Printing Office, 1932. Pp. iii–v.

1933

Allen Johnson. In *Dictionary of American Biography*, vol. 10. Charles Scribner's
  Sons: New York, 1928–37. Pp. 79–81.
The Committee on Americana for College Libraries. AHA, *Annual Report*, 1933.
  2 vols. Washington, D.C.: Government Printing Office, 1936. 1:51.

1934

Early Days of the American Historical Association, 1884–1895. *AHR* 40 (October
  1934): 1–9.

1935

Edward Potts Cheyney as a Member of the American Historical Association. In *Portrait of a Historian, Edward Potts Cheyney,* edited by William E. Lingelbach. Philadelphia: University of Pennsylvania Press, 1935. Pp. 9–13.

Notice of *Friendly Relations: A Narrative of Britain's Ministers and Ambassadors to America, 1791–1930,* by Beckles Willson (Boston: Little, Brown, and Co., 1934). *AHR* 40 (April 1935): 557–59.

1938

[Leland, Waldo G.] John Franklin Jameson. *AHR* 43 (January 1938): 243–52.

Cheyney, Edward P. J. Franklin Jameson. American Council of Learned Societies, *Bulletin* no. 27 (November 1938): 89–94.

1945

Stock, Leo Francis, ed. Some Bryce-Jameson Correspondence. *AHR* 50 (January 1945): 261–98.

1948

Donnan, Elizabeth, and Leo F. Stock, eds. Senator Beveridge, J. Franklin Jameson, and John Marshall. *Mississippi Valley Historical Review* 35 (December 1948): 463–92.

1949

Donnan, Elizabeth, and Leo F. Stock, eds. Senator Beveridge, J. Franklin Jameson, and Abraham Lincoln. *Mississippi Valley Historical Review* 35 (March 1949): 639–73.

Shelley, Fred. The Interest of J. Franklin Jameson in the National Archives, 1908–1934. *American Archivist* 12 (April 1949): 99–130.

1955

Riggs, John Beverley. The Acquisition of Foreign Archival Sources for American History to the Year 1940. Ph.D. dissertation, Yale University, 1955.

1956

Donnan, Elizabeth, and Leo F. Stock, eds. *An Historian's World: Selections from the Correspondence of John Franklin Jameson*. Philadelphia: American Philosophical Society, 1956.

1958

Leland, Waldo Gifford. John Franklin Jameson. In *Dictionary of American Biography*, vol. 22, supplement 2. New York: Charles Scribner's Sons, 1958. Pp. 339–44.

1965

Fisher, Ruth Anna, and William L. Fox, eds. *J. Franklin Jameson: A Tribute*. Washington, D.C.: Catholic University of America Press, 1965.
Van Tassel, David D. John Franklin Jameson. In *Keepers of the Past*, edited by Clifford L. Lord. Chapel Hill: University of North Carolina Press, 1965. Pp. 81–96.

1973

Ginsberg, Alan Harvey. The Historian as Lobbyist: J. Franklin Jameson and the Historical Activities of the Federal Government. Ph.D. dissertation, Louisiana State University, 1973.

1981

Gondos, Victor, Jr. *J. Franklin Jameson and the Birth of the National Archives, 1906–1926*. Philadelphia: University of Pennsylvania Press, 1981.

1982

Rothberg, Morey D. Servant to History: A Study of John Franklin Jameson, 1859–1937. Ph.D. dissertation, Brown University, 1982.

1983

Shrader, Richard A. J. Franklin Jameson. *Dictionary of Literary Biography*, edited by Clyde N. Wilson. Vol. 17. Detroit: Gale Research Co., 1983. Pp. 230–35.

1984

Meier, August, and Elliott Rudwick. J. Franklin Jameson, Carter G. Woodson, and the Foundations of Black Historiography. *AHR* 89 (October 1984): 1005–15.

Rothberg, Morey D. "To Set a Standard of Workmanship and Compel Men to Conform to It": John Franklin Jameson as Editor of the *American Historical Review*. *AHR* 89 (October 1984): 957–75.

1986

Rothberg, Morey D. The Brahmin as Bureaucrat: J. Franklin Jameson at the Carnegie Institution of Washington, 1905–1928. *Public Historian* 8 (Fall 1986): 47–60.

1987

Rothberg, Morey D. John Franklin Jameson at Brown. *Brown Alumni Monthly* (May 1987): 19–22, 29.

1988

Bledstein, Burton J. John Franklin Jameson. In *Historical Dictionary of the Progressive Era*, edited by John D. Buenker and Edward R. Kantowicz. New York: Greenwood Press, 1988. Pp. 226–27.

1993

Rothberg, Morey. John Franklin Jameson and the Creation of *The American Revolution Considered as a Social Movement*. In *"The Transforming Hand of Revolution": Reconsidering the American Revolution as a Social Movement*, edited by Ronald Hoffman and Peter J. Albert. Charlottesville: University Press of Virginia, forthcoming, 1993.

Index

NOTE: John Franklin Jameson made a distinction between "historical writing" (the final product) and "historical scholarship" (the apparatus and organization). We have maintained this distinction in the preparation of the index.

379

Fort Stanwix, 222
Fortune, 240
France, 138, 146, 224; archives in, 300,
318; colonial administration by, 243;
cooperative histories in, 269, 272,
300; documentary publications in,
258, 295, 346; Empire of, 146; and
First World War, 328; foreign policy
of, 345; higher education in, 277,
278; historical journals in, 256, 257,
335; historical scholarship in, 341;
historical societies in, 256, 296; historical writing in, 268; Huguenots
in, 197; July Revolution in, 160;
and Mississippi Valley, 224; and
Moroccan controversy, 312; and
New England Confederation, 237;
and Northwest Territory, 223; population of, 187; national character of,
171; recent history of, 16; Republic
of, 138; and Seven Years' War, 50;
States-General in, 84; and Treaty of
Paris (1783), 224; territorial claims
of, 220–21
Francis, Saint, 169
Franciscans, 174–75
Francis of Assisi, Saint, 171, 176
Francis Xavier, Saint, 171, 174
Frankland, 139
Franklin, Benjamin, 224, 249
Frederick, Md., 195
Fredericksburg, Va., 60
Freeman, Edward, 269
French Broad River, 139
French Revolution, 16, 183, 205, 266,
269, 305; and historical writing, 258,
267–68, 311; and history, 307
Friendly Sons of Saint Patrick, 190
Froissart, Jean, 169
Froude, James Anthony, 271

Gadsden, Christopher, 79
Gallatin, Albert, 141, 148
Galloway, Joseph, 53, 189
Gálvez, Bernardo de, 224
Garcés, Francisco, 173
Gardiner, Samuel Rawson, 269
Gardoqui, Don Diego de, 136, 137

Garland, Hugh, 101
Garrett, W. R., 107
Gedenstukken, 345
Genealogy and social history, 175
General Education Board, 286, 287–88
General Land Office: archives in, 321;
territorial papers in, 320
Georgetown, S.C., 73
Georgia, 59, 130, 142, 143, 144, 163;
colonial constitution of, 74; and
Constitution of 1787, 127–28; and
Constitution of 1798, 128; and Constitution of 1776, 92–93; dispute
over Indian lands in, 157–58; entail
in, 98; finances of, 106; Germans in,
196; growth of democracy in, 162;
historical journals in, 336; and importation of slaves, 216; movement
of state capital in, 227; and Philadelphia Convention, 110; political
parties in, 164; population of, 158;
primogeniture abolished in, 101;
ratification of U.S. Constitution
by, 110; slavery in, 206, 209; state
rights theory in, 158; suffrage in,
150; Supreme Executive Council in,
94; Tories in, 56; western lands of,
107, 108, 139, 143, 144
Georgia Historical Society, 144
German American Historical Society,
297
Germany, 169; cooperative histories
in, 269, 272, 300; documentary
publications in, 258, 295; economic
policy of, 329; Empire of, 196;
higher education in, 277, 278; historical journals in, 256, 335; historical method in, 351; historical
scholarship in, 341; historical societies in, 296; historical writing in,
268; and Moroccan controversy, 312;
national character of, 171; Protestants in, 210; public opinion in,
328; Reichsarchiv in, 346; Social
Democratic party in, 329
Gerry, Elbridge, 38, 124
Gerrymandering, 38
Gervinus, Saint, 169